This book is a translation, in parts augmented and revised, by

JOHN ORR

*Sometime Professor of French in the
University of Edinburgh*

of

INTRODUCERE IN STUDIUL LIMBILOR ROMANICE

by

IORGU IORDAN

*Academician and Professor of Rumanian
Language in the University of Bucharest*

IORDAN–ORR

AN INTRODUCTION TO

ROMANCE LINGUISTICS

ITS SCHOOLS AND SCHOLARS

Revised, with a supplement

THIRTY YEARS ON

by

R. POSNER

Reader in Language, University of York

UNIVERSITY OF CALIFORNIA PRESS

Berkeley and Los Angeles · 1970

University of California Press
Berkeley and Los Angeles, California

ISBN: 0-520-01768-4
Library of Congress Catalog Card Number: 71-122932

Supplement material
© Basil Blackwell 1970

First published in 1937
Second edition 1970

Printed by offset in Great Britain

AUTHOR'S PREFACE

CE livre est la version anglaise de mon ouvrage, *Introducere în studiul limbilor romanice. Evoluția și starea actuală a lingvisticii romanice*, paru à Iași il y a cinq ans. Ecrit en roumain, langue assez peu connue même des philologues, mon livre n'en éveilla pas moins l'attention des spécialistes, et de nombreux comptes-rendus, vingt-cinq au total, lui furent consacrés au cours des trois années qui en suivirent la publication. A de très rares exceptions près, auxquelles, j'en ai la certitude, certains griefs personnels ne furent pas étrangers, ces comptes-rendus furent favorables, souvent même plus que favorables. On s'accorda pour reconnaître et pour louer ma tentative de fournir, sur l'activité scientifique des représentatants les plus marquants de notre discipline du dernier tiers de siècle, des renseignements exacts et détaillés en même temps qu'impartiaux.

Certes, ce travail présentait des lacunes ; il en présente encore sous sa forme nouvelle. Mais il est naturel qu'il en soit ainsi; d'abord parce que la perfection n'est pas de ce monde, ensuite parce que pareil défaut est comme inhérent au caractère même de mon livre. Car, si certaines de ces lacunes se doivent en partie à des nécessités purement pratiques, en partie aussi aux insuffisances soit en périodiques, soit surtout en ouvrages spéciaux, de nos bibliothèques roumaines, d'autres, au contraire, s'expliquent, et se justifient, par le but que je me suis proposé.

En effet, comme je l'ai dit ailleurs, mon but fut de décrire, non pas toute l'activité déployée dans le domaine de la linguistique romane depuis le début du siècle présent, mais seulement celle qui se rattachait plus ou moins étroitement aux écoles et tendances nouvelles, ou qui pouvaient paraître telles. On pouvait ne pas approuver ce project. Mais, une fois admis, il comportait nécessairement certaines omissions. C'est ainsi que, partant du principe que toute discipline vaut surtout par les progrès qu'elle fait réaliser, en méthode ou en doctrine, je me

v

suis cru autorisé à négliger l'activité qui ne faisait que continuer la tradition du dix-neuvième siècle, estimant, d'une part, que celle-ci était plus généralement connue et, d'autre part, qu'elle se prêtait moins à la critique et à la discussion. Cependant, afin que le lecteur soit informé sur les écoles antérieures bases de la linguistique du vingtième siècle, je leur ai consacré un assez long chapitre, le premier du livre.

A côté donc de lacunes matérielles et comme inévitables, des lacunes voulues ou, plutôt, imposées par la nature même de ma tâche telle que je l'avais conçue. C'est ce qui explique, en partie, que pour tel domaine de nos études, pour telle région comme, par exemple, pour la Péninsule Ibérique, les informations sont relativement rares, même dans le present volume, alors que pour telle autre elles sont abondantes, voire même surabondantes.

Mais, même délimités de cette manière, les faits que j'avais à décrire n'en restaient pas moins très complexes. Il fallait trier, classer, choisir dans une matière encore extrêmement touffue. Dans cette opération délicate, opération où, forcément, l'élément personnel joue un rôle très important, comment espérer satisfaire tout le monde ? Ne s'agissait-il pas, dans l'espèce, d'apprécier l'œuvre linguistique de savants pour la plupart encore vivants, et dont l'attitude scientifique, et même la personnalité purement humaine, provoquent chez leurs confrères des réactions trés diverses ? Comment être sûr d'avoir échappé complètement à cette atmosphère de sympathie ou d'antipathie qui entoure et l'œuvre et l'homme ? Comment se flatter d'avoir formulè toujours un jugement purement objectif ? Ces questions que je me pose sincèrement à moi-même, je les pose également à ceux qui, à lire telle appréciation, tel éloge, dans les pages qui vont suivre, pourront èprouver quelque mouvement d'humeur ; qu'ils se disent, eux aussi, qu'en pareille matière, à moins, d'être indiffèrent, il est fort difficile d'être impersonnel.

Qu'il me soit permis à ce propos de citer un exemple spécifique. On sait que l'école dite 'idéaliste' rencontre, surtout en Allemagne, une hostilité des plus acharnées, et qu'il est des romanistes auxquels l'apport scientifique de cette école paraît insignifiant ou même pernicieux. Il est clair que mon attitude à l'égard de cette école semblera trop favorable, sinon partiale, à celui qui partage cette opinion et qui considère un Vossler, un

Lerch ou un Spitzer comme de purs dilettantes. Celui-là, je ne prétends pas à le convaincre de la justesse de mon appréciation de ces trois savants. Je demande seulement qu'il ne fassé pas de son opinion à lui un article de foi auquel, sous peine d'excommunication scientifique, tout le monde doit souscrire ; qu'il ne l'érige pas en axiome pour tout linguiste sérieux, mais qu'il exerce au contraire la tolérance qui est de mise en toute discussion de principes et de méthodes scientifiques, tolérance que j'ai essayé de pratiquer moi-même à l'égard d'écoles ou d'individus dont les œuvres ne m'inspirent pas toujours une admiration sans réserves.

Quant aux deux versions de mon livre, si elles sont assez différentes l'une de l'autre, c'est surtout à mon collègue M. Orr qu'en revient le mérite. Mon rôle personnel en ce qui concerne celle-ci n'a consisté qu'à compléter et à mettre à jour, dans la mesure de mes moyens, la documentation, là où celle-ci se révélait incomplète ou périmée. M. Orr, au contraire, au cours de plus d'une année de travail, n'a cessé de me soumettre des suggestions en vue de rendre cette version anglaise, par la forme et par le fonds, supérieure à la version primitive. Ces suggestions, toujours justes et ingénieuses en même temps que bien documentées, je les ai toutes acceptées. Je lui en suis profondément reconnaissant, surtout en ce qui concerne les améliorations qu'il a apportées aux chapitres III et IV du livre, les plus importants et par l'étendue et par leur portée théorique. Là le traducteur avisé, qui a partout fait preuve d'une connaissance peu commune, hélas, de ma langue maternelle, s'est doublé d'un véritable collaborateur. Je le remercie donc, non seulement d'avoir par cette traduction anglaise contribué à la diffusion de mon livre et d'avoir ainsi, j'ose l'espérer, aidé à éveiller et à propager l'amour de nos communes études, mais aussi de m'avoir aidé à faire de cette édition une édition véritablement nouvelle, revue, augmentée et en partie refondue, ainsi que l'annonce le titre.

IORGU IORDAN

Mínăstirea Agapia,
le 15 juillet, 1937

TRANSLATOR'S PREFACE

I HAD not read many pages of the Rumanian version of this book before I conceived the plan of translating into English what seemed to me a most admirable initiation to the newer Romance scholarship, not only for students of the Romance languages, but for linguists in general. Having secured M. Iordan's ready consent and Messrs. Methuen and Co.'s generous support, I set to work on a task which, though lengthy and, as it proved, laborious, was none the less most congenial in that, apart from a few minor points of appreciation with regard to this or that individual scholar, I found myself completely at one with the author.

At the outset, bearing in mind that *improbe facit qui in alieno libro ingeniosus est*, I applied myself severely to an adequate rendering of the text. But, as the work proceeded, and encouraged, I would add, by M. Iordan's willing acceptance of my suggestions, I allowed myself greater liberties, with the result that in the later portion of the book, as M. Iordan has said above, there is a good deal of my own handiwork, not only in the re-arrangement of the subject-matter, but in the subject-matter itself. As a pure translation, therefore, this English version lacks unity of treatment, although, thanks to the complete conformity of views between M. Iordan and myself, the unity of thought and outlook is, I venture to think, maintained throughout.

I wish to thank my colleagues, Mr. Austin Gill and Mr. W. D. Elcock, for reading the proofs of this edition, and the former also for some valuable suggestions, particularly with regard to the section on Slang Studies, a field in which he has long been working.

JOHN ORR

Edinburgh,
September, 1937

PREFACE TO THE SECOND EDITION

IT has been a source of keen pleasure to me that, among Romanists, English-speaking scholars should have shown the greatest appreciation of the original version of my work on Romance linguistics: *Introducere în studiul limbilor romanice.* That the English translation should now be reprinted is sufficient proof of this: though the Rumanian version has appeared in two editions, none of the other translations has met with such success. The popularity of the 1937 English edition was due to John Orr as translator (incidentally the first foreign Romanist to undertake a translation of the work). Not only did he transpose it into lucid, attractive English, but also, with my consent, he made a number of modifications and improvements. For many years he had planned a new extended edition. Unhappily he did not live to see his plans materialise.

Now it has fallen to Mrs. Rebecca Posner to undertake the task, which she has performed in an excellent manner. After having carefully read the entire text of her supplement, I dare call her contribution *brilliant*. Her up-to-date coverage is virtually exhaustive—which is not true of previous editions. Some linguists of great stature, ignored or almost so by previous versions, here appear in their proper perspective (some of them, it is true were less well-known six or eight years ago). But what has aroused my unreserved admiration is less the information provided than Mrs. Posner's critical attitude, based always on a perfect knowledge not only of the works discussed, but also of the theories, methods and so on, underlying them.

I should like then to congratulate Mrs. Posner on her work. The new edition is a fitting tribute to the memory of John Orr, who will be remembered with affection, gratitude and admiration whenever the book is read.

IORGU IORDAN

Bucharest,
4th September, 1969

ix

CONTENTS

CHAPTER I

ROMANCE STUDIES BEFORE 1900[1]

U NTIL the beginning of the nineteenth century there can be no talk of strictly scientific research upon the Romance languages. As a science in the true sense of the word, that is to say, possessing the necessary evidence to substantiate its affirmations concerning linguistic phenomena, our discipline is scarcely a century old. This does not mean that at an earlier date men were not to be found whose native curiosity, fostered by the general advance of culture, impelled them to seek an understanding of all manner of problems concerning these languages, as far as the knowledge at their disposal allowed. On the contrary, from the remotest times, distinguished minds have concerned themselves with what is to-day the subject matter of Romance linguistics. It merely means that their enquiries, although deserving of every attention from the historical point of view, cannot be set alongside the studies that have taken shape in the course of the nineteenth and of the present centuries. None the less, it is fitting that we should mention here a certain number of authors and works that stand out above the others and have thus a greater claim upon the attention of posterity.

The Middle Ages

Shortly before 1305, in an unfinished work entitled *De vulgari eloquentia*, the great Italian poet, Dante Alighieri, already treated a certain number of questions that are still matters of debate among linguists in general, and Romance scholars in particular, *inter alia*,[2] the origin of speech, the neo-Latin group of languages,—comprising

---

[1] Cf. G. Gröber, *Geschichte der romanischen Philologie*, in *Grundriss der rom. Phil.*, I (2nd edition), Strasburg, 1904-6, p. 1 f. See also, H. Pedersen, *La linguistique au XIX siècle, Méthodes et résultats* (translated from the Danish), 1924 ; English translation, 1931. For reviews of this work, see E. Boisacq, *Revue belge de philologie et d'histoire*, VI (1927), p. 554, n. 1 ; O.D.[ensusianu], *Grai şi suflet*, V (1931, 2), p. 390 ; E. E. Ericson, *Studies in Philology*, XXIX (1932), p. 125 f. ; P. Meriggi, *Die neueren Sprachen*, XLI (1933), nos. 7, 8.

[2] The author is concerned in the main with the problem of literary Italian ; style, versification, criticism and literary history thus take up the major portion of his pages.

for him only the three of which he had personal knowledge, French, Provençal, and Italian—and the Italian dialects, of which he distinguishes fourteen groups, on one side or the other of the Apennines. Dante accepts without question the Biblical story of the origin and diversification of human speech, as was inevitable with the author of the *Divine Comedy*, but when he speaks of the dialectal varieties in Italy he shows himself an excellent observer of the facts of language, and some of his remarks are truly surprising for the period.

The Renascence, that is to say the resumption of close contact with Graeco-Roman antiquity, brought increased interest in **The Rena-** linguistic enquiry and opened up wider horizons. **scence and** Like all men of the Renascence, the authors of **After** grammatical and lexicographical works of the period are distinguished by their many-sided interests and by an erudition which profoundly impresses, not to say bewilders, our over-specialized contemporaries. It is enough to mention the names of Robert Etienne (Robertus Stephanus[1]), Henri Etienne (Henricus Stephanus[2]) and Justus Joseph Scaliger[3] all of them of the XVIth century, and all of them authors of works of outstanding importance in our field of study. The last-mentioned, be it said, treating of the distribution of the languages spoken in Europe, clearly recognizes the kinship of French with Spanish and Italian, assigning all three to the same group.

This renewed linguistic activity continues in the seventeenth century. To this period belongs the foundation of the oldest of our European academies, namely, the Accademia della Crusca, created as early as the end of the preceding century, 1583, and the Académie Française, 1634, whose main purpose was to foster the growth of the national tongue by publishing a grammar and a dictionary.[4] There remains to mention further the famous *Glossarium ad scriptores mediae et infimae latinitatis*, 3 vols., Paris, 1678, the work of the Frenchman Du Cange (Charles du Fresne); this dictionary of

---

[1] *Dictionnaire françois-latin*, 1539 ; *Traicté de la grammaire françoise*, 1559.

[2] *Traité de la conformité du langage françois avec le grec*, 1565 ; *Précellence du langage françois*, 1579.

[3] *Diatribe de Europaeorum lingua*, 1599 ; *De hodiernis Francorum linguis*, 1599 ; *De varia literarum pronuntiatione*, 1610.

[4] The *Vocabolario della Crusca*, in six volumes, appeared in 1612 ; the *Dictionnaire de l'Académie Française*, begun in 1638, took nearly 60 years to complete : it appeared in 1694, in two volumes. The *Grammaire de l'Académie Française* appeared only in 1932. It has been severely criticized by Ferd. Brunot, *Observations sur la Gram. de l'Acad. Fr.*, Paris, 1932.

mediaeval Latin still renders inestimable service to Romance scholars.

In the eighteenth century linguistic studies progress with increased momentum. Philosophic rationalism on the one hand and the encyclopaedic spirit on the other have each a beneficial effect upon our discipline.[1] The former gives rise to works upon the origin of language, the latter, with its strong historical bias, introduces into linguistic investigation that historical outlook which was to be of such great profit to the Romance scholars of the future. One regrets, however, that the attention of the philologists of this century turns with preference to literature, to the neglect of the Romance languages as such. A great name of this period is the Italian Lodovico Muratori, a scholar of prodigious activity who published, *inter alia*, a huge collection of the ' sources ' for the history of the Italian people, an enormous mass of material that has been of great value to Romance studies, supplemented as it is with an inexhaustible store of bibliographical information.

The cosmopolitanism characteristic of the XVIIIth century also shows itself in linguistic studies. Men are interested not merely in their mother tongue, but in the languages spoken beyond their national frontiers. And so we find Italians busy with French or Provençal, Frenchmen with Italian and so on. More than this, in non-Romance lands, in England for example, and particularly in Germany, we note among scholars a similar interest in the neo-Latin tongues. Thus was the ground being prepared for the linguistic achievements of the early decades of the nineteenth century.

We have already stated that as a true science our discipline scarcely exists until after 1800. Its beginnings are to be sought in the romantic movement.[2] It is well known that **Romance Linguistics and Romanticism** one of the essential characteristics of German romanticism was an insatiable thirst for knowledge. Knowledge of self, knowledge of the outer world, or, in short, as they put it themselves, knowledge of the infinite, these were the watchwords of the romantics. This desire to ' know ' gives birth first of all to History, which, inasmuch as it studies the past of humanity, is qualified perhaps more than any other science to gratify our curiosity. The nineteenth century for this reason

---

[1] Cf. G. Harnois, *Les théories du langage en France de 1660 à 1821*, Paris, n.d.

[2] Cp. Gertrud Richert, *Die Anfänge der romanischen Philologie und die deutsche Romantik*, Halle a.S., 1914.

became essentially the century of history. But to ransack the past leads but indirectly to the knowledge of man's soul, the supreme aim of the romantics. So their next recourse was to languages and literatures, as direct sources of information upon the life of the spirit. This was the path that led to the creation of Philology. It began, as was natural, with the more intensive study of the classical languages and literatures, though from the time of Humanism and the Renascence the classics had not ceased for a moment to be read and admired. To these were next added the Sanscrit language and literature, which, for a variety of reasons, held an inevitable appeal for the romantics, with their well-known love of mystery and exotism. It must be remembered, however, that romanticism also came as a reaction against classicism, as a protest against the severity of rules that fettered, if they did not destroy, the liberty of the poet. Hence it is that modern languages and literatures acquire in the eyes of the romantics a peculiar value, and an interest which rapidly led to the creation, first of all of Germanic, and later of Romance philology.

Despite their attitude of hostility towards antiquity, the romantics, in their studies of the modern tongues, had perforce to utilize the **Romance Studies and Classical Philology** methods of classical philology, the only existing linguistic discipline. One of these is the comparative method, the investigation of languages belonging to the same family by comparing them one with the other and taking as a starting-point a so-called parent tongue. This procedure was therefore introduced into Romance linguistics, where it is still applied, and is indeed, in the nature of things, essential, whether in work of a comprehensive character, embracing the various neo-Latin languages in their relationships one with the other and with Latin, or in problems affecting one alone, for recourse must be had to others if we are to bring out the peculiarities of one.

But the Romance scholars did not confine themselves to imitating their Indo-European colleagues ; they went further and took over from the latter a point of view which was quite meaningless in their own particular field. The reader is aware that the language from which Greek, Latin, Sanscrit, Persian, etc., have sprung is unrecorded. Consequently, in order to facilitate the discussion and investigation of these languages, philologists set to work to reconstruct this common Indo-European or Indo-Germanic tongue. After establishing the phonetic, morphological, and other corre-

spondences between the kindred idioms, they proceeded to create
for each particular case, by purely logical methods, an Indo-
European prototype from which the several varieties of sound or
form are supposed to have sprung. This procedure was for them
a prime necessity, which explains its unreserved application in
Indo-European linguistics. The Romance scholars followed faithfully in the wake of the Indo-Europeanists,[1] and thought that they
too must have a similar goal, failing to recognize that their situation
was entirely different from that of their masters, inasmuch as the
starting-point of their languages, namely Vulgar Latin, is comparatively well known, while Classical Latin, forming with
Vulgar Latin a single linguistic whole, which we may call Latin
pure and simple, has yielded up practically all its secrets. Moreover, the Romance tongues are still spoken to-day ; that is to say,
they are living organisms, and can thus be observed and studied
directly, ' in the field ', to use a term borrowed from the natural
sciences, unlike the Indo-European languages mentioned above
which we are obliged to acquire from written sources. None the
less, it took a long time for such obvious truths to gain recognition
and to bring about a change of attitude. To-day, however,
Romance philology has escaped entirely from the guardianship of
the Indo-Europeanists, nay has even become, as Schuchardt
somewhere proudly asserted, a teacher of its fellows. And with
good reason ; for although, like the neo-Latin tongues, the Slavonic
and Germanic idioms are also living languages, and can therefore
be studied on the spot, primitive Slavonic and primitive
Germanic, on the other hand, are entirely unknown to us.

Another peculiarity of Romance linguistics in the XIXth century,
also attributable to the circumstances outlined above, is its excessive

---

[1] The Indo-Europeanists themselves, realizing the difference between the two
disciplines, have more than once striven to condemn the too servile application
of the methods of comparative philology to research in the neo-Latin tongues.
A. Meillet, the regretted chief of French Indo-European scholars, gives his
opinion on this question in a review of P. E. Guarnerio's *Fonologia romanza* (Milan,
1918). He writes : " Les romanistes imitent trop souvent la grammaire comparée
des langues indo-européennes par ses mauvais côtés : en matière d'indo-européen,
on est obligé de juxtaposer des études sur toutes les langues du groupe, parce que
c'est le seul moyen qu'on ait de restituer en quelque mesure la langue initiale. . . .
Les romanistes, qui ont toutes sortes de données pour poser le roman commun,
se sont exercés à mettre sous une même couverture des renseignements se rap-
portant à des développements distincts " ; *Bulletin de la Société de linguistique
de Paris*, XXI (1917–19), p. 230. The error of the ways of those linguists who at
every step reconstructed Vulgar Latin equivalents for Romance forms and words
has become more particularly manifest since the foundation of linguistic geography.
Comparatively recently, L. Sainéan has given us what we may call decisive proof
of this error in his *Les Sources indigènes de l'étymologie française*, 3 vols., Paris, 1925–30.

historical bias. The researches of the Indo-Europeanists, who are chiefly concerned with dead languages, are founded upon texts, their only available source of information. Romance scholars, copying their elders, imagined that they too must give pride of place, not to the spoken idioms, but to written documents ; and the older the document, the greater did its importance appear. There thus came about the truly paradoxical situation that numerous non-French linguists of last century were past masters in their knowledge of Old French and Old Provençal, but unpardonably ignorant of the modern idiom.[1] Against this tendency, which was erroneous in so far as it was excessive, there came a strong reaction towards the end of the XIXth and beginning of the XXth centuries, due in the main, as will be seen later, to the study of linguistic geography (v. Chapter III).[2]

★   ★   ★

Whom are we to call the founder of our discipline ? The answer to this question has long been given, and the matter may now be considered as settled. But there are still heard, from time to time, dissentient voices, which, from motives frequently quite foreign to science, revive discussion of the problem. A short history of the matter would therefore seem to be necessary.

The Foundation of Romance Studies

From the strictly chronological point of view, it is a Frenchman, François Raynouard, who takes first place. Entrusted with

---

[1] The following words of Schuchardt upon this topic are characteristic (v. *Hugo Schuchardt-Brevier*, 2nd edition, Halle a. S., 1928, p. 428 f.) : " Further, there came over me a certain hostility towards Old French, with which for a number of decades we had been somewhat over-fed. Mussafia once told me how on one occasion he set one of his students to write on the board the Old French for ' The emperor called upon Roland '—Li emperere at apelet Rollant. ' Good ! Now write the modern French underneath ! ' ' Sorry, Herr Professor, I haven't got to modern French yet.' As early as 1872, I was told by a colleague qualified to speak, that I would never get on if I did not publish an Old French text. I said to myself : ' I'll risk it ! ' It came off ! " One is given to understand by competent observers (cp. L. Spitzer, *Der Romanist an der deutschen Hochschule*, in *Die neueren Sprachen*, XXXV, 1927) that Mussafia's story is of more than merely historical interest.

[2] Cp. Meillet, *Bull. Soc. Ling.*, XV (1908–9), p. cxix : " D'une manière générale, la linguistique est dominée par une préoccupation d'histoire qui est légitime dans une certaine mesure, mais dont le caractère exclusif surprend et scandalise ceux qui du dehors viennent à y jeter les yeux."

the preparation of the Dictionary of the French Academy, he became convinced. that in order to study seriously the French vocabulary a knowledge of the earlier phases of the language was indispensable. He set himself therefore to investigate linguistic conditions in France in early times, and in doing so, discovered a vast number of literary monuments which he began to publish, and, what is of more immediate interest to us here, to utilize for his *Lexique roman ou dictionnaire de la langue des troubadours comparée avec les autres langues de l'Europe latine*, 6 vols., Paris, 1838–44.[1] He had previously published a series of six volumes of texts, entitled *Choix de poésies originales des troubadours*, Paris, 1816–21. The first of the series is headed *Grammaire de la langue romane* (Paris, 1816), and is of particular importance in the present discussion, inasmuch as it is the first grammar of an ancient Romance language, and is based upon texts. What Raynouard calls ' roman ' we call to-day Old Provençal. And in this error of terminology lies the crux of the problem. For Raynouard imagined that out of Latin there came directly, not the Romance idioms we know, but an intermediate language, common to all the provinces of the defunct Roman empire, and that it was this language which gave birth, at a later date, to Spanish, French, Italian, etc. The idea was not new. In the XVIIIth century there was a like belief in the existence of a unified Romance language, supposed to have been preserved in the *Strasburg Oaths* of the year 842. Raynouard himself believed this text, whose great antiquity renders it of the highest value, to be a Provençal product, and consequently a piece of his early ' roman ', instead of a piece of French as it really is. His conception is thus on all fours with those of his predecessors of the previous century.[2]

Raynouard's *Grammar* impressed, and even astonished, his contemporaries. The latter were able to observe that the characteristics of unity, regularity, and analogy, which, in their belief, were the prerogative of literary languages in their highest stage of perfection, were to be found in the morphology of an archaic and

---

[1] There is a modern reprint of this, without modification, published by C. Winter of Heidelberg. Raynouard's dictionary was completed and corrected by E. Levy, and C. Appel, *Provenzalisches Supplement-Wörterbuch. Berichtigungen und Ergänzungen zu Raynouards Lexique Roman*, 8 vols., Leipzig, 1894–1924.

[2] One must not attach too great importance to such a confusion arising at the period, for in their earliest phases, the neo-Latin tongues, particularly Old French and Old Provençal, have a very great deal in common. [It should be stated, too, that Raynouard sometimes distinguishes between ' langue rustique romane, type primitif ', and ' la romane provençale ' ; cp. *Lex. rom.*, I, p. xiii.—J. O.]

primitive idiom like Old Provençal. But the fundamental error of the work, namely, that a common neo-Latin language had been spoken over the whole of 'Romania', i.e. the Romance area, before the existing Romance idioms, soon became apparent.[1] This in itself would be sufficient for us to refuse to award to Raynouard the title of founder of our discipline. But it is not all, for we have seen that he in fact studies only one Romance language, and therefore does not apply the comparative method, the distinguishing feature of Romance philology as we understand it to-day. It was indeed impossible for this method to be applied in the year 1816, inasmuch as the work which was to lay the foundations of Indo-European linguistics as a science in the real sense, and which later inspired both German and Romance philologists alike, namely, Franz Bopp's *Über das Conjugationssystem der Sanskritsprache, in Vergleichung mit jenem der griechischen, lateinischen, persischen und germanischen Sprachen*, was only published at Frankfurt am Main in the same year, 1816, as Raynouard's *Grammaire de la langue romane*. None the less, despite his shortcomings, there is no challenging Raynouard's achievement as the most vigorous pioneer in Romance studies.

Before passing on to the true founder of the Romance discipline, Friedrich Diez, we must make a brief mention of his predecessors in allied domains. We have just cited the first work of Bopp, which inaugurated the comparative method, and thereby the strictly scientific investigation of the Indo-European languages. In his study of the conjugation system of Sanscrit, Greek, Latin, etc., Bopp formulates the conclusion that the Indo-European flexion is a product of 'agglutination', a term borrowed from W. v. Humboldt. In his view, all words can be reduced to monosyllabic roots, some pronominal, others verbal;[2] to these, flexional endings became attached which were themselves originally independent words, mainly pronouns. But the chief value of Bopp's work is to be sought elsewhere, namely, in the idea, which he upheld with the help of 'physical' and 'mechanical' laws,[3] that the Indo-

---

[1] Already in 1818, A. W. v. Schlegel, in his *Observations sur la langue et la littérature des troubadours*, a work which in certain aspects can be considered as a veritable outline of Romance philology, corrected Raynouard and maintained that the neo-Latin languages came directly from Latin.

[2] From the verbal roots both verbs and substantives were formed, from the pronominal, pronouns, prepositions, conjunctions, and particles.

[3] 'Physical' laws are those which we call to-day 'phonetic' or 'phonological'; 'mechanical' laws concern the relations between vowels and consonants.

European tongues composed a complete unity. Their several developments were of no interest to him, not only in this work, but also in the later *Vergleichende Grammatik des Sanskrit, Send, Griechischen, Litauischen, Gotischen und Deutschen* (1833–52), where he is still solely concerned with their inter-relationships.

Historical linguistics, or, more correctly, language history, we owe to the Germanist Jakob Grimm, who in his *Deutsche Grammatik* (1819 onwards) studies with particular attention the sounds of the Germanic languages, insisting on the relationships between these and the sounds of the classical languages, and showing at the same time that changes in sound are not arbitrary and fortuitous but take place according to definite laws.[1]

Building on the foundations laid by Bopp and Grimm, Friedrich Diez published in the years 1836–43 the three volumes of his *Grammatik der romanischen Sprachen*, in which he applies the comparative method of the former and the historical method of the latter. Romance philology, as a truly scientific discipline, had been founded.[2] Diez divides the Romance languages into two groups, an eastern, comprising Rumanian and Italian, a western, including Old French, Old Provençal, French, Spanish, and Portuguese. He then goes on to show the origin and development of their respective ' forms ', their sounds, flexions, word-formation, and syntax. In the first part, which comprises the phonology of the several languages, sound-change (Lautwandel) is held to be at the basis of all linguistic change. Diez does not confuse sounds with letters, as all his predecessors had done, although he does not hit upon the true reason for phonetic changes, imagining as he does that some of them are conscious and deliberate. We note, too, that he did not make a clear distinction between inherited Latin words and those borrowed from Latin at a later period, although each type has had a different phonetic history. On the other hand, he is fully aware that a sound changes into another sound

Friedrich Diez (1794–1876)

---

[1] It is here that we encounter for the first time the term ' sound-shift ' (Lautver-schiebung) so current in historical grammars of Germanic. It should be stated, however, that the law to which it refers had already been discovered independently by the Danish scholar, Kr. Rask.

[2] Diez is the founder of Romance studies in the fullest sense, linguistics, philology proper, and literary history. Just as his *Grammar* replaced that of Raynouard, so his *Beiträge zur Kenntnis der romanischen Poesie* (1825), his *Poesie der Troubadours* (1826) and his *Leben und Werke der Troubadours* (1829) rendered the similar works of the French scholar superfluous. It was Goethe, whom he met at Jena, in 1818, who encouraged Diez to take up the study of Provençal lyric poetry.

of a kindred type of articulation, and particularly, he is alive to the great importance of analogy in the domain of flexion. It is natural that after a lapse of some hundred years since the first edition, Diez's *Grammar* should have lost much of that outstanding importance which it had at the date of its appearance and for a considerable time after.[1] The first and second volumes (Phonology and Morphology) are to-day only of historical interest ; the third, however, that on Syntax, has lost practically none of its intrinsic value.

In 1854 Diez published, again in Bonn, his *Etymologisches Wörter-buch der romanischen Sprachen*, a natural and necessary corollary to his *Grammar*. Here, he traces the origin of a great number of neo-Latin words, grouping them into (*a*) words common to all the languages, and (*b*) words existing only in one, allotting a section to Italian, a section to Spanish and Portuguese, and another to French and Provençal. What we have said of the *Grammar* holds also for the *Dictionary* : like every work that has been created single-handed, and has formed the basis of subsequent research, it contains much that is imperishable and has become the stock-in-trade of Romance linguistics, beside much that is now only quoted because it comes to us from Friedrich Diez.

The influence of this great scholar soon made itself felt both in Germany and elsewhere. In Italy, in the second half of the last century, we find a figure of the first rank, Graziadio Isaia Ascoli, an Indo-Europeanist and Romanicist all in one, who, although not strictly speaking a pupil of the German linguists, owed a great deal to them, particularly to Bopp and Diez, and who, following in their footsteps, displayed a fruitful and untiring activity in widely varying domains. Here, we are chiefly concerned with his work in Romance, though we can scarcely hope to detach this entirely from his work in the broader field.

Graziadio Isaia Ascoli (1829–1907)

In the first place, it is to this linguist that we owe the setting of Italian Dialectology on a truly scientific basis and, consequently, the foundation of Dialectology as a branch of Romance. studies, for until his day the Romance dialects of all regions had been left to the care of the amateur philologist. In order to publish

---

[1] This is shown by the fact that during roughly 45 years there were five editions of the work, the last in 1882. Of the later editions, the third only was supervised by Diez himself. His *Dictionary* appears to have had even greater success, with its five editions between 1854 and 1887.

his own and his disciples' researches in this field he founded in 1873 the *Archivio glottologico italiano*,[1] an event of signal importance in the history of Romance linguistics. The eighth volume of this journal (1882–85) contains (p. 98 ff.) the famous study entitled *L'Italia dialettale*, in which Ascoli formulated for many years to come the rules and principles to be adopted in the study of Italian dialects.[2] Further, it is thanks to him that a Romance language, until then practically unknown even to specialists, enters the ken of Romance scholars. In the first volume of his journal (pp. 1–556) he published a work which is still of fundamental importance for the dialects of the Rheto-Romance area, his *Saggi ladini*, a model of erudition and breadth of vision despite the inherent aridity of the subject.[3] From the very outset, Ascoli realized the value to general linguistic study that lay in the observation of the popular vernaculars, for he was quick to understand, unlike some of our present-day ultra-fervent supporters of the historical method, that direct observation of living speech illuminates with some certainty the various processes of modification undergone by a language in the past ; whereas the reverse is by no means always true, namely, that the study of the early stages of a language enables us to comprehend with greater ease its present state.

Again, Ascoli attached great importance, when accounting for the peculiarities of a given language, to the ethnical factor or substratum. The idea that racial characteristics manifest themselves in language was not a new one. It is to be found in the works of the earlier empirical linguists, and later in Friedrich Schlegel, von Humboldt, and particularly in Grimm. But Ascoli was the first to work it out at all scientifically.[4] He attributed, for example, the change of the latin long *u* to the sound [y] which we find in France, Northern Italy, and certain Rheto-Romance dialects, to the Celtic populations settled in those areas. Similarly, the change of initial *f* to *h* in Spanish and Gascon was laid at the door of the Iberians. To-day, though there is general agreement

---

[1] Published now in two sections ; one devoted to Indo-European and general linguistics, edited by P. G. Goidànich, the other to Romance, under the direction of M. G. Bartoli.

[2] Cf. N. Maccarrone, *Il concetto dei dialetti e l' " Italia dialettale " nel pensiero ascoliano*, Arch. glott. ital., XXII–XXIII (1929), p. 302 f. To-day the journal *L'Italia dialettale* (Pisa, 1924–), under the direction of the leader of Italian dialect studies, C. Merlo, professor at the University of Pisa, still continues the Ascoli tradition.

[3] The same volume, p. xlii f., contains his system of transcribing sounds.

[4] V. B. A. Terracini, *La Cultura*, VIII (1929), p. 644–5.

among scholars with regard to the principle upheld with such warmth and eloquence by Ascoli, its application to particular cases usually encounters either direct opposition or, to say the least, very lukewarm acceptance.[1]

Finally, we must not forget that Ascoli laid strong emphasis upon the need for intuition in linguistic research. In *Kritische Studien zur Sprachwissenschaft* (Weimar, 1878),[2] pp. iii, viii, xiii, etc., while recognizing that linguistics is at a disadvantage when compared to the exact sciences in its inability to establish laws, and is therefore obliged to confine itself to the methodical observation and close scrutiny of facts, he none the less adds that the task of the philologist is not merely to decant the contents of his card-index, but that he should possess a modicum of fancy, a special flair for what is probable, which alone can lead us to the discovery of what is true. Much more than this : courage and even temerity are required, for without them progress can but be slow.[3]

Ascoli, although not strictly speaking a pupil of Diez, had continued the tradition which the latter had established. A little later, in France, Gaston Paris, who actually **French** studied under Diez in Bonn, began his illustrious **Romanicists** philological career with his *Etude sur le rôle de l'accent latin dans la langue française*, Paris, 1862. With Paul Meyer,

[1] An historical summary of the substratum problem, with particular reference to Italy, will be found in G. Rohlfs, *Vorlateinische Einflüsse in den Mundarten des heutigen Italiens*, Germanisch-romanische Monatsschrift, XVIII (1930), p. 37 f. For subsequent discussions see : V. Bertoldi, *Problèmes de substrat. Essai de méthodologie dans le domaine préhistorique de la toponymie et du vocabulaire*, Bull. Soc. Ling. Paris XXXII (1931), fasc. 2, p. 93 f. ; see also the proceedings of the third congress of Romance linguists in Rome, published in *Revue de linguistique romane*, IX (1933) ; M.-Lübke, in *Archiv für das Studium der neueren Sprachen*, 166 (1934), p. 50 f. (on *f—h* in Spanish) ; P. Kretschmer, in *Glotta*, XXIII (1934), p. 1 f. ; cp. also Meillet, *Les Langues dans l'Europe nouvelle*, 2nd ed., p. 87 f. ; H. Delacroix, *Le Langage et la Pensée*, 2nd ed., p. 202 f.

[2] These *Studien* contain a number of essays which had appeared in Italian in his *Saggi critici*, Gorizia, 1861 (vol. 1) ; Turin, 1877 (vol. 2).

[3] In Chapter II it will be seen how Vossler takes up these ideas of Ascoli's and makes the fullest possible application of them. Ascoli's attitude with regard to sound-laws will be discussed later in the present chapter. The centenary of Ascoli's birth (1829) brought forth a rich harvest of studies concerning the work of this great scholar ; see the list of articles in *Arch. glott. ital.*, XXV (1931–3), sez. riunite, p. 205 ; see also vols. XXII–XXIII of the same journal (1929), dedicated to Ascoli's memory, in particular, the opening article by P. G. Goidànich, *Graziadio Isaia Ascoli* (reviewed by L. Spitzer in *Indogermanische Forschungen*, L (1932), p. 147 f. See further, Fr. D'Ovidio in *Arch. glott. ital.*, XVII (1910–13), p. 1 f., B. A. Terracini, *ibid.*, XIX (1915), p. 129 f. ; L. Spitzer, *Meisterwerke der romanischen Sprachwissenschaft*, I, Munich, 1929, pp. 351–2, 357. Lastly we must mention Paul Meyer's appreciation in *Romania* XXXVI (1907), p. 326 f. He declares that Ascoli represents a progress in method, as compared with Diez, and that the appearance of the *Archivio* was a revelation.

another distinguished name in our annals, he founded, in 1872, the journal *Romania*.[1] Both of these scholars were philologists rather than linguists, that is to say, they were specially interested in the early history of the French language, and in Old French and Provençal literature. But by their methods, and by the spirit which inspired their researches, they created an atmosphere of the most serious scientific endeavour, and thus did much to help on the progress of Romance linguistics in general. A particular tribute must be paid to the memory of Gaston Paris who, directly or indirectly, was the master of all the later French romanicists. It is sufficient to state that Jules Gilliéron, the founder of linguistic geography, of whom more anon (*v.* Chapter III), sat at his feet, and at his instigation began the task of saving from oblivion the popular vernaculars of France.[2]

★　　★　　★

At that period, the natural sciences had made tremendous headway, and had begun to exercise a powerful influence over every field of intellectual activity. The study of language could not escape this influence, particularly after Darwin had published some of his most significant works. Attaching excessive importance to the phonetic side of language, and considering sounds as natural, that is to say, merely physiological products, analogous to other purely physical phenomena, many linguists came under the almost

Linguistics and the Natural Sciences *(marginal heading)*

---

[1] Now appearing, somewhat irregularly, under the editorship of Mario Roques, and still maintaining its early tradition of giving special attention to the language and literature of mediaeval French and Old Provençal.

[2] The purely linguistic studies of this great teacher have been collected by his pupil, Mario Roques, and published in a volume of 700 pages, entitled, *Mélanges linguistiques*, Paris, 1909. The most interesting of them, particularly with regard to the argument of the present book, is that entitled, *Les parlers de France*, a lecture given to the ' Sociétés savantes ' on May 26th, 1888, which is full of good things concerning research upon the vernaculars. It can be said that there is to be found in certain passages of this lecture the basis of the future work of Gilliéron, whose methods of dialect study, as displayed in the *Petit Atlas phonétique du Valais roman (sud du Rhône)*, Gaston Paris praises and recommends.

In the chapter on linguistic geography (Chap. III) the reader will find Gaston Paris' recommendations concerning the study of dialect. It seems however not out of place to reproduce here the following passage, which shows us the founder of Romance studies in France expressing himself according to the prevailing spirit of his day, laying the strongest emphasis, that is to say, upon phonology : " . . . dresser l'atlas phonétique de la France, non pas d'après des divisions arbitraires et factices, mais dans toute la richesse et la liberté de cet immense épanouissement." (*Op. cit.*, p. 440.)

tyrannical sway of naturalist theories, the more readily as, for them, sounds made up the whole of speech. Thus, in 1863, the Indo-Europeanist August Schleicher published *Die Darwin-ische Theorie*, in which he considers the modifications of sounds to be processes that take place according to fixed, immutable laws, identical with natural laws. For each phonetic change, a sound-law was sought out, valid of course only for a single language, while the exceptions were explained either as being ' sporadic sound shifts ', or as resulting from some special laws applicable only to these exceptions. The influence of these theories was not slow to show itself in the Romance domain, much more, be it said, to the detriment of our science than to its advantage. Yet, one good thing the linguists owe to the naturalists. Through Darwin, particularly, the natural sciences had ceased to be a description of nature and had become a history of nature ; phenomena were not merely presented but also elucidated, and brought within the scope of causality. And so the linguists, imitating the naturalists, gradually changed their discipline into a history of language ; they began, that is to say, to concern themselves with even the minutest facts and to trace and explain their evolution.

Side by side with this naturalistic conception of language, the old point of view, which had guided Diez and others, still per-sisted, namely, that human speech, even though it manifests itself in the material form of sounds, is and remains a purely psychical product. More than this, those who favoured this view, by a reaction which was excessive, though natural in the circumstances, against the new school of thought, laid vigorous stress upon the part played by ' analogy', a most important feature in their linguistic doctrine. They contended that a word often changes under the influence of another word or words with which it has no etymologi-cal relationship. They insisted particularly upon ' exceptions '. If certain ' regular ' phenomena could be explained more or less easily with the help of the so-called sound-laws, it was also necessary to discover an explanation for the cases that transgressed the ' rule ', in a word, for all cases without distinction. This tendency of the anti-naturalist school[1] to resort to ' analogy ', particularly in the

---

[1] Their starting-point is to be sought in the works of W. v. Humboldt (1767–1835), who was the first to conceive language, not as something fixed, created once and for all, but as a living thing, that develops and becomes, as an ἐνέργεια not an ἔργον. Before Humboldt, people asked ' what ' was language ; after him, linguists sought to understand language from the genetic point of view, to know the manner, the ' how ' of its becoming. For further reference to W. v. Humboldt, see the chapter on the school of Vossler *infra* (Chap. II).

case of ' exceptions ', is particularly marked with W. Scherer, in his *Zur Geschichte der deutschen Sprache* (1868).

From the conflict between these two points of view there sprang up a new school, which appeared to reconcile even such sharply opposed adversaries as were the advocates of the **The Neo-** ' physical product ' theory on the one hand, and **grammarians** the ' psychical product ' on the other. This is the famous school of the Neo-grammarians.[1] Their views were first set forth with precision and at some length by Hermann Osthoff and Karl Brugmann in the preface to their *Morphologische Untersuchungen*, I. Teil, Leipzig, 1878, which we may therefore consider as the program or manifesto of the new school. The authors observe, first of all, that hitherto too much attention had been paid to language as such, and too little to man, as if language were a separate and independent entity, whereas the life of language is in and through its users, who thus exercise a determining influence upon its development. Similarly, Osthoff and Brugmann reproached their predecessors and contemporaries with having attached excessive importance to the physical side of language to the almost total neglect of the psychical.[2] In order to understand language, they state further, it is not necessary for us to study comparatively the Indo-European tongues, particularly the ancient ones, as is commonly done, chiefly with a view to arriving at a primitive Indo-European that is a pure fiction, but we should study the present-day living languages and their dialects, for these, inasmuch as they are spoken here and now, afford us the opportunity to observe with ease language in its psychological aspects. All these observations and pronouncements are perfectly correct, and any modern linguist would subscribe to them unreservedly. But the gap between theory and practice is apparently not an easy one to bridge. For Brugmann, for example, who at the beginning of this century had become the world's most distinguished Indo-Europeanist, continued to study almost exclusively, against his own avowed opinions,

---

[1] According to H. Schuchardt (*Brevier*, 2nd edition, p. 452, note to p. 451), the name *Jung-grammatiker* was first applied to them by Fr. Zarncke, who had in mind the well-known literary movement of the first half of the nineteenth century, ' das junge Deutschland '. The humorous suggestion in the term was in Zarncke's intention quite a secondary consideration. The term is discussed further at the end of Chapter III of the present book where we deal with M. Bartoli's ' neo-linguistic ' theories.

[2] Among other proofs in support of their assertions they mention the study entitled *Assimilation und Attraktion, psychologisch beleuchtet*, published by H. Steinthal in *Zeitschrift für Völkerpsychologie*, I (1860), p. 93 f., which had not attracted the notice it deserved.

the ancient or dead languages, and to study them of course comparatively, while the majority of his pupils have done nothing but follow their master's example. But let us glance at the other theoretical utterances of the two neo-grammarians. They are of considerable interest, and constitute, according to some, the strength, to others, the weakness of the new school.

For what reason were the languages of to-day to be given preference in linguistic study ? Because " In all living vernaculars, the phonetic changes peculiar to the dialect are put into operation throughout the whole of the speech material, and are observed by all the members of the speech community, with a consistency far greater than might be expected from our study of the older languages, which are accessible only through written media " (p. ix). It is clear that between these words and part of the observations set forth above there is a contradiction, to be detected indeed in the whole system of the neo-grammarians, namely : on the one hand, they protest against the almost exclusive attention paid to the physical aspects of speech, and demand that adequate attention should be paid to the psychical factors, while on the other, they talk with great conviction about the regularity of phonetic change, which equally implies a mechanical, that is to say physical conception of language, as we shall see shortly. Still, Osthoff and Brugmann do not neglect the principle of analogy, which they consider to be purely psychological in character, and award praise to W. Scherer, whose *Geschichte* (see p. 15 above) they quote, for having explained ' analogically ' a number of forms held by others to be the result of phonetic change. The majority of linguists opposed Scherer, but a few followed him, among them A. Leskien, who, in 1876, two years before the *Morphologische Untersuchungen*, published in Leipzig *Die Declination im Slavisch-Litauischen und Germanischen*, where he formulated, for the first time, the principle that sound-laws admit of no exceptions.[1] At the basis of Leskien's doctrine are to be found, according to Osthoff

---

[1] The source of many of the theories set forth in the *Morphologische Untersuchungen* is to be sought in the works of Scherer and Leskien. This is admitted by the adversaries of the neo-grammarians, and is clear from the remarks of Osthoff and Brugmann concerning Scherer and Leskien, and from a confrontation of their respective ideas. The following quotation from Leskien's book illustrates his point of view ; " In my researches I started from the principle that no case-form transmitted to us is the result of a breach of the phonetic laws which are valid elsewhere. . . . To admit haphazard deviations, impossible to coordinate, is to assert in reality that the object of our science, language, is inaccessible to science." *Cit.* Delacroix, *op. cit.*, p. 159.

and Brugmann (pp. xii, xiii), the following ideas : " Firstly, that language is not something outside and above mankind, with an independent life of its own, but that it has its true existence only in the individual, so that all modifications in the life of a language can only come from the speaking individual ; and, secondly, that man's psychical and physical activity, in appropriating to himself the speech inherited from his forbears, and in reproducing and transforming the sound images admitted to his consciousness, must be essentially the same at all periods."[1]

The guiding principles of the neo-grammarians are, according to our authors, the following : (i) " Every change of sound, in so far as it is a mechanical process, takes place according to *laws which admit of no exception* " (p. xiii) ; that is to say, every individual speaker of a language—questions of dialect apart—and all words in identical conditions, are subjected to certain identical laws ;[2] (ii) " the creation of new speech forms by means of analogy plays a very important part in the life of the *modern* tongues " (*ibid.*). In other words, there are two forces which mould man's speech, a physical or mechanical one, Sound-Change, the other, a psychical one, Analogy. Let us enquire to which of these principles the neo-grammarian theorists gave preference.

Judging by the foregoing discussion, and particularly by the reproaches addressed to linguists who saw nothing in language but its material elements, its sounds, we should expect Osthoff and Brugmann to set analogy above sound-change. But no ! To them, too, the rule, that is to say, the prevailing element in the life of language, is the mechanical, the Lautgesetz, while the psychical, for them, Analogie, is exceptional. The function of the latter is but to explain the fragments that fall from the table of the sound-laws. It is not only the practice of the neo-grammarians that reveals them in contradiction with •themselves, but also certain pronouncements of their two leaders. On page xvii of the same preface to the *Morphologische Untersuchungen*, when attempting a reply to those who contended that analogy could only be called in occasionally as an aid in the search for truth, and

---

[1] In a note to the same pages the authors observe that although it had long been recognized that language exists *within* man, in practice the fact had been neglected. A similar neglect of this fundamental fact could be laid at the door cf a great many neo-grammarians.

[2] Elsewhere Osthoff speaks of " the blind necessity with which the sound-laws of a language operate " ; *cit.* A. Darmesteter, *La vie des mots*, Paris, 1928, p. 9, note.

putting up rather a weak defence in its favour, they express themselves as follows : " The principle to which we set ourselves as strictly as possible to conform, is to have recourse to analogy only when the sound-laws *compel* us. To us also association of forms (i.e. analogy) remains a last resort. The difference is, that we find ourselves confronted with it much earlier and much oftener than others, for the very reason that our attitude towards the sound-laws is scrupulous, and because we are convinced that the boldest assumption of analogical influence, so long as it remains within the bounds of possibility, is always more entitled to carry conviction than an arbitrary elusion of the mechanical laws of sound-change."

When we read this manifesto of the neo-grammarian school we are constrained to feel surprise, not at the opposition it aroused among the older linguists, and among some of the later ones, as we shall see later, but at the enthusiasm with which the new doctrine was welcomed by numerous representative scholars in our field. For a long period this outlook prevailed among linguists, and even to-day there are not wanting those who, although they do not make open profession of the neo-grammarian faith, yet reveal themselves as really of their kind by the method of their researches and their conception of human speech. The great success of the school is due, in the main, to the spirit of the times. We have already shown that intellectual activity in all domains was under the sway of the naturalist spirit, which, thanks to the exceptional progress of the natural sciences, had imposed itself everywhere with comparative ease. Now linguistics is concerned, in the majority of cases, with individual facts of detail, from which it seeks to arrive at general principles ; it proceeds, that is to say, inductively, like the natural sciences proper. This point of resemblance certainly accounts in a large measure for the rise of the neo-grammarian school ; particularly as, at the time, language study was in rather a critical condition. An ever-growing mass of material, collected by an increasing number of scholars, in an ever-increasing number of languages and dialects, had strengthened still further that impression of confusion and disorder which living language of itself produces in the observer, and called for the firm intervention of some law-giver. He was not slow to come and to legislate in the manner shown above. The new doctrine was all the more suitable, in that, on the one hand, it reconciled such conflicting tendencies (*v.* p. 14) and, on the other, gave satisfaction to that need for symmetry and harmony which is part of man's nature. The dual formula, ' sound-law ' and ' analogy ', was too reminiscent of the time-honoured distinction between ' body ' and ' spirit ' not to exercise a peculiar attraction upon the minds of men.

It must, however, be admitted that the theories of the neo-grammarians, their preference for the investigation of living languages, their insistence upon the psychological aspects of language, their contention that language had its sole existence in and through the human beings who gave it utterance, marked a real progress. Further, the belief that the science of language was akin to the natural sciences caused the methods of the latter, the direct observation of facts, to be applied to language study, and from the consequent close and minute scrutiny of linguistic phenomena there ensued, as a first result, a more accurate knowledge of human speech, and, in addition, an imposing succession of important works, both in Indo-European philology proper and in other branches, including that with which we are immediately concerned, Romance linguistics.

Before setting forth the effects of the neo-grammarian doctrines upon our discipline, at least a passing mention must be made of the Germanic scholar Hermann Paul, who, on **Hermann Paul** the evidence of supporters and opponents alike of the neo-grammarian school, contributed so conspicuously to the advancement of linguistics, and directly or indirectly prepared the way for its present progress. It can be said that with this linguist there is little or no trace of that contradiction between theory and practice which we have pointed out in our remarks upon the preface to the *Morphologische Untersuchungen*. To Hermann Paul, the importance of the psychical element in language, for example, was no mere matter of doctrine, but a reality which we encounter in his studies at every step. His principal work, from the theoretical point of view at least, is *Prinzipien der Sprachgeschichte* (first edition, 1880, fifth and last, 1920).[1] Paul's importance is well summed up by W. Streitberg in *Indogermanisches Jahrbuch*, IX (1922–3), p. 280 : " In the seventies of last century Paul was the most resolute of the champions of the new linguistic method prepared by Scherer and brought into effect by Leskien. He was the first to expound systematically, with unparalleled clarity and insight, in his *Prinzipien der Sprachgeschichte*

---

[1] A. Philippide's *Principii de istoria limbii*, Iaşi, 1894, is based, in the main, upon Paul's *Prinzipien*, but with examples drawn from Rumanian.

(1880), the principles of linguistic investigation, and thus to lay the foundations upon which, for some fifty years now, research has been building with signal success." Later (on p. 283), he refers to the *Prinzipien* as Paul's masterpiece and ' the code of laws for linguistics', declaring its guiding principle to be the attempt to demonstrate the importance, in the evolution of language, of the mutual influence exercised by individuals, one upon the other.[1]

Among Romanicists, the neo-grammarian doctrine found numerous adherents, and, through a number of contributory causes, one of its most enthusiastic advocates was soon to take the lead in guiding Romance studies in this direction. We refer to Wilhelm Meyer-Lübke, whose importance in the history of Romance philology during the last forty or fifty years has been quite outstanding. It so happened that he received his training just when the star of the neo-grammarians was in the ascendant. It would have been difficult, if not impossible, for a young man to resist the appeal of the new theories, and all the more difficult for Meyer-Lübke, whose works, from first to last, from his smallest pamphlet to his bulkiest volume, show a mind predisposed to order and routine, enamoured of regularity and discipline, a scholar prone to see in language a more or less rigid phenomenon, where creativeness or fancy has no place, the sober product arising from man's inexorable need of communing with his fellows. Endowed with such characteristics, it was inevitable that Meyer-Lübke should embrace wholeheartedly the doctrine of the neo-grammarians. Corrected at times, as circumstances required, it remained the linguistic creed of his whole life. When, further, we take into account other qualities of the great Viennese professor, namely, his astonishing resourcefulness and unusual gifts of construction when dealing with the most complex linguistic problems, we can readily understand how he won recognition at his first venture in our field of study, and at an early age wielded a profound influence even over men older than himself.

Wilhelm Meyer-Lübke (1861-1936)

An important point to be remembered in this connection is the fact that before completing his thirtieth year Meyer-Lübke began to publish his monumental *Grammatik der romanischen Sprachen* (I.

---

[1] Schuchardt was of the view (cp. *Schuchardt-Brevier*, 2nd ed., pp. 452-3) that Paul's declaration, like those of Osthoff and Brugmann in the *Morphologische Untersuchungen* (see above), in attributing changes in language to the individual, was in flagrant contradiction to the dogma of the invariability of the sound-laws.

Lautlehre, Leipzig, 1890 ; II. *Formenlehre*, 1893 ; III. *Syntax*, 1899 ; IV. *Register*, 1902)[1] which represents a distinct advance upon the similar work by Diez, especially in wealth and variety of material.[2] With this work, and with numerous others : *Italienische Grammatik*, Leipzig, 1890, *Einführung in das Studium der romanischen Sprachwissenschaft*, Heidelberg, 1901 (2nd edition 1909, 3rd 1920),[3] *Historische Grammatik der französischen Sprache* (I. *Laut- und Flexionslehre*, Heidelberg, 1909, 2nd edition 1913 ; II. *Wortbildungslehre*, 1921), *Romanisches etymologisches Wörterbuch*, Heidelberg, 1911–20 (revised edition 1935), *Das Katalanische*, Heidelberg, 1925, etc. etc., not to mention innumerable studies, articles, and reviews in journals, presentation volumes, and the proceedings of learned societies, Meyer-Lübke, until his death in 1936 at the ripe age of seventy-five, continuously kept alert the attention and interest of scholars.[4] We must not forget, finally, the academic activity of this ' prince of Romanicists ' as one of his celebrated disciples, M. Bartoli, has called him. For a period of twenty-five years, and those the best and brightest in life, Meyer-Lübke was a professor in the University of Vienna, where the flower of the youth of that great agglomeration the Austro-Hungarian monarchy gathered to study before the war. This it is that explains the numbers of the master's pupils, some of whom are now, in their turn, leaders of Romance studies in Austria, Germany, Italy, Rumania and elsewhere.

The strength of Meyer-Lübke, for the period between 1885 and 1905, and, be it said, his weakness for the present generation, lies in the very fact that he espoused with such ardour and conviction the neo-grammarian doctrine, applying it regularly and consistently, not only at the beginning of his scientific work, but right to the end. It was characteristic of his attitude with regard to linguistic problems that he should identify himself with the theories of Gröber regarding the reconstruction of Vulgar Latin by a comparison of the Romance languages. Gröber's hypothesis,

[1] A French translation in four volumes, by E. Rabiet (vol. I), and A. and G. Doutrepont, was published, in Paris, from 1890 to 1906.

[2] Cp., from another angle, the remarks of Schuchardt concerning the two grammars in *Schuchardt-Brevier*, p. 99 f.

[3] An improved version in Spanish by Américo Castro (*Introducción a la lingüística románica*) appeared in 1926 in Madrid.

[4] It should be observed that the principal works of Meyer-Lübke are grammars and dictionaries, that is to say, book that no Romanicist can be without—another reason for his universal fame. At the opposite extreme one thinks of the case of Schuchardt who, in his sixty years of intense scientific activity, published only one ' book ' in the strict sense of the word, confining himself for the rest to studies, articles, and reviews. A similar instance is that of J. Jud (*v.* Chap. III).

although devoid of any real foundation, could not fail to appeal by its very ingenuity and its rigorously mathematical construction, to a mind like Meyer-Lübke's with its strongly ' geometrical ' bias. In the *Grundriss der romanischen Philologie*, vol. I, 1st ed., p. 359, Meyer-Lübke attributes to all sources of our knowledge of popular Latin, other than the comparison of the Romance languages themselves, very scanty significance, and maintains with conviction that in cases of conflicting evidence, credence should only be given to the latter.[1] It is true that the passage in question disappeared from the second edition of the *Grundriss ;* but this does not signify that Meyer-Lübke had given up reconstructing Vulgar Latin words and forms with the help of the neo-Latin tongues. His works, even the most recent of them, are full of linguistic material obtained by this method. As an example, we may quote, primarily, his *Romanisches etymologisches Wörterbuch*, where we notice, more clearly than in his other works, a further neo-grammarian characteristic, namely, that of attributing an excessive importance to phonetic factors in framing etymologies, to the detriment of semantic considerations.[2] Similarly, we find in Meyer-Lübke a lack of sympathy for theoretical questions surprising in a linguist of such prolonged experience and such wealth and variety of scholarship. Again we quote the *Romanisches etymologisches Wörterbuch*, whose 1200 odd pages are accompanied by an introduction of a bare eight pages, in which no attempt is made to inform the reader concerning the problems of Romance etymology, which even a neo-grammarian would, we believe, have expected. More than this, in *Das Katalanische*, p. vii, Meyer-Lübke openly declares himself averse to discussions of theory. These are his words : " Thus the reader might expect me to make some more detailed pronouncement as to my reason for believing in dialect boundaries, and in larger and smaller language groups, standing in varying degrees of relationship to their neighbours. I forgo doing so, however, not only because I feel a certain dislike for theoretical discussions, which tend all too readily to become purely academic, but also because the booklet contains so much material relating to the question that I can safely leave it to the reader to form his own judgment."[3]

---

[1] Cp. A. Philippide, *Un specialist romîn la Lipsca*, Iași, 1909, p. 116 f.

[2] The *Französisches etymologisches Wörterbuch*, by E. Gamillscheg (Heidelberg, 1926-9), a pupil of Meyer-Lübke, has similar characteristics.

[3] This passage also attracted the attention of Schuchardt : cp. *Schuchardt-Brevier*, 2nd ed., p. 421.

It is true that Meyer-Lübke did publish an *Einführung in das Studium der romanischen Sprachwissenschaft*, in which questions of principle are discussed, yet here too the historical, that is to say, the neo-grammarian point of view predominates, as is made clear, for example, by such chapter-headings as the following : exterior boundaries and internal repartition of the Romance languages ; the material of Romance philology ; palaeontological problems (pre-literary phonology, morphology, word-formation and syntax, foreign influences, etc.). We are far from the attitude, not only of a Schuchardt, with regard to the multiple and diverse problems with which human language confronts us, but even of a Saussure, who, although in certain respects a neo-grammarian, none the less felt and understood that language is a thing of flux and that therefore our pronouncements upon it must always be more or less of purely relative value.

It must be recognized, however, that Meyer-Lübke did not show himself uniformly hostile to new ideas ; on the contrary, he accepted them, but only so far as the innate propensities of his mind and his strictly historicist and comparativist convictions allowed. Thus we find that in his more recent work he adopted, with his own modifications of course, something of the sociological conception of language, and something, too, of the geographical method, to say nothing of that of ' Word and Thing ' (*vide infra*) which, fitting in as it did with his own linguistic outlook, attracted him right from the outset. It may therefore be said that Meyer-Lübke represented in our day an eclectic point of view on matters appertaining to the linguistic doctrine of our subject, for, just as he covered the whole domain of Romance,[1] not merely by writing his *Grammar* and *Dictionary* but also in the investigation of problems of detail concerning nearly all the Romance languages, so too we can distinguish in his more recent attitude towards human speech

---

[1] With regard to Meyer-Lübke's scientific activity, cp. *Beiheft* 26 to *Zeitschrift für romanische Philologie*, Halle a.S., 1910, p. ix f. ; J. Jud, *W. Meyer-Lübke* in *Neue Züricher Zeitung*, 1911, on the occasion of Meyer-Lübke's fiftieth birthday ; A. Zauner, *Germanisch-romanische Monatsschrift*, IX (1921), p. 1 f. : L. Spitzer, *Meisterwerke der romanischen Sprachwissenschaft*, I, Munich, 1929, p. 353 f., 363 f., and *ibid.*, II, Munich, 1930, p. 346 f. ; and, finally, the obituary notices by Jud in *Vox Romanica*, II (1937), pp. 336–44 ; E. Winkler, *Wörter und Sachen*, XVII (1936), pp. v–viii ; Elise Richter, *Archiv f. d. Stud. der neueren Spr. u. Lit.*, CLXX (1936), p. 196 f. ; E. Gamillscheg, *Zeitschr. f. franz. Spr. u. Lit.*, LX (1936–7), pp. 385–406 ; G. Reichenkron, *Zeitschr. f. neusprachlichen Unterricht*, XXXVI (1937), pp. 32–4.

a variety of elements that belong to one or other of the newer schools of linguistic thought.[1]

We cannot close this section devoted to the neo-grammarian trend in our studies without mentioning the names of a few other scholars who may rightly be apportioned to this school : Adolf Tobler, whose work on French Syntax, *Vermischte Beiträge zur französischen Grammatik*, in five series (2nd ed., Leipzig, 1902–12), is still invaluable and universally appreciated,[2] and whose store of lexicographical material is slowly being published by E. Lommatsch in dictionary form (Tobler-Lommatsch, *Altfranzösisches Wörterbuch*, Berlin, 1925–) ; Hermann Suchier, like Tobler, an untiring editor of Old French texts, with introductions that incorporate the results of minute and extensive study of the Old French dialects (cp. also his geographical treatment of the distribution of French and Provençal features in Gröber's *Grundriss der romanischen Philologie*, 2nd ed., I,[3] pp. 712–840) ; and Antoine Thomas, the famous French etymologist, whose rigid adherence to and strict application of the neo-grammarian conception of the regularity of the sound-laws is visible on every page of his *Essais de philologie française* (1897), *Mélanges d'étymologie française* (1902), and *Nouveaux essais de philologie française* (1904).

★ ★ ★

[1] Linguistic geography, although according to Meyer-Lübke himself it has points of contact with the older school of thought, does not find any particular favour with him. The most recent proof of this is his article in vol. I (1925) of the *Revue de linguistique romane*, p. 22 f. This it is which explains not only the dissatisfaction of Gilliéron himself, who in the preface to one of his studies replied with excessive violence to Meyer-Lübke's review of *L'Abeille* in *Literaturblatt f. germ. u. rom. Phil.*, XL (1919), col. 371 f., but also that of his pupils ; a dissatisfaction which, though rarely explicitly expressed, frequently manifests itself in a significant coolness of attitude towards the work of the Bonn scholar. Witness, for example, Jud's review of the *Einführung* in *Archiv für das Studium der neueren Sprachen und Literaturen*, CXXIV (1910), p. 383 f.

[2] The work of Adolf Tobler in the field of syntax, with its already discernible stylistic bias, finds grace even in the eyes of the modern followers of Vossler (see p. 110). E. Lerch, an old pupil of Tobler's, and now an avowed ' idealist ' in his approach to language, may be said to link up the two schools of thought in his great work *Historische Französische Syntax*, of which the third volume appeared in 1934 at Leipzig. Tobler's *Beiträge* were translated into French, with the title *Mélanges de grammaire française*, by M. Kuttner and L. Sudre, Paris, 1905. There has been a third edition of the first series of the German version, Leipzig, 1921.

[3] Translated into French by P. Monet : *Le français et le provençal*, Paris, 1891.

We have already stated that from the first the neo-grammarians encountered opposition, and of a very serious order. Their first **Opponents of** opponents were the adherents of existing schools, **the Neo-** who studied the various languages without concern **grammarians** for ' laws ', contenting themselves with explaining as far as possible each problem independently as it arose. Among these, the great majority, if not all, were Indo-Europeanists, like the innovators themselves. We shall mention some of the more distinguished among them and their principal theories.[1]

In his work *Zur Kritik der neuesten Sprachforschung*, Leipzig, 1885,[2] G. Curtius directs his offensive chiefly against the doctrine of **Georg Curtius** ' analogy ' to which the neo-grammarians attached excessive importance, mainly, it must be said, in theory, as we have seen above (*v.* p. 17 f.). Analogy, according to Curtius, was not a discovery of the present day, but was as old as the Greeks, and was present to the minds of the founders of linguistic studies in the early nineteenth century. But the predecessors of the neo-grammarians were prudent folk, and sought to avoid overworking a factor which, although *possible* everywhere, is *necessary* nowhere ; witness so many cases where analogy remains without effect, although the conditions are exactly the same as in cases where it applies.[3] Beside analogy there exists a contrary tendency in language that causes numerous forms to remain practically unchanged for centuries. F. Misteli, an admirer of the neo-grammarians, had already affirmed, in *Steinthals Zeitschrift*, IX,

---

[1] The problem of sound-laws and analogy has not ceased to be a matter of concern to scholars, as is proved by the study, *Lautgesetz und Analogie*, by Ed. Hermann, in *Abhandlungen der Gesellschaft der Wissenschaften zu Göttingen*, phil.-hist., Klasse, N.F. 23, 3, Berlin, 1931, and the reviews by L. Bloomfield, *Language*, VIII (1932), p. 220 f. ; A. Meillet, *Bull. Soc. Ling.*, XXXIII (1932), fasc. 3, p. 3 f. ; F. Maurer, *Anzeiger f. deutsches Altertum*, LII, no. 1-2, p. 1 f. ; G. Rohlfs, *Deutsche Literaturzeitung*, LV (1934), col. 2171 f. ; cp. also the article by A. Debrunner, *Lautgesetz und Analogie* in *Indogerm. Forschungen*, LI (1933), p. 269 f. ; Kaspar Rogger, *Vom Wesen des Lautwandels*, Leipzig, 1934 (reviewed by E. Hermann, *Arch. f. d. St. d. n. Spr.*, CLXIX (1936), p. 105 f., and M. Sandmann, *Rev. de filología española*, XXIII (1936), p. 76 f.).

[2] Cp. B. Delbrück, *Die neueste Sprachforschung, Betrachtungen über Curtius' Schrift, Zur Kritik der neuesten Sprachforschung*, 1885.

[3] The chief offender, according to Curtius, was A. Leskien, who claimed that analogy should always have the first say in the explanation of grammatical forms. K. Brugmann was at first of the same opinion (*v. Curtius Studien*, IX, p. 317), although later, in his *Morphologische Untersuchungen* (*v. supra* p. 15 f.), he recanted to some extent. The forerunner of the neo-grammarians himself, W. Scherer, combated such exaggerations in the second edition of his *Zur Geschichte der deutschen Sprache*, as did also J. Schmidt, who was in general favourable to the new school (*v. infra*).

p. 444, that analogical formations are the result of a conflict between the conservative and the levelling tendencies in language, of which now one, now the other, is victorious, for what reasons, and in what way, it is impossible to say. Analogy, Curtius goes on to state, is a chance happening, like a disease. He advises us therefore, first of all, to study ' healthy ' forms, and then those that are ' diseased ' or analogical. Similarly, he protests against the equation, ' analogy=psychology,' showing that the psychical factor comes into play even when forms are preserved unchanged, inasmuch as their preservation is due to memory, which is a faculty of the mind. This identification of the analogical and the psychological was also contested by Misteli, and later by Ascoli, and even Brugmann himself was constrained to admit something of a psychical process even in certain phonetic changes, as for example in cases of assimilation. Consequently, the dualism : sound-change or phonological law (physiological), on the one hand, and analogy (psychical) on the other, falls to the ground. Another weakness of the neo-grammarians, according to Curtius, is that although they consider analogy to be the result of an unconscious impulse of the human mind, they make a conscious factor of it when applying it to any given phenomena, just as the grammarians did in the past. With the help of numerous examples, chosen in the main from Greek and Latin, Curtius discusses the conditions in which we are entitled to have recourse to analogy, enquiring, for example, if a great number of forms are necessary in order for analogy to operate, or again whether it operates more readily in the earlier or later stages of a language's development. Finally, he presents a number of cases that are to be explained neither by sound-laws, nor by analogy, such as haplology (the omission of a syllable that is repeated in the same word), the shortening of proper names and of certain appelatives, the duplication of a group of sounds (the opposite process to haplology), and other phenomena.

In his *Epilog*, p. 154, Curtius strikes home at the very foundation of the neo-grammarian doctrine, when he maintains that " they have endeavoured, through a misguided imitation of the natural sciences, to formulate definite laws for linguistics, and to establish their invariability, only in the domain of phonology," and contends that the forms of a language deserve to be studied quite as thoroughly as the sounds, a fact which the neo-grammarians did not or would not understand.

Still more serious were the objections raised by G. I. Ascoli, who had a great advantage over all the Indo-Europeanists, whether neo-grammarians or not, in that he knew a vast number of living dialects and was able to conduct direct observations upon them. Ascoli fully realized, unlike many linguists even of the present day, that living idioms, from the very fact that they are. there for us to see, are full of instruction with regard to the languages of the past. It is they that can enlighten us concerning the dead languages, and concerning the earlier stages of living languages, whereas the adherents of the historical method imagine that the reverse is the case. Thus dialectology was for Ascoli of the first importance, inasmuch as it was the way of approach to general linguistics. His ideas concerning the problems raised by the neo-grammarians are to be found in *Prima lettera glottologica, Rivista di filologia e d'istruzione classica,* X (1882), p. 1 f., and in *Due recenti lettere glottologiche,*[1] of which the second, entitled *Dei Neogrammatici,* is accompanied by a *Poscritta nuova, Archivio glottologico italiano,* X (1886–8), p. 1 f. Let us follow his main argument.

G. I. Ascoli

Ascoli scoffs at the neo-grammarians for making such a pother about psychology, or analogy. The latter are merely big words, ' paroloni ' ; in reality, various linguistic phenomena had long been explained on similar lines (for example, the diphthong *ie* of *mietiamo* is a levelling due to the diphthong in *mieto*, where it represents a stressed Latin *ĕ*), except that there had been no talk of ' psychical moment ' or ' psychical action '. With regard to ' exceptions ', which the new school refused to recognize, the Italian linguist makes an important declaration : " Neither in my writings nor my teaching do I ever speak of exceptions. I propound and expound that a given sound or group of sounds can have different developments within the same language or the same dialect, and I search for the causes of this difference. Frequently I discover them ; and when I fail to do so, I conclude as follows : It does not appear possible that such and such a sound or group of sounds should have another etymological basis than the one I assign to it, but the reason which determines its special phonology is not yet apparent."[2] Such an affirmation signifies, not only the negation

---

[1] Published earlier in *Miscellanea di filologia e linguistica in memoria di Napoleone Caix e Ugo Angelo Canello,* Firenze, 1886, p. 425 f. All the letters appeared in a German translation entitled *Sprachwissenschaftliche Briefe,* Leipzig, 1887.

[2] *Riv. di fil. e d'istr. class.,* X, p. 7–8, note.

of phonetic laws, as the neo-grammarians understood them, but a recognition of the individual element in sound-change, and of the fact that one and the same sound can change differently in different words, because the conditions in which it is found are not identical. There is but a step between this standpoint and that of Gilliéron, that " each word has its own history." But this step Ascoli was not bold enough to take. On the contrary, he appears to have felt impelled to make a declaration of orthodoxy, to counteract the over-subversive spirit of his previous statement. On page 46 of the same journal, when discussing the possibility of certain sound-changes being due to individual causes, he shows himself disposed to believe that isolated methods of pronunciation can create disturbances in the linguistic tradition of a whole people, and destroy the specific characteristics of regional dialects. But were we to suppose that the effects of such individual action in the past had been considerable, we should have to assume that they had rendered impossible or even inconceivable any natural or rational history of languages, an admission which the realities of speech forbid us to countenance.

What the neo-grammarians call ' analogy', and set in opposition to sound-change, is, says Ascoli, in fact also a modification of sound, either by an analogical extension, e.g. the *ie* of It. *chiedo* to *chiedete*, or an analogical elimination, e.g. O.F. *chevauchier* becoming *chevaucher*, on the analogy of the majority of first conjugation verbs which end in -*er*, or, finally, by an analogical creation, e.g. It. *esco*, *esci*, etc., instead of *escio*, etc., after the model of *cresco*, *cresci*, etc., or *uscita* for *escita* under the influence of *uscio*. The principal novelty of the neo-grammarians, the setting of the phonetic against the psychological, is really quite an old thing in Romance philology, and dates from the time of Diez, who himself made a distinction between ' historical ' forms, i.e. inherited from Latin and ' analogical'. The same Diez, moreover, was conscious of the importance of the ethnical factor in linguistic evolution, for he notes that Basque has a dislike for the sound *f*, and that therefore the change of initial *f* to *h* in Spanish might be attributed to the ethnical substratum. Inasmuch as our discipline has at its disposal such sure methods for explaining linguistic phenomena, it has no need for the innovations of the neo-grammarians, which are either unrealities or old things under new names. Constantly, Ascoli takes up the defence of the so-called ' old linguists ', to whom he himself claims to belong, against the new school, affirming, *inter alia*, that the former had already achieved what the latter were striving to attain, and that not through anything they owed to their younger rivals, who at bottom were scarcely distinguishable from their predecessors. He insists time and again that the neo-grammarians had brought to light nothing that was new. Thus, on p. 70 of vol. X of the *Archivio*, he writes, in so many words : " Having denied any real originality to the new school, either of principle or of method, we dared to ask ourselves the question whether any reasoned controversy upon the matter of scientific principles was really admissible." And, farther on, p. 70, he states : " Those who usually take the name of neo-grammarians (it is well to state it once again) have two important things to their credit. They have continued with great energy the analytical and reconstructive work of their predecessors or contemporaries, and they have grasped and upheld with unusual vigour a number of sound principles, thereby contributing greatly to their diffusion and observance." In other words, Ascoli praises the neo-grammarians for having developed and propagated the doctrine of their predecessors,[1] though thinking the while that they had created

---

[1] It is here that is to be sought the source of the misunderstanding between the neo-linguists (*v. infra*, Chapter III, pp. 273–278) and the Italian neo-grammarians of to-day, with regard to their attitude towards Ascoli. The former, in the person of M. Bartoli, consider him at every step as their master, inasmuch as, amongst other things, he was an opponent of ' laws ' in relation to language. The latter see in him an illustrious representative of the old school, prior to 1900. (Cp. C. Merlo, *G. I. Ascoli e i cànoni della glottologia*, *Arch. glott. ital.*, XXII–XXIII (1929), p. 587 f. ; and P. G. Goidànich, *L'Ascoli e i Neogrammatici* and *L'Ascoli e lo Schuchardt, ibid.*, p. 611 f.). As we have seen from Ascoli's own utterances, something can be said for both points of view, seeing that Ascoli's attitude towards the neo-grammarians was not trenchant, and that he considers them, at bottom, very like the representatives of the earlier school ; he commends them in so far as they were like the latter and opposes them where he thinks they go astray. It would seem however just as unjustifiable to make of Ascoli a kind of premature neo-linguist, as to classify him as a neo-grammarian. Against the latter opinion, we have the fact that Ascoli showed himself delighted with Schuchardt's criticisms (*v. infra*) which he declares to have left an ' indelible mark ' (cp. the *Poscritta*, quoted above). Still more significant is the following detail from the second letter, entitled *Dei Neogrammatici*. Ascoli begins the discussion by referring to the following statement by K. Brugmann in *Zum heutigen Stand der Sprachwissenschaft*, Strasburg, 1885, p. 125 : " I personally have always considered the newer attitude as the natural and logical outcome of earlier works, and this conviction has grown stronger with me yearly." The Italian rejoices in this declaration " coming from, so to speak, the opposite camp," and hopes that Brugmann's companion in arms, H. Osthoff, will do likewise. Clearly, Ascoli considers the two champions of the neo-grammarians as his adversaries, and himself as a member of the older school. We may compare also the views expressed in *Schuchardt-Brevier*, 2nd ed., p. 451–2, note, which show that the disagreement among Italian scholars with regard to Ascoli is natural. Schuchardt declares that the method of the neo-grammarians existed before they themselves came upon the scene, and further, that Brugmann and others later gave up certain of their exaggerated ideas, so that the distinction between the neo-grammarians and the older linguists grew less marked as time went on.

something new. He intervened in the controversy, prompted by a desire to put matters into correct focus, blaming as he did the excessive importance they attached to their ' discoveries ', and the errors into which they were led by their self-glorification, and which have left such unpleasant memories.

In his *Poscritta* (*ibid.*, p. 73 ff.), Ascoli adds a number of supplementary details to the ideas propounded in the ' letters '. He remarks, for example, that one and the same phonetic change can take place in several languages, frequently of different origins, inasmuch as the change in question can be brought about everywhere, almost instantaneously, through ethnical causes or for other reasons. Nevertheless, there are cases of sound-changes which, although instantaneous and general, yet present fluctuations, or rather gradations in intensity in different areas ; thus the Vulgar Latin close *u* becomes [y] in Gaul, Northern Italy and Rhetia, but goes to *i* in the Suprasilvan dialect. Such variations may also arise from the fact that the prototype of a given set of sounds may have changed at different times, and consequently in different ways, in examples which in other respects are in identical or almost identical conditions ; thus, to Classical Latin *tl* there corresponds a Vulgar Latin *cl*, which, in its turn, is found in a variety of forms in all the Romance languages, although in certain Rheto-Romance dialects we encounter the opposite phenomenon, *cl>tl*, and similarly, *gl>dl*. But the causes by which a phonetic change can undergo variations as between one dialect and another, or between one word and another, are manifold, viz. stress, the nature of preceding or following sounds, syntactical grouping (' syntactical phonetics '), the influence of neighbouring dialects, and the like.[1]

Among the other Indo-Europeanists who combated the neo-grammarians a passing mention should be made of A. Bezzen-

---

[1] In connection with Ascoli's views two further quotations may be made, which show him again in rather a hostile attitude to the neo-grammarians. On p. 10 of the *Kritische Studien zur Sprachwissenschaft* mentioned above, we read : " In the life of language, as in that of every natural organism, such a rigid and constant uniformity is in every respect a Utopia." The second is still more conclusive : " I would never dream of contesting the principle that in a given language a fundamental sound or group of sounds must give directly the same result in all examples in which it is under the same conditions. *But it is not always easy to be clear whether the realities of language give us a true identity of conditions or not.*" (Quoted by B. A. Terracini in *Atti della Società Italiana per il progresso delle scienze*, XVIII Riunione, Firenze, settembre, 1929 ; Pavia, 1929, p. 7 of offprint). It would seem that the words italicized practically deny the conditions under which, theoretically, the laws of sound-change can operate, which amounts to a denial of these sound-laws themselves.

berger, for having brought forward, in *Göttingische gelehrte Anzeigen*, 1879, p. 641 f., an argument which, as we shall see later, is of the greatest importance, namely, that it frequently happens that a phonetic change takes place with one or more individuals, and that from these it may spread to others, and thus become general. The spread of the phenomenon from its individual source depends upon a variety of circumstances, which the author seeks to illustrate by examples drawn from a number of languages.

But the most determined adversary of the neo-grammarians was the Romanicist Hugo Schuchardt. It is not a mere coincidence that the most bitter opposition came from **Hugo Schuchardt** a representative of our own discipline. We have already seen (*v.* p. 5) that the Romanicists find themselves in an exceptionally favourable position, not only by comparison with the Indo-Europeanists, but also with Germanicists, Slavonic philologists, and others. Not only are they concerned with living languages, but they have the unique advantage of knowing thoroughly the language from which these living languages have sprung. It follows, in theory at least, that the Romanicist is qualified to discuss and to solve with greater competence questions of general linguistics of the type raised by the neo-grammarians. And, indeed, they have shown themselves superior to their colleagues in other fields ; if not at first, for reasons set forth above (p. 4 f.), at all events in the last twenty or twenty-five years. To-day our discipline is the leader of its fellows, and Schuchardt's desire (*v. Schuchardt-Brevier*, 2nd ed., p. 320) that the study of the Romance languages should serve as a model for kindred studies may be said to have been fully realized.

Not long after the publication of what we have called the manifesto of the neo-grammarians, namely, the preface to Osthoff and Brugmann's *Morphologische Untersuchungen*, appeared Schuchardt's *Über die Lautgesetze*, with its very eloquent sub-title *Gegen die Junggrammatiker* (Berlin, 1885).[1] The arguments brought forward in this brochure against the new doctrine are both theoretical and practical, the theoretical contentions being backed up with linguistic facts. Schuchardt contests first of all the notion of ' law ' as conceived by the neo-grammarians, pointing out at the same time that the neo-grammarians themselves might well have been more explicit concerning the exact nature of their phonetic

---

[1] Reprinted in *Hugo Schuchardt-Brevier*, 1st ed., p. 43 f., 2nd ed., p. 51 f.

laws. In the life of languages there can be no question, he says, of blind laws as in nature, for the norms of language, unlike those of nature, do not apply universally and absolutely. Further, the relativity of the so-called sound-laws is conditioned, and in no simple fashion, both in time and in space : in the same period of time, and over the same area, the same phonetic ' law ' does not present the same extension, in a series of examples of the same type. Their extension is unconstant and fortuitous.

Another question, closely related to the foregoing, is that of dialects. Schuchardt enquires " What is dialect ? "—the neo-grammarians having used the term in formulating their theories—and shows that it is an abstract notion, with no real existence. Within the same linguistic community, or dialect, we encounter innumerable individual forms of speech, that vary according to sex, age, temperament, culture, and the like. And these individual speeches influence each other reciprocally, without, however, eliminating or losing completely their peculiar characteristics. Here, too, fashion plays an irresistible part ; the manner of speech of outstanding individuals is continually imitated, and this inevitably results in a modification of the language and in a mingling of forms of speech that would appear from the outset to exclude any attempt at law-making in such a domain.[1] Schuchardt pays considerable attention to language mixture, a phenomenon to which, at a later date, he frequently turned with the most lively interest, and which, for him, included not only the blending that comes of race mixture, as, for example, that of the native peoples with the Roman colonists in Iberia or Gaul, but also that which takes place even in the most homogeneous speech communities, by the movement of individuals of the same stock from one area to another, or from one social category to another, or merely by imitation in the manner described above.

[1] An excellent example of direct observation, extending over a considerable period of time, of the influence of particular persons in changing the speech of a community is given by A. Duraffour in *Bulletin de la Société de linguistique de Paris*, XXVII, fasc. I, p. 68 f.

Schuchardt had already contended as early as 1870, before there was any talk of the neo-grammarians, that the division into languages and particularly into dialects and sub-dialects was more or less artificial. This was in his *Leipziger Probevorlesung*, ' *Über die Klassifikation der romanischen Mundarten* ', of which he deferred publication for 30 years, as if waiting till later research should confirm conclusions which he had reached chiefly by intuition (*v. Schuchardt-Brevier*, 2nd ed., p. 166 f.). It was suggested above that to admit sound-laws presupposes an acceptance of the existence of dialects ; inasmuch as the boundaries of dialectal areas are fixed by means of certain phonetic and, of course, other features, peculiar to them. Schuchardt also discusses this question in *op. cit.*, 2nd ed., p. 91 f.

With similar vigour Schuchardt opposes the notion of ' linguistic periods ', which the neo-grammarians had availed themselves of to affirm that during one and the same phase in the life of a language, sound-laws admitted of no exceptions. Just as there are no fixed boundaries between different vernaculars, so the chronological limits between the successive periods of a language are purely fictions of our minds ; the transition from one to another is imperceptible, like the transition from one dialect to another, and we can no more say when one period of a language begins or ends than we can point out with accuracy the frontiers between one dialect and another. Further, the neo-grammarians spoke of ' identical phonetic conditions ', as being necessary to enable the sound-laws to operate without exceptions. But Schuchardt maintains that such identity is impossible inasmuch as each word has its own peculiar environment, even when it would appear to us to be similar to other words which contain the same sounds.[1] In phonetic change, frequency of use of the linguistic material plays a great part ; a word in constant use is exposed to more numerous and more fundamental modifications than one which occurs only at rare intervals in our speech ; but again, a sound-change introduced from outside may leave untouched the words we use most frequently.

At the end of the discussion Schuchardt gives his own views concerning the problem raised by the neo-grammarians. In view of his complete awareness to the complexity and diversity of linguistic phenomena, we are not surprised to find that his attitude is undogmatic and non-committal. Schuchardt does not maintain that the so-called laws of sound-change admit of exceptions, but affirms that there are sporadic changes of sound, and even that every change of sound, in a certain sense, is sporadic, that is to say individual. If we must talk of laws without exceptions, that, he maintains, is the only one. The dogma of the invariability of the laws of sound-change has its source in the linguistic doctrine of the predecessors of the neo-grammarians, who considered language as an entity apart, extraneous to man. It has its origins in the mysticism of the romantics, but received a strong dash of naturalism at the hands of A. Schleicher, who applied the theories of Darwin to linguistic studies (cf. *supra*, p. 14). He has great praise for H. Paul, who, although a neo-grammarian, gave proof in his *Prinzipien*

[1] How close we are here, with this affirmation of Schuchardt's, to the dictum of Gilliéron : " Each word has its own history " ! (*v. infra*, Chap. III.)

der Sprachgeschichte of deep penetration and great understanding of the true nature of language. Finally, Schuchardt pleads for a unity of method in all branches of linguistic study, and protests against those who would set a gulf between, for example, Indo-Germanic and Romanic, or who are only interested in languages related to the language or languages which they themselves study. Human speech is everywhere the same, and between one language and another there are always points of resemblance, so that to study one is a step towards understanding others.[1]

★   ★   ★

The opposition to the neo-grammarians which we have very incompletely outlined above did not have immediate results. It could not check the enthusiasm of the majority of linguists for the new doctrine, which, in view of the circumstances under which it arose, could not fail to be extremely attractive. It was only after a long period of struggle, and particularly after much research upon dialects, conducted upon the spot, and bringing in a rich store of material, that the ideas sprung from the intuitive genius of a Schuchardt could gain ground and finally shake the convictions of the neo-grammarians.[2] In some of their replies, however, even from the outset, there are signs of a partial yielding of ground in certain adjustments and definitions they are constrained to give to their doctrines. Some details of these may be mentioned.

[1] Schuchardt's treatment of the question of sound-laws is most comprehensive in the work analysed above. He reverted to the matter more than once as can be seen from the bibliography given in *Schuchardt-Brevier*, p. 79 f. (2nd ed., p. 87 f.).

[2] It is an interesting sidelight upon the prevailing atmosphere to find the philosophers of the time taking part in the discussion upon sound-laws. Thus L. Tobler, in *Vierteljahrsschrift für wissenschaftliche Philosophie*, III (1879), p. 30 f., maintains, in opposition to the neo-grammarians, that what the latter call sound-laws are essentially different from natural laws, e.g., of physics or chemistry. Linguistic norms are of value, inasmuch as they put a check to arbitrary and subjective methods, but they should not be so construed as to mechanize our conception of language. In reality, phonetic laws, considered as of general application, and invariable, are merely recordings of facts, and give no information whatever either upon the cause or even upon the nature of the respective phenomena. The latter observation, together with the admission of the need for certain rules in the study of language, is of exceptional importance. We shall see later that a linguist of the calibre of A. Meillet, and many who follow him, have a standpoint similar to that of L. Tobler.

In the second edition of his *Zur Geschichte der deutschen Sprache* (1878), W. Scherer, the precursor of the neo-grammarians, states expressly that " the laws of sound-change are not true laws but merely empirical ". Further, H. Paul, after having previously spoken of the ' absolute necessity ' inherent in the sound-laws, and having compared or rather likened them to the laws of physics or chemistry, admits the contention of the philosopher L. Tobler (*v.* note 2, above) and writes in his *Prinzipien* that the laws of sound-change are not natural laws. Finally, J. Schmidt, who, in general, had accepted the theories of the neo-grammarians, states in the *Zeitschrift für vergleichende Sprachforschung*, XXV (1884), p. 134, that the existence of phonetic laws which do not admit of a single exception, that is to say, which have no exceptions beyond such as can be completely explained away, is an occurrence of the very rarest order. In the following volume of the journal, on p. 371, the same J. Schmidt observes that, in addition to the phonetic laws known to us, there are others which operate upon language but escape our notice.[1] In other words, the neo-grammarians themselves were constrained to curtail much of the importance they had at first attributed to the laws of sound-change, and to consider them chiefly, at least in theory, as a practical device, a kind of indispensable guide, enabling us to keep under control the enormous mass of linguistic material to be investigated, and to introduce some sort of order into the medley of such intricate and diverse phenomena.

A further limitation to the incidence of the laws of sound-change is implied in their admission that in every type of human language there are survivals of earlier linguistic states, which have been transmitted from one generation to another, and have evaded, so to speak, the sound-laws. This adjustment of their doctrine signifies a further reduction of the principal dogma of the neo-grammarians to proportions more nearly in harmony with the realities of language.

★

---

[1] Cp. the remark in *Schuchardt-Brevier*, 2nd ed., p. 452, note, that Leskien, Brugmann and the rest " dressed up the sound-laws in less pretentious attire, and cut out the expression ' with no exceptions '."

But the heaviest blow was to come from elsewhere, although, indirectly, it owed its power to the founders of the new school themselves. We have seen that Osthoff and Brug-

Dialect Studies

mann insisted upon the need for studying languages and dialects spoken at the present day, as our only means of securing enlightenment, by direct observation, upon the functioning of that complex organism we call human speech. Their wish began to be realized towards the end of the last century. It is true that the popular vernaculars had already received attention at the hands of a number of men who, by a kind of echo of democratic romanticism, had been attracted by life in all its manifestations, and particularly by the speech of the anonymous masses. But the majority of these had lacked the necessary training, and their work could not be taken seriously. Dialectology as a scientific study begins, we may say, with Ascoli. His numerous disciples set to work with enthusiasm, and soon the Italian dialects, which had already received much more attention and were more widely known than those of other regions, loomed very large in the minds of linguists, both in their home land and abroad. Yet even Ascoli's pupils failed to detect the facts of greatest interest with regard to those problems of general linguistics raised by the neo-grammarians. Their observations lacked minuteness and, consequently, accuracy, and they had not acquired the habit of sharing for a certain length of time the life of the people of the country-side. Moreover, the science of phonetics had not yet reached that state of perfection indispensable for dialect research, whose most difficult and delicate problems were and still remain in the domain of sound. It was a considerable time before these deficiencies, and others not so serious, could be made good. And it must be admitted that the progress in this direction has been due, for the major part, to the movement initiated by the neo-grammarians. In particular, their very exaggeration of the material, physical side of language gave an extraordinary impulse to phonology, i.e. the historical study of sounds, and to phonetics, their descriptive study, and thus facilitated to a remarkable degree the scientific investigation of dialect.

Circumstances willed it that the change should come about, not in Italy, the home of dialect study, but in France and Switzerland,

Abbé Rousselot

where a number of works upon the popular vernaculars had been published intermittently since the beginning of the nineteenth century. The first piece of really valuable and important dialect research is that of Abbé P.-J. Rousselot, entitled *Modifications phonétiques du langage étudiées dans le patois d'une famille de Cellefrouin*[1] *(Charente)*, and dated 1891. The exceptional importance of this work, from the theoretical point of view, is the author's conclusion that human speech lacks uniformity even within a single family, the members of which are all found to differ in their speech according to age, sex, occupation, and the like. Moreover, the linguistic material collected by Rousselot was so rich and so reliable that the argument was no longer in the air, as heretofore, but solidly substantiated. It followed that if unity of speech did not exist in that most restricted of human communities, the family, whose members are in daily association and can thus influence one another with ease, it was all the less likely to exist in the increasingly wider communities of the village, the commune, the district, and the province.

Rousselot's work represents the first serious blow inflicted upon the school of the neo-grammarians, a blow that came not from theorists but from facts. The attacks soon became more numerous and more insistent. We shall only mention here two studies by L. Gauchat, the well-known Zürich scholar, which may be said to continue the work of the French phonetician, inasmuch as they follow the same direction and lead to almost identical results. The first is an article with the very significant title *Gibt es Mundartgrenzen?* which appeared in the *Archiv für das Studium der neueren Sprachen und Literaturen*, CXI (1903), p. 305 f. On the basis of material collected in the field, Gauchat comes to the conclusion that the realities of speech are much more

Louis Gauchat

---

[1] Cellefrouin is a locality in the Charente department, where the author's native village was also situated. Rousselot collected his material not by using a questionnaire, as was done later by the linguistic geographers (see Chap. III), but by conversing with the villagers, with whose dialect he was perfectly familiar. Like the linguistic geographers, he gives us all manner of information concerning his ' subjects ' or informants.

It should be stated that Rousselot had begun to busy himself with French dialects some ten or twelve years previously. In 1887 he founded, in conjunction with Jules Gilliéron, the *Revue des patois gallo-romans*. Gilliéron, the future founder of linguistic geography, had published as early as 1880 his *Patois de la commune de Vionnaz* (Bas-Valais), with a map, and in 1881 a *Petit Atlas phonétique du Valais roman (sud du Rhône)*, inspired by his master and fellow-countryman, the Swiss J. Cornu, whose *Philologie du Bagnard* appeared in *Romania*, VI (1887), p. 369 f. In 1887 another Frenchman, L. Clédat, founded the *Revue des patois*, which two years later took the name of *Revue de philologie française et provençale*, and was also devoted in the main to dialect study. It became extinct in 1934. Rousselot, who died in 1924, at the age of 78, continued to work in the field of dialect, and particularly of phonetics, until his death. It is to him that we owe the foundation of Experimental Phonetics, which has proved such a valuable aid to linguistic study (cp. *Principes de phonétique expérimentale*, Paris, 1897–1908, 2nd ed., 1923). A chair in the subject, and a laboratory, were founded, and entrusted to Rousselot, at the Collège de France.

complicated than a merely theoretical knowledge would lead us to believe. Dialectal differences between one area and another exist, but in some cases they are sharply marked, in others they are gradual. The boundaries between them are not always determined by topography ; hilly country, for example, may constitute a linguistic frontier, or again it may form no kind of barrier to linguistic change ; similarly, it may be frequently observed that the more important topographical features do not form a boundary between one vernacular and another, while lesser features do. The determining factors would appear to be the political and administrative boundaries. Gauchat quotes the case of two villages, quite close to each other, and joined by an easy road, which showed remarkable differences of speech. On investigation, the cause of this curious state of affairs was found to be a matter of local history ; each of these communities had belonged to a different political unit, and consequently had had no communication with the other, with the result that their respective languages had become increasingly differentiated. In a word, matters are far from being as simple and straightforward as we are prone to think them.

Gauchat's second article, concerned, like the first, with speech conditions in the Franco-Provençal-speaking area of the canton of Fribourg, is entitled *L'unité phonétique dans le patois d'une commune*—Charmey, a large village in the east of the Gruyère valley—and is to be found in *Aus romanischen Sprachen und Literaturen, Festgabe für Heinrich Morf*, Halle a.S., 1905, p. 174 f. The conclusions arrived at with regard to the village are identical to those of Rousselot with regard to the family : speech differs according to age, sex, social standing, occupation, and the like. The following observations of detail are of particular interest : (i) Immigrants from other areas never completely acquire the speech of their new home, but their children are indistinguishable in speech from the children of natives ; (ii) variations and evolutions of sound can be observed according to age, though some families are more conservative in speech than others ; (iii) the beginnings of phonetic modifications are found among the adults, and not among the children, as P. Passy and Rousselot had maintained ; (iv) these changes are not to be explained solely by the transmission of speech from one generation to another, for it is words, rather than persons, that play the most important part in occasioning speech-change. Gauchat is convinced that over a period of thirty years it is possible to detect and examine such change, in successive generations, both in pronunciation, syntax, and vocabulary, and comes to the general conclusion, not unlike that of Rousselot, that a close and minute scrutiny of the speech of a given community proves it to be lacking in unity as a whole, but that unity exists in the speech of individuals belonging to the same generation.[1]

We reserve a fuller treatment of the work of Romance scholars in the field of dialect for the chapter on linguistic geography, confining ourselves at this stage to the above mention of works which, coming as they did before Gilliéron's geographical studies, seriously shook the neo-grammarian positions and prepared the way for what was to provide the *coup de grâce*.[2]

★

To sum up, we have seen that from the date of appearance of the neo-grammarian school this problem formed the main subject of linguistic controversy. It is indeed of some considerable importance, not only to Romance studies, but to the whole of linguistics. For, inasmuch as the object of scientific research is to discover the laws determining the phenomena investigated, the question of linguistic laws in general, and sound-laws in particular, raises in fact the whole problem of the extent to which the study of human language can be called a true science. It is this that explains why the last fifty years have seen such a vast number of studies, of every size and quality, devoted to this question, which has not yet received a solution satisfactory to all linguists or even to the majority of them. It is outside the scope and purpose of

Present Position of the Sound-laws Problem

---

[1] Cp., for a morphological approach to the problem, A. Terracher, *Les aires morphologiques dans les parlers populaires du nord-ouest de l'Angoumois*, Paris, 1914 ; and for a lexicographical one, W. Wenzel, *Wortatlas des Kreises Wetzlar und der umliegenden Gebiete*, in F. Wrede's series, *Deutsche Dialektgeographie*, Marburg, 1930. Wenzel concludes, on a basis of some 500 notions studied, that, in general, there are no word boundaries, save that from time to time certain terms group themselves in a manner corresponding usually to the configuration of territorial units (cf. the review by A. Scheiner in *Siebenbürgische Vierteljahrsschrift*, LVI (1933), p. 292 f.).

[2] Reference may be fittingly made at this point to two periodicals, although of somewhat later date, viz. the *Revue de dialectologie romane*, and the *Bulletin de dialectologie romane*, both of them organs of an international society with its centre in Brussels. They ran from 1909 till 1914. After the war, in 1925, a *Société de linguistique romane* was founded with similar aims, with its organ the *Revue de linguistique romane*, to which we will return later.

this work to set forth in detail half a century's opinions upon this very ticklish matter, nor indeed are we convinced that such an array of conflicting views would bring clarity to a discussion that would appear, at times, to become more and more beclouded the more it is pursued. We shall confine ourselves therefore to giving a short summary of the views of a number of representative scholars whose ideas seem to us to be sound, not excluding those outside the field of Romance studies, inasmuch as it is undesirable, as Schuchardt taught, and indeed impossible, to set a barrier between one branch of linguistic study and another.

The soundest views upon this matter would appear to be those of the French linguists of the school of F. de Saussure (*v.* Chap. IV), **M. Grammont** namely, M. Grammont, A. Meillet, and J. Vendryes. Of these, the first has made sounds his special study, but he has not confined himself to a certain group or family of languages, nor are his methods historical or comparative, nor again can he be called an experimental phonetician in the strict sense. With a rich and varied equipment both on the experimental and the historical side, Grammont concerns himself with the sounds of human language in general, and the modifications which they undergo, or may undergo, in various idioms throughout the world. He is particularly interested in the changes of sound which, irrespective of limits of time and place, take shape when and wherever certain similar conditions are to be found. " We seem to forget ", he says in words reminiscent of those of Schuchardt, " that language is a human phenomenon, that all men who dwell upon the surface of the earth are, organically, roughly the same, and that under the influence of similar causes they may impart to their language, which is one of the functions of their organism, exactly the same modifications, in any place whatever, in the antipodes even, and entirely independently " (*Revue des langues romanes*, XLII (1911), p. 323 ; *cit.* Al. Rosetti, *Grai și suflet*, II (1925-6), p. 179, note). Thus Grammont has succeeded in creating a system of general phonetics applicable to human speech as a whole, which he has propounded in numerous *Notes de phonétique générale* published in the *Mémoires de la Société de linguistique de Paris*, XIX (1914-16), p. 245 f., XX (1916-18), p. 213 f. ; *Bulletin de la Soc. de ling. de Paris*, XXIV (1923-4), p. 1 f., and elsewhere, and which have been for the most part incorporated in his recent *Traité de phonétique*, Paris, 1933.

Grammont draws a distinction between phonetic laws and

phonetic formulae. The former are general tendencies present in every language, such as dissimilation, assimilation, metathesis, etc. ; the latter are the application of general tendencies to a particular language or a particular case. We are reminded here of F. de Saussure's distinction between ' la langue ' and ' la parole '.[1] The phonetic laws belong to ' language ', they exist, that is to say, solely in the mind, which is the abode of that system of sounds, forms, etc., which compose a language, or, in other words, their existence is latent, and they await the occasion to become manifest ; the phonetic formulae, on the other hand, appertain to ' speech ', and have consequently a real existence, but unlike the phonetic laws, which are the same everywhere, they may vary from one idiom to another, and in particular cases.[2]

An attitude closely resembling that of Grammont is taken up by J. Vendryes in his *Réflexions sur les lois phonétiques* (*Mélanges linguistiques offerts à M. Antoine Meillet*, Paris, 1902,

J. Vendryes p. 115 f.). After alluding to the possibility that a sound-change may have its origin with the individual, and spread from him to the community, provided of course that it is in harmony with the system of articulation prevailing in the language at the time, the author speaks of phonetic ' tendencies '. The so-called ' sound-law ' is nothing more than the enunciation of a certain modification of sound which, for its part, is a particular fact in the development of certain phonetic tendencies at a particular time. He alleges (p. 122) that the instances he quotes show clearly that the notion of ' phonetic tendencies ' is theoretically more accurate, and more fruitful in practice, than that of ' phonetic laws '. There follows a classification of these ' tendencies ' into (*a*) General and External, viz. those which are not confined to a particular language, but are met with everywhere and appear to be natural to human kind, such as, for example, onomatopœia, dissimilation, metathesis, etc., all of which have their source in the psyche of the speaker ; and (*b*) Particular and Internal, i.e., those which are peculiar to a given language and have nothing psychological about them, inasmuch as they depend solely upon

---

[1] Cf. *Traité de phonétique*, pp. 166–179.

[2] The first scholar to speak of ' phonetic tendencies ' as understood by Grammont appears to have been Paul Passy, in his *Etude sur les changements phonétiques et leurs caractères généraux*, Paris, 1890, where he dwells upon certain impulsions within man as being the source of sound changes. Hermann Paul, and other neogrammarians after him, have also admitted the existence of some internal psychological impulse in accounting for sound change, but only in the case of exceptions to the sound-laws.

the physiological factors of speech articulation. The latter tendencies are as numerous as the several individuals of any speech community, but in practice differences are levelled out by the interaction of the individuals one upon the other, so that each social group has tendencies that are peculiar to itself. The linguist must first concern himself with the results of this type of ' tendencies ', that is to say the phonetic modifications brought about by them ; after analysing the physiological features of the changes he will then proceed to determine the ' tendency ' to which they owe their origin.[1]

Still more cautious was the attitude of Antoine Meillet, who considered the so-called sound-law as merely the expression of a **A. Meillet**   certain correspondence between sounds. When we speak of the fact, let us say, that where we have a short stressed *e* in Latin, we find a diphthong *ie* in Romance, we are not to understand that *ĕ* stands to *ie* in a relation of cause to effect, nor even that *ie* is the necessary successor to *ĕ*, but merely that Romance *ie* corresponds to Latin *ĕ*.   In other words, the sound-law does not express a relation of causality, like a natural law, nor even a relation of succession, like a historical law, but merely a relation of correspondence ; it is but the statement of a connection between one phenomenon of the common language and one phenomenon of the derived languages, or of one phase of a language with an earlier phase, and, although it postulates a regularity of relationship between these successive phenomena or phases, it leaves open the question of the various causes which may have brought about this regularity, and which may differ widely in different cases (cp. *Les méthodes de la linguistique*, in *Revue du mois*, 1910, juillet-décembre, p. 155 f.).

It is clear from the above that the chief of French Indo-Europeanists of recent times considered the sound-laws as merely practical devices, indispensable if we are to study historically and

---

[1] Cp. the observations of the same scholar in *Le Langage*, Paris, 1921, p. 50 f, where, owing to the nature of the work, which has as its sub-title *Introduction linguistique à l'histoire*, the historical point of view is predominant, and where, in the use of the term ' phonetic correspondences ' the influence of Meillet is also revealed.

Vendryes' terminology is also used by G. Millardet, in his *Linguistique et dialectologie romanes*, Montpellier–Paris, 1923, p. 270 f. Like Vendryes, he sees in the ' phonetic tendency ' a hidden force of which the phonetic law is the particular manifestation. The phonetic tendency can have both physiological and psychological causes, interacting one upon the other. It is not every ' tendency ' that succeeds in manifesting itself in the form of a ' law '. For this to take place, a number of favourable circumstances are necessary, which are frequently extremely complicated.

comparatively the sounds of one or more languages in relationship with those of an earlier language. To this extent, he is ready to defend the sound-laws anywhere and everywhere occasion offers. Thus, to take an instance ready to hand, in his review of certain studies by P. G. Goidànich (see below), in the *Bulletin de la Société de linguistique de Paris*, XXVI (1925), fasc. 3, p. 25, Meillet praises the Italian scholar for upholding the sound-laws, because, he goes on to say, " the principle of the regularity of ' phonetic correspondences ' remains fundamental in linguistics." Elsewhere, however, speaking of the dispute between supporters and opponents of phonetic laws, Meillet asserts that both parties are right, or, if you will, both are wrong, inasmuch as the latter are considering ' la parole ', the former ' la langue '.[1]

A point of view somewhat akin to that of the French philologists is represented by S. Puşcariu, who, in *Despre legile fonologice*, *Dacoromania*, II (1921–2), p. 19 f., draws a dis-
S. Puşcariu tinction between ' phonetic laws ' and ' phonological laws '. The former are more or less unconscious modifications of sounds, which appear in one or several individuals, either once or recurrently ; the latter are usual and general changes, which appear regularly and constantly and affect all similar cases alike, either in the speech of one individual or, more especially, in that of one geographical or social unit. The phonological laws have their source in the phonetic laws ; when departures from the traditional pronunciation have the support of certain psychological factors—for man is a conscious being who compares his own speech with that of his fellows, and endeavours to associate himself with them by a constant relationship—these modifications tend to become general and thus are transformed from phonetic into phonological laws.[2] Every modification of sounds is of individual origin, and is brought about in general by men whose language

---

[1] " La querelle ne s'apaisera jamais : les partisans de la constance des lois phonétiques envisagent ' la langue ', et leurs adversaires ' la parole '. Ils ne parlent pas de la même chose." (*V. Bull. Soc. Ling.*, XXIX (1929), fasc. 2, p. 16.)

[2] On pages 28–30, Puşcariu explains his terminology, which is different from that usually employed. Phonetics, or the physiology of sounds, is concerned with the description of articulated sounds in general, of whatever language. Phonology (and we might say, in a certain sense, historical phonetics also), studies the modifications of sounds within a given language. Consequently, the phonetic laws are met with in several idioms (theoretically, in all of them), and have a purely physiological cause ; the phonological belong, in general, to a single language, and are by nature both physiological, psychological, and sociological. Cp. the article by the same author entitled *Phonetisch und Phonologisch* in *Volkstum und Kultur der Romanen*, III (1930), p. 16 f. Cp. also N. Trubetzkoy, *La phonologie actuelle*, in *Psychologie du langage*, (=*Journal de Psychologie*, 1933), p. 227 f.

sense is strongly developed (or, as Puşcariu puts it, "who have a gift for language"), but only a certain number of these changes become generalized, through the working of the psychological factors mentioned ; the great majority of them disappear and leave no trace. Our author comes to the conclusion therefore that phonological laws exist, that they are not merely a means of avoiding errors in etymology, or of giving precision and assurance to our methods of linguistic research, that they are not mere abstractions or inventions of grammarians, but linguistic realities, formulae present in the mind of speakers, just as 'plural', 'conditional', or 'tense concord' are grammatical terms corresponding to constant relationships which really exist, or have at some given time existed, in the consciousness of the users of a language (pp. 82–3).[1]

More or less similar opinions to those set forth hitherto are to be found in *Schuchardt-Brevier*, 2nd ed., p. 417, Fr. Schürr, *Sprachwissenschaft und Zeitgeist*, Marburg a.L., 1922, p. 39 f., M. Bartoli, *Introduzione alla Neolinguistica*, Genève, 1925, p. 54 f., 93 f., and R. Menéndez Pidal, *Orígenes del español*, I, 2nd ed., Madrid, 1929, p. 559 f.

On page 561 of his *Orígenes* the great Spanish scholar[2] expresses himself as follows : " Clearly, there exists in the development of **R. Menéndez Pidal** each sound tendencies of collective origin, which frequently succeed in transforming themselves into general norms, and in thus becoming regular phonetic laws. But it must be added that such a transformation is not the work of a moment, but of a very long period of time. Those who observe the living language of a locality realize that it

---

[1] Puşcariu's study was reviewed by Ronjat, *Revue des langues romanes*, LXI (1921–2), p. 402 f., who, while praising the author, takes up the defence of the neo-grammarians because of the gain to linguistic studies resulting from the sound-laws. Other reviewers were O. Densusianu, *Grai şi suflet*, I (1923–4), p. 157 f., K. Jaberg, *Literaturblatt f. germ. u. rom. Philologie*, XLV (1924), col. 97 f., Fr. Schürr, *Zeitschrift f. rom. Philologie*, XLVI (1926), p. 291 f., etc. The latter discusses the matter in detail in the form of an article entitled *Lautgesetz oder Lautnorm?* and affirms *inter alia* that no one, or practically no one, now believes that phonetic laws are of the same nature as mechanical laws. For the term 'sound-law' he proposes the term 'sound-norm', i.e. a generalized sound change, to which he attributes a scientific value, not in the naturalist sense, but in the historical sense.

[2] Menéndez Pidal, now far advanced in years, is one of the recognized masters in Romance studies. His enormous activity in philology, literary history and linguistics, his wide influence, and the general admiration in which he is held for his scholarship and breadth of outlook, are well illustrated by the fact that his presentation volume, *Homenaje ofrecido a D. R. M. Pidal*, Madrid, 1925, contained 2,276 pages, from the pens of 135 contributors. The bibliography of the master's works up to 1925 takes up pages 655–674 of the volume. A supplement to this bibliography was brought out in 1931. (Cf. *Zeitschrift f. rom. Phil.*, LIV [1934], p. 326 f.)

takes several generations to make a sound-change effective. Yet their own observations are limited to a moment, and they are obliged to study the various generations simultaneously, old, mature, and young together. This space of time is a mere trifle where the development of a sound-change is concerned ; to give its full fruit, dialect study would need a series of observations conducted repeatedly at sufficiently long intervals in the same locality. An attempt has been made to see in the changing generations the origin of changes in speech ; but the generations do not change at fixed periods but are born and renewed at every hour of the day. Every change in traditional collective activity, whether in language, folk songs, legal customs or what not, has behind it the fact that many *successive* generations have a share in the same innovation, and are persistent in helping it towards realization, despite minor differences in their manner of conceiving it. They build up a new tradition in conflict with the old. Even where we would least expect this continuity, in poetic invention, which is to us such a personal thing, we find proof of this persistence of an innovatory idea over centuries and throughout numerous generations. The latter apply themselves to preserving and developing a certain variant in the character of some poetic hero, or in a description, or in the contamination of two ballads, whose verses they mingle again and again, and in a variety of ways. This continuity is all the more evident in language,[1] because its changes are less subject to the initiative of the individual. A phonetic change is not the exclusive achievement of the three or four generations into which we arbitrarily divide any given population, but is the outcome of a traditional idea or preference which persists throughout many generations of speakers. The duration of a phonetic change is usually extraordinarily long ; it may take centuries, for the reason that the tradition which it has to overcome is the strongest of all, being rooted in the immeasurable daily repetition of the collective act of language. Saussure speaks of the three hundred years taken by a certain linguistic change to become established as a remarkably long period, yet this is short compared to some."

---

[1] J. M. Manly, in his study entitled *From Generation to Generation* (*Jespersen Miscellany*, Copenhagen, 1930, p. 287 f.) finds the reason for this continuity of trend towards a certain linguistic change in the fact that younger children are influenced by children slightly older. It is not a matter of a new generation of speakers arising, so much as of new speakers acquiring the language under the influence of representatives of the most advanced stages of speech ; cp. *Indogermanische Forschungen*, LI (1933), p. 207.

The most vehement supporters of the sound-laws conceived after the fashion of the neo-grammarians are to be found among the Italians. We have, already made mention of C. Merlo, and quoted his article in defence of Ascoli against the attempts of the so-called neo-linguists (*v.* Chap. III) to annex him as a predecessor, and to remove him from the ranks of the neo-grammarians, where Merlo would have him at all costs (p. 29 n.). Merlo's attitude to the question we are considering is still more clearly revealed in his numerous studies upon the Italian vernaculars, and particularly in the bias he gives to the journal *L'Italia dialettale*, published in Pisa from 1924 onwards.

Clemente Merlo

If Merlo has taken little part in theoretical discussions, and shares, as he declares himself in the article mentioned, Meyer-Lübke's avowed dislike for them (cp. p. 22), his fellow-countryman, P. G. Goidànich, on the other hand, professor in the University of Bologna, and co-director of the *Archivio glottologico italiano*, has recently devoted an extensive study to the sound-law problem, entitled, *Le alterazioni fonetiche del linguaggio e le loro cause*, and printed in the *Archivio*,[1] in the section of which he himself is editor, vol. XX (1926), p. 1 ff. Goidànich accepts the existence of sound-laws as understood by the neo-grammarians, blind, mechanical, unconscious laws which he brings into relation with the faculty of hearing, with the organs of speech and with defects of memory. Similarly, and this goes without saying, he contests the theory of the individual origin of phonetic change. And finally, he considers even the changes brought about by analogy to be unconscious phenomena, though even the neo-grammarians had seen in them a psychological and therefore in some degree a conscious element. As an appendix to his article, Goidànich publishes, p. 60 f., a criticism of Gauchat's study, *L'unité phonétique*, etc. (*v. supra*, p. 38 f.), in which he interprets in favour of his own contentions the material examined by Gauchat. His attitude is all the more surprising in view of the fact that at an earlier period we find him taking what is practically the opposite side. In vol. XVII (1910–13), p. 36 f., and vol. XVIII (1914–22), p. 362 f., of the *Archivio*, are to be found two small articles entitled respectively *Le sintesi linguistiche* and *Ancora delle sintesi linguistiche*,

P. G. Goidànich

---

[1] Goidànich's article was reviewed by A. Meillet in *Bull. Soc. Ling.*, XXVI (1925), fasc. 3, p. 25, and, rather severely, by G. Bertoni in *Archivum Romanicum*, IX (1925), p. 492.

in which Goidànich urges that all linguistic phenomena of similar character, at whatever period of the development of a language they occur, should be studied together, as well as corresponding phenomena in other languages ; only so can we hope to understand the true nature of a linguistic fact and discover the ' tendency ' which gives it birth.

Other Italian linguists, although professing a belief in phonetic laws, have a conception of them which is more in harmony with the latest trend of linguistic thought. Thus, G. E. Parodi, in a lecture delivered in 1909, but published in *Nuovi studj medievali*, vol. I (1923-4), p. 263 f., with the title *Questioni teoriche : le leggi fonetiche*, after giving an account of the history of the discussion, formulated his credo as follows : " Our fundamental contention is that the sound-laws exist, though they are in no sense mechanical but purely psychological ". Parodi's successor to the chair of Romance languages in the University of Florence, C. Battisti, comes still closer to what may be termed the modern view in his inaugural address, *Ernesto Giacomo Parodi e la valutazione della legge fonetica*, published in the journal *La Parola*, November, 1925. After discussing the ideas propounded by Parodi in the article mentioned, he concludes : " While asserting that every change or evolution of sound arising from the organic functions is of individual origin, we believe that it is from the community that comes the adoption of such of these changes as are felt intuitively to be in harmony with the peculiar genius of the language."

We would mention finally the views expressed by the Dutch scholar, J. van Ginneken, in an article, *Die Erblichkeit der Lautgesetze*, in *Indogermanische Forschungen*, XLV

J. van Ginneken (1927), p. 1 f.[1] After remarking that before a sound-change becomes established the language goes through a period of transition during which the old form continues to live beside the new, he asks how it is that all departures from the traditional norm do not become generalized, but only a certain number. The reply to this enquiry, he boldly asserts, can come to us, not from psychology, or sociology, but from biology and the study of heredity. The majority of children come into the world with certain identical inborn phonetic tendencies. It is these inborn tendencies that set the path for the linguistic

[1] Cp. also, by the same author, *La biologie de la base d'articulation*, in *Psychologie du langage* (*Journal de Psychologie*, 1933), p. 266 f., and *Atti del III Congresso dei Linguisti*, Florence, 1935, p. 29 f.

innovations to follow. It is clear that we have to do here with a theory not far removed from that of the ' ethnical substratum ' so eloquently championed by Ascoli.[1]

★   ★   ★

From the foregoing pages it is clear that the end of last century and the beginning of the twentieth was a period in which the chief activities of Romance scholars centred around the theories of the neo-grammarian school. Supporters and opponents of these theories fought each other with equal conviction and determination, according to their varying powers and temperament. The main object of attack was the sound-law, conceived by its exponents as analogous to the blind, mechanical laws of nature. But protests, though not so numerous or bitter, were also raised against the whole method of the neo-grammarians, with its strongly historical and comparative bias, a method which, like the sound-law theory with which it is closely related, was also a product of the Indo-European philologists.

Romance Linguistics at the End of the XIXth Century

It is clear that the historical method becomes a necessity when we are concerned with the study of the development of a language over a given period of time. It is equally obvious, further, that we cannot forgo making comparisons between related languages, even when we are specially concerned only with one of them, still less when we are dealing with a family or a group. But there are none the less obvious cases when the historico-comparative method may and must be dispensed with, namely, when the object of study is the present state of a spoken tongue. Here the historical aspect recedes into the background, and comparison, though necessary,

---

[1] According to Goidànich, Rousselot, in the work mentioned above, p. 37, already considered the possibility of an influence of heredity upon phonetic development.

As further material for the study of the sound-laws problem, the reader may consult : O. Jespersen's three articles on the sound-laws, published in 1886, 1904, and 1933 respectively and reprinted in *Linguistica : Selected papers in English, French, and German*, Copenhagen, 1933 ; Ed. Wechssler, *Gibt es Lautgesetze ?* in *Forschungen zur romanischen Philologie, Festgabe für Hermann Suchier*, Halle a.S., 1900, p. 349 f., a critical and historical account of the problem up to 1900 ; E. Herzog, *Streitfragen der romanischen Philologie*, I. *Die Lautgesetzfrage. Zur französischen Lautgeschichte*, Halle a.S., 1904 ; A. Philippide, *Originea Romînilor*, I, Iaşi, 1925, p. 371 f. The latter considers linguistic laws in general, though the sound-laws claim his chief attention.

is applied not with a view to reconstructing some common tongue of which that studied is a variety, nor even in order to establish the greatest possible historical links with kindred speeches, but merely to widen the field of observation, and to achieve a clearer understanding of the nature of living speech, which, in its essentials, is the same everywhere. And to this end, comparison is frequently made with languages belonging to widely different families, for the more different the languages the more fruitful these comparisons become.

The opponents of the neo-grammarians thus concentrated more and more on the observation of living language and the spoken vernaculars, following, in this, the advice of their own adversaries, and achieved results which brought about an entirely new outlook in the whole discipline of Romance and, subsequently, of other linguistic fields. Some of these results we have already briefly outlined. But before giving a complete account of the present state of Romance studies, and of the new atmosphere which pervades them, we must dwell for a moment upon the work of a number of scholars who prepared the ground, and enabled the new tendencies or rather the new spirit—for that is the important matter—to develop. Similarly, it will be necessary to make a passing reference to certain doctrines of current philosophy that have had their influence upon contemporary linguistic thought.

Among the men who have done most to forward the advance of linguistic science there is one who stands out as worthy of our most unstinted respect and admiration. We have already **Hugo Schuchardt** spoken of him when dealing with the opposition to the neo-grammarians, and we shall mention him again in subsequent pages, for if we are to give due attention to all that he has done to change the outlook of linguists, in the course of an unusually long and productive life, we shall be obliged to quote him at every step. The man is Hugo Schuchardt.[1]

---

[1] B. 1842 ; d. 1927. Studied under Diez at Bonn ; privat-dozent at Leipzig, 1870 ; professor at Halle a.S., 1873, at Graz, 1876–1900. Among the numerous appreciations written at his death, giving interesting biographical details as well as comments upon his work, may be mentioned those of : A. Zauner, *Grazer Tagespost*, April 27th, 1927 ; K. v. Ettmayer, *Germanisch-romanische Monatsschrift*, XV (1927), p. 241 f. ; E. Herzog, *Revista filologică*, I (1927), p. 339 f. ; Iorgu Iordan, *Arhiva*, XXXIV (1927), p. 209 f. ; Bruno Migliorini, *La Cultura*, VI (1926–7), p. 305 f. ; R. Riegler, *Archivum Romanicum*, XI (1927), p. 270 f. ; S. Puşcariu, *Dacoromania*, V (1927–8), p. 880 f. ; M. Friedwagner, *Zeitschrift f. rom. Phil.*, XLVIII (1928), p. 241 f. ; A. G[riera], *Buttletí de dialectologia catalana*, XVI (1928), p. 76 f. ; Meyer-Lübke, *Almanach der Wiener Akademie*, 1927, p. 247 f. ; Elise Richter, *Die neueren Sprachen*, XXXVI (1928), p. 35 f., *Archiv f. das Studium der neueren Spr. u. Liter.*, CLIV (1928), p. 224 f., and *Neue österreichische Biographie*,

To follow closely the whole of his scientific activity would be impossible for us here, where we are concerned with a survey of the more conspicuous moments in the history of Romance scholarship, impossible if only on material grounds, inasmuch as the multitude of Schuchardt's studies, and their most varied themes, far exceed the limits we have set ourselves in this book, and because, further, the great majority of them appeared in periodical publications which are often difficult to procure. His work is indeed remarkable both for its complete continuity and for its entirely fragmentary character. It is as it were inspired with the same conception as his attitude towards language, which to him was a continuous entity in process of unceasing development and elaboration.[1] Thus the last word was never spoken on any question. He realized that the phenomena of language are too complex, too protean, to be enclosed, much less to be finally tabulated, in any set formula. He frequently reverted to the same problem with fresh material and a changed point of view, arguing not only with those whom he had not succeeded in convincing, but also, and even more readily, with himself. With the exception of his three volumes entitled *Der Vokalismus des Vulgärlateins*, which, though a work of his youth, may still be consulted with profit, Schuchardt did not write a single book ; the 770 items which compose his literary output are made up of studies, articles, reviews, and discussions ; they comprise no books, and naturally no grammars, dictionaries, or manuals. Thus the service which Leo Spitzer has rendered to scholarship by publishing an anthology of extracts from Schuchardt's writings—on the occasion of his eightieth birthday—is of no mean order. This anthology, entitled *Hugo Schuchardt-Brevier, Ein Vademekum der allgemeinen Sprachwissenschaft*, Halle a.S., 1922,[2] is

I. Abteilung, Band VI, Wien, 1929, p. 122 f. (the second of these is extremely rich in biographical detail, and written with great delicacy of feeling and deep understanding of Schuchardt's personality as a man) ; M. R[oques], *Romania*, LIV (1928), p. 606 f. Further reference can be made to L. Spitzer's preface to his *Hugo Schuchardt-Brevier*, 1922 (2nd ed., 1928) ; L. Spitzer, *Meisterwerke der romanischen Sprachwissenschaft*, I, Munich, 1929, p. 357 f. ; R. Riegler, *Hugo Schuchardt als Lehrer*, in *Die neueren Sprachen*, XXX (1922), p. 45 f. ; H. Steiner, *Zu Hugo Schuchardt's 80. Geburtstag*, in *Zeitschr. f. rom. Phil.*, XLII (1922), p. 1 f. ; A. Castro, *Lengua, enseñanza y literatura (Esbozos)*, Madrid, 1924, p. 155 f.

[1] " Language is a unity and a continuity "—*Brevier*, 2nd ed., p. 318. " . . . the sum total of languages is inexhaustible ; irrespective of unity or multiplicity of origins, it forms a continuous whole."—*Ibid.*, p. 323.

[2] A second and enlarged edition, with *Vademekum* changed to *Vademecum*, appeared in 1928. The following reviews of the book may be mentioned : J. Ronjat, *Revue des langues romanes*, LXI (1921-2), p. 409 f. ; A. Wallensköld, *Neuphilologische Mitteilungen*, XXIII (1922), p. 150 f. ; S. Puşcariu, *Dacoromania*,

grouped by the compiler under the following headings, sufficient of themselves to give an idea of the wealth and variety of the problems Schuchardt treated : Sound-change (concerning the sound-laws) ; Etymology and Word History (with a sub-heading ' Words and Things ') ; The Mingling of Languages ; Linguistic Kinships (the ' Wave Theory ', the Classification of the Romance Languages) ; Primary Affinities and Formations (' Historical or Elementary Kinship? ') ; The Origin of Language ; General Linguistics ; Language and Thought ; Historical and Descriptive Linguistics ; Linguistics in relation to Ethnography, Anthropology, and the History of Civilization ; Language and Nationality ; Politics and Language Teaching ; Linguistic Therapy (i.e. Purism) ; On Science in General (Individualism in Linguistics).[1]

Let us consider briefly some of Schuchardt's ideas. We have already stated his views upon the sound-laws (*v.* p. 31 f.) and will not repeat them. It should be made clear, however, that he reverted to this topic constantly, ever bringing forward new arguments and a fresh point of view. Thus in *Das Baskische und die Sprachwissenschaft*, a study written as late as 1925 (*Brevier*, 2nd ed., p. 204 f.), he maintains that the so-called phonetic laws are of great convenience inasmuch as they facilitate linguistic research, in particular etymology, and that consequently scholars will not readily dispense with them.[2] But this does not signify that language conforms to fixed laws like the laws of nature, that it exists as a thing unto itself, nor even that it conforms to physiological laws, although language is a process (Vorgang), not a ' thing ' or an ' essence '. Language is subject solely to the laws of sociology, or

II (1921–2), p. 702 f. ; E. Lerch, *Archiv f. d. Stud. d. neueren Sprachen*, CXLV (1923), p. 134 f. ; Ed. Hermann, *Zeitschr. f. rom. Phil.*, XLIV (1924), p. 122 f., and XLIX (1929), p. 118 ; A. Meillet, *Rev. crit. d'hist. et de litt.*, XCVI (1929), p. 306 ; Iorgu Iordan, *Arhiva*, XXXVI (1929), p. 289 f. ; E. Lewy, *Zeitschr. f. vergleich. Sprachforschung*, LXIII (1936), p. 271 f. For other reviews, see the preface to the second edition, p. 11.

[1] For an understanding of the personality of Schuchardt, both as a man and a scholar, the reader is referred particularly to Spitzer's article in the *Rev. internationale des études basques*, XXI (1930), 29 pages in off-print, and to Schuchardt's own article, *Der Individualismus in der Sprachforschung*, Brevier, 2nd ed., p. 416 f.

[2] " It is true," he says, " that there has been a certain amount of demolition but it has been confined to accessories, and conducted with too great caution ; the old structure [set up by the neo-grammarians] has been left standing, for convenience' sake " ; *loc. cit.*, p. 205. And further : " That the code of sound-laws is as indispensable to the philologist as the table of logarithms to the mathematician goes without saying ; but the convenience of this aid to reckoning should not lead him to a misunderstanding of true values." Similarly, p. 135 : " ... phonology is merely an adjunct, the sound-laws are landmarks guiding us through the thick forest ".

rather to the effects of these laws upon the individuals who speak. In every language we start from individual ' styles ', which spread and become generalized through imitation. Language is the product of a speaking individual, and depends in the highest degree upon that individual, whose whole mode and conditions of life, as well as his temperament, culture, age, and sex, exercise their influence upon it. But the linguist can only have cognizance of the state of a language when individual styles have already become generalized. Schuchardt, more than any other linguist, sought to set in evidence the fluctuating and fortuitous character of phonetic phenomena, the instability of pronunciation with one and the same individual, the spreading of linguistic innovations by a process of radiation, the ceaseless process of change which language undergoes, etc., all with a view to showing, *inter alia*, the complete absence of ' Law ', a conception entirely inconsistent with such characteristics of human speech.

Similarly, we have shown how Schuchardt contested the existence of linguistic boundaries, in the strict sense of the word, a natural outcome of his ideas concerning language. Given the fact that language is in a continual state of flux, no truly unified linguistic communities can be formed : " Local vernacular, sub-dialect, dialect, and language are entirely relative notions ", he asserted as early as 1866 (*Brevier*, 2nd ed., p. 164). The passage from one to another is gradual and almost imperceptible, because of human intercommunication. Schuchardt compares them to the waves from a stone thrown into a pool : " Let us represent language in its unity like a stretch of water ; its shining surface is set in motion by the formation of wave centres, whose oscillations intercross, varying in extent according to the force that is behind them."[1]

---

[1] This comparison, which occurred to Schuchardt when writing the third volume of his *Vokalismus* (1868), is at the basis of the so-called ' wave-theory ' developed by Johannes Schmidt in *Die Verwandtschaftsverhältnisse der indogermanischen Sprachen*, Weimar, 1872 (cp. A. Philippide, *Principii de istoria limbii*, p. 7 f.). As this assertion has given rise to a certain amount of misunderstanding (cp. Meyer-Lübke, *Revue de linguistique romane*, I [1925], p. 11 f., it is worth while reproducing here Schuchardt's own statements upon the matter, as quoted in *Brevier*, 2nd ed., p. 431 f. " In 1868 (*Vok. des Vulgärlateins*, III, 32 . . .) I announced, briefly, it is true, but clearly, my theory of the geographical differentiation of human speech, while in 1870 I made it the subject of my inaugural lecture in the University of Leipzig (*Über die Klassifikation der romanischen Mundarten*) at which were present, among others, G. Curtius, A. Ebert, Fr. Zarncke, A. Leskien, H. Paul, E. Sievers, K. Brugmann, H. Suchier. By this, I mean to say that it was not confined to a narrow circle, although indeed it was about 1900 before it appeared in print. In May, 1872, the 28th congress of philologists was held in Leipzig, where Joh. Schmidt delivered a lecture entitled : *Die Verwandschaftsverhältnisse der*

For the same reason, namely, the bonds of every description that link men together, and cause them to ignore political boundaries in the satisfying of their material and cultural needs, languages are unceasingly mingled. This fact was of such importance to Schuchardt that it is for ever recurring in his works. " There is not ", he says, " a single language that is free from the blending of foreign elements " (loc. cit., p. 153) ; and again, p. 151, " Of all the problems with which linguistics is at present concerned, there is surely none of greater import than that of speech mingling." But Schuchardt is not thinking merely of the influences exercised one upon the other by languages proper, although many of his most important studies deal with this question.[1] He sees speech everywhere blended with extraneous elements, " even in the language that is held to form a complete unity, that, namely, of one and the same individual ". There is no limit to the possibility of speech blending, inasmuch as " each individual learns and modifies his language in his intercourse with a series of other individuals ". " This mingling of languages can be grasped only if we take into account, on the one hand, the present as we see it, and on the other, that real speech unity, the speech of the individual."

A conspicuous part of Schuchardt's scientific activity was devoted to etymological investigations. In this domain, too, he opened up fresh paths by the originality and fertility of his ideas. To the great majority of his contemporaries, as to many philologists of to-day, an etymology was a kind of mathematical formula, the shorter and simpler, the better. With Schuchardt it becomes a

---

indogermanischen Sprachen, published the same year. I informed him verbally that I had come to the same conclusions concerning the mutual relations of the Romance languages. He reminded me of this in a letter in 1874, asking me where my lecture had been published. To this I could of course give no satisfactory reply ". Schuchardt then goes on to say that he and Schmidt had been fellow students at Bonn for three semesters, but had not met. It is impossible however that they both should have been inspired from the same source, for example, as has been supposed by some, by the lectures of A. Schleicher, whom they both had as a professor ; because Schleicher was an adherent of the ' genealogical ' theory (Stammbaumtheorie) which is in direct opposition to the ' wave ' theory. Shuchardt further rules out as a possible common source a conversation with Schleicher, who, when asked during an excursion with some of his students his opinion upon the gradual differentiation between various languages, made a reference to botanical geography. His conclusion is that " the idea of geographical differentiation was in the air ".

[1] Cp. for example Kreolische Studien, 1882, and following years, in Sitzungsberichte der Wiener Akademie ; Slawo-deutsches und Slawo-italienisches, Graz, 1884 ; Beiträge zur Kenntnis des kreolischen Romanisch (a series of studies published in reviews from 1888 onwards); Beiträge zur Kenntnis des englischen Kreolisch, 1888 ff. ; Die lingua franca, 1909 ; cp. also his numerous researches upon the Basque language (v. infra) where he discusses similar problems.

real history of the word, in its depth and breadth : a wealth of material must first be collected,[1] giving all the dialect variants of the word under investigation, in addition to the various phases of its development from the remotest times to the present ; similarly, we must find out its synonyms, both in the dialect or language to which it belongs, and in other languages as well, inasmuch as the manner in which an idea finds expression in a number of languages frequently puts us on the track of the etymology we are seeking.[2] As an opponent of the sound-laws, as understood by the neo-grammarians, Schuchardt distinguishes himself from his fellows by concentrating, not upon the sounds of a word, but upon its meaning, because it is meaning, not sounds, that gives a word life.[3] For this reason, he would have us study words and things in conjunction.[4] The better we know the latter, their form, uses,

---

[1] " In view of the instinctive dislike with which many appear to regard such a piling up of material, I must emphatically state that it is never the over-much but only the over-little in this direction that constitutes an error of method " (*ibid.*, p. 116).

[2] Cp. his etymology of Fr. *mauvais*<Lat. *malifatius*, *loc. cit.*, p. 135 ff.

[3] " We smile at the etymologists of other days who, in the matter of sounds, considered any sort of resemblance as sufficiently convincing ; but in the matter of meaning our methods to-day are scarcely better " (*op. cit.*, p. 108).

[4] A brilliant example in confirmation of Schuchardt's point of view is his celebrated etymology of Fr. *trouver*, It. *trovare*, etc. It will be remembered that in the Middle Ages the word meant ' to compose poetry ' as well as ' to find ', whence Fr. *trouvere*, *troveor*, Prov. *trobador*, etc., ' a poet '. Hence many linguists thought of deriving the word from *tropus*, ' a figure of rhetoric ', ' metaphor ' ; ' song ' ; others from *tropa*, ' a game with dice ', others again from *contropatio*, ' a comparison ', etc. (*v.* Meyer-Lübke, *Roman. etym. Wörterbuch*, no. 8992). All of these were perfectly satisfactory from the point of view of phonetic laws, although semantically they were open to criticism, inasmuch as meaning usually develops from the concrete to the abstract, and not the reverse. Schuchardt came forward with an explanation of the word which satisfied this semantic requirement but which to the neo-grammarian eye presents phonetic difficulties. He adopts Diez's solution<L. *turbare*, ' to disturb ', and explains it as having been first of all a fisherman's expression : ' to disturb water, in order to catch fish ', then ' to take or find fish ', then ' to find ' in general, before taking on the special meaning of ' to find rimes ', ' to versify '. It will be readily understood that this etymology did not convince the majority of scholars, despite the wealth of illustration adduced by its author, who, conforming to the watchword ' Words and Things ', had made for this purpose a special investigation of fishing methods. Even Meyer-Lübke, although setting the words *trouver*, *trovare*, etc., under the rubric *Turbare*, expresses certain doubts. But in 1921 there appeared a book by M. L. Wagner, entitled, *Das ländliche Leben Sardiniens im Spiegel seiner Sprache*, where we discover (p. 93, note 2) that the semantic evolution of the word *turbare* which Schuchardt, with the intuition of genius, had only divined, corresponded to the facts. Sard. *truðar* means (1) to frighten fish in streams and drive them into a place where the water has been poisoned with mullein or spurge ; (2) to rouse game, whence *sas truðas*, ' the chase ', *truðadores*, ' hunters ' (cp. also Corsican *trovate*, ' a kind of hunt ') ; (3) ' to drive cattle '. All these meanings can be explained only in the manner suggested by Schuchardt. It is therefore with some astonishment that one reads in *Revue des langues romanes*, LXV (1927-8), p. 135, the following words of

method of construction, etc., the more easily will we succeed in discovering the origin of the former. But to a more detailed discussion of the method of ' word and thing ' we will return later, in the section devoted to R. Meringer.[1]

Schuchardt was also extremely interested in onomatopœic formations, in the broadest sense of the word. In his investigations of the numerous languages which he had made his domain, he had frequent occasion to note that certain expressions of an onomatopœic character recurred in idioms which historically were quite unconnected, and frequently in identical or almost identical form. Thus, it frequently occurs that demonstrative particles which indicate proximity contain the vowel *i*, and those which denote remoteness the broader vowel *a* or *o* ; for example : Fr. (*i*)*ci* and *là*, Rum. (*a*)*ici* and (*a*)*colo*, Sp. *allí* and *allá*, *aquí*, and *acá*, etc. Similarly, *i* occurs in words which convey the notion of ' smallness ' : Rum. *mic*, beside *mare*, Fr. *petit* and *grand*, It. *piccolo*, *piccino* and *grande*, etc. Again, in the case of onomatopœic expressions proper, which may be said to depict two successive movements or sounds of an object, the sharper vowel is heard in the first part of the word, which is nearer in time and therefore in space, the heavier vowel in the second, which is more remote ; thus : *tic-tac*, *pif-paf*, *zig-zag*, *ping-pong*, *misch-masch*, *bimb-bamb*, *ding-dang*, *pimp-pamp*, etc.[2] In like fashion, Schuchardt remarks that certain sound formulae or phonetic groups occur in the most widely different languages to express the same idea. The word for ' to thunder ', for example, almost everywhere contains a plosive consonant plus an *r*, accompanied of course by other less significant sounds which vary from one language to another ; or again the group $f(v) + l(r)$

P. Fouché : " Faire une gloire à Schuchardt de son étymologie : It. *trovare*, Fr. *trouver*<Lat. *turbare*, surprend un peu en 1928." But see further the note by E. Gamillscheg in *Revista de filología española*, XIX (1932), p. 120, n. 4 (<*contropatio*, *contropare*) ; see also G.-G. Nicholson, *Recherches philologiques romanes*, p. 1 f.

[1] General directions with regard to Romance etymology are to be found in an article by L. Spitzer, *Aus der Werkstatt des Etymologen*, in *Jahrbuch für Philologie*, I (1925), p. 129 f. (Cp. Iorgu Iordan, *Un catéchisme étymologique*, in *Rev. de ling. rom.*, I [1925], p. 162 f.) Compare further the controversy between Spitzer and E. Gamillscheg called forth by the publication of the latter's *Etymologisches Wörterbuch der französischen Sprache*, Heidelberg, 1926–9. This controversy, which appeared in *Zeitschr. f. rom. Philol.*, XLVI (1926), p. 563 f., XLVIII (1928), p. 75 f. (Spitzer), and in *Zeitschr. f. franz. Sprache u. Liter.*, L (1927–8), p. 216 f. (Gamillscheg), concerns etymological method in general, and French etymology in particular, and is of special importance inasmuch as the two antagonists represent exactly opposite points of view, Spitzer being a follower of Schuchardt, Gamillscheg of the neo-grammarians.

[2] Other examples are to be found in M. Grammont's *Traité de phonétique*, and in H. Güntert, *Grundfragen der Sprachwissenschaft*, Leipzig, 1925, p. 29.

recurs again and again in words which convey the idea of motion round a fixed point, cp. Fr. *flotter, flatter (un cheval)*, Engl. *flutter*, Rum. *fluture* ('butterfly'), etc. It is clear from the above that Schuchardt understood the term onomatopœia in the widest sense, identified it in fact with what he calls elsewhere (*loc. cit.*, p. 246) *Schallwortbildung* or *Lautmalerei*, or with what has perhaps more fittingly been named S o u n d S y m b o l i s m,[1] in recognition of the fact that, spontaneously and unconsciously, there may arise in human speech an association between an idea and a sound so intimate, that the one automatically evokes the other in the speaker's mind, giving rise to the type of word we have mentioned above.

With observations of this character as his starting-point, Schuchardt arrived at a conception of the kinship of languages widely different from that to which we are accustomed. We find it formulated in the most pregnant fashion in the following passages of the *Brevier :* " . . . in contrast to historical kinship of both kinds [i.e. based on ethnical origins or borrowings of words], there may be set the non-historical 'elementary' kinship " (*loc. cit.*, p. 248) ; and, lower down (p. 248–9), " We recognize this elementary kinship most clearly in languages for which there is no evidence of mutual relationship in the narrower sense, or of any historical contact." Not that Schuchardt in the least contested the value of ethnological criteria, or of loan-words, in accounting for coincidences between one language and another, when these have a common origin or have been in close relationship over a long period of time. But he protests against the exaggerated application of these criteria, and insists that we should take into account, as well, the possibility of 'elementary' relationship. Inasmuch as man's mental make-up is fundamentally the same at all times and in all places, we are entitled, he says, and even obliged to enquire, in cases of linguistic resemblance, whether these

---

[1] The question of Sound Symbolism (*Lautsymbolik*) was much discussed at the third international congress of linguists ; cp. *Atti del III Congresso internazionale dei Linguisti*, p. 119 f. ; cp. also A. Debrunner, *Lautsymbolik in alter und neuester Zeit*, in *Germ.-roman. Monatsschrift*, XIV (1926), p. 321 f. ; A. Philippide, *Principii de istoria limbii*, p. 79 f. ; H. Müller, *Experimentelle Beiträge zur Analyse des Verhältnisses von Laut und Sinn*, Berlin, 1935.

Mention should also be made of O. Jespersen's article, *Symbolic value of the vowel i*, reproduced in Spitzer, *Meisterwerke der romanischen Sprachwissenschaft*, vol. I, p. 53 f., in which he endeavours to show that the vowel is widely used to denote things that are small, delicate, insignificant or weakly. This, according to Spitzer, *loc. cit.*, p. 355, was the first attempt to study systematically the symbolical value of a single sound.

are not due to this permanent and general psychological kinship that unites human kind. As for him, he gives a preference to this latter factor, not merely in order to throw light upon coincidences between languages that are, geographically and historically, widely remote, nor to explain certain onomatopœic expressions they share in common, but he would have us think of this ' elementary ' kinship between languages even when we encounter some linguistic phenomenon shared by a group of languages that belong actually to the same family. For example, the origin of the article in all the Romance languages is a matter that still remains obscure ; we do not know when it first came to be used, nor from whence it spread.[1] Now we also find the article in widely different languages, in Basque, German, and Hungarian, for example ; so Schuchardt believes that even if we are convinced that there has been borrowing from one language to another, we must still admit that the borrowing has come about as the result of an ' inner tendency ' shared in common (*loc. cit.*, p. 250). And he would apply this to numerous other cases as well (cp. *loc. cit.*, p. 250 f.).

The investigation of problems of the type touched upon above leads naturally to that major and ultimate problem of linguistics, the origin of language. Schuchardt could not but concern himself with this, and it became the subject of a number of his studies, particularly in the later years of his life. Though it is impossible for us to set forth in detail the views expressed upon this topic by the one linguist most qualified to discuss it, a few points call for mention. An Italian scholar, A. Trombetti,[2] had advocated with profound conviction and a great wealth of material, drawn from languages as widely different as possible, the theory of monogenesis : just as mankind appeared first in one spot only and not in several, so human language, he held, had a single origin, and had spread over the surface of the world from a single area. In this theory Schuchardt detected a survival of the naturalistic conception of language, and therefore opposed it, without claiming, however, that the reverse hypothesis of polygenesis was in any degree a certainty. He is well aware that convincing proof cannot be adduced in favour of either theory, but that the matter would

---

[1] Cf. E. Gamillscheg, *Zum romanischen Artikel und Possessivpronomen*, Berlin, 1936.

[2] Trombetti's researches, after appearing in fragmentary form in reviews, brochures, etc., were grouped together under the title *Elementi di glottologia*, Bologna (1922–3). Cp. the reviews by C. Tagliavini, *Dacoromania*, III (1923), p. 852 f., O. D.[ensusianu], *Grai şi suflet*, I (1923–4), p. 353 f., and A. Meillet, *Bull. Soc. Ling.*, XXIV (1923–4), fasc. 2, p. 8 f.

be better propounded in the form 'both—and', rather than
'either—or'.[1] In any case, those numerous and frequently very
close resemblances between widely different languages do not
presuppose, as Trombetti would have it, a common origin, but can
be explained on the basis of that 'elementary' kinship of which
we have spoken above.

Another important point of some relevance here is the following.
Language, to Schuchardt, represented first and foremost a means
of communication between men.[2] Hence, to him, the fundamental
element in any human speech is the proposition, which, primevally,
would, of course, consist of but a single word. The proposition, he
says, is the simplest form that we can give to things thought, felt,
or willed by us. From the proposition sprang the word, just as
the 'notion' grew out of thinking. The single component of
primitive propositions could express nothing but 'happenings'
(*Geschehnisse*) ; that is to say the verb (*Vorgangswort*) was anterior
to the noun or name (*Dingwort*).[3] This contention he based on
his observation of present facts, of the speech of children, and,
particularly, of primitive types of language like that of the Creoles,
with which he was so familiar.

Schuchardt here raises an important question of method, not
only with regard to problems of the type discussed, but in general,
maintaining that our starting-point should always be the present ;
for the present we know, or can know, better than the past.[4] But
our most immediate present, in linguistic matters, is our mother
tongue : " The deeper the scholar is rooted in his mother tongue,
the deeper will his scientific understanding of foreign languages
become " (*ibid.*, p. 292). For we possess, or can possess, through

---

[1] Here are his own words (*Brevier*, p. 258) : " In any case only a very scanty
number of words can be held to speak in favour of monogenesis ; by far the
greater number of primitive words appear to be of polygenetic origin." And
further : " I must not be taken as admitting expressly the theory of polygenesis ;
taking a broad view, monogenesis, and polygenesis are constantly found associated."

[2] He was not, however, oblivious to the aesthetic side of language: "Born of
necessity ", he says, " language reaches its climax in art " (*op. cit.*, p. 265).

[3] Schuchardt makes a judicious criticism of the lack of precision and of the
ambiguity of current grammatical terminology in his study entitled : *Prädikat,
Subjekt, Objekt* (*op. cit.*, p. 272 f.).

[4] " It will surely be admitted on every hand that the fundamental method in
linguistic enquiry is to start from the present, from what is here and now ". " The
days when the schools, from reasons of high policy, refrained from teaching the
history of the present, or even of the recent past, are over, yet, even among men
of science, there is a prevailing tendency to withdraw into the quiet of the study,
and in doing so, to leave outside things which appear to smack too much of the
present, but which not only are available for research, but which actually invite
research, before they have put on the dignity of rust " (*loc. cit.*, p. 291).

our mother tongue a far stronger sense of language ; and a " ' feeling for language ' is more valuable than a knowledge of the grammatical categories. The former is acquired in early childhood, is almost inborn in us, the latter is learnt much later, and, when acquired at all, is often imperfect and at times erroneous " (*op. cit.*, pp. 293–4).

For similar reasons, Schuchardt is a declared believer in the descriptive method of language study. Admitting that the present state of a language offers, as we have seen, the greatest scientific interest,[1] it follows that it calls for our special attention. Clearly, in this case, a strictly historical method of approach is inapplicable ; the linguistic phenomena that are taking place before our eyes can best be observed, described, and then explained, not by harking back to an original language, but by their psychological analysis, not by referring to earlier states of the language, but by tracing their source to the workings of the individual human mind. It must be said, however, that Schuchardt did not consider the two methods as mutually exclusive ; they must go hand in hand whenever this is possible (cp. his attitude with regard to the question of monogenesis and polygenesis, *supra*, pp. 57–8). Casting round for a name for this linguistic discipline, which is entitled to aspire to the rank of a science, on an equal footing with linguistic history, he suggests the term ' linguistic psychology ' (*Sprachpsychologie*), asserting at the same time that he does not set it in opposition to linguistic history, but links the two together, since both have reference to the phenomena of language (*ibid.*, p. 330). He is of the view that this method of approach is in complete harmony with the precepts of Hermann Paul, who set as the aim of linguistic study both the understanding of the various language phenomena and the apprehension of their relationships. The descriptive method, " far from falling outside the domain of linguistic science, forms the fundamental part thereof, and for this very reason links it up with other branches of science, the investigation of sounds and groups of sounds with physiology, that of word- and sentence-meaning with psychology " (*ibid.*, p. 329). Schuchardt is thus aware of the abusive use to which the historical method can be put, and of the unjustified claims that are made for it. " It would appear ", he says, " that of recent years there has been some misunderstanding of the term 'historical';

---

[1] Schuchardt takes every opportunity of driving this home. Cp. the following passage (*Brevier*, p. 328) : " If the present, with its inexhaustible abundance of facts, which we can even, to some extent, modify experimentally, does not enlighten us upon the laws of language, the past can never do so ". Cp. also *loc. cit.*, p. 331 f., and the views of Saussure and some of his pupils set forth below, Chap. IV.

applied in its widest possible connotation it was first of all held to imply the study of facts, not only in their essence, but especially in their ' becoming ', a thing which in itself has of course no time limitation. But now, many believe they are working ' historically ' when they simply record the facts of the past annalistically, at the same time refusing the title of ' historical ' to any investigation of relationships " (*op. cit.*, pp. 328–9).

From the foregoing discussion, the wealth and variety of the problems that attracted Schuchardt have been made abundantly clear. Yet although we have accorded this scholar, not indeed all the attention he deserves, but at least a place worthy of his importance in the history of our discipline, it has not been possible to touch upon all the questions he treated in the course of his almost superhuman activity. The list of headings on p. 51 will give some idea of these. What we must finally throw into relief is the spirit in which he worked, his tolerance in face of contradiction, his entire freedom from preconceptions, his equally attentive concern for great issues and minute detail, his patience and pains to understand the phenomena of language in their remotest recesses, his realization of the relativity of all opinion in a matter so indeterminate as human speech, his eagerness to walk in unbeaten paths—these are the qualities that mark the scholar Schuchardt. These characteristics help us to understand at the same time how he came to tackle problems that have left other linguists of repute indifferent, or which have caused them to adopt at times an unscientific, even an indignant attitude. Thus, over a long period Schuchardt took part in discussions concerning artificial languages, *Volapük*, *Esperanto* and the like, justifying their existence with solid linguistic arguments, unlike the great majority of language specialists whose attitude, at least until quite recent years, has been in general decidedly hostile.

Schuchardt's interest in the Creole languages, as he informs us himself in *Brevier*, 2nd ed., p. 430, was prompted by reasons similar to those that attracted him to the problem of artificial languages. Like the latter, the Creole languages are quite different in type from the ordinary run of languages, and specialists may from these very peculiarities draw helpful conclusions concerning matters of general linguistics. It was from the Creole languages, which he calls ' languages born of necessity ' (*Notsprachen*), that Schuchardt drew many valuable suggestions concerning the origin of language in general, and received enlightenment upon a number of problems which normally constituted languages, *Natursprachen*, as he calls them, were unable to explain. Schuchardt's linguistic curiosity took him into yet other fields. He was attracted particularly by the Basque language, whose relationship with other human idioms still remains an unsolved problem. Not only did he devote to Basque a considerable number of special articles, but he did it the signal honour of writing an introduction to the study of the language, *Primitiae linguae Vasconum*, Halle a.S., 1923, a remarkable favour from one so averse to anything in the nature of manuals and grammars. His researches into the mysteries of Basque brought him into two domains of study equally foreign to the Romanicist and the Indo-Europeanist, namely, those of the Hamitic languages, particularly Berber, and of the Caucasian languages, as the former has certain lexicographical features in common with Basque, the latter certain similarities of grammar. Again, the study of Berber brought him into contact with Arabic, which he was at pains to acquire in Egypt, and lastly, his appointment to the University of Graz in Austria awoke in him an interest in the Slavonic languages, and also a particular interest in Hungarian.

In 1923, a few years only before his death, Schuchardt published a short article that contained the following words : " A splendid gift from the hands of Chance is of less worth than a modest possession which is the reward of Toil. Let us follow the advice of the husbandman in La Fontaine's fable, who left what he gave out to be a hidden treasure to his three sons : *Creusez, fouillez, bêchez !* (For the real treasure is work ") (*op. cit.*, p. 437). This motto can be considered as Schuchardt's legacy to science. He was faithful to it throughout his whole life. It is this which, in a large measure, accounts for the extreme wealth of ideas contained in his works ; for ever seeking, enquiring, investigating, he became the greatest linguist of his day. But in order to do him full justice, we must also take into account the personal factor, in the narrower sense of the word, to which Schuchardt himself was not slow to give consideration when occasion arose. His admirable study, *Der Individualismus in der Sprachforschung*, written in the last year of his scientific activity, and full of personal reminiscences that singularly enlighten our understanding of Schuchardt the scholar (*loc. cit.*, p. 416 f.) is evidence of this awareness. Elsewhere, too, we find him voicing his views upon science in general, and consequently, indirectly, upon her servants. We cannot resist the temptation to reproduce a certain number of these pronouncements, which have an added interest in that Schuchardt himself was the first to conform to the advice he gave to others. " Scientific work needs continual rejuvenation. Even when dealing with old material it can discover new aspects. The way we are obliged to begin should not determine the way we end " (*loc. cit.*, p. 111). " No one has the right to consider the material he handles as something precious in itself. It should be always considered as fragments for the erecting of a loftier building, itself in turn to become a fragment, and so on and on : Excelsior ! For it is the task of science to simplify not to multiply " (*ibid.*, pp. 436–7). " It always does me good when from beneath the cool breast-plate of objectivity I feel upon me a warm breath of subjectivity, which indeed is never entirely absent. It brings my fellow-worker closer, and I understand him better " (*ibid.*, p. 421). " Science does not lie before us like a fortress, or a field, or a temple ; it lies within us " (*ibid.*, p. 408). " Science is not founded on knowledge alone, but also on feeling. Our work prospers only when we work with love ; it is love alone that begets new and original thought " (*ibid.*, p. 317).

Such a man could not found a school in the ordinary sense of the word. He was indeed an indifferent teacher, and retired from his chair ten years before his time. But for this very reason he was to become the master of the majority, at least, of the linguists of to-day, old and young, for in Schuchardt there is something to learn for all of them. What he says of Diez can be applied equally well to himself : " Diez did not form a school, in the sense in which so many philologists and historians have done, and so many ambitious professors strive to do ; . . . he never exercised any pressure or restraint upon the development of younger men, never strove to turn science into one channel. . . . We are his disciples in the best and widest sense, and it is our boast that we have learnt from him never to swear by the word of the master " (*op. cit.*, p. 407).

★   ★   ★

We have already had occasion to mention the word and thing method. This approach to the study of the vocabulary of a lan-

The Method of ' Word and Thing ' guage may be described briefly as follows. It is an observable fact that many words when they pass from one language into another do not do so

alone, but in company with the thing which they denote. A

garment, or an agricultural implement, etc., borrowed by a community to which it was previously unknown, is taken over with the name it bears in the region from which it came.[1] The borrower thus enriches at one and the same time his language and his material culture. What could be more obvious therefore than the desirability of investigating jointly the representatives of both sides of this dual process, the words and the things ? By this method we remain close to reality, and avoid separating two aspects of human activity that are closely bound together. The history of the language thus keeps step with the history of culture, to the mutual advantage of both.

But this combination of word and thing study is not necessarily confined to loan words. The method can also be applied with advantage to the study of the indigenous vocabulary of a given region. In this case the profit we draw from a sound knowledge of ' Realien '[2] is of course of a somewhat different order, though it is clear that even the autochthonous words of a language can inform us concerning the cultural history of its speakers. Suppose, for example, that we wish to ascertain the etymology of some obscure word, say the name of a plant or an animal. Whatever may be our mastery of the ' sound-laws ' of the language in question, and of the whole specialized equipment which such an investigation requires, we shall not succeed in discovering the origin of the word unless we avail ourselves of the information that is to be drawn from botany or zoology. Many plants and animals owe their names to their external appearance, to their mode of life or their uses, and it is information under these heads that will give us a

---

[1] We must beware of applying this principle too generally, and thus exaggerating a perfectly legitimate conception. As a matter of fact, words do not always circulate in conjunction with things, even when they are the names of material objects. It frequently happens that the name of a thing which has always existed in the life of a given community is replaced by a foreign word, which, in this case, of course, comes unaccompanied from the language to which it belongs. Here, the cause of the change is fashion. Similar happenings are observable, and even in greater measure, within a single linguistic community, as between one social category and another. The lower classes are continually tempted to borrow from the higher all manner of terms, even for notions that have names of long standing in popular speech. It is a case here of psychological motives rather than of historical cultural relationships ; cp. H. Naumann, *Jahrbuch für Philologie*, I (1925), p. 58.

[2] This German term is conveniently used to indicate everything relating to material condition of life, the shape, dimensions, uses, methods of construction of objects, and the like ; cp. the numerous works in German entitled *Reallexikon* (*des klassischen Altertums, der indogermanischen Altertumskunde, der Vorgeschichte*, etc.), *Handwörterbuch des deutschen Aberglaubens*, etc., all of them indispensable to linguists.

likely starting-point for the etymology we are seeking. To take a case in point. The present author, discussing the etymology of the Rumanian plant name *dediță* (a kind of 'anemone'), in *Arhiva*, XXIX (1922), p. 431 f., derived it rightly from Slavonic *dĕdŭ*, 'old man', 'grandfather', but argued, more or less fancifully, that it had been given this name jocularly in popular parlance because it was the *earliest* flower to bloom ! But the name is due to quite other and more realistic reasons. As was shown by L. Spitzer, in *Dacoromania*, III (1923), p. 649 f., who quotes similar names from other languages, the plant owes its name to its fruit, which is covered with a thick white down and thus resembles the head of an old man (cp. the author's supplementary remarks in *Arhiva*, XXXII (1925), p. 73).

Although this method of linking up word and thing has its most obvious application in the case of material objects, it is by no means confined to these. Indeed, L. Spitzer suggests, in *Meisterwerke der romanischen Sprachwissenschaft*, I, Munich, 1929, p. 370, that in future more and more attention will be paid to the more purely cultural elements of vocabulary. The founder of the method, R. Meringer himself, of whom we are about to speak, drew no distinction, in theory, between ' objects ' and ' ideas ' ; for him, they were equally things (*Sachen*), to be investigated in similar fashion. " By things ", he says, " we understand, not material objects alone, but also any thoughts, ideas, and institutions, which find their linguistic expression in a word . . . ; the psychological phenomena that are the basis of speech are also to be reckoned as ' things ', just like spatial objects, for the latter, too, we can only know by their mental images."[1]

Professor of comparative philology at Graz, Rudolf Meringer devoted over thirty years of unceasing labour to expounding and establishing the new method.[2] In 1909, in con-

Rudolf Meringer (1859–1931) junction with a number of other scholars, prominent among whom was Meyer-Lübke, he founded the journal *Wörter und Sachen*, which was to be devoted exclusively

---

[1] *Wörter und Sachen*, VII (1921), p. 50 ; cp. L. Weisgerber, *ibid.*, XII (1929), p. 197. In fact, however, Meringer and his followers concentrated upon material objects, as being more tangible and more readily comprehensible, particularly in the early stages of their work, when their method was not entirely stabilized and had not yet won general acceptance.

[2] Cp. his obituary notice in *Wörter und Sachen*, XIV (1932), p. iii–iv, and the complete bibliography of his works, *ibid.*, p. v f.

to this field of study.[1] His own works in the field are very numerous, and comprise, to mention only the more important and better known, *Etymologien zum geflochtenen Haus*, in *Abhandlungen zur germanischen Philologie, Festschrift für Richard Heinzel*, Halle a.S., 1898 ; *Das volkstümliche Haus in Bosnien und Herzegovina*, Wien, 1901 ; *Wörter und Sachen*, in *Indogermanische Forschungen*, XVI (1904), p. 101 f. ; *Das deutsche Haus und sein Hausrat*, 1906 ; *Zu französisch landier*, in *Zeitschrift f. rom. Philologie*, XXX (1906), p. 414 f. ; *Preface* to *Wörter und Sachen*, I (1909), (in conjunction with the other editors) ; *Die Werkzeuge der pinsere-Reihe und ihre Namen, ibid.*, I, p. 3 f. ; *Sprachlich-sachliche Probleme, ibid.*, I, p. 164 f. ; *Beitrag zur Geschichte der Öfen, ibid.*, III (1911–12), p. 137 f. ; *Omphalos, Nabel, Nebel, ibid.*, V (1913), p. 43 f., etc. etc.

Meringer's conception of the word and thing method can be gathered from the following pronouncements. " Just as linguistic innovations have spread far afield, so have ideas, whether political, religious or artistic, and so also have the things of material civilization, the implements of husbandry, of the house and the household. Side by side with speech waves, we can observe waves of things (*Sachwellen*). Combined, we can call them waves of culture ; for every innovation, every improvement, takes effect in conformity with the wave theory, to which I first drew attention in *Archiv für slavische Philologie*, XVII (1895), p. 504." (*Indogermanische Forschungen*, XVI (1904), p. 191.) " The future of the history of civilization lies in the linking together of the science of words and the science of things."[2] " The history of language is the history of civilization."[3] " Of the sciences that deal with things, those of most use to the linguist are ethnography and ethnology."[4] And finally, to show how strongly he felt the need for the linguist to keep in touch with the realities of life, we have the following trenchant remark : " I would add that to me the mere bookworm is often no more of a researcher than the pen-pusher,

---

[1] Since 1933 the tendency of the review, as announced in vol. XV (1933), p. iii, is to devote increasing attention to questions of general linguistic theory, a trend due, no doubt, to the influence of L. Weisgerber, a distant follower of von Humboldt, and since 1933 one of the editors of the journal.

[2] *Apud* L. Spitzer, *Meisterwerke*, I, p. 370.

[3] *Cit.* H. Sperber, *Sprachwissenschaft und Geistesgeschichte, Wörter u. Sachen*, XII (1929), p. 173 f. The article is of interest inasmuch as it discusses, *inter alia*, the attitude of a number of linguists, in particular of O. Behaghel, towards Meringer's theories.

[4] *Germanisch-romanische Monatsschrift*, I (1909), p. 597.

entrapping his own blobs of ink with blotting-paper, is a big game hunter."[1]

In our description of Schuchardt's scientific activity we have already alluded to the importance he attached to the study of things in conjunction with words. He applied the method whenever occasion offered, witness his investigation of the devices used by fishermen in his study of the word *trouver* (*v.* p. 54 *supra*). Among the articles reproduced in the *Brevier* there is one dating from 1912, entitled *Sachen und Wörter*,[2] which gives us more or less completely his doctrine upon this matter. The following extracts will serve as an outline of his views, and will show at the same time certain divergences between them and those of Meringer. " To achieve an all-round advance, it is not enough that the study of things and the study of words should stand side by side, even in complete readiness to give mutual assistance, they must be interwoven, and must lead to results of a twofold character " (p. 124). " Thus, in relation to the word, the thing is the primary and stable factor ; the word is linked with it and revolves round it " (p. 125). "Just as between fact and proposition there stands thought, so between thing and word stands the idea, in the measure, indeed, in which it too is not also a representative of the thing ; or, as the mediaeval schoolmen put it : *Voces significant res mediantibus conceptibus* " (p. 126). " . . . And so we must picture them [*sc.* things and words in conjunction] not as parallel, but as interwoven lines, the things, so to speak, forming the warp, and the words the woof " (p. 129). " To fix the fundamental relationships between things and words is at the same time to establish in its essentials the method to be followed in this field of research ; it teaches us to know the terrain on which we are to move. The individual paths we shall subsequently follow depend on all kinds of considerations, conditioned in the main, as I have stressed earlier, by our own particular powers " (p. 133). In like manner, in the same article, he discusses various cases of modifications in things or in words, then proceeds from the discussion of the meaning of things, in the strict sense, to the signification of words in general, showing us *inter alia* how in process of time homonyms and synonyms arise.

Hugo Schuchardt

[1] In *Meisterwerke*, I, p. 370.
[2] Note the intentional inversion of the two terms, corresponding with the actual priority in time of ' things ' over ' words '.

Schuchardt's interest in the word and thing method, however, goes much further back than 1912. Already in 1902 he had written : " Words are not always to be set before things, but rather things before words, for that is where they have been from the beginning " (p. 112). A year later, we find him dwelling upon the need for thorough semantic as well as phonetic investigation in the case of words of obscure origin, and, where ' things ' are concerned, upon the necessity for a similar minute scrutiny of their history ; for, as he goes on to say in the same article, " it is in the nature of things, or rather it *is* the very nature of things, that when our representation of an object or the object itself changes, its sound image should also change " (*ibid.*, p. 118). Again, in 1904, he stresses the need for an atlas accompanied by photographs and sketches of the ordinary objects of daily life, and also for an ethnological museum for each neo-Latin country, as well as for a general museum for the whole Romance area, where the linguist might become acquainted with ' things ', and thus reach a completer understanding of the names they bear (*ibid.*, p. 119). Further, in the bibliography of Schuchardt's work prior to 1912 we find a number of articles the titles of which are sufficient proof of his activity in the ' Wörter und Sachen ' field ; for example : *Sichel und Säge ; Sichel und Dolch* (1901, with illustrations) ; *Gezähnte Sicheln*, and *Fischnetzknoten* (1902, the latter illustrated) ; *Sachen und·Wörter* (1905) ; *Sachen und Wörter : Furca, bifurcus* (1909) ; *Sachwortgeschichtliches über den Dreschflegel* (1910) ; *Cose e parole* (1911).[1] The dates of some of these articles clearly raise the question of priority as between Meringer and Schuchardt in introducing the new method. It would appear from two articles published, one in 1908, the other in 1910, and both entitled *Gegen R. Meringer*, that Schuchardt claimed to have been the first in the field, but as we have had no access to these articles nor to Meringer's replies, we are prepared to accept the view expressed by L. Spitzer in *Meisterwerke der rom. Sprachwissenschaft*, I, p. 370, with regard to this ' painful contro-

---

[1] As usual, Schuchardt inverts the customary order of the two terms. Meringer, in *Wörter u. Sachen*, III (1911–12), p. 32–3, combats this attitude of Schuchardt, affirming that the ' thing ' only precedes the ' word ' in the case of entirely new inventions, of things hitherto unknown. In the great majority of cases, old terms are given to new types of objects. Schuchardt's practice, he says, would make word history a mere adjunct of the history of things ; cp. L. Weisgerber, *W. u. S.*, XVI (1934), p. 106. Weisgerber's article, it may be stated here, is of great importance with regard to the whole question of the ' word and thing ' method. It is entitled : *Die Stellung der Sprache im Aufbau der Gesamtkultur*, *W. u. S.*, XV (1933), p. 134 f., and *ibid.*, XVI (1934), p. 97 f.

versy '.[1] He is of the opinion that the " discussion is of no practical importance ; the ' word and thing' method is so completely inherent in the conception that both Meringer and Schuchardt had of language that each of them has a right to be considered the father of the new tendency ". To this we would only add that the close association between word and thing, irrespective of any systematic doctrine, is far from being an entirely new idea. Schuchardt himself (*v. Brevier*, 2nd ed., p. 122 f.) informs us that not only in the nineteenth century, but earlier, there were scholars who were well aware of the facts underlying the ' word and thing' method. The motto of the journal *Wörter und Sachen* itself, namely, the remark of J. Grimm's : " The study of language, of which I am an adherent, and which is my starting-point, has never given me such entire satisfaction that I did not always gladly revert from words to the things themselves ", takes us back a hundred years or more. And for the remoter past, we may recall, with L. Weisgerber (*Wörter und Sachen*, XV (1933), p. 136), that as early as 1623, Francis Bacon in his *De dignitate et augmentis scientiarum*, had the idea of a " grammatica quae non analogiam verborum ad invicem, sed analogiam inter verba et res, sive notionem, sedulo inquirat ".

To return to more recent times, G. Baist, late professor of Romance philology in the University of Freiburg in Breslau, has been considered by some specialists to have claims to be ranked among the founders of the new method.

Gottfried Baist

As A. Zauner pointed out in his obituary notice of Baist, in *Archiv für das Studium der neueren Sprachen*, CXLVII (1924), p. 102 f., before the slogan ' Wörter und Sachen ' had been launched, Baist had frequently applied the method, though only indirectly, when investigating the origin of obscure words. A similar assertion is made by Fr. Schürr, in *Zeitschrift f. rom. Phil.*, XLVI (1926), p. 132, who states : " He [*sc.* Baist], together with Schuchardt, belongs to the group of linguists who very early gave up the study table method of etymologizing, which relied solely upon the ' sound-laws ', in order to follow the path of ' words and things ', in other words, he is among the chief founders of this method."

---

[1] Spitzer refers to *Wörter u. Sachen*, II (1911–12), p. 31 f., for Meringer, and *Zeitschrift f. rom. Philologie*, XXXIV (1910), p. 257 f., for Schuchardt. Cp. also Meyer-Lübke, *Aufgaben der Wortforschung*, in *Germ.-rom. Monatsschrift*, I (1909), p. 643 f.

Having discussed the origins of the ' word and thing ' method and its underlying principles, let us now turn to some of the works in the field of Romance linguistics in which it has been applied. In the front rank of these we must set M. L. Wagner's *Das ländliche Leben Sardiniens im Spiegel seiner Sprache*, Heidelberg, 1921.[1] As is well known, the language of Sardinia, for historical, geographical, and political reasons, is extremely conservative. This is also true of the social life of the islanders, especially of the peasants, and both the language and the culture of the Sardinians have thus constantly attracted the interest of scholars. Wagner, the greatest expert in this field, after publishing a number of articles on the language of the region, decided to investigate the primitive aspects of its peasant life on a linguistic basis ; as he puts it himself : " to depict the peasant life of Sardinia in its most important manifestations, and to study words and things in the closest relationship, and both, as far as possible in their historical connection " (*Preface*, p. v). In over two hundred quarto pages, including the indexes, the author treats of such things as agriculture and agricultural implements, baking, flax-growing, the cultivation of the vine, bee-keeping, pastoral pursuits, weaving, clothing and ornaments, the household and its implements, family life, infancy, marriage, and death. Over one hundred photographs and sketches enable the reader to follow the investigation with ease, and the whole treatment is characterized, not only by a complete mastery of the material, but by a comprehensive consideration of every possible source of kindred information calculated to throw light upon the problems investigated. Indeed, the author may be said to have applied *every* method in this piece of work : his material is as copious and as reliable as the most exacting ' positivist ' could require ; the conclusions he draws with regard to Sardinian culture are used in their turn to throw light upon certain linguistic phenomena, in the approved Vosslerian fashion (cp. Chap. II) ; and, finally, in the case of borrowings between the various dialects, he applies to the study of the extension of words the methods of the linguistic geographer.

Max Leopold Wagner (side note)

---

[1] Published as a supplement to the review *Wörter u. Sachen*, like a number of other studies of the same order, e.g., W. Gerig, *Die Hanf- und Flachskultur in den frankoprovenzalischen Mundarten, mit Ausblicken auf die umgebenden Sprachgebiete* (1913) ; G. Huber, *Les appellations du traîneau et de ses parties dans les dialectes de la Suisse romane* (1919) ; Fr. Hobi, *Die Benennungen von Sichel und Sense in den Mundarten der romanischen Schweiz* (1926) ; each of these studies is accompanied by photographs and sketches.

It is not surprising, therefore, that Wagner's book met with a very favourable reception.[1] In the words of J. Jud, *Romania*, L (1924), p. 605 : " C'est le modèle d'un travail où se combinent l'étude simultanée des choses et des mots et, si je ne me trompe, c'est l'unique monographie que nous ayons jusqu'ici où l'auteur essaye de nous donner une vision complète de la vie, des ouvrages et de la langue d'une région romane."[1]

As the name of M. L. Wagner will recur more than once in subsequent pages, it is fitting that the reader should have some further information upon the remarkable work of this scholar, one of the leading Romanicists of the present day. Not only is he the greatest expert on Sardinian, on which he has published further studies comparatively recently (*Studien über den sardischen Wortschatz*, Geneva, 1930 ; *Die sardische Sprache in ihrem Verhältnis zur sardischen Kultur*, in *Volkstum und Kultur der Romanen*, V [1932], p. 21 f.), but also on the language of the Spanish Jews (cp. *Beiträge zur Kenntnis des Judenspanischen von Konstantinopel*, Vienna, 1914, and *Caracteres generales del judeo-español de Oriente*, Madrid, 1930). He has made numerous linguistic journeys throughout the whole of the Romance area, including Rumania and the Balkans, during which he acquired a practical knowledge of several of the languages. He writes Spanish and Italian like a native, and is the leading German authority on Spanish, particularly on the Spanish of the Americas. He is at once a philologist, an ethnologist, and a literary historian, witness his *Die spanisch-amerikanische Literatur in ihren Hauptströmungen*, 1924. This is how he is characterized by L. Spitzer, who considers him to be the most versatile of Romance linguists, in the practical sense of the term, since Schuchardt : " He combines, with an amazing mastery of languages, the widest theoretical equipment and training, and a knowledge of Romance taken direct from the source. To this he adds a delight in what is popular, autochthonous, particular, and strange, in foreign cultures, and not least in travel itself, in the exploring of outlying and unhospitable regions ; hence his predilection for peripheral linguistic fields, like Sardinian, Jewish Spanish, American Spanish,

---

[1] Among other reviews of Wagner's book may be mentioned those of : K. Vossler, *Literaturblatt f. germ. u. rom. Phil.*, XLIII (1922), col. 192 f. ; G. Rohlfs, *Die neueren Sprachen*, XXX (1922), p. 201 f. ; L. Spitzer, *Zeitschr. f. rom. Phil.*, XLIII (1923), p. 486 f. ; G. Giuglea, *Dacoromania*, II (1921–2), p. 816 f. ; B. A. Terracini, *Archivio storico sardo*, XV (1924), p. 220 f. ; G. Bottiglioni, *Rev. de ling. romane*, II (1926), p. 240 f. ; cp. also *Butlletí de dialectologia catalana*, X (1922), p. 147 f.

etc. In these special fields he has increased our factual knowledge, both of Romance speech and of Romance culture, that is to say, he is, in the best sense of the word, an investigator of civilization, even though his bent is towards the individual and the concrete rather than the general and the ideal." (*Zeitschr. f. rom. Phil.,* XLIII [1923], p. 486.)

The number of studies in Romance linguistics based upon a more or less systematic application of the ' word and thing ' method has much increased of recent years, but it would be impossible in a work like the present to enumerate more than a few of these. First of all, we should mention certain works, not all of them very recent, of a comprehensive character, that provide a rich stock of material, and are to a greater or less degree inspired by the method we are considering. Thus, for France, there is E. Rolland, *Faune populaire de la France,* Paris, 1877–1911 (13 volumes), and *Flore populaire de la France ou histoire naturelle des plantes dans leurs rapports avec la linguistique et le folklore,* Paris, 1896–1914 (11 vols.), and for Italy, A. Garbini, *Antroponomie ed omonimie nel campo della zoologia popolare,* Verona, 1919–25,[1] and O. Penzig, *Flora popolare italiana,* Genoa, 1924 (2 vols.). Though not the work of linguists in the strictest sense of the term, these volumes are mines of factual information concerning plants and animals for use in linguistic research, and provide, though only incidentally, a good deal of linguistic matter as well.[2] But a number of qualified linguists have also made the domains of popular botany and zoology their special study, investigating the names of plants or animals through the peculiar features of their life and habits, or studying on the same basis certain popular expressions and various popular practices and beliefs, with regard to the flora and fauna of the countryside. Among such linguistic naturalists we may mention R. Riegler and V. Bertoldi, the former a specialist in the animal world, and author of *Das Tier im Spiegel der Sprache* (Dresden-Leipzig, 1907), and of numerous articles in *Archiv für das Studium der neueren Sprachen und Literaturen, Die neueren Sprachen, Wörter und Sachen,* and *Archivum Romanicum,* the latter a specialist in flora, and author *inter*

---

[1] See K. Jaberg, *Zeitschr. f. rom. Phil.,* XLVIII (1928), p. 166 f. The work, together with that of Penzig, was also reviewed, from the linguistic point of view, by J. Jud, in *Romania,* LII (1926), p. 516 f.

[2] Rolland, in particular, quotes a great number of dialect terms and numerous popular proverbs, riddles, etc., relating to plants and animals. Garbini actually gives etymologies. Penzig confines himself to registering names, and does not even describe the plants he mentions.

alia of *Un ribelle nel regno dei fiori*, Geneva, 1923,[1] and of a number of extensive studies published in *Archivum Romanicum, Revue de linguistique romane* and elsewhere.

Of particular importance in this connection is the present association of the ' word and thing ' method with linguistic geography (*v.* Chap. III), which we find exemplified in the linguistic atlas in course of publication by K. Jaberg and J. Jud, *Sprach- und Sachatlas Italiens und der Südschweiz.* This impressive work, to which we will revert later, devotes, as the title indicates, particular attention to the domain of ' things ', providing sketches of implements, utensils, etc., to accompany and illustrate the linguistic maps, and is to be completed by a volume of photographs, some 3000 in number, in the manner advocated so warmly by Schuchardt (*v.* p. 67 *supra*). It would seem that in their teaching Jaberg and Jud have insisted upon the application of the ' word and thing ' method more than might be expected from their own published work. Numerous indeed are the theses and studies by linguists who have passed through the active seminars at Berne and Zurich dealing with questions relating to this domain, or applying the method whenever occasion arises.[2]

Among other centres that have been active in this field should be mentioned the Seminar of Romance Philology in the University of Hamburg. Here, since 1928, under the direction of Professor F. Krüger, to whom we owe, *inter alia, Die nordwestiberische Volkskultur* (*Wörter u. Sachen*, vol. X) and *Die Gegenstandskultur Sanabrias und seiner Nachbargebiete*, Hamburg, 1925, a review entitled *Volkstum und Kultur der Romanen* has been published, containing a considerable number of treatises dealing with the terminology and ' Realien ' of neo-Latin cultures.

Dutch linguists, too, have a good deal of similar work to their credit, thanks to the school of research inspired by the Romanicist J. J. Salverda de Grave, to whose reputation as a scholar the

---

[1] Reviewed by G. Pascu, *Revista critică*, V (1930), p. 15 f. One of Bertoldi's articles in *Revue de linguistique romane*, II (1926), p. 137 f., entitled, *Parole e idee : Monaci e popolo, " calques linguistiques " e etimologie popolari*, is of considerable theoretical importance, both with regard to the ' word and thing ' method itself, and to its association with the methods of linguistic geography of which we are about to speak.

[2] Jaberg himself has published in this field : *Dreschmethoden und Dreschgeräte in Romanisch-Bünden, Bündnerisches Monatsblatt*, 1922, p. 33 f. (cp. also Meyer-Lübke, *Über die Dreschgeräte*, in *Wörter u. Sachen*, I [1909], p. 211 f.), and *Zur Sach- und Bezeichnungsgeschichte der Beinkleidung in der Zentralromania, Wörter u. Sachen*, IX (1924–6), p. 137 f. (cp. his discussion of the same problem in *Die Sprachgeographie*, Aarau, 1908, p. 13 f.).

presentation volume, *Mélanges de Philologie*, Groningue, 1932, bears ample testimony. Though it is true that the bias of the Dutch school is distinctly towards lexicography, as can be seen from the titles of some of Salverda de Grave's own works (*De Franse woorden in het Nederlands*, Amsterdam, 1906 ; *L'influence de la langue française en Hollande d'après les mots empruntés*, Paris 1913), yet their researches imply the investigation of a variety of cultural influences and exchanges which entitles them to be associated, if only indirectly, with the Wörter und Sachen movement.[1]

In closer association with the movement is the work of certain Rumanian scholars, in particular the study entitled *Cuvinte şi lucruri, Elemente vechi germane în Orientul romanic*, published in the journal *Dacoromania*, II (1921–22), p. 327 f.,[2] by Gheorghe Giuglea. In this article, the author discusses a number of Rumanian words such as *strúngă, a băgà, a zgribulì, nástur*, etc., to which he ascribes a Germanic origin.[3] Though some of his etymologies are unconvincing, the article is of significance not only for the importance which the author attaches to the Germanic element in Rumanian, but for the wealth of material collected, and

---

[1] Among other productions of the Dutch school we may mention : D. C. Hesseling, *Les mots maritimes empruntés par la Grèce aux langues romanes*, Amsterdam, 1903 ; J. J. Becker Elringa, *Les mots français et les gallicismes dans le ' Hollandsche Spectator '*, Leyde, 1923 ; B. H. Wind, *Les mots italiens introduits en français au XVIe siècle*, Deventer, 1928 : M. Valkhoff, *Les mots français d'origine néerlandaise*, Amsterdam, 1931 ; B. E. Vidos, *La forza d'espansione della lingua italiana*, Nimègue, 1932 ; and a study of the Italian sea-words borrowed by French from Italian by the same author, which is to appear shortly in the *Archivum Romanicum*.

[2] Among more comprehensive studies similar to those mentioned above for French and Italian should be mentioned : F. Damé, *Incercare de terminologie poporană romînă*, Bucharest, 1898 ; S. Fl. Marian, *Ornitologia poporană romînă*, Cernăuţi, 1883, and *Insectele în limba, credinţele şi obiceiurile Romînilor*, Bucharest, 1903 ; Z. Panţu, *Plantele cunoscute de poporul romîn*, Bucharest, 1906 (2nd ed., 1929) ; Gr. Antipa, *Fauna ichtiologică a Romîniei*, Bucharest, 1909, and *Pescăria şi pescuitul în Romînia*, Bucharest, 1916. A more strictly linguistic study is that of G. Pascu, *Nume de plante*, in *Revista critică*, III (1929), and later vols.

[3] His derivation of *strúngă*, ' defile ', from Germ. *stanga* +Lat. *ruga*, for example, is somewhat artificial, particularly in view of the quite acceptable etymology proposed by A. Philippide, *Originea Romînilor*, I, p. 442 f., who associates it with the root *sru-, stru-*, ' to flow ', as in the names of rivers *Strumon* and *Istrus* : cp. the synonyms *gîrliciŭ*, derived from *gîrlă*, ' river ', and Macedorum. *arîstóăcă* from the Slavonic root *tok-, tek-*, ' to flow ' ; cp. P. Skok, *Zeitschr. f. rom. Phil.*, LIV (1934), p. 444. Giuglea's study, despite its merits, suffers from the same weakness that L. Spitzer detects in Meringer's study, ' *Zu französisch landier* ', reproduced in *Meisterwerke der rom. Sprachwissenschaft*, I, p. 221 f. " I do not consider Meringer's results to be certain, none the less it is instructive to note how the observation of things conducted by a realist like Meringer can lead to the building up of linguistic hypotheses, and how it may also come about, supposing that Meringer's etymology is wrong, that the observation of things may become a source of confusion and preconceptions.

for the entirely praiseworthy attempt to apply the ' word and thing ' method to the problems of Rumanian speech.

Finally, inasmuch as it deals with a territory in close relationship to the Rumanian area, and touches the history of Rumanian at so many points, we would mention a fine piece of work by N. Jokl, *Linguistisch-kulturhistorische Untersuchungen aus dem Bereiche des Albanischen*, Berlin–Leipzig, 1923.[1] The titles of the four main sections of this book are sufficient evidence of its right to be incorporated among the products of the ' Wörter und Sachen ' trend in modern linguistics ; they are : (1) Law, Customs, Beliefs ; (2) The house and its equipment ; (3) Landscape and Vegetation ; (4) Flocks and Herds and Animal Names.[2]

★　★　★

R. Meringer made further contributions to the renewal of linguistic studies, beyond his enthusiastic advocacy, and prolonged **Speech and Feeling** practice, of the study of things in conjunction with words. He devoted almost as much attention to those changes in language that have their source in the varying phases of the emotional life of the individual. He begins by recognizing that a speaker may make use of one and the same word in all manner of circumstances that are never completely identical. These differing circumstances affect him in different ways and thus bring about a modification, at first unnoticeable, then increasingly pronounced, in the very material of language. Further, regardless of the question of exterior circumstances, our minds receive certain stimuli which vary according to the psychological and physiological condition of the whole organism ; these, too, may result in modifications of our daily speech, modifications

---

[1] The book was reviewed (to confine ourselves to Rumanian scholars) by : Iorgu Iordan, *Arhiva*, XXXI (1924), p. 75 f. ; S. Puşcariu, *Dacoromania*, III (1923), p. 817 f. ; O. D.[ensusianu], *Grai şi suflet*, I (1923–4), p. 335 f. ; and G. Pascu, *Archivum Romanicum*, IX (1925), p. 300 f.

[2] With regard to other Romance and kindred fields, mention may be made of P. Rokseth's *Terminologie de la culture des céréales à Majorque*, Barcelona, 1923, W. Bierhenke, *Ländliche Gewerbe der Sierra de Gata, Sach- und wortkundliche Untersuchungen*, Hamburg, 1932, and G. Rohlfs' *Baskische Kultur im Spiegel des lateinischen Lehnwortes*, published in *Philologische Studien, Festschrift für Karl Voretzsch*, Halle a.S., 1927, p. 58 f. Cp. also the same scholar's *Sprache und Kultur*, Braunschweig, 1928. This work, which also concerns the theories of Vossler (*v.* Chap. II), was reviewed, unfavourably, by Vossler in *Deutsche Literaturzeitung*, XLIX (1928), col. 421 f. To this review Rohlfs replied in *Zeitschr. f. franz. Spr. u. Lit.*, LI (1928), p. 355.

both in sounds and in the meaning of words. Thus, to take one example among the semantic transformations pointed out by Meringer, the terms employed by various languages to convey the idea of ' to be necessary ' had, originally, a widely different meaning, and only gradually took on the notion of ' compulsion '. Similarly, in allied words like ' labour ', ' task ', ' lesson ', ' corvée ', etc., owing to the fact that the activities which such words denote are usually exercised under obligation, whether to a master, a teacher, a superior officer or what not, the displeasure that accompanies the action colours the meaning of the words themselves, and may even end by changing it entirely.[1]

Meringer treated both phonetic and semantic changes brought about through emotional influences. The following are a few of his studies in this domain : *Versprechen und Verlesen : Eine psychologisch-linguistische Studie*, Stuttgart, 1895 (in collaboration with K. Mayer) ; *Aus dem Leben der Sprache : Versprechen, Kindersprache, Nachahmungstrieb*, Berlin, 1908 ; *Sprache und Seele*, in *Wörter und Sachen*, VII (1921), p. 21 f. ; *Die innere Sprache in der Erregung, ibid.*, p. 40 f. ; *Die täglichen Fehler im Sprechen, Lesen und Handeln*, in *Wörter und Sachen*, VIII (1923), p. 122 f. In the first two of these, the author discusses a considerable number of errors in speaking and reading, interpreting them in the sense of the ideas set forth above. The second contains, in addition, a rich store of material drawn from the speech of children, who, as is well known, make numerous mistakes in talking, mainly due in their case to the fact that they have not yet achieved mastery over their language. Meringer is of the view (which A. Meillet contests in *Bulletin de la Société de linguistique de Paris*, XVI [1908–10], p. lxvii f.), that many changes in a language are to be attributed to errors of the type he describes and discusses in these two books. Similar questions are treated in the *Wörter und Sachen* articles, where he examines also the work of other scholars in the same field, and their interpretation of the facts he himself had brought forward. For numerous investigators, linguists and non-linguists alike, have been attracted by the problems raised by Meringer. First and foremost among these must be mentioned the founder of psycho-analysis, S. Freud,

---

[1] Cp. the origin and meaning of words for ' work ' in various languages ; see for example Iorgu Iordan, *Noţiunea ' muncă ' în limbile romanice*, in *Arhiva*, XXIX (1922), p 216 f.

On the ' affective ' side of language, see H. Delacroix, *Le langage et la pensée*, 2nd ed., Paris, 1930, p. 391 f. See also the discussion (p. 315 f. *infra*) of the work of Bally, whose point of view is a good deal different from that of Meringer and his school.

not on account of his present fame, but because his attitude towards errors of speech has had an influence upon certain representatives of our own studies.

In the journal *Monatsschrift für Psychiatrie und Neurologie*, X (1901), p. 1 f., Freud published a study, entitled *Zur Psychopathologie des Alltagslebens (Vergessen, Versprechen, Vergreifen) nebst Bemerkungen über eine Wurzel des Aberglaubens*, in which he makes use of material drawn from Meringer's *Versprechen und Verlesen*, though he gives it quite a different interpretation. Meringer attributed the majority of errors in speech and writing to the influence of other words in the same sentence.[1] Freud, on the other hand, in keeping with his well-known doctrine, attaches exceptional importance to those so-called *Nebengedanken*, the secret thoughts that dwell in the subconscious mind and influence the thoughts we are about to utter. Meringer, too, attributed certain mistakes to this cause. But Freud greatly exaggerates its importance, seeking to make it the source of nearly all such phenomena, and maintaining that here, too, we have to do with the repression of certain psychical conditions, which find an outlet despite our efforts, unconsciously influencing our thoughts and consequently our modes of expression. To take an example, our forgetting and subsequent mangling of certain proper names, which Meringer explained linguistically, as due to the influence of words whose mental pictures intervene at the moment when we are about to pronounce these names, is put by Freud to the account of other similar names, which arise in our consciousness and for various reasons are distasteful to us. At other times, the name we forget is one that touches some personal complex in the psyche of the speaker. Freud himself, for example, has difficulty, in the ordinary way, in remembering the name *Nervi*, for the reason that he has so much to do with nervous disorders, and on one occasion forgot the name of the locality *Rosenheim*, because at that very time he had been visiting his sister Rosa at her ' home ' (German ' *Heim* ').

---

[1] A further proof of the accuracy of this point of view is the fact that many words when syntactically related influence each other, particularly when they have certain phonetic features in common. The fun that ordinary folk get out of tongue-twisters of the type ' *She sells sea-shells on the sea-shore* ', and from spoonerisms has a definite bearing on this point. For German examples of this apparently universal phenomenon see H. Güntert, *Grundfragen der Sprachwissenschaft*, pp. 32, 33. A satisfying example from Rumanian is quoted by A. Philippide, *Viaţa romînească*, Iulie–Septembrie, 1915, p. 161, from I. Zanne, *Proverbele Romînilor*, II, p. 539 ; it runs : Nu-i anevoie a zice bou breaz bîrlobreaz, dar e anevoie a dîrlobîrlobrezi dîrlobîrlobrezitura din oile dîrlobîrlobrezeanului.

Meringer had contested this kind of interpretation, as being improbable and one-sided, in his *Aus dem Leben der Sprache*, but as Freud repeated his views in the later editions of his works, Meringer returned to the attack in *Wörter und Sachen*, VIII (1923), p. 122 f.

A middle view, though with visible leanings towards Freud, is represented by the Germanic scholar H. Sperber in his *Über den Einfluss sexueller Momente auf Entstehung und Entwicklung der Sprache*, published in *Imago*, Vienna, 1912, no. 5 (cp. L. Spitzer, *Wörter und Sachen*, V [1913], p. 206 f.), his *Über den Affekt als Ursache der Sprachveränderung*, Halle a.S., 1914, and his introduction to semantics (*Einführung in die Bedeutungslehre*), Bonn-Leipzig, 1923 (in particular p. 38 f.). Meringer also opposes Sperber, insisting (*Wörter und Sachen*, VII [1921], p. 21 f.) that the majority of errors in speech are of a purely phonetic character, and have nothing to do with the repression of our thoughts. In the same article of his journal he deals with other linguists who have treated similar problems, like F. N. Finck (*Der deutsche Sprachbau als Ausdruck deutscher Weltanschauung*, Marburg, 1899, *Die Klassifikation der Sprachen*, Marburg, 1901, *Die Haupttypen des Sprachbaus*, Leipzig, 1910), and E. Lewy (*Zur Sprache des alten Goethe : Ein Versuch über die Sprache des Einzelnen*, Berlin, 1913).[1] The former has attempted a classification of the languages of the world according to the temperament of the peoples who speak them, the latter applies the theories of psycho-analysis to the study of certain stylistic peculiarities discernible in the works of Goethe's later years. Meringer is ready to admit the rightness of a point of view common to all these works, the recognition that in the production of speech our individuality, and our emotional condition (our *Erregung*, as Meringer calls it), play a very active and indeed an indispensable part. It is from a kindred source that another factor arises to determine, in an important degree, the characteristics of human speech, namely, fashion and imitation. The cool reserve of the English, that is so widely extolled, is to be explained much less by temperament—their parliamentary debates prove that they are by no means apathetic—than by education, and the will to appear phlegmatic. Similarly, according to Meringer, the German of Germany proper was strongly influenced by the officer class, who, before the war, enjoyed extraordinary

---

[1] It is significant that this work appeared in a preliminary form in the *Zeitschrift für Sexualwissenschaft*, 1930 (cp. L. Spitzer, *Meisterwerke der romanischen Sprachwissenschaft*, I, p. 345).

prestige, and whose language was manifestly imitated by the great mass of their fellow-countrymen.[1]

Of particular interest is Meringer's article, *Die innere Sprache in der Erregung* (*Wörter und Sachen*, VII [1921], p. 50 f.). Here we find him expressing opinions not far removed from those of Freud, whose generalizations he had opposed. Even when we do not utter a single word, he states, there exists within us a kind of inward speech. Certain things come to our minds which would seem to have found expression within our thoughts. As soon as we begin to talk, these reminiscences, which are in full vitality in the depths of our consciousness, exercise an influence, unknown to ourselves, upon the thoughts to which we give utterance.

We shall revert to the question of speech and feeling later, in the paragraphs on Ch. Bally's work and on ' argot ', when we come to discuss the French school of linguists (Chap. IV) ; there we shall see that the problem can be approached from another angle. We would only add here that, among Romance scholars, L. Spitzer pays the greatest attention to the affective element in language, in all its manifestations, as is indeed to be expected in a scholar who shows a special predilection for stylistics and etymology. But, generally, it can be said that there is an increasing tendency to take this emotional element into consideration, particularly as its influence can be detected in every constituent of human speech. It plays its part in pronunciation as is shown for example by J. Marouzeau in his study, *Accent affectif et accent intellectuel* (reproduced in *Meisterwerke der romanischen Sprachwissenschaft*, I, p. 69 f.),[2] and in grammar generally ; cp. E. Gamillscheg, *Zur Einwirkung des Affekts auf den Sprachbau*, in *Neuphilologische Monatsschrift*, I (1930), p. 14 f. In the latter study, which is copiously illustrated with examples from French, Gamillscheg, after first showing how emotional speech makes great play with the quantitative value of sounds, affirms that it is just this departure from the normal which, in general, characterizes emotional and expressive speech, not only in sounds, but also in syntax. The adjective, for example,

---

[1] Nietzsche (cp. *Fröhliche Wissenschaft*, II, p. 104 : *cit.* H. Sperber, *Wörter u. Sachen*, XII [1929], p. 183), had already noted that the speech of German officers was widely imitated by Germans of almost every age, particularly by civil servants, professors, business men, women and even girls.

[2] The same author has published a short article on an allied topic entitled *Deux aspects de la langue vulgaire : langue expressive et langue banale*, in *Bulletin de la Soc. ling. de Paris*, XXVIII (1927-8), fasc. 2, p. 63 f.

usually placed after the noun, where it has an entirely neutral descriptive value, appealing solely to the intellect, acquires, when set before the substantive, an emotional ' subjective ' colouring. And a further characteristic of this type of speech is that it soon loses its expressive value and becomes accepted as normal and colourless. In other words, affectivity is a creator of grammar.[1]

★   ★   ★

From the foregoing pages it is clear that the dissatisfaction with the conceptions and methods of the neo-grammarian grows stronger as we approach the end of the nineteenth century,
Romance Linguistics and Philosophy
and increased efforts are accordingly made to bring about a change. In order as far as possible to complete our information concerning the evolution of Romance studies, round about the year 1900, and the causes of this evolution, it remains for us to say something of the more or less similar developments that came about in other fields of intellectual activity, and have directly or indirectly influenced the science of linguistics generally.

It is well known that the naturalism which, in conjunction with historicism, held sway over our discipline during the course of the past century, was just as preponderant in the domains of philosophy, literature, and art. Determinism and materialism in philosophy, and their various offshoots, positivism, pragmatism, monism, etc., realism proper, and its offspring impressionism, in literature and painting, are nothing more than so many manifestations of one and the same principle, whereby, in science, philosophy, literature, and the arts, facts were to be given precedence over ideas, and matter over mind. The greater the accumulation of material, and the more detailed its description, the more fully, apparently, did each

[1] Cp. the discussion of Bally's work in Chap. IV *infra*. Among other Romanicists who might be mentioned in this connection are Gustav Gröber, who was among the first to show the importance of the psychological study of syntax, and who, in *Grundriss der romanischen Philologie*, I, 2nd ed., p. 272 f., draws a sharp distinction between logical speech, ' objektive Darstellung ', as he calls it, and affective, ' subjektive Darstellung ', thus pointing the way for future research (cp. L. Spitzer, *Meisterwerke*, II, pp. 66 f. and 335–6) ;   Elise Richter, *Grundlinien der Wortstellungslehre*, in *Zeitschr. f. rom. Phil.*, XL (1920), p. 9 f.; and E. Lerch, *Typen der Wortstellung*, in *Idealistische Neuphilologie, Festschrift für Karl Vossler*, Heidelberg, 1922, p. 85 f.

discipline achieve its ideal. Thus, philosophy, which in general strikes the note that is taken up by the other moral sciences, had become entirely empirical, and had consequently broken with metaphysics, our sole guide to an understanding of the causes and signification of the phenomena of this world.

A reaction was inevitable. It began, as was to be expected, in philosophy, and its aim was to throw off the tyranny of conceptions that had been borrowed from the experimental sciences. Against naturalism in psychology, the efforts of the German philosopher, Edm. Husserl, were particularly conspicuous, while, in philosophy proper, his compatriots, W. Windelband and H. Rickert, strove against the tendency to construct a conception of the universe on conclusions drawn from the results of the natural sciences, insisting particularly on the essential differences between the latter and the historical or moral sciences, not only in method, but also in purpose. Although both, they maintain, are based on the observation of individual facts, the natural sciences seek to arrive at general principles, to discover certain laws, and to do so must leave out of account the particular, whereas it is just with what is particular that the moral sciences are in the main concerned. But it does not therefore follow that the latter must needs confine themselves to the presentation and interpretation of even the more characteristic facts studied in isolation. Here, too, relationships must be established between one case and another, on the basis of some guiding principle that sets in evidence what is essential among the multitude of individual facts. This principle is constituted, according to Windelband and Rickert, by what they call ' cultural values ', which have in them something absolute and permanent, like the laws of science, without, however, in any degree being identifiable with the latter. Thus, the distinction between the two categories of scientific discipline lies really in their methods of forming notions. Windelband and Rickert give pride of place to the historical over the natural sciences when it is a matter of framing a conception of the world, inasmuch as the former, from the point of view of forming notions, is in closer contact with visible realities than the latter. But neither the ' laws ' of the one group, nor the ' cultural values ' of the other, can lead us to the discovery of the real and ultimate causes of things. Which is tantamount to recognizing that the intelligence, the source of all our notions, is incapable of providing an explanation of the phenomena of the world around us.

But it was the French philosopher, H. Bergson,[1] who was to deal the severest blow to intelligence as an instrument of knowledge. The function of the intelligence, according to Bergson, is analytic ; it breaks down phenomena into their constituent elements, and presents them to us piecemeal, and thus falsifies reality. At the same time, it destroys everything that constitutes the true life of things, that is to say that character of instability, of perpetual flux, possessed by those moments which make up a given phenomenon, and which are never identical one with the other. This defect is more marked, and consequently more dangerous to the ascertaining of truth, when we seek to account for things pertaining to the domain of consciousness, for here we are confronted in a still greater measure with that element of instability, of continual movement and change, which is one of the essential features of life. It follows that with the intelligence alone it is impossible to grasp the true nature and the causes of things. The notions we frame through the intelligence, and apply to the various domains of scientific enquiry, suffer from the same defects, and like it are rigid, limited and isolated, unsuited, in a word, to reconstruct the relationships between those elements which constitute a phenomenon, and which, when taken severally, by the only method open to the intelligence, are torn from their natural place, and from the organic order to which they belong.

To understand things as they really are, to preserve their essential character, which is one of unceasing movement, flux, and life, we need another faculty. Bergson finds this in instinct, which is opposed to intelligence, inasmuch as it possesses characteristics very like those of life itself : it is mobile, protean, without beginning and without end. It is as distinct from intelligence as the sense of sight is distinct from the sense of touch. " Intelligence is, primarily, the power to establish relations between two points in space, and between two material objects. It can be applied to all sorts of tasks, but it remains outside them, and in any deep causal relationship never sees beyond a disintegration of it into a series of co-existing effects. Whereas instinct perceives phenomena by working from within to without, by means quite different from those of a process of knowing ; its perceptions are living experiences, rather than representations, springing from intuition, which is of the same nature, assuredly, as what we call

---

[1] For Bergson's ideas upon language, v. H. Delacroix, *Le langage et la pensée*, 2nd ed., p. 61 f.

sympathetic understanding." Bergson is thinking, that is to say, of instinct which has become conscious of itself, and which, though aided in this by intelligence, has succeeded, by the properties we have mentioned, in rising above the latter as a perceptive faculty. Instinct, awakened to life and consciousness, enables us to contemplate phenomena in their entirety and absolutely, because its functions, unlike those of the intelligence, are synthetic. Wherefore, whenever we are concerned with totality, with organized and unified wholes, we are obliged to call upon intuition, that is to say, upon instinct conscious of itself.

Bergson's doctrine found an echo far beyond the field of philosophy, especially as there is no essential difference in the instrument of knowledge between the latter and science proper. His ' intuitivism ' made itself felt in a special degree in the domains of art, literature, and criticism. Here it found an ally in the doctrine of B. Croce, who, although in philosophy a rationalist, makes intuition the determining factor in matters of literary or artistic appreciation, as we shall see in the following chapter, when discussing the idealistic or aesthetic school of Vossler. As for linguistics, it was impossible that the study of language should remain unaffected by the philosophical doctrines outlined in the preceding pages. On the one hand, as a scientific discipline, it needs must set its own special means of attaining to a knowledge of reality in agreement with the theories of philosophy concerning this task ; as a branch of philology, in the widest sense of the term, it is obliged, on the other, to borrow from allied disciplines, such as literary history and criticism, certain methods of work, particularly as it frequently happens that one and the same scholar is a student both of language and of literature ; witness the cases of Fr. Diez, Gaston Paris, H. Morf, R. Menéndez Pidal, K. Vossler, L. Spitzer and others.[1]

★

[1] The foregoing discussion is based almost entirely upon the work of Fr. Schürr, *Sprachwissenschaft und Zeitgeist*, Marburg a.L., 1922, p. 3 f., to which the reader is referred for further details. The trend of his brochure is sufficiently indicated by the following quotations : " Science also is conditioned by the spiritual attitude of the period." " Science cannot avoid taking its stand in the conflict that is going on in the fields of philosophy and modern art between divergent conceptions of the universe." With regard to intuition, Schürr is aware of the dangers inherent in its use as a method of research. To avoid becoming too subjective, we must call in intelligence to guide it, as was admitted

We are now at the end of the chapter dealing with the development of Romance linguistics during the course of the nineteenth century. We have seen its beginnings as a properly constituted science, named its most illustrious representatives, and discussed a number of problems with which it has been concerned, and the attitude adopted with regard to these by various Romance scholars. It will readily be understood that we have been unable, so far, to separate our discipline from the wider discipline which gave it birth some hundred years ago, namely, Indo-European philology ; not only because, theoretically, it is prejudicial to set up hard-and-fast boundaries between the various branches of linguistic study, but also for another reason, namely, that until the end of the past century Romance studies did actually evolve in dependence, and at times in very close dependence, upon Indo-European philology, which, as a much longer established discipline, and for other reasons, continued to enjoy exceptional prestige in the eyes of scholars. Similarly, we have been obliged to belie the title of the present chapter and trespass upon the period of the present century, for the obvious reason that the older representatives of our discipline, whether supporters or opponents of those neo-grammarian doctrines that held sway during the last quarter of the nineteenth century, did not cease their scientific activity in the year 1900.

It now remains for us to describe the principal currents that prevail in Romance linguistics at the present time. Before doing so, in order to avoid possible misunderstandings,[1] two points must be made clear with regard to the scheme of the present treatise.

---

by Bergson himself. A second edition of Schürr's work, dedicated like the first to Vossler, whose attitude to problems of linguistic theory he may be said to share, appeared in 1925. It contains a number of additions particularly in the concluding portion, p. 81 f. His concluding remark is worth quoting : " The present conception of linguistics requires from its adepts both personal intuition and creative powers in the highest degree ; it demands that the researcher should be at the same time an artist. More than ever before it is a matter of creative personality." For reviews of the book, see A. Wallensköld, *Neuphilologische Mitteilungen*, XXII (1922), p. 152 f.; K. Vossler, *Deutsche Literaturzeitung*, XLIII (1922), col. 1041 f.; Fr. Karpf, *Die neueren Sprachen*, XXXI (1923), p. 232 f. ; L. Spitzer, *Literaturblatt f. germ. u. rom. Phil.*, XLIV (1923), col. 81 f. ; A. M.[eillet], *Bulletin de la Société de linguistique*, XXIV (1923–4), fasc. 2, p. 15 f. ; Ed. Hermann, *Zeitschr. f. rom. Phil.*, XLIV (1924), p. 123 f. ; A. Kluyver, *Neophilologus*, VIII (1922–3), p. 221 f.

[1] Of the type apparent in Meyer-Lübke's article, *Die romanische Sprachwissenschaft der letzten zwölf Jahre*, in *Rev. de linguistique rom.*, I (1925), p. 9 f., where the present author is reproached, unjustifiably, with having been unfair to the older schools in an article that was entitled " *Der* heutige *Stand der romanischen Sprachwissenschaft*" and published in 1924, in *Stand und Aufgaben der Sprachwissenschaft, Festschrift für Wilhelm Streitberg* (Heidelberg). The date 1924, and the term *heutige*, should have made any misunderstanding impossible.

In the first place, it must not be concluded, from the fact that no further mention of the neo-grammarians is made in subsequent pages, that the latter have dropped out entirely, or that their work is completely negligible in comparison with that of the adepts of more recent doctrines. On the contrary, a considerable number of Romanicists remain faithful to the older traditions, though it must be said, both to do them justice and to tell the truth, that they too, willingly or unwillingly, have appropriated many of the newer principles and methods. Yet notwithstanding this, we are justified in leaving them out of account henceforth, because, in the present chapter, we have already amply discussed their doctrines and given a sufficiently conspicuous place to their more distinguished representatives.

The second point to be made clear is the following. By no means all the linguists to be mentioned in subsequent chapters have broken new ground, or can be described as revolutionary. F. de Saussure, particularly, and the majority of those we shall group round him, are to be considered in many respects as the successors to the neo-grammarians of last century. None the less, beside much that they inherit from their predecessors, they have succeeded in introducing into their work so many fresh features that we are justified in recording them among the renewers of our discipline. Moreover, certain elements of their doctrine, for example, the sociological outlook upon language, represented particularly by A. Meillet, or again the importance given to the affective factor in language by writers like Ch. Bally, which has resulted in the founding of an entirely new linguistic discipline, namely stylistics, have exercised an extremely beneficial and widening influence upon our studies, and kept them more completely in touch with the spirit of the times.[1]

[1] The following bibliography on the question of the present state of Romance studies contains a certain number of articles to which the author has not had access : J. J. Salverda de Grave, *Quelques observations sur l'évolution de la philologie romane depuis* 1884 (noted in *Moyen-Âge*, Nov.–Dec., 1907, p. 355, by G. Huet) ; S. Puşcariu, *Probleme nouă în cercetările lingvistice*, in *Convorbiri literare*, XLIV (1910), pp. 452 f. and 523 f. ; O. Schultz-Gora, *Die deutsche Romanistik in den zwei letzten Jahrzehnten*, in *Archiv f. das Stud. der neueren Spr. u. Lit.*, CXLI (1921), p. 208 f. ; S. Puşcariu, *Probleme nouă in cercetările lingvistice*, in *Cugetul romînesc*, I (1922), p. 73 f. ; O. Densusianu, *Orientări nouă în cercetările filologice*, in *Grai şi suflet*, I (1923–4), p. 1 f. ; W. Meyer-Lübke, art. *cit. supra* ; S. Puşcariu, *Dicţionarul Academiei*, in *Memoriile Academiei Romîne*, secţia literară, seria III, t. III, p. 208 f. ; G. Bertoni, *Indirizzi e orientamenti della filologia romanza*, in *Archivum Romanicum*, XIII (1929), p. 209 f. ; W. Meyer-Lübke, *Romanische Philologie*, in *Aus 50 Jahren deutscher Sprachwissenschaft. Fr. Schmidt-Ott dargebracht*, Berlin, 1930, p. 232 f. (cp. *Arch. f. d. Stud. d. neueren Spr.*, CLIX [1931], p. 150) ; S. Puşcariu, *Lingvistica modernă*

We shall discuss the three chief schools of contemporary Romance linguistics in the following order : (1) The Idealistic school of K. Vossler ; (2) J. Gilliéron and Linguistic Geography ; (3) The French school (F. de Saussure and his followers). A final chapter will be devoted to certain less important branches, which are either direct offshoots from the above, or closely related to them.

şi evoluţia ei, in *Jara Bîrsei*, an. 1931, no. 1 (13 p. in off-print) ; G. Bertoni, *I nuovi problemi della linguistica romanza*, in *Rev. de ling. rom.*, IX (1933), p. 169 f. ; G. Ipsen, *Sprachphilosophie der Gegenwart*, Berlin, 1930 ; L. Spitzer, *L'Etat actuel des études romanes en Allemagne*, in *Rev. d'Allemagne*, VI (1932), p. 572 f. ; Manuel de Paiva Boléo, *Orientações da Filologia románica na Alemanha e o Seminario Românico de Hamburgo*, in *Biblos* (Coimbra), May–June, 1931 (93 p. in off-print) : Ed. Hermann, *Der heutige Stand der Sprachwissenschaft*, in *Zeitschrift f. Deutschkunde*, XLV (1931), p. 145 f. ; A. Schiaffini, *Linguistica neolatina*, in *Nuova Antologia*, 1 July and 16 September, 1932 ; H. Hatzfeld, *Neuere Aufgaben der romanischen Philologie*, in *Neue Jahrbücher f. Wissenschaft u. Geistesbildung*, VIII, p. 432 f. ; N. Maccarrone, *Principî e metodi nella linguistica storica*, in *Revue de ling. rom.*, VI (1931), p. 1 f. ; B. Terracini, *Correnti vecchie e nuove nella linguistica storica contemporanea*, in *Atti della Società Italiana per il progresso delle scienze*, XVIII Riunione, Firenze, September, 1929, Pavia, 1929 ; G. Bertoni, *Nuovi orientamenti linguistici*, in *Leonardo*, II (1926), fasc. 2.

CHAPTER II

THE IDEALISTIC OR AESTHETIC SCHOOL OF K. VOSSLER

ONE of the keenest opponents of neo-grammarianism is Karl Vossler, professor of Romance Philology in the University of Munich. Inspired by the theoretical pronouncements of von Humboldt and of Schuchardt, by the conclusions drawn by such as Rousselot or Gauchat from their observations of the facts of language, by the aesthetic doctrines of Croce, and withal by his own convictions, Vossler, for some thirty years now, that is, from the beginning of his linguistic activity, has taken up an attitude of hostility to the older school. His views upon the problems around which, as we have seen, theoretical controversy has centred among the workers in our field, are to be found in a series of studies that have appeared at intervals from 1904 to the present time. We shall analyse these succinctly, in chronological order.

He opens the attack with *Positivismus und Idealismus in der Sprachwissenschaft*, Heidelberg, 1904, which in many respects can be considered as the manifesto of the idealistic school. To Vossler, as to the neo-grammarians, linguistics is a historical discipline, as being one of the moral sciences (Geisteswissenschaften), and as concerning itself with the development or evolution of the phenomena it investigates. But in our observations of phenomena we must be guided by idealistic, not positivist principles. Positivism, to Vossler, signifies research into linguistic phenomena as an end in itself, the piling up of the greatest possible wealth of material; idealism, on the other hand, aims at determining relations of causality between the facts of language.[1] The

---

[1] Vossler opposes positivism only as an attitude of the mind, the outlook that confuses linguistic facts, i.e. the product of certain inner forces of the language, with those forces themselves. He is naturally no opponent of positivism in method, i.e. the basing of our investigations upon the securest documentation possible.
The Indo-Europeanist W. Porzig, who, though not belonging to Vossler's

positivists believe that the dividing up of grammar into phonology, morphology, syntax, etc., is something much more than a practical device for the more convenient and more systematic study of language. They lose sight of an essential fact, namely, that sounds, words, and sentences, are merely articulations of human speech that enable it to move with freedom. In reality it is the spirit of the language that is the force which constitutes and integrates the sentence, with its component parts, words and sounds. To the idealist, language appears as an expression of the human spirit ; and the history of language signifies consequently a history of the forms of expression, that is to say artistic history, in the widest sense of the term. It follows from this definition that grammar belongs to the history of style and of literature, which in turn forms a branch of the history of culture. Consequently, the best method for the study of a language is, after describing in detail its grammar, to explain the respective phenomena stylistically.[1] To illustrate these purely theoretical assertions Vossler gives us examples from every branch of grammar.

Thus, it is generally asserted that the disappearance of the Latin declension in the Romance languages is due to the fall of the final consonants. Old French and Old Provençal, which kept final *s* up to the thirteenth century, preserved therefore a two-case declension till about the same date.[2] But why is it that Spanish, which also preserves final *s*, even to-day, shows no trace of a formal distinction between objective and nominative ? Just as erroneous is the positivist contention that the disappearance of the two-case

school, has a similar approach to language, defines positivism and idealism as follows : " By positivism we understand that scientific attitude which, taking the isolated fact as a starting-point, considers the function of science to be the exact co-ordination of all such facts. Idealism, on the other hand, looks upon the world as a system made up of perceptible forms, whose nature is solely determined by their function within the whole which they compose. Single phenomena have their value in the positivist's eyes because they exist, for the idealist, because they have a meaning."—*Sprachform u. Bedeutung, Indogermanisches Jahrbuch*, XII (1928), p. 2 f.

[1] The question of ' Stylistics ' will be treated more fully below, with reference to the work of L. Spitzer and Ch. Bally. We can define it provisionally as the branch of linguistic study which concerns itself with those phenomena that display most clearly the life or spirit of a language, whereas syntax and grammar in general investigate linguistic phenomena which have become set formulae, and have lost their expressive vitality.

[2] Latin *murus* becomes, phonetically, *murs* in Old Fr. and Old Prov. ; *murum* gives *mur* ; similarly *muri* gives *mur*, and *muros*, *murs*. This system is extended by analogy to most masculine nouns, in both languages. On the question of the disappearance of the Latin case endings and other flexions, *v.* Ch. Bally, *Linguistique générale et linguistique française*, Paris, 1932, p. 175 ; cp. also Delacroix, *Le langage et la pensée*, 2nd ed., p. 50 f.

declension in French brought with it the fixed order, subject—verb—object, in place of the freedom of word order which once prevailed. The order of words, as we now recognize, has its source in the spirit of the language, that is to say, in the minds of its individual speakers. The Frenchman's love for logic and regularity created the usage, which first of all must have been the work of an individual, but which became generalized as the genius of the language gave it strength, until finally it became a set syntactical norm. Thus the disappearance of final *s* and the existence of the two-case declension are, in fact, merely accessory phenomena, not *causes* of the order, subject—verb—object, and all three are to be set to the account of the psychological make-up of the French people. Even the most insignificant linguistic developments are to be accounted for in the same manner, such for example as the gender of substantives in different languages—compare the words for ' sun ' and ' moon ' in Germanic and Romance—which, it has been contended, is merely conditioned by the phonetic development of the several words, inasmuch as there is no *logical* justification for such a distinction. This contention contains, according to Vossler, a further error, more serious than that of a merely wrong explanation, inasmuch as it speaks of ' logic ' in an investigation into the facts of language. Language is a-logical, and words are merely symbols or metaphors which never fully coincide with the notions they are used to express. It will be seen that Vossler's starting point is ' Speech ' rather than ' Language ', ' la Parole ' rather than ' la Langue ', to use the Saussure terminology (*v.* Chap. IV), for it is the actualization of language in ' la Parole ' which is really a-logical.

With regard to syntax, the positivists speak of objective and subjective tendencies, that is to say, of tendencies springing from reason and reflexion, and of tendencies that are emotional and affective, resulting in ' regular ' syntax on the one hand, and ' irregular ' on the other. This conception implies two errors : the first, that of giving absolute values to what are merely relative terms, since what appears irregular to-day may ultimately become a perfectly regular construction ; the second, and much more serious, that of proceeding from Syntax, or the general and normal, to ' Style ', or the irregular and individual. In reality language follows the reverse direction. Every linguistic utterance is of a purely individual character. Even when we repeat the words of another, we cannot be said to reproduce them, because, as we repeat them, we create them anew, giving them something of our own personality, which is essentially different from the personality of other men. Thus, modifications in language, of whatever kind, are individual in their origin. They are the work of certain individual speakers who are speech-creative, and spread from them to the remainder of the linguistic community.[1] Hence, for Vossler, dialects and sub-dialects do not exist. He recognizes only individual speeches : so many individuals, so many separate languages, so many ' styles '.[2] Nevertheless, these marked differences between one individual and another allow of a general resemblance in expression and content, and at the same time similarity of content leads to similarity of linguistic forms. Thus, in other words, through and from individual ' style ' we are led to syntax. Stylistic is the only true linguistic study in the strict sense of the word, inasmuch as speech, says Vossler, is always representation and intuition : " Language is in its essence an inner activity, intuition ".[3] The linguist must therefore create anew the language he is studying, just as a critic recreates a work of art.

As for semantics, the psychological factor is important enough to be recognized even by the positivists, who themselves distinguish between the usual or general meaning attached to words, and their individual or exceptional usage, which may in turn give rise to a new general acceptation. But here again the positivists go astray, inasmuch as they have recourse to all manner of terms to designate the various modifications of meaning, which, despite their great variety, are in reality nothing more than divers aspects of the sole genuine source of semantic modification, namely metaphor. And, as metaphor alone is the product of intuition, or of language—remembering Vossler's equation : Language=expression=intuition—whereas the so-called ' figures of rhetoric ' are matters of logic, it is metaphor which must be the sole concern of the linguist in his investigation of semantic change.

---

[1] It is clear that Vossler has points of resemblance with Schuchardt, and with Meringer (cp. certain ideas expressed in *Aus dem Leben der Sprache*). It will be seen later that he has also points of agreement with Gilliéron. The notion of speech-creative speakers is to be found also in Puşcariu, *Despre legile fonologice* (*v. supra*, p. 43 f.).

[2] Vossler's ideas on this point call to mind those of Schuchardt, Rousselot and Gauchat, mentioned above. We shall find similar ideas, with convincing proofs, expressed by Gilliéron. It should be added that Vossler's convictions are rather deductive and intuitive, than, as with the other scholars, the result of direct observation.

[3] " Das Wesen der Sprache ist innere Tätigkeit : Intuition " ; *op. cit.*, p. 50.

The Munich scholar, further, pays considerable attention to the question of Sound-Laws, with regard to which his attitude is fundamentally at variance with that of the positivists. To demonstrate the weakness of the latter Vossler makes a detailed analysis of Wechssler's study *Gibt es Lautgesetze ?* (*vide supra*, p. 48, n.), which he considers the best pronouncement upon the question up to the year 1904. Wechssler's first mistake, he says, is to consider language as a physical or psycho-physical phenomenon, and not primarily as the product of some spiritual activity. Hence he speaks of the painful process of acquiring a language and the striving towards phonetic regularity. Such conceptions are clearly erroneous, seeing that spiritual activity constitutes the very life of a language, and that a trend towards phonetic uniformity, where it exists, spells the death of language. It is well known, moreover, that persons of mature age, who possess to a greater or less degree a personality of their own, have greater difficulty in reproducing the sounds of a foreign tongue as perfectly as do children, whose personality is undeveloped. As for the term ' Sound-Laws ', considered in themselves, Vossler holds that it rests upon a circular argument : first of all, he says, it is decided that all modifications of sound that have their source in a shifting of the basis of articulation or of stress are general, and then each phonetic change is taken separately and declared to be without exception, because it depends upon the basis of articulation or stress ! Yet, in spite of this, the positivists are obliged to recognize a considerable number of exceptions, which they explain away by having recourse to analogy, contamination, or borrowing. In reality, Vossler declares, all modifications of sound are individual, and the difference between ' popular words ' and ' learned words ', i.e. words taken over from Latin into the Romance languages at a later date, and not part of the original inheritance, is merely a quantitative, not a qualitative difference.[1] It must not be thought, however, that to combat the Sound-Laws is tantamount to asserting that all changes of sound are arbitrary. To the idea of ' Law ' we must set in opposition the idea of ' freedom ' : phonetic changes are to be envisaged as taking place along certain lines which are determined by the genius of the language, and it is this which it is the task of linguistics to discover.

The distinction made by the positivists between ' sound-change '

---

[1] Here again Vossler's views approximate to those of Gilliéron (*v. infra*, p. 173) although he reaches them by a very different path.

and 'analogy' is of merely practical value : in the latter, the meaning of the word plays an important part, whereas in the former stress or accent is a predominant factor. But stress and meaning are two names for the same notion, namely, the spirit of the language.[1] There are no phonetic phenomena which are the exclusive products either of sound-shifting or of analogy ; the so-called 'Sound-Law' is the effect of the levelling tendency in language. Sound-change takes place where a word has preserved its individuality ; analogy operates when a word is compared with others, that is to say particularly in flexions. Stress is not of a variety of types, as is generally stated. In reality there is but one, the rhetorical, or, better, the artistic stress, which varies from one language to another, as is seen by comparing Romance with Germanic languages, or Romance languages among themselves. At the same time, stress or accent, like style, is individual, differing not only from man to man, but also in the speech of the same individual according to his mood and mental condition.

In a word, every linguistic expression is the result of individual activity, and becomes generalized through acceptance by other individual speakers. When a linguistic innovation takes place there is absolute progress of the language, for the latter is active ; when the innovation spreads, there is relative progress, for here there is no longer creation, but development. Every person is guided by two impulses, one constraining him to make use, as far as possible, of the language of his fellows,[2] the other prompting him to possess a style of his own. A matter of absolute progress in language can only be studied from the aesthetic point of view, while relative progress is to be studied both aesthetically and historically, or, to use the positivist terminology, in the first case we have to do with descriptive grammar, in the second with historical grammar. These two methods of approach are not mutually exclusive, and are to be applied comparatively ; in the first case, the forms of expression are compared with the underlying intuition, in the second with other forms of expression.

The creative and the evolutive phases of language are further

---

[1] Accent is taken as the real modifying factor in language by Elise Richter in her study, *Der innere Zusammenhang in der Entwicklung der romanischen Sprachen* (*v.* 27 *Beiheft zur Zeitschrift f. rom. Philologie*, Halle a.S., 1911, p. 57 f.).

[2] Vossler goes so far as to state explicitly that language is not a means of communication between men, and only serves as such, not because of some linguistic convention, but because individuals who speak the same language have a common linguistic capacity.

explained in another work of Vossler's entitled *Sprache als Schöpfung und Entwicklung*, Heidelberg, 1905. Whereas, in the first work, he had taken the positivists to task, he is here concerned with what is called linguistic psychology (*Sprachpsychologie*) whose chief representative is the German philosopher, W. Wundt, in *Völkerpsychologie*, I. Band, *Die Sprache*.[1] Vossler opposes the latter's contention that all linguistic research should be based upon psychology. Psychology, he maintains, is an empirical and descriptive science, which studies the human mind as something conditioned, and has therefore little to do with language. It may be of use in explaining certain phenomena of analogy, when they are already in being (as has been proved, for example, by the experiments conducted by the linguist, A. Thumb, and the psychologist, K. Marbe),[2] whereas what is needed is a discipline that will enable us to understand each and every analogy when in the making. It is only Aesthetics, in the fullest sense of the term, that can render this service, inasmuch as Aesthetics and Logic are the only sciences that investigate the human mind as a creative and unconditioned force.[3]

[1] First edition, Leipzig, 1900 ; second and third editions, Leipzig, 1904 and 1911–12.

[2] *Experimentelle Untersuchungen über die psychologischen Grundlagen der sprachlichen Analogiebildung*, Leipzig, 1901 ; reviewed by : H. Schuchardt, in *Literaturblatt f. germ. u. rom. Phil.*, XXIII (1902), col. 393 f. ; W. Kinkel, *ibidem*, col. 400 f. ; A. Meillet, *Revue critique*, vol. LIII (1902), p. 64 f. ; E. Herzog, *Zeitschrift f. franz. Sprache u. Literatur*, XXV (1903), pt. II, p. 124 f.

[3] Wundt's theories on language are discussed by H. Delacroix in *Le langage et la pensée*, 2nd ed., p. 56 f. Delacroix also discusses the relation between linguistics and psychology in the same work, p. 25 f. ; cf. also the section devoted to A. Sechehaye, *infra*, Chap. IV.
Other linguists beside Vossler have criticized Wundt's ideas, for example, B. Delbrück, in *Grundfragen der Sprachforschung*, Strasburg, 1901 ; L. Sütterlin, in *Das Wesen der sprachlichen Gebilde*, Heidelberg, 1902 ; and H. Paul, *Prinzipien der Sprachgeschichte* (preface to the fourth edition, 1909), although from more or less different points of view. Paul, for instance, will not accept Wundt's attempt to explain changes in language by collective psychology, but holds that they are the result of changes in the individual mind. (Cp. A. Philippide, *Originea Romînilor*, II, p. 258 f., *passim*). Wundt's theories have been taken up unreservedly by his pupil, O. Dittrich, *Grundzüge der Sprachpsychologie*, I. Band : *Einleitung und allgemein psychologische Grundlage* (mit einem Bilderatlas), Halle a.S., 1903 (cp. L. Sütterlin, in *Zeitschr. f. rom. Phil.*, XXX, 1906, p. 592 f.). Dittrich has also published *Die Probleme der Sprachpsychologie*, Leipzig, 1913. Among kindred works must be mentioned J. van Ginneken, *Principes de linguistique psychologique, Essai synthétique*, Amsterdam–Paris–Leipzig, 1907 (a revised version of the Dutch original, Lier, 1904-6), which was reviewed very favourably by J. Ronjat, in *Revue des langues romanes*, LIII (1910), p. 197 f., on account of the importance the author attributes to 'feeling' in his conception of language, and also for his sensible attitude towards both positivists and idealists, combining as he does the soundness of method of the former with the breadth of view of the latter. Van Ginneken's work receives also great praise from A. Meillet, in *Bulletin de la Soc. ling. de Paris*, XV (1907–8), coupled, however, with serious reservations with regard to some of van Ginneken's facts.

Analogy is generally considered to be a linguistic phenomenon which disturbs and interrupts the working of the laws of sound-change. Vossler contends, however, that numerous examples can be quoted to refute this conception. Thus, in French, every *au* becomes *o*, and every *u* becomes *ü*, the later borrowings following the model of the inherited Latin words. In cases like these, analogy has made use of a sound-change, which it has spread and generalized. Again, it is affirmed that analogy is an instantaneous occurrence, while sound-change is progressive. Yet the displacement of French *r* from the tongue position, where it was pronounced during the sixteenth century, to the uvula, where it is articulated by the modern Parisians and their imitators in the provinces, was a sudden displacement, and happened at a time when the language, following a general tendency towards a rearward pronunciation, possessed relatively few other sounds articulated in the front of the mouth. On the other hand, we meet with cases of analogy that have been quite gradual, for instance, the levelling of the conjugation of French verbs, as in the verb *aimer*, for example, the elimination of the unstressed first syllable *am-* in all tenses. Finally, it is maintained that sound-change operates throughout all words that are liable to its incidence, while analogy only affects isolated cases. But it is well known that in French every word is stressed on the final syllable, and what sound-change could be more general than an analogy of this kind which in certain cases even leads to a conflict between stress and meaning, as in *plaît-il* (beside *il plaît*) or *puissé-je* (beside *que je puisse*), where the stress shifts from the verb to the pronoun, or from root to ending ? On the other hand again, there are cases of sound-change that are quite sporadic, as for example Fr. *larmes*<*lermes*, *harlequin*<*herlequin*, beside *ferme*, *merlette*, etc., where the *e* remains unchanged.

These and similar facts have compelled scholars to search for a causal difference between sound-change and analogy, and to maintain that the former is of physiological, the latter of psychological origin. But the sounds of human speech are articulated sounds ; in other words they presuppose some spiritual activity, and therefore, in order to explain them, we must take into account this psychological factor. A sound-change takes place in certain determined conditions, that is to say it is individual, but its spread is due to the workings of analogy. Both phenomena are of the same order, inasmuch as they have their common origin in the genius of the language. In other words, we have on the one hand creative sound-change (Schöpfung), on the other, historical or evolutive change (Entwicklung). The former is conscious, like every spiritual activity, the latter unconscious, in the sense that we are not conscious, when we speak, of making use of linguistic material imparted to us by others. Through not having made the necessary distinction between these two types of sound-change, grammarians have either, on the one hand, confined themselves to the study of evolutive change, or, on the other, endeavoured to explain aesthetically or, with Wundt, psychologically, the so-called sound-laws ; a vain endeavour, inasmuch as the scope of the sound-laws is solely that which is conditioned and common in a language, and the object therefore of historical, not of descriptive or analytical grammar. By way of illustration to his theoretical argument Vossler brings forward concrete examples ; in particular he analyses a number of passages from French classical poetry, by which he seeks to prove the great importance of the stylistic or artistic stress (*v. supra*, p. 91) in the production of sound-change, insisting withal on the close relationship between the study of stress and stylistics, inasmuch as artistic stress is shown by the syntactical moulding of the expression.

After studying language as a creative activity, Vossler analyses the notion of language as an evolution, a matter exclusively of linguistics, and no concern of psychology. Here we are in the domain of analogy, which is particularly potent in word-formation and in flexions. The first question we ask ourselves is the following : From what source do we receive that linguistic material which is constantly fashioned and transformed creatively by the individual ? From the linguistic community, which, in its turn, is composed of the individual speakers. In other words, we find ourselves in a vicious circle. Hence the attempt to seek the origin of language in dialogue. Thus, for example, Wundt asserts that language is a psycho-social phenomenon, because, on the one hand, he says, it is impossible to detect any activity of the individual, and, on the other, language presents certain general evolutive laws, and the nature of these it is the task of psychology to discover. Vossler vigorously opposes this contention. In the first place, a man often talks to himself, both literally and figuratively, that is to say, in poetry, and, secondly, the fact that we cannot in every case of modification of language determine what is the contribution of the individual does not justify us in creating an entirely new science. Wundt himself recognizes that historical grammar is adequate to the task of investigating linguistic change, but claims at the same time for psychology the part played by physics in regard to the natural sciences, namely, that of illuminating the reciprocal relationships between the linguistic community and its members, and of the individual members among themselves, and of discovering at the same time the laws that regulate these relationships.

A great number of instances can be alleged to refute Wundt's ideas, and to prove convincingly the great importance of the creative activity of the individual in the evolution, and, implicitly, in the birth of language. The part played by analogy in the speech of children, for instance, is well known. Vossler quotes examples from the talk of his own children, who were equally fluent in Italian and German. In place of the form (*io*) *piango*, they used a form (*io*) *piangio*, because the majority of the forms of this verb which they had heard had a soft *g* sound. Similarly, they used the imperfect form *ti recordevi* instead of the present *ti ricordi*, because their mother frequently recalled to their minds certain events with questions of the type : *Ti ricordi? Come* facevi *al nonno? Che* facevi? *Ti ricordi?* Similar analogical phenomena are everywhere extremely numerous[1] and the linguist has no need to call in any extraneous science to explain them. Dialect research, moreover, has proved that phonetic unity is not to be found anywhere in one and the same locality.[2] It is clear therefore, from the foregoing and other considerations, that language has its source in isolated individuals, but develops within a community ; everything that is particular and distinctive in it comes from the individual, while everything that is general and devitalized has been spread by

---

[1] The present author can quote similar examples from children's speech. One of his nephews invented for the form (*eu*) *sînt* (' I am ') special forms of his own, on the model of the second person of the indicative present, and of the present imperative (or subjunctive), namely, *escu* and *fiu*. Being frequently addressed by his elders in the traditional manner : *dece nu eşti cuminte ?* (' Why aren't you good ?') or (*să*) *fii cuminte !* (' Be good ! '), he naturally replied : ' *Escu cuminte* ' or ' *Fiu cuminte* ' (' I are good ! or ' I be good ! '). The fact that *escu* and *hiu* are the current forms in Macedo-Rumanian brings striking support to Vossler's contentions. To take another case, a little girl, the daughter of a friend, a very wide-awake and enquiring child, was puzzling over the problem of the nationality of Adam and Eve. She solved it as follows : God having made them of clay, in Rumanian *lut*, they must have been *Luteni*, seeing that the people of *Moldova* are *Moldoveni* and of *Basarabia*, *Basarabeni*. Similarly, a boy who had a great deal to put up with from his elder sister, gave vent to his wrath with what to him was the last word in insults, *derbedea*, a feminine formed on the word *derbedeu*.

[2] L. Gauchat, for example, has shown in *L'Unité phonétique dans le patois d'une commune* (*v. supra*, p. 38) that the younger generation in one village have speech more different from that of their elders in the same village than from that of speakers of the same age elsewhere.

intercommunication. The linguistic community is therefore not a cause but merely a condition of language development. There is in the minds of men a tendency towards analogical formations, which are nothing more than an artificial grouping and classification of our representations. The workings of analogy have consequently something volitional and practical in them, whereas creative linguistic activity is purely intellectual or ' theoretical '. This ' theoretical ', ' spiritual ' activity is to be found only in specially gifted individuals, that is to say in ' artists ' ; ' practical ' activity is the lot of the common kind.

After voicing his linguistic doctrine in the manner we have described above, Vossler attempts to apply his principles to the study of a given language in a famous work entitled, *Frankreichs Kultur im Spiegel seiner Sprachentwicklung*, Heidelberg, 1913,[1] in which, as the title indicates, he aims at showing how French civilization, or the genius of the French people, is manifest in the development of its language. In other words, this work is a history of the French literary language, from its origins up to the classical period, and endeavours to explain the diverse transformations it has undergone in the course of centuries by means of what Vossler calls the ' genius of the language ' (see above). It goes without saying that a history of the French language, as the Munich scholar then understood it, is incomplete. In the first place, because it does not go beyond the seventeenth century. This the author justifies by saying that French had attained its maximum development in the classical period, and taken on in many respects its final shape. But in addition to this the author does not investigate *all* the changes which took place during the eight centuries of development which he surveys. The reason for this deficiency is to be found in the very nature of Vossler's doctrine, for it will have been seen from our analysis of his theoretical works that the idealistic method is not applicable to each and every linguistic phenomenon, but only to such as clearly reveal the action of the ' genius of the language '.

It is outside our scope to give a complete summary of this book. We shall merely mention certain points which appear characteristic of the author's approach. The general principle from which he starts is the following : There is a close relationship between the evolution of the French language and the political and literary

[1] A supplement (*Nachtrag*) to this work, published in 1921, discusses the criticisms of reviewers, and provides, together with certain emendations and additions, an index of words and a general subject- and author-index.

history of France. Hence, for each linguistic period, the Old (up to the middle of the thirteenth century), the Middle (till about 1500), and the New (till the end of the seventeenth century), Vossler enquires first of all into the social, political, literary, and artistic condition of France at the time ; for by studying these cultural manifestations we can learn to know the prevailing spirit of the French people, by which, in its turn, the language is influenced and transformed. After showing us in this manner the spirit underlying the language, at a given period, that is to say, the trend of French civilization in general, he proceeds to analyse the concurrent linguistic changes and to explain them in terms of these social, political, or literary activities.

To take the first period, the characteristic feature of the French spirit was then the intimate association of national with religious feeling, which finds admirable expression in the *Chanson de Roland*, with its rhetorical style, and its paratactic, impressionist technique. This same unity, which is the outcome of the social organization of the time, is to be found likewise in the contemporary language, marked as it is by a complete harmony between word accent and sentence accent, between the structure of its rhythm and the grouping of ideas, between syntax and phonetics, between the analogical and the spontaneous, and it is this spirit of unity and harmony that gives us the key to a number of changes which the language underwent during the Old French period.

Proceeding to the Middle period, we note that during its first half (up to 1339) there is a very strongly marked class-consciousness. All the social categories are organized, and are frequently at strife one with another. Between 1339 and 1500, on the contrary, the class feeling weakens and gives way to a nationalist sentiment which little by little finds material support in the power of the monarchy. In both cases, however, we find an eclipse of the individual consciousness, which is the chief characteristic of the French people during the whole of this epoch. The consequence of this state of things is a predominantly practical, objective, and realistic turn of mind, that finds scope particularly in the observation of the outer world, with little concern for the things of the spirit. In language, this tendency finds its counterpart in an enrichment of the stock of words, coupled with considerable disorder in phonology and flexion. The language takes on thus a practical, intellectual, and documentary bias which threatens to endanger its artistic qualities.

7

The later period, which comprises the sixteenth and seventeenth centuries, may also be subdivided into two parts, the first ending with the Edict of Nantes (1598), the second comprising the whole of the seventeenth century. As a whole, it can be well characterized by what F. Brunot calls " efforts pour constituer une grammaire ". Individualism, which in the preceding period had been held in check, now reasserts its rights and manifests itself in the Renascence and the Reformation, though at the same time the nationalist spirit thrives with the growth of absolute monarchy, and is powerful enough to induce the individual to find satisfaction in serving the national ideal. The sixteenth century is naturalist, and the seventeenth is the age of reason, but both are essentially nationalist, and thus have features in common. On the one hand, we find writers advocating the enrichment of their mother tongue, in order to equip it for every possible task, and to raise it to the level of the Greek and Latin languages, to which they believed it was in no way inferior, others we find intent upon making it wholly national, a tendency which is manifest in the modifications made in borrowed materials in order to adapt them to the spirit of the French language. The majority of the linguistic changes that take place at this period are to be found in the domains of syntax and morphology, for the reason that here the liberty, or rather the licence, of the middle period called for drastic treatment, all the more drastic in view of the excessive individualism of the sixteenth century itself. It took all the efforts of the seventeenth century, with its salons and its rationalist grammarians, to bring about the reign of law and order in the language. The close association, not to say complete fusion, between humanism and nationalism in the sixteenth century, and between rationalism and nationalism in the seventeenth, led the way to the equilibrium and perfect taste to be found in the works of the great poets of the age of Louis XIV, Molière, Racine and La Fontaine. It can thus be said that in the classical period the French language attained the linguistic ideal of the French people.

Comparatively recently Vossler published a new edition of the work we have been describing, entitled : *Frankreichs Kultur und Sprache. Geschichte der französischen Schriftsprache von den Anfängen bis zur Gegenwart*, Heidelberg, 1929. The differences between the two versions of the book are considerable. In addition to numerous changes in points of detail, e.g. a fuller bibliography and fresh illustrative examples, the author has given us three entirely new chapters, entitled respectively : " From Latin to French ", " The Encyclopaedists ", and " From Romanticism to the Present Day ". The book has thus become a complete history of the French literary language, beginning with the written and spoken Latin of Gaul. The method followed in the last two chapters is as before, an investigation of the main cultural trend of French life during the periods in question, and the explanation of the principal linguistic changes by the prevailing cultural atmosphere of the times. The author comes to the general conclusion that despite the many disturbances that have taken place since 1700, classical French, as we know it from the works of the great writers of the seventeenth century, has remained essentially unchanged to this day " with all its rules of flexion and syntax, with its clear and refined sense of order, with a spelling of which the phonetic basis is partly of the twelfth, partly of the seventeenth century, with a system of versification which had already begun to be antiquated about the year 1500, and with a pronunciation which occasionally, on the stage, can combine features of three different centuries : a proof that the conservative forces are still in being, that in fact they are more vigorous than those which make for change " (p. 381).

Briefly, the eighteenth century, he tells us, is ' journalistic ', both in the strict sense of the word, inasmuch as periodical literature throughout the period increases in scope and volume, and figuratively, in that the writers, as encyclopaedists, are concerned with a great variety of topics, and write for an extensive public. As a consequence, the French language spreads widely, both at home, where it causes the dialects to recede, and abroad, where it becomes the universal language of cultured men. This is accompanied, internally, by an enrichment of the vocabulary with foreign elements, scientific borrowings from Greek and Latin, loan-words from English and from languages further afield, particularly from the colonies overseas, with new formations, notably an extraordinary number of pretentious and pedantic derivatives, a goodly number of which have survived, and finally with technical terms. This thorough-going transformation was inevitable on the eve of 1789, although the political revolution has no counterpart in the basic forms of the language. These remain practically untouched. The respect for the rules of grammar and style seems all the more marked and astonishing in view of the intellectual anarchy which became a veritable dogma in so many other domains. We even find certain pedants, of quite minor importance be it said, claiming to discover incorrect expressions in the great writers of the preceding century, and setting up as censors of Racine, Boileau, and their like, so far is this period from disturbing the foundations of the language laid down in the classical school.

Romanticism, says Vossler, with all its ramifications and prolongations in the nineteenth and twentieth centuries, gave rise, among other things, to an exaggerated concern for style. At this period everyone, even the most mediocre of the wielders of the pen, aims at writing well and handsomely. Simultaneously, there is a deliberate confusion of styles and literary genres, a consequence of a similar medley and confusion in the social and political spheres. The effacement, or at least the attenuation, of class distinctions has its counterpart, from the linguistic point of view, in an almost complete solidarity between the author and the public. Tendencies which govern the evolution of the language as spoken in popular circles are to be observed in the poets and novelists, for example a discarding of ' active ' modes of expression in favour of passive and reflexive forms, an avoidance of the subjunctive, particularly the imperfect, and of the preterite indicative, a liking for pleonasm, abbreviation, emphasis, parataxis, etc., an effacement of the distinction between the parts of speech (the use of noun for adjective, of adjective for noun, of adverb for adjective, etc.), and a predilection for concrete as against abstract forms. It goes without saying that the origin of these common tendencies is different in each case. In the spoken language they are spontaneous, a natural outcome of the popular spirit ; with the writers, they are due to a deliberate attitude, and frequently prompted purely by fashion or snobbery. With regard to extraneous influences upon the language, we note a strong and important influence from foreign sources (English, German, Scandinavian, Russian, American, and African), which is exercised not only on the vocabulary but also, though naturally to a less degree, on stress, sentence rhythm, and syntax. Finally, the all-powerful authority of Paris, the political and cultural centre, increases daily, a significant fact if we take into account the number of foreigners who reside in the French capital and the weakened vitality and resistance of the provincial dialects.

Vossler also discusses certain theoretical problems in a series of review articles which he subsequently published in book form, with the title *Gesammelte Aufsätze zur Sprachphilosophie*, Munich, 1923. We shall examine their contents as briefly as possible. Given that the history of a language is in close relationship, on the one hand, with grammar, and on the other with literary history, Vossler endeavours to throw light on this relationship from the view-point of his linguistic theories, as he is dissatisfied with the manner in which it is usually understood. Grammar, as a purely formal discipline, confining itself to the mere recording of phenomena from the point of view of correctness, and to their superficial explanation, has no reason to exist, although it continues to be taught in schools and colleges. It should be set to the service of language conceived as art, and should instruct us in the technique of linguistic beauty. According to Vossler, a construction or grammatical form can only be correct or incorrect aesthetically, because ' correct ' and ' incorrect ' are in fact synonymous, in this connection, with ' beautiful ' and ' ugly '. And when grammar seeks to explain its facts it must have recourse to the history of language, which, as conceived by Vossler (see above), is a history of linguistic taste, based on a knowledge of the whole cultural activity of a given people, that is to say, on an understanding of the genius of the language. As to the history of literature, its relations with the history of language are so intimate that each must take into account the existence of the other, and consider it not as a rival but as an ally.[1] Similarly, a close association should be maintained between the history of civilization and linguistic history, inasmuch as all three disciplines have as their aim an understanding of the human spirit, and this by means of phenomena which, though superficially distinct one from the other, are fundamentally akin, in that they spring from the same source.[2] None

---

[1] Vossler himself complies with this requirement inasmuch as he is equally active in the study of Romance literatures. His works in the history of literature, such as *Poetische Theorien in der italienischen Frührenaissance*, Berlin, 1900 ; *Italienische Literaturgeschichte (Sammlung Göschen* ; numerous editions since 1900, the date of the first) ; *Die philosophischen Grundlagen zum " süssen neuen Stil " des G. Guinizelli, G. Cavalcanti und Dante Alighieri*, Heidelberg, 1904 ; *Die Göttliche Komödie, Entwicklungsgeschichte und Erklärung*, 2 vol., Heidelberg, 1907-10 (2nd ed., 1925) ; *Salvatore Di Giacomo, ein neapolitanischer Dichter in Wort, Bild und Musik*, Heidelberg, 1908 ; *Italienische Literatur der Gegenwart*, Heidelberg, 1914 ; *La Fontaine und sein Fabelwerk*, Heidelberg, 1919 ; *Dante als religiöser Dichter*, Bern, 1921 ; *Giacomo Leopardi*, Munich, 1923 ; *Die neuesten Richtungen der italienischen Literatur*, Marburg a.L., 1925 ; *Jean Racine*, Munich, 1926 ; *Lope de Vega und sein Zeitalter*, Munich, 1932, etc., have received the warmest praise from the critics. In this respect Vossler may be said to continue the tradition set up by the founder of Romance studies, Friedrich Diez, and continued by Gaston Paris and H. Morf.

[2] On the relation between the history of language and of culture, cp. Bruno Migliorini, *Storia della lingua e storia della cultura*, in *La Cultura*, XI, no. 1 (Jan.–March, 1932), p. 48 f. Migliorini takes to task the too servile disciples of Ascoli, in particular C. Merlo, founder of the journal *L'Italia dialettale*.

of them has the right to consider itself superior to the others or to seek to make these subservient to itself.[1]

The problem of the relation between grammatical and psychological forms has also been treated by Vossler, in an important article in which he takes as his starting-point W. von Humboldt's famous assertion that language is not an object or thing (ἔργον), but an activity, a living force (ἐνέργεια). This Vossler interprets as signifying that the value of language as a spiritual activity lies in the intention to which the speaker desires to give expression. The nature of the grammatical and of the psychological categories had been well elucidated by Hermann Paul, when he showed that the former are a petrification of the latter, but he is at fault when he sets out to determine rules by means of which we may discover the psychological categories ; for a general grammar, over and above historical grammar, does not exist, and the number of psychological categories is unlimited. The latter, according to Vossler, can be accounted for only on the basis of certain grammatical tendencies, though, at the same time, they do show us the direction in which the individual speaker may overstep the bounds imposed upon him by the grammar of his mother tongue. Another article of the *Gesammelte Aufsätze* deals with grammar, and is entitled *Das System der Grammatik*. Here Vossler attacks the attitude of grammarians whose works reveal a conception of language as being something mechanical, schematic, and devoid of life. He maintains that the methods of the linguistic historian, to whom linguistic phenomena are the outcome of the spiritual life of a people and of its whole civilization, should be applied to grammar. It thus becomes a historical and comparative study, and in the true sense scientific.

Two other important articles deal with somewhat similar problems. In one, we are shown the situation of the individual with regard to language, the other enquires into the limitations of so-called linguistic sociology. The members of any community,

---

[1] Friedrich Schlegel, in *Geschichte der alten und neuen Literatur* (1812), had already discussed the manner in which the spirit of a people is reflected in its literature. The chief of German romanticism also examines the influence of literature upon life, from the national and religious angle. Though the approach is different, the principle is already there. The conception that linguistic and literary history should go hand in hand is becoming ever more widely recognized by modern philologists. Not only Vossler's disciples like E. Lerch (see below), or adherents to his doctrine like Leo Spitzer or Fr. Schürr, who investigate Romance literature as well as language, but also certain of his opponents, for example J. Brüch, in *Literaturgeschichte und Sprachgeschichte (Hauptfragen der Romanistik. Festschrift für Ph. Aug. Becker*, Heidelberg, 1922, p. 195 f.) uphold a similar point of view.

taken separately, enjoy a far greater freedom in speech than does the community as a whole. This freedom gives birth to all manner of figures of style, which, springing as they do from the individual genius, are only to be explained psychologically, that is to say, stylistically. When they spread, however, and become generalized, we are obliged to take into account both psychological and purely linguistic factors. On the other hand, the external modifications in language, such for example as analogy, contamination, differentiation, grammatical crystallization, general semantic change, etc., have their origin solely in the speech community and are purely linguistic in character. We have thus both individual and collective activity in the life of a language. The former is creation, expression, or artistic intuition, the latter gives general acceptance to the individual innovation and makes language into an instrument of mutual understanding between men. The sociological conception of language, that sees in human speech merely a means for the intercommunication of ideas and feelings, is justifiable only in so far as it confines itself to purely linguistic phenomena, that is to say, to the work of the community. At the point where language ceases to be merely communication and becomes expression, linguistic sociology ceases to have any standing.

To complete this survey of Vossler's doctrines we would mention the last work in which this productive scholar[1] discusses problems of general linguistics, namely, *Geist und Kultur in der Sprache*, Heidelberg, 1925.[2] Whereas, in his previous works, the author had concerned himself particularly with questions of method, he here investigates the manner in which human speech comes into contact with other fields of spiritual activity and the reciprocal influences which flow from these contacts. The chapter-titles, with their subdivisions, are as follows : (*a*) Speech, dialogue, and language ; (*b*) Language and religion ; (*c*) New modes of thought in popular Latin ; (*d*) Language and nature ; (*e*) Language and life ; (*f*) Linguistic communities [(1) The metaphysical and the empirical linguistic community ; (2) The mother tongue as the language of experience ; (3) Language and national sentiment ; (4) National languages as styles ; (5) The linguistic community as a community of interests ; (6) The linguistic community as a

---

[1] A complete bibliography of Vossler's output from 1897 to 1932 is given by Th. Ostermann in *Festgabe zum 60. Geburtstage Karl Vosslers*, Munich, 1932, pp. 164–205. It comprises 481 entries.

[2] Translated into English by O. Oeser, with the title, *The Spirit of Language in Civilization*, London, 1932.

community of convictions] ; (*g*) Language and science ; (*h*) Language and poetry. Having set forth in sufficient detail the author's conception of language, there is no need for us to discuss this work further. The reader will find little that is new from the purely linguistic standpoint, as Vossler is here concerned with the external conditions under which language develops, rather than with language itself.

★

The Munich scholar's theories have raised very keen discussion, and the attitude of the experts has ranged from the wildest enthusiasm to the bitterest antagonism. In reviews of his work, the attitude adopted seems often to be determined by the age of the reviewer, and all manner of personal and partisan considerations have been allowed to enter and darken counsel.

Vossler's Critics

In general, youth has been on the side of Vossler. Leaving out of account Vossler's own pupils, for example, V. Klemperer, *Studi di filologia moderna*, VII (1914), p. 93 f., mention must be made in this connection of L. Spitzer's reviews in *Zeitschrift f. französische Sprache und Literatur*, XLII (1914), pt. II, p. 139 f., and in *Literaturblatt f. germ. und rom. Philologie*, XLIII (1922), col. 246 f., and, among less well-known scholars, those of R. Rübel in *Archiv f. das Studium der neueren Sprachen und Literaturen*, CXXXI (1913), p. 220 f., and of O. Weidenmüller, in *Die neueren Sprachen*, XXVI (1918), p. 552 f. When we consider the inspired and inspiring quality of Vossler's temperament, we are far from wondering at the praise he wins from these younger scholars. But older men have shown a similar enthusiasm, for example E. Bovet, in *Archiv f. das Studium der neueren Sprachen und Literaturen*, CXXIII (1909), p. 430 f., a proof that approval of Vossler's doctrines does not presuppose, as some have suggested, an absence of critical faculty.[1] Other reviewers have adopted a more or less reserved attitude, endeavouring to point out with complete impartiality the good and the bad sides of the theories, as, for example, Ed.

---

[1] The following is a passage from Bovet's review : " No system can permanently check the growth of new forms of life. Positivism is dead, and a new faith quickens us, which in its turn will die. So long as it is alive, let us work ! That is the heart of the matter. That is what gives Vossler's study (*Positivismus und Idealismus*) its great significance " (*loc. cit.*, p. 432).

Wechssler, in *Literarisches Zentralblatt für Deutschland*, LVI (1905), col. 137 f., and L. Sütterlin, in *Literaturblatt f. germ. u. rom. Philologie*, XXVI (1905), col. 265 f., and XXVII (1906), col. 297 f. But the majority of the critics of Vossler's works have been decidedly hostile. Some, indeed, have been so led astray by passion that they have preferred to remain anonymous (cf. *Frankreichs Kultur*, Nachtrag, p. 371, note 1), while others have accused him openly of being a perverter of student youth.[1] It goes without saying that among his bitterest antagonists were the so-called positivist scholars, who could not sanction the intrusion of intuition into the field of linguistic study. Among the more unprejudiced of these reviewers may be quoted O. Dittrich, *Zeitschrift f. rom. Philologie*, XXX (1906), p. 472 f., and E. Herzog, *Zeitschr. f. franz. Sprache u. Literatur*, XXXIII (1908), pt. II, p. 1 f. (on Vossler's first two works), and *Literaturblatt für germanische und romanische Philologie*, XLII (1921), col. 24 f. (on *Frankreichs Kultur*).[2]

In order to understand, at least in part, the hostile attitude of the majority of linguists to the leader of the Idealistic school, we must realize the spirit that prevailed in linguistic circles at the end of last century, and in the early years of the twentieth, a spirit directly resulting from the progress philology had made under the

---

[1] O. Schultz-Gora, at the 17th congress of German philologists, held in October, 1920, at Halle a.S. Schultz-Gora's paper was printed in *Archiv f. d. Studium der neueren Spr. u. Lit.*, CXLI (1921), p. 208 f., though without the remark referred to above.

[2] To complete the bibliography of references to Vossler's works we append the following : J. Ronjat, *Revue des langues romanes*, LXI (1921–22), p. 406 f. ; G. Rohlfs, *Sprachgeist und Zeitcharakter*, in *Die neueren Spr.*, XXXI (1923), p. 65 f. (*Fr. Kultur*) ; V. Klemperer, *Deutsche Literaturzeitung*, LI (1930), col. 356 f. ; A. Zauner, *Zeitschr. f. franz. Spr. u. Lit.*, LIII (1929–30), p. 94 f. (*Fr. Kultur*, 2nd ed.) ; Leo Jordan, *Archivum Romanicum*, IX (1925), p. 83 f. ; C. Appel, *Zeitschr. f. franz. u. engl. Unterricht*, XXIII (1924), nr. 3, p. 264–5 ; Jul. Stenzel, *Deutsche Literaturzeitung*, XLV (1924), col. 579 ; E. Lerch, *Zeitschr. f. vergleichende Sprachforschung*, LIII (1925), p. 269 f. ; H. J. Pos, *Neophilologus*, X (1924–5), p. 310 f. (all on *Gesammelte Aufsätze*) ; A. Meillet, *Bull. de la Soc. de linguistique*, XXVI (1925), fasc. 3, p. 26 f. ; L. Spitzer, *Literaturblatt f. germ. u. rom. Phil.*, XLVII (1926), col. 81 f. ; E. Lewy, *Zeitschr. f. Völkerpsychologie u. Soziologie*, III, March, 1927, p. 101 f. ; W. E. Collinson, *Litteris*, IV (1927), p. 100 f. ; A. Bussenius, *Neuphilologische Mitteilungen*, XXVIII (1927), p. 40 f. ; A. Kastil, *Arch. f. d. Stud. d. neueren Spr. u. Lit.*, CLII (1927), p. 97 f. (all upon *Geist und Kultur in der Sprache*) ; F. Schalk, *Die neueren Sprachen*, XXXIX (1931), p. 238 f. ; K. Glaser, *Literaturblatt f. germ. u. rom. Phil.*, LII (1931), col. 125 f. (both on *Fr. Kultur*). See also studies entitled *Karl Vossler*, by V. Klemperer and L. Spitzer, in *Jahrbuch f. Philologie*, II (1927), p. 3 f., and in *Der Lesezirkel* (Zurich), XVII (1929–30), no. 6, p. 59 f., respectively. Vossler's first two works, *Positivismus*, and *Sprache als Schöpfung* were also reviewed by Ph. Aug. Becker, in *Deutsche Literaturzeitung*, XXVI (1905), col. 2568 f., and, quite recently, the second edition of *Frankreichs Kultur* by E. Lerch, in *Zeitschr. f. rom. Phil.*, LVI (1936), p. 459 f., where, *inter alia*, the reviewer draws an interesting parallel between Vossler and von Humboldt.

guidance of the neo-grammarians. Despite the opposition put up by Schuchardt and others (see above, p. 25 f.), it was a generally accepted conviction that the phenomena of language could only be studied on the basis of the laws of sound-change as conceived by the neo-grammarian school. A young man like Vossler who had the hardihood to oppose them could not fail to be met with incredulity, contempt, or indignation, especially in view of the importance he attached to intuition, a subjective, and consequently entirely ' unscientific ' factor, as was generally held, but also in view of certain of his outbursts, as violent as they were unjustified, at the expense of the positivists themselves.[1]

Since the war period, it can be said that the air has cleared and his theories awaken less animosity. The excitement which their novelty aroused in the years immediately following the publication of *Positivismus* . . . and *Sprache als Schöpfung* has now quietened down, and a cool unbiased judgment upon them is now possible, and that, not only through lapse of time, but because many of Vossler's views have proved their worth. In particular, his antagonism to the sound-laws as conceived by the neo-grammarians is held almost universally to be entirely justified.[2] The researches of Gilliéron and his pupils have led to the same conclusions as were reached by the leader of the idealistic school, so to speak, by intuition, for, despite their differences, both in doctrine and method, the linguistic geographers and the ' idealists ' have much in common, although there can be no question of any influence of

---

[1] The following are a few specimens : " For positivist philology, that is to say, mere collection of material, it is enough to have five or maybe only four senses, and an adequate stock of patience. For true linguistic investigation, however, what the Italians call *bernoccolo* (' a bump ') is required " (*Positivismus*, p. 43). " Certain witty laymen have bestowed upon those philologists who, by their ' strict empiricism,' claim to have established phonology as an independent science, the appropriate name of ' Sound-shifters ' " (*ibid.*, p. 63). In *Sprache als Schöpfung*, we do not encounter this kind of remark. The author tends on the contrary to revise in a sense more favourable to the positivists some of his earlier utterances (cp. p. 63, and in another direction pp. 96, 97).

[2] The Munich professor is not an out-and-out opponent of the sound-laws. In his review of E. G. Parodi's *Questioni teoriche* : *le leggi fonetiche* (see above, p. 47), in *Literaturblatt f. germ. u. rom. Phil.*, XLVI (1925), we come across expressions like the following : " . . . the notion of Laws of sound change, as perplexing as it is definitely useful " (*loc. cit.*, col. 3) ; or, again, " . . . that Sound-Laws and Analogies have their purpose and genuinely serious significance when we are concerned with a survey of the various phases of one or more languages in time and space, when we seek to view these phases comprehensively, to relate and compare them and to measure their divergence, in a word to orientate them ; but that these self-same Sound-Laws and Analogies become meaningless and a hindrance, and should be forgotten, as soon as it is a question of understanding language in its activity and its progress, and of watching these with discernment."

one group on the other. Both Vossler and Gilliéron insist upon
the individual character of linguistic phenomena, and upon their
psychological causes,[1] and both consider that in reality there are
no such things as clearly marked dialects, sub-dialects, and the
like. Again, ' idealism ' and the ' word and thing ' method of
Meringer meet on common ground in their effort to study language
concurrently and in close relationship with the civilization of a
given people. It is true that Vossler insists more upon culture in
the strict sense of the term, upon literary, artistic, and scientific
activity, and the like, while Meringer and his followers dwell more
upon the material factors in human life, it is true also that the former
pays scant attention to vocabulary, which is Meringer's almost
exclusive interest, and, further, that the ' idealists ' study civilization
in order to discover facts accounting for the development of language
in a given direction, whereas the exponents of the ' word and thing '
method put language and civilization on the same plane, as if both
were equally the concern of linguistics ; but all these differences,
and others that might be pointed out between the two tendencies,
relate to matters of detail and are in no sense fundamental.[2]

[1] Certain of Vossler's ideas are almost identical, at least in spirit, if not in actual
wording, with some of those we find in Gilliéron. For example, in *Positivismus*,
p. 39, we read that every expression has its own specific source or origin, and must
consequently be studied apart from other expressions, that is to say, stylistically,
not grammatically or syntactically. This reminds us of the famous principle which
forms the basis of Gilliéron's doctrine, namely, that every word has its own history,
distinct from that of all other words, no matter how closely related with them it
may be. As for the importance attached by both scholars to the psychological
factor in language, we may compare with what has been said above concerning
Vossler's ideas the following words of Gilliéron : " Les phonéticiens . . . ne
perçoivent guère dans l'évolution d'une langue que celle qu'y produisent les organes
phonateurs et négligent celle qui se produit dans le cerveau " (*Faillite de l'étymologie
phonétique*, p. 67) ; " La vie du français n'est pas dans les organes phonateurs, elle
est dans le cerveau " (*ibid.*, p. 102).

[2] Certain appreciations by H. Güntert, co-editor of the review *Wörter und Sachen*,
are worth reproducing here. They are from the volume of the review dedicated
to Meringer on his seventieth birthday (vol. XII, 1929). Coming from the pen of
one of the directors of this journal they are very pertinent to our discussion.
" To have insisted vigorously on language as an artistic product, at a time when
only its purely phonetic elements were taken into account, is Vossler's lasting
contribution ; from this starting-point he launched a first assault on the neo-
grammarian position. It is true that his work errs on the side of excessive aestheti-
cism, which is quite out of place in the domain of popular speech " (*loc. cit.*,
p. 389). And again : " The days of mere ' Sound-shifting ' are over, and goals
are beckoning to us that are loftier than those to be attained by an exclusive
concern with the letters of the alphabet. On the solid foundations laid by the neo-
grammarians, which must never be abandoned, we must now build further and
give a content to the form ! " (*ibid.*, p. 393). Güntert's article, entitled *Zum
heutigen Stand der Sprachforschung*, has a further interest for us, in that he broaches
the subject of ' Linguistic notions ' (*Sprachbegriffe*), which, a hundred years ago '
W. v. Humboldt had duly recognized under the name of ' innere Sprachform ''

But Vossler's ideas have made headway not only when they have been in agreement with those of other linguists and in circles that were neutral or favourably disposed. His attitude towards the positivists, those scholars who see the be-all and end-all of linguistics in the collecting and cataloguing of material, has spread more rapidly than perhaps Vossler himself would have expected, and has been taken up even by certain scholars whom one might have considered to belong to the class he scoffed at. In any case, the term ' positivism ', with all manner of derivatives, has become current to signify a quality that strikingly few are now willing to claim as their own.[1] It is significant that in a journal like *Indogermanische Forschungen*, which was founded by one of the leaders of the neo-grammarians, Karl Brugmann, and continued by one of his pupils, W. Streitberg, ' positivism '[2] is spoken of in a manner

The point is, that language not only serves for self-expression and as a means of communication between man and man, but that it is at the same time the most important part of the mechanism of thought itself : just as numbers help us to calculate, so words help us to think. Güntert would therefore like to see a new branch of linguistics, an ideological branch, whose aim would be to investigate the origins, transformations and developments of linguistic notions by comparison between one language and another. This would complete the ' word and thing ' method, which hitherto has concerned itself almost entirely with concrete ' things ', to the neglect of the spiritual, despite the fact that Meringer (see above, p. 64), had set ideas and institutions on the same level as ' things ' in the narrower sense of the word.

In the same volume of *Wörter und Sachen*, p. 253, A. Nehring also discusses the relations between the Vossler school and that of Meringer, and urges both branches to widen their methods, the idealists by extending their enquiries to a number of languages, and not confining themselves as is their wont to one, in order to reach more general conclusions concerning the spirit of language, the ' word and thing ' workers by taking a leaf from the ' idealists' ' book, and concerning themselves more with the domain of ideas, applying the methods they have evolved to more spiritual factors than those with which they have dealt hitherto.

[1] L. Spitzer has sized up the situation admirably in his article, *Der Romanist in der deutschen Hochschule, Die neueren Sprachen*, XXXV (1927), p. 5 of the off-print, where he writes : " Karl Vossler has set up an ironical tomb-stone to the zealous and somewhat aimless scholarship and industry of positivism. It is true that his idealism is not proof against all attacks, but, thanks to him, ' positivist ' is a thing that none of us would like to be called to-day." Except, we would add, some who are still pertinacious enough to close their eyes and to profess a ' pride ' in still adhering to the old faith (cf. E. Gamillscheg, *Die romanischen Ortsnamen des Untervinschgaus*, in *Festschrift zum 19-ten Neuphilologentag*, Berlin, 1924, p. 2 of off-print, note). As Schuchardt, who was in a certain sense both a positivist and an idealist, says, in a letter quoted by L. Spitzer, *H. Schuchardt als Briefschreiber, Revue internationale des études basques*, XXI (1930), p. 24 of off-print, " At least in science one should profess no religion ; despising none, we should combine them all." Cp. also *Brevier*, 2nd ed., p. 418 f., where the same idea is expressed in a discussion of the various ' schools ', and in particular of ' idealism ' and ' positivism '.

[2] Cp. a review by G. Ipsen in vol. XLII (1924), p. 1 f., in which the author speaks of the positivists with all the hostility and disdain of a disciple of Vossler. In the same volume, a contributor displays antagonism to the linguistic psychology of Wundt, which, as we have seen (p. 92 f. *supra*), the Munich scholar criticizes so sharply.

that Vossler himself would not disown, while in the supplement to
the journal, *Indogermanisches Jahrbuch*, XI (1926–27), p. 1 f., there
is an article by G. Ipsen, entitled *Besinnung der Sprachwissenschaft*
(*Karl Vossler und seine Schule*), which shows complete understanding
of the idealistic doctrine ; it concludes as follows : " Language
research is at the cross-roads and must make its choice. Vossler
has been the first to raise the question, and to point the way. May
the renewal soon become a reality " (*loc. cit.*, p. 32). Even a
linguist of long experience like A. Meillet, who, in general, had
shown little liking for Vossler's theories, and had at times criticized
them with some severity, was constrained to find a certain merit
in them : " Et, tout en tenant pour dangereuses les ' anticipations '
de M. Vossler, il faut lui savoir gré d'avoir affirmé que le problème
[the relation between language and culture] existe, et qu'il y a lieu
de l'étudier, en somme d'avoir largement contribué à ouvrir une
fenêtre et à donner de l'air à la linguistique " (*Bulletin de la Société
de linguistique*, XXIX [1928–9], fasc. 2, pp. 34–5).[1] Moreover,

---

[1] That the idealistic doctrines, which might have been thought to have now
entered the domain of history, are still capable of awakening keen controversy, is
seen by the vigorous campaigning in recent years on the part of scholars like
G. Rohlfs and Leo Jordan. The former has massed all his forces particularly
against E. Lerch, who was his rival for a linguistic prize (see below), and has
attacked him with unusual violence in an article entitled ' *Idealistische* ' *Neuphilologie*, *Zeitschrift f. franz. Sprache u. Literatur*, XLVIII (1925–6), p. 121 f. Lerch's
reply is to be found in *Jahrb. f. Philologie*, II (1927), p. 298 f., and Rohlfs' rejoinder
in *Zeitschr. f. franz. Spr. u. Lit.*, LI (1928), p. 309 f. Rohlfs has also drawn swords
with Vossler himself, in the same volume of the journal, p. 355 f., where he defends
the views on the relation between speech and civilization expressed in his pamphlet
Sprache und Kultur, Braunschweig, 1928, and criticized by Vossler in *Deutsche
Literaturzeitung*, XLIX (1928), col. 421 f. It should be said that Rohlfs himself
is the author of studies which investigate the relations between speech and culture,
though from an entirely different point of view from that of Vossler ; cp. *Baskische
Kultur im Spiegel des lateinischen Lehnworts*, in the *Voretzsch Festschrift*, Halle a.S., 1927,
p. 58 f.

L. Jordan has not indulged in any polemics with the idealists, but has treated
similar problems and criticized their outlook, in particular that of Vossler whose
doctrine he characterizes as a form of neo-romanticism, the origins of which go
back to Jean-Jacques Rousseau (cp. his article, *Studium der Lautgewohnheiten und
Erkenntnis*, in *Zeitschr. f. rom. Phil.*, XLVII [1927], p. 219 f.). Jordan's studies and
reviews hostile to the idealistic school are to be found mainly in the *Archivum
Romanicum* and in the *Zeitschr. f. rom. Phil.* He also treats general linguistic problems
in a sense antagonistic to the Vosslerians in *Kunst des begrifflichen Denkens*, Munich,
1926, and in *Les idées, leurs rapports et le jugement de l'homme*, Geneva, 1926.

The criticisms directed by K. Jaberg in *Germanisch-romanische Monatsschrift*, XIV
(1926), p. 1 f., and by A. Philippide in *Originea Romînilor*, II, p. 256 f., against
Vossler's linguistic system are of an entirely different character. Although they
are hostile, they are entirely objective and, especially in the case of Jaberg, give
recognition to the good points in the system and are thus illuminating and instructive. Among other recent references to the system may be mentioned those of
Fr. Schürr, *Sprachwissenschaft und Zeitgeist*, Marburg a.L., 1922 (2nd ed., 1925),
p. 29 f., and Hugo Pipping, *Sprachwissenschaft und Metaphysik*, *Neuphilologische
Mitteilungen*, XXV (1924), p. 125 f., the latter hostile to Vossler.

with regard to *Frankreichs Kultur* . . . , which met with much severe criticism, and at times even protest, from certain Romance scholars, Meillet, who, as leader of the sociological school of linguists, tended naturally to appreciate Vossler's view of language as a mirror of civilization, expressed himself in the following favourable terms : " Voici l'un des rares livres sur l'histoire des langues qu'on lit d'un bout à l'autre avec plaisir, où l'on admire le goût d'un auteur qui a le sentiment des choses dont il parle et le sens des styles ; où fourmillent les idées et où partout on voit le talent " (*Bull. Soc. ling.*, XVIII [1912–13], p. cclxxxvii f.). Meillet gives decided approval to the historical side of the work, particularly to the parts dealing with the social background and its influence upon the language, but opposes the attempt to attribute specific concrete changes in forms and sounds to aesthetic causes. He goes on to say, however : " Mais il [Vossler] présente les faits dans leur mouvement, il en fait saisir les actions et réactions, et, même quand on ne sera pas convaincu, on aura profit à le lire et à réfléchir avec lui. Car il a le mérite de ne pas se contenter de formules mécaniques. Il veut partout saisir les actions et les causes " (p. ccxc).

★

To return to the ' positivist ' reception of Vossler's theories, we are all the more surprised at its hostility when we reflect that many of his ideas had been voiced by earlier scholars. It is true that the latter were of undoubted orthodoxy in regard to the neo-grammarian doctrines, or, at least, were so looked up to by their colleagues that they ran no danger of any rash or over-severe criticism. Vossler himself quotes names like those of H. Osthoff, W. Wundt, A. Tobler,[1] G. Gröber, J. v. Rozwadowski, and others, who have understood and appreciated the creative and stylistic values in language development. The merit of these scholars, says Vossler, in *Sprache als Schöpfung*, p. 113, is that they " have thrown into relief the arbitrary and relative character of formal grammar, and shown the necessity for bringing every expression into relation with its psychological environment ". It is possible, further, to

---

[1] See above, p. 24. Tobler's famous essays on French grammar, published in Leipzig, have seen a great number of editions and been translated into French. The author lays considerable stress upon the stylistic and psychological factors in accounting for a great number of syntactical and other problems in French.

quote other predecessors from whom Vossler, on his own admission, has borrowed certain essential elements of his doctrine, and to show that he is not so exceptional in his views as has been thought.

His opponents have seized upon this 'discovery' and made capital out of it, but one may express surprise that things that passed unnoticed, or were accepted without question, when said by others, have suddenly become dangerous after passing through the mind of Vossler. It should be added, however, that from opinions only incidentally expressed by certain predecessors, together with views that are entirely his own, the Munich scholar has succeeded in framing a system of linguistic philosophy that bears the stamp of real originality. Having given much serious thought to linguistic problems, he has imparted to his thoughts, both to those that are entirely new and to those he shares with others, a strongly personal character, and has not hesitated to draw from principles once established the fullest conclusions.

Among the scholars who contributed to the building up of the Vosslerian doctrine two are worthy of special mention : W. von Humboldt and Benedetto Croce. The former **Wilhelm von Humboldt** has played a pre-eminent part in the history of linguistic thought, although the fact that he lived a century ago, when the science of language was scarcely constituted, and also the novelty and originality of his views upon the majority of linguistic problems, have caused him to receive rather scanty recognition from present workers in the field. Recently, however, his name has come very much to the fore, and a whole school of general and Indo-European linguistics[1] may be said to go back to him. It is fitting therefore that we should give some account of his ideas, particularly on the question of the *innere Sprachform*, alluded to above, p. 107, n. 2, irrespective of whether they have been incorporated or not in the Vosslerian system.[2]

A word first of all upon the 'innere Sprachform'. By this von

---

[1] The 'neo-romantic' school (so styled by O. Funke, in *Studien zur Geschichte der Sprachphilosophie*, Bern, 1928, who considers them as the successors of the romantic school founded by von Humboldt, and continued by H. Steinthal and W. Wundt), represented by E. Cassirer, W. Porzig and Leo Weisgerber. Cp. L. Weisgerber, *Neuromantik in der Sprachwissenschaft, Germanisch-romanische Monatsschrift*, XVIII (1930), p. 241 f.

[2] The account is based in the main on the summary of von Humboldt's theories given by B. Delbrück, in *Einleitung in das Studium der indogermanischen Sprachen. Ein Beitrag zur Geschichte und Methodik der vergleichenden Sprachforschung*, 6th ed., Leipzig, 1919, p. 47 f. Cp. also J. Gaudefroy-Demombynes, *L'œuvre linguistique de Humboldt*, Paris, 1931.

Humboldt understands " that constant and homogeneous element in the working of the mind which raises articulated sound to the expression of thought, and which we must comprehend as completely as possible in all its connections and endeavour to set forth systematically ". This constant element is not a pure abstraction, but is a prompting of the spirit and constitutes a well-integrated unity. " Language is present in the mind in its totality ; that is to say, every separate portion of it is conditioned by the rest, even by what awaits clear formulation, everything stands related to a whole, which is determined by the totality of experience and the laws imposed upon the mind, or rather to a whole whose process of creation the latter have made possible." Moreover, " language could not have been invented, if its prototype had not already been inherent in man's understanding ". In other words, this inner ' form ' of language is a fundamental constituent of the human mind. It follows that it is identical in all peoples. The differences which may exist in this respect between one race and another, differences which are due to lesser linguistically creative gifts, or to variety in the interplay of feeling and fancy, are infinitely less than the differences in utterance, i.e. in the ' external form ', apparent between one language and another. " The ' inner form ' of all languages is essentially the same, and has the same general purpose. The differences lie entirely in the means by which this purpose is attained, and are confined within the limits which are set by its attainment."[1]

Man's faculty of speech, therefore, springs from his innermost being and corresponds to a necessity of his nature which cannot be repressed. And just as genius exists in isolated individuals, so it is to be found in certain ethnical groups. It is this ethnical genius which gives rise to sudden progress in the evolution of a language, which otherwise could not be explained. Language represents a sphere of activity in which a people participates as a whole, and by which it manifests its character as a people. " Languages are the outward manifestations of peoples ; their language is their soul, and their soul is their language."[2] Even though the contribution

---

[1] It is clear that the ' elementary kinship ' between languages, which forms such an important part of Schuchardt's linguistic doctrine (see above, p. 56 f.), has its source in the ' innere Sprachform ' as understood by von Humboldt. A certain parallel could also be drawn between von Humboldt's ideas and F. de Saussure's conception of ' la langue ' as opposed to ' la parole ' (see below, Chap. IV).

[2] Quoted by L. Weisgerber, in *Wörter und Sachen*, XV (1933), p. 196.

of individuals may be considerable, the fact that the members of an ethnical group, irrespective of their particular value as individuals, show themselves, quite unconsciously, to be in harmony with the essential character of the group to which they belong, is proof that the soul of the most gifted, as of the most insignificant individual, is nothing more nor less than a component of the collective soul of the community.[1] Language in its essence contains an important artistic element, which is a necessary consequence of its specific character and not due to any conscious tendency in men. The feeling for language, to be found in certain individuals, is born with them, and proceeds, not from any spiritual force peculiar to them, but from the fullest application of man's spiritual capacity to the formation and utilization of language.

Von Humboldt holds further that language is the creative organ of thought. Through being expressed, our ideas, which remain entirely subjective until communicated to others, take on a concrete objective character and, thus transformed, return to the mind, where they become the material from which fresh thought is made. Language is not a thing, but an activity, and an unbroken activity, even when it is fixed in writing, where its, so to speak, dead parts have to undergo anew a process of spiritual elaboration. A living language is continually creative, thanks to a special aptitude of the human spirit. Thus it comes about that the individual speaker always has at his disposal the necessary expression, which comes to him not so much from memory as from that spiritual faculty which instinctively preserves unaltered the key to the formation of words. The word, in its turn, does not communicate something pre-existent, nor does it contain a notion that has already taken shape ; what it does, is to suggest the formation of notions, by methods peculiar to themselves, though naturally prompted in a certain fashion by the word in question ; on hearing the word, a key is touched in the instrument of our minds which gives birth to a notion that corresponds but is not identical with the word.

After identifying these two elements in language, the inner

---

[1] According to this view, linguistic innovations spread because of the spiritual identity to be found in all the speakers composing a linguistic community, the result, not of leading a common life, but of sharing as it were a common soul. It is clear that Humboldt had drunk deeply at the fount of romanticism. Weisgerber (*loc. cit.*, pp. 137-8), quotes passages from Herder's work to proves that Humboldt owed much to him, and states that Herder was the first to give definite expression to the idea that language is closely associated with the other manifestations of spiritual activity.

' form ', and the sounds, which he calls the material part of language (under which head he also includes all the physical impressions, together with that automatic functioning of the spirit that precedes the formation of ideas with the aid of language), von Humboldt proceeds to analyse them in detail, and arrives at a conclusion extremely important with regard to the present trend of linguistic thought, namely, that the exterior form of language is of far less significance than its inner form,[1] that is to say, in present-day terminology, we should give pride of place in our scientific investigations to psychical rather than to psycho-physical factors, or, to take a specific instance that frequently arises, semantics should have pride of place over phonetics, as indeed is constantly the case in the works of Schuchardt and others. Nevertheless, given the great resemblance that exists in the inner forms of languages, the sounds are of capital importance, as it is through them that, in general, one language is distinguished from another. Hence a classification of the various tongues would have to be based upon their formal phonetic elements, that is, on their distinctive features ; but such a classification is impossible, for the reason that there is an infinite variety of sounds. It remains for us therefore to take into account the inner form as well, not so much because a classification of languages would be more readily achieved on this basis, but for another reason, namely, that " Language is the very organ of a people's being, is indeed its very being, as it grows slowly to consciousness of itself and finds expression . . . hence the structure of the languages of mankind is different in so far as the peoples differ in their spiritual characteristics ".[2] According to von Humboldt, there are two phases in the evolution of languages : " the first, when the sound-creating impulse is still in full active growth, the second, when a pause intervenes after at least the outer form of the language has been fully constituted ; this is followed by a period of obvious decay of the creative physical force, save that during this period of decay new sources of life and successful linguistic

---

[1] Von Humboldt goes even further and considers sounds actually as an obstacle, which the ideas must surmount in their effort to take shape in language. Here we observe the very great resemblance that exists between his views and those of another of Vossler's masters, Benedetto Croce (see below).

[2] A. Trombetti has pointed out, in his *Elementi di glottologia*, Bologna, 1922–23, p. 5, that Leibnitz had already maintained that language was the mirror of a nation's spiritual life. This would give us a still earlier ancestor to Vossler, in whose doctrine the interdependence of language and culture in all its branches as kindred manifestations of the spirit of a people is of such fundamental importance.

change may also come into being ".[1] Finally, in the formation of sounds, that is to say, in constituting the ' outer form ' of language, two factors come into play, one entirely organic or physical, which is the product of the vocal organs working together, and is conditioned by ease or difficulty in utterance, and therefore by the natural affinities of the various sounds, the other psychical, which prevents the organs from obeying solely their natural propensities or their natural inertia.   Thus, fifty years before the period of the neo-grammarians, we find von Humboldt formulating the doctrine of the participation of the mind in the development of sounds, a doctrine which even to-day some scholars openly or tacitly contest.

From this summary it may be seen that there is more similarity between the theories of von Humboldt and those of Vossler than is usually admitted.   K. Jaberg, for example, in a thoughtful article published in *Germanisch-romanische Monatsschrift*, XIV (1926), p. 1 f., went so far as to claim that Vossler owed to von Humboldt only the idea that language is the expression of an ethnical character, with the corollary that the history of a language is the history of a nation's culture.   The reader will be able to judge for himself, from the evidence we have supplied, how much more far-reaching and fundamental is the kinship that unites the two writers.   Let us now turn to the influence exercised upon Vossler by the Italian philosopher and aesthetician, Benedetto Croce.[2]

According to K. Jaberg (*loc. cit.*, p. 5), Croce discusses questions relating to the philosophy of language in the following works :

Benedetto Croce   *Estetica come scienza dell' espressione e linguistica generale*, *Breviario di estetica*, 1912, pp. 43–6 (reprinted in *Nuovi saggi di estetica*, Bari, 1920), and *Filosofia del linguaggio* (published in *Conversazioni critiche*, 1st series, 2nd edition, Bari, 1924, p. 87–113).   In summarizing Croce's theories on language we shall confine ourselves to the earliest and most important of these works, *Estetica come scienza*, quoting from the fifth edition, published at Bari in 1922.[3]

---

[1] These two periods remind us of Vossler's distinction between ' Sprache als Schöpfung ' and ' Sprache als Entwicklung ', although, it should be added, von Humboldt, in the passage quoted, is discussing specifically the evolution of flexions.

[2] Cp. H. Friedrich, *Croces Ästhetik und Vosslers Sprachphilosophie*, in *Zeitschr. f. franz. und englischen Unterricht*, XXXI (1932), p. 201 f.   Croce's linguistic theories have been discussed also by M. de Montoliu, *El llenguatge com a fet estètic y com a fet lògic*, Biblioteca filològica de l'Institut de la Llengua catalana, XIII, Barcelona, 1921, p. 134 f. ;   cp. also, by the same author, *El lenguaje como fenómeno estético*, Buenos Aires, 1926, in vol. I of the publications of the Institute of Philology in the Faculty of Letters and Philosophy, p. 201 f.

[3] The first edition was published at Palermo, 1902.

In the preface to the first edition of the work we already meet with the principle conveyed by the title, that language and art, and so linguistics and aesthetics, are one and the same thing : " If language is the earliest of all spiritual manifestations, and if aesthetic form is nothing but language understood in the purest sense of the term, and in all its true and scientific extension, we cannot hope to understand the later and more complex forms of spiritual life if the earliest and simplest remains ill-known, or is mangled and disfigured " (p. viii). In the preface to the fifth edition, again, we read, " Art is expression, not, of course, immediate and practical expression, but ' theoretical ', that is to say, intuition " (p. xi–xii). And so the first chapter of his discourse treats of expression or intuition. Intuition is neither perception, nor sensation, nor even representation, if by representation we understand a complex sensation. It is the purest activity of the spirit, in which neither reflection nor judgment have any part. It may be distinguished from other and inferior forms of spiritual activity by the following sure criterion : " Every true intuition or representation is at one and the same time expression " (p. 11).[1] " There is no intuition by the spirit except when it is creating, fashioning, and expressing." " In intuitive activity expression and intuition go hand in hand " (*ibidem*). Thus, as understood by Croce, ' expression ' has the widest possible extension, and includes not only expression by means of words, but also expression by colours, tones, and lines. Moreover, expression and intuition are identical because they take place simultaneously ; when we have intuited an object or a sentiment, etc., at the same time we give them a form in our consciousness. We cannot intuit a thing without representing to ourselves at the same time the form which it possesses. And if its form is clear in our minds, it follows from this very fact that we have expressed it, irrespective of whether this expression we have given it takes on a material shape, so as to become knowable by others, or remains solely within our own consciousness.[2] Further, intuition, being identical with expression, is at the same time identical with art, for art signifies expression.

---

[1] It should be made clear that Croce is ' intuitionist ' only in aesthetics, unlike Bergson, for example, who founds on intuition a whole system of philosophy. In philosophy, Croce is a rationalist (cp. G. Esposito's article in the journal *Etudes italiennes*, Jan.–March, 1925, p. 21 f.).

[2] We have seen above, p. 94, that to Vossler it is a matter of no concern whether a man speaks aloud in the presence of others, or to himself ; in both cases, from the theoretical point of view, we have the same spiritual phenomenon.

Between the intuition of the artist and that of the ordinary man the differences are merely quantitative and empirical, and are no concern of aesthetics, which is a science of qualities. " Intuitive or artistic genius (*genialità*), like every form of human activity, is always conscious, otherwise it would be merely blind mechanism. What the artist may lack is reflective consciousness, the added consciousness of the historian or the critic, which is inessential " (p. 18).

In his sixth chapter, Croce reverts to the idea that intuition implies expression, but that we must not understand expression solely as a material manifestation of our intuitions, and develops it further. Among other things, he states : " The aesthetic fact exhausts itself in the expressive elaboration of our impressions. When we have laid hold of the word within us, or achieved a clear and lively conception of a figure or a statue, or invented a phrase of music, the expression is known and complete. Whether we later open our mouths, and *will* to open our mouths to speak, or our throats to sing, that is, whether we say aloud and with full throat what we have already said and sung silently to ourselves, whether we stretch out the hand, and *will* to stretch out the hand to play, is a supplementary fact, which obeys quite other laws than that which preceded it, and which, at present, is not our concern, though we may observe forthwith that it signifies a production of ' things ' and is a practical fact, pertaining to the will " (pp. 56–7).[1] Croce is just as categorical upon the same topic in Chap. XIII, where he is concerned with physical beauty in nature and art : " The complete process of aesthetic production can be symbolized in four stages : (*a*) impressions ; (*b*) expression, or aesthetic synthesis within the spirit ; (*c*) a hedonistic accompaniment, or pleasure in the beautiful (aesthetic pleasure) ; (*d*) translation of

---

[1] It might be objected against this point of view, which Vossler has adopted with regard to language, that aesthetic intuitions, so long as they remain un-expressed by means of sounds, colours, etc., are inexistent for other men, and therefore are incapable of being known and analysed by them, for they only become an object of study from the time they have taken on material form, that is, when they have lost, according to Croce, their theoretic and scientific interest, and preserve merely that ' practical ' character which is of no real scientific importance. It would seem to follow that the aesthetician (and the linguist) is on the horns of a dilemma. Croce, and Vossler after him, have found a way of escape from this position by exhorting us to study the work of art (and language) as if it had no material existence, to use it, in other words, as a means of reproducing in our minds the intuition to which it corresponds, and then to judge this in itself without taking into consideration its material elements. Hence the study of stylistics, as conceived by Vossler, and practised with success particularly by Spitzer (see below).

the aesthetic fact into physical phenomena, sounds, tones, movements, combinations of lines and colours, etc. It is clear to all that the essential element is (b), the only strictly aesthetic and truly vital element, and that this is absent from the mere act of manifestation or naturalistic construction, which is by metaphor also given the name of ' expression ' " (p. 105).

To judge a work of art is to reproduce it within oneself, that is, to put oneself in the author's place, and to create anew the process of elaboration of the work in question by the help of its material form. If we wish to appreciate it historically, we must take into account the time at which it appeared and the personality of its author ; we must possess, in other words, in addition to an aptitude for transposing ourselves into the author's mind, the necessary historical knowledge, so as to judge it fittingly both in relation to the author and to his times. It follows that a work of art cannot be compared with others which it might appear to us to resemble, but only with itself.[1]

Croce's conclusion with regard to the identity between linguistics and aesthetics is to be found in the final chapter (XVIII) of the theoretical part of the work : " The science of art and the science of language, aesthetics and linguistics, conceived as true sciences in the strict sense of the word, are not two distinct things, but one only. Not that there is no such a thing as specialized linguistics ; but the true science of language, general linguistics, to the extent to which it may be reduced to a philosophy, is no other than aesthetics. The worker in the field of general linguistics, that is, philosophical linguistics, has to deal with aesthetic problems and vice versa. Philosophy of language and philosophy of art are one and the same thing " (pp. 155–6). For language, like art, employs material means with a view to the expression of intuitions, and that the means are different in both is a detail of practice which is without importance. The essential feature is intuition, and with it of course pure expression, and here there is absolutely no difference. Consequently, artistic and linguistic expression being identical, it follows that they are both the concern of the same discipline. Croce then proceeds to criticize various conceptions concerning linguistic expression, and discusses such terms as interjection, association or convention, onomatopoea and the like, showing that only very few linguists

---

[1] We remember that Vossler affirms the same thing with regard to language, asserting that a linguistic expression is to be compared, not with others, be they like it or not, but with itself.

have come near the truth, namely, those who have seen in language
a creative spiritual act. But even these have gone astray when they
have maintained that language has developed and grown through
association. The formation of new words with the help of old,
says Croce, is also creation, not association, for the old words
become *im*pressions which give birth to new *ex*pressions, just as with
an artist, impressions from without are transformed into expressions,
that is to say, into works of art. Similarly, the Italian aesthetician
protests against the division of linguistic elements into categories
(substantives, verbs, etc.), for language, that is to say, expression,
forms an indivisible whole. The only linguistic reality is the proposition, which he defines as an expressive organism completely
intelligible in itself. Consequently, according to this conception,
a mere interjection, on the one hand, or an entire poem on the
other, are both propositions. Nor is there any reason in the classification of languages, because they in their turn do not constitute
distinct genera or species, but a single complex of facts in its various
phases of development. Another absurdity is normative grammar,
with its attempts at laying down the rules of speech ; real grammar
can only be theoretical, that is to say aesthetic, so that normative
or technical grammar is a contradiction in terms. The case is
different if we understand by grammar merely an empirical
discipline, or in other words, a series of schemata necessary in the
learning of a language. Here, we may even allow the division of
words into substantives, verbs, adjectives, etc., seeing that it helps
us to attain the practical end we are seeking. " Outside aesthetics,
through which we know the nature of language, and empirical
grammar, which is a pedagogic device, nothing remains but the
history of languages in their living reality, that is, the history of
concrete literary products, which is identical in substance with the
history of literature " (p. 162). Just as he opposes the grammatical
categories, so he protests against the so-called linguistic elements,
sounds, syllables, etc., which are in reality physical facts, with no
intellectual content, and consequently non-linguistic, and also
against ' roots ' about which the philologists of the past puzzled
themselves so much. Yet another aberration, according to Croce,
is the idea of a model standard, or of a unity of language, discussed by some linguists, for to him language signifies uninterrupted
activity, whereas a ' model ' language is something fixed and
unchanging. Linguists may, if they like, discuss such questions, but
they are no real concern of linguistics, that is to say, aesthetics. A

similar absurdity is the problem of a universal language, an artificial product even more perverse in character than that of a fixed standard.[1]

★

No great exception can be taken to the principles that underlie Vossler's linguistic doctrine. No one would contest that language **Notes on the** is the product of a people's spirit, and that it mani- **Idealistic** fests the idiosyncrasies of thought and feeling **School** peculiar to a given ethnical community. It follows therefore that the causes of linguistic change are to be sought in the psychology of the individual speaker, and not in his vocal organs. Further, language is only one aspect of the spiritual activity of a community. Beside it, we have literature, art, etc.,

---

[1] In the second part of his book, Croce discusses the history of aesthetics and, of course, linguistics. Certain details which have some relation to the doctrines of Vossler are worth mentioning. Two centuries ago, G. B. Vico maintained that language and poetry are identical. Half a century later Herder, in *Abhandlung über den Ursprung der Sprache*, defines language as " the mind's understanding of itself " (p. 283). Croce pays special attention to von Humboldt's linguistic system, which though not entirely free from the influence of his predecessors, brings us much that is new and true. He approves von Humboldt's objections to dividing language into so-called parts of speech and grammatical rules, which kill what is living in language and destroy its natural unity. Humboldt, too, speaks of man's linguistic activity in a manner that shows he also was aware of the kinship between art and language. Further, his notion of ' innere Sprachform ' is not far removed from what Croce and Vossler call ' intuition ', and the inner synthesis, that is, the combination of the inner speech-form with physical sound utterance, which, according to Humboldt, constitutes the essence of language reminds us of Croce's and Vossler's ' expression '. The difference lies in the fact that to von Humboldt the artistic and the linguistic are comparable, not completely identical, as they are held to be by Croce and Vossler.

A disciple of von Humboldt's, H. Steinthal, also has ideas which approximate closely to those of our two scholars. He asserts, for instance, that thoughts can be expressed without words, by signs, and that hence a deaf-mute using his gestures is no different in this aspect from a man talking ; that logic has no right of interference in language, which is its own master ; that there is no difference between primitive speech-creation (Urschöpfung) and its daily repetition. Croce has also words of praise for Hermann Paul, for having, among other things, re-introduced into language study the philosophical outlook, which had been lost under positivism and naturalism. " For Paul, though a little shaky on the relations between logic and grammar, has the merit of having re-established von Humboldt's contention that in its origin and its present nature speech is the same, by asserting that language is created afresh every time we speak. He has also the further merit of having provided a decisive criticism of the ' folk-psychology ' of Steinthal and Lazarus, by showing that there is no such thing as a collective soul, and that there can be no language save of the individual." (On Croce's linguistic ideas, see further M. Bartoli, *Introduzione alla Neolinguistica*, Geneva, 1925, p. 101, and M. Bartoli and G. Bertoni, *Breviario di Neolinguistica*, Modena, 1925, p. 4.)

which possess an essential kinship with language, coming as they do from the same source. It behoves us therefore to study these manifestations of the human spirit as well, in order to attain a better understanding of the development of language itself; the cause of its modifications, that is, ' the genius of the language ', or, what is the same thing, the genius of the people speaking it, can be the more readily understood if we follow it in these other domains of intellectual activity. The history of language thus becomes identical with the history of culture, or, more precisely, a chapter thereof.[1]

Nor can the idea that language is an aesthetic fact, like literature and art in general, be rejected in its entirety. Human speech certainly has its aesthetic side. Most writers, in particular the poets, whose primary concern is with the beautiful, of necessity make it an important feature of their language. But even in our daily talk there can be observed, not, perhaps, a permanent and strictly aesthetic trend, but, at all events, a marked tendency towards something we may rightly consider to be of an aesthetic character. How could we explain otherwise the use of so many metaphors and figures of speech, or our preference for those words that are felt to be the most expressive, particularly in moments of strong emotion ? ' Idealism ' goes astray only in so far as it overstresses the importance of this aesthetic element. It is true that, compared with Croce, who only recognizes the ' theoretical ' part of language (see above, p. 116), Vossler represents a very real progress ; being a linguist, not a philosopher, he does take into account its practical element, that is to say, its material expression which takes shape in words and sentences. Yet he, in his turn, as good as abolishes it again when he urges the linguist to concern himself in principle solely with what is individual, that is to say, the aesthetic aspects of language, and to leave its ' practical ', its mechanical and general elements, to the consideration of those workers who, being devoid of intuition, are incapable of understanding the higher linguistic forms. Moreover, even if we admit, in theory, that man speaks solely to give concrete expression to his intuitions, which otherwise are devoid of any practical purpose, we observe that in reality the necessity of communicating to the listener certain thoughts or feelings does come into

---

[1] W. von Wartburg, who cannot be suspected of having any close personal or academic connection with the idealists (see next chapter), asserts in *Zeitschr. f. rom. Phil.*, XL (1920), p. 509, that *Frankreichs Kultur* . . . is the only, or at least the most significant attempt to understand linguistic changes concurrently with, and as a part of, the general trend of culture.

play, to a greater or lesser extent. In other words, language *is*, in fact, a means of communication between men. For this reason, the purest intuitions become clouded, and lose their exclusively theoretical character to take on a practical garb, to which the linguist is obliged to give consideration. In the same order of ideas, Vossler commits a further error in not making a distinction between ' language ' (' la langue ', in Saussure's terminology ; see below, Chap. IV) and ' speech ' (' la parole '), or, as Jaberg says, between the linguistics of ' language ' and the linguistics of ' speech '. Jaberg (*loc. cit.*) addresses this objection to Croce, who entirely casts aside ' language ' as appertaining to the domain of practical things, but the same might be said of Vossler, inasmuch as ' la parole ', not ' la langue ', is the basis of his linguistic doctrines. The very fact that Vossler and his pupils confine their studies to the Romance literary languages would seem to confirm this, inasmuch as in literary works we are dealing with individual styles, with individual applications of the linguistic system, not with the system itself. Though this does not prevent them from giving out their conclusions as valid, and applicable to the system as a whole.

We have seen in the course of this discussion the important place given to intuition in the doctrines of the idealistic school. Here, too, the linguist can agree with them, at least in theory. For it is without question that just as the literary critic cannot have a true understanding of a poetic composition through scholarship alone, so the linguist requires, in addition to his learning, an innate gift, a feeling for language, to give him a quick and accurate perception of the origin and growth of a given linguistic phenomenon. We have only to think of Schuchardt, for example, among the older generation of scholars, or of Leo Spitzer among the younger.[1] But here, too, we are confronted with a difficulty, when we come to apply intuition to the explanation of specific phenomena. As, by definition, we have to do with an entirely personal factor, it is inevitable that this factor should differ as between one scholar and another, and

---

[1] Even K. Jaberg (*loc. cit.*) declares himself to be, in principle, a believer in intuition, particularly as von Humboldt, a hundred years ago, and Bergson in our own day, have shown the usefulness of this faculty of the human spirit. But he goes on to say that intuition, to be fruitful, must be accompanied by great linguistic experience, as was the case with von Humboldt or Schuchardt, or by a temperament like that of Gilliéron, who had " all the linguistic possibilities, so to speak, at his finger tips ", and was possessed of an exceptional mastery of the methods of research. Despite the fact that Jaberg seems a little exacting in his demands, we can accept his point of view, interpreting it to mean that intuition must be backed up by a thorough scientific training.

consequently discussion will be apt to take on a markedly subjective character, to the detriment, as has more than once been the
case, of that purely scientific outlook which should prevail in our
studies.   Differences of opinion, and even flat contradiction upon
the selfsame linguistic topic, were frequent enough before.   By this,
so to speak, compulsory introduction of intuition into language
research we run the risk of something like anarchy, and of prejudic-
ing in consequence the scientific character of linguistic study.

   But there are still more serious dangers inherent in this subjectivism that is such an integral part of the Vosslerian doctrine.
Suppose we are studying a given language, and attempting to understand its development with the help of what we know of the national
genius from its other manifestations.   If, for any reason, we are
unfavourably disposed towards this national genius, there is a
danger that we may be led to interpret the linguistic facts in the
light of our own feelings, and to discover everywhere traces of this
spirit we dislike.   In such a case, language study, which should
help to bring peoples together, leads to quite opposite results, and
its representatives sin alike against truth and against humanity.[1]
(Cp. what is said below concerning E. Lerch's study, *Das romanische
Futurum*. . . .)

   Idealistic philology suffers, further, from a certain one-sidedness.
In its endeavour to explain the phenomena of language by what is
characteristic of the spirit of a given people, it tends to pass over
those features that many idioms, not necessarily related to one
another, may possess in common, and, by doing so, to provide an
interpretation of linguistic facts that may hold good for one
language, but be entirely inapplicable to those that have similar
or even identical phenomena.   Schuchardt, in particular, about
whose theory of ' elementary kinship ' between languages we have
spoken above (p. 56 f.), has proved time and again that in idioms
widely remote from one another, geographically and historically,
entirely similar innovations appear, which it is therefore impossible
to account for by the specific genius of the peoples concerned ;
for that would mean postulating certain identical psychological
peculiarities in a number of peoples of entirely different origins,
whereas the real explanation lies in that common humanity which

---

[1] The mission of philology as a means of international understanding has long
been recognized.   It may be of interest, none the less, to quote the views of Ascoli
as reproduced by A. Trombetti, in *Elementi di glottologia*, Bologna, 1922–23, p. 6 :
" by disclosing the affinities between races apparently widely apart, it helps on
the principles of mutual forbearance and the fraternity of nations."

forms a spiritual bond between all peoples, and a basis of union rather than differentiation between the nations. It is clear, for example, from the numerous studies that have appeared in recent years upon the language of the soldiers during the war, that the mentality of the soldier is astonishingly alike as between one nation and another, and that we have to take into account, therefore, not only ethnical characteristics, in our observation and explanation of the facts of language, but also the psychology of classes and professions, irrespective of political or national frontiers.

As can be seen from the foregoing discussion, the objections that can be framed against the idealistic movement in linguistics affect the application of its principles to specific cases, while leaving the doctrine itself unshaken. Hence it is, that of the numerous criticisms directed against Vossler by his opponents, it is chiefly those which concern matters of detail, namely, the interpretation of specific points of language, that have found their mark. Herein, clearly, lies the real weakness of the Munich school. Thus, Jaberg, whose study quoted above is extremely impartial, and who is ready to recognize many good features in Vossler's work, accuses the idealists of frequently taking their linguistic material not directly from the source, but from the works of other scholars who have studied the same problems. To certain of the adherents of idealism he even applies the name of dilettanti.[1] Indeed, Vossler himself has admitted, directly or indirectly, that his opponents are sometimes in the right with regard to certain precise points ; compare, for instance, the modifications he accepts in his supplement to *Frankreichs Kultur* . . . , or the two editions of the same book, the first in 1913, the second in 1929. Similarly, a change of attitude, at times quite fundamental, can be observed in *Sprache als Schöpfung* . . . when confronted with *Positivismus und Idealismus* . . . , and a fresh point of view applied to problems that had been treated in the earlier work. But all these vacillations do not prove the fragility of the idealist doctrine, but merely a certain shakiness in method, aggravated by the rather lively temperament of the man applying it. They are indeed natural, and almost inevitable, in any attempt to revolutionize the methods of scientific enquiry, and can be corrected in process of time, as is proved by the many excellent

---

[1] He quotes as a piece of dilettantism E. Lerch's article, *Zu den Anfängen der altfranzösischen Literatur*, in *Vom Geiste neuer Literaturforschung. Festschrift für Oskar Walzel*, Wildpark-Potsdam, 1924, which G. Rohlfs has also criticized severely (cp. p. 109, note).

studies we owe to Vossler himself and to his disciples, or by the researches of L. Spitzer, who, after beginning on quite different lines, has adopted what was sound in the Munich scholar's theories, and has won admiration and almost general approval by the innovations he has shown to be possible in the practice of our craft (see below).

It should be said, too, that the defects of the Vosslerian doctrine lose much of their importance when we set them beside its virtues. By insisting upon the psychological factor in the evolution of language, linguistics becomes a deeper study, for the effort towards discovering ' the genius of the language ', even though it may at times lead us astray in our interpretations of specific facts, none the less brings us closer to what constitutes the essence of human speech. At the same time, the task of the linguist becomes more difficult and more delicate, for while research on positivist lines required merely skill and application, talent, or an intuitive understanding of the spirit of language, becomes a necessary adjunct if work is to be produced of the kind desired by Vossler. It thus means, as Spitzer says in *Italienische Umgangssprache*, p. 293, that the investigation of speech becomes the investigation of the human spirit. By giving due appreciation to the psychical factors in language, fresh air and a new life have been made to circulate in the field of linguistic research, where, by the piling up of huge quantities of material, particularly phonological, the atmosphere had too frequently been that of the lumber-room. It must be understood, of course, that the credit for this is not entirely due to Vossler, but his share is considerable, particularly as the temperament and revolutionary attitude of the idealists have helped in a large measure to awaken the representatives of the older schools from the torpor into which they had gradually fallen.[1]

Inasmuch as the genius of a language is more manifest in the domains of syntax and style, the representatives of the idealistic school have shown a preference for work in these branches of grammar, which, indeed, are so closely related that they may be said to compose one linguistic discipline ; a stylistic phenomenon becomes syntactical when it becomes a fixed form, or in other words, grammaticalized, and, inversely, every syntactical form was,

---

[1] As Jaberg, says, *loc. cit.*, p. 4, " The great and indisputable service rendered by Vossler towards a new orientation of Romance philology, lies in the stirring effect of this slogan [*viz.* that matter is nothing and the spirit everything] rather than in the formulation of fundamentally new linguistic ideas."

originally, stylistic or individual. But the cultural life of a people, or, what is the same thing, the genius of its language or of the linguistic community, can be readily traced in its vocabulary as well, and neither Vossler nor his pupils have paid adequate attention to the lexical elements of the languages they have investigated. This rather surprising fact has been seized upon and cast up to them by their opponents, though it would seem excessive to expect the idealistic, or any other school for that matter, to make every possible practical application of its theoretical principles.[1]

Another merit of Vossler's is that, having realized that language is a phenomenon of the same nature as literature and art, he has placed linguistic study in its natural setting beside, and in intimate association with, the history of literature and of art and the history of culture in general. The barriers which separated the history of language from kindred disciplines, and which previously were rigorously observed as a matter of principle, have thus been broken down, at least in the case of certain Romanicists, and the old narrow and prejudicial specialization becomes a thing of the past. Although it may be held impossible for the same individual to devote himself with equal success to the history of language and to the history of literature, none the less an interest has been awakened in both camps in things that were once considered quite distinct, and even incompatible. The linguist now shows an interest in literature, and the literary historian in language. The result has been a widening of both horizons, and a more complete understanding of the matter of research, a thing which, particularly in linguistics, was very much to be desired.

There is a final point to be remembered. We have mentioned more than once the preference displayed by the idealists for the language of literature, as against the popular language of everyday life. Now, it is common knowledge that during the last quarter of a century, Romance scholars, particularly since the extraordinary advances registered by Linguistic Geography (see next chapter), have shown a very keen interest in matters relating to dialect;

---

[1] The explanation of this is probably to be found in the fact that, of the two fundamental conceptions, namely, language as a history of culture and language as a history of art, Vossler has strong personal preferences for the latter. It is for this reason that he concerns himself entirely with written language, that is to say, artistic language, employed by authors in literary works. For the same reason, he has been a continuous, and, be it said, most successful worker in the field of literary history. The same preferences are, in general, to be noticed in his pupils. The relations between stylistics and literary history, in the widest sense of the term, are, of course, very close indeed.

and the more the vernacular speeches tended to monopolize the energies of investigators, the greater, naturally, was the tendency to neglect the written language. The efforts of Vossler and his disciples came as a healthy reaction. Interesting as the dialects are as living, spontaneous, and unshackled forms of speech, they cannot be held to represent the whole of a people's language. If we are to comprehend the whole life of a given idiom, and appreciate its evolution to the full, a knowledge of the literary tongue is an immediate necessity. But the idealistic school, when dealing with the literary language, does not confine itself to the older periods as the positivists tended to do. Like the majority of German Romanicists, Vossler and his followers have chosen to specialize more particularly in French, but the present author is unaware of any purely linguistic study from their pens which is confined entirely to the early stages of that language. Here, too, their attitude is entirely to be praised.[1]

★ ★ ★

Vossler's pupils, in the strict sense of the term, are not over-numerous.[2] On the linguistic side, one of the most distinguished

---

[1] Another point to the credit of the idealists is the style in which they clothe their ideas. It can be said that the German positivists neglected on principle the 'form' of their scientific writings. Whoever has followed their activiites closely knows from experience with what difficulties he has had to contend in order to get at their meaning, and that, not because of any great abstruseness in their ideas, or even from a lack of the necessary knowledge of German. Here, too, Vossler is responsible for a salutary reaction. His own works are not only readable, but enjoyable, precisely because of their brightness, their wealth of words, and their artistic phrasing. The same, to a lesser degree, is true of his disciples. We may conclude our appreciation of Vossler with a quotation from L. Spitzer's *Meisterwerke der romanischen Sprachwissenschaft*, II, p. 340–1 : " Perhaps the leading German romanicist. More than that : a renewer of the philology of the turning century. Still more than that : a man bold and gifted enough to see, and to win through to the essential and to finality. He is one of the few scientific workers who look beyond their speciality and are able to survey a culture in its entirety. His influence consequently is most marked in a domain where the traditions of narrow specialization, and an aversion for all breadth and comprehensiveness of vision, were ingrained most deeply—in the science of language."

[2] Although we are here exclusively concerned with linguistics, it would appear appropriate to mention the names of two of Vossler's pupils who, like their master himself, have distinguished themselves in other domains. They are : Leonardo Olschki, the author of a number of works on the history of literature and culture, particularly relating to the Renascence and pre-Renascence periods, and Viktor Klemperer, a literary historian of great powers, who has published a number of studies on French literature, apparently fragments of a complete history in course of preparation. Both are collaborators in the *Handbuch der Literaturwissenschaft*, a prodigious work, embracing the literature of all peoples, published in

is Eugen Lerch, until 1935 a professor in the University of Münster, in Westphalia, whose speciality is syntax, particularly

Eugen Lerch French syntax. We shall mention only a certain number of his numerous and extensive publications, giving some idea of their contents and of the reception they have received at the hands of critics. In 1919, Lerch published at Leipzig a study entitled *Die Verwendung des romanischen Futurums als Ausdruck eines sittlichen Sollens*, the burden of which is as follows. It is known that in certain conditions the future plays the part of an imperative. This future Lerch calls the imperative, or ' Heischefuturum,' and gives as its characteristics that, on the one hand, it expresses a conviction on the part of the speaker that what he desires is sure to come about, and, on the other, that it differs from the ordinary future only by receiving a special intonation. After discussing various significations of this verbal form, in a first section which he calls ' systematic ', and where he adduces a rich collection of examples from all the Romance languages, the author endeavours to provide a ' stylistic ' explanation of the phenomenon, in the Vosslerian sense. From this stage onwards he confines himself to French, not only because it is more widely known, but for another reason, namely, because he considers the use of the future as an imperative more characteristic of French, where, indeed, it is more frequently met with, particularly in popular speech,—a proof that there can be no question of any Latin influence, as might be the case in the other Romance languages. The explanation of the phenomenon is to be sought, therefore, in the genius of the French language, that is to say, in the spirit of the French people, whose predominant feature, as we get to know it from its other manifestations, is an impulsiveness that gives rise to a depreciative and overweening attitude with regard to others ! Hence, the imperative future, we are told, presupposes that the speaker who uses it regards the men he is addressing in the nature of mere objects, devoid of a will and personality of their own, and incapable of resisting his injunctions.

Wildpark-Potsdam under the direction of O. Walzel. A nation's literature, in Klemperer's view, signifies the linguistic expression of the people's ideals. Hence the title of one of his books : *Idealistische Literaturgeschichte*, Bielefeld-Leipzig, 1929, where the epithet ' idealist ' characterizes, not so much the method, but the contents of literary history as understood by the author. (Cp. K. Vossler, *Deutsche Literaturzeitung*, LI, 1930, col. 18 f.). Lerch and Klemperer were the founders, in 1925, of a review, *Jahrbuch für Philologie*, which can be considered as the organ of the idealist school. After changing its title to *Idealistische Philologie* in its third year, it ceased publication. (Cp. *Neuphilologische Mitteilungen*, XXVII [1926], p. 14 f.)

Lerch's explanation of the phenomenon cannot, in general, be said to have satisfied the critics,[1] although they gave hearty approval to his grammatical treatment of the material in the earlier part of his book. What particularly disturbed the reviewers was his neglect of the other languages, Romance and non-Romance, where a similar use of the future as an imperative is encountered. Clearly, if the same verbal function exists elsewhere, it follows that other peoples also are guilty of ' impulsiveness ', which thus ceases to be a prerogative of the French, unless indeed, as is more likely, a psychological explanation of the usage different from that propounded by Lerch must be sought. Even Vossler is constrained to disown his pupil's[2] exaggerations when he writes, in the 1921 supplement to *Frankreichs Kultur* . . . , p. 384 : " There is no doubt that Lerch, in his moral and psychological interpretation of the French use of the future as an imperative, has overstepped the mark." While Spitzer, in an article entitled *Eine Strömung innerhalb der romanischen Sprachwissenschaft*, *Archiv für das Studium der neueren Sprachen und Literaturen*, CXLI (1921), p. 111 f., calls attention to the unfriendly atmosphere that studies of this character are apt to generate.[3]

---

[1] Among the reviews of Lerch's study may be mentioned those of A. Debrunner, *Deutsche Literaturzeitung*, XLI (1920), col. 377 f. ; K. Vossler, *Literaturblatt f. germ. u. rom. Philologie*, XLI (1920), col. 101 f. ; A. Wallensköld, *Neuphilologische Mitteilungen*, XXI (1920), p. 153 f. ; A. Franz, *Zur galloromanischen Syntax*, Jena-Leipzig, 1920, p. 87 f. ; V. Klemperer, *Archiv f. d. Stud. der neueren Spr. u. Lit.*, CXL (1920), p. 125 f. ; W. v. Wartburg, *Zeitschr. f. rom. Phil.*, XLI (1921), p. 364 f. ; W. Meyer-Lübke, *Revue de linguistique romane*, I (1925), p. 17 f. The same problem was treated by G. Rohlfs in competition for a prize awarded by the Munich Academy. Rohlfs, whose study, entitled *Das romanische habeo-Futurum und Konditionalis*, appeared in *Archivum Romanicum*, VI (1922), p. 105 f., concerns himself more particularly with the manner in which the future and the conditional came into being. For reviews on Rohlfs' study see E. Gamillscheg, *Zeitschr. f. rom. Phil.*, XLIII (1923), p. 722 f. ; J. Ronjat, *Revue des langues romanes*, LXII (1923–4), p. 444 f. ; Elise Richter, *Zu Gerhard Rohlfs' Das romanische habeo-Futurum*, in *Zeitschr. f. rom. Phil.*, XLIV (1924), p. 91 f. ; A. Meillet, *Bull. Soc. Ling.*, XXIV (1923), fasc. 2, p. 85 ; Eva Seifert, *Die neueren Sprachen*, XXXII (1924), p. 111 f. ; K. Sneyders de Vogel, *Neophilologus*, X (1924–5), p. 223 ; W. Meyer-Lübke, *Rev. de linguistique romane*, I (1925), p. 17 f.—More or less similar topics are discussed by W. Esser, in *Beiträge zur Geschichte des Irrealis in Italien*, *Romanische Forschungen*, XXXIX (1951–5), p. 267 f. (the conditional only), and by P. Meriggi, *Parralleli nell' evoluzione del sistema verbale romanzo e germanico*, in *Zeitschr. f. rom. Phil.*, L (1930), p. 129 f.

[2] It should be made clear that Lerch began as a pupil of Tobler, in the University of Berlin, and only later became a whole-hearted follower of Vossler. This explains why, from the point of view of wealth of documentation, his works remind us of the earlier school ; indeed some of them, for example *Französische Syntax*, despite or because of their subject matter, have in them little that can really be styled ' idealistic '.

[3] It would appear from a review by Leo Jordan in *Zeitschr. f. rom. Phil.*, LI (1931), p. 112 f., that a similar attitude to that of Lerch in his *Futurum* . . . is

The other works by Lerch, to consider only those that have appeared in volume form, namely *Die Bedeutung der Modi im Französischen*,[1] Leipzig, 1919, and *Historische französische Syntax*, vol. I, Leipzig, 1925 ; vol. II, *ibidem*, 1929 ; vol. III, 1934, have enjoyed a more favourable reception at the hands of the critics.[2] Under the title of *Hauptprobleme der französischen Sprache*, Lerch has recently published two volumes[3] of collected essays on the French language

to be found in Klemperer's *Romanische Sonderart*, Munich, 1926. This kind of animosity is doubtless to be attributed to the bitterness aroused by the war, which unfortunately spread to the world of scholarship. There is apparent, for instance, in Ed. Wechssler's voluminous work, *Esprit und Geist. Versuch einer Wesenskunde des Deutschen und des Franzosen*, Bielefeld, 1927, a jingoist attitude which actually called forth a smarting rebuke from Klemperer himself, in a long review of the work in *Literaturblatt f. germ. u. rom. Phil.*, XLIX (1928), col. 89 f. It is true that Wechssler is a declared opponent of the Vosslerian school. To be just, it should be said that this attitude, which is now almost entirely a thing of the past, was not confined to German scholars. No less a linguist than A. Meillet, in an article entitled : *Ce que la linguistique doit aux Allemands*, could go so far as to maintain that linguistic science owes nothing of really great importance to the Germans ! (Cp. Spitzer's protest in *Literaturblatt f. germ. u. rom. Phil.*, XLIV [1923], col. 297 f.)

[1] Reviewed by K. Vossler, *Literaturblatt f. germ. u. rom. Phil.*, XL (1919), col. 246 f. ; A. Wallensköld, *Neuphilologische Mitteilungen*, XX (1919), p. 124 f. ; K. Sneyders de Vogel, *Neophilologus*, V (1919–20), p. 81 f. ; W. v. Wartburg, *Zeitschr. f. rom. Phil.*, XL (1920), p. 721 f., etc. Von Wartburg calls it the first really profound treatment of the French moods in their psychological correlations. As, in a sense, complementary to this work we may mention a number of studies by M. Regula, *Über die modale und psycho-dynamische Bedeutung der französischen Modi im Nebensatze*, in *Zeitschr. f. rom. Phil.*, XLV (1925), p. 129 f. ; *Die Modi des Französischen in erfassungstheoretischer Beleuchtung*, ibid., XLIX (1929), p. 676 f. ; *Zum französischen Konjunktiv*, in *Jahrbuch für Philologie*, II (1927), p. 209 f. ; and *Über die Beziehungen zwischen Erfassungsart, psychologischem Gewicht und Modalität des Denkinhaltes*, ibid., III (1927–8), p. 273 f.

[2] Vol. I, which aroused considerable discussion among many of the leading linguists, who frankly recognized its value, was reviewed by, among others, L. Spitzer, *Literaturblatt f. germ. u. rom. Phil.*, XLVII (1926), col. 19 f. ; A. Meillet, *Bull. Soc. Ling.*, XXVII (1926–7), fasc. 2, p. 100 f. ; K. Sneyders de Vogel, *Neophilologus*, XII (1926–7), p. 291 f. ; E. Gamillscheg, *Göttingische gelehrte Anzeigen*, CLXXXIX (1927), p. 25 f. ; O. Bloch, *Revue critique*, yr. LXII (1928), p. 138 f. ; N. Drăganu, *Dacoromania*, V (1927–8), p. 698 f. The preface to the volume is of considerable extent and discusses theoretical questions, in particular ' idealism '. The author makes clear his standpoint with regard to the Munich school, which he extols above all others. Vol. II has been reviewed by E. Bourciez, *Revue critique*, LXIII (1929), p. 313 f. ; El. Richter, *Literaturblatt f. germ. u. rom. Phil.*, LI (1930), col. 107 f. ; Iorgu Iordan, *Arhiva*, XXXVII (1930), p. 306 f. ; K. Sneyders de Vogel, *Neophilologus*, XV (1929–30), p. 279 f. ; M. Regula, *Die neueren Sprachen*, XXXVIII (1930), p. 430 f. (the last two are not directly known to the author) ; and O. Schultz-Gora, *Arch. f. d. Stud. der neueren Spr. u. Lit.*, CLVII (1930), p. 310. On vol. III, see : E. Bourciez, *Rev. crit.*, yr. LXIX (1935), p. 143 f. ; Iorgu Iordan, *Bule . Inst. de Fil. Rom.*, II (1935), p. 244 f. ; A. Meillet, *Bull. Soc. Ling.*, XXXVI (1935), fasc. 2, p. 57 f. ; M. Regula, *Literaturblatt f. germ. u. rom. Phil.*, LVI (1935), col. 500 f. ; G. Rohlfs, *Archiv f. d. Stud. d. neueren Spr.*, CLXVII (1935), p. 152 f. ; E. Seifert, *Zeitschr. f. neusprachl. Unterricht*, XXXIV (1935), no. 5 ; E. Staaf, *Studia neophilologica*, VIII, nos. 2–3.

[3] Vol. I, ' *Allgemeineres* ', Braunschweig, 1930 ; Vol. II, ' *Besonderes* ', ibid., 1931. Reviewed by Kr. Sandfeld, in *Archiv f. d. Stud. d. neueren Spr. u. Lit.*,

which had appeared in various journals and presentation volumes. One of the best of them, and deserving of special mention, is that entitled " *Die ' halbe ' Negation* ", in which we find an explanation of the fact that in French the first part of the negation (*ne*) is occasionally used instead of the customary *ne . . . pas*. The construction without *pas* is extremely frequent in Old French, whereas the nearer we get to modern times the rarer it becomes. Lerch attributes the difference between the two forms of expression to the greater affectivity of the forms without *pas*, which causes the stress to be placed on the verb, whereas, in the other form, which is less affective, the stress is carried over to the second element of the negative. Though this explanation is far from being generally accepted,[1] the author must be given credit for the manner in which, following the example set by Vossler in *Frankreichs Kultur . . .*, he has traced historically the phases through which the negative has passed, and linked them up with the spiritual development of the French people. The same Vosslerian trend is manifest in recent studies like : *Die spanische Kultur im Spiegel des spanischen Wortschatzes, Neuphilologische Monatsschrift*, I (1930), p. 525 f., where the history of Spanish civilization is studied on the basis of the loan-words in the Spanish vocabulary,[2] *Nationenkunde durch Stilistik*, in

CLX (1931), p. 283 f. ; K. Lewent (first volume only) in *Neuphilologische Monatsschrift*, II (1931), p. 249 f. ; A. Meillet, *Bull. Soc. Ling.*, XXXI (1931), p. 136 f., and XXXII (1931), p. 27 f. ; H. Oppenheim, *Die neueren Sprachen*, XLI (1933), nr. 1 ; E. Bourciez, *Rev. crit.*, yr. LXIV (1930), p. 427 f. ; O. Bloch, *ibid.*, LXVI (1932), p. 128 f. ; P. Fouché, *Revue des langues romanes*, LXVI (1929–32), p. 428 f., and, finally, by E. Winkler, who devotes an extensive study to this work, entitled, *Aus dem Denksystem des Französischen*, and published in the *Zeitschrift für französische Sprache und Literatur*, LIV (1930–31), p. 423 f. Against Lerch's contention that the sole method of syntactical investigation is the historical, Winkler upholds the view that, as is proved by Lerch's own practice throughout the two volumes, the historical and the descriptive methods can be combined, and that in fact preference should be given to the descriptive, or psychologically interpretative method, which is of necessity at the basis even of a so-called historical investigation ; for in order to understand any syntactical phenomenon it is necessary to grasp first of all the psychological causes underlying it. Winkler's study was, in its turn, reviewed by M. Regula, in *Literaturblatt f. germ. u. rom. Phil.*, LIII (1932), col. 169 f.

[1] The article, which appeared first in *Die neueren Sprachen*, XXIX (1921), p. 6 f., and has been reproduced in *Meisterwerke der romanischen Sprachwissenschaft*, II, p. 98 f., by Spitzer, who considers Lerch " the greatest investigator in the field of syntax since Tobler ", has been criticized, among others, by G. Rohlfs, *Zeitschrift f. rom. Phil.*, XLII (1922), p. 80 f., and M. Kuttner, *Die neueren Sprachen*, XXX (1922), p. 440 f. Kuttner contends, (1) that the full negative is a very early phenomenon, and (2) that the presence or absence of *pas* depends upon the stress or rhythm of the French sentence : if the verb is the psychological predicate, i.e. the most important element in the sentence, *pas* is not necessary ; if, on the other hand, the negation is more important, *pas* is indispensable, as it carries the stress.

[2] Criticized by Rohlfs in *Archiv f. d. Stud. d. neueren Sprachen*, CLX (1931), p. 100 f.

vol. II, p. 5 f., of his *Hauptprobleme, Spanische Sprache und Wesensart*, in *Handbuch der Spanienkunde*,[1] Frankfurt a.M., 1932, p. 147 f., *Der Einfluss des Christentums auf den französischen Wortschatz*, in *Neuphilologische Monatsschrift*, III (1932), p. 65 f. and 108 f., and *Französische Sprache und Wesensart*,[2] Frankfurt a.M., 1933. Again like Vossler, but less frequently and with less distinction, Lerch has published studies in literary history, while, in conformity with his early training, we find him elsewhere engaging in work of the traditional philological type, for example in an edition of the *Chanson de Roland*, published at Munich in 1923.

★

In a chapter that is devoted to the idealist school of Romance philology it is indispensable that we should discuss two scholars
Etienne Lorck
who, though not actually pupils of Vossler, have so identified themselves with his doctrines and methods that we can rightly consider them as belonging to his group. One of them is E. Lorck, late professor in the University of Cologne, who, having written comparatively little, remains practically unknown even to workers in our own field. Lorck's name is associated particularly with the question of ' erlebte Rede ', which he raised in a book entitled *Die " erlebte Rede "*, *Eine sprachliche Untersuchung*, Heidelberg, 1921. The phenomenon may be explained briefly as follows. In order to communicate what has been said by another, we dispose of three methods of procedure : (*a*) we may reproduce it exactly in the words of the speaker, accompanying them, when writing, with inverted commas,—in other words, by ' direct speech ' ; or (*b*) we may preface it with a formula like " So-and-so said that," etc., using our own words, and not claiming to render the statement exactly as we heard it,—by ' indirect speech ',

---

[1] Reviewed by R. Ruppert y Ujaravi, in *Literaturblatt f. germ. u. rom. Phil.*, LIV (1933), col. 257 f.

[2] Reviewed by : A. Dauzat, *Le français moderne*, II (1934), p. 169 f. ; E. Bourciez, *Rev. critique*, yr. LXVII (1933), p. 372 f. ; A. Meillet, *Bull. Soc. Ling.*, XXXIV (1933), fasc. 3, p. 96 f. ; P. Fouché, *Rev. des langues rom.*, LXVII (1933-4), p. 201 f. ; K. Glaser, *Literaturbl. f. germ. u. rom. Phil.*, LV (1934), col. 236 f. ; St. Papp, *Neuphilologische Mitteilungen*, XXXV (1934), p. 193 f. ; E. Seifert, *Zeitschr. f. franz. u. engl. Unterricht*, XXXIII (1934), no. 4 ; G. Gougenheim, *Romania*, LXI (1935), p. 227 f. ; K. Sneyders de Vogel, *Neophilologus*, XXI (1935-6), no. 1 ; F. Schalk, *Indogermanische Forschungen*, LIV (1936), p. 133 f. ; El. Richter, *Zeitschr. f. rom. Phil.*, LVII (1937), p. 108 f.

in other words ; or (c) we may render it by words which would appear to be our own but in such a way that we are obviously identifying ourselves with the speaker's experience and acting as his mouthpiece. A concrete example of the three methods applied to a single instance of reported speech would be : (a) " Humble myself before such a man ? Never ! " (b) " X says he will never humble himself before such a man " ; (c) " Humble himself before such a man ? Never ! " The psychological process underlying (c) when used in narrative, for example, in a sentence of the type : " He had acted unfairly, but it was not his fault, and in any case no one would be any the wiser ", is that the narrator, without warranting the truth of the statement, identifies himself for the time being with the point of view of his hero, and speaks or writes accordingly. A characteristic of this stylistic device is that it is but rarely met with in everyday speech, but is a favourite device with modern authors—from Balzac onwards, it would appear, in French literature, and much later elsewhere. It gives exceptional vividness to narrative, the writer entering into and to some extent making his own the thoughts, feelings, and words of his characters, while the reader realizes at the same time that the author does not commit himself but reserves his right to an objective judgment. The ' erlebte Rede ', or ' substitutionary narration ', as we may call it, is thus a kind of poetic fiction, which serves to give the reader the particular pleasure of appreciating at once the reality of the narration, qua narration, and the possible irreality of the facts.

The matter has attracted the attention of quite a number of linguists, particularly among those interested in stylistics. If we leave out of account A. Tobler, Vermischte Beiträge zur französischen Grammatik, vol. II, edition II, p. 7 f., and others of less repute, we may say that it was Ch. Bally who was the first to call attention to it in recent times, in a series of articles entitled ' Le style indirect libre en français moderne ', which appeared in the Germanisch-romanische Monatsschrift, vol. IV (1912), pp. 549 f., 597 f., and vol. VI (1914), pp. 405 f., 456 f. He has been followed by E. Lerch, Die stilistische Bedeutung des Imperfektums der Rede (style indirect libre), ibid., VI (1914), p. 470 f., and Ursprung und Bedeutung der sogenannten ' Erlebten Rede ' (" Rede als Tatsache "), ibid., XVI (1928), p. 459 f. ; Gertraud Lerch, Die uneigentlich direkte Rede, in Idealistische Neuphilologie. Festschrift für Karl Vossler, Heidelberg, 1922, p. 107 f. ; Marguerite Lips, Le style indirect libre, Paris, 1926 ; W. Günther, Probleme der Rededarstellung, Marburg a.L., 1928 ; Th. Kalepky, Verkleidete Rede, in *Neophilologus*, XIII (1927–8), p. 1 f. ; E. Låftman, *Stellvertretende Darstellung, ibid.*, XIV (1928–9), p. 161 f. ; Fr. Todemann, *Die erlebte Rede im Spanischen*, in *Romanische Forschungen*, XLIV (1930), p. 103 f.[1] Lorck himself has reverted to the topic in *Die neueren Sprachen*, XXXV (1927), p. 456 f., in an article entitled *Noch einiges zur Frage der " erlebten Rede "*, and also incidentally in *Jahrbuch für Philologie*, II (1927), p. 175 f., in a study called *Sprache als Medium und als Mittel*, where he endeavours to investigate language as a product both of the intelligence and of fancy.

In addition to his illuminating studies on the ' erlebte Rede ', Lorck has given us psychological, or, to use the Vosslerian term now generally current, ' stylistic ' interpretations of certain forms of the French verb, for example, in *Passé indéfini, imparfait, passé défini*, Heidelberg, 1914,[2] and in *Die Sprachseelenforschung und die französischen Modi*, two articles which appeared in *Jahrbuch für Philologie*, I (1925), p. 24 f., and II (1927), p. 188 f. In all his works Lorck lays particular stress upon fancy as a source of new syntactical constructions,

---

[1] To complete the bibliography on this topic the reader is referred to p. 82, note 1, of Günther's study mentioned above, where additions to the list provided by Mlle. Lips are to be found ; cp. also a review of the latter's book by N. Drăganu, *Dacoromania*, V (1927–8), p. 714 f., where (pp. 716–17) the more important studies are mentioned. Later articles are by Ch. Bally, *Antiphrase et style indirect libre*, in *A grammatical Miscellany offered to Otto Jespersen on his seventieth birthday*, Copenhagen-London, 1930 ; Fr. Karpf, *Die klangliche Form der erlebten Rede*, in *Die neueren Sprachen*, XXXIX (1931), no. 3 ; cp. also H. Frei, *La grammaire des fautes*, Paris–Genève–Leipzig, 1929, pp. 242–3 (" style direct figuré ") ; Th. Heinermann, *Die Arten der reproduzierten Rede*, Münster i.W., 1931 ; J. Bayet, *Le style indirect libre en latin*, in *Revue de philologie littéraire et histoire anciennes*, LVII, 1933, p. 327 f.

In an article entitled ' *Zur entstehung der sogenannten " erlebten Rede* "', published in *Germanisch-romanische Monatsschrift*, XVI (1928), p. 327 f., L. Spitzer gives a kind of summary of the various opinions that have been expressed concerning the phenomenon and states his preference for the views of A. Thibaudet in his book, *Gustave Flaubert*, Paris, 1922.

Thibaudet uses the term ' style indirect double', adding yet another to the long list of names collected by Günther, *op. cit.*, p. 85, note 3 ; for example, ' berichtende Form ' (Behaghel), ' verschleierte ' or ' verkleidete Rede ' (Kalepky), ' Imperfekt der Rede' (and ' Rede als Tatsache ') (E. Lerch), ' pseudo-objektive ' or ' halbdirekte Rede ' (Spitzer).

[2] Reprinted from *Germanisch-romanische Monatsschrift*, VI (1914), and reviewed by E. Lerch, *Literaturblatt f. germ. u. rom. Phil.*, XXXVI (1915), col. 208 f. ; El. Richter, *Archiv f. d. Stud. d. neueren Sprachen*, CXXIV (1916), p. 209 f. ; and Th. Kalepky, *Zeitschr. f. rom. Phil.*, XLVIII (1928), p. 55 f. Among other studies on the Imperfect, which is more frequently used than other tenses in the ' erlebte Rede ', may be mentioned a lengthy article by E. Lerch, *Das Imperfektum als Ausdruck der lebhaften Vorstellung, Zeitschr. f. rom. Phil.*, XLII (1922), p. 311 f. and 385 f., and one by E. Winkler, *Die seelische Grundlagen der Imperfektverwendung im Romanischen, Germ.-rom. Monatsschrift*, XII (1924), p. 233 f. ; cf. also J. Damourette et Ed. Pichon, *Le tiroir type Saviez et la notion de l'actualité dans le français d'aujourd'hui*, *Revue de philologie française*, XLII (1930), p. 1 f. ; and Ed. Pichon und H. Hoesli, *Über den Ausdruck der Vergangenheit im Französischen, Neuphilologische Monatsschrift*, II (1931), p. 481 f. and 555 f.

finding in it an explanation for a great number of phenomena which earlier writers had sought to account for on rational psychological principles, either historically, like Tobler in his *Vermischte Beiträge* already mentioned, or naturalistically, like J. Haas, in his *Neufranzösische Syntax*, Halle a.S., 1912, and *Französische Syntax*, Halle a.S., 1916.

★

The other romanicist who, although not, strictly speaking, a pupil of Vossler's, has adopted his theories and methods, is Leo Spitzer, who succeeded Lorck in the chair of Romance philology in Cologne University, and later migrated to a similar post in Constantinople, and subsequently to Baltimore. His position with regard to the ' idealistic ' school becomes clearer if we remember that his first scientific work, *Die Wortbildung als stilistisches Mittel, exemplifiziert an Rabelais*, Halle a.S., 1910, was undertaken in the field of stylistics quite independently of Vossler's influence, at a period when stylistics, as a separate branch of linguistic enquiry, was still in its infancy. It was after writing this book that Spitzer underwent the influence of the leader of the idealistic school, to whom he was attracted not only by the new and wide horizons opened up by Vossler's theories, but also by marked spiritual affinities. Of the two conceptions which form the essential basis of the Vosslerian system, namely, language as a cultural fact, and language as an aesthetic fact, Spitzer has identified himself particularly with the latter, to which, however, he has given a much wider interpretation. Making no fundamental distinction between the language of the cultured class and that of the common folk, he has studied from the stylistic angle both literary and familiar speech, considering them both as articulate manifestations of the human spirit, springing thus from a common source which is essentially the same, at all times and in all places. His ' positivist ' training as a pupil of Meyer-Lübke, and his own marked individuality, have enabled him to detect the weak points in the Vosslerian doctrine, more particularly apparent in the writings of Vossler's pupils, and on occasions he has severely, though impartially, criticized the exaggerations and shortcomings of the school. His *Eine Strömung innerhalb der romanischen Sprachwissenschaft*, called forth by Lerch's book on the imperative use of the future, we have already

Leo Spitzer

mentioned (see above, p. 129). Moreover, in a review of the work of H. Hatzfeld, another of Vossler's pupils, *Meisterwerke der spanischen Literatur*, Munich, 1923 (cp. *Zeitschrift für romanische Philologie*, XLIV [1924], p. 373 f.), he contrasts the serious labour and solid learning of the old school of philologists, the positivists, with the haste and shallow offhandedness of the ' idealist ' Hatzfeld. Spitzer himself has in more than one place defined his attitude towards Vossler, notably in reviewing a number of his works (cp., for example, *Literaturblatt f. germ. u. rom. Phil.*, XLIII [1922], col. 246 f.), in a review of Fr. Schürr's *Sprachwissenschaft und Zeitgeist* (*ibid.*, XLIV [1923], col. 81 f.), or, finally, in some of his own studies, e.g. *Italienische Umgangssprache*, p. 290 f., and *Stilstudien*, II, p. 503.[1]

Another respect in which Spitzer differs from the ' idealists ' is by his versatility. We have seen that the latter are open to the charge of being rather one-sided in their scientific work. Vossler himself, and Lerch as well, have confined themselves almost entirely to French. Further, they have, in the main, been content to apply the idealistic method alone, which is doubtless natural in the founder of the school and his most faithful follower. Spitzer has no such limitations. It would be difficult to find a Romanicist more many-sided, both for variety of interests and versatility of method. French, Spanish, and Italian studies alike, owe much to this exceptionally productive worker. Nor has he neglected the ' lesser ' languages like Catalan or Rumanian. Here, too, he has contributed and continues to contribute important work on etymological and other problems. Not only does he take into account all the Romance languages, but, as occasion demands, he has recourse as well to languages outside the group, Germanic, Slavonic or Hungarian, and uses them as an expert. In fact, the words he uses with regard to M. L. Wagner in *Meisterwerke der romanischen Sprachwissenschaft*, II, p. 344, namely, that " he knows more languages than any Romanicist since the death of Schuchardt " (*v. supra*, p. 70) may be applied with singular aptness to himself.

With no special predilection for any of the Romance regions, he is just as catholic in the branches of philology which he practises. He

[1] Vossler, writing in the *Deutsche Literaturzeitung*, XLV (1924), col. 1963 f., says of Spitzer's studies of the style of various authors (see below) that they belong rather to the field of literary history than of linguistics, and he would prefer to see the two disciplines kept apart. He admits, however, that such studies have their value, inasmuch as they show that linguistics has its own contribution to make towards the appreciation and understanding of a work of art by elucidating its individual linguistic features.

has worked in all fields, phonology, morphology (here least of all, however), word-formation, syntax, stylistics, and lexicography, giving unity to his work by his constant concern for the psychological individuality underlying the facts he investigates. A convinced adherent of Vossler in this respect, his governing tendency is to give a stylistic interpretation to every linguistic phenomenon, whatever its nature, endeavouring to understand from the standpoint of the psychology of the individual how a given linguistic innovation may have come about, and the circumstances under which it may have arisen or became generalized, irrespective of whether the innovation is recent or of long standing, or whether it belongs to the standard written or spoken language or to the vernacular of the country-side. A similar universality characterizes his method. Although we are discussing him in a chapter devoted to the idealistic school, he has not the idealist's disregard for all other means of acquiring truth. We shall see below that he has done important work in linguistic geography, a field which he knows in its minutest details. He has also treated problems of ' linguistic politics ' and ' therapeutics ', to use the titles he gives to the relevant pages in his *Hugo Schuchardt-Brevier*, for instance, in his pamphlets *Fremdwörterhatz und Fremdvölkerhass. Eine Streitschrift gegen die Sprachreinigung*, Vienna, 1918, and *Anti-Chamberlain. Betrachtungen eines Linguisten über Houston Stewart Chamberlains " Kriegsaufsätze " und die Sprachbewertung im allgemeinen*, Leipzig, 1918. Although a Vosslerian in his effort to reduce linguistic phenomena to their individual origins, he draws upon all schools and methods to attain this end, leaving no aspect of the life of a language out of account, its earlier stages, its geographical distribution, historical and social conditions, etc., whenever these are likely to provide the least material necessary to elucidate his theme. He reminds us in this respect of Schuchardt, and like him, he frequently returns to a question afresh, when his earlier solution, or the solution proposed by others, has ceased to satisfy him.

The stylistic method, as understood and advocated by Vossler, and applied by him, and even by a few predecessors, to syntactical studies, has been given wider application by Spitzer, who has introduced it into the field of etymology, for which he has shown a particular predilection, especially of recent years. It is this that explains his great interest in the spontaneous formations of a language, that is to say, not only in onomatopœia, but in everything which the idiom may produce from within by utilizing its own native resources. And it must be said that in these resources languages are a good deal richer than is generally allowed.[1] Conscious of this fact, Spitzer has formulated an etymological principle, namely, that in endeavouring to throw light upon any word of obscure origin, we should look for the solution in, and by, the language in which it exists, before having recourse to other languages. The majority of his etymological studies, which are extremely numerous, are to be found in journals like the *Zeitschrift für romanische Philologie*, *Archivum Romanicum*, *Neuphilologische Mitteilungen*; *Revista de filología española* (for the Ibero-Romance languages) *Dacoromania* (for Rumanian), etc. From the point of view of etymological method particular mention should be made of the following : *Aus der Werkstatt des Etymologen*, in *Jahrbuch für Philologie*, I (1925), p. 129 f.,[2] and *Ein neues " Französisches Etymologisches Wörterbuch,"* in *Zeitschr. f. rom. Phil.*, XLVI (1926), p. 563 f., with its sequel, *Zur Methodik der etymologischen Forschung*, *ibid.*, XLVIII (1928), p. 77 f.[3]

Spitzer, like Vossler, is of the view that the study of the history of a language should be conducted in close relationship with that of the history of literature, but his manner of conceiving this relationship is different. He is persuaded that between the author of a poetical work and an ordinary individual there is merely a formal difference, one expresses himself artistically, the other says what he thinks and feels with no strictly aesthetic preoccupations ; in other respects they are alike, particularly in the fact that both openly manifest their temperament and mentality in what they say. It follows, therefore, that by analysing the language of a poet or of an ordinary man we may know their mental states at a given moment. The method of procedure will be the same in each case, the form of expression used giving us the psychological key to the mind of writer or speaker. It is on this basis that Spitzer has composed his numerous stylistic studies in which he investigates the language, or certain linguistic peculiarities, of various authors and literary

---

[1] L. Sainéan, in *Les sources indigènes de l'étymologie française*, 4 vols., Paris, 1925–30, and Florence, 1935, has endeavoured, with some success, to show this for French.

[2] Analysed by Iorgu Iordan, with the title, *Un catéchisme étymologique*, in *Revue de linguistique romane*, I (1925), p. 162 f.

[3] Both contain a very severe but impartial, and, in the belief of the present writer, generally well-founded criticism of the first fascicules of Gamillscheg's *Etymologisches Wörterbuch der französischen Sprache*, Heidelberg, 1926–9, and a detailed discussion of the etymological principles applied in this work. Gamillscheg's reply is to be found in *Zeitschr. f. franz. Spr. u. Lit.*, L (1927–8), p. 216 f. His method may be said to be diametrically opposed to that of Spitzer.

works, such as *Studien zu Henri Barbusse*, Bonn, 1920, *Der Unanimismus Jules Romains' im Spiegel seiner Sprache*, *Zu Charles Peguy's Stil*, *Zum Stil Marcel Proust's*, *Zur Kunstgestalt einer spanischen Romanze*, *Über zeitliche Perspektive in der neueren französischen Lyrik* (*Anredelyrik und evokatives Präsens*), etc., all of which have been reprinted and included in *Stilstudien, II : Stilsprachen*, Munich, 1928. We mention them here because they belong more to the domain of linguistics than of literary criticism, for, unlike the majority of literary critics, Spitzer defines the personality of a writer in the first place by means of his language, and then proceeds to consider the contents of his work. It should be made clear that his conception of a stylistic investigation of an author is different from that which prevailed formerly, and which is, unfortunately, not unknown even to-day, in that, firstly, his approach is purely linguistic, that is to say, based on the psychology of the individual and not on any rules of formal rhetoric, and that, secondly, he is not only concerned with the so-called figures of style, in the wide sense of the word, but also, and even to a greater degree, with the more usual modes of expression (cp. *Stilstudien*, II, p. 510).[1]

We insert here a list of the specifically linguistic works published by Spitzer in volume form, accompanying them with references to a number of reviews in which they have been discussed : *Aufsätze zur romanischen Syntax und Stilistik*, Halle a.S., 1918 ;[2] *Über einige Wörter der Liebessprache*, Leipzig, 1919 ;[3] *Die Umschreibungen des*

---

[1] Spitzer has continued this line of investigation in his two volumes entitled *Romanische Stil- und Literaturstudien*, Marburg a.Lahn, 1931, although here the aesthetic, that is to say the literary interest, is predominant. Cp. the reviews by Iorgu Iordan in *Arhiva*, XXXIX (1932), p. 115 f. ; E. Auerbach, *Deutsche Literaturzeitung*, LIII (1932), col. 360 f. ; H. Hatzfeld, *Zeitschr. f. rom. Phil.*, LII (1932), p. 624 f. ; E. Seifert, *Zeitschr. f. französischen u. englischen Unterricht*, XXXI (1932), p. 249f.; Ulrich Leo, *Arch. f. d. St. d. n. Spr. u. Lit.*, CLXII (1932), p. 246 f.; W. Petersen, *Boletín bibliográfico del centro de intercambio intelectual germano-español*, IV (1932), p. 9 f. ; A. Meillet, *Bull. Soc. Ling.*, XXXII (1931), p. 14 f. ; A. Rosenblat, *Revista de filología española*, XXI (1934), p. 285 f. ; J. Fransen, *Museum*, XL (1933), col. 158 f. ; G. Gougenheim, *Rev. de philologie française*, XLIV (1932), nos. 1 and 2.
On recent Romance stylistic work, see H. Hatzfeld, *Die romanistische Stilforschung in den letzten Jahren*, *Germ.-rom. Monatsschrift*, XVII (1929), p. 50 f., and *ibidem*, XX (1932), p. 453 f.

[2] Cp. K. Vossler, *Literaturblatt f. germ. u. rom. Phil.*, XL (1919), col. 242 f. ; E. Lerch, *Archiv f. d. Stud. d. neueren Spr. u. Lit.*, CXL (1920), p. 282 f. ; X., *Butlletí de dialectologia catalana*, VIII (1920), p. 79 f. ; A. Meillet, *Bull. de la Soc. de ling.*, XXII (1920–21), p. 73 f. ; G. Rohlfs, *Zeitschr. f. rom. Phil.*, XLII (1922), p. 509 f. ; W. Meyer-Lübke, *Revue de linguistique romane*, I (1925), p. 20, etc.

[3] Cp. E. Lerch, *Arch. f. d. Stud. d. neueren Spr. u. Lit.*, CXL (1920), p. 167 f. ; E. Herzog, *Literaturblatt f. germ. u. rom. Phil.*, XLII (1921), col. 30 f. ; R. Riegler, *Zeitschr. f. rom. Phil.*, XLII (1922), p. 246 f. ; and W. Meyer-Lübke, *Rev. de ling. rom.*, I (1925), p. 30 f.

Begriffes " *Hunger* " *im Italienischen*, Halle a.S., 1921 ;[1] *Italienische Kriegsgefangenenbriefe*, Bonn, 1921 ;[2] *Lexikalisches aus dem Katalanischen und den übrigen ibero-romanischen Sprachen*, Genève, 1921 ;[3] *Beiträge zur romanischen Wortbildungslehre* (in collaboration with E. Gamill-scheg), Genève, 1921 ;[4] *Italienische Umgangssprache*, Bonn-Leipzig, 1922 ;[5] *Puxi. Eine kleine Studie zur Sprache einer Mutter*, Munich, 1927 ;[6] *Stilstudien* (vol. I *Sprachstile*, vol. II *Stilsprachen*), Munich, 1928.[7]

[1] Cp. J. J. Salverda de Grave, *Neophilologus*, VII (1921–2), p. 272 f. ; E. A. Saarimaa, *Neuphilologische Mitteilungen*, XXII (1921), p. 156 f. ; G. Rohlfs, *Archiv f. d. St. d. n. Spr. u. Lit.*, CXLIII (1922), p. 311 f. ; G. Giuglea, *Dacoromania*, II (1921–2), p. 827 f. ; Iorgu Iordan, *Arhiva*, XXX (1923), p. 123 f. ; and Fr. Schürr, *Literaturblatt f. germ. u. rom. Phil.*, XLV (1924), col. 127 f.

[2] Cp. G. Rohlfs, *Archiv f. d. St. d. neueren Spr. u. Lit.*, CXLIV (1922), p. 286 f., and Fr. Schürr, *Literaturblatt f. germ. u. rom. Phil.*, XLV (1924), col. 127 f. This work of Spitzer's links up his strictly linguistic studies on what F. de Saussure calls ' la langue ' with those mentioned above, p. 139, where he studies the language of a particular author, or work, in other words, ' la parole '.

[3] Cp. W. v. Wartburg, *Zeitschr. f. rom. Phil.*, XLI (1921), p. 619 f., and X., *Butlletí de dialectologia catalana*, IX (1921), p. 97 f.

[4] Cp. S. Puşcariu, *Dacoromania*, II (1921–2), p. 693 f. ; W. v. Wartburg, *Zeitschr. f. rom. Phil.*, XLIII (1923), p. 109 f. ; M. L. Wagner, *ibid.*, p. 121 f. ; W. Meyer-Lübke, *Rev. de ling. rom.*, I (1925), p. 19. Spitzer's contribution to this volume, which is not a collaboration in the strict sense of the term, is a lengthy study entitled *Über Ausbildung von Gegensinn in der Wortbildung*, and begins at p. 81.

[5] Cp. El. Richter, *Die neueren Sprachen*, XXXI (1923), p. 426 f. ; Iorgu Iordan, *Arhiva*, XXX (1923), p. 399 f. ; B. Wiese, *Indogermanische Forschungen*, XLIII (1925), Anzeiger, p. 60 f. ; Leo Jordan, *Archivum Romanicum*, IX (1925), p. 77 f. ; A. Meillet, *Bull. Soc. Ling.*, XXVI (1925), fasc. 3, p. 105 f. ; K. Rogger, *Literaturblatt f. germ. u. rom. Phil.*, XLVI (1925), col. 371 f. ; and Aline Pipping, *Neuphilologische Mitteilungen*, XXVI (1925), p. 123 f. A pupil of Spitzer's, W. Beinhauer, has published on similar lines a *Spanische Umgangssprache*, Berlin-Bonn, 1930, cp. also, *Spanischer Sprachhumor (Augenblicksbildungen)*, Bonn-Cologne, 1932, by the same author. The earlier work was reviewed by W. Giese, *Die neueren Sprachen*, XXXVIII (1930), p. 614 f. ; M. L. Wagner, *Volkstum und Kultur der Romanen*, III (1930), p. 109 f. ; A. Hämel, *Zeitschr. f. rom. Phil.*, LI (1931), p. 740 ; and R. Riegler, *Literaturblatt f. germ. u. rom. Phil.*, LII (1931), col. 373 f.

[6] Reprinted from *Jahrbuch für Philologie*, III (1927–28). Cp. K. Jaberg, *Literaturblatt f. germ. u. rom. Phil.*, XLVIII (1927), p. 329 f. ; B. Migliorini, *Archivum Romanicum*, XI (1927), p. 413 f. ; Jos. Schrijnen, *Neophilologus*, XIII (1927–8), p. 70 ; El. Richter, *Die neueren Sprachen*, XXXVI (1928), no. 4, p. 305 f. ; and A. Debrunner, *Indogermanische Forschungen*, XLVI (1928), p. 192 f.

[7] Cp. H. Hatzfeld, *Literaturblatt f. germ. u. rom. Phil.*, XLIX (1928), col. 420 f. ; M. Kuttner, *Deutsche Literaturzeitung*, XLIX (1928), col. 2159 f. ; Iorgu Iordan, *Arhiva*, XXXVI (1929), p. 65 f. ; A. Meillet, *Bull. Soc. Ling.*, XXIX (1928–9), fasc. 2, p. 10 f. ; El. Richter, *Die neueren Sprachen*, XXXVII (1929), p. 344 f. ; N. Drăganu, *Dacoromania*, V (1927–8), p. 719 f. ; O. Densusianu, *Grai şi suflet*, IV (1929–30), p. 184 f. ; C. Tagliavini, *Studi rumeni*, IV (1929–30), p. 190 f. ; A. Barth, *Zeitschr. f. franz. Spr. u. Lit.*, LIV (1930–31), p. 487 f. ; G. Rohlfs, *Zeitschr. f. rom. Phil.*, LII (1932), p. 122 f., etc. Kuttner, who opposes Spitzer, has devoted a special article to the subject, entitled ' *Stilstudien* ' *und Studienstil*, published in *Archiv f. d. St. d. n. Spr. u. Lit.*, CLV (1929), p. 229 f., to which Spitzer replied in *Archivum Romanicum*, XIII (1929), p. 195 f.

An endeavour to give a systematic account of stylistic problems and solutions has been made by E. Winkler in a small volume entitled *Grundlegung der Stilistik*, Bielefeld-Leipzig, 1929 ; cp. also, by the same writer, *Seelische Energie und Wortwert*.

We have seen elsewhere (p. 50 f.) that Spitzer has also published an anthology from the works of Schuchardt, and has thus rendered an inestimable service to all students of language, who would otherwise find it difficult to have access to the teachings of this great scholar and renewer of our discipline. He has done the same with respect to the letters he himself received from Schuchardt over a period of many years, extracting from them the passages which were of scientific interest, or which expressed views not always represented in the *Brevier*, and grouping them according to subject-matter as in the latter collection. They compose the article entitled *Hugo Schuchardt als Briefschreiber*, published in the *Revue internationale des études basques*, XXI (1930), and run to twenty-nine pages of the journal. He has thus contributed greatly towards giving us a complete and well-defined picture of the scholar whom we may call the grand old man of Romance philology and of general linguistics. For Spitzer, despite his somewhat revolutionary attitude, is ready to admire any scholar, past or present, who works, or has worked, with devotion and success in the Romance and kindred fields of study. It was this admiration, together with a desire to acquaint the young Romanicist with what he considers to be the outstanding contributions of his predecessors, which prompted him to publish the two volumes entitled, *Meisterwerke der romanischen Sprachwissenschaft*, Munich, 1929, 1930,[1] a veritable anthology of Romance philology, comprising forty-two studies from the pens of its leading representatives, including its founder, Friedrich Diez, and present-day scholars like E. Lerch and W. von Wartburg. It goes without

---

Ein Kapitel Stilistik, in the *Voretzsch. Festschrift*, Halle a.S., 1927, p. 1 f., and *Sprachtheoretische Studien*, Jena, 1933. Winkler's book was reviewed by H. Kuen, *Deutsche Literaturzeitung*, L (1930), col. 1284 f., and in articles by E. Gamillscheg, *Grammatik und Stilistik, Die neueren Sprachen*, XXXVII (1929), p. 89 f. ; El. Richter, *Sprachpsychologie und Stilistik, Arch. f. d. St. d. n. Spr. u. Lit.*, CLVI (1929), p. 203 f. ; Leo Jordan, *Äusserlich phantasiemässig anschauen oder begrifflich-wertig denken und fühlen?*, ibid., p. 237 f. ; M. Regula, *Zu Winklers Grundlegung der Stilistik, Zeitschr. f. franz. Spr. u. Lit.*, LIV (1930–31), p. 160 f. ; and E. Glässer, *Göttingische gelehrte Anzeigen*, CXCIII (1931–2), p. 473 f. Winkler's reply to Jordan's criticisms entitled *Kritik, Logik und Ethos. Leo Jordan als Rezensent*, is to be found in *Zeitschr. f. franz. Spr. u. Lit.*, LV (1931–2), p. 224 f. An earlier study by Winkler, *Die neuen Wege und Aufgaben der Stilistik*, appeared in *Die neueren Sprachen*, XXXIII (1925), p. 407 f., and was reviewed by Spitzer in *Literaturblatt f. germ. u. rom. Phil.*, XLVII (1926), col. 89 f.

[1] Cp. Iorgu Iordan, *Arhiva*, XXXVI (1929), p. 291 f. ; E. Otto, *Literaturblatt f. germ. u. rom. Phil.*, LI (1930), col. 261 f. ; H. Rheinfelder, *Die neueren Sprachen*, XXXVIII (1930), p. 606 f. ; A. Meillet, *Bull. Soc. Ling.*, XXX (1929–30), p. 127 f.; E. Gamillscheg, *Zeitschr. f. franz. Spr. u. Lit.*, LIV (1930–31), p. 127 (vol. I), LV (1931–2), p. 126 f. (vol. II) ; O. Schultz-Gora, *Zeitschr. f. rom. Phil.*, LII (1932), p. 492 f. ; H. Rheinfelder, *Die neueren Sprachen*, XL (1932), p. 54 f. ; and F. Schalk, *Volkstum u. Kultur der Rom.*, V (1932), p. 246 f.

saying that we miss certain names which ought to have been represented in such a collection, while, on the other hand, representatives of other domains, for example, Germanic and Indo-European, have been given a place, but Spitzer himself, in the first volume, p. 1 f., explains the principle on which he has made his choice. The work is given an added value by the information it contains concerning the scholars represented and by the commentary he provides upon the several articles included. His appreciations of the work of others show that he is full of admiration and respect for sound scholarship, to whatever school it may belong, and that he possesses the rare quality of understanding, not merely intellectually, but intuitively, the entire personality of the worker whom he sees grappling with a linguistic problem. This quality, which the Germans call ' Einfühlung ', is indeed a distinctive trait of Spitzer's, as has been recognized by every critic, without exception, and is still more manifest in his studies of language, whether it be that of some author or the ordinary speech of everyday life.[1]

★

To conclude our discussion of the idealistic school some mention must be made of a book by Giulio Bertoni, entitled *Programma di filologia romanza come scienza idealistica*, Geneva, 1923. Bertoni, at present professor of Romance philology in the University of Rome, understands by 'idealism' a good deal more than Vossler. It is true that the major part of Vossler's ideas are to be found in Bertoni's book, and there is evidence, both in the preface, and in various quotations throughout the work, that the author is inspired by Croce and by his quondam disciple Gentile, which again does not differentiate him much from the leader of the idealistic school. But Bertoni's doctrine also includes a great deal that is taken from the theories of Gilliéron[2] and Schuchardt. The *Programma* thus becomes an eclectic system founded on principles taken from widely different

Giulio
Bertoni

[1] A number of Spitzer's works have been discussed by O. J. Tallgren, in *Neuphilologische Mitteilungen*, XIX (1918), p. 78 f., and XX (1919), p. 38 f.

[2] In an inaugural lecture delivered in Rome, and published in *Archivum Romanicum*, XIII (1929), p. 209 f., with the title *Indirizzi e orientamenti della filologia romanza*, Gilliéron is annexed as an ' idealist', which proves a much wider understanding of the term than was ever given to it by Vossler.

sources, if not actually contradictory. But Bertoni goes much farther, and makes certain concessions even to ' positivism ', not merely from the point of view of method—we have seen that even Vossler recognizes the need of amassing a rich store of material, to be worked up subsequently on ' idealistic ' lines—but also with regard to certain fundamental ideas of ' positivist ' doctrine. We are therefore not surprised that in a review of the book (*v. Literaturblatt f. germ. u. rom. Phil.*, XLIV [1923], col. 225 f.), Vossler expressed a certain disapproval of Bertoni's point of view. It should be stated that the term *filologia*, as used in the *Programma*, has a very wide connotation, and the author discusses matters pertaining to literary history and criticism as well as purely linguistic questions. More recently, Bertoni has become an adherent of the so-called ' neolinguistic ' doctrine, to which we shall refer in the following chapter. But it may be said forthwith that as between the *Programma* and the *Breviario di neolinguistica (Parte I ; Principî generali)* the differences are of much less account than might appear at first sight from the terminology employed ; in fact, the ' idealism ' of the former work recurs with only slight and unessential modifications in the latter.[1]

[1] A complete bibliography of Bertoni's works up to January, 1933, is to be found in *Annuario della Reale Accademia d'Italia*, the purely linguistic works on p. 24 f. His theory of language is elaborated particularly in *Linguaggio e poesia*, Rieti, 1929, and in *Lingua e pensiero*, Florence, 1932.

CHAPTER III

LINGUISTIC GEOGRAPHY

B Y Linguistic Geography we understand the cartographical study of the vernaculars. The method,[1] being
essentially confined to dialect, and not applicable directly
to the spoken or written standard, is called by some ' Dialect
Geography '. The Germans use both terms, *Sprachgeographie* and
Dialektgeographie,[2] but chiefly the former, which is the name that
those who actually work in the field would appear
to use exclusively, the latter being preferred by
those who themselves do not practise the method.
The French, on the other hand, use only the term *Géographie
linguistique*, on which the other neo-Latin countries have modelled
their equivalents, and, as the new method came from France, we
shall do likewise and adopt what is now the general Romance name
for the subject.

Linguistic
Maps

We have shown in Chapter I (p. 15 f.) that one of the essential
points contained in the manifesto of the neo-grammarians was that
investigation of dialects, of the living vernaculars, should be undertaken, with a view to arriving at a more precise understanding of
human speech and receiving new enlightenment on the nature of
language. But it is a long road from theory to practice and the
neo-grammarians were unable to travel it. Before their day,
however, as we have seen, the scientific study of dialect had already
been inaugurated, though without any theoretical manifesto, by
the great Italian linguist Ascoli, whom Jaberg and Jud, the most
authoritative representatives of linguistic geography at the present

---

[1] We say ' method ' advisedly, as there is no justification for claiming it as a
new ' science ', despite the revolution it has brought about in our linguistic
outlook, and the remarkable results it has achieved.

[2] Cp. H. Sköld, *Deutsche Literaturzeitung*, LI (1930), col. 1454 f., in a review of
A. Terracher, *L'Histoire des langues et la géographie linguistique.* ' Dialektgeographie '
is also the term consistently used by H. Güntert, in *Zum heutigen Stand der Sprachforschung, Wörter und Sachen*, XII (1929), p. 386 f.

day, consider as the most distinguished among early workers in the vernacular field.[1] At about the same period, we find the French philologist Paul Meyer advocating, in *Romania*, IV (1875), p. 295, a geographical approach to the study of dialect peculiarities : " faire en quelque sorte la géographie des caractères dialectaux bien plus que celle des dialectes ".[2] The method of the early investigators was the following. One or several localities of a chosen area were visited, and, after conversation with the local inhabitants, the dialect peculiarities that from various points of view were considered of interest were recorded. Most attention was paid to sounds, morphology came next, and last of all, and very rarely, syntax. Scarcely any account was taken of vocabulary. The material thus collected was worked up according to the customary methods : the linguistic features of the dialect were set beside those of the standard language, at times beside those of other dialects, and were always explained according to the accepted principles of historical grammar. It was thus possible to obtain a good knowledge, in part at least, of the various dialects of a language, but the relations between them, their resemblances and differences, and the reasons why some of them were more, or less, alike remained entirely obscure. Frequently, too, the material used was of a very restricted order and of doubtful quality, and researches were based upon such inadequate material as glossaries compiled by amateurs without any scientific training. Needless to say, conclusions drawn from such material, even by competent linguists, could only be of very limited value.

A step forward was made when it occurred to investigators to present the results of their enquiries in the form of a map or a collection of maps, called a ' linguistic atlas '. It was, so to speak, an obvious device, once an investigator concerned himself with several dialects at a time ; for in order to compare them without difficulty it was desirable that a given phonetic or morphological peculiarity could be followed at a glance in all the dialects of a region, and the best way to do this was to display the phenomenon on a map of the area under investigation. Instead of referring to

---

[1] In an article entitled *Ein Sprach- und Sachatlas Italiens und der Südschweiz*, *Wörter und Sachen*, IX (1924–6), p. 126.

[2] Gilliéron's first dialect study, *Petit Atlas phonétique du Valais roman* (*sud du Rhône*), 1881, was conducted on these lines. Paul Meyer himself, according to Jaberg and Jud (*loc. cit.*), seems to have been inspired by suggestions of Ascoli's in his *Schizzi franco-provenzali*, published in *Archivio glottologico italiano*, III (1878–9), p. 61 f. Cp. also G. I. Ascoli, *P. Meyer e il franco-provenzale*, *ibid.*, II (1873–6), p. 385 f.

a dozen or more glossaries, when available, to observe how a given sound or flexion behaved in a dozen or more dialects, it was enough now to refer to the map on which the phenomenon was recorded. This not only meant a great saving of time in obtaining a complete survey of the situation, but also, quite unexpectedly, led to other important results which we shall describe later. A linguistic map is thus a synoptic picture of a linguistic phenomenon in its geographical distribution.

The first attempt at a linguistic atlas was made by the German scholar Georg Wenker. Inspired by the doctrines of the neo-

Wenker's Atlas

grammarians, he set to work with the intention of proving the existence of dialect boundaries, and, implicitly, of dialects themselves. Being concerned exclusively with phonetic features, he composed a questionnaire of forty short sentences with the sole aim of studying varieties of sound development. The questionnaire was sent to school teachers and to others of the more enlightened dwellers in the country-side, and Wenker began to draw up his maps on the basis of their replies. But various circumstances, into which we need not enter, prevented publication of the projected atlas.[1] A single fascicule appeared in 1881, entitled *Sprachatlas von Nord- und Mittel-deutschland, auf Grund von systematisch mit Hülfe der Volksschullehrer gesammeltem Material aus circa* 30,000 *Orten, bearbeitet, entworfen und gezeichnet von Dr. G. Wenker*. Abteilung I, Lieferung I, 23 S. 8° Text. 6 Karten gr. Folio, Strasburg, 1881.[2] It is worth noting, as a fact of considerable bearing upon our discussion, that Wenker reached conclusions directly opposed to those he had been seeking,

---

[1] Details of this investigation by correspondence, as opposed to the direct investigation, ' enquête directe ', of later times, are to be found in Jos. Schrijnen, *Essai de bibliographie de géographie linguistique générale*, Nimeguen, 1933, p. 19 f. ; cp. also K. Jaberg, *Aspects géographiques du langage*, Paris, 1936, p. 13 f.

[2] Reviewed by O. Behaghel, *Literaturblatt f. germ. u. rom. Phil.*, II (1881), col. 434. The material collected and partly worked up by Wenker was deposited in the Berlin Academy. It has been extended, again by the correspondence method, to some 14,000 fresh localities, in order to include areas omitted by Wenker, and is being published by Ferd. Wrede, professor at Marburg a.L., where a veritable institute of linguistic geography has been founded. Wrede's atlas, of which some eight fascicules have now been published, bears the title : *Deutscher Sprachatlas auf Grund des von Georg Wenker begründeten Sprachatlas des Deutschen Reiches und mit Einschluss von Luxemburg in vereinfachter Form bearbeitet bei der Zentralstelle für den Sprachatlas des Deutschen Reiches und deutscher Mundartenforschung unter Leitung von Ferdinand Wrede*, Marburg, 1926–. (Cp. also, F. Wrede, *Der Sprachatlas des Deutschen Reiches und die elsässische Dialektforschung*, in *Arch. f. d. St. d. n. Spr. u. Lit.*, CXI [1903], p. 29 f.) The first fascicule of the atlas was reviewed by O. Behaghel, *Literaturblatt f. germ. u. rom. Phil.*, XLVIII (1927), col. 401 f., and by A. Hübner, *Deutsche Literaturzeitung*, XLIX (1928), col. 565 f. ; the latter review is of particular theoretical importance.

and found that dialect boundaries, and consequently dialects themselves, did not exist. He discovered that the phonetic lines or **isophones** which were to mark the divisions between the various vernaculars ran in a strangely irregular fashion and were without stability ; more than this, it frequently happened that no real lines could be drawn at all, inasmuch as almost every word had its own peculiar position differing from that of words with which it was thought it must of necessity coincide. In particular, the so-called ' sound-shift,[1] presented extremely marked differences as between one case and another, proving that in the development of dialects speech mingling and speech transference plays a most important part.[2]

Among other similar undertakings which preceded that of Gilliéron we must dwell a moment upon G. Weigand's *Linguistischer Atlas des dacorumänischen Sprachgebietes*, Leipzig, 1909, which marked a distinct advance upon earlier works. The author, in collecting his material, employed the method of the ' enquête directe ', conducting his enquiry himself, on the basis of a questionnaire established beforehand. There is no need to stress the advantages of this method over the correspondence method for accuracy and reliability in the perception and recording of the sounds of the vernaculars ; it will be readily understood that a trained linguist, even of foreign origin, will render the words he hears from his informers much more accurately than the village schoolmaster or the parish priest, whose sole qualifications are, at best, keenness and goodwill.[3] But we must beware of exaggerating Weigand's merits in the history of linguistic geography.[4] Even taking into account, not the date of publication of his atlas, 1909, but the year he began his survey of the Daco-Rumanian territory, namely,

G. Weigand's Daco-Rumanian Atlas

---

[1] That is, the *second* sound-shift, which took place during the sixth and seventh centuries and affected chiefly the voiceless plosives *p*, *k*, *t*, changing them into spirants or fricatives.

[2] Cp. O. Behaghel, *Die Alten und die Jungen*, in *Germanisch-romanische Monatsschrift*, XIV (1926), p. 385 f. The article is also of interest with regard to the strife between ' positivists ' and ' idealists '.

[3] The two methods and their respective advantages and disadvantages are discussed by S. Pop, *Buts et méthodes des enquêtes dialectales*, Paris, 1927 (*Mélanges de l'Ecole Roumaine en France*, II-e partie, 1926), p. 11 f. We shall revert to the topic later in the chapter.

[4] Cp. the reviews of the Daco-Rumanian Atlas by Kr. Sandfeld-Jensen, in *Revue de dialectologie romane*, II (1910), p. 403 f. ; A. Zauner, in *Literaturblatt für germ. u. rom. Phil.*, XXXI (1910), col. 291 f. ; and M. Roques, *Romania*, XXXVIII (1909), p. 310 f.

1895, we cannot award him the exclusive credit for the introduction of the new method of direct work in the field ; for before him, Gilliéron had applied it in his *Petit Atlas phonétique du Valais roman* (1881), and Rousselot as well, in his *Modifications phonétiques du langage étudiées dans le patois d'une famille de Cellefrouin* (1891). It is true that neither of them had made use of a systematic questionnaire as Weigand did, but, in 1895, when the German scholar began his dialect investigations in the regions of Dacia, the idea of drawing up lists of words for the purpose of direct enquiry in the field was already current in linguistic circles ; witness the fact that only two years later Gilliéron's fellow-worker, Edmont, started on his journeys with a questionnaire which must of necessity have been drawn up a considerable time before. Moreover, in 1909, when Weigand began printing his atlas, almost the whole of Gilliéron's atlas, conceived on a much bigger scale and far richer in content, had already been published. All questions of priority apart, any comparison of the two works is entirely to the disadvantage of Weigand, who set out on his enquiry with a list of only 114 words, and who only concerned himself with the sounds of the dialects he investigated. Even so, his phonetic investigation was not complete ; as he did not cover all the sounds, nor were those he studied examined in every position. Further, his atlas contains only 67 maps, and of these three give information upon the extent and distribution of the Daco-Rumanian dialects, and sixteen are what he calls ' übersichtskarten ', giving a kind of summary of the contents of the remainder.

★

The first atlas which met most, if not all, the needs of science, and which has therefore served as a model for later workers, was **The Linguistic Atlas of France** the *Atlas linguistique de la France*, by J. Gilliéron and E. Edmont, Paris, 1902–10. The chief author, Jules Gilliéron, set to work after a prolonged period of training and preparation. A native of Switzerland, where, thanks to the prevailing linguistic conditions, the feeling for everything pertaining to language, and particularly to dialect, is very acutely developed, Gilliéron was also temperamentally the very man for sharing the life of the peasants and investigating their speech. In 1880–81 he had published his two studies, *Patois de la commune de Vionnaz (Bas-Valais)* and *Petit Atlas phonétique du Valais roman (sud du Rhône)*, which, although far from satisfying all the requirements of present-day dialectology, marked a distinct progress on all earlier work, and, in particular, gave proof on the part of the author, who had collected his material on the spot, of an exceptional understanding of popular speech. In 1883 he was appointed lecturer in French dialectology at the Ecole Pratique des Hautes-Etudes in Paris, a post he held till his death in 1926. Four years later, in 1887, in collaboration with Abbé Rousselot, he founded the *Revue des patois gallo-romans*, a journal confined exclusively to dialect studies.[1] Gilliéron was thus by training and equipment, as well as by his own special bent, the obvious person to undertake the linguistic survey of the French vernaculars, and it is not a mere matter of chance that, of all the French linguists, he alone took fully to heart the advice given by Gaston Paris in 1888 : " Il faudrait que chaque commune d'une part, chaque mot de l'autre, eût sa monographie, purement descriptive, faite de première main et tracée avec toute la rigueur d'observation qu'exigent les sciences naturelles "[2] A further consideration gave special urgency to the need for closer study of the dialects. The spread of education among the masses, and the strong centralizing tendency of French institutions and administration, were bringing the speeches of the country-side increasingly under the influence of the national tongue, and threatening to destroy their integrity and indeed their very existence. In order to save them from oblivion, the work of collecting their linguistic material, and of preserving it in an atlas, like flowers in a herbarium, had to be undertaken with all speed. This was what Gilliéron took upon himself to do.

He proceeded as follows. He first of all compiled a questionnaire to be used in his enquiry. It ran to over 1900 words, a huge number when compared with those of his predecessors. Moreover,

---

[1] Other less important studies, like *Remarques sur la vitalité phonétique des patois* (in *Etudes romanes dédiées à Gaston Paris*, Paris, 1891, p. 459 f.), or *Notes dialectologiques*, *Romania*, XXV (1896), p. 424 f., also show the leanings of the future creator of linguistic geography. The former already contains one of the fundamental ideas of the Gilliéronian doctrine, namely, that the phonetic development of the patois is impeded by the ever-increasing influence of the French standard as well as by that of neighbouring dialects.

[2] Quoted by S. Pop, *op. cit.*, p. 102. The passage is taken from Paris' famous article, *Les Parlers de France*, published in *Revue des patois gallo-romans*, II (1888), p. 161 f., and reprinted in *Mélanges linguistiques*, p. 432 f. (*vide supra*, p. 13, note 2).

unlike the latter, who had confined themselves exclusively to problems of sound, Gilliéron realized that all the other characteristics of the dialects needed investigating as well. And so he included in his questionnaire words which would elicit information concerning morphology, syntax, and vocabulary. With regard to the latter, he did not confine himself to words of strictly popular origin, but included in his list a number of neologisms, in order to discover how these were accepted by the dialects and the lines of their expansion or radiation from Paris, the political and cultural centre. Among words of definitely popular origin he gave preference to the terminology of common everyday objects, so that the enquiry might bring out the wealth and variety of dialect nomenclature, it being natural to suppose that a familiar object would have more numerous and more varied names than an unfamiliar thing.[1]

After completing his questionnaire, at the cost of much patient effort, plans were made for the survey. Of the 37,000 localities in pre-war France, only 639 were chosen,[2] a comparatively small number, to enable the survey to be completed within a reasonable time, and yet large enough to make the meshes of the observer's net sufficiently close, and to include representatives of all the French, Provençal, and Franco-Provençal dialects and their main subdivisions. The Breton-speaking parts of Brittany, the Flemish-speaking corner of North-eastern France, and the Basque area in the south-west were omitted, as Gilliéron was concerned solely with the Gallo-Romance dialects. On the other hand, the survey included those areas outside the French frontiers where French dialects are spoken, namely, the southern half of Belgium, where they speak Walloon, the west of Switzerland or the so-called ' Suisse romande ', where the dialect is Franco-Provençal, and certain border areas of Italian territory in Piedmont, where the villagers speak either Franco-Provençal (in the north) or Provençal (in the south).

The actual survey in the field was entrusted to Gilliéron's fellow-worker, Edmond Edmont,[3] a fact which has given rise to much

---

[1] For further details concerning the questionnaire, v. S. Pop, op. cit., p. 105 f.

[2] Including the villages in French-speaking Belgium and Switzerland.

[3] It is of interest to note that Edmont was not a linguist but a shop-keeper. He had a passion for his native dialect of St.-Pol (Pas-de-Calais) and, what was more, an excellent understanding of linguistic problems. He became a friend of Gilliéron when he began work on his Lexique St.-Polois, St.-Pol, 1897, a part of which (A.G) Gilliéron published in the Revue des patois gallo-romans, I f., describing

discussion. Gilliéron's opponents have made it a matter of reproach that Edmont should have been allowed to make the survey alone. His reply would seem to be entirely reasonable. He maintained that to ensure unity as well as accuracy in the perception and transcription of dialect words, it is not only advisable but indispensable that the ear of only one person should come into play. Gilliéron was so convinced that this was an essential condition that he would even prefer one defective hearer to a number of more acute observers. But, in reality, Edmont was endowed with very exceptional powers of audition. Moreover, in the eyes of Gilliéron, who, though a linguist by profession, had no great belief in the ' objectivity ' of his colleagues, he possessed a further and inestimable quality : he was not only not a specialist, but actually lacked all strictly philological training, and was thus exempt from all those preconceived theories and ideas which frequently prevent us from seeing or hearing linguistic realities, as they exist, living and undistorted, on the lips of the individual speaker. It goes without saying that Edmont had been thoroughly trained by Gilliéron in the use of the phonetic alphabet specially devised for transcribing the replies to the questionnaire, as well as in all other devices and methods requisite for the enquiry.

Edmont's journeyings lasted approximately four and a half years, from the 1st of August, 1897, to the end of 1901, without an interruption. For each of the 639 localities investigated he had a notebook containing the complete questionnaire arranged always in the same order. On arriving in a village his first task was to select an informant, preferably a native of the locality, whose dialect was unadulterated, and who had the minimum of education called for by the nature of the enquiry and necessary for ready conversation. The informant was on principle left entirely free. Only in those cases where no positive result was forthcoming was Edmont to prompt him with supplementary questions. In other words, the replies had to be spontaneous, not extorted, in order to reproduce the vernacular as it really was, with no intervention on the part of the investigator, who otherwise, by making use of current French in his conversation with his informants, might run the risk of influencing their response and thus falsifying the linguistic

it as " le meilleur, le plus réel de nos lexiques patois." Edmont's zeal for dialectology was so overpowering that at the age of fifty he set out upon his survey, giving up for a prolonged period his home and his customary employment. Cp. the obituary notice by M. R[oques] in *Romania*, LII (1926), p. 220 f.

facts.[1] Moreover, by insisting upon eliciting information at all costs, informants are unduly influenced, and often force themselves to express what, strictly speaking, does not really exist in their own particular dialect. The replies were inserted in the notebook opposite the corresponding question, and when the enquiry was complete the notebook for the particular locality was sent off to Gilliéron in Paris, who immediately set to work to record the material. Thus, Edmont never went back over his notes, even when occasionally he had the impression that he had been mistaken in his hearing or recording of the replies, nor could he be influenced when investigating the next dialect by the results obtained previously elsewhere. Only by this method could the necessary impartiality and open-mindedness be guaranteed for every fresh enquiry.[2]

After all the notebooks were complete the atlas was begun. For each word or notion a map was constructed, with numbers standing for each locality investigated. At the top, on the left, the standard French equivalent is inserted as a title, and on the map itself, opposite each number, the corresponding dialect word used in the locality to which the number is allocated. If the idea is unknown and therefore no word exists in a given locality, the space is usually left blank. When the title runs to more than one word two sheets are occasionally used to cover the whole territory, as one would have left insufficient space for inscribing the replies in full, so that, strictly speaking, there are rather more maps than the 1920 questionnaire headings. It should be stated further that the maps from No. 1422 onwards are confined to the southern half of France and those from 1748 onwards only to the eastern and larger portion of this area.[3]

---

[1] Fault has been found with Gilliéron because Edmont put his questions in French. But what alternative was possible? French was the only language which all or at least the great majority of his informants might be expected to know. And Edmont had to converse with them all. It would have been impossible to find an observer able to speak all the dialects and sub-dialects that had to be investigated.

[2] Gilliéron was so convinced that this was the only possible method of procedure that he preferred to insert in the maps erroneous replies, that is to say, where hearing or transcription was obviously at fault, rather than to ‘ rectify ’ them on any theoretical basis, and thus run the risk of introducing a certain subjective element which might traduce the facts.

[3] In order to facilitate the use of the Atlas the authors published an explanatory brochure, entitled : *Atlas linguistique de la France. Notice servant à l'intelligence des cartes*, Paris, 1902. They also compiled a complete alphabetic index to all the words, both French and dialect, contained in the Atlas : *Table de l'Atlas linguistique de la France*, Paris, 1912, and, further, a supplementary volume containing material collected incidentally during the survey but not included in the questionnaire : *Suppléments*, tome premier, Paris, 1920.

The publication of the *Atlas linguistique de la France* made a great impression in all quarters. Many linguists saw in it the beginning of a complete revolution in our field of study, destined to transform the whole character of language history, either because of new problems which the atlas raised, or by the changed solutions it brought to problems of long standing. Hence the incredulity, and even hostility, with which it was received by certain scholars, the majority of them French,[1] strongly imbued with the spirit of tradition. In Switzerland and in Germany, however, the enthusiasm was great and almost unanimous, and the new discipline, as we shall see below, forthwith attracted workers and continues to flourish vigorously to-day. The studies published by Gilliéron himself and by others, on the basis of the material collected and presented in the manner we have described, confirmed in no small measure those expectations which the atlas had raised. But new as was the method of collecting and recording the dialect material which Gilliéron had conceived and achieved, the full fruits of the enterprise are even now coming in but slowly. The exceptional number of dialect words and forms which the atlas contains, needed, and still need, interpretation, if the science of language is to profit fully by them ; the maps must be read and elucidated, and their present configuration explained, by tracing the earlier evolutions which lie behind and beneath them. Then only will the new discipline of linguistic geography have come fully into its own.[2]

★

[1] In the front rank of the critics stood the late Antoine Thomas, professor at the Sorbonne, who wrote a famous review of the Atlas in the *Journal des Savants*, 1904, p. 89 f. Gilliéron replied in a brochure entitled *Atlas linguistique de la France, compte-rendu de M. A. Thomas*, Paris, 1905. Other opponents were E. Bourciez and M. Grammont, of whom more anon. It should be said, however, that there were scholars in France who appreciated Gilliéron's gigantic work, and rated it as a scientific event of national importance ; among them stand first and foremost Antoine Meillet, and next Mario Roques (see below).

[2] A. Meillet, in one of his remarks, maintains that the founder of linguistic *geography* was really Abbé Rousselot, in his study *Les modifications phonétiques* . . . which we have already mentioned (*v.* p. 37). According to Meillet, Gilliéron and his pupils were concerned with linguistic *geology*. The import of this distinction will become clearer later on.

Before proceeding to study the fundamental principles of Gilliéron's doctrine it seems fitting to mention forthwith certain, so to speak, self-evident observations and conclusions which the maps provided the moment they met the specialist's eye.[1] It was evident, for example, that words, like individuals, migrate ; leaving their native environment, as it were, they spread to other areas, near or far afield, according to circumstances. In their journeyings they encounter many difficulties, occasioned, either by the rivalry of other words with which they have to compete, or by material conditions, and their victory or defeat in the struggle is determined by the adequacy of their powers of resistance. Many words, however, have disappeared, merely because their rivals hailed from Paris, the political and cultural centre of the country, which confers an overwhelming superiority upon any term it sponsors, and reduces local resistance to a minimum. Paris and its neighbourhood are thus almost invariably the centre from which by various routes new words spread over the land, and the closer the relations between this centre and any given area, the more favourable are the conditions for their expansion. Regions that are geographically remote, or that are out of touch with the capital, are, in general, less exposed or less well disposed to the Parisian invasion. Thus, the South of France, in particular the departments along the Atlantic and those over against Italy, and, further, certain territories of some size in Franche-Comté and Burgundy show the greatest powers of resistance in the struggle with standard French, the former because they are distant from the capital, the latter, on the one hand, because they remained politically independent over a long period and, on the other, because difficulty of communication has prevented them from having very close relations with the national centre. In contrast to this, the whole valley of the Rhone, right to its mouth, is strongly influenced by central speech, despite its distance from Paris, because the river and its tributaries, and later the roads and railways along their banks, have provided the easiest means of communication with the political capital.

But these strictly geographical facts are not the only conditions which fortify or undermine dialect traditions. The fate of words in their migrations is often determined by factors of a cultural order. A regional cultural centre is more ready to accept linguistic

[1] The details given in this part of the chapter are taken from K. Jaberg, *Sprachgeographie. Beitrag zum Verständnis des Atlas linguistique de la France*, Aarau, 1908. Cp. E. Herzog's review in *Literaturblatt . . .*, XXXII (1911), col. 234 f.

innovations hailing from the capital than a locality of no cultural pretentions, just as, among men, the uneducated or semi-educated are, in general, less ready to welcome new ideas. That is why, despite its distance from Paris, despite, to use the accepted terminology, its 'peripheral' position, the area round the town of Bordeaux undergoes appreciably the influence of standard French, whereas, further north, the intervening territories, although closer to Paris, still preserve many of the characteristic features of their local vernaculars.

A few concrete examples will illustrate these points. The substantive *soif*, which comes from Latin *sĭtis*, *sĭtem*, is represented in Old French by a nominative *soiz* and an accusative *soi*. Towards the end of the twelfth century, possibly on the analogy of *nois* (<Lat. *nĭvis*)—*noif* (*nĭvem*)—a new accusative *soif* came to be used. To begin with, this was confined to the language of Paris and its vicinity, but gradually the pronunciation with final *f* gained ground, until now it covers the greater part of Northern France where French dialects, in the strict sense of the word, are spoken,[1] and its victorious advance still continues. Again, the word *blaireau*, ' badger ', is of comparatively recent origin, and appears only towards the end of the fourteenth century.[2] But to-day it is current in a great many regions of Northern France, where it has supplanted the descendants of the Germanic **thahs* (cf. mod. Germ. *Dachs*) which is still preserved as *tais*, *taisson*, etc., in the South, in Franche-Comté, Burgundy, Lorraine, and the Walloon area. Similarly, the word for the carpenter's ' bench ', *établi*, has ousted from roughly the same areas the earlier ' *banc de menuisier* '.

In other cases, the propagation of a word or words reveals that where, to begin with, a single word was in use over a great extent of territory, or even over the whole of Gaul, a new word has arisen to oust it from certain territories, and then a third to supplant the second (or the first where it still survived) and so on. In these cases we speak of different *linguistic strata*.[3] This phenomenon is well illustrated by the history of the words for ' trousers ', like *braie, chausse, culotte, pantalon*, etc.,[4] and also by the names for the

---

[1] Cp. E. Gamillscheg, *Etymologisches Wörterbuch der französischen Sprache*, p. 804, col. 2.

[2] According to Gamillscheg, *op. cit.*, p. 112, col. 2, in the thirteenth.

[3] The terms ' linguistic stratification ', ' linguistic stratigraphy ', and ' linguistic eruptions ' (see below), have been aptly borrowed from the terminology of geology.

[4] K. Jaberg has devoted a special study to this topic in *Wörter und Sachen*, IX (1924–6), p. 137 f. (see end of present chapter).

' cauldron ' or ' boiler ', *chaudière, chaudron, grap, pairol, pairolo,* etc.
In the South of France, it would appear that either the large
boiler was unknown, or was not different in shape from the smaller
vessel, hence there was only one word for both notions. Later,
the large boiler was introduced into the southern areas, and gave
rise to a number of linguistic complications. With the thing, came
the name—in Latin, *caldaria,* which we find with its initial *k-* in the
south-west, but with an obviously French *ch-* in the south-east.
The forms with *ch-* clearly came from the north, the origin of
those with *k-* cannot be determined with certainty. But all areas
did not behave in this manner. Some of them took over the new
utensil and gave it the old name, either unqualified (*pairol*), or
coupled with an adjective (*grand pairol*). Others again modified
the local word to meet the new situation, and gave, for example,
the old name *pairolo* to the large boiler, and created a diminutive,
pairulet, to indicate the smaller vessel, this in territories situated
between the south-western areas with their *k-* forms and the south-
eastern with their palatalized *ch-* equivalents.

At other times, the innovations take the form of linguistic
' eruptions '. New words, or sound-changes in words already
existing, crop up in isolated places with no apparent relationship
between them, like volcanoes far apart but subterraneously connected. Such eruptions can be observed if we study the names of
the ' hawthorn '. The Latin *alba spina* and its masculine variant,
albus spinus, French *aubépin(e),* underwent considerable changes
when once the Latin adjective *albus* had been replaced, as an
independent word, by the Germanic *blank,* and the initial syllable
of the French word had thus ceased to have any semantic value
of its own. The transformations of the French word are numerous
and varied, and can be divided into several groups : (*a*) some
of them are based on the word *épine,* for example *épinette, épinar,*
etc. (the word *buisson,* too, probably belongs here, as it occurs
as a name for other ' thorny ' shrubs) ; (*b*) elsewhere, the old Latin
adjective has been replaced by its Germanic equivalent, and thus
the white flowers of the shrub account anew for the forms *blanche
épine, épine blanche,* and the like ; (*c*) elsewhere the fruit has been
the determining factor and we have forms like *asañe, asaña, cenélier,*
etc. Along with these names, and others like them, called forth
by certain characteristics of the hawthorn itself, there is another
category based upon phonetic variations of its older name, such as
ebopĕ, bopè, epopĕ, and the like, due to metathesis, assimilation, etc.,

of *obépẽ* (*aubépin*), or *noble épine*, a popular etymology provoked by the agglutination of the final *n* of the indefinite article. All these names are to be found disseminated more or less irregularly over the French area, as is well demonstrated by the coloured map provided in Jaberg's *Sprachgeographie* (map XIII).[1]

★　★　★

We have shown in the preceding pages the great advantages which the geographical study of dialect presents in comparison with that based upon glossaries and the customary collections of living linguistic material. We have further given some idea, from certain of Jaberg's studies, of the kind of problem which linguistic geography sets the linguist. We now turn to a more fundamental matter. The investigation of dialect on the spot, conducted scientifically, has made plain a fact of which the more enlightened representatives of our discipline had already been more or less dimly aware,[2] namely, that spoken language is a much more varied and complicated phenomenon than investigations based upon texts, and conceived in the neo-grammarian spirit, would lead us to suspect. The so-called historical method leads to simplification, and therefore gives us a false picture of what language really is. The linguistic atlas, on the other hand, takes us, so to speak, into the laboratory of living speech, and enables us to witness the difficult and even painful elaboration of human language. It is a depository of the results of a linguistic experiment, both interesting in itself, and of particular import to scholars by the horizons which it opens up. As we study the processes of expansion, and the manner in which the zones of the various linguistic phenomena are juxtaposed and stratified, we are enabled to reconstruct the successive phases of the language, and even work back to its earliest

Gilliéron's Studies in Linguistic Geography

---

[1] In studies of linguistic geography the areas covered by the various words investigated are indicated by colouring or hachuring on the respective maps. The colour method, though more difficult to reproduce, provides a very clear and striking survey of the distribution.

[2] Ulrich Leo, in *Dialektgeographie und romanische Sprachwissenschaft* (*Archiv f. d. St. d. neueren Sprachen*, CLXII [1932], p. 203 f.) holds that Gilliéron's conception of linguistic geography is already to be found, broadly, in Schuchardt's *Die Klassifikation der romanischen Mundarten*, 1870. Cp. *Schuchardt-Brevier* (2nd ed.), p. 167.

condition. We might entitle this process linguistic geology, reserving the term linguistic geography, in the strict sense of the word, for the investigation, by means of the language maps, of the conditions under which the migrations of linguistic phenomena take place.[1] In any case, language history proper finds a new base of operations in the mere fact that frequently two newer linguistic forms present approximately the same area of expansion and thus afford an opportunity of demonstrating their underlying relationship.

No one could have been more obviously fitted for such investigations than Gilliéron. Not only because he had planned and brought into being the *Linguistic Atlas of France*, nor because, as we have shown above, he had both the scientific training and the temperament necessary for understanding the nature of vernacular speech. To a degree unknown in any other representative of Romance studies, Gilliéron was endowed with a truly exceptional faculty, an intuitive apprehension of the living element in language. He seemed to feel, step by step, and moment by moment, every phase in the evolution of a word and the circumstances of its present existence, just as a chemist, watching an experiment, sees and appreciates the transformations taking place before his eyes. This faculty of Gilliéron's is revealed in all his works but was particularly conspicuous in the lecture-room. Whoever has had the opportunity and privilege of listening to him for any length of time has been struck by the extraordinary ease with which he moved through the maze of living language. One had the impression that he actually heard and saw the whole turmoil in the life of a word, its struggles to survive, and the difficulties which barred its way to existence. This it is that accounts for his curiously abrupt and metaphorical style,[2] a style that would cause surprise in an ordinary linguist, but which in his case appears and is so perfectly natural. When we consider, further, that Gilliéron had a perfect knowledge of spoken French and its dialects, as well as of the material collected under his own guidance in the Atlas, we can readily understand how his studies have a power of conviction that we do not find elsewhere ; he combines the intuition of a Vossler with the ' positivist ' documentation of a Meyer-Lübke. His linguistic visions are always based

---

[1] The distinction is more apparent than real, as, in practice, the two investigations can scarcely be kept apart. Linguistic ' geology ' is merely linguistic ' geography ' viewed historically.—*Translator's note.*

[2] His style has been compared to that of the post-war expressionists, who endeavour, not to picture to us their own life with the help of external objects, but the life of these objects themselves.

upon facts, and the facts have the added merit of being new and unexpected. Consequently, his theories have made a deep impression in the linguistic world, and it is to him that linguistic geography owes its high position as a branch of the science of language.

Let us now examine the essential principles of Gilliéron's doctrine, confining ourselves in the main to his most extensive and most important work,[1] *Généalogie des mots qui désignent l'abeille.*

[1] The following is a list of his principal studies, in chronological order. (The earlier works were published in collaboration with other linguists, possibly in order to secure attention from those who had been sceptical or hostile to his undertaking, possibly for another reason. Gilliéron, as he himself admitted, was not an expert in the use of literary French, or rather he had a way of introducing into his prose, either purposely or not, a number of the peculiarities of his native Swiss French which he jokingly called " français fédéral ". It may have been that he felt the need of a collaborator in order to tone these down and to give shape and order to his demonstrations).

J. Gilliéron et J. Mongin, *Etude de Géographie linguistique* : ' *Scier* ' *dans la Gaule Romane du Sud et de l'Est*, Paris, 1905. Reviewed by: A. Dauzat, *Romania*, XXXIV (1905), p. 621 f. ; L. Vignon, *Revue de philologie française et de littérature*, XIX (1905), p. 308 f. ; L. Gauchat, *Zeitschr. f. franz. Spr. u. Lit.*, XXIX (1906), pt. II, p. 273 f. ; J. Jud, *Literaturblatt f. germ. u. rom. Phil.*, XXIX (1908), col. 332 f. etc.

J. Gilliéron et M. Roques, *Etudes de Géographie linguistique d'après l'Atlas linguistique de la France*, Paris, 1912. Reviewed by A. Meillet, *Bulletin de la Soc. de linguistique*, XVIII (1912–3), p. cclxxxiv f. ; A. Dauzat, *Annales du Midi*, XXV (1913), p. 354 f. ; and *Romania*, XLII (1913), p. 287 f. ; L. Spitzer, *Zeitschr. f. franz. Spr. u. Lit.*, XLII (1914), pt. II, p. 25 ; E. Winkler, *Zeitschr. f. rom. Phil.*, XXXIX (1919), p. 108 f. Cp. also, for some of the earlier studies in the volume, previously published in reviews, J. Jud, *Literaturblatt f. germ. u. rom. Phil.*, XXXII (1911), col. 330 f.

J. Gilliéron, *L'Aire Clavellus, d'après l'Atlas linguistique de la France*, Neuveville, 1912. Reviewed by A. Dauzat, *Revue de phil. fr. et de litt.*, XXVI (1912), p. 228 f. ; L. Spitzer, *Zeitschr. f. franz. Spr. u. Lit.*, XL (1912–13), pt. II, p. 139 f. ; W. v. Wartburg, *Zeitschr. f. rom. Phil.*, XXXVIII (1914–15), p. 490 f., etc.

J. Gilliéron, *Pathologie et thérapeutique verbales*, I and II (separate pamphlets), Neuveville, 1915. Reviewed by A. Meillet, *Bull. Soc. Ling.*, XX (1916), p. 65 f. ; J. Ronjat, *Revue des langues romanes*, LIX (1916–17), p. 138 f. ; W. Meyer-Lübke, *Literaturblatt f. germ. u. rom. Phil.*, XXXVII (1916), col. 238 f. ; J. J. Salverda de Grave, *Neophilologus*, I (1915–16), p. 306 f., etc.

J. Gilliéron, *Généalogie des mots qui désignent l'abeille d'après l'Atlas linguistique de la France*, Paris, 1918. Reviewed by A. Terracher, *Bull. Soc. Ling.*, XXI (1918–19), p. 231 f. ; W. Meyer-Lübke, *Literaturblatt f. germ. u. rom. Phil.*, XL (1919), col. 371 f.; K. Jaberg, *Romania*, XLVI (1920), p. 121 f., etc. Cp. also Terracher's article, *A propos de la Généalogie des mots qui ont désigné* (sic) *l'abeille*, in the same volume of *Bull. Soc. Ling.*, p. 147 f.

J. Gilliéron, *Etude sur la défectivité des verbes. La faillite de l'étymologie phonétique*, Paris, 1919. Reviewed by L. Spitzer, *Literaturblatt f. germ. u. rom. Phil.*, XLI (1920), col. 380 f. ; A. Meillet, *Bull. Soc. Ling.*, XXII (1920–21), p. 70 f., etc.

J. Gilliéron, *Pathologie et thérapeutique verbales*, III and IV (separately), Paris, 1921. Vol. IV was reviewed by A. Meillet, *Bull. Soc. Ling.*, XXII (1920–21), p. 228 f., and by V. Bogrea, *Dacoromania*, III (1923), p. 856 f.

J. Gilliéron, *Les conséquences d'une collision lexicale et la latinisation des mots français*, in *Cinquantenaire de l'Ecole pratique des Hautes-Etudes. Mélanges publiés par les directeurs d'études de la section des sciences historiques et philologiques*, Paris, 1921, p. 55 f. Reviewed by M. Roques, *Romania*, XLVIII (1922), p. 455 f.

J. Gilliéron, *Ménagiana du XXe siècle*, Paris, 1922.

J. Gilliéron, *Les étymologies des étymologistes et celles du peuple*, Paris, 1922. Reviewed by A. Meillet, *Bull. Soc. Ling.*, XXIII (1922), fasc. 2., p. 32 ; V. Bogrea,

Sound-change and analogy, to which, as we have seen, the neo-grammarians had recourse exclusively, in order to explain historically the linguistic material to which they were accustomed, are entirely inadequate when we seek to understand and explain the extremely complicated phenomena presented by popular or vernacular speech. Gilliéron is thus compelled to look elsewhere for the causes of language change, and discovers that one of the main factors in its production is the effort of the individual speaker to express himself with clearness, and to avoid any possible confusion in the mind of his hearer. Of the conditions that give rise to change, the most fertile are those produced by homonymic clash and popular etymology.

The phonetic changes of all kinds to which a word is exposed are frequently destructive in their action, and the body of the word may be slowly worn away, almost to nothing. The shorter the word, the more exposed it is, naturally, to this destructive attrition. A striking example of this, among many others that might be quoted, is the Latin dissyllable *apis*, which becomes, in various French dialects, *ep*, *ef*, *es*, *e*, etc. A similar reduction has befallen monosyllabic French words like *mai*, *mars*, *août*, etc., which Gilliéron considers (*Abeille*, p. 153) to be " prédestinés à la mutilation, et, par conséquent, à l'homonymie." Words reduced to these minute proportions are either entirely inadequate as vehicles for the idea they should convey, or they may become identical in sound with other words, and thus create confusion in the minds of those who hear them. To both of these awkward situations the language, that is to say, the individual speakers, seek a remedy, and apply all kinds of methods to that end. To prevent the complete disappear-ance of a word whose sound volume has been worn away, new sounds may be added, at the beginning or the end of the word as, and if, circumstances allow. These additions come from other words which precede or follow the word which is in danger, in some closely knit syntactical group. Thus *ep* or *ef*, quoted above, become

Dacoromania, III (1923), p. 858 ; A. Dauzat, *Revue des langues romanes*, LXII (1923-4), p. 184 f.
    J. Gilliéron, *Thaumaturgie linguistique*, Paris, 1923. Reviewed by A. Meillet, *Bull. Soc. Ling.*, XXV (1925), fasc. 2, p. 95 f. ; A. Dauzat, *Revue des langues romanes*, LXII (1923-4), p. 193 f.
    The above list may be completed by reference to M. Roques, *Jules Gilliéron. Notes biographiques, et bibliographie*, in *Annuaire de l'Ecole pratique des Hautes-Etudes*, section des sciences historiques et philologiques, Paris, 1926-7, p. 3 f. (reviewed by L. Spitzer, *Literaturblatt f. germ. u. rom. Phil.*, XLVIII [1927], col. 111 f.), and to M. Roques, *Bibliographie des travaux de J. Gilliéron* (Société de publications romanes et françaises, No. 1), Paris, undated.

nep or *nef* by annexing the *n* of the preceding indefinite article. But such therapeutic devices, to use a Gilliéronian term, are in most instances either inapplicable or only effect a temporary cure of the ailing word. In such cases, the language has to cast about for a new term to replace the old.

The question of homonymy or homophony[1] is likewise of particular importance in Gilliéron's system of linguistics. Homonymic clash can take place between words of any kind, irrespective of whether they have similar meanings or not. It would appear even that the greater the difference in the meaning of two homonyms the greater the inconvenience and confusion that is likely to arise from their identity of sound. This confusion the language naturally strives to avoid. Thus, to take a concrete example, although *héroïne* and *héroïsme* are preceded by *l'*, and treated like all words beginning with a mute *h*, the word *héros* is preceded by *le* as if the *h* were aspirated, the reason being that in the plural, *les héros* or *des héros*, if pronounced with a liaison *z*, would be heard as *les zéros* or *des zéros*, with the disastrously comic or unseemly effect of identifying a band of 'heroes' with a band of 'nonentities'.[2]

The patois, which develop more freely than the standard language, are at the same time more exposed to the dangers of homonymic collision. In certain regions of France the nouns corresponding to the standard words *sable*, *savon*, *sève*, and *sel* have become identical in sound, despite the fact that it would be difficult to imagine a greater discrepancy in meaning between any given pair, or more, of nouns in the same language. Again, the possibility of homonymic clash is enormously increased by the fact that the constituents of speech do not occur in isolation, but in the form of sentences or phrases ; words which, when employed alone, are incapable of being

---

[1] The former is the term which has found general acceptance and which Gilliéron seems to prefer. There is a case for preserving them both, and for using *homophony* for the cases where two words, different originally, in sound and in meaning, have taken on the same pronunciation, and *homonymy* for cases where one and the same word has acquired a variety of different meanings (see below).

[2] The following are a few similar instances : *Christ*, when preceded by *Jésus* is pronounced *cri*, when used alone or with an article (*le Christ*, *un Christ*) it is pronounced *crist*, to avoid confusion with *le cri*, *un cri* ; *sens* is pronounced with final *s* to avoid clashing with *cent* or *sang* (cf. A. Dauzat, *Histoire de la langue française*, Paris, 1930, p. 97) ; the sounding of the final *s* in *mars*, and of final *t* in *août*, or the preference for *mois de mai*, *mois d'août*, as against *mai* and *août* alone, the differentiation between *fait* the noun and *fait* the participle by pronouncing the *t* in the former, the distinction between *un lis* and *un lit* (pronounced *lis* and *li*), *une vis* and *une vie* (*vis* and *vi*), and between *tous* and *tout* are all analogous phemonena. Cp. J. U. Hubschmied, *Revue celtique*, L (1933), p. 269 note ; H. Frei, *La grammaire des fautes*, p. 70, 71.

confused with others, come into homonymic collision as soon as they are used in certain closely knit syntactical groups. The interplay of syntactical phonetic conditions is thus a factor of supreme importance in the life of language, inasmuch as man talks not in isolated words but in groups of words, a fact which is frequently overlooked. Thus the dialect word *ep* for ' bee ' (< Lat. *apem*) when preceded by the indefinite article is identical in sound in certain areas with *une nep*, ' a medlar '. Or again, elsewhere, the plural *és* (< *apes*), preceded by the plural article, clashes with the plural of *ézé*, the local equivalent for *oiseau* (< Lat. *aucellum*), so that the group *le vol des és* can be understood either as ' the flight of the bees ' or ' the flight of birds '.[1]

But every case of homonymy is not equally detrimental to the clarity of human discourse. Certain conditions, either material or linguistic, combine to obviate confusion or, on the other hand, to make it inevitable. Thus Gilliéron speaks of ' homonymies supportables ', that is to say, which are tolerated because they give rise only occasionally to misapprehension, and ' homonymies insupportables ' which must be got rid of at all costs. He is similarly led to consider words which for various causes have acquired a great variety of meanings. Here also it is a case of homonymy in the Gilliéronian sense, inasmuch as the possibility of confusion in the mind of the hearer is as great with these homonyms of semantic origin as with those that have come about phonetically. The substantive *pomme*, for example, means both ' apple ' and ' potato ', for the standard adjunct *de terre* is not always made use of to convey the latter meaning, e.g. *biftek aux pommes*. In ordinary circumstances there would be little risk of confusing the two senses, but in the language of the kitchen misapprehension might well arise, hence we find the cooks using *pomme* for ' potato ' and *pomme-pomme*, *pomme de l'air*, or *pomme fruit* for ' apple ' ! It has thus come about that *pomme* (< Lat. *poma*), ' apple ' has yielded up its traditional name to a

---

[1] In *L'Abeille*, passim, and particularly on pages 218 f., the problem of homonymy is given extraordinary prominence. Elsewhere, it would seem that Gilliéron viewed the phemonenon with other eyes, for in *Etudes de Géographie linguistique*, Paris, 1912, p. 149, we read the following words : " L'homonymie n'est pas une force qui va fatale, inéluctable, détruisant sans merci tout ce que lui livre une phonétique aveugle : pour qu'elle ait à agir, encore faut-il qu'il y ait rencontre, et la rencontre ne se produit que pour des mots engagés dans les mêmes chemins de la pensée." But the work from which this is taken was written in conjunction with M. Roques, and at a lecture heard by the present author in 1925, Gilliéron, referring to a remark contained in *Stand und Aufgaben der Sprachwissenschaft. Festschrift für W. Streitberg*, Heidelberg, 1924, p. 598, note, declared that he was not the author of that particular passage.

comparative late-comer on European soil, because of the greater culinary importance of its rival. On the other hand, a word like *truffe*, which means both ' truffle ' and, in certain areas, ' potato ', constitutes a much less disturbing homonymy, inasmuch as, in the regions where this homonymy exists, either truffles are not used for cooking, or are used in a manner which excludes the possibility of any confusion. In Gilliéron's words : " Nous avons de plus en plus le sentiment que le rôle destructeur de l'homonymie n'apparaît que lorsque le parler a pleine conscience du caractère intolérable des conflits ; on n'essaye d'y remédier qu'après expérience d'une gêne intolérable." (*Abeille*, p. 58.)

In order to avoid ' intolerable ' homonyms all sorts of devices come into play. At times, for example, a difference in gender or number suffices to keep the words apart. Thus *livre*, ' book ', and *livre*, ' pound ', can live together with little inconvenience because the first is masculine and the second feminine and both are frequently accompanied by the article. Similarly, (*le*) *moule*, ' mould ', and (*la*) *moule*, ' mussel ', (*le*) *foie*, ' liver ', and (*la*) *foi*, ' faith ', can live together with impunity.[1] And a further point which makes confusion between these pairs of words still more unlikely is the fact that neither of the homonyms can possibly be envisaged as the masculine or feminine of the other. But this is not always effective, as is shown by the case of (*la*) *moisson*, ' harvest ', and dialectal (*le*) *moisson*, ' sparrow '. As the sparrow can be either a ' cock ' or a ' hen ', the differentiation in gender here brings no remedy to the situation, and, as a result, in an area stretching from Paris to Boulogne, *moisson*, ' sparrow ', has given way to *moineau*, a diminutive of *moine*, ' monk '. The following example will serve to illustrate the avoidance of misunderstanding by a difference in number. From the word *moucher*, ' to snuff a candle ', a substantive *mouchettes* has been formed, to designate the tongs used for snuffing candles in the church. The word can subsist without inconvenience beside *mouchette*, a derivative of *mouche*, ' fly ', both because of the different domain of the vocabulary to which it belongs, and because it is only used in the plural, whereas the ' diminutive ' *mouchette* is used at least as frequently in the singular as in the plural.

Having mentioned the word *mouchettes*, which strikes us at first

---

[1] Even in the last case inconvenience may arise. In a recent work of Bergson's, the author, who would have no scruple about writing ' *une crise de conscience* ' writes ' *une crise de* la *foi* ', because *une crise de foie*, ' a liver attack,' was in the offing! (*Translator's note*).

sight as a diminutive, we must explain, if only in passing, that formations of this kind are frequently resorted to in order to obviate homonymic clash. The Latin words *napus*, ' turnip ', and *navis*, ' ship ', have become homophones by regular phonetic change to *nef* in many Gallo-romance dialects. In fact, a third homophone has arisen in some areas where ' a bee ' is *une ef*, which is identical in pronunciation with *une nef*. It would appear that this homonymy was of the ' intolerable ' order, for to avoid it the language has created new words on the basis of the old : *nef*, ' turnip ', has been replaced by *navet*,[1] and *nef*, ' ship ', preserved in the technical sense of ' nave ', has given way to *navire*, or to other equivalents. Although *navet* may be considered a true diminutive, both in form, and, originally, in meaning, such formations are frequently diminutives only in appearance. This is the case with *mouchettes*, quoted above, with *pommette*, ' potato ' (in Lorraine), with *soleil* from Latin *sol*,[2] *hirondelle* from *hirundo*, etc. All these words have the full value of the simple forms from which they are derived, and which they have replaced to avoid confusion.

Theoretically, all words are exposed to the danger of ' homonymy ', since they are all equally liable to undergo the destructive action of phonetic change. Even the most recent words, whether borrowed by the vernaculars from the standard language, or created spontaneously to take the place of those eliminated by homonymic collision, are exposed to the same fate, and, being treated on the same footing as the existing elements of the vocabulary, may sooner or later find themselves identical in form with,

---

[1] In Old French there was already a derivative *navel*, still to be found as *naveau*, *naviau*, in numerous dialects ; cp. Gamillscheg, *op. cit.* s.v. *Navet*.

[2] *Sol, solis*, ' sun ', clashed with *solum*, ' soil ', and *solidum*, ' sou ', in Gaul and Catalonia ; cp. A. Griera, *Homenaje a Menéndez Pidal*, p. 689 f., and *Etudes de géographie linguistique*, Ière série, Barcelona, 1933, p. 38 f.
The Latin derivatives *auricula*, for *auris*, *avicellus*, for *avis*, *cauliculus*, for *caulis*, *ovicula*, for *ovis* are of similar character to the French words mentioned above, and have left more representatives in the Romance idioms than their base forms ; similarly the Rumanian place name, *Tecucel*, a stream in the district of Tecuciu, beside *Tecuciu*, the chief town in the same district, situated on the banks of the stream, or Rumanian *umăraş*, the part of a garment which covers the shoulders, *umeri*, or a ' hanger ' for clothes ; in all these cases the words are only ' formally ' diminutives, and the suffix is used for purposes of differentiation. With regard to *pommette*, Gilliéron, in *Les étymologies des étymologistes* . . . , p. 38, states that it signifies a tuber " ressemblant à la pomme ", just as *mouchette*, ' bee ', means an " insecte ressemblant à la mouche ". Cp. also L. Spitzer, in *Miscellanea linguistica dedicata a Hugo Schuchardt*, Geneva, 1922, p. 143, where *corset* (<O.F. *cors*, ' corps '), *œillet*, *petit-fils*, *roitelet*, etc., are similarly explained. For a similar phenomenon in place-names, *v.* Iorgu Iordan, *Rumänische Toponomastik*, Bonn-Leipzig, 1924-6, p. 276 f.

and therefore confused with others. However, as we have shown above, the greatest risk attends those whose sound volume is small, particularly those of one or even two syllables. Again, of two or more homophones, theoretically, any one or all may be eliminated to avoid confusion ; the language need show no preference in its treatment of them. Or, again, there may be conditions which weigh the scale in favour of one or another. We quoted above (p. 163) the words (*la*) *moisson* and (*le*) *moisson* and saw that where the co-existence of these terms was a cause of misapprehension, (*le*) *moisson* had been supplanted by *moineau*, it having been found easier to find a substitute to render the idea of ' sparrow ' than to discover a new term for ' harvest '. Similar considerations doubtless account for the victory of *avena*, ' oats ', over *habena*, ' bridle ', which by the loss of *h* in Vulgar Latin and the popular confusion of intervocalic *b* and *v*, was pronounced like *avena* ; a new name was apparently more readily forthcoming for the bridle than for the cereal.[1] This hypothesis would appear to find corroboration in a passage from *L'aire Clavellus* . . . (p. 2), where Gilliéron writes : " Chronologiquement et phonétiquement *clavis* et *clavus* ont dû être égaux et la création d'un substitut incombait à celui des deux qui était le plus apte ou le plus invité à le produire." It would appear from this passage that, in Gilliéron's view, there exist linguistic circumstances (" le plus apte ") and factual circumstances (" le plus invité ") which decide which of two homonyms is to give birth to the new word destined to supplant it.

In addition to homonymy,[2] there is another cause which saps

---

[1] This example comes from J. Jud, *Probleme der altromanischen Sprachgeographie, Zeitschr. f. rom. Phil.*, XXXVIII (1914–15), p. 1 f. Cp. what was said above, p. 162, concerning *pomme* : ' apple ' and ' potato '.

[2] On the topic of homonymic conflicts see further : A. Meillet, *Sur les effets de l'homonymie dans les anciennes langues indo-européennes*, in *Cinquantenaire de l'Ecole des Hautes-Etudes*, p. 169 f. (quoted by V. Bogrea, *Dacoromania*, IV [1924–6], p. 1057) ; H. Hatzfeld, *Über Bedeutungsverschiedenheit durch Formähnlichkeit im Neufranzösischen*, Munich, 1924 (reviewed by V. Bogrea, *ibid.*, p. 1045 f.) ; Elise Richter, *Über Homonymie*, in *Beiträge zur griechischen und lateinischen Sprachforschung. Festschrift für Univ.-Prof. Hofrat Dr. Paul Kretschmer*, Berlin–Vienna–Leipz ig–New York, 1926, p. 167 f. Frau Richter shows some reserve in admitting the wholesale destruction wrought by homonymy. She notes two causes of the phenomenon, namely, (*a*) phonetic evolution, by which two words etymologically unrelated come to be pronounced alike, and (*b*) semantic evolution, by which one word acquires a great number of meanings and undergoes a kind of semantic plethora or inflation. Homonyms, in the strict sense of the word, are few in number, because the context of the sentence and the syntax make understanding easy. It is only in cases of real homonymy that a word falls into disuse. She discusses a number of cases to prove her contention, among them that of *clavus-clavis-clavellus*, treated by Gilliéron.

The principle of homonymic interference as applied to morphology has been discussed by P. Skok, *Du rôle de l'homonymie dans les changements phonétiques et morphologiques*, in *Časopis pro moderni filologii a literatury*, XII (1925–6), p. 273 f., XV (1928–9), the vigour of words and causes them to disappear, namely, that of semantic hypertrophy, or semantic overload as it has been called, to which we have alluded above. As time goes on a word

pp. 39 f., 147 f., 265 f., XVI (1929-30), pp. 44 f., 276 f., XVII (1930-1), p. 133 f. Cp. also Ch. Bally, *Linguistique générale et linguistique française*, Paris, 1932, p. 142 f.

Upon the question of homonymic clashes in Rumanian the following points may be of interest. D. Caracostea, in an article entitled : *Wortgeographisches und Wortgeschichtliches vom Standpunkte der Homonymität*, in *Mitteilungen des rumänischen Instituts an der Universität Wien*, published by W. Meyer-Lübke, Heidelberg, 1914, p. 79 f., accounts in similar fashion to that explained above for the complete or partial disappearance of certain Rumanian words like *păcurar* 'shepherd', in conflict with *păcurar* 'petroleum-seller' or 'petroleum extractor', or Old Rum., *a deşira*, with its variant *a deşidera*, from Lat., *desiderare*, in conflict with *a deşira*, 'to undo', derived from *şir*, or Lat. *basiare*, which is found in Macedo-Rumanian as *băşare* 'to kiss', but which has been replaced in Daco-Rum. by *sărutare* because of its clash with the representative of Lat. *vessire*. He also discusses cases which had attracted the attention of Ascoli and S. Puşcariu, namely the disappearance of *centum*, which became a homophone of the representative of *quinque* (Vulg. Lat. *cinque*) and was replaced by the Slavonic *sută*, or the creation of the past participle *fost*, to which corresponds Macedo-Rum. *futâ*, a form which in Puşcariu's view is too reminiscent of certain forms of the verb *futuere* which has been preserved in Rumanian. Puşcariu also treats similar problems in his article *Dicţionarul Academiei*, in *Memoriile Academiei Romîne*, Secţia Literară, Seria III, Tom. III, Bucharest, 1926, p. 213 f. He attributes to insufficiency of sound volume the disappearance, either total or partial, of the Rumanian representatives of *ire*, *lavare* (found only in certain areas and with very restricted meaning), *uva*, *limus*, *nivem*, etc., and to homonymic clash the substitution of other words for *amo* (confused with *am*[habeo]), *audet* (in conflict with *aude<audit*), *carus* 'dear' (identical with *car<carrum*), *labrum* 'lip', which would have become *laur* and therefore identical with *laur<laurum*, etc. Further examples are to be found in *Studii istroromîne*, II, Bucharest, 1926, § 200, by the same author, and in an article by I. A. Candrea, in *Grai şi suflet*, I (1923-4), p. 192. This study, which is entitled *Constatări în domeniul dialectologiei* (*loc. cit.*, p. 169 f.), has a bearing on most of the problems of linguistic geography. The present author has also called attention in his lectures to the following similar cases : Latin *altus* is represented by *înalt* (<*inalto* or *inaltum*, according to S. Puşcariu, *Dacoromania*, IV [1924-6], p. 690, note), to avoid confusion with *alt<alter* ; *aratrum* (preserved in Macedo-Rumanian as *arat*) has given way to Slav. *plug* because of the participle and verbal substantive *arat* 'ploughed (land)' ; *macru* 'lean' has been kept only in the expression *carne macră*, because in the frequently used group *om *macru* it was indistinguishable from the adj. *acru* ; *miere* 'honey', which tends to be pronounced without the *i*, has become entangled with *mere* the plural of *măr*, 'apple', with the result that the need for an explicative adjunct has been felt, and while *mere* alone is used for the fruit, 'honey' is now 'bee-honey' *mere de albine* ; the feminine plural of *nou*, 'new', is pronounced by many speakers *noi* instead of the 'correct' form *nouă* which is in collision with the numeral *nouă* 'nine' ; in the Wallachian dialect the word *porumb* 'pigeon' is nearly always *porumbel* to distinguish it from *porumb* 'maize'. An exactly similar example is *pescăruş*, the name of an aquatic bird, which is also called, though rarely, *pescar*='fisherman'. It is likely too that the formation of the numerals from 11 to 19 with the help of the prepositional infix *spre*, on the Slavonic model, has been partially due to homonymy. Without the preposition there would have been confusion with the multiples of ten ; thus the feminine of *twelve* would have been *două zeci*, or at least *două zece*, similarly *trei zeci* ọr *trei zece*, etc. Compare finally the common saying *seamănă, da' nu răsare* ; when it is said of a man that he is like ('*seamănd*') another man, a person not of this opinion seizes upon the identity of the verbs *a semăna*, 'to sow' and 'to resemble' to make the grotesque reply *seamănd da' nu răsare*, 'he sows but it doesn't grow'. [Cp. in French "*Il en a l'air mais pas la chanson*."] Similar examples from Rumanian are given by Tache Papahagi in *Grai şi suflet*, III (1927-8), pp. 84 f. and 96 f., and IV (1929-30), p. 87 f.

may take on a great variety of meanings, metaphorical uses that we, as speaking individuals, would perhaps not have conferred upon it if we had kept in view in a strictly logical fashion its original meaning and function. A word which thus occurs with undue frequency in speech, loses little by little its expressive power, becomes, so to speak, worn out and jaded. Moreover, such a plethora of meanings to one word may lead to confusion, and the hearer of the word come to hesitate as to what meaning the speaker has in mind. The results are therefore similar to those occurring in the cases we have been discussing, though it is here the semantic, not the phonetic side of the word which has, as it were, become diseased. The remedies which the language applies to meet the situation are also similar. Just as we have seen attempts made to save the victims of phonetic attrition by adding on extra sounds from various sources, so the victims of semantic overload are frequently given a new lease of life by changes which at times make them unrecognizable. French *vaisseau*, for example, which has many other meanings besides that of Latin or Rumanian *vas*, once had the meaning of ' swarm of bees ', in certain parts of Northern France (*v.* points 282 and 283 of the *Linguistic Atlas*), after previously meaning ' hive '. Being super-saturated with meanings it was doomed to disappear, but before its demise shifts were made to save it by creating the form *maisseau*,[1] where the *m* is due to the influence of *mouche*, the local word for ' bee ', or again the variant *faisseau*[1] with an *f* that spread from syntactical groups where the word followed a voiceless consonant.

When all such devices fail, or cease to be available, the language simply gives up the words affected and replaces them by others more expressive and in more vigorous health, whether phonetic attrition or semantic plethora be the destructive factor. When two words come into collision and cause intolerable confusion one may disappear, or both, in acute cases usually both, according to Gilliéron. A famous example is the case of Lat. *aestimare* and *amare* which in French take on an identical pronunciation [*eme*] ; *aestimare* having become first *esmer*, with an *s* that soon ceased to be pronounced (cp. Engl. *aim*) and the old verb *amer* ' to love ' having generalized by analogy the early diphthong *ai*, at first only used where the stem bore the stress (cf. the old participle *amant*, which survives as a noun). In the dialect of St. Pol the verb

---

[1] The spelling of these dialect words has been standardized for the sake of convenience.

émer, which had the meanings both of *aestimare* and *amare*, has ended by disappearing entirely, whereas, in standard French, *amare* has vanquished its rival but, according to Gilliéron, not without showing some traces of the conflict.[1]

The replacement of words which hinder the lucid flow of speech by the misapprehensions to which they give rise is achieved by a variety of means, according to the psychological and phonological circumstances prevailing in each case. The phonetic qualities of the word, the greater or less sensitiveness of a particular linguistic group to homonymic difficulties, the availability of suitable substitutes, all such considerations must be taken into account. Further, when a number of alternatives are ready to hand there may be all manner of hesitation before a choice is made and one of the competitors proves finally to be better armed for existence than its rivals. But different as the therapeutic devices may be, they have one inportant feature in common, namely, they are all the result of a psychological process, applied to a situation which, in the case of phonetic homonymy, is of physical origin. Thus, to Gilliéron, phonetic change is the mechanical and at the same time the destructive force in language, whereas the spirit of the individual speaker is its life-preserving power. His standpoint is thus fundamentally different from that of the neo-grammarians, or from the ' phonétistes ' as he frequently styles them, whom he accuses of seeking to explain everything by means of the so-called soundlaws. These two principles, so fundamentally opposed, the pathology of words, on the one hand, produced by phonetic change, and, on the other, the therapeutic treatment meted out to them by the psychological reaction of the speakers, recur like a leit-motiv throughout the whole of Gilliéron's teaching.

To revert to the vernaculars, we find them frequently endeavouring to get out of the difficulties due to phonetic attrition or homonymy by their own efforts. Thus, a word whose sound content has been reduced excessively may receive an *s* even in the singular ; thus é, the ' regular ' development of *apem*, may be pronounced *es*, which, with its fuller sound volume, will have a somewhat greater power of resistance in the struggle for survival. Similarly, *ou*, from Lat. *ovum*, has in some places become *ous*. We even find this cura-

---

[1] Gilliéron claims that in the construction, *j'aime mieux danser que me reposer*, as against *j'aime à danser*, the use of *mieux* is only explicable on the basis of *aimer*= *aestimare*. Von Wartburg, *Französisches etymologisches Wörterbuch*, I, p. 46, col. 1, disputes this view.

tive *s* applied to words which, unlike those quoted, are less frequently used in the plural than the singular, but only when a
dialect, for various reasons, is unable to coin a derivative, or find
a convenient substitute for the ailing term. But, as a rule, these
therapeutic devices only give temporary relief, and the dialect, to
replace the word threatened with effacement, looks for help to a
neighbouring patois or to the standard language. At an earlier
period, when the standard did not enjoy its present undisputed
sway, and the old provincial dialects were still vigorous,[1] the
patois were under the control of the regional centres, many of the
patois forming a comparatively unified group and forming a single
dialect area around some central point. Moreover, educated
people did not, as now, despise the local vernacular, and this gave
added prestige and consequently greater vitality to the regional
dialect and helped to maintain its unity. But with the passage of
time the written language asserted itself with increasing vigour,
and now reigns supreme over the whole of France, so that, at
present, a patois almost invariably has recourse to the national
standard when it finds itself in difficulties. It is the national tongue
that brings order into the disorder of popular speech, which is
unceasingly exposed to the destructive action of sound-change and
semantic ' super-saturation '. But it frequently occurs that the
literary language does not provide a satisfactory way out, and the
old word persistently lingers on. Representatives of *apis*, to take
a conspicuous example, despite the pathological attrition which
they have undergone, are still to be found on the fringes of the
Gallo-Romance area, where they lead an obviously puny and
precarious existence.

In their endeavours to secure order and clarity, the vernaculars
throw up a wealth of new formations, whose history and phonetic
constitution are usually extremely complicated, and which the
so-called sound-laws are absolutely powerless to explain. It is to
the inability of the phoneticians to cope with such chaotic conditions that Gilliéron refers when he says : " Aussi ne paraîtra-t-il
pas inutile que nous donnions en appendice un exemple du grand
déploiement et de la vanité de leurs efforts critiques pour expliquer
des faits qui découlent de la façon la plus naturelle d'une lutte
entre mots associés et d'où les vainqueurs apparaissent actuellement

---

[1] Gilliéron distinguishes between ' patois ' and ' dialect ' as follows : " Les
patois ne sont que les débris des dialectes, organes tombés en déchéance par la
défection des classes intellectuelles."

munis des dépouilles des vaincus et les vaincus dépossédés de ce qui constitue le trophée des vainqueurs."[1] (*Abeille*, p. 115.)

This inapplicability of the ordinary laws of sound-change to the problems of living speech he crystallized in the famous formula ' the bankruptcy of phonetical etymology ', ' *la faillite de l'étymologie phonétique* ', a sub-title of one of his linguistic studies.[2] The grave error of the neo-grammarians lay in insisting that a single phonetic law, determined by themselves, applied to all words similarly constituted and situated. The realities of language, however, as they are revealed in the studies of Gilliéron and his disciples, prove that there can be no talk of applying a phonetic norm to a series of words, because we never find two words identically situated. Words which at first sight seem to share the same conditions show themselves, in fact, to have each a life of its own, different, to a greater or less degree, from that of all the rest. This is the inwardness of another fundamental principle of the Gilliéronian doctrine, namely, that every word has its own history—' chaque mot a son histoire '.[3] A pretty example in support of this maxim is to be found in the treatment of final *s*, which shows us that when we are working on the basis of the so-called phonetic laws we are frequently confronted with ' mirages phonétiques '.[4] In reality,

---

[1] The quotation concludes a discussion, the main point of which is as follows. In the turmoil of their struggle for existence, it frequently occurs that the dialects throw up words or forms which have only a momentary existence, but which none the less leave some trace upon the words with which they have come into contact or collision, phonetically or semantically, and which they have contaminated. Ephemeral words of this type are naturally not attested in any document, but their existence can be deduced with almost mathematical certainty by the traces they leave behind. " Les romanistes ", Gilliéron goes on to say, " n'ont guère rencontré, que nous sachions, ces irréalités linguistiques que la géographie transforme en réalités " (*Abeille*, p. 114).

[2] Gilliéron has explained his understanding of the term ' bankruptcy ' in *Pathologie et thérapeutique verbales*, III, p. 19 : " Je veux chercher à convaincre que ' La faillite de l'étymologie phonétique ' n'est pas un titre de réclame, mais qu'il renferme l'expression exacte de ma pensée, que je résume ainsi : l'étymologie primaire [i.e. the original source of a word] n'a souvent qu'une valeur fugitive ; une fois embarqué, le mot français vogue où le pousse le français, obéit à l'étymologie populaire, devient papillon, de chrysalide qu'il était et à l'état de quoi il reste selon les lexicographes."

[3] A corollary of this proposition is that dialect boundaries, in the phonetic sense, do not exist, nor, consequently, dialects (cf. above, pp. 32, 52). We are of necessity reminded, at the same time, of the idea stressed so strongly by Vossler, namely, that linguistic innovations come from the individual.

[4] This is the title of a chapter in *Etudes de Géographie linguistique* (written in collaboration with M. Roques), p. 49 f., where the Gallo-Romance representatives of words with initial *cl-* and *fl-* are discussed. Although the meaning of the expression is clear, a few explanatory passages may be quoted, which give further illustration of Gilliéron's attitude to phonetics and the ' phonétistes ', who are no other than our friends the neo-grammarians : " Dès maintenant la phonétique

linguistic geography proves conclusively that the extension of the form *Jacques*, for example, does not coincide with that of *diables*, and that both of these differ again in extension from the word *Dieus*. Similarly, *pays*, *pis*, *plus* and *prix* all differ among themselves. A like observation is to be made with regard to words where *s* has a flexional value, namely, that of indicating the plural of substantives, adjectives, etc. (cf. *arbres* and *autres* among those that figure in the *Atlas*) or the second person singular of verbs, e.g. *tu as*, *tu vas*.[1]

In lieu of the laws of sound-change, which is a purely physiological and, as we have seen, destructive phenomenon, other principles of language are brought into play, forces which are psychological in their origin and which are beneficial and, one might say, creative in their action. Such principles are contamination and popular etymology. As examples of the former we may quote the following. In certain French patois Lat. *apis* is represented by *op*, which, in its turn, comes from an earlier *ap*. Gilliéron believes, and undertakes to demonstrate in most convincing fashion, that the *p* in this word results from contamination with the successor

nous a suffisamment révélé ses faiblesses : puissante comme instrument d'observation, pour nous permettre de découvrir les marques physiques d'origine étrangère ou récente que peut présenter tel ou tel mot, elle n'est pas un instrument d'épreuve certain ; elle ne nous donne pas le moyen de reconnaître dans un parler les étrangers et les nouveaux-venus qui se déguisent : elle se laisse tromper et nous trompe." " . . . le langage n'est pas seulement le miroir fidèle d'une activité qui lui est extérieure, il sollicite encore pour lui-même l'attention et l'activité du sujet parlant. A tous les degrés, le langage est l'objet de préoccupations où se mêlent à la volonté d'être pleinement intelligible, la conscience de la diversité des parlers individuels ou locaux, le sentiment confus d'une hiérarchie des parlers et des formes, un désir obscur de mieux-dire." " Le langage est ainsi l'objet d'une étude incessante, d'un travail d'amélioration et de retouche, qui paralysent la liberté de son développement . . ." (*op. cit.*, pp. 73, 74).

[1] Cf. *loc. cit.*, p. 102 f. A Rumanian example in support of the principle that each word has its own history may be quoted. The substantives *păreche* (<Lat. *paricula*) and *părete* (<Lat. *parietem*) present exactly ' the same phonetic conditions ', the *k'* of the one and the *t* of the other being so alike that in certain circumstances the sounds may be confused. It would follow therefore that they should everywhere undergo the same treatment. Yet, in the south of Moldavia, at Tecuciu, they pronounce *părete* and *pereche*. Clearly the latter word has undergone vowel assimilation ; *ă—é* has become *e—é*, as in the Wallachian dialect, where the phenomenon, however, has affected both words. Why, in spite of this ' identity of conditions ', has *părete* kept its *ă* ? Phonetics cannot give us the answer, as it is not a phonetic phenomenon. In reality, *pereche* is a word that has come to Tecuciu from elsewhere, a form from the standard language introduced by merchants who are most of them strangers and do not speak the local dialect. The dwellers in the outskirts of the town and the peasants from the neighbouring woods have borrowed the words first in familiar contexts like ' o *pereche de ghete* ', ' a pair of shoes ', etc., and then generalized it to all uses. The geographical position of Tecuciu, which is near Wallachia, where the dialect has much in common with standard, facilitated the adoption of the new form, which has found no foothold in parts of Moldavia further afield. The word *părete*, being of a different type, has retained its popular form and escaped any ' cultural ' influence.

to Latin *vespa*, ' wasp ', or its Germanic equivalent.[1] *Maisseau*, arising from a contamination of *vaisseau* and *mouche*, has already been mentioned. *Mouchette*, also quoted above, which means ' bee ' in certain regions, is not a diminutive of *mouche*, according to Gilliéron, because, *inter alia*, the ' bee ' is *not* smaller than the ' fly ', if we start from the original meaning of the substantive *mouche*, and because the idea does not lend itself to diminutivization, admitting, as we must, that the basis of *mouchette* is *mouche*=*mouche à miel*, the widespread dialect equivalent of *abeille*.[2] The word *mouchette* springs from an earlier but unattested *mouche-ep, a fusion of *mouche* and *ep* (<*apem*), which has become *mouchette* on the analogy of the numerous substantives ending in -*ette*. Similarly, in *essaim*, ' swarm ', Gilliéron detects, not a successor to Lat. *examen* which fits it so well both in sound and meaning, but a derivative of *es* <*apis*, due to the one-time *living* association of the word *es* with the first syllable of the word *essaim*.

Popular etymology, the second of the forces mentioned above, is also of great importance in the elaboration of language, particularly in the case of the patois, and is closely allied to what we have called contamination.[3] When Gilliéron states, for

---

[1] Where Latin initial *v*- is represented by *g*- or *gu*- in French words, e.g. *vastari*> *gâter*, it is generally held that there has been fusion between the Latin word and its Germanic equivalent, as *g*- or *gu*- is the standard French representative of Germanic *w*-. But the question is complicated by the fact that *g* for Lat. *v* is found in certain words and place-names for which no Germanic equivalent can be quoted.

[2] It is important to note that *muscă*, ' bee ', is also to be found in Rumanian. As far as the author is aware, it is used in the singular with a kind of collective value. When it is found that the hives in spring are well stocked with bees, the bee-keepers will say ' *este muscă multă anul acesta* '. Cf. also H. Tiktin, *Rumänisch-deutsches Wörterbuch*, p. 1024, col. 1.

[3] On popular etymology, see, for example, A. Philippide, *Principii de istoria limbii*, p. 106 f. ; Iorgu Iordan, *Viaţa romînească*, July, 1923, p. 119 f. ; W. v. Wartburg, *Zur Frage der Volksetymologie*, in *Homenaje ofrecido a R. Menéndez Pidal*, Madrid, 1925, vol. I, p. 17 f. Popular etymology, according to von Wartburg, is " essentially, the grouping of words, in the consciousness of the speaker, into families, which differ according to times and places ". A. Dauzat, *La géographie linguistique*, Paris, 1922, p. 72 f., calls it by the name of ' homonymic attraction '. He claims that it is not a matter of ' etymology ' in the real sense of the term, although it is true that the common folk possess what Ch. Bally calls somewhere ' the etymological instinct ', but of the attraction exercised by one word upon another with which it shares more or less similar phonetic characteristics. Elsewhere, in *Les patois*, Paris, 1927, p. 109, Dauzat puts forward an alternative term ' paronymic attraction ', which is preferable, seeing that the two terms associated are, to begin with, not strictly speaking homonyms but paronyms, i.e. have merely a certain formal resemblance. It should be made clear that Dauzat does not differentiate between ' popular etymology ' and ' contamination ', which to him are one and the same phenomenon. He rejects the term ' contamination ' because of its ' pathological ' associations, which are inappropriate, inasmuch as the word which exercises the attraction is more vigorous and

example, that the word *essaim* has as its first part the popular form *es* <*apis*, the phenomenon to which he refers may be considered either as a contamination of the representative of Lat. *examen* by the word *es* or as a case of popular etymology, the first syllable of *essaim* having been felt by speakers to be the word *es*, which comes to saying that they etymologize and ' derive ' *essaim* from *es*. Thus, in all Gilliéron's works, and particularly in *L'Abeille*, we find him at every step calling in the principle of popular etymology to explain either the changes in old-established words or new formations, which the need for clarity and for the avoidance of misunderstanding has caused the vernaculars to bring forth. Unlike the majority of philologists, he does not consider that popular etymology affects only rare, technical or foreign words which, having no support in the minds of speakers, are liable to undergo all kinds of transformation. Consequently, popular etymology is, in his eyes, far from being the pathological process[1] which it is to the ' phonétistes ', " qui ne voient guère dans la constitution de la langue que l'élément mécanique et ne se sont pas suffisamment préoccupés de l'autre élément, de l'élément psychologique." (*Abeille*, p. 224.) Among the many errors into which the neo-grammarians have fallen in this connection none is more serious than the distinction they set up between popular and learned words, for no such absolute distinction can be justified. Each so-called ' learned ' word must be investigated separately. Popular etymology has been at work upon human speech at every phase of its development, and has saved hosts of words which sound-change has menaced with destruction. It is for ever striving to give significance to elements of the language

---

' healthier ' than the word which undergoes it. According to E. Boisacq, *Revue belge de philologie et d'histoire*, V (1926), p. 535, the term ' popular etymology ', which is still almost universally employed, occurs first in an article by E. Förstemann in *Kuhns Zeitschrift für vergleichende Sprachforschung*, vol. I (1852). The term was objected to by Wundt, *Die Sprache*, I, pp. 474-5. Recently, by M. Runes (*v. Actes du II*e *Congrès international de linguistes* [Geneva, 25-29 August, 1931], p. 208), the alternative ' word-analogy ' has been suggested. Cp. also : M.-Elisabeth Houtzager, *Unconscious Sound- and Sense-Assimilations*, Amsterdam, 1935 ; *v.* A. Sommerfelt, *Bull. Soc. Ling.*, XXXVII (1936), fasc. 3, pp. 23-4.

[1] Cf., for example, F. de Saussure, *Cours de linguistique générale*, Paris, 1916, p. 247 : " L'étymologie populaire est un phénomène pathologique ; elle n'agit que dans des conditions particulières, et n'atteint que des mots rares, techniques ou étrangers, que les sujets s'assimilent imparfaitement." The first phrase was dropped in the second edition (1923), p. 241. None the less it is clear from the comparison set up between popular etymology and analogy that the former continues to be considered as something abnormal, unlike analogy " qui appartient au fonctionnement normal de la langue ".

that are obscure, creating formal connections between words which though semantically associated are etymologically unrelated. " L'étymologie populaire est, si l'on veut, un parasite de l'étymologie phonétique d'un mot, mais un parasite qui peut supprimer en entier la vie de celle-ci (Ex. *fermer*), ou vivre collatéralement (Ex. *dégoûter*) et, alors, nous venons de voir quelle conséquence il peut résulter de cette intime association, de cet attelage sous le même joug (Ex. *dégoûtant* ébranlé, caduc)."[1]

The following examples show us popular etymology at work. Latin *cubare*, ' to lie down ', has had its meaning restricted in French *couver*, ' to hatch ', because the popular mind brought it into relationship with the *ovum* family, and its derivative *ovare*, ' to lay ', when intervocalic *b* had changed into *v*. This is proved by the disappearance of *ovare* from all regions where *cubare* has survived (cp., however, Prov. *coar* beside *ovar* registered by Meyer-Lübke, *Romanisches etymologisches Wörterbuch*, nos. 2351 and 6128). Again, in certain areas of France, of the old names for the days of the

---

[1] From *Pathologie et thérapeutique verbales*, III, p. 26. In this study, p. 20 f., Gilliéron explains *fermer* as a ' semantic derivative ' of *fer*<Lat. *ferrum*, not as the successor of Lat. *firmare* (like *essaim* from *es*, above) ; the speakers having felt the first syllable of the verb as identical with the noun *fer*, not only because of the identity of sound, but more particularly because doors were once, and are still in some parts, closed with an iron nail (cf. Rum. *încuia* ' to lock '<*cuiu*, ' nail '). He also states that *dégoûtant*, which to the phoneticians is merely a derivative of *gustum*, is in reality at the same time identical with *dégouttant*, participle of *dégoutter* ' to drop '<*goutte*, the idea of ' droppings ' being closely associated with the word *dégoûtant* in certain contexts. Elsewhere we find similar explanations of familiar words ; for example, in *Pathologie et thérapeutique verbales*, IV, p. 124 f., he derives *maison*, in those dialects where it means ' kitchen ', from *maie*, ' kneading trough ', as being the room where this utensil is kept and used. This etymology he calls the ' French ' etymology of the word (étymologie II) as distinct from the derivation from Lat. *mansionem* (étymologie I). The present author remembers him, in a lecture, in 1925, considering *adorer* as now in etymological relationship with *abhorrer* (pronounced *aborer*) and as its semantic opposite, this fact being, according to Gilliéron, the only satisfactory way of explaining such expressions as " *j'adore les huîtres* ", etc. Similarly, in his lectures, he explained the current meaning of *fruste* ' coarse, unpolished, etc.' (cf. Ital. *frusto*,. ' worn ') as a semantic derivative of ' rustre '. (J. Vendryes, in *Le Langage*, Paris, 1921, p. 232, has also discussed this word : " L'adjectif *fruste* ne se disait à l'origine que d'une monnaie dont l'effigie était effacée ; *monnaie fruste* a été compris comme désignant une monnaie grossièrement frappée, dépourvue d'art et de fini. Par extension le mot s'est dit d'un homme grossier, sans culture, rude. C'est un faux sens qui a prévalu, favorisé peut-être par une vague similitude de sons avec les mots *rustre* et *rustaud*." The word has been adopted in Rumanian with its new. meaning.) At times similar phenomena occur in literary French ; for example, this sentence quoted by Gilliéron from a newspaper article : *les maisons se sèment sur la plaine* where *se sèment* (from *semer*, ' to sow ') stands for *s'essaiment* (from *essaimer*, ' to swarm ').' In support of the general truth of Gilliéron's theory the author can quote an example from Rumanian as it affects his own personal linguistic sense. The verb *a forfeca*, ' to clip into small pieces ', is, to him, in semantic association with the noun *ferfeniță*, ' rag ', ' tatter ', and entirely dissociated from the word *foarfece*, ' scissors ', to which it ' etymologically ' belongs.

week beginning with *di-*, only *dimyèk* (=*dimercre*), 'Wednesday', has survived ; the others have all given way to the central forms ending in -*di*. It is popular etymology which, according to Gilliéron, has caused *dimyèk* to be preserved, the word having been brought into association with *demi-*, inasmuch as Wednesday is the middle day of the week (cp. Germ. *Mittwoch*, 'Wednesday', and also Slav. *srĕda*, which, according to Fr. Miklosich, *Etymologisches Wörterbuch der slavischen Sprachen*, p. 292, col. 2, owes its meaning of 'Wednesday' to the influence of the German word). Standard French *absinthe*, to take another case, becomes in certain dialects *herbe sainte*. And though Gilliéron's opponents have made merry over his and Edmont's gullibility in admitting this as a *bona fide* form, it has become clear that *herbe sainte* for *absinthe* exists, but only where *herbe* is pronounced *arb* and where *ab* is felt as a vulgarism for *arb* (cp. *arbre*, pronounced *abr* in dialect). In other words *arb* (' herbe ') for *ab* is a ' hyper-urbanism ' or what Gilliéron calls a ' faux retour '.

The etymologizing ' instinct ' works so strongly upon the minds of speakers that it has come about at times that a number of words have taken a certain direction under the influence of popular etymology and then carried with them other words showing similar phonetic characteristics, but quite unrelated semantically. Thus, *femer* (<Lat.* *fimare*) ' to manure ', and *femier* (<**fimarium*) ' dung-heap '. having become *fumer* and *fumier* under the influence of *fumée* ' smoke ', other words beginning with *fem-* are caught up in the movement and *femelle*, for example, becomes in places *fumelle*.[1] " L'étymologie populaire ", says Gilliéron (*Abeille*, p. 230), " épie les mots, les épluche, son visa est nécessaire pour qu'un mot parvienne jusqu'à nous, et souvent elle en modifie la destination."[2]

---

[1] According to some, this is a purely phonological phenomenon due to the rounding influence of *f* and *m* on the *e*. Cf. Rumanian dial. *fomeie*, from *fămeie* (<Lat. *familia*).

[2] To throw further light on the workings of popular etymology the following Rumanian examples are appended, most of them hitherto unnoticed : *Adagiu*, ' adage ', used by a professor with the meaning of *adaus*, ' appendix, addition ', a case of ' semantic derivation ', from the verb *a adăugi* ; *buratic*, for *broatec*, ' kind of frog' influenced by *bura*, ' drizzle ', these frogs being frequent in wet weather ; *căprar*, popular form of *caporal*, which after assimilation (>*căpurar*, a variant heard by the author) has been attached to the family of *capră*, ' goat ' ; *ciocantin*, ' a kind of maize ', from Ital. *cinquantino*, ' maize which sprouts and ripens in 50 days ', but influenced by *ciocan*, ' dry reed of maize ' in Tecuciu ; *cîrni* for *cîrmi*, ' to steer ' under the influence of *cîrn*, ' flat-nosed ', used first, no doubt, in expressions like *a cîrni din nas*, ' to make a wry face ' ; *filigram* for *filigran*, influence of -*gram*, a common element of technical words ; *holercă* for *horilcă*, ' cheap spirit ', with a metathesis of consonants helped out by association with *holeră*, ' cholera ' (cf.

It must not be inferred that these phenomena are confined to dialect or popular speech, and that the literary language is immune from or unaffected by them. The distinction which is usually drawn between the popular and the written tongue is as illusory and unfounded as the distinction between popular and learned words. From the moment when any component enters the language, the same forces come to bear upon it irrespective of its age, and consequently, when the same phenomenon is found to occur, as frequently happens, in both the phonetics of the learned and the popular tongue, it is courting error to maintain this distinction. As Gilliéron rightly urges (*Abeille*, p. 289) : " Cessons de considérer la langue littéraire comme d'une essence supérieure et comme étant en dehors des atteintes de la loi commune aux parlers populaires." The written language also strives towards clarity, even more persistently than the dialects ; it, too, struggles with all its power to avoid phonetic and semantic collision. It is true that it is less sensitive to homonymy, or, more exactly, appears less prone to use the therapeutic devices which we have seen applied to avoid homonymic difficulties, but this is because its resources are greater.[1] On the other hand, it suffers more readily than the

---

the variant *bolearcă*, explained by the *Dicţionarul Academiei*, t. I, pt. ii, p. 401, col. 1, as due to *holercă+boală*, ' disease ') ; the old preposition *întru*, ' in, into ', has become extremely rare through identification with *între*, ' among ', or *într'o*, ' in a ' (cf. the common version of the prayer " Come and dwell within us and lead us not into temptation " : *vino şi te sălăşluieşte* într*e noi, şi nu ne duce* într'o *ispită*) ; *normă* for *noimă*, ' sense ', a would-be learned form ; *palmac*, ' a measure of length ', is Turkish *parmak*, influenced by *palmă*, ' palm of the hand, span ' ; *patvagon*, ' luggage-van of a train ', is Germ. *Packwagen*, influenced by *pat*, ' bed ', the van being fitted with a bed for the luggage guard ; *privinţă* for *prevenţie* from *privi*, ' to watch ', *închis în prevenţie*, ' imprisoned for preventive reasons ', thus becomes, popularly, *închis în privinţă* ; *prenume*, ' Christian name ', becomes *pronume*, a form not confined to the uneducated or semi-educated ; *ruşfert*, Moldavian for *ruşfet*, ' bribe, tip ' (Turkish *rüşvet*), is due to the influence of *sfert*, ' tax ', pronounced *şfert* in Moldavia ; *săricică*, ' citric acid ', is pronounced in Tecuciu *sărăcică*, under the influence of *sărac*, ' wretched ' ; *stor*, ' window-blind ', is commonly pronounced as *stol*, ' mass, swarm ' ; *strănuta*, ' to sneeze ', becomes in certain areas, at Tecuciu for example, *strămuta*, by popular association with *muta* (<Lat. *mutare*) ; *sirepe*, ' wild, not broken in ', used in the formula *iepe sirepe*, ' unbroken mares ', has become in places *sure iepe* (<*sur*, ' grey ') ; *uger*, ' udder ', is pronounced at Tecuciu and elsewhere *unger* through the influence of *a unge*, ' to grease ' ; *v.* for further details and examples Iorgu Iordan, *Etimologii populare*, in *Arhiva*, XXXIX (1932), p. 34 f., and V. Bogrea, *Dacoromania*, II (1921-2), p. 437 f., and IV (1924-6), p. 892 f.

[1] " La langue littéraire possède, à côté de la langue parlée, une langue écrite pleine de traditions étymologiques—légitimes ou illégitimes—qui constitue en quelque sorte une autre vie linguistique, tolérant les phonèmes proscrits par la phonétique de la langue parlée, en même temps qu'un réservoir où celle-ci peut se régénérer et se prémunir des accidents qui la menacent " (*Pathologie et thérapeutique verbales*, II, p. 16).

popular tongue from semantic hypertrophy, because of the greater wealth of ideas it is called upon to express.

To ward off the dangers with which it also is threatened the literary language looks for help, above all, to Latin, with which it has been continuously in contact, though more particularly since the period of the Renascence.[1] It is Latin that has enabled French, not only to enrich its vocabulary, but also to acquire that clarity which is the admiration of the world. But French has not disdained at times to call in the help of popular speech as well, to eliminate some source of phonetic or semantic confusion. Here again we find Gilliéron at variance with traditional doctrine. As is well known, the existence of dialect words or forms in the standard language is usually explained by the ' word and thing ' method,[2] i.e. the provincial name of an object, it is claimed, is accounted for by the provincial origin of the object itself. The words *avoine* and *foin* are cases in point. They come respectively from *avēna* and *fēnum*, and according to the regular ' sound-laws ' should be *aveine* and *fein*, forms which are found in early texts (cp. *plein<plēnum*, *pleine<plēna*). In certain regions, however, in Burgundy for example, the forms with *oi* are phonetically ' regular '. And as Burgundy has always been for Paris a provider of oats and hay, we find Meyer-Lübke, in his *Grammatik der romanischen Sprachen*, I, p. 104, § 89, expressing the view that for this reason the Burgundian forms for these two words were finally adopted by the Parisians, and the old forms in *ei* discarded. Gilliéron waxes merry over this explanation,[3] and puts forward one of his own in conformity with the principles drawn from linguistic geography. The cause of the substitution of *oi* for *ei*, which occurs also in *moins<minus*, a case not explained by Meyer-Lübke, is homonymic. The old form *aveine* clashed with *veine*, in *l'aveine*, *s'aveine* (=*son avoine*), *fein* clashed

---

[1] As early as the reign of Charlemagne, when French was in its infancy, there was a revival of Latin learning, a first Renascence.

[2] See above, Chap. I, p. 62 f.

[3] " Quelle raison pouvait avoir la langue de Paris d'abandonner sa tradition phonétique, sa tradition légale (pour *foin* et pour *avoine* parce que Paris tirait son ' foin ' et son ' avoine ' de la Bourgogne !), elle, qui, à l'époque où se seraient produits ces emprunts, était consciente de sa supériorité et de l'infériorité des patois congénères ? Troquer l'habit pour la blouse quand on va se présenter à la cour ? " (*Abeille*, p. 202–3). A. Dauzat, *Histoire de la langue française*, Paris, 1930, p. 102, note 1, says that Meyer-Lübke's explanation is not only unlikely but is without basis in fact. It is known that Paris got its hay from the districts of Poissy, Pontoise, l'Ile–Adam, etc., and not from Burgundy.

with *fin*, *faim*, and *meins* with *main*, *maint*, etc.[1] The modification came about at a period when in words of this type both pronunciations, *ei* and *oi*, were concurrent in the territory of French proper, as is evidenced to-day by the coexistence of *François* and *français*, originally the same word, and by *français*, *japonais*, beside *danois* and *suédois*, where, in both cases, the suffix goes back to *-ensis*.[2] Hence, Gilliéron also rejects the purely phonetic explanation which others have brought forward, namely, that *ei* has become *oi* in these words because of the labial consonants (*v*, *f*, *m*) which precede it and which have caused it to be rounded. Why, if this is the case, he asks, have so many words kept the *ei* although preceded by a labial consonant?[3] Thus, in the present instance, the literary language has escaped from its difficulties by using the resources offered by current standard speech conditions, and not by calling in the help of the dialects. But Gilliéron is far from denying the contribution of the dialects to the standard tongue, and their help in the cause of order and clarity; on the contrary, he gives them full recognition in this respect as well. What he is protesting against is the undue stressing of the ' material ' factor; he believes that the literary language accepts from the dialects any element which it can use in its efforts towards clarity and intelligibility, irrespective of the material associations of ' word ' and ' thing '. Gilliéron, in

---

[1] Gilliéron does not say with what word *minus* > *meins* would have clashed, but he invents a sentence to show what would have been the position if the forms in *ei* had not been dropped : *Le cheval mange s'aveine et aussi du fein fin, mais meins*, instead of as at present : *Le cheval mange son avoine et aussi du foin fin, mais moins*.

[2] Von Wartburg, *Franz. etym. Wörterbuch*, vol. III, p. 290, and E. Gamillscheg, *Etym. Wörterbuch der franz. Sprache*, pp. 12–13, derive *danois* from *danisk* (*daniscum). As for *français*, von Wartburg (*s.v. France*, note 10) hesitates between *-ensis* and *-iscus*. Cp. also : W. Meyer-Lübke, *Rom. etym. Wörterbuch*, no. 3483, and E. Gamillscheg, *Romania Germanica*, I, Berlin–Leipzig, 1934, p. 228, and II, *ibid.*, 1935, p. 203.

[3] Leo Jordan, *Altfranzösisches Elementarbuch*, Bielefeld–Leipzig, 1923, pp. 74–5, reverts to the problem discussed above and attempts a phonetic or neo-grammarian solution. Accounting for *avoine*, *foin*, and *moins* by the influence of the labials, he explains that *moine* for *mène*, which, he says, is found in early texts, was discarded in favour of *mène* through the influence of *mener* and other forms with final stress. *Poine* yielded to *peine* through Latin influence from ecclesiastical sources. *Veine*, for which Jordan can find no early example in *oi*, he considers a technical medical word and therefore learned. G. Rohlfs, reviewing Jordan's book in *Literaturblatt f. germ. u. rom. Phil.*, XLVI (1925), col. 297 f., approves this view, with certain reservations as to detail. Von Wartburg, *Franz. etym. Wörterbuch*, I, p. 187, col. 2, casts doubt on Gilliéron's theory, alleging that other Romance languages and even certain French dialects tolerate the clash in question. The force of this argument may be gauged from the remarks to follow. Cf. also on the present topic, C. B. Lewis, *A purely traditional explanation of foin, moins, avoine* in *Revue belge de philologie et d'histoire*, IX (1930), p. 801 f.

fact, is rather disposed to deny the importance of these associations in accounting for such phenomena.[1]

★　★　★

Having made some acquaintance with the principles of linguistic geography, and Gilliéron's application of them to problems raised **Criticisms of** by the *Linguistic Atlas*, let us see how his studies **Gilliéron's** were received by the specialists. We have already **Theories** mentioned that the majority of French philologists were, from the beginning, frankly hostile. An outstanding opponent was the late Antoine Thomas, who published a severely critical review of the *Atlas* in the *Journal des Savants*, 1904, p. 89 f.[2] Next to him come M. Grammont (cp. *Indogermanische Forschungen*, XVI [1904], Anzeiger, p. 12 f. ; cp. also *Revue des langues romanes*, XLVIII [1905], p. 377 f.), E. Bourciez,[3] J. Ronjat, and G. Millardet. The latter is the author, *inter alia*, of a biggish volume entitled *Linguistique et dialectologie romanes. Problèmes et Méthodes*, Montpellier–Paris, 1923, the main purpose of which, although it touches matters of method as applied to all domains of Romance philology, including phonology, morphology, syntax, etc., may be said to be to combat linguistic geography as represented by Gilliéron and his French disciples, O. Bloch, Ch. Bruneau, and A. Terracher.[4] Certain of

---

[1] Cf. K. Jaberg, *Aspects géographiques du langage*, Paris, 1936, p. 27.

[2] Reprinted by the author in *Nouveaux essais de philologie française*, Paris, 1904, p. 346 f.

[3] In his review of the Rumanian edition of the present work, *Rev. crit.*, yr. LXVII (1933), p. 176, M. Bourciez protests at being classed among the " contempteurs " of the *Atlas*. He says' that the work brings the greatest honour to French scholarship, but that a large share of the credit for it is Edmont's. He goes on to say that he expressed the most serious reservations concerning Gilliéron's methods and his studies (like *l'Abeille*), and that he criticized Gilliéron's hostility to the phoneticians and particularly his style !

[4] Millardet's book was reviewed by : S. Puşcariu, *Dacoromania*, III (1923), p. 827 f. ; E. Bourciez, *Rev. crit.*, vol. XC (1923), p. 145 f. ; O. Densusianu, *Grai şi suflet*, I (1923–4), p. 150 f. ; A. Meillet, *Bull. Soc. Ling.*, XXIV (1923–4), fasc. 2, p. 80 f. ; N. Maccarrone, *Revue de linguistique romane*, VI (1930), p. 20 f. ; J. Ronjat, *Revue des langues romanes*, LXIII (1925), p. 152 f. ; O. J. Tallgren *Neuphilologische Mitteilungen*, XXVI (1925), p. 185 f., etc. Cf. also a very flattering notice in an article by J. Feller, *Quelques aspects récents de la philologie romane en France* in *Revue belge de philologie et d'histoire*, V (1926), p. 759 f. On behalf of those attacked, A. Terracher made a stinging reply in an article entitled *Géographie linguistique, histoire et philologie*, in *Bull. de la Soc. ling. de Paris*, XXIV (1923–4), p. 259 f., to which Millardet rejoined in *Revue des langues romanes*, LXII (1923–4). All questions of personal animosity apart, the controversy is of great interest with

the comments made by Gilliéron's opponents are so severe as to make us suspect their good faith, especially when we remember that the writers were not personally on good terms with Gilliéron. As a sample, we may quote the remarks of M. Grammont in *Revue des langues romanes*, XLVIII (1905), p. 377 : " Or, si nous avons fait voir (*Indogermanische Forschungen*, XVI, Anzeiger, s. 12 ff. [*sic*]) quels services peut rendre cet atlas et quelle est l'étendue de ces services, nous n'avons pas moins nettement montré que pour ce qui est des mots et de la forme des mots tout doit être considéré *a priori* comme faux. Rien ne saurait être accepté qu'après une minutieuse vérification." Elsewhere, in the same journal, LIV (1911), p. 323, we find him saying : " Quant à la géographie linguistique, dont on fait grand tapage, ce n'est pas une discipline nouvelle ; ce qui est nouveau, c'est l'abus qu'on en fait aujourd'hui." G. Millardet, likewise, shows a similar attitude (*Revue des langues romanes*, LXII [1923–4], p. 168), in a review of two books of Bourciez', when he says : " Il [Bourciez] s'est donc gardé d'accepter sans réserves la théorie brutale de l'homonymie et du polysémantisme qui fait le fond de la doctrine de M. Gilliéron et de son école, doctrine des exagérations de laquelle M. Bourciez a fait justice ailleurs [*Revue critique*, 1923, p. 145 f.], et dont il déclare une fois pour toutes dans sa préface[1] qu'il la connaît, mais ne s'en embarrassera pas." It was doubtless of such criticisms as these that A. Meillet was thinking, in his discussion of Gilliéron's *Pathologie et thérapeutique verbales*, I and II, in *Bulletin de la Société de linguistique*, XX (1916), p. 65 f., though he feels constrained to refute Gilliéron's accusation of actual bad faith on the part of his opponents. He too detects certain blemishes in Gilliéron's work, which we shall discuss later, but he ends by declaring (p. 67) :

---

regard to the whole subject of linguistic geography. It should be stated that Millardet began as a worker in the field of linguistic geography and is thus to some extent a pupil of Gilliéron's. We are not surprised therefore that the best part of his book is that in which he reveals himself in this light. When he opposes Gilliéron, he is really opposing himself. By his conception of phonology, however, which he exalts beyond measure, and by his apology for ' comparativism ' as represented by Bourciez and Meyer-Lübke, and in other respects as well, he belongs rather to the school of the neo-grammarians.

[1] In the preface to *Eléments de linguistique romane*, ed. II, Paris, 1923, pp. viii–ix : " . . . j'ai à dessein laissé de côté certains articles de Revues ou certains livres parus soit à l'étranger, soit chez nous, et qui concernent notamment la syntaxe ou la répartition géographique des mots: les uns, en dépit d'une terminologie nouvelle, n'ajoutent pas grand'chose aux résultats depuis longtemps acquis; les autres m'ont paru procéder d'une méthode trouble et vraiment trop aventureuse. Je les connais, j'ai jugé inutile de les signaler ici où je ne pouvais même pas mentionner tout ce qui en eût valu la peine."

" . . . M. Gilliéron a fait progresser d'une manière importante la théorie du vocabulaire." It should be said that, from the very beginning, Meillet's attitude towards linguistic geography and the works of its founder had always been most scrupulously unbiased.

Outside France, Gilliéron's doctrine was received with enthusiasm or at least goodwill, another proof of the well-worn adage : ' No man is a prophet in his own country '. The most serious reservations were made by Meyer-Lübke, who has given an opinion on various studies by Gilliéron in reviews already quoted (v. above, p. 159, note) and who, on a number of occasions, has discussed linguistic geography in general, for example in a review of K. Jaberg's *Sprachgeographie*, in *Göttingische gelehrte Anzeigen*, CLXXI (1909), p. 138 f., in an article entitled *Aufgaben der Wortforschung* in *Germanisch-romanische Monatsschrift*, I (1909), p. 634 f., and in *Einführung in das Studium der romanischen Sprachwissenschaft*, ed. III, § 65, p. 80 f.[1] He has been followed by some of his older pupils, like E. Herzog and K. von Ettmayer. Herzog, in *Literaturblatt f. germ. u. rom. Phil.*, XXXII (1911), col. 234 f., reviewing Jaberg's *Sprachgeographie*, and discussing linguistic geography in general and the theories of Gilliéron, makes a defence of the sound-laws and refers the reader to the views expressed in his *Streitfragen der romanischen Philologie*, Halle a.S., 1904. Von Ettmayer, in a review of the same work in *Zeitschrift f. rom. Philologie*, XXXV (1911), p. 250 f., represents a point of view which may be considered as characteristic of the whole Meyer-Lübke school, namely, a strictly ' historical ' attitude with regard to the laws of sound-change. To quote his words, *loc. cit.*, p. 255 : " In linguistics, there is in my opinion only one standpoint which preserves us from false thinking, and that is the strictly historical." In like manner, Herzog, too, in the review mentioned above, protests against the assertion made by the linguistic geographers that the sound-laws are just so many fictions ; while Meyer-Lübke himself, in *Archiv für das Studium der neueren Sprachen*, CL (1926), p. 82, at the end of an article prompted

---

[1] The allotting of merely two pages to linguistic geography, out of nearly 300, in a book devoted to questions of theory, is proof that the author does not attach anything like the necessary importance to this approach to language. This was pointed out more than twenty years ago by J. Jud in his review of the second edition, in *Archiv f. d. Studium d. neueren Spr. u. Lit.*, CXXIV (1910), p. 383 f. Meyer-Lübke has also discussed linguistic geography in a very favourable review of the first fascicule of the *Atlas linguistique de la France* in *Literaturblatt f. germ. u. rom. Phil.*, XXIII (1902), col. 219 f., in *Zeitschr. f. rom. Phil.*, XXXIII (1909), p. 431 f. (in connection with J. Jud's study of Fr. *aune* mentioned below), and in *Revue de linguistique romane*, I (1925), p. 22 f., etc.

by G. Rohlfs' *Griechen und Romanen in Unteritalien*, Geneva, 1924, uses words to the following effect : Linguistic geography, although it renders great service, does not always suffice to explain the phenomena of language. This is proved by the case before us, Rohlfs' exploration of the Southern Italian dialects having been solely ' horizontal ', i.e. geographical, and not at the same time ' vertical ' or historical. It is only the much-maligned phonetic method which can solve our difficulties in circumstances like the present.

Let us consider the chief objections that have been raised against linguistic geography. In the first place, doubt has been cast upon the accuracy of the material contained in the *Linguistic Atlas of France*. Various critics have compared the information given by the *Atlas* with what they themselves knew concerning a given French dialect or dialects, and, discovering considerable points of disagreement, have concluded that the replies given by Edmont's informants were inaccurate, or had been inaccurately reproduced. But even if these points of disagreement were more numerous or more serious than they are, we should not be entitled to consider them as other than quite natural occurrences. It must not be forgotten that a linguistic atlas, compiled in the manner described above, registers the popular speech of the several localities as represented by certain definite individuals, chosen as ' subjects ', and in certain psychological conditions.[1] When the conditions are not the same, that is to say, when the ' subject ' is different, or when the whole situation is changed, it is inevitable that the response should vary to some extent, even to the same questions. It is a well-known fact that, with one and the same individual, pronunciation, and often even grammar and vocabulary, are modified according to the circumstances prevailing, and particularly according to the speaker's mood. Such variations are clearly still more likely to occur when investigations have been conducted at different periods, and when other informants have been questioned. Supposing even we were to admit, what is on the face of it an absurdity, namely, that of several enquiries conducted in a given locality only one will give results that are in accordance with the facts, what means have we of deciding which is that particular

---

[1] In other words, to use the Saussure terminology, a linguistic atlas reproduces ' la parole ', not ' la langue '. This is recognized by the authors of the *Linguistic Atlas of Italy and Southern Switzerland*, K. Jaberg and J. Jud, when they say : " Wir geben Sprechen wieder, nicht Sprache," *v, Der Sprachatlas als Forschungsinstrument*, Halle a.S., 1928, p. 214.

one? What right, in other words, have Gilliéron's opponents to believe that they have perceived and recorded more accurately than Edmont the speech of a particular locality? Would they allege that they are specialists in the matter and that he was without philological training? Such an argument would not only be frivolous but to their own detriment, inasmuch as an enquiry conducted by means of a questionnaire demands no equipment beyond an acute ear and the ability to transcribe accurately what is heard in reply to the questions put. Edmont possessed this equipment to a remarkable degree and, in addition, he had a greater knack of ingratiating himself with peasant folk than the average linguist, being himself of comparatively humble origin. But not only theory but facts can be alleged in support of the *Atlas linguistique de la France*. As we shall see later, a number of Gilliéron's pupils (O. Bloch, Ch. Bruneau, and others) have repeated their master's experiments over less extensive areas, and have applied his method more minutely to the vernaculars of certain special regions of France. They have thus been able, so to speak, to use a finer mesh in their researches than was possible for the larger atlas. All of them have acknowledged that, apart from a few points of no significance, the results they have obtained confirm in the most striking fashion those of Edmont. More than that, the necessarily few localities investigated by the latter in a given area can be considered as authentic representatives of the dialect of the whole area, and their vernaculars as typical of the speeches of those villages which Edmont could not visit, but which they, with a more limited territory to explore, could include in their survey.

As for the criticisms called forth by the studies published by Gilliéron on the basis of material taken from the *Atlas*, they are more numerous and just as harsh. He is reproached, for instance, with having too frequently had recourse to reasons of homonymy to explain the disappearance or the transformation of words. It is true that in the works of the founder of linguistic geography and of certain of his followers we encounter the word ' homonymy ' at every step, and, what is more, in cases where we least expect it to arise, to the astonishment of many. But what is important, surely, is not the number of cases of homonymic clash in a given language, but the principle itself, and would anyone deny that a word may be supplanted, or made to undergo all kinds of modification, if it is identical in sound with another word? If this is generally admitted, the numerical question is a detail of little or no importance. Another fact too must not be lost sight of. When once the language, through its speakers, has become aware that a certain case of homonymy is disturbing and leads to confusion, it may eliminate it by a variety of means, but the extent to which any one of these means may be applied is a question which really does not arise ; a language does not proceed with the logical method of the scientist, nor can we apply to its workings our own individual standards. But there is a further point. Those who protest against the ' abuse ' of the homonymic explanation, either provide no other, or, if they do, fail to convince us. Why indeed should they be more entitled to credence than Gilliéron ? Of two impressions, one of them that of the founder of linguistic geography, the other that of a linguist who, however well he may know the *Atlas* and the French dialects, cannot sustain comparison with Gilliéron in this respect, why should we not accept that of the latter, particularly when it is supported by geographical arguments, as we have shown in a number of the words quoted above ? We have already alluded to a rare faculty which, as everyone admits, Gilliéron possessed, namely, his peculiar gift of entering into what we may call the life of language, of finding his way into the laboratory of human speech, and of observing processes which to other linguists are more or less completely inaccessible. May it not be that, at least in some cases, Gilliéron's so-called ' abuse ' of homonyms is, in reality, an inability on the part of his adversaries to see the truly living realities of language ?

But the objections to the theory of homonyms go further. Not only is it alleged that Gilliéron went too far in his use of this explanation, but it has been also urged against him, sometimes by the same opponent, that both in French and in other languages numerous homonyms continue to exist. It is clear that between this and the former allegation there is something of a contradiction, particularly when they both emanate from the same critic—an interesting example of the relativity of human judgments ! Gilliéron has not let this latter objection pass unnoticed. In his typically fresh and expressive way he says : " C'est par centaines que se chiffrent les substitutions à des mots ' indésirables ' pour cause de pléthore sémantique, par centaines même celles qui ont pour cause la collision homonymique. Cette dernière catégorie de substitutions est généralement niée, et cette négation repose sur la constatation que l'homonymie est fréquente dans la langue.

Singulier raisonnement : la catastrophe n'a pas eu lieu, parce qu'il y a eu de nombreux rescapés ! " (*L'Abeille*, p. 263). It is true that numerous homonyms are to be found in the language to-day, and that they cause no great hardship and are consequently allowed to remain. But to attach any force to this argument would be tantamount to admitting that the French language—the object of Gilliéron's studies—has reached a stagnation point in its evolution, and has ceased to live, at least in this respect. For who can argue that the existing homonyms are not destined slowly to disappear, and that at this very moment some kind of effort is not being made to eliminate one or other of their number ? Does the fact that we are able to observe a linguistic phenomenon, not while it is in gestation, but only when it has actually come to light, entitle us to affirm that a particular phenomenon is not actually taking place or that it never will ? A language encounters all manner of difficulties in its efforts towards clarity, and often these difficulties are insurmountable at the moment, or even over a long period. We have seen above that it is no rare thing for a word that has been changed for homonymic reasons to be unable to survive in its new guise, and for it to become entangled again with some other word in the language. That is one cause, and a very potent one, of the retention of homonyms. For the objection to be taken seriously, each set of homonyms would need to be examined individually, on the principle that every word has its own history ; only then could the reason for their persistence be discovered.

Another error can be laid at the door of those who allege the case of other languages as an argument against the theory of homonymic incompatibility. If every word is entitled to be treated as an individual and examined on its merits, how much more is this the case with a language ! More than this, only for French do we possess at the present moment a full-fledged atlas ; the atlases for other languages are either only in the making or in process of publication, and in Gilliéron's day the French atlas stood entirely alone, as that of Corsica (see below), and of Dacia, by Weigand, can for various reasons be left out of account. Can it be considered a sound proceeding, from the point of view of method, to compare the French material housed in the *Atlas* with the material for other languages to be found only in texts or glossaries ? We have seen, and every scholar would subscribe in some measure at least to our contention, that one of the contributions made by linguistic geography to the renewal of our studies is just this new picture of language which it gives us, so fundamentally different from that we receive from texts and dictionaries. But supposing we had atlases for all the Romance languages, and that, consequently, a comparison between them on the basis of the same criteria were possible. Could the fact that Italian, Spanish, etc., were seen actually to contain fewer homonyms than French be alleged as proof that homonymic theory is false? Are all human idioms equally sensitive to homonymic clashes? And does not such sensitiveness depend on psychological factors which may vary from people to people?[1]

Here, indeed, we have reached the main point at issue in the discussion concerning homonyms. The French language is in a peculiar position when compared to its neighbours. Gilliéron himself and some of his followers have insisted more than once upon one of the outstanding characteristics of the French mind, namely clarity. It would appear that nowhere do we find this quality as highly developed as in France. Further, we have seen that the avoidance of homonyms is due to just that need for clarity without which a language cannot adequately fulfil its purpose of providing us with a means of mutual understanding. We would not venture to contest the existence of this characteristic feature of French psychology, conspicuous as it is in every field of intellectual activity, but we are of the belief that it is not of primary importance in the matter at issue, though it may be the best means of accounting for the modification or elimination of homonyms in the standard language. We need not dwell upon the important part played, precisely when the literary language was being finally constituted, by the grammarians, the salons, and the French Academy, whose aim was to ' purify ', in every sense of the word, the language of cultured society, to frame rules for it, as well as to solve all kinds of linguistic difficulties, the whole on an exclusively rational basis. Among these difficulties homonymy certainly figured. But the vernaculars of the country-side were outside the control of such grammatical or social standards. For a long period of time they developed in perfect freedom, so that the conscious will of the individual speaker or speakers played but a small part in their evolution.

---

[1] Cf. on the kindred subject of semantic overload, K. Jaberg, *Aspects géographiques du langage*, Paris, 1936, p. 50 : " On voudrait savoir si les différentes langues sont également réfractaires ou accessibles à la polysémie, et on voudrait connaître les facteurs qui, dans chaque cas particulier, déterminent la solution du conflit."

The reason why homonyms are more plentiful and consequently less easy to tolerate in French is to be sought elsewhere. The historical and comparative study of Romance phonology reveals at the first glance that the most numerous and most radical transformations of Latin sounds have occurred in French.[1] To take a few examples, voiced and unvoiced plosives (*t* and *d*, *c* and *g*) first became identical in sound when between two vowels, and finally disappeared (*vita*>*vie*, *mica*>*mie*), *p* and *b* in the same position are both reduced to *v*, both the closed and the open *o* sound become [œ] in open syllables under the stress, final vowels are worn down to [ə] now generally silent, etc. etc. French has thus gone far ahead of its neo-Latin sisters in the paths of phonetic change, and that from the earliest times, as almost all the innovations that arose in the Romanic period, before the break-up into the several Romance languages took place, seem to have originated on Gallo-Roman territory, and to have radiated from this revolutionary centre into the other provinces of the late empire. This being the case, we can readily understand why homonyms have arisen more frequently in French than elsewhere, and at the same time why Gilliéron had recourse so frequently to the ' homonymic ' explanation. At every stage of the development of French homonymy has played an important part, but its occurrence certainly increased in frequency from the end of what is called the Old French period, the second half of the XIIIth century, onwards, when the final consonants began to be no longer pronounced and *s* ceased to be heard before another consonant. If we were to investigate the older language with an eye to homonymic influences, as Gilliéron urged more than once, we should discover, no doubt, that French sensitiveness to this phenomenon has increased since 1300. The peculiar affection for clarity thus takes on another light ; there is no denying that it is so to speak organically inherent in the French mind, but one has the impression that in the field of language, and, in particular, in the matter of homonymy, its vigorous application has been due to the purely linguistic causes outlined above. In what Romance idiom, other than French, has, for example, Latin *mulgēre*, ' to milk ', collided with *molere*, ' to mill ' (both of them becoming *moudre*, via the intermediate stage *moldre*), then to disappear and be replaced by makeshifts like *traire* (lit. ' to draw '), *tirer*, *ajuster*, and the like ?

[1] Cf. E. Gamillscheg's observations in *Die Sprachgeographie* . . . , Bielefeld–Leipzig, 1928, p. 42.

The other Romance languages have been brought into the argument by Gilliéron's adversaries for a further purpose. He is reproached with confining himself to French and of neglecting entirely Italian, Spanish, and the rest. The only possible grounds for this reproach would be an attempt to make use of the results obtained by Gilliéron from the *Atlas* to draw conclusions applicable to the whole of the Romance group. In such a case, naturally, his theories would lose entirely, or at least appreciably, their demonstrative value. But, as far as we are aware, Gilliéron had no ambition to impose his doctrine upon areas outside the French territory ; in none of his works, to our knowledge, can any assertion be found that might be capable of such an interpretation. On the contrary, he was at pains to make plain, whenever occasion arose, that the field of his activity was Gallo-Romance dialectology, and that he was not concerned with other neo-Latin languages or dialects. " Dans mes dernières études ", he says, in *Pathologie et thérapeutique verbales*, III, p. 27, " je crois m'être soigneusement abstenu d'aborder tout problème dont la solution aurait pu être conditionnée par son existence au-delà du territoire que comprend l'Atlas linguistique de la France—lequel n'est qu'une ébauche d'un travail restant à faire—j'ai écarté tout problème dont la solution exigerait la connaissance personnelle d'autres langues romanes que le français. Je crois ainsi m'être préservé des erreurs inévitables qui découleraient d'une documentation très incomplète sur les parlers romans qui me sont inconnus." It might be alleged that by this frank and straightforward declaration Gilliéron merely eludes the obligation to study in certain cases the linguistic situation as it appears in other Romance areas, for it cannot be denied that at least some problems are common to several languages and require a solution applicable to all. But was any such alternative open to him ? As we have shown, Gaul was the only country to possess an atlas worthy of the name. For the other territories, the customary sources of information would have had to be used, which from the point of view of method was inadmissible. Rather would we see, in these words of Gilliéron, a reflection upon those Romanicists who claim the right to publish work upon several languages with which they are more or less superficially acquainted. We refrain from quoting here the names of distinguished writers whose books have been shown, by specialists really competent in the language, and some of them natives of the country concerned, to be full of mistakes, often of a quite elementary kind. We have the conviction that

Gilliéron had a better knowledge of certain Romance languages than many a scholar who boldly airs his views on some of their most intricate problems. But he knew how to master the field in which he felt drawn to work as completely as he was master of his own tongue, and realized likewise the need for a thorough know-ledge of the present-day vernaculars of Gaul, linguistically one of the key provinces of the empire. Only thus, he believed, could words of any weight or fruitfulness be spoken, words worthy of note in themselves and at the same time likely to serve, should occasion arise, in other linguistic fields. Whoever has read even one of Gilliéron's books knows what the knowledge of his material meant to him. It was not a matter of knowledge in the strictly intellectual sense, but of that almost instinctive comprehension, based on an innate linguistic sense, which, in the ordinary way, one can only have, if at all, in regard to one's mother tongue.

Similarly, Gilliéron has been charged with neglecting the earlier stages of the language and of taking no count of the past. Here again he confesses himself that the previous phases of the patois are not his concern. Writing on the topic of the alternation of *we* and *e* in the later development of the early French diphthong *ei*, *oi*, he says : " L'étude de cette question doit reposer avant tout sur une exploration des textes et, pour cette raison, n'est pas de notre ressort. Mais le fait qui constitue la question, sa nature de flotte-ment, la marge chronologique dans laquelle s'est mû le flottement sont certains, et ce sont là précisément les points qui intéressent l'histoire des mots désignant l'abeille " (*Abeille*, p. 196). The accusation appears this time to be justified, but not if it becomes an assertion, as it does with some of his opponents, that Gilliéron was lacking in historical sense. It should be made clear that this allegation, like that discussed above, is made by representatives of the comparativist and historical point of view, who hold that a language can only be investigated in conjunction with its kindred languages and by tracing it from its origins, from the parent tongue, to use a common, though not very scientific term. But Gilliéron has his own conception of the comparative method, and this he does apply in all his works. While his opponents attempt to study the language and dialects of France in comparison with those of other Romance lands, he is content to study the French vernaculars for their own sake, comparing them one with the other, and at the same time with the standard medium, or, more exactly, showing their mutual relations, how one dialect influences others, how all undergo the influence of the written language, how the latter accepts words from the dialects, and so forth. And it is clear that he is justified in so doing, if we are mindful of the following fact, one of the most important of the conclusions arrived at by linguistic geography, namely, that not a single dialect of present-day France goes back directly to Latin as is usually held. Is there then any reason for comparing them with this or that Romance dialect which has probably likewise undergone considerable modification and lost its direct connections with the parent tongue. And the comparison would be no less irrational even were we to admit that in other Romance territories the Romance dialects have been less influenced by the literary medium, and consequently preserve various features which we should be entitled to consider as directly continuing corresponding features of popular Latin. But this argument is of no value against the accusation that Gilliéron refrained almost on principle from comparing historically present linguistic phenomena with those of the past. It is certainly true that the method which he inaugurated has as its essential object the investigation of popular speech as it exists to-day, and it was certainly this he had in mind when making the declaration quoted above. But linguistic geography does not confine itself to a surface description of the vernaculars, but, as we have seen, develops into linguistic geology, and traces, by means of its cartographic material, the linguistic strata that lie beneath the surface. This subterraneous exploring implies a delving among increasingly ancient linguistic states, and is analogous to the work of a philologist who, in a historical study of a given language, traces in all its phases the past history of a sound, a form, or a construction. These underlying linguistic strata Gilliéron reconstructed almost exclusively from the materials provided by the *Atlas*, although, to ensure that the picture they present should still more faithfully represent the facts, it would have been advisable, nay indispensable, to utilize the knowledge obtainable concerning these earlier periods by recourse to texts. In this manner it would have been frequently possible, though, of course, not always, to determine to which period in the evolution of the French language this or that linguistic stratum, as revealed by the respective maps, corresponded. A close association of the geographical and the historical methods would undoubtedly be of benefit to both disciplines.[1] We shall see later

[1] This question was discussed at the International Congress of Linguists held at The Hague, in April, 1928, as appears from the titles of two articles published

what fine results have been achieved by Jud, working on these lines.

Among the other objections that have been raised against Gilliéron and his methods we shall discuss two that have been brought forward by L. Spitzer, himself the author of studies in linguistic geography (see below) and a great admirer of the founder of the subject. In accordance with his ' stylistic ' conception of human speech, which we have expounded above, Chap. II, p. 137 f., Spitzer accuses Gilliéron of neglecting, in his assessment of the processes of language development, the creative element, which is always in its essence individual. In an article entitled *Zur Bewertung des " Schöpferischen " in der Sprache*, in *Archivum Romanicum*, VIII (1924), p. 383,[1] the then Cologne professor of Romance philology discusses the following problem. The Béarn dialect of south-western France has lost the Latin word for ' the cock ', *gallus*, which in this region had become identical with the word for ' the cat ', *gat*. In place of *gat* from *gallus*, forms corresponding to literary French *faisan*, ' pheasant ', and *vicaire*, ' curate ', are utilized. Gilliéron notes the fact and explains it naturally as the result of the homonymic clash, and as due to the necessity for the language, if it is to fulfil its function as a means of communication and understanding between men, to eliminate the possibility of confusion between notions so familiar, and belonging both of them to the same domain of ideas, namely, those relating to the household. But he does not ask himself why it occurred to the Béarnese to resort to the names of ' pheasant ' or ' curate ' in order to designate ' the cock '. It is certain that before the confusion in the two names came about the terms ' pheasant ' and ' curate ' had already been humorously applied to ' the cock ' sporadically, and it was only when the need was felt for avoiding misapprehension that the language settled finally upon them and installed them (for an indefinite period) as the normal name of the bird without any humorous suggestion. In a word, Spitzer would have us distinguish

by G. Neckel in the Proceedings (*Actes du premier Congrès . . .* , Leiden, 1930) : *Dialektgeographie und Sprachgeschichte müssen enger zusammenwirken als bisher*, and *Sprachgeschichte und Sprachgeographie*. Again, in *Wörter und Sachen*, XII (1929), p. 390, H. Güntert talks of the desirability of a ' historische Lautgeographie ', with a view to the study of the sounds of the ancient languages on a combined historical and geographical basis, inasmuch as it is certain that linguistic zones existed also in ancient times.

[1] Cf. also *Meisterwerke der romanischen Sprachwissenschaft*, I, p. 368, where Spitzer repeats his objection that Gilliéron has an ' economic ' view of language, seeing in it nothing more than a means for satisfying a need, that of communicating ideas.

between the ' creative ', the spontaneous outcome of fancy, and the ' fixative ', the product of necessity.[1] The same linguist, *loc. cit.*, p. 350, expresses certain reservations with regard to Gilliéron's theory of ' verbal pathology ' occasioned by plethora of meaning. It does not always occur, according to Spitzer, that a word ' grows sick ' and is threatened with extinction because of the many meanings it is made to bear. Spitzer quotes as an example the word *facere*, which although it possesses innumerable meanings in the various Romance languages, has come to be used in certain circumstances instead of the word *dicere* which is semantically far from being so heavily laden. Some revision, or, at least, some limitation of the ' pathological theory ', would therefore appear to be called for.[2]

[1] Spitzer borrows this terminology from H. Sperber (see above, Chap. I, p. 77). It reminds us also of Vossler's distinction between ' language as creation ' and ' language as evolution ' (*vide supra*, p. 91 f.).

[2] Certain critics have found fault with the actual term, though it is quite in its place in the Gilliéronian doctrine. As we have seen, in Gilliéron's view, sound-change, with all its consequences, homonymy, polysemia, and the like, are causes of disease in words. Through their action the material of speech slowly but surely undergoes a process of destruction, which may be compared to the action of disease upon the human frame. This is indeed one of his most fruitful ideas, leading him as it does to study not only living words, like all linguists, but also those that are dead or dying. He thus creates a veritable biology of language, embracing its whole development, inasmuch as life presupposes death. At the same time, by investigating those words which have perished in the process of time, he discovers the causes of this destructive action. The founder of linguistic geography thus gives us a complete picture of language as it is, in its minutest details. His own reply to those who accused him of being, in his attitude to language, too like a doctor with a patient, is typical and worth quoting : " On m'a reproché (à propos de ma brochure Pathologie et thérapeutique verbales) de conduire de jeunes linguistes dans une salle d'hôpital. Qui dit mort, dit maladie ; qui dit transformation, dit guérison ; qui dit vie, dit nécessité de vivre ! Où devais-je donc les conduire ? Au bal masqué, où tourbillonnent les mots, et où les maîtres de danse, à chaque entrée et à chaque départ, enregistrent des noms sans autre formalité d'enquête sur les causes de départ ou d'arrivée, pas plus d'ailleurs que sur celles qui font changer de masque aux premiers participants ? " (*Pathologie et thérapeutique verbales*, III, p. 34). Other passages from Gilliéron relating to the biology of language are to be found quoted in H. Frei's *Grammaire des fautes*, p. 66.

It is pointed out by V. Bogrea, *Dacoromania*, III (1923), p. 856, with regard to the use of the term ' pathology ' in linguistics, that the ancient grammarians already spoke of πάθη τῆς φωνῆς. In modern times we find Ascoli, in *Corsi di glottologia*, Turin, 1870, p. 28, speaking of " continuatori etimologici ", that is resulting from ' regular ' linguistic change, and " fenomeni patologici " which transgress the ' rule '. But the term was given a certain currency in French by Littré, the author of the famous French dictionary who was a doctor before he became a lexicographer, and who used it in an article entitled *Pathologie verbale ou lésions de certains mots dans le cours de l'usage*, published subsequently in the volume *Etudes et glanures (pour faire suite à l'Histoire de la langue française)*, Paris, 1880, p. 1 f. " Sous ce titre ", he explains, " je comprends les malformations (la *cour* au lieu de la *court*, *épellation* au lieu *d'épelation*), les confusions (*éconduire* et l'ancien verbe *escondir*), les abrogations de signification, les pertes de rang (par exemple quand un mot attaché aux usages nobles tombe aux usages vulgaires ou vils), enfin les

But whatever, and however numerous, may have been the criticisms brought to bear upon the doctrine of Gilliéron, it is not to be disputed that linguistic geography has brought about a radical and beneficial revolution in linguistic studies and in our conception of the nature of language. It was not until Gilliéron's day that the plea of the neo-grammarians, formulated some fifty years ago, that pride of place should be given to the study of living language, came to be realized in such a manner as to bring our ideas of language in closer approximation to reality. Thanks to the *Linguistic Atlas of France*, and to the studies which it has inspired, we have acquired a real understanding of language life, of the unceasing movement and turmoil which goes on within it, and of the spirit which at every moment pervades it, and of which, formerly, much was spoken but little clearly understood. It is only now, thanks to linguistic geography, that Schuchardt's dictum that language is a ' continuum ' has become for all of us a palpable reality. Similarly, it has brought striking confirmation of another pronouncement of the great German linguist, who is in so many respects a precursor of Gilliéron, namely, that there are no languages that are unmixed, for the manner in which the popular dialects influence each other, and modify and are modified by the literary tongue, could not be more convincingly illustrated than has been done in the works of Gilliéron. By following up in every direction the cross-currents that weave their way through human speech, linguistic geography has shown us the part played by political, religious, and cultural circumstances, while, by seeking for the causes of change, not in the outward components of words, that is, their more or less mechanical constituents, but in the mind of the individual speaker, it has humanized language and led us back to its true and only source. Finally, it has brought us the solution of a number of problems hitherto deemed inexplicable, and that in a manner so natural as to force conviction. We may therefore subscribe whole-heartedly to Gilliéron's claim in *Pathologie et thérapeutique verbales*, II, p. 10 : " En voulant soustraire la

---

mutilations de signification " (*op. cit.*, p. 1). Darmesteter, following upon Littré, uses it in the preface to his *La vie des mots*, p. x, to designate the restriction of meaning suffered by certain French words. Though neither in Littré nor in Darmesteter do we find any trace of Gilliéron's use of the term, it is worth pointing out that one is at times reminded of Gilliéron by certain points in Darmesteter's chapter, *Comment meurent les mots*, *op. cit.*, p. 151 f., and particularly p. 162 f. of the 1928 edition. Some influence of Darmesteter on Gilliéron is therefore fairly safely to be presumed. Cp. also, on this question of terminology and the attitude it implies, what we have said above, pp. 25–6, on Curtius's conception of ' analogy '.

linguistique à l'examen de la géographie on la diminue d'un facteur puissant—le plus puissant peut-être—qui peut lui donner le droit d'être considérée comme une véritable science."

Gilliéron's doctrine has points in common, now with one, now with another of the linguistic schools which we are discussing in the present volume. In Chapter II we have already insisted upon similarities it possesses with the 'idealism' of Karl Vossler, in the importance it awards to the psychological factor in the creation and evolution of linguistic forms. A further point of resemblance between Gilliéron and the 'idealistic' school is that both concern themselves with speech ('la parole', 'das Sprechen'), not with language as a system ('la langue', 'die Sprache'), or, in other words, both study the human activity of language at a given moment, under well determined conditions, Vossler on the basis of the language of literary artists, as his interests are aesthetic, Gilliéron on the basis of the patois, as represented by his informants and their reaction to his enquiries, the only direct source of information open to him. L. Spitzer, *Meisterwerke der romanischen Sprachwissenschaft*, I, p. 368, finds yet another resemblance between the two scholars. After observing that Gilliéron, on his 'Columbus voyage', had sought to discover the real life of language among the dialects, but had landed on the banks of the literary language, which in reality flows into and feeds the dialects, Spitzer goes on to say : " The dialectologist Gilliéron—and this from the point of view of theory speaks against the study of folk culture and dialect in combination—has led us to an insight into the nature of the ruling standard tongue, and latterly his investigations have assumed a stylistic bent similar to those of Vossler, though he lacks the latter's aesthetic sense." Again, there are points in common, both in outlook and method, between linguistic geography and the doctrines of F. de Saussure of whom we shall speak more fully in the next chapter. Like Saussure, Gilliéron concerns himself in the main with the static aspects of language ; his linguistic is descriptive, or, in the Saussurian terminology, 'synchronic' ; he does not study language in its earlier phases, nor see it in its past development. If he frequently does take into consideration earlier conditions, it is due to the need for distinguishing one linguistic stratum from another. His conception of language is also analogous to that of Saussure, in the sense that they both envisage human speech as a mere means of comprehension between individuals, taking no thought for the artistic features which it undeniably possesses. In this respect they are both akin to the neo-grammarians. They are at the same time, both of them, avowed rationalists, appreciating man's linguistic activity solely from the angle of reason. One is inclined to attribute this common bias to their common French origin, for, as we shall see in the next chapter, almost all the representatives of the sociological conception of language are Frenchmen, and, with few exceptions, all of them see in it an instrument for the communication of ideas, and that alone. It may be that here is to be sought the reason why homonymy plays such an outstanding part in the Gilliéronian system ; not because the French as speaking individuals are more keenly intent than other folk upon clarity, the need for which has its source clearly in common reason or reasoning consciousness, but that Gilliéron, a Frenchman, and consequently a rationalist, both by temperament and education, discovers the working of reason in the life of language where the rest of us would not be disposed to admit it.

To terminate our account of the founder of linguistic geography we would quote appreciations of him and his work by a number of specially qualified scholars. A. Terracher, discussing *L'Abeille* in *Bulletin de la Société de linguistique de Paris*, XXI (1918–19), p. 147 f., after observing that there is no one to compare with Gilliéron in knowledge of the *Linguistic Atlas of France*, goes on to say : " Voilà sans doute pourquoi les travaux de M. Gilliéron sont si riches et les études similaires [i.e. of others who have worked in the field of linguistic geography] si pauvres, par comparaison. Voilà aussi pourquoi les raisonnements de M. Gilliéron apparaissent souvent touffus : des rapprochements qui déconcertent à première vue ne sont que le signe d'un commerce intime, prolongé et unique avec l'*Atlas*." (*Loc. cit.*, p. 148.) M. Terracher then speaks of certain criticisms voiced by Gilliéron's opponents upon his drawing conclusions concerning the speech of a whole locality from the answers of a single individual, or upon his reconstructing the history of words not within the bounds of a single dialect but for the whole of France : " En réalite ", he says, " ce sont deux conceptions fondamentalement opposées qui se heurtent : l'une, celle de M. Gilliéron, affirme que les détails ne s'éclairent que par l'ensemble (cf. pp. 118–19, etc.) ; l'autre, la conception courante, espère inconsciemment construire l'ensemble avec les détails." " Les romanistes, dialectologues ou non, seraient en tout cas particulièrement mal venus à protester contre le point de vue de M. Gilliéron, car presque toutes leurs études de détail ne font que mettre en œuvre une conception d'ensemble . . . qu'ils n'ont pas inventée, qu'ils n'ont, pour la plupart, jamais examinée ni discutée, dont trop souvent ils n'ont même pas conscience. Si M. Gilliéron se trompait entièrement, il rendrait encore aux études romanes un service immense en apportant de la romanisation, de la vie des parlers populaires et des langues littéraires, et même de la phonétique, une idée générale très différente de celle qu'on accepte d'ordinaire et qui, depuis Diez, s'est beaucoup moins heureusement modifiée qu'on ne pourrait croire ou souhaiter." (*Loc. cit.*, p. 151.) " Parce que Diez a constitué—et était tenu de constituer—la linguistique romane sur le patron de la linguistique indo-européenne de son temps, les romanistes préfèrent encore reconstruire le latin au lieu de l'étudier, et semblent vraiment refuser un peu trop aux langues romanes toute puissance vitale, alors qu'elles vivent pourtant depuis un nombre respectable de siècles." (*Loc. cit.*, pp. 152–3.) " Au total, il ne s'agit de rien moins que d'un renversement des méthodes reçues : M. Gilliéron en arrive à peu près à mettre au premier rang des lois qui président aux transformations lexicologiques et phonétiques l'étymologie populaire, les mots dits savants, la conscience linguistique, etc., que les ouvrages faits ' selon la bonne méthode ' mentionnent ordinairement comme des exceptions aux lois ; et ces lois traditionnelles de correspondance phonétique lui apparaissent—du moins sous la forme courante qu'elles revêtent—comme un leurre qui, dans le cas du français littéraire, s'expliqueraient principalement par la ' reprise de contact ' avec le latin, surtout à l'époque de la Renaissance (pp. 14, 59 *sqq.*, 200, etc.)." (*Loc. cit.*, pp. 153–54.) " Depuis le triomphe universel, légitime et nécessaire des idées et des méthodes de Diez (ou de J. Grimm ?), il ne s'est trouvé que de trop rares romanistes pour faire des réserves sur ce que le développement de la linguistique y a encore ajouté de mécanisme : si la plupart des dissidents (notamment Ascoli et Schuchardt, dont les idées offrent plus d'une analogie avec celles de M. Gilliéron)[1] ont été surtout préoccupés des influences ethnographiques qui ont pu agir sur le développement phonétique des langues romanes, c'est bien à eux, au fond, que se rattache le créateur de la ' géologie linguistique ', quoiqu'il élève sa protestation sur un tout autre terrain et qu'il la fasse au nom de principes moins fugitifs s'appliquant à des faits plus tangibles. *Opportet haereses esse.*" (*Loc. cit.*, p. 156.)

Gilliéron's study of the names of ' the bee ' also called forth an

---

[1] On these analogies cp. N. Maccarrone, *Rev. ling. rom.*, VI (1930), pp. 5–6.

important review from K. Jaberg, published in *Romania*, XLVI (1920), p. 121 f., of which we shall summarize or quote certain characteristic passages. " D'ailleurs l'importance extrême qu'il faut attribuer au livre de M. G. me paraît résider moins dans les solutions qu'il donne à des problèmes particuliers, quelque passionnante qu'en soit la discussion, que dans la méthode qu'il emploie pour y parvenir et dans les idées générales que lui suggère l'étude de ces problèmes " (p. 121). Gilliéron's volume realizes in the completest manner possible the etymological ideal expressed by Schuchardt in the words : ". . . We do not etymologize as though we were seeking to solve a riddle or to guess a charade, the goal which is ever before us is a continuous word-history." (*Zeitschrift f. rom. Phil.*, XXV, 1901, p. 615.) " Chercher le noyau des idées de M. G. dans Diez (Meyer-Lübke, *Literaturblatt f. germ. u. rom. Phil.* 1919, p. 372), c'est attribuer à Léonard de Vinci le mérite d'avoir inventé l'aéroplane. Ni Léonard ni Diez n'ont besoin d'être grandis par l'amoindrissement de leurs successeurs " (p. 123, note 1). The principles set forth with some detail in the preceding pages were arrived at by Gilliéron by methods that grew out of the use of the *Atlas*, and these are based on two essential ideas : the coincidence of the area of extension of two linguistic phenomena and geographical solidarity or interdependence. Thus, in the south-west of France the words *épi* and *épine* have both disappeared : the area of their disappearance coincides with that of the fall of intervocalic *n*. The latter phenomenon is thus the cause of the loss of these two words, for *épine* became a homonym of *épi* when the *n* ceased to be pronounced. Geographical interdependence is further illustrated by the following example. At points 184 and 191 of the *Atlas* the word for ' a bee ' is *mouche*, and nowhere else in France is this term to be found. Between these points is No. 190, which gives us *mouche* with the meaning of ' midget ' (Fr. *moucheron*) ; again, in no other locality on the *Atlas* do we find this usage. This implies that there is some connection between the phenomena presented by the first two points and by the third, a geographical interdependence or solidarity, the explanation being, in the light of all the facts, that *mouche* ' abeille ' is a ' dediminutivized ' throw-off from *mouchette* ' abeille ' (see above, p. 192), and that *mouchette* ' midget ', in the neighbouring patois, has somewhat mechanically followed suit. ". . . Personne n'a jamais eu une intuition aussi profonde de la vie intime du langage, intuition basée sur une expérience de quarante ans passés à pénétrer les secrets des parlers

populaires de la France." " L'isolement scientifique dans lequel
vit le maître a ses dangers ; mais puisque c'est cet isolement qui
lui a permis d'ouvrir de nouveaux horizons à la science, qui oserait
lui en faire un grief ? " (p. 130).

We have already stated that from the very beginning the significance of Gilliéron's work had been appreciated by A. Meillet,
who consequently supported him and encouraged him in every
way. As an Indo-Europeanist, Meillet was of necessity a comparative and historical philologist, the comparative and historical
method being the only one applicable to the Indo-Germanic tongues,
so many of which have long since ceased to be spoken. This has
not prevented him—unlike a number of Romanicists who, as
students of living languages, might have shown a little more
receptiveness—from recognizing the great importance of the new
discipline, from the point of view both of method and of results,
and its value, not only to general linguistic theory, but also as
applicable to Indo-European philology, despite the fact that the
latter, when compared with Romance philology, is, or appears
to be, quite differently circumstanced. We proceed to quote some
of Meillet's observations from *La méthode comparative en linguistique
historique*, Oslo, 1925, pp. 60–71. They carry particular weight,
especially as they concern the relations between linguistic geography
and the comparative and historical study of the Indo-European
languages. " C'est que la comparaison a trouvé, dans ces enquêtes
[*sc.* dialect enquiry, conducted in the field] un instrument de
travail supérieur à tout ce qu'elle possédait et précisément adapté
à ses besoins. Pour la première fois, on avait, clairement présenté,
un ensemble de données immédiatement comparables entre elles,
et réparties sur tout le domaine étudié. Quiconque a fait des
travaux de grammaire comparée sait combien on souffre de ce
que les faits rapprochés offrent des différences de niveau dont il
faut faire abstraction : le comparatiste qui travaille sur les langues
indo-européennes se sert de données dont les dates s'étendent sur
un espace de quelque trois mille ans, qui abondent à certains
moments et manquent tout à fait à d'autres, qui existent pour une
région, alors que pour tel autre domaine toute indication manque.[1]
Avant de faire un rapprochement, il en faut critiquer en détail

---

[1] These remarks are also applicable, in a certain measure, to the comparative
grammar of the Romance languages. We have to take into account that there
are written documents in French dating from the ninth century, whereas there is
nothing in Rumanian before the sixteenth. Seven hundred years is a large gap
in the comparatively short period covered by our studies.

tous les éléments. Dans la grammaire comparée des langues indo-européennes, il y a peu de rapprochements qui ne boitent pas de quelque côté " (*op. cit.*, p. 65). " Partout où l'on a pu appliquer la méthode géographique, elle a donné lieu à des progrès décisifs. Elle exige des enquêtes aussi étendues qu'il est possible et l'utilisation de toutes les données qu'on possède sur l'ensemble d'un domaine linguistique. La méthode comparative gagne par là une précision, une étendue et une aisance jusqu'alors imprévues " (*ibid.*, p. 70). Already at an earlier date, in *Linguistique historique et linguistique générale*, Paris, 1921, Meillet had made many judicious and pointed observations concerning Gilliéron's *Abeille*, some of which we cannot refrain from reproducing. " Mais il n'y a pas d'homme qui, depuis qu'il enseigne, ait eu plus d'action sur tous ceux qui ont étudié l'histoire des parlers gallo-romans, l'histoire des langues romanes, et, finalement, toute la linguistique historique en général " (*op. cit.*, p. 305). " En une certaine mesure—il ne faut naturellement pas exagérer—chaque village de France a eu, depuis l'époque latine, son développement linguistique propre " (*ibid.*, p. 306). " Dès lors, si, au lieu de comparer quinze ou vingt dialectes fortement distincts les uns des autres, mal localisés et dont les rapports mutuels sont mal connus ou inconnus, on peut comparer des centaines de parlers très voisins, ayant conservé d'une manière certaine leur ancienne répartition géographique, on dispose d'un moyen de recherche bien supérieur, et l'on a chance de déterminer avec une précision toute nouvelle l'histoire de l'ensemble des parlers étudiés." " Jusqu'ici on a fait la grammaire comparée des langues romanes avec la méthode qu'imposent les conditions de fait, assez fâcheuses, où se trouve la grammaire comparée des langues indo-européennes : aucune donnée sur la langue initiale ; un petit nombre de groupes de langues très différentes entre elles ; ces quelques données permettent surtout de saisir certaines grandes lignes, le détail n'étant perceptible que dans quelques rares cas spécialement favorables " (*ibid.*, p. 308).

Leo Spitzer, in *Meisterwerke der romanischen Sprachwissenschaft*, I, p. 368, after bringing forward certain theoretical objections to linguistic atlases, and pointing out that Gilliéron's conception of language as a mere means of understanding between men was one-sided, goes on to say : " All the attempts, such for example as those made by Meyer-Lübke in his Romance Grammar, or by Ascoli in his dialect investigations, to link up dialect with Latin and to make of it a purely autochthonous development of the latter, have thereby [*sc.* by linguistic geography] been brought to nought—Gilliéron has produced practical proof of Schuchardt's theoretical conception of word migration and of ' sound-laws '. He was the first to propound the question : ' Why in just this locality does just this linguistic phenomenon occur ? ' A comparison of his book on the genealogy of the names for ' the bee ' with, say, Meyer-Lübke's essay on Prov. *beko,* ' bee ', ' wasp ' (*Zeitschr. f. rom. Phil.,* 29, p. 402 f.), where material from Gilliéron's *Atlas* is also used, and where the effort is all towards making the forms appearing in the *Atlas* ' etymologically transparent ', is illuminating. We are thus led to the conviction that it was Gilliéron's philosophy of language which prompted him to compose his *Atlas,* rather than that his philosophy of language is a result of the *Atlas* which he ' just happened ' (?) to construct on geological lines.''

Finally, we quote certain words of one of Gilliéron's fellow-workers, Mario Roques : '' Que ceux dont Gilliéron a parfois parlé avec rudesse fassent aujourd'hui effort pour imaginer cette lutte intime de son esprit contre les vieilles idoles linguistiques, son éblouissement devant la vérité entrevue . . . il restera de lui deux magnifiques dons qu'il a fait à la France et à la science : l'Atlas, la plus sûre enquête qui ait jamais été faite sur le langage, base nécessaire de toute autre enquête sur les parlers de France, de toute étude future sur l'évolution de ces parlers, et premier modèle de toute enquête ultérieure sur quelque parler que ce soit ; et ce principe, dont il est un peu vain de se demander s'il fonde une science ou une méthode nouvelle, mais auquel la linguistique ne pourra plus désormais faillir, que la répartition des faits du langage est elle-même un fait qu'il faut expliquer et par elle-même est génératrice d'explications '' (Cit. L. Spitzer, *op. cit.,* pp. 367–8).

★　　★　　★

NOTE.—We append, in chronological order, a list of books, articles, etc., some of which have already been mentioned, as a contribution towards a bibliography of the subject of linguistic geography.

E. Tappolet, *Über die Bedeutung der Sprachgeographie, mit besonderer Berücksichtigung französischer Mundarten,* extract from *Aus romanischen Sprachen und Literaturen. Festgabe für Heinrich Morf,* Halle a.S., 1905 (32 pages) ; K. Jaberg, *Sprachgeographie. Beitrag zum Verständnis des Atlas linguistique de la France,* Aarau, 1908 ; J. Huber, *Sprachgeographie. Ein Rückblick und Ausblick,* in *Bulletin de dialectologie romane,* I (1909), p. 89 f. ; G. Bertoni, *A proposito di geografia linguistica,* in *Atti e memorie della R. Deputazione di Storia Patria per le Provincie Modenese,* Serie V, vol. VII, Modena, 1911 (ten-page extract) ; A. Bayot, *La géographie linguistique,* in *Bulletin du dictionnaire wallon*, VI (1911), p. 65 f. ; M. de Montoliu, *La geografía lingüística* in *Estudio*, I (1912), p. 24 f., and II (1913), p. 76 f. ; K. Jaberg, *Die neuere Forschung auf dem Gebiete der romanischen Sprachgeographie*, in *Die Geisteswissenschaften*, I (1913–14), col. 487 f. ; L. Spitzer, *Die Sprachgeographie. Kritische Zusammenfassung (1909–14)*, in *Revue de dialectologie romane*, VI (1914), p. 318 f. ; G. Bertoni, *Studî di geografia linguistica*, in *Archivum Romanicum*, I (1917), p. 258 f. (this article is a kind of general survey of a number of studies) ; J. Feller, *L'évolution de la géographie linguistique*, in *Bulletin du dictionnaire wallon*, XII (1917), p. 73 f. ; L. Gauchat et J. Jeanjaquet, *Bibliographie linguistique de la Suisse romande*, II, Neuchâtel, 1920, p. 158 f. ; K. Jaberg, *Romania*, XLVI (1920), p. 121 f. ; A. Meillet, *Linguistique historique et linguistique générale*, Paris, 1921, p. 305 f. ; B. A. Terracini, *Questioni di metodo nella linguistica storica*, in *Atene e Roma*, nuova serie II (1921), Nos. 1–3, 4–6 (38-page extract) ; Fr. Schürr, *Sprachwissenschaft und Zeitgeist*, Marburg a.L., 1922, p. 72 f. ; A. Dauzat, *La géographie linguistique*, Paris, 1922 ; W. von Wartburg, *Französisches etymologisches Wörterbuch*, Bonn, 1922, p. 1 f. ; J. Feller, *L'évolution de la géographie linguistique*, Liège, 1923 (*Extrait du Bulletin du dictionnaire général de la langue wallonne*) ; I. A. Candrea, *Constatări în domeniul dialectologiei*, in *Grai şi suflet*, I (1923–4), p. 169 f. ; G. Bertoni, *La geografia linguistica*, in *Rivista della Società filologica friulana*, V (1924), p. 214 f. (reprint of an article published previously in *La Cultura*, III [1923–4], p. 404 f.) ; A. Meillet, *La méthode comparative en linguistique historique*, Oslo, 1925, p. 60 f. ; W. Meyer-Lübke, *Revue de linguistique romane*, I (1925), p. 22 f. ; A. Philippide, *Originea Romînilor*, I, Iaşi, 1925, p. 380 f. ; Fr. Ribezzo, *Metodo storico e metodo geografico allo stato presente della scienza del linguaggio*, in *Rivista indo-greco-italica di filologia-linguaantichità*, IX (1925), p. 277 f. ; Johs. Brøndum-Nielsen, *Dialekter og Dialektforskning*, Copenhagen, 1927 ; A. Dauzat, *Les patois*, Paris, 1927 (this book may be considered as complementary to the author's *La géographie linguistique*, mentioned above) ; Sever Pop, *Buts et méthodes des enquêtes dialectales*, Paris, 1927 (reviewed by L. Spitzer, *Literaturblatt f. germ. u. rom. Phil.*, XLIX [1928], col. 189 f., and C. Tagliavini, *Archivum Romanicum*, XIII [1929], p. 579 f.) ; G. Bertoni, *Geografia linguistica*, in *Archivum Romanicum*, XII (1928), p. 333 f. ; A. Dauzat, *Les atlas linguistiques et la cartographie*, in *Mercure de France*, 15 déc., 1928, p. 592 f. ; E. Gamillscheg, *Die Sprachgeographie und ihre Ergebnisse für die allgemeine Sprachwissenschaft*, Bielefeld–Leipzig, 1928 ; E. Platz, *Géographie panlinguistique*, in *Jahrbuch der luxemburgischen Sprachgesellschaft*, 1928, p. 63 f. ; W. J. Doroszewski, *Betrachtungen über die Methode der Linguistischen Geographie*, in *Prace filologiczne*, XIV (1929), p. 154 f. ; Al. Rosetti, *Jules Gilliéron şi geografia linguistică*, in *Viaţa romînească*, Jan., 1929, p. 20 f. ; O. Bloch, *J. Gilliéron et l'Atlas linguistique de la France*, in *Revue de Paris*, 1er févr., 1929 (16-page extract) ; A. Terracher, *L'histoire des langues et la géographie linguistique*, Zaharoff Lecture, Oxford, 1929 ; Th. Frings, *Sprachgeographie und Kulturgeographie*, in *Zeitschrift für Deutschkunde*, 1930, p. 564 f. ; F. Karg, *Mundartgeographie*, in *Archiv für Kulturgeschichte*, XX (1930), p. 222 f. ; Al. Rosetti, *Linguistica în cercetarea monografică*, in *Viaţa romînească*, July–August, 1930, p. 69 f. ; N. S. Trubetzkoi, *Phonologie und Sprachgeographie*, in *Travaux du Cercle linguistique de Prague*, IV (1931), p. 228 f. ; G. Bottiglioni, *Le inchieste dialettali e gli atlanti linguistici*, in *Atti della XX riunione della Società Italiana per il progresso delle scienze*, Milan, 1932, and *Il valore unitario e quello obiettivo degli atlanti linguistici*, in *Annali della Scuola Normale Superiore di Pisa*, ser. II, vol. I, Bologna, 1932 ; Ulrich Leo, *Dialektgeographie und romanische Sprachwissenschaft*, in *Archiv f. das Studium der neueren Sprachen*, CLXII (1932), p. 203 f. ; Jos. Schrijnen, *Essai de bibliographie de géographie linguistique générale*, Nimeguen, 1933 ; K. Jaberg, *Aspects géographiques du langage*, Paris, 1936.

On the occasion of Gilliéron's death a number of obituary notices were published, many of them of considerable interest both with regard to his teachings and to his remarkable human qualities. The following are particularly worthy of mention : K. Jaberg, in the newspaper *Der Bund*, Berne, 4th May, 1926 ; J. U. Hubschmied, *Neue Zürcher Zeitung*, 6th May, 1926 ; E. Tappolet, *Basler Nachrichten* (date unspecified) ; L. Spitzer, *Zeitschrift f. fr. Spr. u. Lit.*, XLVIII (1925–6), p. 506 f. ; B. A. Terracini, *Archivio glottologico italiano, sezione neo-latina*, XX (1926), p. 151 f. ; L. Clédat, *Revue de philologie française et de littérature*, XXXVIII (1926), p. 87 f. ; Iorgu Iordan, *Arhiva*, XXXIII (1926), p. 223 f. ;

A. Terracher, *Revue de linguistique romane*, II (1926), p. 1 f. ; M. Roques, *Romania*, LII (1926), p. 219 f. ; idem, *Jules Gilliéron. Notes biographiques et bibliographie*, in *Annuaire de l'Ecole Pratique des Hautes-Etudes* (section des sciences historiques et philologiques), 1926–7, p. 3 f. (reviewed by L. Spitzer, *Literaturblatt f. germ. u. rom. Phil.*, XLVIII [1927], col. 111 f.) ; S. Pop, *Dacoromania*, IV (1924–6), p. 1531 f. ; A. Griera, *Butlletí de dialectologia catalana*, XVI (1928), p. 72 f. Cp. also the reviews of studies in linguistic geography and of atlases mentioned later in the present volume.

★   ★   ★

The influence exercised by linguistic geography as conceived and practised by Gilliéron appears in its full light when we consider the attention it has received, and is still receiving, **Other French Studies in Linguistic Geography** at the hands of a number of specialists of all countries, who are vigorously using the tools that the master forged. We shall pass under review the principal studies which treat of the Romance languages, and the attempts that have been made to apply the method to other domains, and shall mention finally a number of Atlases which are in process of publication or in the making. We can naturally not attempt to exhaust the subject, as this would be a wellnigh impossible task. It will suffice if we are able to show, on the one hand, the extraordinary influence already exercised upon linguistic science by the new method, and thus justify the assertion that since the time of Diez there has not been a more fundamental revolution in our field of study, and on the other, the innovations which Gilliéron's disciples and successors have introduced into the subject, in their endeavour to give still greater perfection to his handiwork, and to ensure its growth and progress in conformity with the demands of our time.

Of pupils in the strict sense of the word, having actually followed the famous lectures in the Ecole des Hautes-Etudes, Gilliéron had no great number. The subject matter of his classes was arid and abstruse, unattractive therefore, and the manner of his exposition was awkward and completely devoid of form. That is why, no doubt, the majority of his audience was composed of foreigners.[1] The French are too keen in their appreciation of the purely formal

---

[1] In 1925, his audience of ten students was made up as follows : 5 Swiss, 1 Pole, 1 Russian, 1 Anglo-Saxon, 1 Rumanian, and 1 Frenchman ! Even the latter, judging by his name, must have been either of Swiss or Alsatian origin. Cf. on this topic the remarks of Gilliéron himself, in *Pathologie et thérapeutique verbales*, IV, p. 20, note.

qualities of a lecture, as of printed studies, for them to have enjoyed those difficult ' lectures ', which Gilliéron, with his almost barbarous style, delivered weekly in the ' Salle Gaston Paris ', for two hours on end. We shall begin, however, with his French pupils, particularly as they have shown themselves, in the main, to be close followers of the master.

The oldest of Gilliéron's French disciples, though not actually his pupil, is Georges Millardet, who later was to reveal himself as

Georges Millardet

an opponent of linguistic geography (cp. above, p. 179, where we discussed his *Linguistique et dialectologie romanes*). He was a student of E. Bourciez's, to whom he dedicates one of the studies mentioned below, which explains both his affection for ' la phonétique ' and the historical method, that dates from the foundation of our studies, and the fact that he could become so lukewarm, nay even hostile to Gilliéron and to linguistic geography.[1] Hence, too, the combination we find in his work of the traditional methods with the new. He began with a comprehensive linguistic study of the Landes region, in south-west France, publishing in the same year : *Petit Atlas linguistique d'une région des Landes. Contribution à la dialectologie gasconne*, Toulouse-Paris, 1910 ; *Etudes de dialectologie landaise. Le développement des phonèmes additionnels*, Toulouse, 1910 ; *Recueil de textes des anciens dialectes landais*, Paris, 1910.

The *Atlas* comprises 573 maps of the Landes area, where the local vernaculars belong to the Gascon dialect. In choosing this area, the author hoped, by investigating an extensive stretch of country devoid of political, geographical, and economic unity, to find all the more readily a solution to the vexed question of the existence of dialects. His questionnaire contained 800 items : 400 single words, and, in addition, 400 phrases, which shows his particular interest in syntax and meaning development. The enquiry lasted four years, with interruptions, and was conducted on the spot. The replies recorded numbered 68,000. As the basis of the investigation he took the communes (85 all told), with the principal ' bourg ' acting as a nucleus. Smaller hamlets were not neglected, but they are not numerous in this part of France. In addition to the maps, the *Atlas* contains a number of sound-charts ; as the author puts it,

---

[1] Despite this, we find in the earlier books by Millardet expressions of warm appreciation of the *Atlas linguistique de la France*, which he calls ' magnifique ', of Gilliéron's method of collecting the material, " the drawbacks to which should not be exaggerated ", of the questionnaire, on which he based his own, and the like. Cp. also N. Maccarrone, *Rev. ling. rom.*, I (1925), p. 20 f.

he used the methods of the natural sciences, observation and experiment. The maps are the result of the former, the sound-charts of the latter, for he conducted his investigations with the help of the artificial palate and a recorder, as used by Abbé Rousselot in *Les modifications du langage* . . . and *Principes de phonétique expérimentale*. The whole is preceded by an introduction, giving information concerning the area explored, the inhabitants and their speech, the methods adopted, his informants, and the like.

The material thus collected was worked up, from the phonetic point of view, in the second volume, although the author confined himself to a particular set of phenomena, namely, sound-insertion, epenthesis, prothesis, glide-sounds, and supporting sounds. These phenomena, which are all ' additional ' in character, are to be attributed, when they are not extra-phonetic in their origin, to one common source, namely, the tendency inherent in the majority of sounds towards segmentation. The simplest sound sets in motion a number of speech organs, and if these do not function in complete concordance one with the other, as indeed happens in the majority of cases, gradually new sounds are brought into being. Or, again, it may happen that the speech organs do not cease to function in time, and continue to articulate, producing embryos of sounds which with the help of neighbouring sounds take on ultimately an independent existence. Finally, the author attempts to date these phenomena by means of the texts contained in his third volume. As he says himself, in *Etudes de dialectologie landaise*, he has thus applied all the methods of linguistic enquiry, with a view to discovering to what conclusions they would lead him : (*a*) the critical study of historical or literary documents (" la plus ancienne des trois méthodes, celle à qui la science doit la plupart de ses certitudes actuelles ") ; (*b*) the experimental method, new but indispensable ; (*c*) the geographical method (" rajeunie aujourd'hui par une école qui lui a communiqué une impulsion et une portée nouvelles "[1]) (*op. cit.*, pp. 12–13). The first of these enabled him to determine the chronology of the phenomena, the second helped him to understand the mechanism of the formation of the new sounds, the last disclosed the extension in space of the linguistic facts.

[1] This would appear to imply that Millardet did not consider Gilliéron as the founder of linguistic geography. Cp. the remarks of Meillet (quoted above, p. 153, n. 2), who sees Rousselot as the founder of linguistic geography and Gilliéron of linguistic geology.

The author's conclusions are of interest (*ibid.*, p. 215 f.). He observes everywhere an infinite variety in the phenomena investigated, although the territory explored was comparatively restricted. He notes, similarly, an almost complete disorder and absence of regularity. He attributes the diversity to the following causes : either an old ' law ' had ceased to operate, or a new tendency had arisen, but had not reached its full development. But despite the disorder and diversity, certain general ' laws ' concerning the spread of the ' organic ', or physiological phonetic phenomena, can none the less be established, as is proved by the ' isophones ', or soundlines drawn across the maps. Millardet would explain the existence of such ' laws ' as follows : The physiological modifications of sound are produced unconsciously, but they develop and ultimately become conscious ; thenceforward they tend to stabilize and become general, thus giving rise to certain norms or ' laws '.

It is plain from the foregoing account[1] that Millardet endeavours to reconcile the traditional methods with those adopted by Gilliéron, and at the same time the traditionalist outlook with that of the linguistic geographer. Whether, and in what measure he succeeds, we cannot here discuss. In any case, it cannot be doubted that the author's leanings are all towards the older school, or more exactly, the new method has merely served to buttress up with new arguments the accepted doctrines. His attitude towards Gilliéron and linguistic geography, as manifested later in *Linguistique et dialectologie romanes*, thus comes as no surprise.

Ch. Bruneau shares with Millardet a special interest in sounds, and, like him, also investigates both the past and present phases of the dialects he explores. On the other hand, he

Charles Bruneau shows himself to be a much more faithful adherent of Gilliéron's doctrine, although he does not abandon the traditional manner of presenting the dialect material in glossary form. He too explored his field personally, and used a questionnaire supplemented by experimental work, as Millardet did. His results were published in two volumes, entitled *Enquête linguistique sur les patois d'Ardenne* ; volume I, containing the words from *A*

---

[1] Millardet's books were reviewed by, among others, A. Meillet, *Bull. Soc. Ling.*, XVI (1909–10), p. cccxxvii f., M. Grammont, *Rev. des langues romanes*, XLVI (1913), p. 481 f., and E. Bourciez, *Annales du Midi*, XXIII (1011), p. 79 f. Meillet praises the wealth of material collected, but regrets that the author did not pay more attention to ' objects ', as distinct from mere names. The use of the term for ' barley ' to designate ' corn ', for example, is obviously a matter of ' Realien '.

to *L*, came out in 1914 (Paris), volume II (*M–Y*) in 1926. The author visited 93 villages in the Ardennes department, and the Belgian provinces of Namur and Luxemburg, using the questionnaire compiled by Gilliéron for the *Linguistic Atlas of France*, but with modifications to fit the special requirements of his own area. In his enquiry he departed from the Gilliéronian principle of never extorting a reply, and did all in his power to obtain a definite answer to every question put. Further, when he thought it necessary or interesting to do so, he availed himself of material contained in certain ' mémoires ' composed by school teachers in the Ardennes, on the occasion of an education conference held in 1910. He has thus, so to speak, combined the methods of direct personal investigation and of enquiry through correspondence. The replies to the questionnaire are grouped alphabetically, as in a dictionary ; at the head of each article figures the standard French word, then follow the dialect equivalents, each with a number standing for the village where it occurs. Many of the articles are very substantial, as the author does not confine himself to reproducing the words, but adds a good deal of linguistic information about them. In this manner an article has the same value as a linguistic map, from which it differs only in the method of presentation. Indeed, from time to time we are actually provided with a small map (89 in all) showing the distribution of certain phonetic or lexical features, similar to some of the maps in Millardet's *Atlas* mentioned above.

The material of the *Enquête* was worked up in a book entitled *Etude phonétique des patois d'Ardenne*, Paris, 1913, the general plan of which is described by the author as follows (p. 3) : " J'ai donc étudié successivement les différents phonèmes que présentent, à l'époque actuelle, les patois d'Ardenne, et, après une description aussi précise que possible de ces phonèmes, j'ai indiqué les principaux cas dans lesquels on les rencontre." But he concerns himself also with the past history of the vernaculars he investigates, and is thus led to draw upon ancient documents belonging to the region, a number of which he publishes at the end of the volume under the heading *Chartes de Mézières en langue vulgaire*. Thus, as he goes on to say, " L'Etude phonétique des patois d'Ardenne présente donc un tableau complet des principaux caractères dialectaux de la région ardennaise à l'époque ancienne et à l'époque moderne. J'essayerai, après avoir étudié successivement chaque fait, de faire la synthèse des conclusions de détail que j'aurai établies et de dégager les tendances phonétiques générales qui ont dominé toutes les évolutions particulières " (*ibid.*, p. 7). These ' general tendencies ' of the phonology of the region are set out in his conclusion, p. 534 f.

Bruneau's third work, *La limite des dialectes wallon, champenois et lorrain en Ardenne*, Paris, 1913,[1] is closely related to the two mentioned above. This study is of considerable interest in regard to certain problems raised by linguistic geography. The dialects of the Ardennes region are proved to be the outcome of a threefold series of causes, linguistic, social, and historical. Linguistically, they are independent in phonology and morphology, but in other respects, particularly in vocabulary, they are not clearly outlined ; they lack stability and have been continually undermined by the standard literary language. Socially, they form a group continually influenced by neighbouring areas with which they are in close contact, while, historically, they have been conditioned and constituted in a large measure by the migrations of peoples and other vicissitudes which have befallen the territory they occupy. Owing to their geographical position, the dialects investigated by Bruneau fall into three groups, belonging to three distinct linguistic zones, Walloon, Champenois, and Lorrain, whose boundaries, once well defined, are now shifting and uncertain. " La limite dialectale d'un caractère phonétique n'est pas nette. Les villages voisins de la frontière phonétique mélangent, ou échangent, les formes : les différences d'articulation s'atténuent ; des voyelles intermédiaires créent entre deux voyelles extrêmes une sorte de transition. La limite d'un caractère phonétique dépend aussi de la vitalité du mot étudié : elle varie sensiblement avec chaque mot " (*loc. cit.*, p. 179). Like the sounds, the morphology, which, as we have seen, the author also investigates, reveals itself as more or less autonomous. But here, too, he bears witness to ". . . la confusion des formes dans l'intérieur de chaque dialecte et entre les différents dialectes. Cette confusion provient de trois causes principales : l'invasion des formes françaises ; les évolutions phonétiques, qui ont multiplié, par exemple, les évolutions d'une voyelle unique (-*o*, désinence de la 3ᵉ personne du pluriel de l'indicatif présent) ; et surtout les créations analogiques " (*ibidem*, p. 230). His conclusion with regard to the much-discussed question of dialect boundaries, and the existence of dialects is set forth quite early in the book : " Il n'y a donc pas de dialectes ; et, s'il y en avait, nos cartes seraient impuissantes à les

---

[1] Cp. also, Ch. Bruneau, *La Champagne* : *dialecte ancien et patois moderne* (*Bibliographie critique*), in *Revue de linguistique romane*, V (1929), p. 71 f.

reproduire dans leur réalité. L'unité apparente, purement abstraite, de dialecte, se résout à l'analyse en une multitude de groupes linguistiques " (*ibid.*, pp. 9–10). " Il peut donc y avoir des limites de dialectes, et il est nécessaire de les déterminer : mais ces limites n'ont qu'une existence scientifique et abstraite ; elles ne correspondent à rien de réel dans la conscience du sujet parlant " (*ibid.*, p. 19). The ' Conclusion ' to the work expresses the same ideas, in different language (p. 231 f.).[1]

Millardet and Bruneau, though favourably disposed towards the methods of linguistic geography, have, as we have seen, made considerable concessions to the traditional schools, chiefly in that they have studied more particularly the phonetics of rural speech. A. Terracher, on the other hand, another of Gilliéron's pupils, made a complete break with tradition and chose as the field of his research dialect morphology. In addition to this innovation, he makes a further advance, by associating in his work the methods of the linguistic geographer with a sociological conception of language that has its origin in the tenets of the French school (*v.* Chap. IV), to whom human speech is essentially a social fact, conditioned in its evolution by other social facts. Thus, Terracher studies the modifications which certain dialects have undergone through influences brought in by local marriages with speakers of a different dialect, applying withal a principle inherent in this sociological outlook upon language, namely, that where two patois confront each other, a strong influence is always exercised by the one which, from some particular circumstance, enjoys the greater prestige. In view of this happy alliance of the sociological doctrine as represented by Meillet, with the geographical method, backed up as it is by an extremely acute critical faculty, we may say that of all the French pupils of Gilliéron, the present Rector of Bordeaux University has displayed the most marked originality.

A. Terracher

---

[1] Cp. the reviews by O. Bloch, *Bull. Soc. Ling.*, XVIII (1912–13), p. cclxxiii f., and by J. Ronjat, *Revue des langues romanes*, LX (1918–20), p. 191 f. The latter, an opponent of linguistic geography (*v. supra*, p. 179), acknowledges that Bruneau's work throws fresh light not only on local linguistic problems but on questions of general linguistic importance. If the problems are not completely solved, it is due to the complexity of the facts, not to any fault of method. He admits that the book confirms the view that there are no hard and fast dialect boundaries, and illustrates further Gauchat's observations in *Gibt es Mundartgrenzen?* that the limits between dialects form " un faisceau de traits ", and do not coincide with natural boundaries, as well as giving support to the views expressed by Morf with regard to ecclesiastical divisions (see below). Coming from Ronjat, these remarks are all the more significant.

Terracher made his entry into the field of Romance linguistics with a work entitled *Les aires morphologiques dans les parlers du nord-ouest de l'Angoumois (1800–1900)*, vol. I, Paris, 1914 ; vol. II (sub-title *Appendices*), Paris, 1912 ; vol. III (sub-title *Atlas*), Paris, 1914. It should be made clear forthwith that this *Atlas* does not contain linguistic material, but gives us in cartographical form a wealth of information concerning the region investigated. We quote some of the map-headings : The Prehistorical Period, The Gallo-Roman Period, Toponymy, Agriculture, Trade and Industry, Communications, Fairs and Markets, The Plural of the Definite Article, of Substantives and Feminine Adjectives, The Personal Pronoun *ego*, Personal Flexions, The Perfect Indicative, The Imperfect Subjunctive, Phonetic Boundaries, Morphological Zones, Proportions of Marriages, Density of Marriages, Intermarriages, Settled Population, etc. Volume II contains statistical material, the results of research into departmental archives over the period 1800–1900, with a view to discovering the influence of marriage upon the dialects of the localities investigated. As typical of this material we may quote the following titles : Lists of Marriages and Intermarriages (i.e. when husband or wife comes from another community), Marriage among Natives, Marriage among Outsiders, Calculations for the Matrimonial Charts, etc. It is clear from the foregoing that our present concern will be chiefly with volume I, which gives us the author's observations and ideas.

In the introduction to this volume Terracher discusses general questions relating to linguistic geography and linguistic geology,[1] and shows considerable independence of judgment, particularly with regard to homonymy, and to the results, both positive and negative, accruing from the geographical method. Cartographic investigation of the patois, he claims, as conducted hitherto, has confined itself to registering the phenomena, without explaining them. To become a really scientific discipline, linguistic geography (see the note below) must discover the causes of the topographical distribution of the linguistic facts. This the author sets out to do. It is well known that the existence of dialect

---

[1] The use of these terms is further evidence of Meillet's influence upon Terracher (cp. above, p. 153, n. 2). The latter defines them more precisely as follows : linguistic geography means the presentation of linguistic material in map form, with a view to following the topographical distribution of phonetic phenomena ; linguistic geology, which was founded by Gilliéron, makes use of word-maps and concerns itself with the successive superposings of lexical elements, or, in other words, with the stratigraphy of language.

boundaries has been associated, by some writers, with the difference in type of the populations dwelling in the various provinces of the Roman Empire, by others, with certain geographical or historical circumstances. But although numerous cases of coincidence have been observed, particularly between linguistic and geographical, or political, boundaries, the proposed explanations are unconvincing, inasmuch as they do not establish any real relationship between language and the individuals who speak it. Such a relationship can only be established if we take into consideration " les intermédiaires humains constants entre la répartition du langage et ' l'histoire locale ' " (vol. I, p. xi), and one of these ' constant human intermediaries ' is constituted by marriages in which one of the parties is from another community.[1] Terracher therefore decides to study the dialects of a French territory from the point of view of the impact of the social institution of marriage upon human speech.

His reason for choosing morphology is to be found on page 35 of his treatise. It is the morphological elements of a language, he says, which are most characteristic of it : they have stability, particularly when they compose a well-defined system, and they are used unconsciously, and thus, being less exposed to outside influences, can be observed more readily and with greater security than the other linguistic instruments. He has, for preference, based his enquiries upon morphological types, the second person singular of verbs, the plural of nouns, and so forth, rather than upon individual flexional forms, with particular reference to those types whose distribution is such as to constitute well-defined morphological areas. The investigation proved that intermarriage can bring about changes even in flexional forms, when the latter are not part of a well-defined system, as, for instance, the definite article, the infinitive or the participle. These changes are in the nature of a cross between two types of speech (' Sprachmischung ') : the individuals who have entered the community by marriage adapt their morphological system to that of the new patois, for a variety of reasons, although imperfectly ; one contributory cause

[1] To illustrate his point, Terracher quotes the case of a Swedish area which speaks a dialect sharply differentiated from that of the surrounding territories. The inhabitants of this area never marry outside it, as the arable land is always divided equally among all the children, and marriages are arranged almost exclusively between neighbours, in order to prevent excessive disintegration of the holdings. The language of the area has thus undergone no outside influences, and has become increasingly differentiated from that of neighbouring regions, which are in constant association one with the other.

being, possibly, the ability to read, which helps the speaker to realize the difference between one patois and another ; another, perhaps, the consciousness that one dialect is, as Terracher puts it, " moins patois ", or " plus patois " than another, in which case the latter is inevitably exposed to the influence of the former. But change is not confined to the language of the immigrant speaker. The children born of such marriages tend to give up their traditional speech more quickly and more completely than children of pure local stock, and to adopt another type. As an illustration, Terracher quotes the case of the tiny village of Blancheteaux, which, with its total population of 46, he chooses as representing a community midway in size between the family studied by Rousselot and Gauchat's commune.[1] He records the following observations : The vernacular of this locality shows a general tendency to replace its older forms by new forms, not, however, taken from standard French, but from neighbouring (western) dialects. The substitution has gone farther with some forms than with others. The causes of the breaking down of the morphological type appear to be chiefly related to immigration resulting from marriage with men from elsewhere ; for, from the point of view of their local origin, the 46 inhabitants are divided as follows : 20 are from another locality, 18 had one immigrant parent, and only 8, i.e. less than 20 per cent of the whole community, are of purely local parentage. On the other hand, in villages where the ' native ' population is numerous, such a breakdown of the morphological type cannot be observed.

We may conclude therefore that there are matrimonial zones which coincide with morphological areas. " Donc, il est aisé de mettre en rapport avec les faits de résistance ou de désagrégation morphologiques des faits démographiques et matrimoniaux strictement parallèles. Par contre, je n'ai pu relever, pour aucune des rares communautés dont il n'a pas été fait mention dans les notes qui précèdent, un manque de coïncidence entre cette double série de faits " (op. cit., p. 220). But Terracher does not stress unduly the results of his investigations. He is fully aware of the imperfections of the system he has applied, and shows true scientific restraint in his conclusions. In particular, he is not forgetful of the fact that the area he has explored is a boundary

---

[1] Terracher expresses disagreement in principle with the views of these investigators, who, we have seen (p. 37 f.), have maintained and proved that linguistic unity does not exist in any community of speakers, however small.

region between the French and Provençal territories, and that its great linguistic variety is in part due to this. But, none the less, the facts cannot be gainsaid, and it is difficult to believe that the coincidence, both broadly and in detail, between marriage movement on the one hand and resistance or disintegration of the morphological types on the other, is due to mere chance. The processes of linguistic change as revealed in the region explored by Terracher throw valuable light upon the linguistic history of the past, when similar substitutions have taken place—for example, the eviction of Celtic by the Roman colonists—and for similar psychological causes, namely, the tendency, when two idioms are in conflict, for speakers to give up the one that is judged inferior, and to adopt the one held to be superior, or with the greater social prestige. This tendency, however, is again conditioned by the special circumstances of the case, otherwise how are we to explain the often extremely vigorous resistance put up by so many dialects which preserve, to a greater or less degree, their traditional form, despite the pressure of other idioms in many respects their superiors? Terracher has shown convincingly that among the circumstances which encourage or hinder linguistic substitution must be reckoned marriage. What is there to prevent us from supposing that in the past this social institution had similar effects upon the evolution of language? The supposition would appear all the more justifiable in that the author has investigated marriage movement in his territory previous to 1800, and has discovered that, contrary to the assertions made by Rousselot and Dauzat,[1] marriage outside the village community was practised on a considerable scale in earlier times. There was, however, a restriction, which was laid down by the old feudal ' coutumes ' : marriage was only permitted between villages belonging to the same fief, not with natives of villages beyond its borders. The geographical distribution of present-day morphological types confirms the statistical and historical data, so that Terracher establishes a relation between linguistic boundaries and the confines of the old feudal divisions ; the morphological areas, in the region investigated by him, do not correspond to ancient administrative or ecclesiastical divisions, as Boehmer and Morf had asserted in the case of other Roman territories, but with the feudal divisions

---

[1] The former in the book already quoted, *Les modifications phonétiques* . . . , the latter in his geographical linguistic studies of the dialects of Basse-Auvergne (see below).

the coincidence is frequent. These feudal divisions are set out on the last map of his *Atlas*, under the heading : ' Limite des fiefs (XIIe–XIIIe siècles).'[1]

Last among Gilliéron's French pupils, in chronological order of published work, comes Oscar Bloch,[2] who has succeeded his master **Oscar Bloch** as lecturer in Gallo-Romance dialectology at the Ecole des Hautes-Etudes. He has taken as the region of his dialect investigations a part of the mountain area of the Vosges, where the vernaculars belong to the Lorrain group. His work differs from that of his predecessors in that he, on the one hand, concerns himself with every aspect of the patois, sounds, flexions, syntax and vocabulary, and, on the other, pays particular attention to the influences exercised upon the patois by the French standard language. His material is set forth in the *Atlas linguistique des Vosges méridionales*, Paris, 1917, and in his *Lexique patois-français des Vosges méridionales*, Paris, 1917. It was collected in twenty-two localities, on the basis of a questionnaire modelled upon that used by Edmont for the *Atlas linguistique de la France*. Bloch's *Atlas* contains 810 maps (quite minute in size, because of the restricted area investigated, eight of them going to the quarto page), together with explanatory matter, both with regard to the circumstances of the investigation and to the utilization of the *Atlas*. An interesting

[1] Terracher's studies were well received by the critics. A. Meillet, *Bull. Soc. Ling.*, XIX (1914–15), p. 28 f., praises unreservedly not only the material and the ideas, but also the critical spirit shown by the author, both towards others and towards himself. Certain of Meillet's appreciations have a bearing on linguistic geography in general, and are worth reproducing. " C'est que depuis le livre de M. Rousselot [see preceding note], la géographie linguistique est devenue une force." " La nouveauté du mot et de l'aspect sous lequel se présentent les choses a trop dissimulé le fait que la géographie linguistique représente simplement la perfection de la méthode comparative." " Mais il n'y a rien d'essentiellement nouveau dans la méthode ; il ne s'agit que d'appliquer à des masses de faits beaucoup plus grandes la vieille méthode comparative, la seule avec laquelle on puisse faire l'histoire des langues " (*loc. cit.*, p. 30). The review by J. Ronjat, in *Revue des langues romanes*, LX (1918–20), p. 194 f., is equally eulogistic : " Les travaux de M. Terracher complètent ou modifient beaucoup d'idées admises et apportent des vues nouvelles extrêmement précieuses. Leur intérêt dépasse le cadre du romanisme, et c'est à bon droit que dans la IVe édition de son *Introduction à l'étude comparative des langues indo-européennes* M. Meillet indique *Les aires morphologiques* . . . comme un ' livre capital ' pour une bonne orientation en linguistique générale " (*loc. cit.*, p. 194). Cp. also the review by J. Anglade in *Annales du Midi*, XXIX–XXX (1917–18), p. 99 f.

Other studies by Terracher which call for mention here are : *Aveille<apicula à Paris ?* in *Mélanges Antoine Thomas*, Paris, 1927 (14 pages in off-print) and *La Rencontre des langues entre Loire et Dordogne* (extract from *Centre-Ouest*), Paris, 1926 (7 pages). Terracher is also the general editor of the *Revue de Linguistique romane* which may be considered as the organ for linguistic geography. Its first number appeared in 1925.

[2] Obiit April 15th, 1937.

detail is that among the villages investigated by Bloch, two figure as points 66 and 67 respectively in the *Linguistic Atlas of France*. In view of the doubts that had been expressed as to the reliability of the larger work it is not to be wondered at that Bloch used his own enquiry to check Edmont's results. It so happened that he was able actually to interrogate one of Edmont's own informants. This is the conclusion at which he arrives : ". . . Il résulte de l'examen précédent que, si les graphies des consonnes de M. Edmont et les miennes sont divergentes dans un certain nombre de mots, ce désaccord, dans la plupart des cas, s'explique de différentes façons, sans que l'on puisse l'attribuer à une erreur de l'audition de M. Edmont " (*Atlas*, p. xxi). And, lower down : " En somme, que ressort-il de cet examen minutieux des données de l'AL [the French Atlas] ? Quelques formes, en petit nombre, proviennent des méprises que les témoins ont commises sur le sens de la question ; quelques autres sont des formes individuelles, ou sont d'origine étrangère, ces dernières plus nombreuses à Val-d'Ajol qu'à Ramonchamp, pour des raisons propres aux parlers de cette localité. Tous ces faits sont inhérents à la méthode de l'enquête, dont j'ai parlé plus haut. Quelle est à son tour la part des erreurs de l'audition de M. Edmont ? En vérité, on l'a vu, peu considérable. Les différences de nos graphies sont sans doute assez nombreuses, concernant surtout les voyelles. Mais beaucoup sont menues, beaucoup attribuables à une insuffisance de système graphique, pour plusieurs l'erreur peut être de mon côté aussi bien que de celui de M. Edmont ; il reste au compte de M. Edmont une insuffisance dans l'audition des voyelles nasales brèves de Ramonchamp, un nombre très réduit d'erreurs sur les consonnes, plus important sur le timbre des voyelles dans des mots qui ont été obtenus en groupe. En conclusion finale, les données de l'AL méritent, dans l'ensemble, toute notre confiance " (*ibid.*, p. xxiv).

The linguistic material which could not be inserted in the *Atlas*, either because the replies were too simple to require mapping or too complex to be incorporated on a single map, were published in the *Lexique* . . ., together with an alphabetical list of the localities explored (p. 145 f.) and forty patois texts with translations into Standard French (p. 155 f.). In a word, Bloch has combined the two methods of presenting dialect material, the cartographical and the old lexicographical and documentary method.

The material housed in these two volumes is worked up in a further work entitled, *Les parlers des Vosges méridionales* (*Arrondissement de Remiremont, Département des Vosges). Etude de dialectologie,* Paris, 1917. The purpose of this volume is set forth as follows : " On se propose de montrer comment les systèmes phonétique et morphologique de nos parlers se sont formés, et d'où procède l'étonnante variété de ces systèmes ; en outre une troisième partie, consacrée au lexique, montre que l'activité lexicale n'est pas moindre. Dans cette étude on a pris comme base l'état actuel des parlers " (p. xvi). The study is " essentiellement linguistique ", although " la géographie a aussi sa part dans ce travail : étant donné la configuration de notre domaine et l'existence du centre prépondérant que Remiremont a été à toute époque, il convenait d'examiner quelle action le parler de cette ville a exercée sur ceux des localités environnantes " (*ibid.*, p. xvii). About half the book is devoted to phonetics (pp. 1-150), then come morphology and syntax (pp. 151-243), and finally vocabulary (pp. 244-319). A point of interest, with regard to the latter, is the existence of a considerable number of Alemannic elements of recent date, which the author attributes, not to purely geographical causes, namely, the nearness of the Germanic dialects of Alsace, but to the immigration of Alsatian settlers, and to the progress of industry and consequent borrowing of technical nomenclature and equipment from the highly industrialized regions to the east. The conclusion of the work (p. 320 f.) is of particular interest inasmuch as the author here discusses a number of points of general linguistic import on the basis of his detailed information. He discovers that no single patois resembles closely any of its neighbours, and not only that, two or even more linguistic developments may be observed in one and the same locality. It is thus impossible to trace exact boundaries between the different types of patois, although all are closely related. Val d'Ajol alone offers certain well-marked individual features, owing to its excentric situation with regard to the others. There are, however, certain cases of coincidence which it is important to note. A group of ' isophones ' and ' isomorphs ' passes exactly through the point where the two valleys which make up the area investigated join each other. Again, the repartition of the linguistic phenomena has not taken place in the past according to parishes, as was asserted by Rousselot and Dauzat, nor does it correspond, at the present day, with the communes ; that is to say, the observations made by Terracher (see above, p. 212) are here confirmed. Despite their close relationship one with the other, the dialects studied by Bloch display a strong tendency towards disintegration, to which many causes contribute, some purely local, for example, the preponderance of the dialect of Remiremont, which, as the speech of a town, is considered socially superior, and thanks to this greater prestige, undermines that of the villages, others of wider origin, and in particular the ever-increasing penetration of the standard language, which causes the vernaculars to become ' local ' in the strictest sense of the word, and confined to their own respective communities.

This spread of standard French is discussed by Bloch in a special treatise, entitled *La pénétration du français dans les parlers des Vosges méridionales*, Paris, 1921, where he enquires into the methods of its infiltration into the patois, which, as we have seen, are continually losing ground. Its action, he says, is both direct and indirect ; ' direct ' when it takes the form of deliberate borrowing on the part of the patois speakers, ' indirect ' when these speakers use French instead of dialect. Neglecting its ' indirect ' action, as of lesser linguistic interest, the author confines himself to its ' direct ' or internal action. A few significant facts of a material order may be quoted. The town-dwellers use dialect only in conversation with the peasantry, or, among themselves, for a joke ! The country-dwellers, as a general rule, speak in dialect, although they are clearly irresistibly attracted to the use of French, which all of them understand, with the exception of a very small minority. In by far the most families the children are spoken to in French by their parents. The standard language is spread by the schools and by military service, by economic contacts with the town, by the important cotton industry, etc. But the major part of the book, which is some 150 pages long, is devoted to the strictly linguistic phenomena brought about by the infiltration of French, and describes the manner in which the dialects assimilate and adapt the forms, sounds, and words which they receive from the official language. As is habitual in such cases, the ' grammar ' of the dialects, that is, the morphology and syntax, suffers least, the greatest havoc being wrought in the sounds and particularly in the vocabulary.[1]

---

[1] Bloch's work has been reviewed by, among others, A. Meillet, in *Bull. Soc. Ling.*, XX (1916), p. 182 ; A. Terracher, *ibid.*, XXI (1918–19), p. 88 f. ; M. Grammont, *Revue des langues romanes*, LX (1918–20), p. 121 f. ; and A. Horning, *Romania*, LI (1925), p. 581 f. A recent study in linguistic geography by Bloch, *Se taire en gallo-roman, d'après la carte 1277 de l'ALF*, appeared in *Etudes de dialectologie romane, dédiées à la mémoire de Charles Grandgagnage*, Liège, 1932, p. 39 f., and another, entitled *Une frontière linguistique entre les Vosges et la Haute-Saône*, in *Festschrift für Ernst Tappolet*, Bâle, 1935, p. 42 f.

Editor in chief of the recently founded review, *Le français moderne*, and author of a number of valuable linguistic works of a semi-popular type, A. Dauzat, like Bloch, a director of studies at the Ecole des Hautes-Etudes, can scarcely be called a pupil of Gilliéron's in the domain of linguistic geography, as he had passed out of Gilliéron's classes before the new method had been launched. He would be the first to admit, however, that he has learnt a great deal from Gilliéron, whom he mentions as one of his masters in the preface to his *Histoire de la langue française*, Paris, 1930. Although he may have lost some of his early enthusiasm for the geographical method, and although he has not always seen eye to eye with Gilliéron,[1] he has to his credit a long list of works of a geographical linguistic character, some of them of quite recent date : *Géographie linguistique phonétique d'une région de la basse Auvergne*, Paris, 1906 (one of four volumes devoted to the dialect of this region of which Dauzat is a native, the others being *Phonétique historique du patois de Vinzelles*, Paris, 1897 ; *Morphologie du patois de Vinzelles*, Paris, 1899 ; *Glossaire étymologique du patois de Vinzelles*, Paris, 1915) ; *Essais de géographie linguistique. Noms d'animaux*, Paris, 1921 ; *La géographie linguistique*, Paris, 1922 ; *Les Patois*, Paris, 1927 (like the preceding work, more for the general public than for specialists) ; *Essais de géographie linguistique. Deuxième série ; Problèmes phonétiques*, Paris, 1929 ; *Essais de géographie linguistique. Nouvelle série, I. Pièges phonétiques et extension de formes*, in *Revue des langues romanes*, LXVI (1929–32), p. 45 f., and *II. Aires phonétiques*, *ibid.*, LXVII (1935), p. 1 f. Mention also should be made of his doctorate thesis, *Essai de méthodologie linguistique dans le domaine des langues et des patois romans*, Paris, 1906, where questions relating to linguistic geography are discussed, particularly in the second part which treats of the study of dialects.[2]

★　★　★

[1] Dauzat has reviewed certain of Gilliéron's studies, for example, *Les étymologies des étymologistes et celles du peuple*, in *Revue des langues romanes*, LXII (1923–4), p. 184 f., and *Thaumaturgie linguistique*, *ib.*, p. 193 f. Some of his observations are in reply to criticisms of his own work by that rather ruthless combatant Gilliéron. Dauzat's own criticisms and rejoinders show no theoretical disagreement with Gilliéron and his methods, but relate only to specific points of detail.

[2] On French dialect study cp. O. Bloch, *La dialectologie gallo-romane*, in *Le français moderne*, III (1935), p. 109 f.

Linguistic geography was taken up enthusiastically by a number of Swiss scholars for reasons which are easy to discover. In the first place, there is in Switzerland, with its varieties of official idioms and remarkable diversity in vernacular speech, a highly developed feeling for matters concerning language in general, and dialect in particular, and, secondly, with the exception of the Geneva group, of whom we are to speak later in connection with the French School (*v.* chapter IV), the majority of the Swiss philologists are themselves from country or peasant stock, and have therefore a particular interest and affection for rural speech and rural life. This twofold affection is indeed manifest in the particular bias they have given to their geographico-linguistic studies, namely, as we shall see, the linking together of the study of words with that of the objects which they designate. As pointed out by Professor Jud in a letter to the present author, the true city-dweller has, as a rule, a certain disdain for the language and customs of the country-side. And to the town-bred linguist the language of literature, the artistic and aristocratic medium, will generally have a greater appeal than the humble dialect of the peasant. The Geneva group, Saussure, Bally, and Sechehaye, for example, or the Viennese Spitzer, are cases in point. But affection and interest must be backed up by a sound professional training, if they are to produce results useful to science. This training, too, was not lacking, thanks to the labours of a number of teachers, of whom we shall single out for special mention H. Morf and L. Gauchat.

The Swiss School

Almost all the Swiss linguists of present note have been pupils of Morf and Gauchat. It is true that neither of them, strictly speaking, worked in the field of linguistic geography, nor have they made any significant pronouncements concerning the new method, having confined themselves to dialectology in the traditional acceptation of the term. But the distinction between the two disciplines is in no sense fundamental, and the training they gave their students stood the latter in good stead when they came to the new method and, fortifying their native understanding and sympathy for things of the country-side, enabled them to adopt and apply it with the most fruitful results. Before proceeding to discuss these two scholars individually, however, we must make a passing reference to another, J. Cornu, who has a particular claim to our attention inasmuch as he was one of Gilliéron's masters, and, like him, hailed from French-speaking Switzerland. Cornu also was a dialectologist (cp., for example, his *Phonologie du Bagnard*, in *Romania*, VI [1877], p. 369 f.), and an independent thinker, whom Gilliéron, who owed not a little to his teaching, always held in great respect.

★

Morf,[1] as a dialectologist, had none of the true explorer's spirit, but used material collected by others as a basis for discussions of a general theoretical character upon the formation

Heinrich Morf

and distribution of dialects, a problem which has been, and is still,[2] much discussed and one which likewise comes within the purview of the linguistic geographer. The works in which Morf examines questions of dialectology are the following : *Ein Sprachenstreit in der rätischen Schweiz* (*Aus Dichtung und Sprache der Romanen*, I, p. 418 f.), *Deutsche und Romanen in der Schweiz* (*ibid.*, II, p. 220 f.), *Die romanische Schweiz und die Mundartenforschung* (*ibid.*, II, p. 288 f.), *Mundartenforschung und Geschichte auf romanischem Gebiet* (*ibid.*, III, p. 295 f.), and *Zur sprachlichen Gliederung Frankreichs*, in *Abhandlungen der Preussischen Akademie der Wissenschaften*, Berlin, 1911 (37 pages and 7 maps in offprint).[3] The distinctive feature of Morf's treatment of dialect distribution is the great importance he attaches in accounting for it to the organization

---

[1] Morf was professor in Berne, Zürich, Frankfort, and finally Berlin, where he died early in 1921, while still on the active list. He was a literary historian of distinction as well as a philologist, witness his *Geschichte der französischen Literatur im Zeitalter der Renaissance*, Strasburg, 1898 (ed. II, 1914), *Die romanischen Literaturen*, in *Die Kultur der Gegenwart*, Teil I, Abteilung XI, 1, Berlin, 1909 (ed. II, Berlin–Leipzig, 1925), and the admirable essays which, with a number of linguistic studies, compose the three volumes entitled *Aus Dichtung und Sprache der Romanen :* I, Strasburg, 1903 ; II, *ibid.*, 1911 ; III, Berlin–Leipzig, 1922.

[2] Cp., for example : A. Horning, *Über Dialektgrenzen im Romanischen, Zeitschr. f. rom. Phil.*, XVII (1893), p. 160 f. ; Karl Haag, *Mundartgrenzen, Arch. f. d. St. d. neueren Sprachen*, CXV (1905), p. 182 f. ; K. Bohnenberger, *Über Mundartgrenzen*, in Verhandlungen der 49. *Philologenversammlung in Basel*, 1907 ; Karl Haag, *Sprachwandel im Lichte der Mundartgrenzen*, in *Teuthonista*, VI (1929), p. 1 f. ; W. v. Wartburg, *Die Entstehung der Sprachgrenzen im Inneren der Romania*, in *Beiträge zur Geschichte der deutschen Sprache und Literatur*, LVIII (1934), p. 209 f.

[3] We would also mention a lecture delivered to the *Berliner Gesellschaft für das Studium der neueren Sprachen*, on the *Linguistic Atlas of France*, and summarized in *Archiv f. d. St. d. neueren Spr. u. Lit.*, CXXVIII (1912), p. 212 f., and a notice of J. Gilliéron et Roques, *Etudes de Géographie linguistique, ibid.*, CXXXI (1913), p. 268. Morf's admiration for the *French Atlas* is also expressed in *Aus Dichtung und Sprache der Romanen*, II, p. 314 f.

of the Roman provinces into dioceses.[1] He has concerned himself in the main with certain topics that have constantly attracted the attention of scholars, namely, the boundaries between the languages and dialects of the Gallo-Roman area, the position of the Franco-Provençal group of patois, and of Catalan. A few examples will illustrate his point of view. Tracing the various modifications of the consonant *c* before the vowels *a*, *e*, and *i*, in their geographical distribution, he discovers an ancient linguistic unit composed of Normandy, Picardy, and the Walloon area. In like manner, he observes that the Picard and Walloon dialects preserve the nasal *e* resulting from Latin *en*, whereas the ' Francien ' or Ile-de-France dialect, and later Norman, have changed it to a nasal *a*. The distribution of these phenomena shows that between the Picard dialects and the speech of the Ile-de-France and Champagne there runs a clear-cut boundary of some 200 kilometres in length, and that this boundary coincides almost exactly with the boundaries of the ancient dioceses of Beauvais, Noyon, and Cambrai, on the one hand, and of Rouen, Paris, and Laon, on the other, which in their turn are identical, in the main, with the boundaries of the old Gallo-Roman ' civitates ', the Bellovacensis, Noviomensis, and Cameracensis. We have to do, therefore, in this instance, with territorial divisions which go back some two thousand years.

Similar considerations are advanced to account for the localization of the Franco-Provençal group of dialects. On the basis of the treatment of Latin *a*, Morf observes that the linguistic boundary coincides in the south and west with those of the territories of the bishoprics of Vienne and Lyons respectively, which again are based on administrative divisions dating from Roman times. A like importance is attached by Morf to the great Roman lines of communication, around which he groups the old Gallo-Roman ' civitates ' in three great linguistic units, corresponding, roughly, with the famous ' tres partes ' we find in Caesar.[2]

---

[1] In the *Revista de filología española*, III (1916), p. 82 note, it is stated that the idea of associating dialect boundaries with ecclesiastical divisions occurred to Salvioni, in 1901, and was mentioned also by R. Menéndez Pidal in 1906 and 1908.

[2] J. Ronjat, whose review of Morf's *Zur sprachlichen Gliederung Frankreichs*, in *Revue des langues romanes*, XLV (1912), p. 418 f., we have made use of for the above summary, is of the opinion that the dioceses determined the boundaries of dialects, to any noteworthy extent, only in the plains, whereas, in the hilly regions, the basis is the Roman pagus, or the valleys and parts of valleys.

With regard to the coincidence of linguistic with administrative or ecclesiastical boundaries the remarks of Menéndez Pidal, *Orígenes del español*, I, ed. II, Madrid, 1929, p. 572 f., are worth quoting. After showing that the necessities of human

Any outline of Morf's scientific personality would be incomplete if it were not made clear that this great scholar, from the very beginning of his career, displayed an attitude in complete conformity with the spirit which at present prevails in Romance studies. In 1889, in his inaugural lecture as Professor of Romance Philology in the University of Zürich, he already protested against the undue prominence given to the study of Old French by the Romanicists of the period, asserting at the same time that linguistic changes have their source in the individual, and are psychological in origin (*v. Aus Dichtung und Sprache der Romanen*, II, p. 331 f.).

Gauchat's name is already known to us as the author of studies which contributed in a great measure towards changing the prevailing conceptions concerning dialect and dialect boundaries. We refer the reader to what has been said above under this head on pages 37 f. At present, we shall confine ourselves to providing some information concerning an imposing piece of dialect work of which the Zürich scholar is the founder and principal director. Taking as his model the dictionary of the Germanic dialects of Switzerland, the *Schweizerisches Idiotikon*, which began publication in 1881 (in 1924 it had reached the letter *S*), Gauchat decided to undertake the compilation of a similar corpus for the dialects of ' la Suisse romande,' those, that is to say, spoken in the cantons of Geneva, Vaud, and Neuchâtel, and in the western portions of those of Valais, Fribourg, and Berne, and belonging to the Franco-Provençal group mentioned above. This was in 1890, when, as a student of Morf's, he was awarded his doctorate for a study of the dialect of Dompierre in

Louis Gauchat *(margin note)*

relations cannot be overcome by administrative territorial divisions, inasmuch as the former are conditioned by factors of greater permanence than any political or religious convenience, he goes on to say (p. 574) : " The Roman political divisions, and the ecclesiastical dioceses which continued them, may account for certain linguistic boundaries, but are powerless to explain the dialect distribution in Romania as a whole. And the same can be said, and with still greater force, of mediaeval political divisions, by which many have sought to explain the present framework of the dialects. Finally, we must take into account that the stability of a linguistic boundary, the existence of which we have been able to verify or which we have reason to suspect, is unlikely to be absolute. The probabilities are that a boundary, however stable it may remain, has been changed or reconstituted by currents of a later date than that which originally determined the expansion and boundaries of the phenomenon concerned." Conspicuous among contemporary linguists who adhere to and consistently apply Morf's theory of the coincidence of linguistic and ecclesiastical boundaries is the Catalan scholar, A. Griera (see below). On the topic of relations between administrative and linguistic divisions with regard to France, see further, A. Rosenqvist, *Limites administratives et division dialectale de la France*, in *Neuphilologische Mitteilungen*, XX (1919), p. 87 f.

the canton of Fribourg. Five years later, having received official support, he was able to set about organizing the undertaking. The collecting of the material was begun in 1899, and lasted twelve years. Realizing that the work was beyond the powers of a single individual, and wishing at the same time to make it, so to speak, more national in character, Gauchat secured the collaboration of two Romanicists trained in the same school as himself, E. Tappolet and J. Jeanjaquet,[1] professors, respectively, at Bâle and Neuchâtel. The methods of collecting the material were twofold. Questionnaires were sent to a great number of correspondents, and the editors themselves conducted enquiries in the field, mainly with a view to verifying the replies from correspondents and to making an exact record of the phonetic peculiarities of the various dialects. The existing regional glossaries were likewise utilized, and other written documents, published and unpublished, together with old and modern texts. No less than a million and a half slips have been accumulated. Proper names, both place names and family names, were ultimately included in the investigation, both for the sake of completeness, and also because they provide valuable information on the common speech, from which they are very often derived. To this end a fourth collaborator was called in, in the person of E. Muret, professor at Geneva, who has made a special study of toponymy and anthroponymy. In 1924 the first fascicule of this truly monumental work appeared. It bore the title, *Glossaire des patois de la Suisse romande, élaboré avec le concours de nombreux auxiliaires et rédigé par* L. Gauchat, J. Jeanjaquet, E. Tappolet, *avec la collaboration de* E. Muret.[2] The preface and introduction to the work gave a great deal of interesting information concerning the undertaking in general, the methods of compiling and presenting the material, and the like. In the latter respect the authors comply to the fullest extent with every requirement of modern linguistics. For each word in the glossary, they give (*a*) its form and place of origin, (*b*) its function and meaning, with examples of its usage, (*c*) historical and encyclopaedical notes concerning word and thing.

---

[1] Tappolet has written an article on dialect work in the ' Suisse romande ' field, in *Die Schweiz. Ein nationales Jahrbuch* 1931. *Herausgegeben von der neuen Helvetischen Gesellschaft*, Erlenbach–Zürich (cp. *Literaturblatt f. germ. u. rom. Phil.*, LIII [1932], col. 31). (For a description of some of Tappolet's other works, see p. 248, note 2.) A characterization of the dialects of the Valais canton by Jeanjaquet appeared in *Revue de linguistique romane*, VII (1931), p. 23 f.

[2] Other collaborators have since been enlisted : P. Aebischer, from fascicule V onwards, and O. Keller, fasc. IX and X (*v. Gloss. pat. Suisse rom., 34ᵉ rapport annuel*, Neuchâtel, 1933, p. 4, and *35ᵉ rapport, ibid.*, 1934, p. 5).

Objects of particular interest are illustrated by photographs or sketches, and the geographical distribution of words or flexional types is frequently set forth in map form. The work is thus carried out on lines which represent all the main tendencies of modern linguistic investigation, historical, geographical, and ethnological.[1] The reception which it met with at the hands of scholars was therefore most enthusiastic, and reviews were both laudatory and extremely numerous.[2] If there is one fault to be found with this great ' glossary ', it is that its publication is extremely slow, proceeding as it does at the rate of some sixty-odd pages a year.

The example set by Gauchat and his collaborators has borne fruit and led to similar undertakings, both at home and abroad. Thus, in 1904, R. v. Planta and Florian Melcher set to work on a corpus of the Rheto-Romance dialects of Switzerland (*Rätisches Idiotikon*), and their work is to be continued by the recently announced *Dicziunari rumantsch-grischun* by C. Pult, which, judging by the prospectus fascicule published in 1933, is to be similar in character to the *Glossaire*. For the Ticino canton, where the dialect is more closely related to the North Italian group, there is the *Vocabolario della Svizzera italiana*, begun by C. Salvioni[3] († 1920) in conjunction with P. E. Guarnerio († 1919) and C. Merlo, on which periodical bulletins are published in the journal of the last named, *L'Italia dialettale*. Outside Switzerland, the most active investigation on similar lines has perhaps been that pursued by Belgian scholars in the Walloon area to which we shall refer below (*v.* p. 267 f.), though mention may be made here of the

---

[1] Mention should be made of a number of publications which are, so to speak, satellites of the *Glossaire*, namely, *Bibliographie linguistique de la Suisse romande*, vol. I, Neuchâtel, 1912 ; vol. II, *ibid.*, 1920, *Bulletin du Glossaire des patois de la Suisse romande*, *ibid.*, 1902–15, and *Tableaux phonétiques des patois suisses romands*, *ibid.*, 1925. The purpose of the second of these was to keep up a close connection between the correspondents and the compilers of the Glossary ; the third contains comparative tables of some 500 words phonetically transcribed, and representing sixty-two typical patois.

[2] Of the score of reviews known to the author the following are mentioned as being among the most important : those of G. Millardet, in *Revue des langues romanes*, LXII (1923-4), p. 492 f. ; E. Gamillscheg, *Zeitschr. f. rom. Phil.*, XLIV (1924), p. 610 f. ; K. Jaberg, *Romania*, LI (1925), p. 571 f. ; Meyer-Lübke, *Literaturblatt f. germ. u. rom. Phil.*, XLVI (1925), col. 159 f. The whole of vol. I of the *Glossaire* (fasc. I-X) was reviewed by the last-named, *ibid.*, LV (1934), col. 398 f. Cp. also an interesting discussion of questions of theory on the basis of the *Glossaire* by one of the editors, E. Tappolet, *Neuere Aufgaben der Wortforschung*, in *Germanisch-romanische Monatsschrift*, XIII (1925), p. 130 f.

[3] On Salvioni's philological work, see the obituary notice by B. Terracini, in *Archivio glottologico italiano*, XVIII (1914-22), p. 586 f.

Enquêtes du Musée de la vie wallonne with its *Bulletin-Questionnaire Trimestriel* published under the direction of J. M. Remouchamps (Tome Iᵉʳ, Années 1924 à 1926, Liège, 1927, viii+422 pp., avec 470 illustrations, etc.) ; cp. *Volkstum und Kultur der Romanen*, III (1930), p. 98 f.[1]

It was natural that after the interest in dialect displayed and encouraged by teachers like Morf and Gauchat, linguistic geography should find numerous and worthy adherents among the Swiss philologists. We shall confine ourselves here to the most distinguished of their number, and to their principal works, discussing them in chronological order. K. Jaberg, Professor at the University of Berne, came early to the Gilliéronian doctrine. Like Gilliéron himself, and unlike the French scholars mentioned above, he bases his investigations on the material supplied by the *Atlas linguistique de la France* and, latterly, also on that contained in the Italian and Southern Swiss Atlas of which we are to speak below : the map for a given notion is analysed, and all the words which are used to express the notion are investigated thoroughly in their geographical relationships. It should be stated, however, that Jaberg finds room for certain considerations which Gilliéron either neglects or eliminates from his investigations. In the first place, he works on both comparative and historical lines, taking account of the past phases of the language as well as of kindred phenomena in other domains, and, secondly, he devotes adequate attention to cultural history, and the relations between ' words ' and ' things '. This particular bent is to be detected to a greater or less degree in all his writings, but particularly in such studies as *Kultur und Sprache in Romanisch-Bünden*, Berne, 1921, *Dreschmethoden und Dreschgeräte in Romanisch-Bünden* (in *Bündnerisches Monatsblatt*, 1922), and *Zur Sach- und Bezeichnungsgeschichte der Beinkleidung in der Zentralromania* (*Wörter und Sachen*, IX [1924–6], p. 137 f.).[2] Finally, Jaberg also concerns himself with the psychological side of language, and the modifications which arise

(In the left margin: **Karl Jaberg**)

---

[1] Other studies by Gauchat which should be mentioned here are : *Über die Bedeutung der Wortzonen*, Bâle, 1907, *Les noms gallo-romans de l'écureuil*, in *Mélanges . . . Wilmotte*, Paris, 1910, p. 174 f., *Régression linguistique*, in *Festschrift zum XIV. allgemeinen deutschen Neuphilologentage in Zürich*, 1910, p. 335 f., and *Sprachforschung im Terrain*, in *Bulletin de dialectologie romane*, II (1910), p. 93 f.

[2] As the title indicates, this study covers not only France but also the whole of the central Romance area. The question is treated from the Gallo-Romance point of view in a shorter study in *Sprachgeographie*, p. 13 f. A detailed review by S. Puşcariu of *Kultur und Sprache . . .* and *Dreschmethoden . . .* and another of Jaberg's studies is to be found in *Dacoromania*, II (1921–2), p. 714 f.

therein from affective states in the individual.[1] His study entitled *Sprache als Äusserung und Sprache als Mitteilung, Grundfragen der Onomasiologie*, and published in *Archiv für das Studium der neueren Sprachen und Literaturen*, CXXXVI (1917), p. 84 f., can be considered as a very happy attempt at combining the psychological and the geographical methods. None the less, Jaberg would have the linguist concern himself primarily with purely linguistic problems, for only thus can such a combination of methods give results that are beneficial at the same time both to linguistics, to psychology, and to the history of cultures.

From this summary account of his activity something can already be gathered of the variety and breadth of Jaberg's interests. If we consider, further, other writings of the Berne scholar, such as *Idealistische Neuphilologie*, where he discusses the Vosslerian school (*v.* pp. 109 n., 133 f.), and his numerous reviews of works on all manner of topics concerned with Romance studies, we can confidently assert that there are few Romanicists who show a more lively interest in linguistic problems than Jaberg, and few who can claim to possess his insight and breadth of understanding. We append a list of other studies by this indefatigable worker : *Peiorative Bedeutungsentwicklung im Französischen, mit Berücksichtigung allgemeiner Fragen der Semasiologie*, in *Zeitschr. f. rom. Phil.*, XXV (1901), p. 561 f. ; XXVII (1903), p. 25 f. ; XXIX (1905), p. 57 f. ; *Sprachgeographie*,[2] Aarau, 1908 ; *Sprachgeographische Untersuchungen*, in *Archiv f. d. Studium der neueren Spr. u. Lit.*, CXX (1908), p. 96 f. (on Fr. *arocher, garocher, garoter, rocher, rucher*, ' to throw ') ; CXXVI (1911), p. 371 f. (on Fr. *s'asseoir*) ; *Sprachgeographisches.* " *Soif* " *und die sprachliche Expansion in Nordfrankreich*, in *Zeitschr. f. französische Spr. u. Lit.*, XXXVIII (1911), p. 231 f. ;[3] *Der Sach- und Sprachatlas Italiens und der Südschweiz und die Bezeichnungsgeschichte des Begriffes* " *anfangen* ", in *Revue de linguistique romane*, I (1925), p. 118 f. ; *Una pera mezza*,[4] in *Festschrift Louis Gauchat*, Aarau, 1926, p. 52 f. ;

---

[1] Jaberg's penetrating grasp of such questions is well evidenced by his review of Spitzer's *Puxi, eine kleine Studie zur Sprache einer Mutter*, in *Literaturblatt f. germ. u. rom. Phil.*, XLVIII (1927), col. 329 f.

[2] Cp. p. 154 n., above. It should be pointed out that when this booklet was published the whole of the *French Atlas* had not been issued and Gilliéron had as yet only published his work on ' *scier* '. None the less, we find the geographical method applied by Jaberg with great skill and understanding.

[3] Cp. E. Herzog, *Aus dem Atlas linguistique*, in the same review XXXVII (1911), p. 134 f., and by the same writer, *Noch einmal* " *soif* ", *ibid.*, XL (1912-13), p. 213 f.

[4] This and the preceding study were based on material from the *Italian and Swiss Atlas* which had not yet begun publication.

Sprache und Leben,[1] in *Revue de linguistique romane*, II (1926), p. 3 f. ; *Spiel und Scherz in der Sprache*, in *Festgabe für Samuel Singer*, Tübingen, 1930, p. 67 f. ; *Beitrag zur Geschichte der französischen Schriftsprache und ihrer Beziehung zu den Mundarten*, in *Revue de linguistique romane*, VI (1930), p. 91 f. ; *Sprachtradition und Sprachwandel*, Berne, 1932 ;[2] *Aspects géographiques du langage*, Paris, 1936.[3] Further works, produced in collaboration with J. Jud, of whom we are now to speak, will be mentioned below.

The name of Jaberg inevitably calls up that of Jud, professor at the University of Zürich, who, like him, is one of the most outstand-

Jakob Jud   ing representatives of linguistic geography, not only in Switzerland, but in the world. These two scholars have long worked together for the advancement of Romance studies in the most perfect understanding, and with the finest results, the most noteworthy fruit of their collaboration being the monumental *Atlas of Italy and Southern Switzerland* which we shall describe shortly. What we have said regarding the linguistic activity of his colleague applies in the main to Jud as well. There are, however, certain minor differences that are worth noting. Jaberg extends his investigations wider afield than Jud, both territorially and in the substance of his researches. Jud, on the other hand, delves more deeply, and investigates the problems he tackles in the minutest detail. There is no Romance scholar to compare with him in wealth and reliability of documentation and in exhaustiveness of treatment, particularly in matters of lexicography. Not only is his own work evidence of the completeness of his information, but the numerous expressions of gratitude he earns from other scholars bear eloquent testimony, as much to his generosity, as to the inexhaustible store of material housed in the drawers of his ' fichier '. Indeed, of all Romance scholars Jud would appear most qualified to write an etymological dictionary of the Romance languages and dialects, to take the place of the useful but in many respects unsatisfactory works at present available. A further detail

---

[1] Apropos of Ch. Bally's booklet, *Le langage et la vie*, of which we are to speak in the next chapter.

[2] *Sprachtradition* . . . , which, like the preceding study, treats of important theoretical questions, was reviewed by Ulrich Leo, *Deutsche Literaturzeitung*, LIV (1933), col. 535 f. ; W. Petersen, *Boletín bibliográfico del centro de intercambio intelectual germano-español*, V (1932), p. 76–7 ; and A. Meillet, in *Bull. Soc. Ling.*, XXXIV (1933), fasc. 3, p. 7 f.

[3] Reviewed by : G. Rohlfs, *Arch. f. d. St. d. n. Spr.*, CLXX (1936), p. 145 f. ; Iorgu Iordan, *Bul. Inst. Fil. Rom.* " *Alexandru Philippide* ", III (1936), p. 202 f. ; O. Bloch, *Le franç. mod.*, V (1937), p. 83.

is of importance in this general characterization of Jud's activities, namely, that the Romance Seminar of Zürich University is a veritable nursery of well-trained and industrious linguists, a fact which bodes well for the future progress of our studies.

To turn now to his methods of work, we observe forthwith that he devotes as much attention to the historical aspects of his problems as to the geographical. The reproach which the partisans of the historical method have often addressed to Gilliéron, namely, his disregard for history, is in no sense applicable to Jud. On the contrary, in the latter's studies the heritage from ancient literary monuments is happily associated with the fruits of the linguistic atlases, not only in complete harmony, but in active and astonishingly fertile collaboration. Jud has proved in most brilliant fashion that the historical and the geographical approaches to language are complementary, and not antagonistic, as the more fanatical supporters of either school had claimed. His work is thus of very considerable theoretical value, as well as being, intrinsically, of great scientific importance. This predilection for the historical view, which seems to be characteristic of the man, rather than the result of any specialized training, has led him to investigate the most remote periods in the development of the Romance languages. In *Probleme der altromanischen Sprachgeographie*, for example (*Zeitschr. f. rom. Phil.*, XXXVIII [1914–15], p. 1 f.), we find him using the methods of the linguistic geographer to probe into what we may call the pre-Romance state of spoken Latin, and discovering in the non-Romance dialects bordering on the Romance domain evidence of the early existence of words which the Romance languages or dialects have since lost. Elsewhere, in *Problèmes de géographie linguistique romane* (*Rev. de ling. rom.*, I [1925], p. 181 f.), he uses the geographical method to enlighten us upon the linguistic cleavages which took place as early as the Vulgar Latin era in the various regions of the empire, and to break down the dogma of the uniformity of their speech. Or again, like the most authentic representative of the historical school, he will reconstruct the non-Latin elements, in particular, the Gaulish words, which, though unattested in any document, were certainly in current use in pre-Romance times and have left their traces in the modern dialects. In this regard, Jud can suffer comparison with the recognized master of the reconstructive method, Meyer-Lübke, both for historical flair and etymological ingenuity. We would refer more particularly to his series of articles, entitled, *Mots d'origine gauloise?* which have appeared at intervals in *Romania* (I, vol. XLVI [1920], p. 465 f. ; II, vol. XLVII [1921], p. 481 f. ; III, vol. XLIX [1923], p. 389 f. ; IV, vol. LII [1926], p. 328 f.).

To complete our appreciation of Jud's scientific personality we may quote certain remarks made by Spitzer in *Meisterwerke der romanischen Sprachwissenschaft*, I, p. 369 : " He has brought Gilliéron's doctrine into line with the accepted results of Romance Philology and, in his lexicographical works, particularly in the essay we reproduce [*sc.* on Fr. *dru* ; see below], he brings us a synthesis of all the prevailing methods, the reconstruction of etymons, the comparative method, that of ' word ' and ' thing ', the study of stylistic values and of geographical distribution, the whole applied from a historico-cultural angle, not so much, as with Vossler, to show speech merely as a mirror of cultural phenomena, but to stress the closely interwoven causal relationships between the linguistic and the cultural." After finding some fault with Jud's confidence in the complete accuracy of his etymological reconstructions, Spitzer proceeds to compare him with Schuchardt, and concludes that in wealth of material he frequently surpasses the latter ; he also finds him more convincing in his arguments and more easy to follow, from the fact that his examples, both ancient and modern, are presented geographically and are thus more readily surveyed and remembered by the reader.[1]

In addition to those already quoted the following studies by Jud call for mention : *Sprachgeographische Untersuchungen*, in *Archiv f. d. St. d. neueren Spr. u. Lit.*, CXX (1908), p. 72 f. (on Fr. *poutre*) ; CXXI (1908), p. 76 f. (on Fr. *aune*, ' alder ', and N. It. *barba*, ' uncle ') ; CXXIV (1910), p. 83 f. (on Fr. *aune*, ' alder ', Part II) ; CXXVI (1911), p. 109 f. (on Fr. *son*, ' bran ') ; *Zur Geschichte der bündner-romanischen Kirchensprache* (extract from *XLIX. Jahresbericht der historisch-antiquarischen Gesellschaft von Graubünden*, Coire, 1919) ;[2]

---

[1] A similar appreciation by W. v. Wartburg of Jud's comprehensive technique is to be found in *Zeitschrift f. rom. Phil.*, XL (1920), p. 508 f. Cp. also L. Spitzer's remarks in *Revue de dialectologie romane*, VI (1914), p. 322 f.

[2] Reviewed by S. Puşcariu in *Dacoromania*, I (1920–1), p. 434 f., particularly from the Rumanian angle. This work, despite its title, takes account of other domains and may be considered as a preliminary sketch of the history of Romance Christian terminology in general, which Jud has taken further, in his recent article in the *Revue de linguistique romane* (see above), for the French and Italian domains. In the latter study and a number of earlier articles in the same review Jud lays the basis of a general linguistic geography of Romance, an important extension of his scientific activity and one which he is particularly qualified to undertake. Indeed, one might with singular appropriateness apply to Jud himself, with but a few inessential changes, the words with which he and his collaborator, A. Steiger, have characterized the trend of Swiss linguistics as a whole, in the

Zur Geschichte zweier franzözischer Rechtsausdrücke, in *Zeitschrift für schweizerische Geschichte*, II (1922), p. 412 f. (on Fr. *corvée* and Fr. dial. *verchère*) ; *Zur Geschichte und Herkunft von franz. dru*, in *Archivum Romanicum*, VI (1922), p. 313 f. ; *Problèmes de géographie linguistique romane* : I. *Introduction ; Problèmes lexicologiques de l'Hispano-roman ;* II. *Eteindre dans les langues romanes*, in *Revue de linguistique romane*, I (1925), p. 181 f. ; *Zum Schriftitalienischen Wortschatz in seinem Verhältnis zum Toskanischen und zur Wortgeographie der Toskana*, in *Festschrift Louis Gauchat*, Aarau, 1926, p. 298 f. ; *Problèmes de géographie linguistique romane :* III. *S'éveiller dans les langues romanes*, in *Revue de linguistique romane*, II (1926), p. 163 f. ; *La valeur documentaire de l'Atlas linguistique de l'Italie et de la Suisse méridionale*, in the same review, vol IV (1928), p. 251 f. (' à suivre ') ; *Sur l'histoire de la terminologie ecclésiastique de la France et de l'Italie*, ibid., vol. X (1934), p. 1 f. Finally, his reviews in journals like the *Archiv f. d. St. d. neueren Spr. u. Lit.*, etc., should not be forgotten, as they are of exceptional importance, particularly for the fresh material they bring to fill the gaps in that of the books or articles reviewed.

Another of Gilliéron's Swiss followers is J. U. Hubschmied. He has written little, both because he is severely self-critical and

J. U. Hubschmied because of the calls made upon his time by his work as a schoolmaster in Zürich. None the less, he stood very high in the esteem of his master and, in general, reviewers have endorsed the latter's appreciation of the work of this modest but thorough investigator. Of the linguists we have mentioned so far, it is with Jud that he would appear to have most in common, both in his historical bias and his affection for the Celtic elements in the neo-Latin languages. In his search for these Celtic relicta he has paid particular attention to place-names, where the pre-Roman elements are far more numerous than in ordinary speech. But his concern with place-names is not confined to the vestiges of Celtic which they may contain. He is interested in problems of pre-Roman toponymy in general and, a point which concerns us here, he applies to their investigation the methods of

' Geleitwort ' to the first number of their newly-founded journal *Vox Romanica*, of which the sub-title is, *Annales Helvetici explorandis linguis Romanicis destinati :* " The simultaneous investigation of the Alemannic, Franco-Provençal, Lombard and Rheto-Romance dialects and regional cultures leads automatically to a consideration from a wide inter-Romance standpoint of the problems raised by individual tongues, and at the same time to a comprehensive study of the interplay of borrowing of words and things between the speech zones of Romania and Germania, between ancient Gaul and the Romance lands, and between Southern Romania and Arabia ". (*Vox Rom.*, I [1936], p. 1.)

the linguistic geographer combined with those of the historian. As examples of his toponymical work we can mention : *Drei Ortsnamen gallischen Ursprungs : Ogo, Château d'Oex, Üechtland*, in *Zeitschrift für deutsche Mundarten*, XIX (1924), p. 169 f., and *Gallische Nomina auf -pi-, -pā-*, in *Festschrift Louis Gauchat*, Aarau, 1926, p. 435 f. A longer work, based chiefly upon the material of the *Atlas linguistique de la France*, is his *Zur Bildung des Imperfekts im Frankoprovenzalischen. Die v-losen Formen, mit Untersuchung über die Bedeutung der Satzphonetik für die Entwicklung der Verbalformen*, Halle a.S., 1914, published as the 58th *Beiheft* to the *Zeitschrift für romanische Philologie*. The main purpose of the author is to explain certain flexional changes, not by analogy, of which excessive use had been and continues to be made in morphological studies, but as the outcome of syntactic phonology, the reciprocal influence exercised by words which are commonly combined in the same phrase, and by which not only words, as such, may be modified, but also verbal flexions. The work was reviewed favourably by A. Meillet, in *Bulletin de la Société de linguistique*, XIX (1914–15), p. 33 f., who writes, *inter alia :* " M. Hubschmied n'est pas l'ennemi des ' lois phonétiques ' : en proposant de leur donner la souplesse et la précision qui leur manquent trop souvent, il leur souffle une nouvelle vie, et il les rend vraiment propres à expliquer le développement du langage " (*loc. cit.*, p. 36).[1]

The same concern for history which we have seen to be characteristic of the Swiss school of linguistic geographers is to be found in the works of W. von Wartburg, a pupil of Gauchat **Walther von Wartburg** and Jud in Zürich, and of Gilliéron in Paris. Von Wartburg, now Professor in the University of Leipzig, may even be said latterly to have given precedence in his investigations to historical over geographical factors, an attitude determined doubtless by the nature of the *magnum opus* which his

---

[1] J. Ronjat, an adversary of Gilliéron and the geographical method, in a laudatory review of Hubschmied's book, *Revue des langues romanes*, LVIII (1915), p. 333 f., writes : " Ce livre est dédié à M. Gilliéron, mais il procède plutôt de la doctrine que représente M. Gauchat, et ce n'est pas moi qui m'en plaindrai." This affirmation, and the remarks of Meillet quoted above, may appear surprising in view of Gilliéron's well-known appreciation of Hubschmied. But it must not be forgotten that there is greater unity than is apparent on the surface between the dialect investigations of a Gauchat and the probings of the linguistic geographer, and that there have been critics who have maintained that even between the doctrine of Gilliéron and the school of the neo-grammarians there are definite points of contact and agreement. As instances, we may quote Fr. Schürr in *Sprachwissenschaft und Zeitgeist*, Marburg a.L., 1922 passim, and H. Güntert, in *Wörter und Sachen*, XII (1929), p, 390 f.

name immediately brings to mind, the *Französisches etymologisches Wörterbuch*.[1] A dictionary of this monumental character could scarcely be conceived on other than historical lines, aiming as it does at recording the whole thesaurus of French, both Standard and Dialect, from the remotest times to the present. But notwithstanding this, not only has von Wartburg made ample use of the *Linguistic Atlas*, and all the geographical studies relating to French, in collecting his material, but he has benefited to the full by his contact with the Gilliéronian doctrine, as is obvious from the first pages of the dictionary, which, it is fair to say, has been made possible, in its present form, only by the earlier work of the type we have been describing above.

An interesting light is thrown upon von Wartburg's scientific attitude by the explanatory page which precedes the preface to the first volume of his *Dictionary*. The work is dedicated to Jules Gilliéron and Wilhelm Meyer-Lübke, and the author feels constrained to comment upon this coupling of two names which it is unusual to find associated. After characterizing them antithetically, the former as a romantic, the latter as a realist, he goes on to say : " Thus do both men embody, in a state of purity which is rare in the field of Romance linguistics, those two fundamental forces whose collaboration and interplay are the stuff of which Science is made. The state of our knowledge would have been entirely different but for the rich harvest of these two long scholarly lives, so noble in their simplicity. It is thanks to them, in the deepest sense, that the times were ripe for an Etymological Dictionary of the French Language. Both for the work itself and for me personally, the acquaintance I made with both these men was of the highest significance. It was my particular good fortune to approach one of them more closely in the years of youthful gropings and uncertainties, the other at a maturer age. For these reasons I dedicate my book to both. May Meyer-Lübke find it at his side to help him in his untiring efforts to throw light on the dark places in the history of Romance speech. And though Gilliéron is no longer among us, may it be one of the many witnesses to the undying spirit that lived within him." This moving passage does more than

---

[1] This unique piece of lexicographical work, which began publication in Bonn, 1922, has undergone many vicissitudes, but is now appearing regularly, if somewhat slowly. Vol. I (A–B), 683 pp., and vol. III (D–F), 945 pp., are now complete. A supplement to vol. I, 190 pp., giving a complete list of abbreviations and a number of maps, etc., was published in 1929. The present publisher (from the 21st fascicule onwards) is G. B. Teubner, Leipzig–Berlin.

illustrate the scientific outlook of the author ; it provides, one may hope, a further and instructive delineation to the portrait we have tried to give the reader of the two great scholars whom it commemorates.

Von Wartburg's *Dictionary* met with a very favourable reception from the learned world, and continues to do so. Most reviewers, after pointing out, in general, the outstanding qualities of the work, have sought to fill in certain gaps (no easy undertaking), or to question or rectify certain etymologies, for these are obviously the most subjective element in the work, and thus provide the readiest matter for discussion. Of the more important reviews we would single out for special mention those by : L. Spitzer, *Die neueren Sprachen*, XXX (1922), p. 264 f. (continued in succeeding volumes for the later fascicules) ; S. Puşcariu, *Dacoromania*, III (1923), p. 824 f. ; E. Gamillscheg, *Zeitschrift f. rom. Phil.*, XLIII (1923), p. 513 f. ; W. Meyer-Lübke, *Deutsche Literaturzeitung*, XLV (1924), col. 1957 f. ; H. Pedersen, *Litteris*, II (1925), p. 77 f. (proceeding) ; and Ch. Bruneau, *Romania*, LII (1926), p. 174 f. (proceeding). Of the above, Meyer-Lübke's review deals more particularly with general questions of theory, the others are concerned with more special points of omission or error, that of Pedersen being confined to the Celtic element.

A characterization of von Wartburg's scientific work is to be found in L. Spitzer's *Meisterwerke der romanischen Sprachwissenschaft*, II, p. 343, together with an explanation of the fact that in the works of the Swiss school as a whole there is a marked strain of dialectology. We find evidence of this, not only in von Wartburg's special studies listed below, and in the fact that he is the author of a *Bibliographie des dictionnaires patois*, Paris, 1934 (*Société des publications romanes et françaises*, No. 8), but also in his recent sketch of the history of French, *Évolution et structure de la langue française*, Leipzig, 1933, many of the best pages of which owe their particular savour to the familiarity of the author with dialect words and dialect problems, and his ability to link them up with wider themes and issues. It should be stated, finally, that, as the author of an etymological dictionary, he could not but be concerned with the principles of his craft ; these we find him discussing in an essay entitled *Grundfragen der etymologischen Forschung*, published in *Neue Jahrbücher für Wissenschaft und Jugendbildung*, VII (1931), p. 222 f.

The following is a selection of the more important of von Wartburg's remaining works : *Die Ausdrücke für die Fehler des Gesichtsorgans in den romanischen Sprachen und Dialekten. Eine semasiologische Untersuchung,* in *Revue de dialectologie romane,* III (1911), p. 402 f., and IV (1912), p. 16 f. ; *Zur Benennung des Schafes in den romanischen Sprachen. Ein Beitrag zur Frage der provinziellen Differenzierung des spätern Lateins,* in *Abhandlungen der Preussischen Akademie der Wissenschaften in Berlin,* Berlin, 1918 ; *Zur Stellung der Bergeller Mundart zwischen dem Rätischen und dem Lombardischen* (reproduced in *Meisterwerke der romanischen Sprachwissenschaft,* II, p. 186 f.). In addition to these studies relating to dialectology and linguistic geography the following of a more general character may be quoted : *Das Schriftfranzösische im FEW* (*sc. Franz. etym. Wörterbuch*), in *Festschrift für Dietrich Behrens,* Jena-Leipzig, 1929, p. 48 f., and *Der Einfluss der germanischen Sprachen auf den französischen Wortschatz,* in *Archiv für Kulturgeschichte,* XX (1930), p. 309 f.

Other studies in linguistic geography from the pens of Swiss scholars will be found listed below ; special mention will be made of P. S c h e u e r m e i e r, the chief explorer for the *Italian and Southern Swiss Atlas,* when we come to consider that work.

★   ★   ★

Next to Switzerland, Germany and Austria, which for this purpose we can take together, were the countries to take up linguistic
Linguistic Geography in Germany and Austria
geography with the greatest enthusiasm.[1] Nor is this to be wondered at, when we consider that those cultural circumstances which we have stressed in accounting for the Swiss readiness to adopt the new method (see above, p. 218) prevail, at least partially, in Germany and Austria as well. Also, it must not be forgotten that the earliest

[1] With regard to German linguistic geography, as applied to the study of the German vernaculars, much of interest is to be found in Kurt Wagner's *Deutsche Sprachlandschaften,* Marburg a.L., 1927, published in the series *Deutsche Dialektgeographie* (Heft 23), directed by Professor Wrede, and now comprising some thirty volumes (*v.* Jos. Schrijnen, *Essai de bibliographie de géographie linguistique générale,* p. 24). Wagner's book was reviewed by K. Jaberg, in *Zeitschr. f. rom. Phil.,* L (1930), p. 241 f. Jaberg, as a Romanicist, insists mainly on the relations between Germanic and Romance linguistic geography. He admits that the latter, though more advanced in some directions, has something to learn from its younger rival, particularly in the matter of its association with history, the tendency of the Romance practitioners, influenced by Gilliéron himself and by Saussure, being to confine themselves somewhat too narrowly to undiluted linguistics. In Germany, says Jaberg, thanks to the work of scholars like Ferd. Wrede, and his pupil Th. Frings, professor at Leipzig, great progress has been made in this direction, particularly in establishing the connection between linguistic areas and the ethnical group-

attempts at compiling a linguistic atlas were made in Germany (cp. pp. 146-7 above). We are therefore obliged to consider as inaccurate and prejudiced the explanation put forward by Dauzat, when he states (*La Géographie linguistique*, pp. 23-4) : " Chez les Allemands, au contraire, ce fut dès le début un véritable engouement : avec l'esprit d'imitation qui les caractérise—et aussi avec l'intuition qui leur fait reconnaître la valeur des travaux d'autrui— ils se sont attelés, dès avant la guerre, à des travaux de géographie linguistique." The other reasons alleged by Dauzat to account for the fact that German scholars have not produced work of outstanding importance in this branch of Romance linguistics may be left unnoticed, as they do not concern us here. It is certainly the case that neither Germany nor Austria can bring forward a name to compete with those we have mentioned hitherto, but the reason of this is to be sought elsewhere. As far as we are aware, no German or Austrian Romanicist has devoted the whole, or nearly the whole of his energies to linguistic geography, as is the case with a goodly number of the scholars we have described above. Some of the names with which we are now to deal we have already met with as workers in other domains, to which, like a number of those who are new to us, they have devoted or continue to devote the major part of their activities. Moreover, Germany is the country which led the way in the scientific study of Romance languages, and still holds the

ings and settlements of the past. Jaberg seizes the opportunity of defining with some precision the term ' Sprachlandschaft ', or as he himself, independently of Wagner, had put it, ' sprachliche Landschaft ', in relation to a conception which is assuming increasing importance in linguistic geography. By this term, or its French equivalent, ' type linguistique régional ', Jaberg understands : " An area which is not distinguished primarily by the extension of any particular phonetic, flexional, syntactical, or lexical feature, but which is characterized by a certain unity in its social and linguistic make-up, its greater or less conservatism, its unity or diversity, or by the direction and range of its prevailing speech tendencies, etc." (*Loc. cit.*, pp. 242-3). Something different, therefore, from the ' dialect area ' of which Gilliéron speaks (cp. p. 169, above). It should be made clear, however, that Wagner uses the term with reference rather to well-defined individual features than to any generally prevailing type.

We would also refer under this head to the Leipzig inaugural lecture of Th. Frings (the author, either singly, or in collaboration with his pupils, of numerous studies in linguistic geography, particularly on the region of the Rhine valley), entitled, *Sprachgeographie und Kulturgeographie* (*v. Zeitschrift für Deutschkunde*, 1930, p. 546 f.), where a number of theoretical questions are discussed. Frings has applied Romance methods to German problems in *Germania Romana*, Halle a.S., 1932. Cp. also : L. Jutz, *Grundzüge der Mundartforschung*, in *Zeitschr. f. Deutschkunde*, XLVI (1932), p. 465 f. ; Adolf Bach, *Deutsche Mundartenforschung, ihre Wege, Ergebnisse und Aufgaben*, Heidelberg, 1934 (a useful introduction to the subject) ; W. Pessler, *Deutsche Wortgeographie, Wesen und Werden, Wollen und Weg*, in *Wörter und Sachen*, XV (1933), p. 1 f. (important) ; Paul Kretschmer, *Wortgeographie der hochdeutschen Umgangssprache*, Göttingen, 1918 (a discussion of 350 words belonging to 170 localities).

record by the quantity and quality of her output in Romance philology. It was therefore all the more difficult for her, with her long-established traditions, now a century old, to leave the beaten track. Finally, as a non-Romance country, Germany has no reason to prefer one Romance tongue to the other ; her researches are more evenly spread over the whole field, whereas, until quite recently, material for geographical study was available for France alone. A further point, of more general import, lies in the very nature of this geographico-linguistic study, which requires a feeling for the language which a foreigner, however well informed theoretically, rarely acquires. To conduct it efficiently and convincingly —one thinks more particularly of the work of Gilliéron, Jaberg, and Jud—it would seem indispensable that the worker should confine himself either to his mother tongue or to a language familiar to him from childhood.

To sum up : the German scholars who have worked or are working in this field tend to consider it as a more or less secondary domain of their scientific activity. They have therefore not produced works of exceptional value, nor have they made any great innovations in method or theory. On the other hand, the attitude of German Romance scholars towards the geographical method and towards Gilliéron's theories has been more cordially receptive than that of all others except the Swiss. Neither in Germany nor in Austria was there, or is there to be found, any Romanicist to protest on principle against linguistic atlases and studies founded upon them, as A. Thomas, E. Bourciez, and others have done in France. The geographical point of view is to be met with, to a greater or less degree, in the work of all the German Romanicists, and it may be that this is of even greater value to our discipline as a whole than a richer harvest of more specialized geographico-linguistic studies.

Let us turn now to individuals and their works.

★

These two scholars are the joint authors of a study entitled, *Die Bezeichnungen der " Klette " im Galloromanischen*, Halle a.S., 1915. The

E. Gamillscheg and L. Spitzer work is dedicated to Gilliéron (under whom they both studied for a year in Paris, after graduating under Meyer-Lübke in Vienna), on the occasion of his sixtieth birthday. The authors display a laudable breadth of outlook. They did not confine themselves to tracking down and explaining the various names for the ' burdock ' in the Gallo-Romance dialects, but endeavoured, at the same time, to draw from the facts recorded general conclusions with regard both to the changes and confusion which occur so readily in plant nomenclature, and to linguistic geography as a whole (*v.* p. 73 f.). The work thus met with a favourable reception at the hands of reviewers.[1]

Gamillscheg alone has published in *Archivum Romanicum*, VI (1922), p. 1 f., a very detailed study entitled *Wetzstein und Kumpf im Galloromanischen*. We have the impression in this work that the author overdoes the ' homonymic ' explanation in accounting for the disappearance of certain terms and their replacement by others. None the less, he shows a commendable determination and ability to explore the minutest details of language life, and to set in evidence both the continuous struggle towards greater clarity and intelligibility, and at the same time the great variety of means of which a language can avail itself to meet the difficulties that may beset it.[2]

The same scholar, who recently contributed a study entitled *Essai de géographie linguistique : prov. lavaire ' lavoir'* to the presentation volume, *Omagiu Profesorului Ilie Bărbulescu*, Iași, 1931, p. 77 f., and whose *Romania Germanica*[3] is leavened throughout by the outlook of the linguistic geographer, has published a useful introduction to the subject in a booklet entitled : *Die Sprachgeographie und ihre Ergebnisse für die allgemeine Sprachwissenschaft*, Bielefeld-Leipzig, 1928. In this work[4] on the basis of his own investigations and of the

---

[1] It opened a series entitled *Sprachgeographische Arbeiten*, in which, up to 1930, only one other study has appeared, that of H. Schurter, *Die Ausdrücke für den ' Löwenzahn ' im Galloromanischen*, Halle a.S., 1921. For reviews, see A. Thomas, *Romania*, XLIV (1915–17), p. 274 f. ; W. v. Wartburg, *Literaturblatt f. germ. u. rom. Phil.*, XXXVII (1916), col. 120 f. (' the authors have considerably improved the methods of linguistic investigation ') ; K. Jaberg, *Archiv f. d. Studium d. neueren Spr. u. Lit.*, CXXXIX (1919), p. 110 f. ('Linguistic geography has enabled the authors to discover facts of a historical or biological order ') ; and G. Rohlfs, *Zeitschr. f. rom. Phil.*, XLI (1921), p. 453 f.

[2] Reviewed by : Iorgu Iordan, *Arhiva*, XXX (1923), p. 119 f. ; G. Giuglea, *Dacoromania*, III (1923), p. 971 f. ; A Meillet, *Bull. Soc. Ling.*, XXIV (1923–4), fasc. 2, p. 99 ; J. Jud, *Zeitschrift f. franz. Spr. u. Lit.*, XLVIII (1925–6), p. 158 f.

[3] Ernst Gamillscheg, *Romania Germanica. Sprach- und Siedlungsgeschichte der Germanen auf dem Boden des alten Römerreichs. Grundriss der germanischen Philologie*, XI i. Band I : *Zu den ältesten Berührungen zwischen Römern und Germanen. Die Franken. Die Westgoten*, Berlin and Leipzig, 1934 ; Bd. II : *Die Ostgoten. Die Langobarden. Die altgermanischen Bestandteile des Ostromanischen. Altgermanisches im Alpenromanischen*, ibid., 1935 ; Bd. III : *Die Burgunder. Schlusswort*, ibid., 1936.

[4] Reviewed by O. Bloch, *Rev. crit.*, yr. LXIII (1929), p. 463 f. ; E. Öhmann, *Neuphilologische Mitteilungen*, XXX (1929), p. 45 f. ; W. Schroeder, *Volkstum und Kultur der Romanen*, II (1929), p. 88 f. ; Eva Seifert, *Zeitschr. f. rom. Phil.*, L (1930), p. 244 f., etc.

conclusions of other scholars, Gamillscheg discusses briefly a variety of problems of general linguistics, such as the formation of dialects, sound-change, word-migration, the stratification of words and forms, homonymy, the loss and replacement of words, popular etymology, etc., with a view to showing the contribution made by linguistic geography towards their solution. His attitude towards the discipline is, as one would expect, extremely favourable, although, as befits a linguist with his marked critical faculty, he makes certain reservations, and demands, if errors and hasty conclusions are to be avoided in this type of work, that it should only be undertaken by people adequately equipped.

Leo Spitzer's activity in the field of linguistic geography has been confined, in the main, to the early years of his career, and was at no time very considerable. In addition to the brochure published in collaboration with Gamillscheg already mentioned, he has written *Die Namengebung bei neuen Kulturpflanzen im Französischen. Mit 3 Karten. 1. Mais und Buchweizen. 2. Kartoffel und topinambour*, which appeared in *Wörter und Sachen*, IV (1912), p. 122 f., and V (1913), p. 124 f. Here he combines the geographical with the ' word and thing ' method, in the manner favoured, as we have seen, by the Swiss school. He is also the author of *Die Sprachgeographie (1909–14), Kritische Zusammenfassung*, in *Revue de dialectologie romane*, VI (1914), p. 318 f., which gives a detailed account of the work in the field of linguistic geography during the previous quinquennium. Mention should also be made of his numerous reviews, particularly of Gilliéron's studies, some of which we have already had occasion to cite.

Spitzer, it must be said, had never shown a whole-hearted enthusiasm for the methods of linguistic geography, even from the beginning. He criticized its exclusiveness, and the, so to speak, mathematical and therefore forced and artificial nature of its procedure in a matter so shifting and intangible as the life of language, defects which he discovered particularly in the very founder of the method. But after the war even this qualified enthusiasm began to wane, until finally he has become an outspoken adversary of the Gilliéronian discipline and especially of linguistic atlases. We shall see later that the compilation of an atlas has come to be considered as almost an obligation for every linguistic area, a prospect which, to a revolutionary mind, might well appear an abuse that calls for some repression. Further, in later years, Spitzer has been cultivating a new branch of linguistic studies, namely, stylistics (*v.* Chap. II, p. 137 f.), which has no very apparent relationship with linguistic geography ; whereas, in the old material used by the dialectologist, i.e. dictionaries, glossaries, patois texts, and the like, it finds a plentiful source of information. So we find him now protesting against the whole policy of linguistic atlases, and the investigation of dialect on the spot by means of a questionnaire of the Gilliéronian type, and advocating the composition of glossaries, with grammars and texts annexed. This attitude, already visible in his review of the *Catalonian Atlas*, in *Zeitschr. f. rom. Phil.*, XLV (1925), p. 614, came out strongly in a paper read to the International Congress of Linguists held at The Hague in April, 1928, and published subsequently in the *Revue internationale des études basques*, XX (1929), p. 169 f.[1] Spitzer's reasons for preferring the dictionary to the atlas may be summarized as follows. The picture of a language given by a dictionary accompanied by texts is a natural one ; it is at the same time historical and much more complete than that provided by an atlas. In a dictionary, the creative element in a language is revealed, while an atlas misses this entirely. Atlases offer us a grammaticalized or standardized type of speech, in a more or less artificial form, as it appears or appeared at a single moment of its existence, whereas no moment is exactly like the moment that preceded it or that follows it. The linguistic material contained in an atlas thus reminds one of the representative system in politics : just as millions of citizens send to Parliament a comparatively small number of delegates, so the great mass of popular speech finds itself represented in an atlas by a few chosen hundreds of words or forms, which, as in political life, are not always those most qualified to speak in the name of the multitude. With regard to the collecting of material for dictionaries Spitzer prefers the correspondence method, as being less artificial than that based on direct investigation in the field.[2]

---

[1] Cp. also *Die neueren Sprachen*, XXXVI (1928), p. 440. Spitzer's paper was prompted by a proposal of A. Meillet's, at the same congress, that a linguistic world atlas should be compiled to enable the languages of the earth to be studied comprehensively on a geographical basis.

[2] On this question of Atlases versus Dictionaries, cp. Meyer-Lübke's remarks in his review of von Wartburg's *Franz. etym. Wb.*, in *Deutsche Literaturzeitung*, XLV (1924), col. 1957 f. ; M.-L. shows a preference for dictionaries, though for other reasons than Spitzer, but advocates both methods. K. Jaberg also discusses the point in his review of Griera's *Atlas lingüistic de Catalunya*, *Romania*, L (1924), p. 278 f., insisting on the fact that the material contained in an Atlas is all collected under the same conditions and thus, though not so rich as that provided in dictionaries, is entirely homogeneous and a safer basis of investigation.

Of the remaining German scholars who have worked in the field of linguistic geography we shall only mention at this stage

Karl von Ettmayer

K. von Ettmayer ; to others we shall refer later, when dealing with various Romance atlases, and also in the section relating to onomasiology. Von Ettmayer is the author of a work entitled *Über das Wesen der Dialektbildung, erläutert an den Dialekten Frankreichs*, and published in *Denkschriften der Akademie der Wissenschaften in Wien, philologisch-historische Klasse*, 66. Band, 3. Abhandlung, Vienna-Leipzig, 1924. Beginning with a historical survey of dialect study, in which he discerns a Romantic outlook previous to Gilliéron, and an anti-Romantic outlook due to Gilliéron and his school, von Ettmayer, while admitting the superiority of the linguistic geographers, finds that they also have their deficiencies, which he proceeds to enumerate and analyse. A serious flaw in the Gilliéronian doctrine, from the point of view of first principles (' erkenntnis-theoretisch '), is, according to von Ettmayer, its failure to recognize that a word possesses, in addition to sound and meaning (' Bedeutung '), a further element which he calls ' Sinn ', ' Wert ', or ' Geltung ', and which we may translate by ' emotional ' or ' affective ' value. Thus, Fr. *jurer comme un payen, comme un charretier, voiturier, bourguignon, démon*, etc., are perfectly synonymous from the point of view of affective values, though the intellectual content of the words *payen, charretier*, etc., is entirely different. As a result of this error, many of the maps of the French *Atlas* do not show us, strictly speaking, the boundaries of word distribution (' Wortgrenzen '), but boundaries that have been determined by particular affective values that given words may or may not possess (' Wortgeltungsgrenzen '), as is shown, notably, by such maps as those for *garçon, beau, profond*, etc.

With regard to the causes underlying the formation of dialects, von Ettmayer is of the opinion that they are to be sought, not in local variations in methods of expression, but rather in the trend towards mutual adaptation which is manifest in individual speakers, an idea already to be found in Hermann Paul's suggestion that we should seek to explain, not the peculiarities of a dialect, but the characteristics which the members of a given speech community have in common, and the manner in which the individuals combine to accommodate their language each to that of his fellow-members. The author notes three stages in the existence of a dialect : ' patois ', based on purely local relationship, ' jargon ', presupposing intellectual relationships, and ' idiom '. All three he analyses in the minutest detail, showing how each in turn contributes to the building up of dialect. He has much of interest to say concerning the cultural and commercial channels through which the speech of Paris invades the provinces, and concerning regions which show linguistic innovations, the source and direction of which cannot be traced. When considering the process of accommodation alluded to above, we should pay particular attention to morphology, which in this regard is of more importance than vocabulary. Morphological boundaries, although they frequently coincide over long stretches with lexical boundaries, often sharply diverge from them.[1] With regard to phonetic boundaries, Ettmayer apparently does not share the view of Schuchardt and Gilliéron, who hold that they are fictitious. There are cases, he contends, which strongly contradict this doctrine, for example, the distribution of the palatalized and non-palatalized forms of *ca-* and *ga-*, etc., in France. After discussing this question in detail, the author concludes as follows : " None the less I believe I have proved in the above discussion of the phenomena relating to the development of *k* before *a*, of *g* before *e* and *i*, and of Lat. *j*, that in other cases a certain constancy in the distribution of various phonetic features stands out so clearly from the pages of the *Atlas* that we cannot close our eyes to its existence." And, lower down : " When we survey in their totality the sound-changes which have taken place on French soil, we are obliged to admit that this well-marked delimitation of sound-phenomena is possible in the majority of cases and that, quite definitely, we can enclose with a fairly clear line the areas where final vowels drop, where *d*, from earlier *t*, falls between vowels, where *ct* changes to either *tš* (*ts*) or *it*, where *l* remains before a consonant, be the latter labial or dental, and so forth." " To seek to use the *Atlas* as proof of the dictum that sound-phenomena are incapable of delimitation would be to travesty the facts " (*op. cit.*, p. 54, col. 2). " All the *Atlas* teaches us is that (1) a sound boundary which actually exists is frequently disturbed as a result of word-migration, and (2) that certain individual sound-phenomena do not in fact admit of sharp de-

---

[1] Thus the Limousin dialect of southern France has much in common with French proper in sounds and vocabulary, but in morphology it has kept many of the features of Old Provençal. Cp. also, A. Terracher, *Les aires morphologiques* . . . (see above, p. 209) where the importance of morphology is likewise stressed, though from a different angle.

limitation " (*ibid.*, p. 54, col. 2, 55, col. 1). " Hence it is plain that the so-called ' Sound-laws ' must be a genuine unified product, and no chance outcome of word-migration, and also that, to say the least, despite contradictory individual cases which may occur, as was observable in the treatment of -*aticum* and of the ' palatalized ' labials in Southern France, the uniform treatment which has been applied to a whole series of sound-groups in a given dialect as a result of a great influx of borrowed words with similar features, represents a principle which sets the stamp of unification on such regular sound-changes as well " (*ibid.*, p. 55, col. 1).

As we see, von Ettmayer endeavours to build a bridge between linguistic geography and the neo-grammarian doctrine, or, more precisely, strives to extract from the *Linguistic Atlas of France* arguments in support of the ' sound-laws ', his conception of which differs only in non-essentials from that traditionally held.[1] Whether he succeeds or not is another matter. His study appears to have passed almost unnoticed, and we can quote no reviews of it. Indeed, a similar fate seems to have befallen all the works of Meyer-Lübke's successor in the Vienna chair of Romance Philology. His manner of approach to the problems of language shows real independence and originality of thought, but these he tends frequently to exaggerate, to the point of oddity. Added to this, a certain obscurity of style, reflected, we fear, in the above quotations from his work, accentuates still further the impression of strangeness which his linguistic doctrine leaves with us.

★ ★ ★

---

[1] We find a somewhat similar point of view expressed by E. Gamillscheg, *Sprachgeographie* . . . , p. 10 f., where he takes up the defence of the ' Sound-laws ', and breaks a lance against some of their unnamed opponents. But it must be admitted that the Berlin professor is at least clear in his pronouncements and one of his detailed observations is of particular interest to the present discussion. The sound-laws, he says, are valid for phenomena that form a series, that is, for groups of words or forms which for various reasons go together. Isolated elements, which have either ceased to belong to a series, or which have none in which they can enter, escape from the influence of the sound-laws, and are exposed to other influences, particularly that of popular etymology.

For a more recent expression of von Ettmayer's views on the sound-laws, see his article, *Lateinisch-Romanisches zur Lautgesetzfrage*, in *Glotta*, XXV (1936), p. 79 f.

To complete our information upon the repercussions of linguistic geography outside France, its native country, we must speak of the work conducted in this field in two other Romance lands, Catalonia and Italy. The former is in many respects like Switzerland. In reality, of course, Catalan is a language in itself, which has been used in literary and scientific works for centuries, but, owing to the fact that the territory where it is spoken had lost its political independence, it had been considered by the Spanish rulers as a dialect, an inferior idiom. A consequence of this has been an extraordinary development in Catalonia of philological (and historical) studies, the sense of injustice having awakened and fostered in the Catalans an affection and interest for everything that could be regarded as a specific product of their national soul. This regionalist movement in politics and culture has led to quite remarkable results in the field of Romance studies. It may be said that, taking count of its geographical extent and its population, there is no Romance territory where linguistic activity is more intense. Nor are we surprised to note that, of all the linguistic branches, dialectology has been, and continues to be, cultivated with the greatest ardour. The organ for this dialect activity is the *Butlletí de dialectologia catalana*, founded (in 1913) and directed by A. Griera, M. de Montoliu, and P. Barnils, all of whom had studied abroad, in France, Germany, and Switzerland.

Linguistic Geography in Catalonia and Italy

★

The most active of the three, in the domain which here concerns us, is A. Griera. His dialect studies, like that of the other Catalans, have had as their chief object the question of dialect frontiers.[1] We find here evidence of the influence of Morf and Gauchat, particularly of the former, inasmuch as Griera endeavours to explain the formation of dialects on the

Antoni Griera

---

[1] A. Griera, *La frontera catalano-aragonesa. Estudi geogràfico-lingüístic*, Barcelona, 1914 (reviewed in the *Revista de filología española*, III [1916], p. 73 f., by Menéndez Pidal, who protests against Griera's attempt to fix linguistic boundaries by the sole means of a questionnaire. Pidal also denies the assertion that the boundary between Catalan and Aragonese was conditioned by the extent of the bishopric of Roda and the county of Ribagorza in the XIth century) ; *La frontera del català occidental*, in *Butll. dial. catal.*, VI (1918), p. 17 f. and VII (1919), 69 f. ; *El català oriental*, *ibid.*, VIII (1920), p. 1 f. ; *El català occidental*, *ibid.*, VIII (1920), p. 35 f., and

basis of the ancient ecclesiastical and political divisions of the territories concerned (see above, p. 220). Griera has also treated the problem from the point of view of the Catalan territory as a whole, enquiring into how it was constituted, its special characteristics, and the particular place it occupies in the Romance family. At its beginning, the discussion as to the place of Catalan, as frequently occurs in similar cases, had a definitely political flavour. As is well known, the Spanish are averse to considering Catalan as a separate language, quite distinct from the other languages of the Peninsula, and it was in order to prove its individuality that Griera wrote an article entitled *Afro-romànic o ibero-romànic?*, published in the *Butlletí de dialectologia catalana*, X (1922), p. 34 f. In this he maintains that the Romance languages are to be divided into two groups, one, comprising Spanish, Portuguese, Southern Italian, and Rumanian, which is characterized by a strongly marked African influence (African in a very wide sense, comprising Arabian, Berber, and Turkish as well), the other, to which the remainder of the Romance languages, including Catalan, belong, which is free from such African admixtures. In other words, Catalan stands with French, Provençal, etc., and is thus ' Iberoromanic ', and not ' Afroromanic ' like Spanish or Portuguese.[1]

The discussion concerning the place of Catalan broke out afresh when Meyer-Lübke's booklet *Das Katalanische* was published in Heidelberg in 1925. Griera examined the work in a study of some sixty pages, entitled *Castellà—Català—Provençal. Observacions sobre el llibre de W. Meyer-Lübke*, in *Zeitschrift f. rom. Phil.*, XLV

IX (1921), p. 1 f. ; *El valencià, ibid.*, IX, p. 4 f. ; *El rossellonès, ibid.*, IX, p. 33 f.— P. Barnils, *Die Mundart von Alacant*, Barcelona, 1913, and *Dialectes catalans*, in *Butll. dial. catal.*, VII (1919), p. 1 f.—M. de Montoliu has published, *inter alia*, *La geografia lingüística*, in the journal *Estudio*, I (1912), p. 24 f., and II (1913), p. 76 f. : the first part gives a summary of the views of Morf, Gauchat, and Jud ; the second contains a synthesis of Gilliéron's theories and demonstrates with the help of the *Linguistic Atlas of France* what is meant by word expansion and homonymy.—On the topic of Catalan boundaries, cp. also : B. Schädel, *Mundartliches aus Mallorca*, Halle a.S., 1905, *La frontière entre le gascon et le catalan, Romania,* XXXVII (1908), p. 140 f., *Die katalanischen Pyrenäendialekte, Revue de dialectologie romane,* I (1909), p. 15 f. ; H. Meier, *Beiträge zur sprachlichen Gliederung der Pyrenäenhalbinsel und ihrer historischen Begründung,* Hamburg, 1930.

[1] The study was reviewed by W. v. Wartburg, *Archivum Romanicum*, VIII (1924), p. 487 f. ; J. Jud, *Romania*, LI (1925), p. 291 f. ; and Meyer-Lübke, *Zeitschr. f. rom. Phil.*, XLVI (1926), p. 116 f. All three combat Griera's assertions, to a greater or less degree, alleging that they are based solely on lexical facts, which cannot be decisive in such matters, and criticizing him for making no distinction between old and comparatively new words, and for not taking into account the ' things ' which the words represent, etc. M.-Lübke also replies to criticisms directed by Griera against his own book *Das Katalanische* (see above).

(1925), p. 198 f. Although the Bonn scholar, who, in his *Einführung in das Studium der romanischen Sprachwissenschaft*, ed. III, p. 24, had classified Catalan among the dialects of Provençal, now set it apart as an independent linguistic unity having affinities with Spanish and still closer affinities with Provençal, Griera was not satisfied, and insisted on the status of Catalan as an idiom apart, distinct from the Spanish dialects in the west, and the Provençal dialects to the north. Whoever travels on foot, and not in the train, he adds, is quick to notice the existence of certain definite linguistic boundaries between Catalonia and Aragon on the one hand, and Catalonia and South-West France on the other. The Spanish scholar, Amado Alonso, also took part in the discussion, with a study entitled, *La subagrupación románica del catalán*, published in *Revista de filología española*, XIII (1926), p. 1 f. Alonso disagreed with both Meyer-Lübke and Griera ; the former he accused of exaggerating the resemblances between Catalan and Provençal, the latter he reproves for putting Catalan in the ' Iberoromanic ' group and considering Spanish as ' Afroromanic ' (see above).[1]

Problems related to the above topic are also discussed by Griera in the *Revue de linguistique romane*, V (1929), p. 192 f., in a study entitled *Sur l'origine des langues afro-romanes ou ibéro-romanes*. We may further mention a bibliographical survey of Catalan Philology, published in the same journal, vol. I (1925), p. 35 f., which contains important information on dialect work (p. 70 f.), and *Etudes de géographie linguistique*, I-ère série, *Anuari de l'Oficina Romànica de Lingüística i Literatura*, V (1932), p. 73 f.

But the most important of Griera's works, and the one which is of the most concern to the linguistic geographer, is his *Atlas lingüístic de Catalunya*. This we shall describe at a later stage.

★   ★   ★

The Italians, in general, have shown little enthusiasm for the Gilliéronian method and doctrine. This might appear surprising when we remember that Italy, thanks to the philologist Ascoli, was

---

[1] Cp. Griera's reviews in *Revue de linguistique romane*, V (1929), p. 256 f., and *Zeitschr. f. rom. Phil.*, L (1930), p. 246 f. Alonso represents the views of his master, Menéndez Pidal, who (cp., *inter alia*, *Discursos leídos ante la Real Academia Española en la recepción pública del Excelentísimo Señor Don Francesco Codera*, Madrid, 1910, p. 73 f.) maintains that Catalan should not be kept apart from the other Romance languages of the Peninsula.

the birthplace of scientific dialectology. But it is not improbable that this is the very reason of their attitude, and that the influence of their great and well-remembered scholar is still so powerful that they cannot imagine any other method of investigating vernacular speech than that inaugurated by Ascoli himself. However this may be, their most celebrated dialectologists, like C. Salvioni, C. Merlo, and C. Battisti, are, or have been, distinctly hostile to linguistic geography. Moreover, those scholars who have shown an understanding of the Gilliéronian doctrine have only occasionally published studies in linguistic geography and have confined themselves in the main to using its results as a leaven for their work in other fields.

★

This eminent scholar, now Professor of Romance Philology in the University of Rome, and member of the Italian Academy, showed himself to be a convinced supporter of

Giulio Bertoni

Gilliéron from the beginning. But he has published little himself in the field of linguistic geography, his exceptional activity having led him into numerous other paths, not only linguistic, but literary as well. He is, however, the author of a few studies which concern us here, one of which we single out for special reference, the first in date, and the most important for a variety of reasons, namely, *Le denominazioni dell' imbuto nell' Italia del Nord. Ricerca di geografia linguistica con una tavola a colori fuori testo*, Bologna-Modena, 1909. The author begins with certain theoretical considerations, protesting against the tendency to attach excessive importance to sounds in etymological work, and combating the ' sound-laws ' as understood by the neo-grammarians, by asserting that their hypothesis of ' identity of condition ', entailing identity of phonetic development in all words similarly situated, was a fiction belied by the facts of language. Linguistic geography has proved, he maintains, that every word has a life of its own, differing from that of other words. Bertoni then proceeds with the study proper, which is an attempt to retrace the history of the terms for ' funnel ' on the basis of their geographical distribution, as shown in the replies received from correspondents in forty-seven localities of North Italy. The study is of no great size, but it raised a controversy which is of some importance for the subject we are discussing. It was criticized unfavourably by Salvioni, in *Rendiconti del Reale Istituto Lombardo di scienze e lettere*, serie II, vol. XLIV (1910), pp. 793–4, and Bertoni published a reply, entitled *A proposito di geografia linguistica*, in *Atti e memorie della Reale Deputazione di Storia Patria per le Provincie Modenesi*, serie V, vol. VII, Modena, 1911 (10 pages in offprint), where he takes up the defence of the new discipline and endeavours to show that the point of view of his opponent belongs to a past epoch of etymological and linguistic method.[1]

We have seen above, p. 142, that in his booklet entitled *Programma di filologia romanza come scienza idealistica*, Bertoni finds a place for linguistic geography, and later we shall speak of the part he played for a period in the preparatory work for the Italian *Atlas* in conjunction with M. Bartoli and U. Pellis. We shall therefore defer further consideration of his work until we come to discuss, in the final section of this chapter, the ' neo-linguists ' and their chief, M. Bartoli, the first redactor of the Italian Atlas.

Although, strictly speaking, a classical philologist, B. A. Terracini deserves a place in our survey of geographico-linguistic work, because he is the author of a certain number **B. A. Terracini** of studies which have a direct bearing on our subject, namely, *Il parlare d'Usseglio*, in *Archivio glottologico italiano*, XVII (1910–13), pp. 198 f. and 289 f., *Questioni di metodo nella linguistica storica*, in *Atene e Roma*, nuova serie, II (1921) (38 pages in offprint), *In morte di Jules Gilliéron*, in *Archivio glottologico italiano*, XX (1926), p. 151 f., etc. The first of these studies, of which the earlier part contains the investigation proper of the dialect material collected, and the later, theoretical considerations of a general character based upon the investigation, reveals Terracini as a follower of Rousselot, although he has much that is fresh to say, especially with regard to speech peculiarities due to sex or age. In the second, the author, after setting forth the achievements of the neo-grammarian school, in historical

---

[1] Reviewed also by J. Jud, *Literaturblatt f. germ. u. rom. Phil.*, XXX (1909), col. 294 f. Bertoni's other studies in linguistic geography are : *Geografia linguistica*, in *Fanf. di Domenica*, no. 28, 14th July, 1907 ; a review of Gilliéron and Mongin's ' *Scier* ' *dans la Gaule romane*, in *Studi di filologia moderna*, 1909 ; *Denominazioni del* ' *ramarro* ' (see below, p. 249) ; *Intorno ad alcune denominazioni del* ' *mirtello* ' *nei dialetti alpini*, in *Archivum Romanicum*, I (1917), p. 73 f. ; *Intorno alle denominazioni della* ' *gerla* ' *in alcuni dialetti alpini*, ibid., p. 153 f. ; *La geografia linguistica*, in *La Cultura*, III (1923), p. 404 f. ; together with numerous reviews to be found listed in *Annuario della Reale Accademia d'Italia*, 1933, p. 24 f.

grammar, etymology and semantics, discusses the new methods, particularly that of linguistic geography, and maintains that the opposition between the latter and the older methods is not so fundamental as to make them mutually exclusive, but that on the contrary they can quite easily be reconciled.[1] In other words, Terracini endeavours to build a bridge between Indo-European philology and the Gilliéronian system, of which, in the obituary article mentioned above, he provides an admirable summary.

★   ★   ★

In the latter part of the present chapter we have had occasion to speak of a number of studies in Romance dialectology (e.g. those of Morf, Gauchat, etc.) as if they came under the head-
Dialect Studies ing of linguistic geography, a term more strictly applicable to the work of Gilliéron and his followers. This procedure would seem to need no apology, in view of their common aim, the investigation of vernacular speech. But there is a further point which not only justifies our method of procedure but makes it practically inevitable, namely, the tendency of recent years for the two disciplines to converge. Linguistic geography is an offshoot of dialectology, and though at first sharply differentiated in method and outlook from its parent, it ceases more and more to be so, inasmuch as the dialectologists have modified their methods on the lines of the newer discipline. They, too, conduct their investigations by direct enquiry in the field, and though they may not actually compile atlases, they at least use the cartographical method to show the distribution of various linguistic phenomena, which comes very much to the same thing. Similarly, they also have recourse to the ' word and thing ' method whenever occasion arises.

In view of this convergence of what at one time constituted two distinct disciplines, the reader will find in the following list of recent work studies which belong to both domains without distinction. The list, which we give without commentary, incomplete as it must necessarily be, provides some idea of the very great activity in the

[1] We have already seen in the course of the present chapter that this view is fairly widely held, particularly among the Indo-Europeanists. Some Romanicists, too, for example Gamillscheg and von Ettmayer (see above), trained in the neo-grammarian school, adopt a similar attitude.

field of dialect investigation—on increasingly geographical lines—which is characteristic of present-day Romance linguistics, an activity the scope and intensity of which may not have been realized from the perusal of the preceding pages.

A further word of explanation is necessary. A number of works already mentioned, and many of those about to be listed, have very similar titles : " The names for such and such a thing in the dialects of such and such a region." We find this kind of investigation already in a number of Gilliéron's works, for example, the vernacular words for ' to saw ' or for ' the bee ' are discussed in ' *Scier* ' *dans la Gaule romane*, and in *La généalogie des mots qui désignent l'abeille* respectively. His example has been widely followed, for the very good reason that the material of a linguistic atlas is naturally treated in this manner. A linguistic map is really a map of the various dialect names for a given notion, and the study of a map is, of necessity, a study of the nomenclature applied to such and such an object. Studies of this kind are termed onomasiological. It should not be thought, however, that we are claiming onomasiology as a child of linguistic geography. The latter has merely increased the number of investigations of this type because of the kind of material it provides. Onomasiology[1] has its origin elsewhere, though none the less still in close connexion with dialect study. The works which laid the foundations of this branch of linguistics were, in chronological order, and also, one may venture to say, in order of importance : E. Tappolet's *Die romanischen Verwandtschaftsnamen*, Strassburg, 1895 ;[2] A. Zauner's *Die romanischen*

---

[1] Jud, *Archivum Romanicum*, IX (1925), p. 105, defines the aims of onomasiology as follows : the investigation of a word as the expression of a group of well-defined notions within a linguistic community either great or small, in order to compose, so to speak, an inventory of the means employed by the language to express a given idea. The fundamental principles of this discipline are set forth and discussed by Jaberg in his article already quoted, *Sprache als Äusserung und Sprache als Mitteilung. Grundfragen der Onomasiologie*, in *Archiv f. d. Studium der neueren Spr. u. Lit.*, CXXXVI (1917), p. 84 f.

[2] We have already had occasion to mention this scholar in our description of the *Glossaire de la Suisse romande* (see above, p. 222), in which he took and continues to take a leading part. It should be added that he has shown from the beginning a ready understanding and appreciation of the new tendencies in our discipline. Thus, in an article entitled *Phonetik und Semantik in der etymologischen Forschung* (*Arch. f. d. St. d. neueren Spr. u. Lit.*, CXV [1905], p. 101 f.), we find him insisting upon the importance of the semantic element in proving the etymology of a word, and attempting thus to reconcile the doctrines of Schuchardt and Antoine Thomas. His interest in meaning is further evidenced by his affection for onomasiological studies. Another ' modern ' quality he possesses is that he recognizes the importance in etymological research of ingenuity and imagination by the side of knowledge. He evinces further, in a study called *Die Ursachen des Wortreichtums bei den Haustiernamen der französischen Schweiz*, in *Archiv f. d. St. d. neueren Spr. u. Lit.*, CXXXI

Namen der Körperteile, in *Romanische Forschungen*, XIV (1903), p. 339 f., and C. Merlo's *I nomi romanzi delle stagioni e dei mesi*, Torino, 1904. As the titles indicate, the above works embrace the whole of the Romance area, languages, and dialects. Latterly, as the material available has grown in quantity, owing to linguistic atlases and other collections of dialect matter, investigations tend to be confined to more restricted areas and are consequently more detailed. Scarcely any of those mentioned below cover the whole Romance field.

K. Kemna, *Der Begriff ' Schiff' im Französischen*, Marburg, 1901.

H. Davidsen, *Die Benennungen des Hauses und seiner Teile im Französischen*, Kiel, 1903.

W. O. Streng, *Haus und Hof im Französischen*, Helsingfors, 1907.

E. Tappolet, *Les termes de fenaison, le regain et la pâture d'automne*, in *Bulletin du Glossaire des patois de la Suisse romande*, VIII (1907), p. 26 f., and X (1909), p. 17 f.

J. Callais, *Die Mundart von Hattigny und die Mundart von Ommeray, nebst lautgeographischer Darstellung der Dialektgrenze zwischen Vosgien und Saunois (Lothringen)*, Metz, 1909.

Fr. Fankhauser, *Das Patois von Val d'Illiez (Unterwallis)*, 1911 (extract from *Revue de dialectologie romane*, II–III [1910–11]).

Josef Jordan, *Die Bezeichnungen der Angriffswaffen im Französischen*, Bonn, 1911.

C. Merlo, *Die romanischen Bezeichnungen des Faschings*, in *Wörter und Sachen*, III (1911–12), p. 88 f.

K. Göhri, *Die Ausdrücke für Blitz und Donner im Galloromanischen. Eine onomasiologische Studie*, in *Revue de dialectologie romane*, IV (1912), pp. 45 f. and 140 f.

K. Salow, *Sprachgeographische Untersuchungen über den östlichen Teil des katalanisch-languedokischen Grenzgebietes*, Hamburg, 1912.

A. Chr. Thorn, *Quelques dénominations du ' cordonnier' en français. Etude de géographie linguistique*, in *Archiv f. d. St. d. neueren Spr. u. Lit.*, CXXIX (1912), p. 81 f.

K. Bauer, *Gebäckbezeichnungen im Galloromanischen*, Darmstadt, 1913.

G. Bertoni, *Denominazioni del ' ramarro' (Lacerta viridis) in Italia*, in *Romania*, XLII (1913), p. 161 f.

(1913), p. 81 f., a capacity for appreciating the importance of affective values in the life of languages, and for ranking at their true value logic and conscious will, which in the eyes of so many linguists take on an importance far in excess of their deserts. Tappolet has received the honour of a *Festschrift*, Bâle, 1935.

Fr. Fleischer, *Studien zur Sprachgeographie der Gascogne*, Halle a.S., 1913.

W. Kaufmann, *Die galloromanischen Bezeichnungen für den Begriff 'Wald'. Wortgeschichtliche Studie auf Grund der Karten 'forêt' und 'bois' des Atlas linguistique de la France*, Zürich, 1913.

F. Krüger, *Sprachgeographische Untersuchungen in Languedoc und Roussillon*, Hamburg, 1913 (extract from *Revue de dialectologie romane*, III–V, 1911–13).

A. Chr. Thorn, *Sartre-Tailleur. Etude de lexicologie et de géographie linguistique*, Lund-Leipzig, 1913.

H. Urtel, *Prolegomena zu einer Studie über die romanischen Krankheitsnamen*, in *Arch. f. d. St. d. neueren Spr. u. Lit.*, CXXX (1913), p. 81 f.

C. Volpati, *Nomi romanzi del pianeta Venere*, in *Revue de dialectologie romane*, V (1913), p. 312 f.

P. G. Goidànich, *Denominazioni del pane e di dolci caserecci in Italia*, Bologna, 1914 (in *Memorie della R. Academia delle scienze dell' Istituto di Bologna*, classe di scienze morali, serie I, tomo VIII, p. 23 f.).

A. Griera, *Els noms dels vents en català*, in *Butlletí de dialectologia catalana*, II (1914), p. 74.

F. Krüger, *Studien zur Lautgeschichte westspanischer Mundarten auf Grund von Untersuchungen an Ort und Stelle*, Hamburg, 1914 (with two maps).

S. Merian, *Die französischen Namen des Regenbogens*, Halle a.S., 1914.

C. Merlo, *I nomi romanzi della Candelara o festa della Purificazione di Maria Vergine*, Perugia, 1915.

H. Rotzler, *Die Benennungen der Milchstrasse im Französischen*, in *Romanische Forschungen*, XXXIII (1915), p. 794 f.

O. Schroefl, *Die Ausdrücke für den Mohn im Galloromanischen*, Graz, 1915.

P. Herzog, *Die Bezeichnungen der täglichen Mahlzeiten in den romanischen Sprachen und Dialekten*, Zürich, 1916.

Margot Henschel, *Zur Sprachgeographie Südwestgalliens*, Braunschweig–Berlin, 1917.

C. Merlo, *I nomi romanzi del dì feriale con una appendice sui nomi del dì festivo*, Pisa, 1918.

G. Bottiglioni, *L'ape e l'alveare nelle lingue romanze*, Pisa, 1919.

J. Lazzari, *I nomi di alcuni fenomeni atmosferici nei dialetti dell' alta Italia geografica*, Pisa, 1919.

I. Pauli, ' *Enfant*,' ' *garçon* ', ' *fille* ' *dans les langues romanes, étudiés particulièrement dans les dialectes gallo-romans et italiens. Essai de lexicologie comparée*, Lund, 1919.

W. Gottschalk, *Lat. audire im Französischen*, Giessen, 1921.

W. Hebeisen, *Die Bezeichnungen für Geschirr, Eimer, Krug im Französischen, Oberitalienischen und Rätoromanischen mit besonderer Berücksichtigung des Alpengebietes*, Bern, 1921.

W. Ochs, *Die Bezeichnungen der ' Wilden Rose ' im Galloromanischen*, Giessen, 1921.

H. Schurter, *Die Ausdrücke für den ' Löwenzahn ' im Galloromanischen*, Halle a.S., 1921.

G. Stephan, *Die Bezeichnungen der ' Weide ' im Galloromanischen*, Giessen, 1921.

F. Usinger, *Die französischen Bezeichnungen des Modehelden im 18. und 19. Jahrhundert*, Giessen, 1921.

Alice Brügger, *Les noms du roitelet en France*, Zürich, 1922.

G. Walter, *Die Bezeichnungen der Buche im Galloromanischen*, Giessen, 1922.

E. Weick, *Lat. cadere im Französischen*, Giessen, 1922.

V. Bertoldi, *Un ribelle nel regno dei fiori. I nomi romanzi del Colchicum autumnale L. attraverso il tempo e lo spazio*, Geneva, 1923.

H. Schmidt, *Die Bezeichnungen für Zaun und Hag in den romanischen Sprachen und Mundarten, speziell in der romanischen Schweiz, I. Teil : Westschweiz*, Zürich, 1923.

E. Tappolet, *Les noms gallo-romans du moyeu*, in Romania, XLIX (1923), p. 481 f.

P. Benoit, *Die Bezeichnungen für Feuerbock und Feuerkette im Französischen, Italienischen und Rätoromanischen mit besonderer Berücksichtigung des Alpengebietes*, in Zeitschr. f. rom. Phil., XLIV (1924), p. 385 f.

Fr. Aeppli, *Die wichtigsten Ausdrücke für das Tanzen in den romanischen Sprachen*, Halle a.S., 1925.

Fr. Hobi, *Die Benennungen von Sichel und Sense in den Mundarten der romanischen Schweiz*, Heidelberg, 1926.

E. Hochuli, *Einige Bezeichnungen für den Begriff Strasse, Weg und Kreuzweg im Romanischen*, Aarau, 1926.

N. Maccarrone, *Le denominazioni del ' tacchino ' e della ' tacchina ' nelle lingue romanze*, in Archivio glottologico italiano, XX (1926), sezione neolatina, p. 1 f.

K. Gernand, *Die Bezeichnungen des Sarges im Galloromanischen*, Giessen, 1928.

M. Sandmann, *Die Bezeichnungen der Meise in den romanischen Sprachen*, Bonn, 1929.

Maria Margarete Stangier, *Die Bezeichnungen des Schweines im Galloromanischen*, Bonn, 1929.

H. Kläui, *Die Bezeichnungen für ' Nebel ' im Galloromanischen*, Zürich, 1930.

K. Miethlich, *Bezeichnungen von Getreide- und Heuhaufen im Galloromanischen*, Aarau, 1930.

L. Feiler, *Die Bezeichnungen für den Waschtrog im Galloromanischen*, in *Romanische Forschungen*, XLV (1931), p. 257 f.

A. Chr. Thorn, *Les désignations françaises du Médecin et de ses concurrents aujourd'hui et autrefois*, Jena-Leipzig, 1932 (extract from *Zeitschr. f. franz. Spr. u. Lit.*, LV [1931–32]).

H. Kahane, *Bezeichnungen der Kinnbacke im Galloromanischen*, Weimar, 1932.

Carlo Volpati, *Nomi romanzi degli astri Sirio, Orione, le Pleiadi e le Jadi*, in *Zeitschr. f. rom. Phil.*, LII (1932), p. 152 f.

Miebet Ankersmit, *Die Namen des Leuchtkäfers im Italienischen* (with 9 maps), Zürich, 1934.

Max Steffen, *Die Ausdrücke für ' Regen ' und ' Schnee ' im Französischen, Rätoromanischen und Italienischen* (with 8 maps), Zürich, 1935.[1]

★　★　★

Thanks to the great interest and activity in dialect research which was prompted or encouraged by the existence of the French **Other Linguistic Atlases** *Atlas*, and by the doctrine and methods of its compiler, Gilliéron, a great number of other atlases have either already sprung into being or are in process of construction. Not only is every Romance territory to have its atlas, but, as we shall see, the example of the Romanicists is being widely followed by workers in other fields.[2] Those who

---

[1] To help to complete this bibliographical survey, reference may be made to *Bibliographie linguistique de la Suisse romande*, II, pp. 134 f. and 372 f., to the articles by J. Huber and L. Spitzer (see above, p. 200, note), and to *The Year's Work in Modern Studies*, Oxford, 1930–, particularly vol. V (1935), p. 33 (A. Ewert).

[2] A thoroughgoing discussion of the subject took place at The Hague in April, 1928 ; cp. *Actes du premier Congrès international de linguistes à La Haye*, Leyden, 1929, pp. 19 f. and 134 f. ; and *Rivista di filologia classica*, LVII (1929), p. 342 f., and LVIII (1930), pp. 27 and 32.

are opposed to linguistic atlases have taken alarm at this, shall we say, epidemic of atlases, and have on this account stiffened still further their attitude of hostility. Having referred already to this controversy (p. 237 f., above) we shall only state here our conviction that there can be no scientific justification for pitting the Glossary or Dictionary against the Atlas, as if these two methods of investigating and recording dialect material were mutually exclusive. Both methods have their uses, and even their advantages, and, being complementary one to the other, both are necessary.

A glossary has the advantage of being able to show, conveniently, details about the meaning and use of individual words which an atlas could only display, if at all, by being swollen to quite un-manageable dimensions. Further, a glossary, for practical reasons, can be far more exhaustive, numerically, than an atlas. On the other hand, the cartographical presentation even of a limited number of well-chosen words raises, and helps to solve, problems of which a glossary can rarely reveal the existence, problems which concern, not only the life of individual words, but the whole linguistic life of the communities great or small which compose a language area. In other terms, a glossary gives full value to the individual word, but at the same time isolates it. An atlas enables us to see it in relation to its equivalents in neighbouring areas, and, as no speech community is self-contained, obliges us to investigate those wider factors of linguistic life by which the speech of any community is of necessity conditioned, and which it would be entirely unscientific to neglect.[1]

The ideal method would be to undertake conjointly the com-position both of a general atlas and local glossaries, but in practice this is wellnigh impossible in most cases. Something approaching it, however, was being realized in the case of Catalonia, where, in addition to the *Atlas* of which we are to speak below, there are in course of publication a remarkably complete dictionary of all the Catalan dialects, *Diccionari català-valencià-balear*, by Mn. A. M-a Alcover y Sureda y En Francesch de B. Moll y Casasnovas, Barcelona-Palma de Mallorca (undated), and a *Tresor de la Llengua, de les Tradicions i de la Cultura popular de Catalunya* (vols. I–V

---

[1] On this controversy see also V. Bertoldi, *Vocabolari e atlanti dialettali*, in *Rivista della Società filologica friulana*, V (1924), p. 112 f. The author criticizes the defects of glossaries, and after passing in review a number of atlases, concludes with a paragraph in defence of linguistic geography. Cp. also B. Migliorini, *Atlanti linguistici*, in *La Cultura*, VIII (1929), p. 219 f.

[A-Enfar], Barcelona, 1935–6) by the author of the *Atlas* himself,
A. Griera.

★

The *Atlas linguistique de la Corse*, by J. Gilliéron and E. Edmont,
Paris, 1914–15, is a continuation of the *Atlas linguistique de la France*
by the same authors, and composed on the same
The Atlas of lines. It was again Edmont who collected the
Corsica material, and to do so he learnt Italian, as the
common folk in Corsica still speak an Italian dialect, a variety of
Tuscan. The questionnaire was twice as large as that used for the
French *Atlas*. The enquiry was conducted in forty-five localities
and lasted from the spring of 1911 till the end of the summer of
1912. In each locality investigated at least one dialect text was to
be recorded and reproduced as delivered by the same person who
had served as the local informant for the questionnaire (cp. M.
Roques, *Romania*, XLI, 1912, p. 156). So far, only the first four
volumes, containing 799 maps (*une abeille* to *haïr quelqu'un*), have
been published. There still remain six more volumes of the same
size to be issued, but now that both authors are deceased the
publication seems likely to be deferred indefinitely. The *Atlas*
provoked a good deal of rather acrimonious discussion, for a
number of reasons. Much was made of the fact that the investigator
was linguistically a foreigner in the region investigated. Moreover,
the questions having been put in standard Italian, it was said that
this had influenced the responses, which showed a remarkable
sameness throughout the island. For further details the reader is
referred to P. E. Guarnerio, *Note etimologiche e lessicali corse*, in
Rendiconti del R. Istituto Lombardo, XLVIII (1915), p. 517 f. ;
C. Salvioni, *Note di dialettologia corsa*, Pavia, 1916 (extract from the
same *Rendiconti*, vol. XLIX, p. 705 f.) ; A. Dauzat, *La géographie
linguistique*, p. 149, note, and p. 152 ; and S. Pop, *Buts et méthodes
des enquêtes dialectales*, p. 118 f.

The investigation of the speech of Corsica has also been undertaken from the Italian side, under the auspices of the *Italia dialettale*
group of scholars (see below). The investigators claim to have
improved, not only upon the methods of Edmont and Gilliéron, but
on those applied by Jaberg and Jud to the construction of the *Atlas
of Italy and Southern Switzerland*. The full title of this *Corsican Atlas*,

of which the first volume of 200 maps appeared in 1933, is *Atlante linguistico etnografico italiano della Corsica. Promosso dalla R. Università di Cagliari. Disegni di Guido Colucci.* (*L'Italia dialettale*, Supp. I, Serie IIa.) As the title indicates, the ' word and thing ' method has been very widely applied as in the work of Jaberg and Jud. The localities investigated are more numerous than in the previous *Corsican Atlas*, 49 as against 45, and to these have been added two localities from Sardinia, one from Elba, and three from the mainland, Pisa, Lucca, and Stazzema. The complete atlas[1] is to contain 2000 maps, in ten volumes, each volume to be devoted to one or more groups of correlated ideas ; thus vol. I is devoted to Man, the human body, its parts and functions, physical and moral qualities and defects. G. Bottiglioni, the chief author, is a professor in the University of Pavia.

★

Like Gilliéron and Edmont's *Atlas of Corsica*, the *Atlas lingüístic de Catalunya*, Barcelona (Institut d'Estudis Catalans, Palau de la Generalitat), 1923– , may be considered as a
The Catalonian Atlas continuation of the *Atlas linguistique de la France*, both by the method of its composition and because the Catalonian linguistic territory actually begins on French soil, although its greatest extent is within the frontiers of Spain along the western shores of the Mediterranean. The author of the work is A. Griera, whom we have already had occasion to mention more than once in the course of the present chapter. Unlike the authors of similar undertakings, Griera has worked unaided. He made all the preparations for the enquiry and collected the material single-handed, during vacations from 1912 to 1921, and is also solely responsible for its publication. Hitherto four volumes only have appeared, the fourth in 1926, representing a total of 786 maps (*abans d'ahir–els estreps*). Details concerning the *Atlas* are to be found in the author's *Introducció*, published in *Butlletí de dialectologia catalana*, VI (1918), p. 57 f., and in a review of the first fascicule by Eva Seifert in *Archivum Romanicum*, VIII (1924), p. 337 f. It is to contain some 3500 maps, that is to say, twice the number contained

---

[1] The fourth volume, maps 601–800, came out in 1935, when an introductory volume was also published : *Atlante linguistico-etnografico italiano della Corsica : Introduzione*, Pisa, 1935, 229 pp. Cp. C. Battisti, *L'Atlante ling.-etnogr. della Corsica*, in *L'Universo* (*rivista mensile dell' Istituto Geografico Militare*), June, 1937.

in the *French Atlas*, and is based on a questionnaire similar to that used by Edmont but extended to 2886 items. The investigation covered the whole of the Catalonian speech area, namely, the French Department of the Pyrénées Orientales (the ancient county of Roussillon), Andorra, Catalonia proper (together with certain adjoining points in Aragon, beyond the Noguera Ribagorzana, which forms the linguistic frontier between Aragon and Catalonia), the province of Valencia, the Balearic Isles, and the town of Alghero in Sardinia, where the Catalan spoken is a relic of the Aragonese sovereignty of the XIVth century. The number of ' points ' or localities investigated is 101, representing a density roughly twice as great as that of the *French Atlas*, where an area like Gascony, which is similar in extent to the Catalonian speech area, is represented by only 62 points. With regard to the distribution of these points over the Catalonian territory, the density is greater in the east than the west, which is rather to be regretted, for, as Jaberg says in his review in *Romania*, L (1924), p. 278 f., there is greater uniformity of speech in the east than in the west, which, bordering as it does on other speech areas, offers the characteristic variety and interest of all transitional regions.

The *Catalonian Atlas* was well received by scholars. Of the reviews which greeted its appearance[1] that of Jaberg referred to above is of special importance for the general questions which it raises. Comparing the replies obtained by Edmont, in the Catalonian localities investigated for the purpose of the *French Atlas*, with those recorded by Griera, Jaberg detects certain differences and states, namely, that the notations made by Edmont are more finely differentiated than those of Griera, who tends towards uniformity. Jaberg notes a similar difference between Edmont's recordings of the speech of La Suisse romande and his own ; Gilliéron's henchman there, too, tended to reproduce accidental variations of individual speech (' la parole ', to use the Saussurian terminology), where Jaberg had approximated more to the general scheme of phonology prevailing in the area (i.e. ' la langue '). The reviewer would account for these facts as follows : Edmont was not acquainted either with the Catalonian dialects

[1] Cp. G. Millardet, *Revue des langues romanes*, LXII (1923–4), pp. 177 f. and 500 f. ; Eva Seifert, *Archivum Romanicum*, VIII (1924), p. 337 f. and IX (1925), p. 113 f. ; W. v. Wartburg, *ibid.*, IX (1925), p. 111 f. ; A. Dauzat, *Revue de philologie française et de littérature*, XXXVI (1924), p. 163 f. and XXXVII (1925), p. 167 f. ; K. Jaberg, *loc. cit.* ; J. Jud, *The Romanic Review*, XVI (1925), p. 368 f. ; L. Spitzer, *Zeitschr. f. rom. Phil.*, XLV (1925), p. 612 f. ; A. Terracher, *Autour de l'Atlas lingüístic de Catalunya*, in *Revue de linguistique romane*, I (1925), p. 440 f.

of the Pyrénées Orientales, or with the Franco-Provençal dialects of Western Switzerland ; he was thus struck and attracted by the specific peculiarities of the patois he encountered, and perhaps stressed unduly the distinctive features in the speech of his informers. Griera and Jaberg, on the other hand, were familiar with every detail of the vernaculars of their respective areas, and thus unwittingly had tended to reproduce a kind of mean, and approximate their notations to the local standard. Both methods of procedure have their dangers and their advantages. Over a wide area, with a great variety of dialects, Edmont's method must inevitably be applied ; but Griera's system is permissible when we have to do with a restricted area, where the vernaculars are of a more or less uniform type and the investigator is intimately acquainted with them. Jaberg then proceeds to discuss the question of the variety in lexicographical, phonetic, morphological, and syntactical types which the *Atlas* reveals, and the relationship between these types and the neighbouring linguistic areas, Spanish and French. Catalonia, he says, has served as an avenue for the spread of linguistic innovations entering the Peninsula from Gaul, and has played, with regard to Spain, the part which the north of Italy, and particularly the province of Piedmont, has played in the linguistic relations between the Romance of France and that of Italy. The *Atlas of Catalonia*, Jaberg concludes, is thus of a very special interest to linguists, who owe a debt of gratitude to the author for the new paths he has opened up to science.

★

Despite their great and undeniable value, the atlases described so far are greatly surpassed by the *Sprach- und Sachatlas Italiens und der Südschweiz*, Zofingen, 1928– , the joint work of K. Jaberg and J. Jud. Six volumes of the work have so far been issued containing each some 200 maps, and two more are to follow, making a total of some 1600 maps, all told. An explanatory treatise published by the authors, entitled *Der Sprachatlas als Forschungsinstrument*, Halle a.S., 1928, is a necessary accompaniment, explaining as it does the general economy of the *Atlas* and the sources and methods of compiling the information it contains. Before publishing

The Atlas of Italy and Southern Switzerland

this explanatory volume the authors had inserted a number of preparatory articles in various journals, some of them already utilizing material from the *Atlas* to illustrate its uses and importance. A list of these will be found in the accompanying note below.[1] We shall confine ourselves to reproducing here such details as are necessary to give the reader an idea of those features which make Jaberg and Jud's *Atlas* the best work of the kind so far composed.

The survey embraced 405 localities in Southern Switzerland, Italy, Sicily, and Sardinia. In the north of Italy and the Swiss areas the network is closer than in the *French Atlas*, but somewhat more open elsewhere. The initial plan was to confine the survey to the Rheto-Romance dialects and those of Northern Italy, and to employ a single investigator, but when the enterprise grew in scope and it was decided to include the whole of the Italian speech domain, the number was increased to three. The northern areas were explored by P. Scheuermeier[2] as originally intended, and the central areas were added to his domain. G. Rohlfs[3] undertook

---

[1] *Un Atlante linguistico-etnografico svizzero-italiano*, in *Vie d'Italia* ('Rivista del Touring Club Italiano'), May and November nos., 1923 ; *A Linguistic and Ethnographical Atlas of the Raetian and Italian speech-domain of Switzerland and of Upper and Central Italy*, in *The Romanic Review*, XIV (1923), p. 249 f. ; *Ein neuer Sprachatlas*, in *Indogermanisches Jahrbuch*, IX (1922–3), p. 1 f. ; *Der Sprach- und Sachatlas Italiens und der Südschweiz und die Bezeichnungsgeschichte des Begriffes ' anfangen '*, in *Revue de linguistique romane*, I (1925), p. 114 f. ; *Ein Sprach- und Sachatlas Italiens und der Südschweiz*, in *Wörter und Sachen*, IX (1924–6), p. 126 f. ; *Transkriptionsverfahren, Aussprache- und Gehörsschwankungen*. (*Prolegomena zum ' Sprach- und Sachatlas Italiens und der Südschweiz '*), in *Zeitschr. f. rom. Phil.*, XLVII (1927), p. 171 f.

[2] Scheuermeier was a pupil of Gauchat and Jud at Zürich, where he obtained his doctorate with a valuable thesis entitled, *Einige Bezeichnungen für den Begriff Höhle in den romanischen Alpendialekten (Balma, Spelunca, Crypta, Tana, Cubulum). Ein wortgeschichtlicher Beitrag zum Studium der Alpinen Geländeausdrücke*, Halle a.S., 1920. In addition to an excellent scientific training, Scheuermeier underwent a thorough initiation into all the secrets of linguistic investigation in the field, its methods and peculiar problems. He had, further, a thorough knowledge of the Romauntsh and Italian languages. A Swiss, and an alumnus of Zürich University, he was thus well equipped for the task of investigating the areas assigned to him by the authors of the *Atlas*. He had, too, the necessary physique and temperament for the vicissitudes of a dialect explorer's life. Interesting details on this topic are to be found in his articles : *Im Dienste des Sprach- und Sachatlasses Italiens und der Südschweiz*, in *Festschrift Louis Gauchat*, Aarau, 1926, p. 317 f., and *Observations et expériences personnelles faites au cours de mon enquête pour ' l'Atlas linguistique et ethnographique de l'Italie et de la Suisse méridionale '*, in *Bull. Soc. Ling.*, Paris, XXXIII (1932), fasc. 1, p. 93 f. Scheuermeier is also the author of an interesting study in geographical ethnography : *Wasser- und Weingefässe im heutigen Italien*, Bern, 1934.

[3] Rohlfs, Professor of Romance Philology in the University of Tübingen, is the greatest expert outside Italy in the dialects of Southern Italy and Sicily. He has paid particular attention to the problem of the Greek element in Southern Italy, which he has studied in *Griechen und Romanen in Unteritalien. Ein Beitrag zur Geschichte der unteritalienischen Gräzität*, Geneva, 1924 (Italian version : *Scavi linguistici nella Magna Grecia*, Halle a.S.–Rome, 1933), and in a number of supplementary articles and notes. His thesis is, that this element goes back to the Greek

Southern Italy and Sicily, and M. L. Wagner[1] Sardinia. It is generally admitted by competent authorities that there is a disadvantage in having three investigators, inasmuch as it multiplies by three the personal co-efficient to be taken into account when assessing the quality of the material recorded, and the editors of the *Atlas* themselves were the first to realize this. But no other course was open to them, both on personal grounds—Scheuermeier was unable to give more time to the enquiry—and by the very nature of the task, as it would have been difficult to find a person equally qualified in languages and dialects so diverse as are the speeches of the Rheto-Romance and Italian areas combined.

Jaberg and Jud's *Atlas*, which, as we have said, excels all previous works of the kind, does so, chiefly, by certain innovations which we may now enumerate. In the first place, three questionnaires, instead of one, were made use of. The 'normal' questionnaire, which was used in the great majority of the localities investigated, contained 2000 items, words, forms, and phrases, and was based on that used by Gilliéron for the *French Atlas*, with additions and the necessary modifications imposed by the different linguistic and social conditions prevailing in the respective territories. The second questionnaire was an abridged version of the first, for use in the larger towns (which Gilliéron had neglected), where rural occupations are unknown, but where, on the other hand, there are trades and crafts unknown to the countryside. Finally, the third questionnaire was twice as voluminous as the 'normal', and was destined to determine, as far as possible, the complete vocabulary of each of the chief groups of dialects occupying geographical areas of any considerable extent. Roughly speaking, the augmented questionnaire was used once in every twenty of the localities explored.

colonists of Roman imperial times, and not, as was generally believed, merely to the Byzantine period. Though his theory has been generally approved, it has been vigorously opposed in some quarters, in particular by C. Battisti, *Appunti sulla storia e sulla diffusione dell' ellenismo nell' Italia Meridionale*, in *Revue de linguistique romane*, III (1927), p. 1 f., and *Nuove osservazioni sulla grecità nella provincia di Reggio Calabria*, in *L'Italia dialettale*, V (1930), p. 56 f. (cp. Rohlfs' reply : *Autochtone Griechen oder byzantinische Gräzität*, in *Revue de linguistique romane*, IV [1928], p. 118 f.). Rohlfs is also the author of a 400-page volume entitled : *Etymologisches Wörterbuch der unteritalienischen Gräzität*, Halle a.S., 1930, which contains a comprehensive collection, not only of the Greek words used by the localities which still speak a Greek dialect, but also of those found in the Italian dialects of the region. Latterly, he has turned his attention to the Pyrenean area and has recently published an important work on the Gascon dialect : *Le Gascon, Etudes de philologie pyrénéenne*, Halle a.S., 1935. (Beiheft 85, *Zeitschr. f. rom. Phil.*)

[1] We have discussed this scholar, the greatest living expert in Sardinian, both from the theoretical and practical side, earlier in the present volume (*v.* p. 69 f.).

In their choice of localities, Jaberg and Jud have profited by their own experience and by that of other composers of linguistic atlases, who have soon become aware that the realities of language are not infrequently quite the reverse of what one might expect. For instance, not every town is linguistically progressive, nor every village conservative. Moreover, the vernaculars of localities situated near the great lines of communication are not, in every case, more influenced by standard than those of places more remote. Thus the ' points ' which figure on the *Atlas of Italy and Southern Switzerland* are in many cases materially different in character and situation from those that appear on the *Atlas Linguistique de la France*. The introduction of the larger towns, Turin, Milan, Venice, Genoa, Bologna, Florence, Naples, etc., particularly, provides a striking difference, although here the authors had but to follow the example set by Griera in the *Catalonian Atlas*.

The most important new departure, however, and the key to a number of others, is the predominance of lexical over phonetic phenomena. The authors' main concern has been with the words, the current terminology used in various forms of human activity, by the vernaculars of Italy and Southern Switzerland. To know the varied expressions made use of by the peasant, the craftsman, etc., in his daily task is also to become acquainted with that task and its implements, in a word, to know a civilization. The study of language is thus combined with the study of the material and spiritual conditions of life, as the modern trend of linguistic investigation demands. Further, to mark the interdependence of word and thing the authors have made another innovation. In order to save from oblivion, not only the words, but the things of the countryside, which are fast being supplanted by the products of modern industry, they decided to make extensive use of the pencil and the camera, and to have sketched or photographed the typical implements, utensils, dwellings, etc., of the several areas. These photographs and sketches, some 4000 of the former and 2000 of the latter, are to appear in the form of an album, accompanied by the relevant terminology and descriptive matter. The whole work will thus combine in the most felicitous manner the geographical and the ' word and thing ' methods, as indeed was to be expected from the tendencies manifest in the previous work of the two Swiss scholars.

From the technical point of view, too, namely, in the arrangement of the maps, this wider outlook has produced a change. Instead of being arranged as hitherto, in alphabetical order, the maps are grouped together according to subject matter. Of the eight volumes of which the atlas ultimately is to be composed, six have so far (1937) been published. They are made up as follows : Vol. I : The family and family relationships ; the human body, its parts and functions, physical qualities and defects ; Vol. II : Crafts and implements, trade, numbers, time and space, celestial bodies, atmospheric phenomena, metals ; Vol. III : Minerals, topographical features, animals, hunting and fishing, forestry, plants and trees ; Vol. IV : Sleep, dress, disease, moral and social life, church ; Vol. V : The house, furniture, the kitchen, food, eating and drinking ; Vol. VI : Flocks and herds, the bee, the silk-worm, stable and byre, pasturage, dairying, vehicles.

The authors have also introduced welcome improvements in the construction of the maps. In addition to the words that figure beside the several ' points ' representing the localities explored, many of the sheets contain a rich store of marginal matter, supplementary or explanatory to that displayed cartographically. Sketches, too, are sometimes appended, to serve the same explanatory ends, pending the publication of the ' *Illustrationsband* '. Moreover, whenever possible, in order to facilitate comparison of the Italian and Rheto-Romance nomenclature with that of France or Catalonia, references are given to the corresponding maps in the French and Catalonian Atlases, to the geographico-linguistic works of O. Bloch, Ch. Bruneau, and G. Millardet and also to collections of material relating to popular botany and zoology, namely, those of Rolland for France, and of O. Penzig and A. Garbini for Italy.[1] Jaberg and Jud have thus succeeded, so to speak, in laying the foundations of comparative linguistic geography, and have run no risk of incurring the reproach that was frequently cast at Gilliéron, namely, that he confined his attention exclusively to a single Romance domain.[2]

★

[1] See above, p. 71.

[2] A list of reviews of Jaberg and Jud's *Atlas* (the ' *AIS* ') is to be found in *Archivum Romanicum*, XVIII (1934), pp. 155–6. We need only mention further A. Griera's article, *Entorn de l'Atlas linguistique de l'Italie et de la Suisse méridionale de K. Jaberg i J. Jud*, in *Anuari de l'Oficina Romànica de Lingüística i Literatura*, vol. I, Barcelona, 1928, p. 21 f., which is, in the main, a geographical study of the name of ' the lizard ' in the Italian, Sardinian, Provençal, Catalan, Spanish and Basque domains.

The atlases other than those already described need not detain us long as they are all more or less in the preparatory stage. One of the most advanced would appear to be the rival **Another Italian Atlas** atlas to that of Jaberg and Jud, an atlas of Italy done by Italians and not by foreigners, as a national, not to say nationalist, enterprise. It should be recognized, however, that the project is some twenty years old, although serious work upon it only began when the Swiss *Atlas* was well on the way to completion. The organizing committee was composed originally of the well-known scholars, M. Bartoli and G. Bertoni, Ugo Pellis, director of the *Rivista della Società filologica friulana G. I. Ascoli*,[1] now lecturer in the University of Turin, and, lastly, V. Bertoldi.[2] The first two were to be the chief editors, and Bertoldi was to take part in the survey, if and when the chief explorer, Pellis, should be prevented from carrying on the work. But the constitution of this committee underwent considerable modification. Bertoldi withdrew from it before having taken any effective part in the undertaking, and in 1927 Bertoni did likewise. Consequently, there remain at present one editor, Bartoli, and one investigator, Pellis.

A word now upon the composition of the *Atlas*, its scope and methods. The questionnaire is made up of two parts, one general, containing questions relating to the individual, the family, society, and nature, the other special, dealing with agriculture, vine-growing, hunting, fishing, arts and crafts. For use in certain cases a kind of supplementary questionnaire has been framed to throw light on technical nomenclature, special features of vocabulary, local customs, beliefs, and the science and literature of the peasantry. Finally, there is a morphological appendix, for the registration of grammatical forms. Accompanying the questionnaire is a volume of some 2500 photographs and illustrations, for use when the object for which the name is sought is not ready to hand, and, generally, to avoid misunderstanding between enquirer and informant. The general questionnaire comprises 3630 items, made up of 826 photographs or illustrations, 291 sentences or phrases, and 2513 separate words. The special questionnaire contains 3324 items : 1841 illustrations, 739 phrases, and 744 words, the morphological

---

[1] It should be stated that the whole undertaking was under the auspices of this *Società filologica friulana G. I. Ascoli*, who chose the personnel mentioned above to carry out the work.

[2] See above, p. 71 f.

appendix 1048 items, 861 of which relate to the forms of verbs. The number of the localities to be visited was at first fixed at 730, and the investigation was to take five or six years. The localities now contemplated number 1000, and include villages where foreign tongues are spoken, Albanian, Rumanian, Slavonic, German, Greek, and Tzigane. Of these, in July, 1932, only 328 had been investigated. The explorer was to be free to choose other localities than those prescribed, if circumstances seemed to warrant his doing so, and in the investigation of matters relating to the household he was to have the assistance of his wife.

The enterprise conducted on these lines by Bartoli and Pellis has been the subject of keen controversy among Italian linguists. C. Merlo, in particular, has attacked it violently on a number of occasions.[1] Some of his observations and suggestions are of interest and worth summarizing. The distance between the ' points ' investigated, he says, should not exceed thirty kilometres, nor be less than fifteen. Among the localities with no rail or tramway communication preference should be given to those more than seven kilometres distant from a station. The questionnaire should have a general section, containing current notions common to all Italians, and a special section with four subdivisions : (1) notions familiar to the majority of the peasantry ; (2) those familiar to the townsfolk ; (3) to the dwellers on the coasts ; (4) to the people of the highlands, and the respective groups of questions should be put only to the communities concerned. The localities themselves, further, should be divided into two groups, the mountain and hill areas on the one hand, the plain and coastal areas on the other, the dividing line being fixed at 350 metres. The informants should be interrogated, preferably, concerning their own field of activity, the enquiries in the hill regions being confined in the main to the life of the mountaineers and so forth. Again the ' points ' should be scientifically chosen ; they should be denser in the Alps and Apennines, and near dialect boundaries, sparser where influence of the literary language or of the speech of some important regional centre is strongly felt and makes speech more uniform. Finally, in addition to expressing dissatisfaction with the choice of the localities and their geographical distribution, Merlo disapproves

---

[1] Cp. *Rendiconti della R. Accademia Nazionale dei Lincei*, classe di scienze morali, storiche e filologiche, serie V-a, vol. XXXIII, fasc. 4–6, Rome, 1924, p. 149 f., which contain a communication made by Merlo verbally on the 18th of May, 1924. He returned to the topic at another sitting of the Academy on December the 18th, 1927 ; see also, *L'Italia dialettale*, IV (1928), p. 297 f.

of the employment of a single investigator. He would have one investigator for each dialect area, and would, as far as possible, confine himself to observers who are of local origin, or at least entirely familiar with local speech conditions. With regard to Pellis, he expresses the fear that, being a Friulano, he is not sufficiently at home with the peculiarities of Italian dialects, which are so numerous and so varied.[1]

We have spoken above of the *Corsican Atlas* which is in process of publication, and which is being issued as a supplement to the review *L'Italia dialettale*, of which Merlo is the director (see p. 254 f.). It only remains for us to mention among the Italian activities in this field the projected *Atlante linguistico-folclorico della Lunigiana* announced in the *Zeitschrift für romanische Philologie*, LIII (1933), p. 550, by P. S. Pasquali, who there refers to his article, *Per un Atlante demologico della Lunigiana*, in *Omaggio alla R. Deputazione di S. P. per le Provincie Parmensi adunata a Montelungo il 27 agosto 1930–VIII*, Parma, 1930, pp. 3–4.

★

Rumania has played and is playing an important part in linguistic cartography. At the beginning of the present chapter (p. 147 f.) we gave the reader some description of

Rumanian Atlases

the *Daco-Rumanian Atlas* by Weigand, which we saw was conceived on entirely phonological lines. Mention should also be made of a linguistic atlas of the Banat

---

[1] Merlo's criticisms were endorsed by V. Crescini, then Professor of Romance Philology in the University of Padua, who sought to obtain an official pronouncement from the Accademia dei Lincei on the topic of the proposed atlas, as a matter of national importance. For further details upon the atlas the reader is referred to : M. Bartoli, *Piano generale dell' Atlante linguistico italiano*, extract from *Rivista della Società filologica friulana*, Udine, 1924 (cp. O. Densusianu, *Grai şi suflet*, II [1925–6], p. 184 f.) ; *Per l'Atlante linguistico italiano*, extract from *Atti del IX Congresso geografico italiano*, vol. II, Genoa, 1926 ; *L'Atlante linguistico italiano*, in *Atti della Società italiana per il progresso delle scienze*, vol. XVII (1928), p. 664 f. (cp. *Literaturblatt f. germ. u. rom. Phil.*, L [1929], col. 446 f.) ; and an article by the same author in *Archivio glottologico italiano*, XXI (1927), sezione neolatina, p. 149 f. Cp. also : Il consiglio direttivo, *Per l'Atlante linguistico italiano. Promemoria*, Udine, 1925 ; S. Pop, *Buts et méthodes des enquêtes dialectales*, Paris, 1927, p. 156 f. ; G. Vidossich, *L'atlante linguistico italiano, questioni di metodo e di fini*, in *Bollettino dell' Atlante lingu. ital.*, I (1933), p. 4 f., and *L'Atlante linguistico italiano (ALIt)*, ap. Schrijnen, *Essai de bibliographie de géographie linguistique générale*, p. 73 f. ; G. Bottiglioni, *Le inchieste dialettali e gli Atlanti linguistici*, in *Atti della Società Italiana per il progresso delle scienze*, riunione XX, Rome, 1932, vol. I, p. 413 f., and *Il valore unitario e quello obiettivo degli Atlanti linguistici*, in *Annali della R. Scuola Normale Superiore di Pisa (Lettere, Storia e Filosofia)*, serie II, vol. I (1932), p. 167 f. ; U. Pellis, *Atlante linguistico italiano, relazioni e rendiconti*, in *Ce fastu?*, VII (1931), p. 1 f.

region (*Atlasul linguistic al Bănatului*) which is the work of the Buchar-est philologist, I. A. Candrea. In a study entitled, *Constatări în domeniul dialectologiei*, published in *Grai şi suflet*, I (1923–4), p. 169 f., we read that this scholar has in the course of twenty years explored over 250 localities in the Banat and investigated more than 700 typical words. The material collected has been worked up into an atlas of 130 maps, but up to the present none of it has been published. A number of maps, one of them in colour, accompanied the article quoted above, but they can scarcely be said to give us an idea of the atlas itself, the more particularly as they are presented in a manner which makes it difficult for the reader to follow the distribution of the phenomena concerned.

A much more ambitious enterprise is that now in process of execution under the direction of S. Puşcariu, who for some fifteen years or more, in conjunction with other Cluj linguists, has had in mind a linguistic atlas on a big scale for the whole of Rumania. By means of an extremely detailed questionnaire concerning ' the household ', ' the horse ', etc., which was sent to correspondents throughout the whole of Dacia, the Director of the Cluj Institute of Rumanian studies (*Muzeul limbii romîne*) prepared the ground for a thorough-going investigation in the field ; on the one hand, the replies received made it clear that the vernaculars were of conspicu-ous linguistic interest and, on the other, people became familiar with the idea of a linguistic survey, while at the same time good ' subjects ' for an enquiry were discovered and their names kept in reserve for future use. Puşcariu has profited to the full by the experience of specialists in the field of linguistic cartography else-where, particularly by that of Jaberg and Jud, and of Bartoli, his more recent predecessors, with all of whom he has been in close personal contact. Thus, in the *Rumanian Atlas*, special attention is being paid to ethnography, to ' things ', as in the Swiss work, and to folklore, as in that of the Italians. In addition, an entirely new departure is being made by the inclusion of person and place names. A number of investigators are taking part in the enquiry. The specially linguistic side was entrusted first of all to Sever Pop, but later the services of E. Petrovici were also secured. Pop, who is the author of a work we have already had occasion to mention, *Buts et méthodes des enquêtes dialectales*, Paris, 1927, and of a doctorate thesis on the terminology applied to ' the horse ' (*Cîteva capitole din terminologia calului, v. Dacoromania*, V [1927–8], p. 51 f.), has had considerable experience of the geographical method, particularly as applied in France, and has taken part in dialect surveys in the West. Petrovici is a specialist in phonetics and the author, *inter alia*, of *De la nasalité en roumain*, Cluj, 1930. The section devoted to place and person names has been in the charge of Şt. Paşca, who has likewise had a training in western Europe, and has published work of a geographico-linguistic character, for example : *Terminologia calului ; părţile corpului (v. Dacoromania,* V, p. 272 f.), *Glosar dialectal,* in *Memoriile Academiei Romîne,* secţia literară, seria III, tom. IV, p. 193 f., and *Nume de persoane şi nume de animale in Ţara Oltului,* Bucharest, 1936. Finally, the work relating to ethnography and folklore has been undertaken in close conjunction with the Cluj Ethnographical Institute.

The questionnaire used for the enquiry was framed with great care by S. Pop, on the basis of those already in existence for other Romance areas. It was discussed and modified at numerous sittings of the Cluj Museu by the local linguists, and tried out in a number of experimental surveys before receiving its final form. Like that used for the *AIS,* i.e. Jaberg and Jud's *Atlas,* it is not confined to one version. The ' normal ' questionnaire comprises 2200 items, and deals with what may be called fundamental widespread notions ; the other contains 4800 headings and embraces as far as possible every phase of peasant life, not excluding customs, folklore, superstitions and the like. The shorter questionnaire was entrusted to Pop, who applied it in 350 localities, making use of only one informant in each locality. These 350 points, however, are disseminated over the whole linguistic territory surveyed, and thus unity of perception and recording have been secured for the whole area. Petrovici, who used the larger version, visited 115 localities, all different from those investigated by Pop, but also distributed throughout the whole domain. His investigation not only entailed a longer stay in each locality—twelve days as against four—but was carried out on different lines. Numerous ' subjects ' of both sexes and widely different in age and occupation were interrogated in each village. The information on the maps is thus of two different kinds, elicited in two different ways. This feature, and the inclusion of proper names mentioned above, form interesting innovations in technique, and give a certain stamp of individuality to the *ALR, Atlasul linguistic al Romîniei.*[1] The survey, which

---

[1] Interesting details concerning the *ALR,* and the methods and scope of the survey are to be found in an article by S. Pop, entitled, *L'Atlas linguistique de la Roumanie,* in *Revue de linguistique romane,* IX (1933), p. 86 f. Cp. also *Dacoromania,* VII (1931–3) and VIII (1934–5), *passim.*

began in 1930, is now entirely finished. The first fascicules of the *Atlas* are to appear in 1937, and it is hoped to complete publication by 1945. In its final shape the *Atlas* will contain, in addition to its 2500 full-sized maps, a number of smaller, coloured maps to show the geographical distribution of terms which do not vary sufficiently to justify fuller cartographical treatment. This again forms an interesting and commendable departure. Finally, the work is given a wider appeal by the inclusion of twelve non-Romance specimens comprising Serbian, Ruthenian, Bulgarian, Magyar, German, and Tzigane, in addition to the five Macedo-Rumanian, the two Megleno-Rumanian, and the two Istro-Rumanian localities.

★

From many points of view the southern half of Belgium, whose dialects prolong to the north-east the Gallo-Romance domain, is, linguistically, in a position similar to that of the **The Walloon Atlas** Romance-speaking parts of Switzerland and of Catalonia (cp. pp. 220 and 243, above). It is not to be wondered at, therefore, that the French-speaking Belgians have shown considerable zeal in investigating their local language and culture. As early as 1858 there had been talk among Walloon philologists of a linguistic atlas of their country. But the project was still-born. Some fifty years later, in 1905, the ' Commission du Dictionnaire Wallon ' approved a proposal for a phonetic atlas of the region, but again the matter would have lapsed but for the energy and initiative of J. Haust, of the University of Liège, who has devoted the major part of his scientific activity to research upon the Romance vernaculars of Belgium, and in particular to that of the town and district of Liège. Haust, who is a worthy successor to his great compatriot Grandgagnage, is the author of a number of important dialectological works, mainly of a glossarial and etymological character, of which we may single out for special mention the following : *Le dialecte liégeois au XVIIe siècle*, Liège, 1921 ; *Etymologies wallonnes et françaises*, Liège-Paris, 1923 ; *La houillerie liégeoise. I. Vocabulaire philologique et technologique de l'usage moderne dans le bassin de Seraing-Jemappe-Flémalle*, rédigé avec la collaboration de G. Massart et J. Sacré, Liège, 1925 ; *Le dialecte wallon de Liège. Ière partie : Dictionnaire des rimes ou vocabulaire liégeois-français groupant les mots d'après la prononciation des finales,*

Liège, 1927, *IIième partie : Dictionnaire liégeois, illustré de* 735 *figures documentaires établies par J.-M. Remouchamps, Directeur du Musée de la Vie Wallonne,* Liège, 1933 ;[1] *Enquête sur les patois de la Belgique romane. Notes de géographie linguistique et de folklore* (avec 9 cartes), in *Bulletin de la Commission de toponymie et dialectologie,* II (1928), p. 265 f.

Not content with a purely phonetic atlas, as contemplated by the Commission du Dictionnaire Wallon, in which he is an active collaborator, Haust, taking as a basis the questionnaires used by Gilliéron and Bruneau (see above, p. 205), has compiled a questionnaire of some 2100 headings, containing 4150 words relating to every phase of local life. His plan is to apply this questionnaire to 200 out of the 1400 communes in Wallonia, which represents a density in the number of chosen ' points ' almost twelve times as great as in that part of the French maps which take in the Walloon areas. In November, 1936, the survey was complete for close on 170 localities, and it was hoped to finish the whole work in two further years. A parallel enquiry on ethnographical lines is being conducted by the ' Musée de la Vie Wallonne.'

★

Of these, the Spanish Atlas to be constructed under the auspices of the ' Centro de Estudios Históricos ' in Madrid, was already **Other** well under way before the civil war. In all, 600 **Romance** localities were to be investigated, including 100 in **Atlases** Catalonia, and 135 had been completed in 1934 (cp. *Archiv für das Studium der neueren Sprachen,* CLXVI [1934], p. 86). The director of the enterprise was T. Navarro Tomás, the well-known phonetician, and the chief of Menéndez Pidal's collaborators at the now famous Centro. According to an account given by A. M. Espinosa (hijo), one of the active participants in the survey, at the Fourth Congress of Romance Philologists held in Bordeaux, in 1934, the principle of a single explorer had been abandoned for the Spanish Atlas, and considerable use was being made of mechanical devices for the recording of sounds. The *Revista de filología española,* XX (1933), p. 225 f., contains an article

---

[1] Reviewed by J. Jud, *Archivum Romanicum,* XVII (1933), p. 127 f., and A. Dauzat, *Le français moderne,* II (1934), pp. 368-9. A third part is to follow, namely, a *Dictionnaire français-liégeois.*

by T. N. Tomás, A. M. Espinosa, and L. Rodríguez-Castellano, entitled *La frontera del andaluz*, which already embodies some of the results of the Spanish survey.

Of the project which was on foot for a similar survey of Portugal[1] nothing definite seems to have materialized. Cp. M. Rodrigues, *O Atlas lingüístico de Portugal e Ilhas*, in *A Lingua Portuguesa*, IV (1935), p. 215 f.

Before leaving the Romance domain passing mention should be made of the *Atlas dialectologique de la Normandie*, by Ch. Guerlin de Guer, now of the University of Lille, of which only one fascicule has been published (Caen, 1903), and of the *Atlas linguistique et tableaux des pronoms personnels du Nivernais* by the abbé J.-M. Meunier.[2] Finally, a non-Romance atlas dealing with French territory may be recorded here, namely, the *Atlas linguistique de la Basse-Bretagne* by P. Le Roux, the first volume of which, made up of 100 maps, with a preface and physical map of the area explored, was published in Paris in 1924, the second, also of a hundred maps, in 1927, since when no more parts have been issued.[3]

★

We have alluded above to the decision arrived at by the International Congress of Linguists held at The Hague in 1928 to encourage actively the publication of Linguistic Altases for every country in the world, and to secure if possible the support of the various governments in carrying out this enormous undertaking.[4] Partly as a result of this, atlases are already being prepared in a great number of the non-Romance territories. An account of these projects, and the various stages reached in their fulfilment up to the year 1933, is to be found in Professor Jos. Schrijnen's valuable *Essai de biblio-*

Other Atlases

---

[1] It should be stated that Portugal has acquired considerable standing in the domain of Romance dialectology largely through the achievements of one great scholar, J. Leite de Vasconcellos, who is not only the founder of Portuguese dialectology but a considerable figure in Romance philology generally. His collected studies are now accessible in volume form : *Opusculos*, four volumes, Coimbra (1928–). His valuable *Esquisse d'une dialectologie portugaise* was published in Paris, in 1901.

[2] Cp. Dauzat, *Les Patois*, p. 199 f., and *La géographie linguistique*, p. 194 f.

[3] Details concerning the preparation of this atlas are given by S. Pop, *Buts et méthodes* . . . , p. 134 f.

[4] Cp. W. Pessler, *Atlas der Wortgeographie von Europa—eine Notwendigkeit*, in *Donum Natalicium Schrijnen*, Nimeguen–Utrecht, 1929, p. 69 f.

graphie de géographie linguistique générale, Nimeguen, 1933. According to this account, in addition to the thirteen atlases published or being published, plans were on foot for no less than sixteen others, representing countries as wide apart as Finland and the United States of America. As this world-wide movement is outside our theme it will suffice for us to refer the reader to Professor Schrijnen's book for details concerning what, to the Romanicist, is a gratifying homage to the genius and vision of Jules Gilliéron, the founder of linguistic geography.[1]

The geographical method has proved so fruitful that it was natural that scholars should seek to avail themselves of the possibilities it might offer in other spheres than that to which it was applied by its founder. We have already shown (p. 227) how one of Gilliéron's most distinguished pupils, J. Jud, has used the method to enlighten us upon the submerged past of the Romance languages in relation to neighbouring tongues (*Probleme der altromanischen Wortgeographie*), and upon the later history of Vulgar Latin itself (*Problèmes de géographie linguistique romane*). It is clear, therefore, that although the method is more naturally applicable to states of language which can be investigated comprehensively and upon a uniform basis, it can in some measure be profitably applied to the past. There is thus justification for such exhortations as that of O. J. Tallgren, who, in an article entitled *Un desideratum : L'atlas historique roman* (*Bulletin de dialectologie romane*, V [1913], p. 1 f.), urges the construction of a historical atlas of the whole

Other Applications of the Geographical Method

---

[1] To the bibliography provided by Schrijnen we would add the following items of more recent date : *Jüdischer Sprachatlas der Sowjetunion, zusammengestellt und herausgegeben von der jüdischen Abteilung der Weissrussischen Akademie der Wissenschaften*, Moscow, 1932 (written in Yiddish ; 75 maps) ; K. Donner, *Über sprachgeographische Untersuchungen und ihre Ausführungen in Finnland*, in *Finnischugrische Forschungen*, vol. XXI, p. 138 f. ; A. Meillet-L.Tesnière, *Rapport sur l'activité du comité d'organisation de l'Atlas linguistique slave*, and M. Bartoli, *Atlante linguistico slavo*, communications delivered at the International Congress of ' Slavistes ' in Warsaw, 1934 ; P. Wirth, *Beiträge zum sorbischen (wendischen) Sprachatlas*. I. Lieferung, Text und Kartenband, in *Slavische Abhandlungen im Auftrage der Preussischen Akademie der Wissenschaften*, herausgegeben von M. Vasmer, Leipzig, 1933 ; II. Lief. 1936 ; M. Małecki–K.Nitsch, *Atlas, językowy polskiego Podkarpacia*, Cracow, 1934. I. *Mapy* (500 maps). II. *Wstęp, Objaśnienia, Wykazy wyrazów* (112 pages).

Schrijnen does not record certain atlases mentioned by Dauzat in *La géographie linguistique*, p. 16, viz. : a Swabian Atlas, of only 28 maps, by H. Fischer, Tübingen, 1895, a Danish Atlas, by V. Bennike and M. Kristensen, Copenhagen, 1898–1914 (100 maps), and a Northern Dutch Atlas, begun by J. Te Winkel and now continued by G. Klocke (*v. Zeitschr. f. rom. Phil.*, LV [1935], p. 216). Dauzat also mentions, *ibid.*, an atlas of 500 maps of the Aude, Ariège and Pyrénées-Orientales departments, deposited in manuscript in the library of Halle a.Saale, Germany.

Romance area, showing the political, ethnological, administrative, and ecclesiastical boundaries, the lines of communication, etc. ; for here we are concerned with, so to speak, the physical background of language development, and with known and depictable facts. But whether historical atlases of the type envisaged by O. Densusianu, in *Grai şi suflet*, II (1925–26), p. 184, are feasible is a very debatable matter. " It would be desirable ", he writes, " that linguistic atlases should be published for the past, linguistic atlases which would supplement the dialect atlases of to-day, in so far as they could be founded upon texts of earlier periods, carefully and critically chosen."

When applied to the past, and particularly to the ancient languages, the geographical method requires very careful handling indeed, as its cogency and effectiveness are reduced in proportion to the remoteness, lack of precise localization, and dissimilarity of the material treated. As A. Meillet puts it, in a review of Rein van der Velde, *Thessalische Dialektgeographie*, Nijmegen-Utrecht, 1924, in *Bulletin de la Société de linguistique de Paris*, XXV (1925), fasc. 2, p. 76, " Ce n'est pas la forme de l'exposition qui est l'essentiel en géographie linguistique, c'est l'enquête portant d'une manière égale sur toutes les parties du domaine, et sur toutes les questions posées, qui aboutit à fournir des données immédiatement comparables entre elles." None the less, the Indo-Europeanists, rightly or wrongly, have applied the technique of linguistic geography to a number of their own particular problems. Before Rein van der Velde, another Dutch scholar, no other than J. Schrijnen himself, had attempted, in an article entitled *Italische Dialektgeographie*, in *Neophilologus*, VII (1921–22), p. 223 f., a cartographical study of certain features of Italic phonology, among them the substitution of *F* for *H* and *H* for *F*, which he would attribute to Etruscan influence ; but the localization of his examples is too uncertain for his conclusions to be convincing. Latterly, despite the reservations expressed by Meillet, there has been a study by Erika Kretschmer, entitled *Beiträge zur Wortgeographie der altgriechischen Dialekte*, in *Glotta*, XVIII (1930), p. 67 f., while H. Güntert, in *Wörter und Sachen*, XII (1929), p. 390, asks boldly for a ' historische Lautgeographie ' which will trace historically the distribution and extension of phonetic phenomena.[1]

★

[1] Cp. also, H. Sköld, *Beiträge zur allgemeinen Sprachwissenschaft*. I : *Sprachgeographie und Indogermanistik*, Lund, 1931.

It remains for us to make brief mention of two other applications of the method, namely, to the facts of ethnography and to folklore, either separately or jointly, which would appear to be more securely founded and likely to bring results comparable in their finality to those often obtained by the linguistic geographer. With regard to the former, indeed, we have seen that the ' Word and Thing ' movement demands the close association of linguistics and ethnography, and the very title of Jaberg and Jud's great work, *Sprach- und Sachatlas*, is testimony to the possibility of both recording and representing in a uniform manner the speech and the paraphernalia of daily life. Similarly, among the studies listed on pp. 249–52 f. there are many that combine the geographical and the ' Word and Thing ' methods. There is indeed a frequent correspondence between the distribution of linguistic and ethnographical material. P. Scheuermeier, for example, the chief contributor to Jaberg and Jud's *Atlas*, in his booklet entitled *Wasser und Weingefässe im heutigen Italien*, Bern, 1934, has shown in some eloquent maps this coincidence for the regions of Italy. Similarly, S. Mehedinți, in a lecture published in *Vom Leben und Wirken der Romanen, II. Rumänische Reihe*, Heft 7–12, Jena-Leipzig, 1936, p. 21, displays cartographically those Rumanian areas where the Mediterranean practice of carrying vessels upon the head still survives, and points out the importance of this fact in any discussion of the movements of the Latin-speaking population in the past, and its consequent bearing upon the history of the Rumanian language. It cannot therefore be disputed either that ethnographical material lends itself to cartographical presentation as well, to say the least, as the facts of language, or that the linguist proper stands to gain by the increasing activity of the ethnographic geographer and the numerous surveys at present on foot or contemplated.[1]

[1] Cp. W. Pessler, *Grundzüge zu einer Sachgeographie der deutschen Volkskunst*, in *Jahrbuch f. histor. Volkskunst*, II, p. 44 f. ; Idem, *Der deutsche Volkskunde-Atlas*, in *Geschichtliche Landeskunde, Beilage der Rheinischen Heimatblätter*, Bonn, 1929, p. 75 f. ; Idem, *Volkstumgeographisches aus Niedersachsen auf Grund der Erhebungen des Volkskunde-Atlasses*, in *Niederdeutsche Zeitschrift für Volkskunde*, IX (1931), Nos. 1–2 ; Idem, *Deutsche Volkstumsgeographie*, Braunschweig, 1931 ; Idem, *Die geographische Methode in der Volkskunde*, in *Anthropos*, XXVII (1932) ; Idem, *Der deutsche Volkskunde-Atlas*, ap. Schrijnen, *Essai . . .*, p. 31 f. ; F. Wrede, *Ethnographie und Dialektwissenschaft*, in *Historische Zeitschrift*, Neue Folge, LII (1902), p. 22 f. ; F. Maurer, *Der Atlas der deutschen Volkskunde*, in *Nachrichten der Göttinger Hochschulgesellschaft*, VIII (1931), p. 2 f. ; Th. Frings, *Volkskunde und Sprachgeographie*, Berlin, 1928 ; H. Schlenger, *Methodische und technische Grundlagen des Atlas der deutschen Volkskunde*, Berlin, 1934 ; M. Bartoli, *Analogia di metodo fra la storia dei linguaggi e quella delle tradizioni popolari*, in *Bollettino dell' Atlante linguistico italiano*, I, No. 2, 1934. Cp. also *Instructions d'enquête linguistique*, published by the *Institut d'ethnologie de l'Université de Paris*, Paris, 1928 ; H. R. Weiss, *Die geographische Methode in der Volkskunde*,

The diffusion of the themes of folk songs and stories, as of popular beliefs and customs, appertaining as they do more to the domain of the spirit, offers perhaps even greater analogies with the extension of linguistic forms than does the diffusion of the concrete facts of ethnography ; and here, too, the application of the geographical method, though as yet little developed, has already proved extremely fruitful. An outstanding example is the remarkable study by Menéndez Pidal, *Sobre geografía folklórica. Ensayo de un método* (with three maps), published in *Revista de filología española*, VII (1920), p. 229 f., where the author investigates the geographical distribution of the versions of two Spanish romances, *Gerineldo* and *La boda estorbada*, and proves conclusively, to quote his own words, that " so many close analogies are to be observed in the dissemination of poetic themes and the phenomena of language, that folklore geography, just like linguistic geography, can lead to scientific deductions concerning the propagation of traditional literature." As this subject is strictly outside our scope, we must content ourselves with referring the reader to this article for the details of these analogies and for the very interesting points both of theory and of method which the author expounds. That these methods are gaining ground is proved by the importance given to discussions concerning the relations between linguistic and folklore studies in the Third Congress of Linguists held at Rome in 1933.[1]

★   ★   ★

We shall end this chapter on Linguistic Geography with a reference to the so-called Neo-linguistic School, whose tenets,

Neo-linguistics as will be seen, are little more than a somewhat hard-and-fast formulation of certain of Gilliéron's ideas. The principles and methods of the school are to be found set forth in the *Breviario di neolinguistica*. I. *Princìpi generali* (by G. Bertoni), II. *Criteri tecnici* (by M. G. Bartoli),

---

in *Vox Romanica*, I (1936), p. 370 f., and *Plan und Rechtfertigung eines Kartenwerks der Schweizerischen Volkskunde, ibid.*, II (1937), p. 136 f. (On p. 136 the writer announces the publication of the first fascicule of the *Atlas der deutschen Volkskunde*, containing 21 maps and the list and reference-names of the 20,000 localities investigated.)

[1] G. Vidossi, *Il folklore italiano*, VIII (1933), p. 222 f., applies the technique of the neo-linguists (see next section) to folklore study. He attributes the introduction of the geographical method into folklore research to the Finnish scholar, Julius Krohn, author of *Die folkloristische Arbeitsmethode*, Oslo, 1926. Krohn's priority is also recognized by Menéndez Pidal in the article referred to above. Cp. also a later article by M. Pidal, on similar lines, *Supervivencia del poema de Kudrun*, in *Rev. de filología española*, XX (1933), p. 1 f.

Modena, 1925, and also in Matteo Bartoli, *Introduzione alla Neo-linguistica*, Geneva, 1925.[1] We have already had occasion to describe Bertoni's attitude to 'language in the second chapter of this book (*v.* p. 142 f.), where we discussed briefly his booklet, *Programma di filologia romanza come scienza idealistica*, Geneva, 1923. The ideas he expresses in the *Breviario* are essentially the same as those already expounded in the linguistic portion of the *Programma*. The same eclecticism is characteristic of them both. Bertoni's doctrine is a compound of the ideas of von Humboldt, Croce, and Vossler, on the one hand, and of those of Schuchardt and of Gilliéron on the other, though the mixture varies slightly from one book to the other, possibly to bring his views more into line with those of his collaborator.[2] Thus, Vossler would appear to have been almost left out of account in the *Breviario*, while room has been found for certain considerations unmentioned in the *Programma*, namely, those relating to linguistic zones, centres of irradiation and the like, which play such an important part in the neo-linguistic doctrine. Despite these minor modifications the ' neo-linguist ' Bertoni is really the ' idealist ' Bertoni under another name. We are therefore justified in considering Bartoli as the true representative of the neo-linguistic school, the more so as he is the inventor of its style and title, and had already outlined the fundamentals of its doctrine more than twenty-five years ago in his article, *Alle fonti del neolatino*, in *Miscellanea di studi in onore di Attilio Hortis*, Trieste, 1910, parts of which are actually repeated verbally in the *Introduzione alla Neolinguistica*, published fifteen years later.

First as to the term itself. Bartoli, *Introduzione . . .* , p. v, explains it as follows : " The names ' neo-linguist ' and ' neo-grammarian '

---

[1] Cp. also other works by Bartoli, e.g. *Alle fonti del neolatino* (see below), *La norma neolinguistica dell' area maggiore*, in *Rivista di filologia e d'istruzione classica*, LVII (1929), p. 333 f., *Le norme neolinguistiche e la loro utilità per la storia dei linguaggi e dei costumi*, in *Atti della Soc. Italiana per il progresso delle scienze*, Rome, 1933, p. 157 f. (with a very full bibliography), *La norma delle arie laterali*, in *Bollettino dell' Atlante linguistico italiano*, I (1933), No. 1, p. 28 f. Various specific points are to be found explained incidentally in *Studi italiani di filologia classica*, nuova serie, VIII (1930), p. 21, note 4, and p. 22, note 4, in *Archivio glottologico italiano*, XXI (1927), sezione neolatina, p. 2, in *Rivista di filologia e d'istruzione classica*, LVII (1929), p. 344, and LVIII (1930), p. 39 f., etc. Bartoli does not confine himself to Romance but applies his theories to the classical languages and to Indo-European, e.g. in the two articles last mentioned, and in *Il carattere conservativo dei linguaggi baltici* (*Studi baltici*, III [1933], p. 1 f.).

[2] As we have seen above (p. 262), the collaboration did not last. The *Italian Atlas*, originally a joint undertaking, is now directed by Bartoli alone.

may be said to fit the specific characteristics of the two schools. As will be seen below, on pages 49, 95 f., and 100, the neo-grammarians believe that there is an essential difference between creations and innovations that are purely grammatical and those that are not ; whereas, for the neo-linguist, this distinction between various types of linguistic creation, be they grammatical or lexical, normal or abnormal, popular or learned, does not hold good." In other words, the stress is on the ' -linguist ' and not on the ' neo- ', which latter, being merely a carry-over from the name of the other school, itself also ' new ', may even count as the mark of a certain affinity ; the important thing is the substitution of ' linguist ' for ' grammarian ', intended to imply a wider outlook and a more comprehensive understanding of the facts of language.

Bartoli himself is avowedly an eclectic. In the *Introduzione*, p. v, he states clearly that the neo-linguistic school is founded upon the ideas suggested by Gilliéron's *Atlas* and upon those of certain linguists and philosophers, both Italian and foreign. In the course of the discussion we discover these to be : von Humboldt, Croce, Gentile, Ascoli, Schuchardt, Meyer-Lübke, and others. But an attentive reading of the book does not entirely confirm this. In the first place, Vossler, though he proceeds almost entirely from von Humboldt and Croce, is not only made to contribute nothing to the constructive side of the neo-linguistic system, but is actually rather roughly handled ; for example, on page 64, the German scholar, with his whole school, figures as a ' glottosofo ', who has no concern whatever with linguistics, allied, it is true, with the school of Gilliéron and therefore with the neo-linguists, but an ally from whom Bartoli asks Providence to preserve him. Again, it is true that he has borrowed from the idealist philosophy, i.e. of Croce and Gentile, the idea that the distinction between vocabulary, flexions, and sounds as of things fundamentally apart, is erroneous, and the doctrine that all the elements of a language, being in essence identical, must be investigated and explained on the same footing, a point of view shared as we have been by Vossler (*v.* Chap. II). It is likewise true that, again in common with Vossler (*v.* pp. 88–9, above), he adopts Croce's theory of imitation, namely, that to imitate a new sound, word, or form, is not to reproduce it in its identical shape, but to create it anew with the means at one's own disposal. But the essential feature of the Crocean doctrine, the identification of intuition and expression, that is, of aesthetics and linguistics, is to seek in Bartoli's system. Instead, he has taken from Meillet the idea that linguistic influences flow from a people or a social class who enjoy exceptional prestige, and thus inspire imitation.

It should be said, however, that the above are but the trimmings to the system, and are of more or less secondary importance. Its foundation is primarily linguistic geography, coupled with certain ideas which it owes to Ascoli. Neglecting the really new and original features of Gilliéron's methods and doctrine, his deep soundings into the whole linguistic structure (linguistic stratigraphy or geology), his explanations of the causes of the disappearance and replacements of words (homonymy, contamination, popular etymology, etc.), Bartoli has confined himself to systematizing the exterior, the purely geographical aspects of Gilliéron's teaching, and to formulating certain laws or ' norms '[1] with regard to the spread of linguistic phenomena over territories of greater or less extent, or to the ways of determining their point of departure. Ascoli has supplied him with the means of accounting for certain linguistic innovations, by providing him with the famous notion of the ' ethnical substratum ', that is, of the influence of the native speech habits of the subject races of the Roman empire upon the imported idiom. Bartoli, however, makes certain reservations with regard to some of Ascoli's views, which he endeavours to bring into line with modern ideas. He pays greater attention, for instance, to the effects of the movements of population resulting from the so-called barbarian invasions, of Germans in the west and Slavs in

[1] Bartoli is interested primarily in the question of linguistic innovations, of those differences which in course of time arise in the life of a language or of a group of languages. These changes he investigates from three points of view, age, place of origin, and cause. To establish the age, he has recourse to texts, the other two problems are solved on a geographical and ethnico-linguistic basis. The ' laws ' or ' norms ' he arrives at and systematizes remind us, in their rigidity and apparent certitude, of the laws of the neo-grammarians. We quote a few : Of two linguistic phases, the older is, as a rule, the one that is attested earlier. Isolated areas (such as islands or mountain regions) are more conservative, consequently more archaic in speech than others. Lateral areas (like the Iberian peninsula, or Dacia) are more archaic than central areas (like Gaul and Italy). The forms of speech found over extensive areas (comprising, say, three or four Roman provinces) are earlier than the forms found only in a single area, etc. etc. To each of these ' norms ' Bartoli frames a number of restrictions, which again remind us of the ' exceptions ' of the neo-grammarians. We must recognize, however, that the neo-linguistic ' norms ' carry more conviction than the laws of the neo-grammarians, as they do not give us the impression of having been framed a priori, but seem to follow, more or less naturally, from observation of the facts of language. But they suffer from the same weakness as all formulæ : they are of purely relative value, and when unduly stressed, and their importance and infallibility exaggerated, as they occasionally are by their author, they lose the only real virtue they undoubtedly possess, namely, that of serving as practical criteria for the assortment of certain linguistic innovations.

the east, etc., and takes count also of the influence of Greeks and Osco-Umbrians upon the Latin of Italy. His attitude to such foreign influences, and the importance he attaches to them, rather go to show that he has been attracted by Schuchardt's ideas upon language mixture (*v. supra*, p. 53).

After expounding the neo-linguistic method, Bartoli compares it with that of the neo-grammarians (*Introduzione*, p. 48 f.).[1] The chief difference, and the source of practically all other divergences, lies in the attitude of the neo-linguist towards the ' sound-laws ', in which, unlike the neo-grammarian, he does not believe. In other respects, the two schools are more alike than one might have been led to suppose. Though the sound-laws are rejected by the neo-linguists they have other laws, equally rigid, of their own. Further, Bartoli, at every turn, shows himself to be as much of a comparatist or a historicist as your typical neo-grammarian. He even goes so far as to say somewhere that linguistics in the real sense is impossible without the application of the historical and comparative method. That is why, no doubt, the dialects and popular vernacular of the Romance peoples do not receive, in his system, the recognition to which they would appear to be entitled

---

[1] Bartoli's theories have not been discussed to any great extent in specialist journals. The *Introduzione* has been reviewed by O. Densusianu, *Grai şi suflet*, III (1927–8), p. 253 f. ; A. Meillet, *Bull. Soc. Ling.*, XXVIII (1927–8), fasc. 1, p. 4 f. ; N. Maccarrone, *Rev. de ling. rom.*, VI (1930), p. 23 f. Meillet asserts that the work is far from being as original in its ideas as the author claims, though J. B. Hofmann, *Deutsche Literaturzeitung*, LIII (1932), col. 1022–3, states that Meillet in his *Esquisse d'une histoire de la langue latine*, 2nd ed., p. 285 f., applies Bartoli's ' norm ' of the ' isolated area ' to Indo-European. Bartoli's article, *Alle fonti del neolatino*, is also criticized unfavourably by A. Philippide, in *Originea Rominilor*, I, p. 367 f. Whereas, with Bartoli, it is the lateral areas that are the more conservative, Philippide maintains, in *Originea Rominilor*, II, that the Macedo-Rumanian and Banat areas are the more archaic because they are nearer the region where the Rumanian language developed, whereas Moldavian shows numerous and striking innovations, due to its greater remoteness from the original cradle of the language (cp. the comparison, on similar grounds, of Moldavia and France, both of them innovating areas, made by the present author in *Revista critică*, I [1927], p. 96 f.).
    Reviews of the *Breviario* were more numerous, and the discussion it provoked sometimes heated. An article by Goidànich, entitled *Neolinguistica o linguistica senza aggettivo?* in *Archivio glottologico italiano*, XXI (1927), sezione Goidànich, p. 59 f. (reviewed by Meillet in *Bull. Soc. Ling.*, XXX [1930], p. 23 f.), called forth a sharp retort from Bertoni in *Archivum Romanicum*, XII (1928), p. 344 f. A continuation to Goidànich's article appeared later in *L'Italia dialettale*, VII (1931), p. 146 f., and a reply to Goidànich by Bartoli in *Studi albanesi*, II (1932), p. 1 f. Among other reviews of the *Breviario* we may mention : O. Densusianu, *Grai şi suflet*, II (1925–6), p. 405 f. (favourable) ; C. Tagliavini, *Dacoromania*, IV (1924–6), p. 992 f. ; A. Dauzat, *Revue de philologie franç. et de litt.*, XXXVIII (1926), p. 165 f. ; Leo Jordan, *Zeitschr. f. rom. Phil.*, XLVI (1926), p. 706 f. (favourable) ; A. Meillet, *Bull. Soc. Ling.*, XXVII (1926–7), fasc. 2, p. 7 f., and *Revue critique d'histoire et de littérature*, XCIII (1926), p. 334 f.

from an avowed disciple of linguistic geography. We are not surprised, therefore, to find him annexing as neo-linguists, either past or present, both Ascoli[1] and Meyer-Lübke who, particularly the latter, could with equal justice, to say the least, be classed among the neo-grammarians.

We will conclude, therefore, that the neo-linguistic doctrine is nothing more than a continuation of that of the neo-grammarians, but with certain modifications introduced to bring it into line with modern tendencies, mainly geographical. In fact, its founder would appear to admit as much when he says (*Introduzione*, p. v) : " It is thought by some that the neo-grammarians are mere ' grammarians and not linguists '. But I recognize that they too, in specified cases (pp. 55 and 98), conduct research historically and are thus also linguists. For the same reason I am convinced that ' reconciliation [between the two schools] is not difficult, and is in any case to be desired, and that it will come about at such time as our courteous opponents shall discover, as they will certainly find means of discovering, that for which hitherto they have preferred not to seek ' (*v. Giornale storico della letteratura italiana*, LXIX, p. 383, note 5)."

---

[1] Cp. Merlo's claims with regard to Ascoli mentioned above, p. 29, note.

CHAPTER IV

THE FRENCH SCHOOL

UNLIKE the originators of the idealistic movement and of linguistic geography, with which we have been concerned in the last two chapters, the founder of the French school, Ferdinand de Saussure, was an Indo-Europeanist, not a Romanicist. We are none the less entitled, nay obliged, to discuss his

Preamble

doctrines in a book intended as a theoretical introduction to Romance linguistics, and that for a variety of reasons. We have already seen that it is neither admissible, nor indeed possible, to partition off Romance studies from allied disciplines ; the connections between the different branches of linguistics are so close that the methods and results of one of necessity become operative in the others. Thus, already in the second half of last century, we find scholars like Ascoli or Schuchardt, to quote two names well known to the reader, who explored the fields of Indo-European and Romance with equal assiduity, and who even, particularly the latter, frequently travelled far beyond these very extensive domains. Further, although Saussure was himself an Indo-Europeanist, numbers of those whom he can claim, directly or indirectly, as his disciples are either solely Romanicists or have made serious contributions to Romance studies. To understand them fully we must first understand their master. Finally, as we shall see, many of the Saussurian theories have now become common property among Romance scholars generally, of whatever creed or persuasion, and consequently concern us intimately.

Another preliminary question we may ask is the following : In dealing with Saussure, are we dealing with a breaker of new ground, like Vossler or Gilliéron, or with a traditionalist, a neogrammarian ? In other words, again, are we justified in devoting a separate chapter of this book to the French linguistic school, as we have done for ' idealism ' and linguistic geography ? Without going into details at this stage, we can state here and now that although by no means a revolutionary—no one would call him that—Saussure introduced into the traditional theories of language so many and, in some cases, such essential modifications that they have become scarcely recognizable, while his numerous followers have continued and completed his work, contributing new points of view, or at least elaborating still further the ideas of their master. He is therefore very definitely, as Montaigne says, *notre gibier*.

The school founded by F. de Saussure is s o c i o l o g i c a l, or to be more precise, is based upon the s o c i o l o g i c a l c o n c e p t i o n of l a n g u a g e, namely, that human speech is a social fact, incapable of taking shape except as a product of society, and holds consequently that language is to be studied in relationship with other social facts or phenomena.[1] The exact implications of this outlook will become apparent as we proceed. For the present we shall confine ourselves to two preliminary remarks. It can scarcely be a pure coincidence that this sociological conception of language should have taken shape in the mind of one who, though by nationality a Swiss, was brought up in close association with French culture. That there is, on the contrary, some fundamental relationship between the two facts, as we are inclined to believe, would appear to be abundantly confirmed by the observation that every member of the sociological school we are to discuss is also, either French or, like Saussure, from French-speaking Switzerland. In France, as is well known, the social will, the will of the group, wields a powerful influence in matters which elsewhere are comparatively immune from its interference. Extreme centralization makes itself felt not only in the political and administrative spheres, but also in matters of language ; the capital exercises its control with as much severity in this domain as elsewhere, and the provinces must bow to the linguistic dictates of Paris. The tradition is of long standing, dating from the times of Francis the First at least, and has resulted in smoothing out to a much greater extent than in other Romance lands the peculiarities of dialect. Again, this standard speech, radiated by the political and cultural centre, took on its present form also as the result of close supervision by an ' authority ', that of the famous Salons, which, in the seventeenth century, when classical French received what we may call its

---

[1] On the relations between speech and society, cp. H. Delacroix, *Le langage et la pensée*, 2nd ed., p. 63 f. ; cp. also : W. Doroszewski, *Quelques remarques sur les rapports de la sociologie et de la linguistique : Durkheim et F. de Saussure*, in *Psychologie du langage* (=*Journal de psychologie*, 1933), p. 82 f.

final shape, consulting on the one hand the speech of the court, and on the other the pronouncements of the grammarians, played a decisive part in the work of linguistic standardization. All this could not have happened if it had not been in tune with the French mind, which is the more ready to bow to the will of the community the more evidently social in character is the act to be performed. Now nothing could be more ' social ' than language. We talk to others, not to ourselves. We have continually in view our audience, be it of one or several, and we strive to adjust ourselves to it, and to adopt as far as possible its modes of expression. The Frenchman, so prone to ask, even in regard to his most everyday acts, " What will people say ? ", obeys these inward promptings much more readily and with greater consistency than the majority of his fellows. His rationalism and his love for clarity and precision work in the same direction : talking to be understood, we must do all we can to help our listener to follow what we say. No wonder, then, that with French linguists the idea that human language is a means for the intercommunication of thought, and only that, prevails.

The reader will encounter towards the end of the present chapter a number of linguists whose affiliation to the French school does not go beyond certain similarities in doctrine, or even in method. Some of these are investigators of ' argots ' or ' slangs ', those special forms of language thrown up by certain social conditions or evolved by certain social categories. Others make a study of the characteristic features which differentiate one language from others. Both groups are alike, however, in that they consider language as it is at a given time, not concerning themselves with its earlier phases, and this it is which gives them a kinship with the French school, most of whom, as we shall see, either in practice or theory, also show a preference for what their master termed the synchronistic study of language, i.e. descriptive study, as against the diachronistic or historical method. Moreover, students of ' slangs ' have a further bond with Saussure, in that nothing could provide more patent evidence that speech is a social phenomenon than the existence of these purely social products.

★　★　★

A comparison between Saussure and one of the founders of the schools already studied, Vossler to wit, would provide a striking array of contrasts. Whereas the system propounded **Ferdinand de Saussure** by the Munich scholar appears in the mass as a lofty and audacious structure, but somewhat ill-defined and insecure in points of detail, Saussure's edifice is remarkable for the excessive care which he brings to bear on the analysis of its several component parts.[1] It is as though we had before us a professor, a real teacher, examining calmly and reflectively what he is to say to his pupils, intent at every step upon drawing their attention to the errors to be avoided and upon showing them the path along which they may travel without danger. It is difficult to imagine a more thorough or a more unprejudiced observer of the facts of language than Saussure. The explanations he brings us are thus, in the majority of cases, extremely precise, almost mathematical, and consequently convincing. Only rarely does he arouse contradiction. What interests him above all things is method ; on this his whole powers appear to be concentrated.

To turn now to his theories. The most famous of these is the sharp distinction he makes between 'la langue' and 'la parole', which we may render, imperfectly, by 'language' and 'speech'. 'Language' is a lexical and grammatical system, having a virtual existence in the consciousness of those individuals

---

[1] Saussure's theory of language is to be found in his *Cours de linguistique générale*, Lausanne–Paris, 1916, 2nd ed., Paris, 1923, 3rd, *ibid.*, 1931. The book was published after his death, and was compiled from lecture-notes taken by two of his pupils, Ch. Bally and A. Sechehaye. There is a German translation by H. Lommel, which bears the more appropriate title, *Grundfragen der allgemeinen Sprachwissenschaft*, Berlin–Leipzig, 1931.

Saussure's scientific career was a curious one, in a number of ways. In 1879, when he was scarcely twenty-one, and still a student (he studied in Germany, particularly at Leipzig under those famous neo-grammarians, Leskien, Osthoff, and Brugmann), he published a work entitled *Mémoire sur le système primitif des voyelles dans les langues indo-européennes*, which, even to-day, arouses the unbounded admiration of the experts in this field. In 1881 he was appointed ' Maître de conférences ' at the Ecole Pratique des Hautes-Etudes, in Paris ; ten years later, he transferred to his native Geneva, as lecturer in Indo-European, and in 1896 became full professor of Sanscrit and Indo-European philology ; in 1907 he received in addition the chair of general linguistics, which he held till his death in 1913. He has written very little. In addition to the *Cours de linguistique générale*, his collected works, republished posthumously as *Recueil des publications scientifiques de Ferdinand de Saussure*, Genève, 1922, compose a volume of some six hundred pages. None the less, his influence, not only upon his pupils, but upon philologists in general, has been among the most profound. He was a remarkable teacher, and among his numerous pupils are, or were, some of the leading lights of European linguistic scholarship ; for example, A. Meillet, M. Grammont, and Ch. Bally. Meillet, a world celebrity, did not hesitate to declare that on every page of his own work was to be found something he owed to Saussure (cp. *Bull. de la Société de linguistique*, XVIII [1912–13], p. clxx).

who compose a linguistic community ; without such a group, be it small or great, of speaking individuals, ' language ' is impossible. As a social product, and a means of communication between men, ' language ' does not depend upon the individual who speaks it ; on the contrary, the latter is obliged to apply himself to acquire it, and often does so completely only after much effort. It follows that the study of ' language ' must of necessity be purely psychological. ' Speech ' signifies the act whereby the individual avails himself of ' language ' to express his ideas. Thus, it is individual in its nature. It comprises, too, the emission of sounds. It must therefore be studied both psychologically and physically. It is in ' speech ' that all linguistic changes have their source, but these only succeed in modifying ' language ', that is, the established system, when conditions are favourable for their generalization and they are adopted by the linguistic community as a whole. For this to happen they must of necessity correspond to certain generally prevailing tendencies within the community. Saussure's distinction between ' language ' and ' speech ', it should be added, is not only an essential part of his linguistic system, illustrative of his whole attitude towards human language, but also enables us to understand more completely certain points in the doctrine of Gilliéron and, particularly, of Vossler.[1]

[1] It should be stated here that this twofold conception of the phenomenon of language is not actually of Saussure's invention. Hermann Paul, *Prinzipien* . . . , 5th ed., 1920, p. 31 f. and p. 404 f., speaks of ' (Sprach-) Usus ', i.e. Saussure's ' la langue ', and ' (individuelle) Sprechtätigkeit ' (=' la parole '), and asserts likewise that changes in the ' Usus ' have their source in the speech activity of the individual. A similar conception, according to N. Drăganu, *Dacoromania*, VII, p. 268, is already to be found in the writings of von Humboldt. But no one before Saussure had made it the keystone of his linguistic doctrine, nor elaborated it in such exhaustive detail, for the great good, be it said, of all linguistic thought.

Before leaving this topic it is relevant to mention that Gabelentz, in *Die Sprachwissenschaft, ihre Aufgaben, Methoden und bisherigen Ergebnisse*, Leipzig, 1891, pp. 3–4, establishes a similar distinction between ' Rede ', or language as an individual phenomenon, a means for the expression of certain ideas, and ' Sprache ', the totality of all such means of expression for all manner of ideas, and the totality of all those aptitudes and inclinations which determine the forms of speech, and of all the representations which determine its content. But it is the stress laid upon this dualism by Saussure which accounts for the discussions which it has aroused in recent years. Without going into this in detail, we must mention a further refinement suggested by Delacroix, in his introduction to *Le langage et la pensée* (2nd ed., 1930), where he subdivides further each member of the Saussurian duality, distinguishing between ' le langage ' as a human faculty common to all peoples and races (an idea reminiscent of von Humboldt), ' la langue ', understood as with Saussure, ' la parole ', the psychological activity of the individual in the formulation of words, and finally ' le parler ', or process of utterance. Elsewhere, *ibid.*, p. 74, we find Delacroix quoting with approval the opinion of Jespersen, *Journal de psychologie*, 1927, p. 585, that the distinction between ' la langue ' and ' la parole ' should not be made too absolute. Similarly, Vendryes,

It follows from the foregoing that linguistics is but a branch of semeiology, or the science of the signs and symbols used in society, and is of a kindred nature with the various rituals, signals, formulae of politeness, etc., to which conventional values are attached by the social group. Language should indeed be studied in relationship with these other social phenomena, as well as independently, for its own sake. The relations between language and civilization, social institutions, dialect and so forth appertain to external linguistics, an important branch of language study, inasmuch as it throws light on numerous linguistic problems ; but there is nothing in common between this and internal linguistics, as the facts it studies do not affect in any degree the nature and inward essence of language. Internal linguistics, on the other hand, deals with everything which can modify the linguistic system. In keeping with this novel conception Saussure makes use of a terminology that is also unusual. Language consists of signs, that is to say, unities, which can, however, be decomposed into a ' determinate ', i.e. the notion, and a ' determinant ', the acoustic image, but both of these are so closely interwoven that one of them always calls up the other. The linguistic sign, moreover, has the following characteristics : it is arbitrary, that is to say, there is no real relationship between a word and the notion it embodies, but only a fortuitous connection between name and thing,[1] and, secondly, it is constant, and cannot be modified by the whim of the individual, though subject to change in and by the process of time.

Internal linguistics is static or synchronistic and evolutional or diachronistic. In the former case, we describe a language as it appears at a given moment, taking no account of its earlier phases ; in the latter, we investigate a language over

in a review of Jespersen, *Mankind, Nation and Individual from a linguistic point of view*, Oslo, 1925, in *Bull. de la Soc. de ling.*, XXVII (1926-7), fasc. 2, p. 5, writes that the distinction set up by Saussure is only defensible if we take his two terms sociologically. " La parole ", he says, p. 6, " est la langue en action dans un groupe social donné ". " La parole ne peut être observée et étudiée que dans l'individu. Mais l'usage que fait chaque individu de la parole est réglé par des conventions sociales, celles du groupe auquel il appartient." It is legitimate, therefore, to " considérer la langue comme une entité idéale, indépendante des individus qui la parlent et s'imposant à eux sans restriction ". " La parole a pour résultat de transformer à chaque instant la langue." Cp. also *Travaux du Cercle linguistique de Prague*, I, Prague, 1929, p. 33 f. ; and A. H. Gardiner, *The Theory of Speech and Language*, Oxford, 1932.

[1] The idea that the linguistic sign is arbitrary is an ancient one and goes back to the Thomists, and to Aristotle. It is to be found in Condillac, together with a number of other ideas propounded anew by Schuchardt or Vossler as, for example, the poetic origin of language ; cp. J. Ronjat, *Revue des langues romanes*, LXI (1921-2), p. 394.

one or several periods, tracing it through its successive stages. Both from the point of view of theory and method these two branches of internal linguistics are quite distinct, and must be kept strictly apart in language study. Both are equally legitimate, but the static or synchronistic should have our preference, inasmuch as, on the one hand, to the individual speakers the present state of a language, its static element, is the only reality,[1] and, on the other, the modifications in language are individual in their origin, that is to say, are phenomena of ' la parole ', and only become incorporated in ' la langue ' if circumstances are favourable for their adoption. By definition, diachronistic or evolutional linguistics can only deal with ' la langue ', as only ' la langue ' is a continuum that can change in Time.[2]

[1] That is to say, when we are speaking we are conscious only of the system of expression which prevails at the moment, of the existing syntactical and verbal convention. We do not concern ourselves with earlier modes of speech, or with the origins of our words, not even if we are etymologists by profession.

[2] Alternative terms for those used by Saussure are : descriptive linguistics and historical linguistics respectively. It is the latter which has been and still remains predominant in Romance studies. But the former has not been neglected, especially of late. Thus K. v. Ettmayer has an article in *Prinzipienfragen der romanischen Sprachwissenschaft*, I, Halle a.S., 1910, p. 1 f., entitled *Benötigen wir eine wissenschaftlich deskriptive Grammatik ?*, a question to which he replies in the affirmative. Similarly, we may quote works by E. Herzog, *Historische Sprachlehre des Neufranzösischen. Einleitung. I : Lautlehre*, Heidelberg, 1913, which describes the present state of the French language from the phonetic point of view, or again J. Haas, *Neufranzösische Syntax*, Halle a.S., 1909, and *Über sprachwissenschaftliche Erklärung. Ein methodischer Beitrag*, Halle a.S., 1922 (an extract of this work is reproduced by Spitzer in *Meisterwerke der romanischen Sprachwissenschaft*, II, Munich, 1930, p. 92 f.), where he urges that beside the etymology (i.e. the origin and evolution) of the syntactical elements of the language, the syntactical functions of these elements also call for methodical and scientific treatment. But no linguist makes such a sharp distinction between the historical and the descriptive method as do Saussure and his disciples. Even the authors mentioned above mingle both methods, with a natural leaning towards the historical in view of its time-honoured predominance in our discipline. Herzog, for example, entitles his study historical, because, as he says in the preface, he holds that a knowledge of the past helps to understand the present, while Haas, who combines the psychological (i.e. descriptive) with the historical method in his *Neufranzösische Syntax*, published shortly afterwards a *Französische Syntax*, Halle a.S., 1916, where he deals with Old French. A closer kinship with Saussure is displayed by Ernst Otto, *Zur Grundlegung der Sprachwissenschaft*, Bielefeld–Leipzig, 1919, whose distinction ' Sprechkunde '—' Sprachkunde ' corresponds in a large measure to Saussure's ' Static linguistics '—' Diachronistic linguistics '. The question has been given a certain prominence fairly recently through a study by von Wartburg, *Das Ineinandergreifen von deskriptiver und historischer Sprachwissenschaft*, in *Berichte über die Verhandlungen der Sächsischen Akademie der Wissenschaften zu Leipzig*, phil.-hist. Klasse, 83. Band (1931), 1. Heft, p. 1 f. From the review of this study by Spitzer, *Literaturblatt f. germ. u. rom. Phil.*, LII (1931), col. 401 f., it would appear that von Wartburg maintains that historical and descriptive linguistics, so religiously kept apart by Saussure, have become mingled thanks to Gilliéron, and his work on homonyms (*vide supra*, p. 161 f.). The detecting of incompatible homonyms at a given period is ' descriptive ', but their replacement

Saussure passes at this point to the important problem of language laws. Like every law of a social character these, too, should be imperative and general. But the laws of language, whether synchronistic or diachronistic, do not severally comply with both of these requirements ; the former are solely general, the latter solely imperative.[1] Even the much discussed ' sound-laws ' are in no better case because, being diachronistic, they, too, have no general validity. Moreover, their significance with respect to ' la langue ' is further reduced by the fact that they do not affect what is essential in the material of language.[2]

We have seen above that these two branches of the science of language are distinct in their aims and methods. After analysing the notion of ' la langue ', which is not a ' substance ', but only a ' form ', Saussure concerns himself in detail, first with static linguistics, and then with evolutional. The constituent elements of human language, considered at a particular moment, without taking count of its earlier stages, are related to each other syntagmatically and associatively. Words are combined in syntagmas, which owe their structure to the linear dimension of speech and have a real existence, outside ourselves.[3] Syntagmas are of the domain of ' la langue ', not of ' la parole ', particularly when we have to do with ready-made expressions of the type : *allons donc !, à force de, rompre une lance*, etc., where no change of any of the component parts is permissible. Freedom to change word sequence is a characteristic only of ' la parole '. Association

by other words is a matter of historical linguistics, the effective link between the two phenomena being frequently, as alleged by Spitzer himself (see above, p. 191), the fancy of the speakers. In this connection the reviewer expresses surprise that von Wartburg does not mention Vossler, the champion of ' fancy ' as a creative force in language. Von Wartburg's reply is to be found in *Literaturbl. f. germ. u. rom. Phil.*, LIII (1932), col. 142 f.

[1] The laws, or rules, which govern a language at a given moment are general because they apply to all facts of the same type, but they have no imperative character, in the sense that the language has no means of enforcing their observance, so that, in process of time, one law is replaced by another. The laws which preside over linguistic change, viewed historically, are imperative, from the very fact that they have come about, but they are not general in character, because they fail to exercise their influence upon all words, forms, etc., of the same type, witness, for example, the numerous exceptions to the sound-laws.

[2] In truth, neither the meaning of a word nor the function of a grammatical form is affected by a change in sound.

[3] A syntagma is composed of at least two units in sequence : *relire* (=*re*+*lire*) ; *contre tous* ; *la vie humaine* ; *Dieu est bon* ; *s'il fait beau temps, nous sortirons* ; etc: The study of syntagmas is not to be identified with syntax, which is but a branch of syntagmatology. Thus, of the examples quoted, the first, *re-lire*, belongs to word-formation, to use the current terminology, and in no sense to syntax.

is the process by which a word awakens in our mind the image
of one or more words with which it is in formal or semantic relationship. Thus, the word *enseignement* calls to mind, whether we
will it or not, *enseigner, renseigner*, on the one hand, and *éducation*,
apprentissage, etc. on the other. These two types of relationship
exercise reciprocal influence one upon the other ; the closer their
mutual correspondence, the less arbitrary are the linguistic ' signs '.
Languages differ greatly in respect of this correspondence. In
some [in French for example], the arbitrary character of the
linguistic signs is more apparent (see p. 381), and these Saussure
calls lexicological languages ; in others, where there is greater
solidarity between the semantic and the formal associations [for
example German], the signs appear less arbitrary, and these he
calls grammatical languages. The traditional division of
grammar into morphology and syntax is inaccurate, that is to
say incomplete, inasmuch as vocabulary also forms part of
grammar, for there are words which express all manner of relationships unaided by any grammatical forms. In any case, grammar
can only have as its object the static or coexistent phenomena of
a language, for it can only concern itself with a language considered
as a system of means of expression, and such a system is of necessity confined to a single period. The term ' historical grammar '
is thus meaningless, as it would imply the study of the linguistic
system while in process of evolution, which is impossible, for the
system as it evolves, changes, and becomes another system. What
we usually call historical grammar is no other than diachronistic
linguistics.

It is to this latter domain that the thorny problem of phonetic
changes belongs.[1] Saussure makes a close scrutiny of all the

---

[1] The author attempts a modification of current terminology. Generally,
'phonetics' is used to designate the physiology of sounds, and ' phonology '
the history of sounds. Saussure reverses the use of the two terms, because, as he
says (*op. cit.*, pp. 55–6), ' la phonétique ' was originally used, and is still used, to
mean the study of the evolution of sounds. If we apply this term also to the
physiology of sound production, he goes on to say, we would be confusing two
entirely different disciplines : (1) phonology or the description of sounds,
which is a science ancillary to linguistics, but not part of linguistics, as it is concerned with ' la parole ', and (2) phonetics, an historical science, and an
essential part of linguistics. The distinction is a legitimate one, but the confusion
Saussure would wish to avoid appears more likely if his terminology is adopted.
The great majority of linguists and all the phoneticians (Sievers, Jespersen,
Rousselot, etc.) use ' phonetics ' for the physiology of sounds, and although all
do not adopt the term ' phonology ' for their historical study, those who use the
term ' phonetics ' for the latter avoid confusion by speaking of ' historical
phonetics '. Another way out is to use instead of ' historical phonetics ' the term

theories which have been put forward to account for these changes, such as : race, physical environment, convenience, transmission to children, social and political conditions, the ethnical substratum, and fashion. With regard to all or nearly all, he shows himself sceptical, because although theoretically it is impossible to deny the action of any one of them, it is equally impossible to determine that action with precision. It is worth pointing out, further, that Saussure gives particular prominence to convenience of articulation, to which he attaches far greater importance than other modern linguists. A peculiarity of phonetic change is that it is not limited in time or space. At the same time it may be the cause of much disturbance in grammar.[1]

Special attention is paid by Saussure to analogy, which, to him, as to the neo-grammarians, is a kind of linguistic counterpoise to sound-change. From the point of view of results, analogy is of the domain of ' la parole ', because analogical formations are individual ; but from the point of view of the psychological process underlying it, it appertains to ' la langue ', as the individual speaker breaks up the word into its component parts, real or supposed, and with their help sets about creating new formations. This analysis, applied by men when they speak, is called by Saussure ' subjective analysis ', and is distinguished from the ' objective analysis ' of the linguist, which is based on special historical knowledge, not on a feeling for the language like the former. In a word like *amabas*, he says, a Roman would see three elements (*ama-ba-s*), or possibly only two (*ama-bas*), whereas a linguist picks out four (*am-a-ba-s*). Similarly, a Parisian feels the word *enfant* as a single unit, while the linguist breaks it down into two constituents, *en-* and *-fant*, Latin *in-fans*, *in-fantem*, ' not talking '. In the life of language it is of course only the subjective analysis that matters, because it alone is productive of new, analogical, formations. But objective analysis is not to be disdained, because, for one reason, it springs from the same source as its counterpart.

Saussure devotes a number of chapters to geographical

' history of sounds ', as is frequently done. Cp. Al. Rosetti, *Phonétique et phonologie*, in *Bulletin linguistique* (Bucharest), II (1934), p. 5 f. Cp. also S. Puşcariu's remarks in *Dacoromania*, II (1921–2), p. 28 f., VI (1929–30), p. 211 f., VII (1931–3), p. 437 f., and *Volkstum und Kultur der Romanen*, III (1930), p. 16 f. This matter of terminology has become complicated still further by the special meaning given to ' phonology ' by the Prague philologists. (Cp. *infra*, p. 334, n. 1.)

[1] For example, many forms in the Romance declensions or conjugations that are unknown to Latin have come about because of the confusion resulting from phonetic changes undergone by the Latin endings in popular speech.

linguistics,[1] a branch of external linguistics (see above, p. 284). Here the problem of the differentiation of languages is, in every respect, of quite major importance. The differences between languages, as between dialects, he attributes to the workings of time. Space, on the other hand, accounts for their common elements. Spatial factors cause the differences between one idiom and another to be less marked than they would have been if the action of time had been unimpeded. Through geographical contiguity features peculiar to one idiom may spread to others and thus give rise to so-called isoglosses, or boundaries between dialect features, a term to which Saussure prefers 'waves of innovation', borrowed from J. Schmidt's wave theory mentioned above on p. 52, note. Two conflicting forces preside over the expansion of new linguistic forms, one centripetal, 'la force d'intercourse', or 'force unifiante', the other centrifugal, the 'esprit de clocher'. There are no such things as natural linguistic boundaries ; there are as many dialects as there are localities. When we cast our eyes over a linguistic map, we observe that sometimes two or three 'waves of innovation' roughly coincide, or even merge together over a certain distance. When coincidences of this kind are sufficiently numerous we may, with some measure of justification, speak of dialects.[2] But in any case the causes which differentiate dialects are of a non-linguistic order in the strict sense, be they social, political, religious facts or what not. Nor are there natural boundaries between languages, though in the case of the latter the differences are more noticeable and frequently sharply marked. But these, likewise, are to be attributed to causes foreign to language, above all to migration, movements

[1] Not to be confused with linguistic geography. Saussure only concerns himself with the distribution of the various languages over the globe, the reasons why they are so numerous, the existence, or otherwise, of boundaries between them, etc. His use of the term 'geography' is thus in keeping with its normal connotation, and quite different from the meaning attached to it in Chap. III of the present book. It is true that Saussure does mention the *Atlas linguistique de la France* and its author, but in a manner which shows clearly that he did not realize its exceptional value, particularly to general linguistics. On p. 277, for example, he writes : " Un des avantages des atlas linguistiques, c'est de fournir des matériaux pour des travaux de dialectologie ", having previously stated that the study of dialect features called for the cartographical method. That is all he makes of linguistic geography in the Gilliéronian sense !

[2] Saussure also examines the question : What is language and what is dialect ? From his discussion we gather that these are very relative notions, which, like so much of what we have seen of his doctrine, reminds us of Schuchardt (cp. above, p. 52 f.). The question has been discussed recently by A. Schmidt, *Volksmundart, Gemeinsprache und Schriftsprache, Germanisch-romanische Monatsschrift*, XIX (1931), p. 434 f.

19

of population and the like, which have brought about the disappearance of intermediate forms of speech far less divergent than the languages that are to-day contiguous.[1] A similar obliteration of transitional forms may occur for other reasons, as, for example, the imposition of a standard speech, as in France, to the detriment of the popular vernaculars.

Despite the fact that language is a purely spiritual product, Saussure does not believe that its study can lead us to conclusions concerning the minds of the individuals who speak it. To controvert the view cherished by Vossler (see above, Chapter II), he puts forward two arguments : (1) " Un procédé linguistique n'est pas nécessairement déterminé par des causes psychiques " (op. cit., ed. II, pp. 310–11), (2) " Le caractère psychologique du groupe linguistique pèse peu devant un fait comme la suppression d'une voyelle ou une modification d'accent, et bien d'autres choses analogues capables de révolutionner à chaque instant le rapport du signe et de l'idée dans n'importe quelle forme de la langue " (ibidem, pp. 311–12). These assertions are backed up by a number of well chosen examples, and it follows that, if the facts are as stated, no family of languages is entitled to rank once and for all as belonging to a certain linguistic type. This point of view finds forcible expression in the concluding words of his book, which may be considered as summarizing in its essentials the whole Saussurian outlook upon language, " La linguistique a pour unique et véritable objet la langue envisagée en elle-même et pour elle-même " (ibidem, p. 317).

★　　★　　★

Following upon this account of Saussure's linguistic system, a comparison would appear to be called for between him and certain **Criticism of** scholars already known to us, the more so as his **the Saussurian** place in the history of linguistics has been a matter **Doctrine** of considerable argument. Thus, A. Wallensköld, reviewing in *Neuphilologische Mitteilungen*, XXV (1924), p. 230 f., a study by the present author upon the state of Romance Philology,[2]

---

[1] This is the case with regard to the frontier between Slavonic and German ; between French and Italian, on the other hand, transitional dialects exist.

[2] *Der heutige Stand der romanischen Sprachwissenschaft*, in *Stand und Aufgaben der Sprachwissenschaft. Festschrift für Wilhelm Streitberg*, Heidelberg, 1924, p. 585 f. In this study, the author, while attaching due importance to the innovations in method and outlook introduced by Saussure and his disciples, and setting them forth in as great detail as those of Vossler and Gilliéron, expressly states that Saussure is *not* a revolutionary.

objects to the representatives of the French school and their leader being considered as adversaries of the neo-grammarians whom, it is asserted, they do but follow. Fr. Schürr, again, *Das Wesen der Sprache und der Sinn der Sprachwissenschaft*, in *Deutsche Vierteljahrsschrift für Literaturwissenschaft und Geistesgeschichte*, I (1923), goes so far as to claim (pp. 485–6), that Saussure is in many respects a ' positivist ', inasmuch as he speaks of the ' mechanism ' of language and has an approach to linguistics which is decidedly rationalistic. Other scholars, too, have in like manner set Saussure among the neo-grammarians.

It is indeed true that Saussure very frequently reminds us of them. The great importance he attaches to convenience as a factor in language change, his setting analogy beside and in contradistinction to sound-change, his disregard for linguistic geography, his rejection of the Vosslerian conception of ' the spirit of the language ', etc., are so many ' old ' features in his doctrine. But how many other features, more numerous and more important than these, mark him off from the traditionalist school ! To mention a few : the upholding of the individual origin of linguistic changes, the denial of laws of whatever kind, particularly of the sound-laws (which, to boot, have the further demerit of being quite extraneous to the system, the substance of the language), the assertion of the non-existence of natural linguistic boundaries, of the essentially psychological nature of language, manifest even in the utterance of sounds, the preference for ' static ' linguistics and, consequently, at least in principle, a certain hostility towards the historical approach so cherished by the neo-grammarians. From this concern with the actual ' states ' of language ensue other features characteristic of the Saussurian doctrine, namely, the great importance it allows to syntax[1] and the interest in style which brings into being a new branch of language study, stylistics.[2] In this regard the French school comes near to that of Vossler and his pupils, from which in other respects it is so fundamentally different, particularly by its unconcern, as a general rule (the exceptions will come later), for the aesthetic element in language,

---

[1] It is true that the neo-grammarians also worked in this field, but the great majority of them were concerned with sounds, or at most with flexions, showing, where syntax was concerned, a respectful abnegation. One needs only to think of the multitude of manuals and grammars which treat of phonology and morphology but stop short at syntax.

[2] Not actually in the case of Saussure himself but with his pupil Ch. Bally (see below).

on which the idealists set such great store in their works. As we have seen, the members of the idealist group show, like the followers of Saussure, a marked preference for syntax study, in the broad sense of the term, though naturally from a different angle, holding as they do that the ' spirit of the language ' can be more readily discovered through the study of its grammatical structure. Finally, even the sociological conception of language, although not an entire innovation, has none the less brought fresh fruits by being applied consistently ; many are the linguistic phenomena which have received new and more convincing explanation, because language has been envisaged as a social fact.[1]

We have seen that Saussure differs from Vossler by a diametrically opposite attitude towards the question of ' the spirit ' of language, and by a complete disregard for its aesthetic side. But this is not all. Saussure talks of our ' acquiring ' language ; a man does not begin with a complete understanding of the linguistic system into which he is born, but is obliged to acquire it gradually, a process entailing at times considerable effort. Vossler, on the contrary, looks upon the speaking individual as creative, like the poet, as original, and consequently incapable of imitating others or even himself. The reason of this divergence is to be sought in the fact that Saussure is thinking of ' la langue ' and Vossler of ' la parole '. Each of them is right therefore in his own fashion. We have only to think of the struggles which confront the child and, often enough, the adult even, before he can achieve a complete mastery of the system of his mother tongue, above all of the grammatical forms ; while as regards ' la parole ', or language in actual application by the individual seeking to give utterance to something, it is evident that there can be no question here of ' acquiring ' or of ' imitating ', except in the matter of grammatical formulae and ready-made constructions, for how can we model our speech on that of another, when the thoughts and feelings we seek to express are our own and exclusively our own ? This dualism of ' la langue ' and ' la parole ' explains a further distinction between Saussure and Vossler, namely, that the former studies what is common and general in human language, while the latter is interested in what is individual and particular.

Saussure's affinities with Gilliéron lie more deeply, and are due

[1] For details under this head see below, where we describe the work of A. Meillet, the most authoritative representative of the sociological trend in language study.

not to any fortuitous circumstance, but to a certain intellectual kinship, to be explained partly racially, partly by similarity of training.[1] Like Gilliéron, Saussure is a rationalist, though less obviously. He, too, sees in language solely a means of mutual understanding between men, a product of reason, to the exclusion of any interference on the part of fancy or emotivity. Equally rationalistic is his use of the word ' system ' with regard to language, as though it were a piece of mechanism, a machine, constructed from a number of parts, closely and intricately assembled, a machine, therefore, that we must learn to handle by getting to know its components, and further that we are constantly tempted to take to pieces, by that process of ' subjective analysis ' mentioned above (p. 288). The natural consequence of this rationalistic conception is the important part given to consciousness in the doctrine of both scholars ; Gilliéron, at every turn, calls upon homonymy, popular etymology, and other purely intellectual factors in the development of human speech, while Saussure makes of analogy, again an exclusively rational and conscious phenomenon, a linguistic principle of the first importance.[2]

Among the features which differentiate these two linguists, in addition to the fact already noted (p. 289) of Saussure's entire failure to appreciate the significance of linguistic geography in the domain of language theory, we would point particularly to the following, which is also of considerable import : Gilliéron, a student of dialect, is concerned naturally with ' la parole '—although he does also take into account ' la langue ', for example when his investigations go down into the subjacent strata of vocabulary, or when he discusses linguistic principles—and, further, partly by reason of the nature and object of the discipline he founded, investigates more particularly the vocabulary of the vernaculars, with, as an immediate and natural consequence, their phonology, whereas Saussure, in theory, inclines towards syntax, believing at the same

[1] From 1881 to 1891 they were both of them living and working in Paris.
[2] We may quote a few characteristic passages from the *Cours de linguistique générale*, ed. II : " La langue ne cesse d'interpréter et de décomposer les unités qui lui sont données " (p. 232). " Mais même dans ses tâtonnements l'analogie exerce une influence sur la langue. Ainsi, bien qu'elle ne soit pas en elle-même un fait d'évolution, elle reflète de moment en moment les changements intervenus dans l'économie de la langue et les consacre par des combinaisons nouvelles. Elle est la collaboratrice efficace de toutes les forces qui modifient sans cesse l'architecture intérieure d'un idiome, et à ce titre elle est un puissant facteur d'évolution " (p. 234-5). " . . . pris en bloc, ces continuels remaniements [called forth by analogy] jouent dans l'évolution de la langue un rôle considérable, plus considérable même que celui des changements de sons " (p. 235).

time, for reasons we have shown, that preference should be given to synchronistic or static linguistics over the diachronistic or historical.[1]

Saussure's doctrines have been much discussed by linguistic specialists, particularly on the occasion of his death, and on the posthumous publication of the work we have just summarized. We append a list of the articles or reviews known to us, either directly or indirectly : A. Meillet, *Ferdinand de Saussure* (obituary notice), in *Bull. Soc. Ling.*, XVIII (1912–13), CLXV f. ; Ch. Bally, *Ferdinand de Saussure et l'état actuel des études linguistiques*, Geneva, 1913 ; W. Str.[eitberg], *Ferdinand de Saussure*, in *Indogermanische Forschungen*, XXXI (1913), Anzeiger, p. 16 ; A. Meillet, *Ferdinand*

---

[1] Saussure's ideas are to be met with in the writings of a number of other scholars, particularly in those of Bréal, Henry, and Darmesteter, and, as all of these were his seniors, one might be tempted to speak of Saussure as their debtor. But, as a similar kinship is to be detected between certain of Saussure's doctrines and the teachings of the neo-grammarians, it is more appropriate to consider him as having focused a number of ideas which were taking shape in the linguistic world, and which were, in a sense, common property. His originality, which is indisputable, would thus consist in having evolved a complete and coherent system, all his own, irrespective of the source of any particular ingredient. We quote some of his points of contact with the scholars mentioned. In the following sentence from V. Henry's *Antinomies linguistiques*, Paris, 1896, p. 58, reproduced by A. Dauzat, *Essai de méthodologie linguistique dans le domaine des langues et des patois romans*, Paris, 1906, p. 100, we have a conception of language as a ' system ' analogous to ' la langue ' of Saussure : " Notre langue maternelle, nous la savions virtuellement avant que de naître : je veux dire que les tours de phrase, l'ordre des mots et conséquemment l'agencement des idées constituent un fonds linguistique et logique qui par un vague atavisme doit se transmettre du cerveau de l'ancêtre à celui de ses descendants." With regard to Bréal, as Dauzat also points out, we find in his famous *Essai de sémantique*, Paris, 1897 (5th ed., 1911), the principle of ' utility ' put forward as one of the causes of semantic change, together with an entirely rationalistic conception of language analogous to that of Saussure. Indeed, A. Meillet's summing up of Bréal and his work in *Bulletin de la Société de linguistique*, XX (1916), pp. 16–17, might with equal appropriateness be applied to Saussure : " Présentant le langage comme le résultat de l'activité humaine et des efforts faits par les hommes comme pour s'exprimer clairement et commodément, l'auteur échappe au danger de considérer le langage en lui-même, comme une sorte d'objet ; tout, dans ce livre, est raisonnable et intelligible ; l'espèce de mysticisme latent qui subsiste du fait que la linguistique historique s'est développée au milieu de l'époque romantique en est entièrement banni." As for Darmesteter, a number of Saussure's ideas are to be met with in his famous *La vie des mots*, Paris, 1886, notably that of the individual origin of sound-changes (17th ed., 1928, pp. 7–8), and of semantic and other linguistic modifications (pp. 46 and 89), together with the view that language is solely a means of mutual understanding between men (p. 16). Dauzat, in the work already quoted, which we can recommend as providing a great deal of matter supplementary to the information contained in this and the preceding chapter of the present book, claims that Darmesteter's principle of ' catachresis ' (the process whereby, in an expression like *note noire*, the speaker forgets one of the terms and thus allows the word *noire* alone to take on the meaning of ' crotchet '), as set forth in his *Cours de grammaire historique de la langue française* [and also in *La vie des mots*, p. 67], contains the germ of the theory of psychological interference propounded by Saussure's most distinguished pupil, A. Meillet.

de Saussure, in *Annuaire de l'Ecole pratique des Hautes-Etudes* (1913–14), Paris ; W. Streitberg, *Ferdinand de Saussure*, in *Indogermanisches Jahrbuch*, II (1914), p. 203 f. ; A. Meillet, *Bull. Soc. Ling.*, XX (1916), p. 32 f. ; M. Grammont, *Revue des langues romanes*, LIX (1916–17), p. 402 f. ; B. Bourdon, *Revue philosophique de la France et de l'Etranger*, XLII (1917), p. 90 f. ; A. Meillet, *Revue critique d'histoire et de littérature*, vol. LXXXIV (1917), p. 49 f. ; H. Schuchardt, *Literaturblatt für germanische und romanische Philologie*, XXXVIII (1917), col. 1 f. ; A. Sechehaye, *Les problèmes de la langue à la lumière d'une théorie nouvelle*, in *Revue philosophique de la France*, XLII (1917), 30-page off-print ; A. Dauzat, *L'orientation sociologique actuelle dans la science du langage*, in *Revue de l'Institut de sociologie*, I (1920), fasc. 2, p. 7 f. ; H. Lommel, *Göttingische gelehrte Anzeigen*, CLXXXIII (1921), p. 232 f. ; J. Vendryes, *Le caractère social du langage et la doctrine de F. de Saussure*, in *Journal de psychologie normale et pathologique*, XVIII (1921), p. 617 f. ; V. Bogrea, *Dacoromania*, II (1921–22), p. 777 f. ; H. Lommel, *Deutsche Literaturzeitung*, XLV (1924), col. 2040 f. ; Th. Absil, *Sprache und Rede. Zu de Saussures ' Vorlesungen über allgemeine Sprachwissenschaft '*, in *Neophilologus*, X (1924–5), pp. 100 f. and 186 f. ; M. Bartoli, *Introduzione alla Neolinguistica*, Geneva, 1925, p. 102 f. ; A. Philippide, *Originea Românilor* I, Iaşi, 1925, p. 377 f. ; J. Feller, *Quelques aspects récents de la philologie romane en France*, in *Revue belge de philologie et d'histoire*, V (1926), p. 744 f. (*v. supra*, p. 179, n. 4) ; A. Sechehaye, *L'école genevoise de linguistique générale*, in *Indogermanische Forschungen*, XLIV (1926), p. 217 f. (a study treating of Saussure's theories and of the work of Bally and Sechehaye himself) ; H. Amman, *Kritische Würdigung einiger Hauptgedanken von F. de Saussures ' Grundfragen der allgemeinen Sprachwissenschaft '*, in *Indogermanische Forschungen*, LII (1934), p. 261 f.

Certain views expressed in some of the studies listed above may be appropriately quoted in confirmation or illustration of assertions made in the present chapter. In his obituary notice on Saussure, printed in the *Bull. Soc. Ling.*, XVIII, Meillet dwells upon the great influence exercised by the Geneva scholar, and, speaking for himself, declares that he feels a certain compunction in not inscribing on the cover of his own publications the name of Saussure, who, in a sense, had contributed something to every page. But the same scholar, in his review of the *Cours de linguistique générale* (*Bull. Soc. Ling.*, XX), finds certain deficiencies of principle in his master's work, namely : (*a*) that he concerns himself solely with ' la langue ', which, although of more importance than ' la parole ', as it is a social fact and not dependent upon the individual speaker, cannot be fully known unless we first of all study ' la parole ' ; and (b) that he isolates the modifications of language from the exterior circumstances by which they are conditioned, thus making the evolution of human language appear as something devoid of real life, a kind of abstraction, which must of necessity remain unexplainable.

Grammont's summing up of Saussure's contribution to language theory corresponds with that set forth above on p. 280 and p. 291 f. He alleges, for example, that on the problem of dialect, Saussure's ideas are not entirely new, but goes on to say that no one had ever formulated the problem with such clarity and precision. Similarly, he asserts, with regard to the general questions raised by Saussure, that all linguists were aware of their existence, but that : " aucun ne les avait résolues avec la même sûreté, et beaucoup mêlaient ce qu'il a si judicieusement distingué " (Revue des langues romanes, LIX, p. 404). On the topic of Saussure's influence, and the activity of the French school in general, Grammont has some illuminating remarks in the same volume of the journal (p. 415), when he is discussing Meillet's book, Caractères généraux des langues germaniques, Paris, 1917. They are as follows : " L'école de Ferdinand de Saussure, ou école française, a fait de la grammaire comparée, et avec maîtrise, quand elle l'a jugé à propos ; mais sa spécialité est plutôt la linguistique, c'est-à-dire essentiellement l'étude des caractères généraux soit d'une langue soit d'un groupe ou d'une famille de langues, des tendances qui sont propres à chacune et des phénomènes qui dominent l'évolution de l'ensemble des langues humaines. M. Meillet en offre un bel exemple avec ses Caractères généraux des langues germaniques."

★　　★　　★

Meillet[1] was the most distinguished of Saussure's pupils. A

---

[1] Meillet, who succeeded Saussure as a Director of Studies at the Ecole des Hautes-Etudes, followed Bréal, another of his teachers, as Professor at the Collège de France. He died in 1936 at the age of seventy. Obituary notices by, inter alios, M. Roques, Romania, LXIII (1937), pp. 132-3 ; Al. Rosetti, Revista fundaţilor regale, January, 1937, p. 111 f. ; Ch. Bally, Vox Romanica, II (1937), pp. 334-5 ; P. Boyer, Rev. des études slaves, XVI (1936), p. 191 f.

linguist of world repute, his titles to fame were as numerous as

Antoine Meillet

they were outstanding. Both in scope and volume, his scientific output was prodigious.[1] Although a specialist in Indo-European philology, there was scarcely a single branch of linguistics on which he had not found something of interest to say. Of the Indo-European family of languages, the classical tongues were his field of predilection, a preference to which we owe such works as : *De quelques innovations de la déclinaison latine*, Paris, 1906 ; *Aperçu d'une histoire de la langue grecque*, Paris, 1913 (2nd ed., 1921) ; *Traité de grammaire comparée des langues classiques*, Paris, 1924 (in collaboration with J. Vendryes) ; *Esquisse d'une histoire de la langue latine*, Paris, 1928 (3rd ed., 1933) ; but his activity not only embraced other related languages or groups of languages such as Armenian (*Altarmenisches Elementarbuch*, Heidelberg, 1913), Germanic (*Caractères généraux des langues germaniques*, Paris, 1917), and Slavonic (*Le slave commun*, Paris, 1924), but led him to such comprehensive surveys as *Les dialectes indo-européens*, Paris, 1908 (2nd ed., 1922), and *Introduction à l'étude comparative des langues indo-européennes*, Paris, 1903 (7th ed., 1934). Moreover, he was the author or co-editor of works of still wider range, such as *Les langues dans l'Europe nouvelle*, Paris, 1918 (2nd ed., 1928), with a statistical appendix by L. Tesnière, and *Les langues du monde* (par un groupe de linguistes sous la direction de A. Meillet et M. Cohen), Paris, 1924. To these works in volume form which, numerous as they are, by no means complete the list of his books, must be added the innumerable studies and articles published in journals, both at home and abroad, and finally, the reviews, which must run into thousands, that he contributed to the *Bulletin de la Société de linguistique de Paris* and to other periodicals. Moreover, the reviews signed by Meillet in the *Bulletin*, of which he was editor-in-chief, were by no means confined to purely linguistic publications, but included those relating to allied domains such as history, ethnography, and sociology.

It was inevitable that such fruitful and varied activities should cause Meillet to rank as an undisputed authority, even in our own branch of study, for this vast experience in the field of human language enabled him to speak with entire confidence upon any

---

[1] He also had real gifts as an organizer. He was the moving spirit of the celebrated *Société de linguistique de Paris ;* he founded an *Institut d'études slaves*, with its organ, *Revue des études slaves*, to say nothing of the leading part he took in international linguistic congresses, etc.

problem relating to it. No one, in recent times, has been so completely qualified as he to discuss with authority matters of linguistic principles or method. General ideas on these topics are to be found in practically all his writings, as is natural with a Frenchman, and particularly with one who, by reason of his outstanding position,[1] felt called upon to express an opinion upon every branch of linguistic activity. But he has also written books specially devoted to problems of theory and doctrine, for example, *Linguistique historique et linguistique générale*, Paris, 1921 (2nd ed., 1926), a collection of studies of which more anon, and *La méthode comparative en linguistique historique*, Oslo, 1925, both of them of direct interest to Romance scholars, as the principles they enunciate concern the study of neo-Latin as well as of other languages. But he has closer contacts with Romance studies than this, for, in the first place, his influence was so preponderant that nearly all the French Romanicists of the present day are, to a greater or less degree, his pupils, and, secondly, his numerous reviews of works relating to Romance studies, and his own articles devoted to this or that problem concerning them, almost made him one of ourselves. In the present work, in the chapters on the idealistic school and on linguistic geography, we have had to quote him at every step, for the great majority of the works there mentioned had been discussed by him, particularly from the point of view of their theoretical and methodological significance.

Another characteristic of Meillet's, also due, in a large measure, to the wide range of his activities, is the complete impartiality, the freedom from all prejudice, the broad and penetrative vision which he brought to bear upon the views of linguists whose opinions differed from his own. We have noted his many astute observations with regard to Vossler, and we have also observed that Gilliéron's work, which was criticized by many of his compatriots with such unwonted severity, would have been seriously endangered, and its salutary influence largely frustrated, had it not been for Meillet's warm and authoritative support. This attitude surprises and attracts us all the more in that his own particular field of research, namely, Indo-European philology, made him of necessity a historicist and comparatist. In the nature

---

[1] L. Spitzer, in *Meisterwerke der romanischen Sprachwissenschaft*, II, p. 336, befittingly styles him " *pater patriae* of French linguistics ", " the only linguist of to-day who can survey the development of the science in all its branches, Indogermanic, Semitic, Egyptian, etc., Romance, Germanic, or Slavonic, the only man entitled, on linguistic matters, to speak to ' the ear of Europe ' ".

of things, if one studies the dead languages, and is interested primarily in their mutual relationships, one must perforce take as a basis of comparison language states of extreme antiquity. None the less, Meillet showed an understanding of such anti-comparatists and anti-historicists as Gilliéron and Vossler to which Meyer-Lübke, to take a purely Romance scholar of similar standing, has not always succeeded in attaining. This is not the only point in which he compared favourably with certain Romani-cists. He displayed a keen interest in living speech, in dialect and patois. His convinced belief in and support of Gilliéron's work, his appreciation of the importance of dialect studies, as evinced by his proposal, at the Linguistic Congress held in April, 1928, at The Hague, that every country should subsidize for its own terri-tory a linguistic survey similar to that of Gilliéron for France, all this sprang from his firm conviction that only by concentrating upon the investigation of living speech could many of the major problems of linguistic theory receive a final solution.

A linguist so outstanding could not fail to have a following and to found a school, and, in fact, a Meillet school of linguistics ad-mittedly exists, not fundamentally divergent from that of Saussure, perhaps, but none the less with features definitely its own. The most marked of these is the predominance given to a principle we have already encountered in the *Cours de linguistique générale*, namely, that language is a social fact.[1] This principle is applied and elabor-ated in its fullest implications by the Meillet school, whose members are to be found chiefly in France and in Scandinavia, particularly in Norway. It is therefore of them that we think first when we speak of a sociological trend in linguistic study.[2]

---

[1] On the relations between sociology and linguistics, cp. G. Millardet, *Linguistique et dialectologie romanes*, p. 488 f. See also H. Levy, *Sprache und Wirtschafts-wissenschaft*, in *Neuphilologische Monatsschrift*, II (1931), p. 35 f. According to Delacroix, *Le langage et la pensée*, 2nd ed., p. 63 note, the conception of language as a social fact is already to be found in Whitney. Durkheim and, possibly, Lévy-Bruhl, also influenced Meillet.

[2] This sociological trend has had its critics, for example in Norway, where H. Falk attacked what he called ' the French philosophy of language ' mainly on the grounds of its excessively ' social ' outlook. A pupil of Meillet's, A. Sommerfelt, took up the cudgels in its defence in *Bull. Soc. Ling.*, XXV (1924-5), fasc. 1, p. 22 f., in an article entitled " *La philosophie linguistique française* ", *Réponse à M. Hjalmar Falk*. As Sommerfelt's reply throws light on a number of points in the doctrine of the whole French school we append a summary of a few passages : Social facts, of which language is one, are of various kinds. They exist outside the individual, and at times despite his will, such, for example, as dress, obedience to laws, marriage, purchasing, and the like. Facts of an organic character, like eating, drinking, sleeping, etc., or psychological facts, are different in kind, and, though taking place within society, cannot be called ' social ', being either

As we have stated above, Meillet's discussions of matters of linguistic theory are to be found chiefly in *Linguistique historique et linguistique générale*, and in *La méthode comparative en linguistique historique*. Of these the latter is of special importance to the Indo-European scholar, whereas the former may be said to contain the author's doctrine with regard to language generally, and thus concerns us more directly. We append therefore a brief account of its essential teachings.

The historical method in linguistic research, applied almost exclusively by the scholars of the nineteenth century, and by so many of our contemporaries to-day, has shown itself to be inadequate. There is no doubt that this method can explain much, and that the solutions it brings, taken separately, are often accurate, yet it should be considered solely as a means, never as an end in

dictated by the bodily needs of the individual or confined to the individual mind. The private manifestations of strictly social phenomena do not lose their social character, inasmuch as they reproduce, so to speak, a collective model, although they are conditioned by the organic or psychological make-up of the individual. For this reason, the sociologist Durkheim calls them socio-psychical acts. Language is a social fact in the latter sense, is indeed the typical social fact, representing as it does a part of a common human faculty, and being independent of the individual speaker, and yet only existing where individuals are to be found. The individual use of language is organico-psychical, like all private manifestations of social phenomena, and this is what Saussure called ' la parole '. Linguistic changes have their source in the socio-psychical domain ; they are, that is to say, of an individual character, or better, a particular manifestation of a social fact, and thus conditioned by the organico-psychological make-up of the individual ; but to become linguistic changes in the true sense, that is, to become part of ' la langue ', they must become completely social in character, in other words, they must spread and become general.

Sommerfelt endeavours, further, to give more precise definition to other terms current in the doctrines of the French school, namely, ' law ', ' formula ', and ' tendency '. A ' law ', he says, is the general and constant element in a process. It holds for all languages, and everywhere it has common features as, for example, in such phenomena as dissimilation, differentiation, etc. ; it is thus a pure abstraction. A ' formula ', he defines as a particular application of a law, and a ' tendency ', as the prevailing trend of a series of phonological or morphological changes. With regard to transformations which the sounds of a language may undergo, he affirms that there may be common features of phonetic evolution as between one language and another, but that the actual changes, taken individually, are in essence particular to each. Meillet also took part in the controversy begun by Falk, stating, *Bull. Soc. Ling.*, XXV (1924–5), fasc. 2, p. 15 f., that of the four scholars held to account by Falk, namely, Grammont, Millardet, Vendryes, and Meillet himself, he alone could be accused of attributing a predominating part to social factors in the development of language. No French linguist, on the other hand, had denied the importance of psychology in the study of language, but linguistic science could only investigate psychological processes in terms of linguistic formulae. Moreover, if it is the case that the psychological factor is everywhere constant, while languages differ, the cause of this difference can only be attributed to different social conditions, as between one people and another, or one period and another. Consequently, the common features in languages are due to human psychology, which is more or less alike at all times and in all places ; their peculiarities, on the other hand, have their source in the social milieu.

itself. Preference should be given to the observation of present-day speech conditions, not only because they inform us about the present, but because they make clearer to us the language phenomena of the past, whereas the study of the ancient phases of a language does not always help us to understand aright what is taking place before our eyes. Moreover, a language viewed as a ' system ' (see Saussure's definition, above) can only be known to us when it is investigated as it stands at a given period.

The historian, setting out to explain linguistic phenomena, operates usually by means of sound-changes and analogy, ' historical laws ', and leaves out of account borrowing, which, as linguistic geography has convincingly proved, plays an outstanding part in the evolution of language.[1] Sound-shifting and analogy can account for the phenomena of a given language, but not for those of language in general. The laws which apply to the latter are purely and solely linguistic, and neither physiological nor psychological. To discover them we must take into consideration the two characteristic features of language, namely, (a) that it is a system of means of expression, and (b) that it is a social fact. The first of these implies that individual modifications in language, the importance of which by the way has been much exaggerated, only become adopted if they conform to the system. Hence we should speak in such cases rather of general than generalized innovations, their acceptance proving that all the members of the speech community felt them, so to speak, as necessary ; otherwise, we could not understand how they spread to every member and in such a comparatively short time. Therefore we are dealing here not with a case of imitation, but with a general linguistic tendency, awaiting a suitable moment to become manifest. Only when there is a complete change of language, when, that is to say,

[1] French *loi*, for example, which in Old French was pronounced like the first syllable of English *loyal*, is now pronounced *lwa* (formerly *lwe*). This is a sound-change, a phenomenon of phonetics, which originated in Paris. But the fact that all contemporary Frenchmen pronounce thus is not to be explained as a sound-shift, or as a process of analogy, but as a borrowing, in other words as a social phenomenon, the result of an imitation of Parisian utterance by the Frenchmen of other regions. " . . . en réalité, l'emprunt est un fait normal, et dont l'importance dans le développement linguistique éclate chaque jour davantage." (*Linguistique hist. et ling. gén.*, p. 7. The quotations are from the 2nd ed., which differs from the first only in the two fresh articles, added at the end.) We may compare in this connection Schuchardt's assertion that there are no unmixed languages (see above, p. 53), and Gilliéron's remarks upon the influence exercised upon the vernaculars by standard French, and by neighbouring dialects (Chap. III, p. 169, above).

for whatever reason, a language is displaced by another, are we entitled to resort to imitation to explain the phenomenon. Thus, the Gauls of the leading classes voluntarily abandoned their mother tongue and imitated the Romans, the new rulers of their country.

The second of these characteristics of language, that it is a social fact, has as its corollary that every transformation of the social structure brings about a consequential change in language. Thus it comes about that languages vary considerably among themselves, although they have, at least in part, a common origin, and although the physiological and psychological conditions of human life are everywhere more or less constant (cp. above, p. 300, note). It is in semantic change particularly that the dependence of linguistic upon social phenomena is manifest. The fact that the individuals composing a linguistic community are differentiated socially, causes words to modify their meaning as they pass from one social category to the other. Thus, a word in general use may receive a restricted meaning through its adoption by a small group within the community, and vice versa.[1] Though this principle is not ignored by other scholars, for example Schuchardt and Meringer (for the latter, cp. p. 74 f., above), Meillet is particularly insistent upon it. Every social category, he points out, has its own mentality, and consequently its own language.[2] We thus observe marked

---

[1] To take some concrete examples : Latin *paganus*, means, first of all, ' a dweller in a *pagus* ', a ' peasant '. In the language of the Roman soldiery it came to be used as the equivalent of ' civilian ' as opposed to the ' miles '. Then, in Christian terminology, it was used as the opposite of the ' miles Christi ', and hence ' a pagan '. These changes of meaning are thus due to specialized uses of a general word on the part of groups within the wider community (cp. E. Löfstedt, *Syntactica*, II, Lund, 1933, pp. 468–9, and H. Rheinfelder, *Kultsprache und Profansprache in den romanischen Ländern*, Geneva–Florence, 1934, p. 132). In other cases, a word belonging to the specialized vocabulary of a group becomes generalized. Thus French *niais*, like Italian *nidiace* and *nidace*, represent a Latin form *nidax*, from *nidus*, ' a nest '. They were originally falconry words and were used of the bird in the nest. A *faucon niais* was thus an ' untrained ', a ' callow ' bird ; hence the meaning ' simpleton ' which is now general in French for *niais*, its narrower, technical use having disappeared. Pejorative change in the meaning of French words has been very fully investigated by K. Jaberg in the study already mentioned, *Pejorative Bedeutungsentwicklung im Französischen, mit Berücksichtigung allgemeiner Fragen der Semasiologie, Zeitschrift f. rom. Phil.*, XXV (1901), p. 561 f., XXVII (1903), p. 25 f., XXIX (1905), p. 57 f.

[2] Meillet quotes Bréal's remarks in *Essai de sémantique*, p. 285 f. : " A mesure qu'une civilisation gagne en variété et en richesse, les occupations, les actes, les intérêts dont se compose la vie de la société se partagent entre différents groupes d'hommes ; ni l'état d'esprit, ni la direction de l'activité ne sont les mêmes chez le prêtre, le soldat, l'homme politique, l'agriculteur. Bien qu'ils aient hérité de la même langue, les mots se colorent chez eux d'une nuance distincte laquelle s'y fixe et finit par y adhérer. . . . Au mot d'*opération*, s'il est prononcé par un chirurgien, nous voyons un patient, une plaie, des instruments pour couper et tailler ; supposez un militaire qui parle, nous pensons à des armées en campagne ;

points of resemblance between the speech of the same social classes[1] in the most widely differing linguistic communities, just as, within the domain of a single language, considerable differences are to be noticed between the speech of one social category and another.

From this cause, profound semantic changes must inevitably arise in words which pass from one social group to another, whether higher or lower. Of great interest in this connection are the numerous borrowings which, particularly in these days of wide-spread education, the common language makes from the vocabulary of the scientist or of cultured circles generally. In such cases, modifications of meaning are to be observed similar to that under-gone by French *niais* (*v. supra*, p. 302, n. 1), a technical term borrowed by common speech ; to the uninitiated, technical words, from whatever source, science, literature, or the arts and crafts, must of necessity be somewhat obscure, nor can they keep their earlier values or precision in their new and wider habitat.[2] Like happenings are to be observed when we study borrowings made by languages proper from other languages. Here, again, it frequently happens that one language is felt as superior, and acts as a lexical storehouse on which the other may draw at need. It was thus that Latin enriched its vocabulary from Greek, and, at a later date, the European languages from both Greek and Latin. Meillet pays particular attention[3] to what we may call s e m a n t i c b o r r o w i n g s, when a native word takes on the meaning of a corresponding word in another language. The Latin *causa* is a case in point ; it meant originally ' a thing ', ' an object ', then also ' cause ' in the philo-sophical or theological sense, as a translation of Greek αἰτία. Its old meaning survives in the Romance languages, in inherited popular words like Fr. *chose* or Ital. *cosa*, while in its more philo-sophical acceptation it is represented by the learned forms *cause*, *causa*, etc. Meillet gives a similar explanation of the meanings taken on by various Greek words used in translating the Bible, such as κύριος (' a ruler ', ' God ', to which as in the case of *causa*,

---

que ce soit un financier, nous comprenons qu'il s'agit de capitaux en mouvement ; un maître de calcul, il est question d'additions et de soustractions. Chaque science, chaque art, chaque métier, en composant sa terminologie marque de son empreinte les mots de la langue commune " (cit. Meillet, *Linguistique hist. et ling. gén.*, p. 244).

[1] This is the case with the language of soldiers, schoolboys, criminals, etc. ; in other words, with the different ' slangs ' (cp. the final section of this chapter).

[2] Cp. particularly Meillet's article *A propos de ' qualitas '*, *op. cit.*, p. 355 f.

[3] In *Les interférences de vocabulaires*, *op. cit.*, p. 343 f.

corresponds Lat. *Dominus*, and in other languages *Seigneur, Lord, Herr*, etc.), ἄγγελος, διάβολος, etc., which were ready to hand as the normal equivalents of the corresponding Hebrew words, and consequently enriched their meaning with the special significance attaching to the latter.[1]

The conclusion drawn from all this intermingling of social, cultural, and psychological cross-currents, from these lexical ' interferences ' as Meillet calls them, is at least as interesting as his account of the various transformations which they bring about. This conclusion, it is true, is not to be found in the work we have been examining, but the present author heard it formulated verbally by Meillet in lectures delivered at the Collège de France during the session 1924–25. It was roughly as follows : The semantic transformations which words undergo from the causes mentioned are frequently so profound that little or nothing is left of their original meaning. We are therefore entitled in such extreme cases to speak, semantically, of *new* words, although in other respects they are still the same. What have the French words *bon, bel* and *bien* retained, asks Meillet (in a lecture delivered on March 17th, 1925) of the sense of their Latin prototypes *bonus, bellus* and *bene ?* From the point of view of meaning, they are different words. There is thus frequently a semantic discontinuity between French, or any other Romance idiom, and Latin, a conclusion almost identical with that come to by Gilliéron, when he asserts that the popular vernaculars of France, as at present constituted, cannot be considered as continuations of the vulgar Latin of ancient Gaul, inasmuch as the changes they have undergone, whether through the influence of standard French, or of neighbouring dialects, or through their own efforts to counteract homonymy and other destructive forces, have been so profound that they have been changed almost out of all recognition.

We have already had occasion to make passing mention of another idea which recurs frequently in the works of Meillet and his pupils, that of linguistic prestige, which has also important bearings

---

[1] Meillet rightly concludes his article, *Comment les mots changent de sens*, as follows (p. 271) : " Ces exemples, où l'on a remarqué les plus gros faits et les plus généraux, permettent de se faire une idée de la manière dont les faits linguistiques, les faits historiques et les faits sociaux s'unissent, agissent et réagissent pour transformer le sens des mots ; on voit que, partout, le moment essentiel est le passage d'un mot de la langue générale à une langue particulière, ou le fait inverse, ou tous les deux, et que, par suite, les changements de sens doivent être considérés comme ayant pour condition principale la différenciation des éléments qui constituent les sociétés."

upon the problem of semantic changes. In the exchanges which constantly take place between languages which find themselves in contact, the language which enjoys ' prestige' is usually the creditor, the other the debtor language. But this notion of prestige is entirely a relative matter ; there is no language, however primitive, which may not, on occasions, enjoy this advantage, even with regard to a far more privileged language. All the languages of the earth, indeed, are at once debtors and creditors, according to circumstances. The relative superiority of one or the other may be limited to a narrow domain of experience and be merely momentary. It may arise also from a number of causes. The Romans borrowed from the Greeks, who were their cultural superiors. The inhabitants of the Iberian peninsula, of Gaul, Rhetia, etc., took over the Latin tongue which came with a threefold superiority, cultural, military, and political. The Normans under William the Conqueror brought their language to England, where it spread as the language of a dominant class and of a superior culture. The dialects yield to the standard language also for cultural reasons, sometimes under political pressure. For similar reasons, too, a strong dialect centre sheds its influence over adjoining vernaculars. And finally, within one speech community, the technical terms of specialists are accepted without question by the general public, who recognize their incapacity, their inferiority, in other words, in matters which are outside their competence.[1]

A further question to which the sociological treatment of language gives prominence, and which occurs more than once in the works of Meillet and of his disciples is that of linguistic inhibitions. A quotation will make clear what is meant : " En des points du monde très divers, et dans des langues très variées, on observe des ' tabous' de vocabulaire, . . . dans l'Afrique du Sud, dans le domaine des langues malayo-polinésiennes . . . , en Extrême-Orient et aussi en Europe, notamment dans le Nord de l'Europe, il apparaît que certains mots sont interdits par l'usage, soit à un groupe d'hommes, soit à des individus déterminés, soit durant certaines périodes, en certaines occasions ; on ' taboue' par exemple le nom d'un mort, celui d'un chef, celui des membres de la famille où l'on prend femme, etc. ; et le tabou ne touche pas seulement les noms propres en question, mais il s'étend aux noms

---

[1] The borrowings made by ' civilized' languages from those of savage peoples are to be explained in similar wise ; they are also, in a sense, ' technical' borrowings. On the whole question see Vendryes, *Le langage*, Paris, 1921, p. 330 f.

communs, identiques ou non à ces noms, qui sonnent d'une manière identique ou analogue, ou même partiellement analogue " (*op. cit.* p. 281). The notion of tabou can have a still wider connotation than this, and Meillet himself also points out that the names of certain bodily functions are systematically avoided in polite conversation everywhere, while tabous with regard to the name of the deity account for such euphemisms as French *morbleu, parbleu,* used in avoidance of *mort Dieu, par Dieu,* etc. It is true, however, that among European peoples tabous, as a whole, are relatively infrequent, and usually refer to the names of certain beings, which for various reasons we are afraid to utter, and so either replace by other names or modify. Of more interest to us than the phenomenon itself, which is to be explained on social and psychological grounds, are its linguistic effects, and particularly the light it throws on the strange disappearance of certain words. Thus Meillet, examining the names of the ' bear ' and the ' snake ' in the Slavonic, Germanic and Baltic languages, observes that everywhere the old Indo-European word has been replaced by euphemisms and periphrases, such as ' honey-eater ', ' brown ', etc., for the ' bear ', or ' crawler ', ' repulsive ', etc., for the ' snake ', and can only account for this phenomenon as being the result of a tabou applied to the original names.[1]

Meillet's sociological conception of language also manifests itself in the explanations he gives of certain widespread linguistic

---

[1] The occurrence is frequent in the case of the names of certain animals, for this type of nomenclature is particularly exposed to the influence of primitive psychology, as the most superficial study of animal names will show. The name of the ' weasel ' in various languages is an obvious case, cp. Rum. *nevăstuică,* Mod. Gr. νυφίτζα (lit. ' young woman ') ; Hungarian *hölgy* (' lady '), Fr. *belette* (' pretty one '), etc. (see Iorgu Iordan, *Arhiva,* XXXIII [1926], p. 141 f.). As for the ' snake ', J. U. Hubschmied, in an article in *Der kleine Bund,* 29th Nov., 1931, p. 381, explains the use of the Greek word δρακῶν, as a name for certain streams in the Rheto-Romance area, as a borrowing from the language of Massilia (Marseilles), to avoid the use of the local name for ' snake ' ; another way out was to use periphrases such as ' the winder ' or ' the bender ', as evidenced by the numerous stream names he quotes which go back to words of this type. On the whole question of animal names we may refer the reader to R. Riegler, *Das Tier im Spiegel der Sprache,* Dresden-Leipzig, 1907, and articles by the same author in *Wörter und Sachen, Archivum Romanicum, Die neueren Sprachen,* etc., and also to the monumental *Handwörterbuch des deutschen Aberglaubens,* a collective work on ethnology and folklore published by Walter de Gruyter & Co., Berlin. The general topic of word tabous has been much discussed in works relating to general linguistics ; cp., for example, A. Philippide, *Principii de istoria limbii,* p. 233 f. The subject is discussed also by A. Niceforo in *Le génie de l'argot,* p. 216 f., from a more special angle, but with examples of inhibited words from a great variety of languages ; cp. also O. Jespersen, *Die Sprache,* Heidelberg, 1925, p. 222 f., and O. Vočadlo, *On lexical restriction,* in *Charisteria Guilelmo Mathesio Quinquagenario,* Prague, 1932, p. 105 f.

tendencies, such for example as the simplification of the flexional system in the leading Indo-European languages. We find, for instance, that the past-definite has disappeared, or is by way of disappearing, in a great number of idioms, French, German, Rumanian, Serbian, Slovene, etc. Such a widespread phenomenon must have everywhere a common cause, of a social character. The development of civilization brings with it an abstract method of thought, which, on the one hand, tends to eliminate those grammatical categories that are of a more concrete order, and to foster those turns of expression that are more in keeping with the abstractions of the modern mind. In this regard English has gone farthest because of its rigorous reduction in the number of the flexional forms of the verb, the state of which thus approximates to that of the noun, which both in English and in French has about reached its morphological minimum. Meillet quotes with approval (*op. cit.*, p. 156) Gilliéron's remarks in *La faillite de l'étymologie phonétique*, p. 104, where, speaking of the disappearance of the past definite, he says : " Avec elle [la disparition du passé défini], commence pour les verbes une nouvelle ère, c'est un acheminement vers l'état du verbe où il n'y aura plus comme voiles que des auxiliaires, faisant manœuvrer une coque qui porte l'idée."[1]

Finally, on a still wider scale, the features which the present-day languages of Europe share in common, and which are increasingly numerous and important, irrespective of their historical relationships, are also set to the account of social factors, namely, that

---

[1] On the question of prevailing trends in language cp. H. Delacroix, *Le langage et la pensée*, 2nd ed., p. 259. The question of the disappearance of the preterite has attracted the attention of a number of scholars ; e.g. L. Spitzer, *Über den Schwund des einfachen Perfektums*, in *Donum Natalicium Schrijnen*, Nimeguen–Utrecht, 1929, p. 86 f. ; A. J. F. Zieglschmid, *Der Untergang des einfachen Präteritums in verschiedenen indogermanischen Sprachen*, in *Curme Volume of Linguistic Studies*, Philadelphia, 1930, p. 167 f. ; Ch. Bally, *Linguistique générale et linguistique française*, Paris, 1932, pp. 7 and 193–4 ; Phil. Kaiblinger, *Ursachen des Präteritumverfalls im Deutschen*, in *Teuthonista*, VI (1930), p. 269 f. The latter explains the phenomenon linguistically, attributing it to the irregularity of the forms of the tense, whereas Zieglschmid explains it psychologically (cp. *Zeitschrift f. deutsches Altertum und deutsche Literatur*, LXVIII [1931], Anzeiger, p. 101). Bally is of the view that the Romance languages prefer the compound perfect because in this tense the lexical element, represented by the participle, is postposed, in conformity with the general tendency in the structure of these languages (*op. cit.*, p. 7). With regard to French he invokes also special reasons, like the variety of forms, the difference in the form of the root element in the preterite, as compared with other tenses, or, in the case of the first conjugation, the practical identity in pronunciation of forms like *je chantai* with that of the imperfect *je chantais* (*op. cit.*, pp. 193–4). The problem as it affects Rumanian is discussed by I. Şiadbei, in *Romania*, LVI (1930), p. 331 f. For Portuguese cp. M. de Paiva Boléo, *O Perfeito e o Pretérito em português em confronto com as outras linguas románicas*, Coimbra, 1937.

community of feeling which Meillet calls " le sentiment d'une unité de civilisation."[1]

To complete, if only approximately, our account of Meillet's philosophy of language, we append a few quotations from other works. They are passages that have been culled on various occasions, but are all variations upon the familiar theme that language is a social fact and must be studied as such. " Depuis le début de l'époque historique, et sans doute dès longtemps avant, l'histoire du langage est commandée avant tout par des faits de civilisation. L'extension de grandes langues communes, telles que le latin, l'arabe, l'espagnol, l'anglais, est ce que l'on observe en fait." (*Bull. Soc. Ling.*, XXII [1920–1], p. 39.) " Il lui a seulement échappé [in a discussion of E. Cassirer's *Philosophie der symbolischen Formen. I. Teil : Die Sprache*, Berlin, 1923] que depuis Bréal et F. de Saussure, pour ne parler que des morts, le rôle des conditions sociales a été mis en évidence d'une manière qui renouvelle le problème et que la langue étant de tous les faits humains le plus manifestement social—car ni la langue n'est imaginable sans la société ni la société des hommes sans la langue—les conditions sociales dominent le langage." (*Ibid.*, XXV [1924–5], fasc. 2, p. 2.) " Mais l'unité de parler est nécessaire. Les changements qui survivent sont ceux qui sont conformes aux tendances existant chez la plupart des sujets ou chez les plus influents entre eux et celles qui, répondant aux conditions générales du langage et aux conditions particulières où se trouve le parler considéré, satisfont le mieux aux besoins communs des sujets parlants. Comme beaucoup de lois naturelles, la ' loi phonétique ' résulterait, non d'un changement universel, mais d'une moyenne." (*Ibid.*, XXV, fasc. 2, p. 5.)[2]

★ ★ ★

[1] Another of Saussure's disciples, Ch. Bally, makes a similar observation with regard to style, and speaks of the possibility of ' une stylistique européenne '. One cannot help thinking, at the same time, of the attitude of Schuchardt, who in similar cases invokes the psychology common to mankind, at all times and in all places (cp. Chap. I, p. 56 f., above). Meillet defends his own point of view as follows (*op. cit.*, p. 156) : " On est amené à éliminer toutes les causes qui seraient particulières à une langue, dès l'instant qu'il s'agit d'un fait constaté sur un grand nombre de points : si une même évolution se produit sur deux domaines distincts, ce peut être dû à une rencontre fortuite, mais si on l'observe sur cinq ou six grands domaines, le hasard semble exclu et il faut découvrir des causes qui aient pu agir sur tous les domaines considérés. La généralité même du fait est une donnée de premier ordre pour la recherche des causes."

[2] Meillet's doctrine is also set forth in Delacroix, *Le langage et la pensée*, 2nd ed., p. 48 f. The work we have been examining, *Linguistique historique et linguistique*

It is appropriate at this stage to make some mention of Meillet's most distinguished pupil, J. Vendryes, professor of Indo-European linguistics at the Sorbonne. Like his late master, he is mainly concerned with the classical languages and those most closely connected with them, particularly the Celtic group, on which he is a leading authority. But he also, though not to the same extent as Meillet, gives consideration to matters of linguistic theory, not merely in connection with the problems of historical grammar he discusses in his works, but also in special studies like that already quoted (Chap. I, p. 41 f., above), upon the ' sound-laws '. The work we would dwell upon now for a moment is Vendryes' book *Le Langage. Introduction linguistique à l'histoire*,[1] Paris, 1921, where, it may be said, he touches upon all the major problems of the theory of language. We are indeed entitled, inasmuch as the author makes no departure from the conception of language characteristic of the French school, to consider this work of Vendryes as an epitome of its doctrines, particularly as at the basis of all its principles lies material which is the product of comparative-historical research, as is the case with all the French scholars we have mentioned, briefly or at length, in the present chapter.

It is not possible for practical reasons to give a summary of this work, nor is it really necessary to do so, inasmuch as Vendryes brings us scarcely anything that we are not already acquainted with through the works of other members of the French school.[2] Meillet's ideas and, indirectly, those of Saussure, are to be met

J. Vendryes

---

générale, was discussed by, *inter alios*, H. Delacroix, *Journal de psychologie normale et pathologique*, XVIII (1921), p. 765 f. ; A. Ernout, *Journal des Savants*, 1921, pp. 205 f. and 258 f. ; L. Foulet, *Romania*, XLVII (1921), p. 119 f. ; S. Puşcariu, *Dacoromania*, II (1921–2), p. 686 f. ; D. C. Hesseling, *Neophilologus*, VII (1921–2), p. 76 f. ; and A. Philippide, *Originea Romînilor*, I, p. 387 f. ; while N. Maccarrone, *Revue de linguistique romane*, VI (1930), p. 11 f., discusses from the point of view of Romance studies the other work of Meillet's mentioned above, *La méthode comparative en linguistique historique*. The second volume of *Linguistique historique et linguistique générale* (xiii+235 pp.) came out in 1936.

[1] Published in the series *Bibliothèque de synthèse historique*, in the section entitled *L'évolution de l'humanité* ; the general editor of the series is Henri Berr, director of the *Revue de synthèse historique*. Vendryes has a closer connection with our discipline, in that he contributed to Meillet's *Les langues du monde* (see above, p. 297), the chapter entitled ' Langues indo-européennes ', which has a section on the Romance languages.

[2] This is an observation, not a criticism. It could not be otherwise, the nature of the book, and of the series in which it appeared, compelling the author to confine himself to widely accepted facts. His originality is sufficiently apparent in the dispassionate and penetrating criticism he applies to the ideas of various scholars.

with at every turn : language is a social fact ; it owes its origin
to man's need to communicate with his fellows ; it took on a stable
form, within the first groups of speaking individuals, according to
laws which govern the foundation of any other social institution ;[1]
between word and notion the relationship is merely fortuitous, not
essential, that is, as Saussure says, the linguistic sign is arbitrary ;
the generalization of phonetic innovations only takes place when
they correspond to tendencies that are natural and congenial to all
members of the linguistic community ;[2] between the mentality of a
given people and the grammatical categories of their language there
is no relationship, it is therefore a dangerous proceeding to draw
from grammar conclusions concerning racial psychology ;[3] the

---

[1] On page 20 of *Le Langage*, after stating that linguistics had been wrongly
placed among the natural sciences, Vendryes quotes Bréal's remarks on the last
page of his *Essai de sémantique*, where he compares the Indo-European conjugation
with " ces grandes institutions [Bréal : corps] politiques ou judiciaires—les
Parlements ou le Conseil du roi—qui, nées [Br. : nés] d'un besoin primordial,
ont vu peu à peu se diversifier, s'étendre [Br. : s'étendre, se diversifier] leurs
attributions [Br. adds : au point d'en être surchargés], jusqu'à ce qu'un autre
âge, trouvant cet ensemble de rouages trop lourd [Br. : cet ens. tr. l.], en ait
retranché une part [Br. has not this phrase], en ait divisé le fonctionnement entre
divers corps libres et indépendants, quoique prenant part encore, dans une
certaine mesure, et avec la preuve visible de leur ancienne solidarité, à la destination initiale." The passage is of interest in showing, firstly, the relations between
Vendryes and other French linguists we do not discuss, and secondly, how, as in
this curious parallel of Bréal's, the sociological conception of language can at times
be carried too far. It should be said that Saussure was not one of Vendryes'
teachers, nor did the latter make use of the *Cours de linguistique générale*, as *Le
Langage* was complete in manuscript in 1914, whereas the *Cours* only came out in
1916. The connection between the two, which is very real and close, was thus
entirely through Meillet.

[2] A few quotations on the never-ending question of the sound-laws :
" . . . celles-ci sont des formules qui résument des procès, des règles de correspondance " (p. 51 ; cp. Meillet's remarks quoted above, p. 42 f.). " D'une
part, la loi phonétique ne renseigne qu'imparfaitement sur la nature du changement dont elle enregistre le résultat ; et, d'autre part, elle n'est jamais qu'une
moyenne, en laquelle se résument divers procès compliqués " (p. 53 ; cp. Meillet,
p. 308, above). " Les exceptions aux changements phonétiques sont inévitables "
(pp. 57–8). " Nous avons rencontré, dans l'exposé qui précède, des cas où les
tendances phonétiques régulières se trouvaient en conflit avec des tendances de
caractère différent. Ces cas ont dû se présenter souvent dans l'histoire des
langues ; c'est à eux qu'il faut attribuer les irrégularités de toute histoire
phonétique " (p. 60).

[3] An idea already met with in a slightly varied form in our discussion of
Saussure, where we set it in opposition to Vossler's conception of the ' genius
of the language '. It also runs counter to the belief expressed by F. N. Finck, that
there is a certain relationship between the temperament of a people and the
nature of its language (*v. supra*, p. 77). On the other hand, there would appear
to be a definite connection between this idea and that of the arbitrary character
of the linguistic sign ; in both cases there is a denial that logic takes any part in
the evolution of language ; so that here we discover an agreement with Vossler's
contention that language is alogical. Cp. Vendryes, *loc. cit.*, p. 277 : " Il est aussi
arbitraire de faire sortir la langue de la mentalité que la mentalité de la langue.
Toutes deux sont le produit des circonstances ; ce sont des faits de civilisation."

grammatical categories are of social origin and are thus conditioned by man's life in society ; analogy brings about the disappearance of certain irregular grammatical forms, and thus contributes towards the simplification of morphology (elsewhere Vendryes observes that concrete substantives are more readily lost than abstract, which, like the preceding statement, reminds us of Meillet's contention that the progress of culture develops the powers of abstraction and brings with it the disappearance of certain grammatical forms) ; to understand language in the strict sense, ' la langue ' according to Saussure, we must consider it in its present condition ;[1] there is an avoidance of equivocal forms of speech, of homonymy, Gilliéron would have put it, due to the need for intelligibility and clarity, which are the aims of language ; too much importance should not be accorded to phonology, particularly in accounting for semantic changes, the wear and tear of words being due, in the main, to the action of the social milieu ; words of civilization, Kulturwörter, are more readily borrowed than others (cp. Meillet's views on the levelling effects of the ' sentiment d'une unité de civilisation ') ; in the evolution of language is to be observed a struggle between two rival forces, one tending towards differentiation, the other towards unification (the terminology is Meillet's, but the same idea is expressed by Saussure, see above, p. 289) ; the part played by ' prestige ' in language relationships ; and finally, the phenomenon of language mixing, with a recognition, at the same time, as with Meillet, that however great the number of foreign elements a language may contain, it is still one language, and is felt to be so by the individuals who speak it.

Vendryes also discusses, however, a number of questions which neither Saussure nor Meillet take into account, for example : emotional or affective speech (p. 162 f.), onomatopœia (p. 214 f.), the relations between speech and thought (p. 77 f.),[2] etc. In this

[1] Cp. : " . . . l'étymologie donne une fausse idée de la nature d'un vocabulaire ; elle n'a d'intérêt que pour montrer comment un vocabulaire s'est formé. Les mots ne sont pas employés dans l'usage d'après leur valeur historique. L'esprit oublie—à supposer qu'il l'ait jamais su—par quelles évolutions sémantiques ils ont passé. Les mots ont toujours une valeur actuelle, c'est-à-dire limitée au moment où on les emploie, et singulière, c'est-à-dire, relative à l'emploi momentané qui en est fait " (p. 206).

[2] It should be made clear that Vendryes shows some misgivings with regard to certain of these topics. For example, he holds that the study of affective language is of the domain of psychology and art rather than of linguistics proper (p. 165). Similarly, the relationship between speech and thought is a matter for psychological rather than linguistic investigation (p. 77). In his terminology, also, he shows a certain independence, as compared with Meillet and Saussure. His use of the term ' langage ' both in the title and the body of the book is a case

he displays a kinship with other members of the French school who have specialized in these fields of language study, such, for example, as Ch. Bally, to whom we are soon to turn. If to all this we add the other problems touched upon in this work, some of them of a speculative character, such as the origin or the progress of language,[1] some of them, to use a Saussurian term, problems of external linguistics, such as the constitution of languages (standard, dialect, written language, literary language, slangs, linguistic geography, families of languages and mixed languages), the origin

in point, as the term only occurs incidentally in these authors. He defines it as follows (p. 275) : " Il y a cette différence entre le langage et les langues, que le langage est l'ensemble des procédés physiologiques et psychiques dont l'être humain dispose pour parler, tandis que les langues représentent l'utilisation pratique de ces procédés. Pour arriver à la définition du mot langue, il faut donc sortir du cadre des chapitres précédents et étudier le rôle que joue le langage dans les sociétés organisées." Thus ' langage ' is held to comprise both ' la langue ' and ' la parole ', as in Delacroix' refinement upon the Saussurian terminology mentioned above, p. 283, note. Cp. G. Bertoni, *Linguaggio e lingua*, in *Archivum Ro anicum*, XV (1931), nr. 3.

[1] The notion of progress in language, to which we have alluded briefly in the section upon Meillet, is worthy of fuller explanation. Of those scholars who have given consideration to the question the most outstanding is Jespersen in his book, *Progress in Language*, London, 1898, 2nd ed., 1909. Jespersen adopts an attitude diametrically opposed to that of the nineteenth-century scholars, who held that language evolution was synonymous with language decay, as proved by the superiority of the classical over the modern languages. He maintains that linguistic changes have spelt progress. The further we go back towards the beginnings of a language the more complicated does its structure become. With the lapse of time the system becomes more simple, superfluous forms are discarded, word order takes the place of flexions, etc. To Jespersen, English, which has most radically reduced its grammatical forms, is the most advanced, and the ease and convenience which it offers as a mode of expression make it definitely superior to any other language, at least from the practical point of view, which, he says, linguists are too prone to neglect. Vendryes does not deny the facts, but rebuts Jespersen's interpretation of them. When we study the history of languages we observe, he says, that many of the losses they suffer are compensated by new formations, so that, on balance, there is frequently no deficit at all, or at least no considerable deficit. It is also erroneous to speak of a linguistic ideal, according to which one language is to be set above another. The ideal in this matter is the most complete adaptation of the linguistic material to the needs of the individuals who use it. In this respect every language has its own advantages and disadvantages. If we are to discuss these matters at all, which, he holds, are not strictly the concern of linguistics, the most reasonable view is to consider progress in language as something entirely relative and unstable. With regard to the reasons which bring about the simplification of morphology, Vendryes, like Meillet, finds the social character of language, its dependence upon the life of man in society, adequate to explain them. Thought, with savages and primitive man, is concrete and mystical, and memory well developed ; consequently, their language is characterized by a great wealth of grammatical forms, easily retained by their plastic unworn memories. Civilized man, on the contrary, thinks more abstractly ; his memory is less retentive, as he has other means of recording facts, and this leads, among other things, to a simplification of grammar, to make it correspond more closely to his method of thought.

Jespersen also discusses this question of ' language progress ' in *Die Sprache*, Heidelberg, 1925, pp. 304 f. and 322 f.

of writing, spelling, etc., we have said enough to show that this work of Vendryes' forms a very complete introduction to the whole subject of language study, a book particularly to be recommended to students, inasmuch as, in his discussions of phonological, morphological, and lexical problems, which form the backbone of the book, the author is at pains to explain step by step the terminology he uses. It has a further merit, in that the examples chosen to illustrate the various problems treated are drawn from every type of language ; the reader is thus given some idea of the specific peculiarities of idioms to which many of us find it difficult if not impossible to have access.

Vendryes' *Le Langage* was very favourably received by scholars. Among the reviews which it called forth we would mention those of M. Grammont, *Revue des langues romanes*, LXI (1921–2), p. 369 f. ; A. Ernout, *Journal des Savants*, 1922, p. 134 f. ; H. Delacroix, *Journal de psychologie normale et pathologique*, XVIII (1921), p. 772 f. ; V. Bogrea, *Dacoromania*, II (1921–2), p. 765 f. ; G. Dottin, *Annales de Bretagne*, XXXV (1921–3), p. 496 f. ; A. Debrunner, *Deutsche Literaturzeitung*, XLV (1924), col. 1447 f.[1] Of these, that of Grammont, himself, like Vendryes, a representative of the French school of linguistics (see below), although in the main eulogistic, contains some reservations which are worth our attention. We should not neglect, he says, the aesthetic side of language, because it is of particular importance ; art is one of the higher manifestations of the intellectual activity of a people ; it marks the end and aim of its spiritual development. Grammont also defends the conception of language progress : just as our thoughts can differ

---

[1] The director of the series in which *Le langage* was published, H. Berr, contributed a preface in which he shows that the sociological approach to language, characteristic of Vendryes and his master Meillet, is to be ascribed in the main to the influence of the French sociologists Durkheim and Lévy-Bruhl. Some of Berr's observations concerning essential features in Vendryes' doctrine are worth quoting : " Le langage n'est vraiment social, selon nous, que s'il est une création de la société, une institution inhérente à la société " (p. xvi). " Si donc, en soulignant l'action de la société, comme il le fait en beaucoup de passages, il voulait simplement montrer quelle ressource l'organisation sociale devait trouver dans ce moyen de communication entre les hommes, comment l' ' adaptation ' des facultés humaines aux besoins sociaux a fait progresser tout à la fois la société et le langage, on ne pourrait qu'être d'accord avec lui " (pp. xvi–xvii). " Dire que l'évolution du langage est en rapports étroits avec la civilisation, ce n'est pas méconnaître l'effort logique, le rôle du facteur humain ; et c'est restreindre le rôle du facteur social. Le concept de la civilisation est distinct de celui de la société " (p. xxvi). " De même que le linguiste a besoin de l'histoire, l'historien a besoin de la linguistique—s'il conçoit l'histoire, non comme le récit pur et simple de ce qui a été, mais comme l'interprétation profonde de la vie infiniment complexe " (p. xxviii). This concluding remark of Berr's is particularly applicable to Vendryes' book, whose entire basis is historical.

in quality, so also the means of giving expression to them may differ. Nor does he share the author's views upon the question of the relationship between racial psychology and language, holding that the evolution of a language is not conditioned solely by linguistic factors, as Vendryes would have it, but that it depends also upon the mentality of the people who speak it. Again, Vendryes' statement that of two competing linguistic forms it is the stronger and more influential which prevails is held to be unsatisfactory ; the question being rather : " Why *is* it that one is more influential, and consequently victorious, and not the other ? " Finally, the reviewer, as an inveterate phonetician, considers a mere 64 pages out of 420 devoted to the subject of phonetics a very meagre allowance.[1]

★   ★   ★

From considering members of the French school who discuss the whole domain of linguistic theory, like Saussure, Meillet, and Vendryes, all of them Indo-Europeanists, we now turn to some of its representatives who have made particular study of a special

---

[1] Vendryes has also voiced opinions upon matters of linguistic theory elsewhere, for example, in *Sur les tâches de la linguistique statique*, in *Journal de psychologie* (' *Psychologie du langage* '), 1933, p. 172 f., and in the article already mentioned, *Le caractère social du langage et la doctrine de F. de Saussure*, *Journal de psychologie*, XVIII (1921), p. 617 f. We quote a few passages from the latter study as they throw further light on his own position, as well as on that of Saussure. " L'acte linguistique est dans l'association d'un concept psychique et d'une image acoustique, et l'objet de la linguistique est d'étudier le rapport qui unit les deux " (p. 619). " Les principes de la linguistique synchronique se dégagent de la valeur du signe ; donc la linguistique synchronique ou statique est sociologique par définition " (p. 622). " L'étude de la langue ne peut être que synchronique ou plus exactement idiosynchronique. . . . En revanche, l'étude des faits de langue est nécessairement diachronique, puisque ces faits ne peuvent être considérés autrement que dans le temps. Or, tout ce qui est diachronique dans la langue ne l'est que par la parole " (p. 622). This precise statement helps us to understand certain features in the practice of Vossler and his pupils which aroused opposition, namely, that, confusing ' la langue ' and ' la parole ', they falsified observations which were perfectly accurate with regard to the latter, by claiming that they held good for the former. At the same time, Vossler's affirmation that linguistics can only be historical becomes intelligible ; as he was concerned exclusively with ' la parole ', it is inevitable that he should make this contention. The French linguists, on the other hand, make it clear that historical investigation is only applicable to ' facts of language ', not to ' la langue ' itself. Again Vossler's claim that everything in language is individual, is justifiable from the Saussurian point of view only if ' la parole ' and not ' la langue ' is meant. Thus Vendryes, following, no doubt, Meillet (cp. p. 301), would appear to be justified in speaking of " innovations générales se manifestant dans les individus isolés " in lieu of " innovations individuelles généralisées " (p. 623).

field, and that in direct association with the Romance discipline. All of them are pre-eminently students of French, though, when constructing their theories, they occasionally, but rarely, refer indiscriminately to other languages. They thus put into actual practice Saussure's exhortation to study present states of language, whereas Meillet and Vendryes, as Indo-Europeanists, and not working upon living languages, have been obliged to content themselves with a theoretical support and advocacy of such investigations. These specifically Romance members of the French school have thus been enabled to bring new and substantial contributions of their own upon matters which are but imperfectly treated, if at all, by their Indo-European colleagues. We shall present them in the order of their close connection, or otherwise, with the doctrine of Saussure.

Bally, with whom we begin, succeeded his master in the chair of linguistics at Geneva University. The following are his chief
Charles Bally publications : *Précis de stylistique*, Geneva, 1905 ; *Traité de stylistique française*, 2 vol., Heidelberg, 1909, 2nd ed., 1919–21 ; *Le langage et la vie*, Geneva–Heidelberg, 1913 (2nd and much-augmented edition, Paris, 1926, 3rd ed., 1935) ; and *Linguistique générale et linguistique française*, Paris 1932. It will be seen from this list that Bally's earlier work is in the field of stylistics, a new branch of linguistic study, which, as at present understood, he can be said to have founded. It will be convenient to confine ourselves at present to this, his major contribution to linguistic studies, and to defer consideration of his more recent work to a later stage (see p. 379 f.). We have already had occasion to mention the word ' stylistics ' in our discussion of the work of L. Spitzer (see p. 135 f., above). But as Bally's use of the term differs essentially from Spitzer's, and as the word, unlike the special branch of study to which it is now applied, is by no means of recent origin, it will avoid confusion if we attempt briefly to define it in its present connotation. In the first place, we must not confuse stylistics with the study of style. The latter appertains to aesthetics or literary criticism, because, by ' style ', we understand the manner in which a writer uses the resources of a language to obtain certain effects of an artistic order. It follows, therefore, that style varies from one author to another, and even, with a single author, from one of his works to another ; it is thus in the highest degree individual, even though the instruments it uses are common property. Moreover, style presupposes an intervention of the

consciousness, or, more precisely, of the will ; from among the means which the language places at his disposal for rendering his thought the author, or the orator, chooses those which he considers the most adequate to give it effective or artistic shape. Consequently, we must study style in a single author, or in a single work, and from an aesthetic standpoint. And so it is that literary critics concern themselves almost exclusively with what are called ' figures of style ', to the neglect of other stylistic processes, for the latter are common to a multitude of writers, whereas the former are the particular property of one. In a word, style implies artificiality, a necessary feature of literature as of other arts, and the study of style, when it is confined to strictly formal aspects, to the neglect of the underlying psychological phenomena, tends thus to become a purely schematic and punctilious pursuit. It has been a common belief that style is in the nature of a craft that any man may learn, whatever his gifts,[1] and every period has had its rhetors, its purveyors of recipes for the art of good writing and good speaking. It is because of such as these, men exclusively concerned with its formal aspects, that so many useless and prejudicial ideas still remain to darken counsel, and to hinder or prevent a true understanding of the nature of style.[2]

Stylistics, as the term is used by Bally, is a strictly scientific discipline which studies the means of expression shared by a linguistic community from the point of view of their affective or emotional content.[3] As is well known, many words, in addition

---

[1] Admittedly, a talented writer may, by dint of effort, achieve mastery in style, but that is far from implying that style is something external and superficial, to be acquired merely by toil and application.

[2] Classical scholars, in the nature of things, find it difficult to jettison their ancient cargo of rhetoric. A work like C. Balmuş, *Etude sur le style de St.-Augustin*, Paris, 1930, which applies modern methods to the investigation of the style of an ancient author, is thus particularly meritorious.

[3] To quote Bally's own words : " La stylistique étudie donc les faits d'expression du langage au point de vue de leur contenu affectif, c'est à dire l'expression des faits de la sensibilité par le langage et l'action des faits de langage sur la sensibilité " (*Traité*, I, ed. 2, p. 16). It should be made clear at this point that Bally, probably influenced by Saussure's ' external and internal linguistics ', distinguishes ' external or comparative stylistics ' from ' internal ' stylistics : " Ainsi il y a deux manières très différentes de dégager les caractères expressifs d'une langue : on peut ou bien comparer ses moyens d'expression avec ceux d'une autre langue, ou bien comparer entre eux les principaux types expressifs de la même langue, en tenant compte des milieux auxquelles ils appartiennent, des circonstances où ils ont leur emploi convenable, des intentions qui les font choisir dans chaque cas, et, enfin et surtout, des effets qu'ils produisent sur la sensibilité des sujets parlants et entendants " (p. 105). Just as Saussure leaves on one side external linguistics, so Bally shows a preference for internal stylistics, whose aims he defines as follows : " . . . la stylistique interne . . . cherche à fixer les rapports qui s'établissent

to their intellectual content, that is to say, the notion they express, have affective or emotional values. A speaker using such a word, not only conveys a meaning, but betrays an attitude or a feeling. The more we are under the influence of emotion (admiration, hatred, contempt, etc.) the more readily we have recourse to words or phrases of this expressive type. This particular quality differs from word to word, and also, according to the period, in one and the same word. For too frequent use reduces a word's expressive value, and words of this kind are thus more exposed than others to the wear and tear to which all language is subject. Many of them, having lost in process of time their affective values, are replaced by others which satisfy more fully the constant need for expressiveness, and these too, in their turn, are threatened with the same fate. To take an example from Rumanian, the usual name given to a ' spendthrift' is *risipitor*, a word which is entirely neutral in tone and, in itself, reveals no particular mental attitude on the part of the speaker.[1] But if the speaker is affected by the spending, if, for example, it is his money or the money of someone he cares about that is being spent, he ceases to be indifferent, and will have recourse to a ' stronger' expression, as, for example, *mînă spartă* [lit. ' leaky hand '], to give vent to his feelings. There is thus not a complete equivalence in the two expressions. Intellectually, they are of the same value, but emotionally they are widely different : one is affective, the other colourless.

There are, of course, notions which are entirely neutral, and awake no emotion within us, and the words that render them are

---

entre la parole et la pensée chez le sujet parlant ou entendant : elle étudie la langue dans ses rapports avec la vie réelle ; c'est-à-dire que la pensée qu'elle y trouve exprimée est presque toujours affective de quelque manière " (pp. 110–11). The author himself realizes that internal stylistics, thus understood, approximates closely to the study of style in the literary sense. This is indeed unavoidable, in that, when all is said and done, the writer uses the same means of expression as any other individual, and applies them to the same ends, to giving utterance to certain moods and experiences. The essential distinction between the two lies in the aesthetic intentions of the poet, which are entirely absent from ordinary speech. We find a more precise definition of the aims of internal stylistics on p. 111 : " . . . tout en se confinant dans le langage de tous, de mettre à nu les germes du style, de montrer que les ressorts qui l'actionnent se trouvent cachés dans les formes les plus banales de la langue." See also p. 134 f., where we are shown that the historical point of view has no standing in stylistic enquiries. We would point, finally, to the happy insistence in two of the above passages upon that obvious but much neglected fact that language implies a hearer as well as a speaker. This recurs with great frequence throughout Bally's writings, and with valuable scientific results.

[1] The word *risipitor* must once have had affective value, and meant ' a man who scatters money broadcast ' ; cp. the verb *risipi*, ' to disperse, destroy '.

thus unexpressive and plain, such as *chair*, *table*, *street*, *tree*, *water*, *corn*, *coat*, *flat*, *go*, *stand*, etc. Other notions, however, are always tinged with some sort of feeling and call for names that are correspondingly coloured. One has but to think of the wealth of terms which so many languages possess to render the notions ' head ' (the seat of intelligence and also of folly), ' lazy ', ' simpleton ', ' mouth ' (the voracious and loquacious organ), ' miserly ', ' poor ', ' frivolous ', ' harlot ', etc. etc. Many of these terms owe their expressive value largely to the part played by fancy in their fabrication ; as in the case of the equivalents for French *tête* mentioned in the note, they are often the names of material objects whose image arises in the mind at the same time as the notion concerned.[1] We are therefore, in a sense, justified in comparing them to the stylistic figures of speech used in literature, although the latter, which are willed and wooed, have not the natural spontaneity of the former. It should be said, too, that even when a language has no set term at its disposal to give affective colour to a notion, or when, as more usually happens, the speaker cannot call one quickly to mind, he may obtain much the same effect by giving a special intonation to an otherwise colourless word.[2] But there is no dearth of affective words or affective expressions, comparisons, and the like in any language, and colloquial speech, whether educated or uneducated, is full of them. They are more prevalent, however, in the speech of the uneducated, who speak with greater freedom, and are more completely swayed by their affective impulses. The educated, from various motives, show greater self-discipline and control, and among the words at their disposal choose those which do not offend against convention or shock the sensitive listener. Although these affective elements in speech are more noticeable

---

[1] For ' head ' Rumanian has *bostan*, *dovleac*, *căpăţînă*, *capazon*, *glavă*, *glăvăţînă*, etc. French *tête*, itself originally a very expressive word, representing Latin *testa*, ' potsherd ', etc. (cp. Rum. *ţeastă*, ' skull '), compared with the neutral *caput*>*chef*, has long lost its affective values and is replaced in popular and familiar speech by such ' synonyms ' as *citron*, *betterave*, *soupière*, *carafe*, *boule*, *caillou*, etc., of which some fifty exist in ' argot '. A similar variety of Rumanian equivalents for the remaining words are to be found in the Rumanian edition of this work.

[2] Again to take a Rumanian example : if it is desired to say that a person is ' intelligent ', and at the same time to show disapproval of his use of his intelligence, the only available adjective *deştept* is pronounced with a special musical intonation of the last syllable, which is at the same time lengthened ; or, alternatively, some expressive formula is added, e.g. *dacă-i deştept*, *ce să-i faci !* or *zi-i deştept şi pace !* [' what about it ! ' or ' enough said ! ']. For affective accentuation in French, cp. J. Marouzeau, *Accent affectif et accent intellectuel*, reproduced in L. Spitzer, *Meisterwerke*, I, p. 69 f., and discussed in *Le français moderne*, vol. I (1933), p. 61 f., and II (1934), p. 123 f.

in vocabulary and intonation, they are equally important in syntax and, though here much research has still to be done, probably also in the domain of sounds. As Bally says : ". . . la stylistique embrasse le domaine entier du langage. Tous les phénomènes linguistiques, depuis les sons jusqu'aux combinaisons syntaxiques les plus complexes, peuvent révéler quelque caractère fondamental de la langue étudiée ; tous les faits linguistiques, quels qu'ils soient, peuvent manifester quelque parcelle de la vie de l'esprit et quelque mouvement de la sensibilité "[1] (*Le langage et la vie*, 2nd ed., pp. 113–14).

It should now be clear in what respects ' stylistics ' is distinct from the study of style : the latter is concerned with aesthetic values,[2] the former investigates language from the point of view of its affective quality. Again, stylistics is concerned primarily with the spoken tongue, and only takes count of the written language in so far as it contains expressive words and phraseology taken from familiar speech,[3] whereas the study of style confines itself to the language

---

[1] Bally has perforce comparatively little to say on that scantily investigated topic the expressive values of sounds *qua* sounds, and consequently of their ' stylistic ' values. He is well aware, however, of ". . . la faculté plus ou moins grande qu'ont certains sons de produire des effets, lorsque les valeurs phoniques concordent avec le mouvement de la sensibilité de celui qui entend et comprend " (*ibid.*, p. 116). On the following page, he quotes the French words *goguenard, dégingandé, ratatouille*, etc., and endeavours to account for the particular impression they produce upon us. He concludes : " (1) les sons, surtout les combinaisons de sons qui figurent dans ces mots, ont quelque chose de frappant, qu'on chercherait vainement dans d'autres mots tels que *table, chaise, monter*, etc., et ils sont frappants par eux-mêmes, indépendamment du sens que les mots peuvent avoir ; (2) ces effets phoniques sont dans un certain rapport avec les sentiments provoqués par le sens des mots." We are here reminded of onomatopœic words, and also of Schuchardt's *Lautsymbolik*, see above, p. 55 f.

[2] Bally deliberately leaves out of account the aesthetic element in language and justifies this procedure as follows : ". . . disons que le point de vue linguistique intéresse seul notre étude ; on ne s'étonnera pas de voir négliger ici l'aspect esthétique du sujet, le côté style, poésie, art, et l'on nous pardonnera de prendre nos exemples dans les parties les plus diverses du trésor expressif, d'accoupler même, au nom de principes généraux, des faits qui n'ont pas l'habitude de voisiner. Notre excuse est que nous nous attachons aux procédés, non aux effets qu'ils peuvent produire. Ce n'est pas tout : pour étudier ces procédés il est nécessaire de recourir d'abord à des faits de langage non socialisés, dont le mécanisme est plus apparent, en même temps que leurs effets sont plus évidents " (*ibid.*, p. 154). And elsewhere (*Traité de stylistique française*, I, 2nd ed., p. 181, § 190) : " Le langage spontané est toujours ' en puissance de beauté ', mais sa fonction naturelle et constante n'est pas d'exprimer la beauté ; dès qu'il se met volontairement au service de l'expression du beau, il cesse d'être l'objet de la stylistique ; il appartient à la litterature et à l'art d'écrire ; car nous verrons que l'expression littéraire ne nous intéresse qu'à titre de fait d'évocation."

[3] This distinction between the spoken and the written language recurs as a leit-motiv throughout all Bally's works. In *Le langage et la vie*, for example, a whole chapter is devoted to ' langue écrite et langue parlée ' (*op. cit.*, 2nd ed., p. 126 f.), from which we would quote the following significant passages :

of literature. An immediate consequence of this distinction is, therefore, that stylistics, as understood and practised by Bally, finds its material in what is common to all the members of a linguistic group, while style is a matter of individual peculiarities ; in one case we have to do with a study of ' la langue ', in the other with a study of its individual manifestations in ' la parole '.

We have already stated that this conception of stylistics is not the same as that found in Spitzer's works upon style. Without reverting in detail to the latter's methods (see Chap. II, p. 137 f., above) it should be plain from the foregoing where the difference lies. Spitzer's stylistics stand half-way between those of Bally and the study of style in the traditional sense. The Baltimore scholar is interested both in spoken and written language, though more particularly in the language of specific authors ; he analyses methods of expression from the affective angle, but at the same time he takes account of their aesthetic values, even in the case of the common tongue. His method is based upon the psychology of the individual, even when he applies it to stylistic features that are general. Bally's method is socio-psychological, and aims at drawing general conclusions from the investigation of current

" L'étude des expressions figurées est la pierre de touche de la distinction entre l'écrit et le parler. Quiconque veut connaître la manière dont un peuple voit la vie doit écarter la langue écrite et étudier les images les plus banales du langage courant. Là, tout est fixé, et la base d'observation est sûre ; dès qu'on opère sur les textes littéraires, tout s'embrouille ; . . . ." " En s'attachant aux textes, on néglige aussi les ressources phonétiques de la langue " (p. 131). " La langue écrite ne peut donc faire découvrir les véritables caractères d'une langue vivante, car par son essence même elle est en dehors des conditions de la vie réelle ; . . ." (p. 132). On the same page, however, we read : " Il ne s'ensuit pas que la langue écrite doive rester en dehors de l'étude stylistique ; elle y joue même un rôle fort utile dès qu'elle est étudiée en fonction de la langue parlée." The following quotation brings out a further point in Bally's attitude towards the written language : " D'abord ce caractère conscient et artificiel de la langue écrite explique pourquoi, en s'écartant de la langue populaire, elle obéit à un rythme capricieux, reculant volontiers vers des formes archaïques (cf. le latin de l'âge d'argent), influencée parfois par des langues étrangères (action du grec sur le latin), le plus souvent figée dans une immobilité relative " (p. 196). The literary language is the domain of style, in the strict sense ; it is intellectual, whereas spoken language is affective, another of Bally's recurring antitheses. We see, however, from the passages quoted, that stylistics does not rule out entirely the figures of speech, although it confines itself to those which have ceased to be individual in character (as all figures of speech must once have been), and which have become the common coinage of language, while still preserving affective or expressive values, those, in a word, which have something of the nature of syntactical groups, without being completely crystallized like the latter into mere elements of grammar. The figures of speech used by a writer are, by definition, individual, and remain so. Even when the same figure recurs in a number of writers its value changes, and it may even change when it recurs with the same writer. It is not on such material that general conclusions can easily or safely be based.

emotive words or expressions which manifest the spiritual and mental attitude common to, or prevalent within, a linguistic group. To revert again to the Saussurian terminology, the Swiss linguist is concerned with ' la langue ', Spitzer with ' la parole ', for even when the latter does study methods of expression that are common to a group, he still does so on the basis of individual psychology, endeavouring to discover how a given individual uses the material supplied by his mother tongue to give utterance to his own momentary mood or feeling.[1]

It remains for us now to examine Bally's ideas upon language and to discover how he came to found the study of stylistics as he understands it. As a faithful disciple of F. de Saussure, the Geneva professor gives his whole attention to present linguistic states, and investigates them without enquiring for a moment of what earlier phases they are the outcome. The historical method, he maintains, is more of a hindrance than a help to understanding the true nature of a language, because, for one reason, it conceals from us the actual relationship between thought and speech, whereas if we confine ourselves to the study of a language as it is to-day this relationship is readily revealed, it being sufficient to observe the words of the language in their synchronistic association and to follow our own psychological processes when in the act of speaking it. It follows that the linguist should take as the object of his research, not the language of literature, but the common tongue, familiar, colloquial speech, because this alone is unconscious and, like the spirit which creates it, ' collective ' in character : the more freely and spontaneously we talk, the less we concern ourselves with the manner of our speech, and the more readily we are understood by others, which is what human speech is for. A speaker, however, in this respect is in a different position from a listener. Our hearer is conscious,[2] that is to say he follows

---

[1] Spitzer endeavours to re-create the linguistic act at the moment when a given expression first took shape. Bally is, as a rule, satisfied with the mere recognition of the affective value of an expression without further analysis, either of its origin, or specific function, a legitimate procedure inasmuch as, unlike Spitzer, he deals with quite unsophisticated phenomena. We would call attention, however, to an article in *Le langage et la vie* (2nd ed., p. 141 f.), entitled ' Mécanisme de l'expressivité linguistique,' where he studies the methods which language employs to give expression to affective states.

[2] Familiar speech is unconscious, in the sense that it does not show that conscious effort which the orator or the writer puts forth. It is none the less conscious in so far as every function of the mind is conscious. Similarly, though the will does not intervene in the choice of the affective expressions which spring to the mind to give vent to certain emotions, there is none the less a will to impress

attentively not only what we say, but how we say it, he notices if we conform to the accepted rules of the language, and, if we depart from them, accepts or rejects our innovations. The hearer takes as his standpoint ' la langue ', and may be considered as the representative of the linguistic system under which the conversation is taking place, and by means of which he is able to interpret and understand ' la parole ' of the speaker. Innovations in speech which fit in with the accepted system catch on and become general. These Bally calls ' borrowings ', a term to which he thus gives wider application than did the neo-grammarians, while at the same time attaching more importance to the thing it signifies. ' Borrowings ' of this type, it should be added, can only be sanctioned by adult speakers, who are alone qualified to judge whether they are in keeping with the linguistic system.

The purpose of language is to serve as a means of understanding between men; the social environment, therefore, plays an important part in all matters concerning language. In particular, the affective elements in man's make-up are strongly influenced by his life in society, so that when we perform the social act of speech we are usually to a greater or less degree under their control, and our speech is correspondingly coloured by them. Like Meringer and Sperber (see above, p. 74 f.), Bally makes a sharp distinction between purely intellectual language and the more coloured variety to be found in speech ; and the latter is so important in his eyes that, as we have seen, he creates his entirely new discipline of stylistics to investigate it.[1] To pursue these

the listener. The extent to which consciousness and will intervene in speech varies greatly from one social class to another and is in direct ratio to the degree of education. In *Le langage et la vie*, 2nd ed., a whole chapter deals with this and similar problems, under the heading : ' Langage transmis et langage acquis '. The distinction is between forms that are purely inherited and traditional, and forms which the individual has acquired through his own special experience. In the latter case we have to do with phenomena which are far more conscious in character than in the former. Bally protests against the neo-grammarian conception of language as a purely ' natural ' phenomenon, in which the individual consciousness plays no part at all.

[1] In an article published in 1914 in the *Germanisch-romanische Monatsschrift*, VI (1914), p. 459 f., Bally draws a distinction between ' la langue ' and ' la parole ' on the basis of ' affectivity '. ' La langue ' is the colourless, impersonal, logical, normal, completely organized, and established medium. ' La parole ' is the medium of fancy, individuality, emotionalism, and subjectivism. He adds that ' la langue ', conceived as a purely intellectual mode of expression, does not exist in fact. A living language is always coloured to some extent by the feelings of the person using it, for language is made for life, not for speculative thought. It should be observed that we are here some distance from the Saussurian distinction between ' la langue ' and ' la parole ' as summarized earlier in the present chapter.

investigations we must always be on our guard against assuming the historical bias which would lead us to compare present with past linguistic states, and also against that strong and innate tendency we all possess to connect up words according to their real or supposed relationships, which Bally calls the etymologizing instinct,[1] for both of these attitudes are incompatible with the study of a language, statically and synchronistically, as a system actually in being.

Bally's sociological outlook upon language is apparent in another of his important observations. We have seen above (p. 307) how Meillet spoke of a prevailing European spirit, a ' sentiment d'une unité de civilisation ', to which he attributed the fact that the languages of our continent tend to have more and more in common, despite their widely different origins. Bally makes a somewhat similar contention. He asserts that the close cultural bonds between the European peoples have produced a kind of common mentality which is manifest in their respective languages, and that idioms which, in origin, are entirely remote one from the other thus show striking stylistic similarities that only the similarity of prevailing social conditions can account for satisfactorily. We are thus led to the conception of a European style, and to consider the possibility of a discipline of comparative European stylistics, whose aims would be, on the one hand, to differentiate between languages according to their modes of expression, and, on the other, to observe the features they share in common which might rightly be attributed to this community of social and cultural conditions. Bally, indeed, as we shall see below, in the section dealing with language characterization (p. 379 f.), has recently applied himself with signal success to the first of these problems.

Finally, we find in the works of the Geneva scholar a wholly commendable attitude with regard to sounds, and one which shows him to be in tune with the tendencies of linguistic thought in the Romance field. Hitherto, investigation of sounds, he maintains, has been vitiated by concentration upon their physiological characteristics, to the entire neglect of their psychological aspects. As language in its entirety is a product of the human spirit, it

---

[1] Gilliéron, too, was well aware of this phenomenon. It is the source of those popular etymologies which, as linguistic geography has shown, have played such a potent part in language change.

follows that the so-called sound-laws are also psychical in their origin.[1]

✶

The works of which we have given the gist in the preceding pages have received wide discussion, and appreciations have varied from qualified approval to complete eulogy, according as the attitude of the reviewer towards language differed from or resembled that of the author. M. Grammont, analysing the *Précis de stylistique*, in *Revue des langues romanes*, LIV (1911), p. 103 f., writes : " M. Bally ouvre une voie nouvelle." Similarly, H. Sperber, also a student of ' affective' language (cp. p. 77, above), states, in *Über den Affekt als Ursache der Sprachveränderung*, Halle a.S., 1914, p. iii, that *Le langage et la vie* is the first book on language to give the requisite importance to affective phenomena ; while K. Jaberg, speaking of the second edition of the same work, in an article entitled, *Sprache und Leben*, *Revue de linguistique romane*, II (1926), p. 3 f., regrets that linguists have not given it the attention it deserved, and expresses the hope that it will not be long before a new edition of this "fine and very important book " sees the light of day.

Among the reviewers who voiced objections of any weight to Bally's linguistic theory, mention must be made of A. Meillet, whose remarks are of particular interest, coming from a member of the same school. In the *Bulletin de la Société de linguistique*, XVIII (1912–13), p. clxxix f., in an account of the first edition of *Le langage et la vie*, he declares, *inter alia*, that language, like all natural or social phenomena, can only be studied analytically, and in close relationship with cultural conditions, to which it tends constantly

---

[1] Bally, like Gilliéron, thinks of sound changes as destructive in their action, and contrasts them with ' analogy ', that " action inconsciente et commune des sujets parlants, action qui tantôt conserve ce qui est en train de disparaître, tantôt recrée ce qui est déjà disparu " (*Le langage et la vie*, 2nd ed., p. 40). This antithesis, sound-law on the one hand, analogy on the other, reminds us of the neo-grammarians, but the creative functions which Bally attributes to analogy distinguish his point of view from theirs. He goes so far as to speak of an analogical instinct (*Traité de stylistique française*, I, 2nd ed., p. 38), which he not only sets upon the same footing as the etymologizing instinct referred to above, as being a product of the same mental quality in man, but actually considers to be the same activity in a more pronounced form : one creates new meanings, by detecting etymological connections between very different words, the other creates new forms.

to conform. On the topic of its affective elements, to which Bally assigns such an important place, he writes as follows (p. clxxxii) : " Tout en retenant l'idée fondamentale de M. Bally, on se demandera donc si l'ardeur de son prosélytisme ne l'a pas conduit à exagérer." The same scholar, however, has nothing but praise for the *Traité de stylistique française* (v. *Bull. Soc. Ling.*, XVI, 1909–10, p. cxviii f.), which he considers much superior to the *Précis de stylistique*, for here he is glad to recognize that Bally has attached due importance to the sociological aspects of his problem.[1]

One prevailing characteristic of all Bally's work which should be mentioned finally is its leaning to the didactic. We continually find him calling upon his own professorial experience, and at the same time adjusting his theoretical dissertations to the practical needs of teaching. This is particularly the case in his *Traité de stylistique française*, which has a definitely pedagogical purpose, the second volume being composed entirely of exercises for the use of students and teachers. Bally has not escaped censure for this mingling of things usually kept strictly apart, witness the reproaches addressed to him by Schuchardt in *Literaturblatt f. germ. u. rom. Phil.*, xxxviii (1917), col. 6–7 ; indeed Jaberg, in his article already quoted (*Rev. de ling. rom.*, II (1926), p. 5), expresses the view that had it not been for this didactic bias the importance of Bally's work would have received fuller recognition from the world of scholarship. There is no gainsaying, however, that language teaching has much to gain from ' stylistics ' as understood and practised by Bally, and it is clear that in applying his method, with the necessary modifications, to the study of the several ' mother tongues ', a

---

[1] Other reviews of Bally's writings have been published by : E. Lerch, *Literaturblatt f. germ. u. rom. Phil.*, XXXIII (1912), col. 283 f. ; K. Morgenroth, *Zeitschr. f. franz. Spr. u. Lit.*, XLII (1914), pt. II, p. 1 f. ; J. Ronjat, *Rev. des langues romanes*, LVII (1914), p. 158 f. ; K. Vossler, *Germ.-rom. Monatsschrift*, VII (1915), p. 85 f. (in an article entitled *Das Leben und die Sprache*, reproduced in *Gesammelte Aufsätze zur Sprachphilosophie*, Munich, 1923, p. 97 f.) ; E. Lerch, *Literaturblatt f. germ. u. rom. Phil.*, XXXVI (1915), col. 121 f. ; H. Schuchardt, *ibid.*, XXXVIII (1917), col. 6 f. (actually this review is devoted to Saussure's *Cours de linguistique générale*, but Bally's work is also incidentally discussed) ; A. Franz, *Zeitschr. f. franz. Spr. u. Lit.*, XLVI (1920–23), p. 453 ; Leo Jordan, *Archivum Romanicum*, IX (1925), p. 338 f. ; E. Boisacq, *Revue belge de philologie et d'histoire*, V (1926), p. 973 f. ; O. Densusianu, *Grai și suflet*, III (1927–8), p. 276 f.; W. Porzig, *Indogerm. Forschungen*, XLVI (1928), p. 326 f. ; H. Wengler, *Die neueren Sprachen*, XXXVI (1928), p. 161 f. (under the title, *Ch. Ballys ' Stylistique '*). An appreciation of Bally's whole scientific activity is to be found in a study by A. Sechehaye, entitled, *L'école genevoise de linguistique générale*, in *Indogerman. Forschungen*, XLIV (1926), p. 225 f. ; cp. also, L. Spitzer's characterization in *Meisterwerke der romanischen Sprachwissenschaft*, II, p. 339 f. (Three studies by Bally are reproduced by Spitzer in this volume.) For reviews of *Linguistique générale et linguistique française*, see p. 382, note.

finer feeling for ' la langue ' and a fuller understanding of its peculiar qualities would be developed in the various linguistic communities.[1]

We would conclude this section with a brief mention of studies by two of Bally's pupils, Marguerite Lips and Henri Frei. The former is the author of the work entitled *Le style indirect libre*, Paris 1926, which, as we have shown elsewhere (p. 133), treats of a problem discussed in a number of studies by Bally himself, and was reviewed at some length by various scholars, for example, Elise Richter, *Archiv für das Studium der neueren Sprachen und Literaturen*, CLIII (1928), p. 149 f. ; E. Gamillscheg, *Deutsche Literaturzeitung*, XLVIII (1927), col. 2391 f. ; A. Wallensköld, *Neuphilologische Mitteilungen*, XXVIII (1927), p. 239 f. ; and G. Weöres, *ibid.*, p. 241 f. The latter, Henri Frei, is well known to linguists as the author of an important and interesting book called *La grammaire des fautes*, Paris–Geneva–Leipzig, 1929. In this work the author sets out to investigate from the angle of general linguistic theory the so-called errors which crop up in spoken and written French. The usual attitude towards such errors is either to treat them as due to carelessness or ignorance and as of no significance, or to consider them as symptoms of language degeneracy and decay. Frei sets out to discover the promptings behind the ' error ', enquiring ' en quoi les fautes sont conditionnées par le fonctionnement du langage et comment elles le reflètent." After an introductory chapter in which he explains and justifies the functional as distinct from the normative approach to the problem, he classifies his rich collection of errors according as they manifest (*a*) those conflicting tendencies towards assimilation and differentiation which are constant phenomena in language life, (*b*) economy of effort, and (*c*) a desire for vividness and vigour of expression. One of his important contentions is that " dans un grand nombre de cas la faute, qui a passé jusqu'à présent pour un phénomène quasi-pathologique, sert à prévenir ou à réparer les déficits du langage correct." In other words, what is commonly condemned as a mistake is frequently due to a conscious or unconscious attempt to improve upon the traditional norm, and though some of these

---

[1] Mention should be made of a recent book of Bally's, *La crise du français. Notre langue maternelle à l'école*, Paris, 1930, which would appear to be solely concerned with problems of pedagogics (cp. the reviews by H. Frei, *Archiv f. d. St. der neueren Sprachen*, CLX [1931], p. 270 f., and L. Spitzer, *Indogerm. Forschungen*, XLIX [1931], p. 165 f.), and of his article, *Les notions grammaticales d'absolu et de relatif*, in *Journal de psychologie*, 1933, p. 341 f.

attempts are necessarily still-born, others are destined to survive and receive full rights of citizenship in the language of the future.[1]

★ ★ ★

Also a pupil of Saussure, Albert Sechehaye has worked along lines closely related to those followed by Bally, his colleague at the University of Geneva. Not only do both scholars share the outlook upon language which is common to all members of the French school, but they have deeper and closer relationships, which make them in a sense complementary one to the other. Bally, we have seen, is constantly concerned with determining the relationships between thought and speech ; Sechehaye is even more so. Thought has two sides to it, an intellectual and an emotional. Bally's chosen field is the affective side, which he considers, particularly in his earlier work, as the determining factor in spoken language, and which forms the material of his stylistic studies described above. Sechehaye,[2] on

Albert Sechehaye

---

[1] For reviews of Frei's book see : J. B. Hofmann, *Deutsche Literaturzeitung*, L (1929), col. 2341 f. ; Elise Richter, *Archiv f. d. St. d. neueren Spr. u. Lit.*, CLVII (1930), p. 304 f. ; A. Meillet, *Litteris*, VII (1930), p. 58 f., and *Bull. Soc. Ling.*, XXX (1930), p. 145 f. ; E. Pelkonen, *Neuphilologische Mitteilungen*, XXXIV (1933), p. 42 f. ; A. Grégoire, *Revue belge de philologie et d'histoire*, X (1931), p. 212 f. ; cp. also E. Lerch, *Grammatische Fehler*, in *Die neueren Sprachen*, XXXIX (1931), p. 599 f.

[2] In his *Essai sur la structure logique de la phrase*, Paris, 1926, pp. 211-12, we find a passage which defines in an interesting way the difference between his standpoint and that of Bally. After explaining why he has left out of account syntactical constructions and grammatical forms which ' expriment les mouve-ments de la vie ', such as commands, interjections, interrogations, etc., he states : " Mais notre programme était tout différent. Nous avons voulu mettre en lumière, s'il est permis de s'exprimer ainsi, l'ossature psychologique de la phrase considérée dans son expression grammaticale. Or, c'est la communication des idées, et non l'expression des sentiments, qui a fourni à la grammaire les éléments essentiels de ses constructions. Les bases de l'édifice syntagmatique ont été posées par l'intelligence qui pense, qui essaie de se faire comprendre et qui réagit par la logique devant les difficultés de l'entreprise. Elle crée ainsi la langue, dont la fin propre est, dans ce sens, l'expression de la pensée objective. Si, dans son contact permanent avec la parole et la vie, la langue, création de l'intelligence, est restée mêlée et comme toute pénétrée d'éléments affectifs, cela n'a pas influencé le développement général de ses institutions grammaticales, et c'est sur le canevas d'une grammaire faite pour exprimer une pensée logiquement déduite que l'on a brodé et surajouté sans système, un peu au hasard, les créations de la grammaire affective. Nous n'en voulons pour preuve que nos grammaires et le fait que, dans ces exposés systématiques, quel qu'en soit le plan, ce sont les données de la grammaire objective qui fournissent les têtes de chapitres et les principes de classement : distinction du sujet et du prédicat, distinction du substantif et du verbe, distinction de la proposition indépendante et de la subordonnée, etc. Les chapitres qui traitent de la manière de poser une question, de donner un ordre, d'exprimer une émotion ne sont que des hors d'œuvres ; la grammaire affective se dissout dans une multitude de faits particuliers, les uns assez larges, les autres

the other hand, is chiefly interested in the intellectual aspect of thought, and in language as an intellectual medium. His chosen field will therefore be syntax, those constructions which are fixed both in their form and in their uses, formulae that have become completely grammaticalized and which show no vestige of their ' individual ' origin, or of that subjective quality which, in common with so many peculiarities of language, they must once have possessed. For this reason Sechehaye's work strikes us as being more rigid and abstract than that of Bally. The two disciples of Saussure are clearly different in temperament and in general outlook, and this it is, no doubt, which not only accounts for the different impression we receive from the work of each, but also actually determined the choice of their respective fields of study.[1]

très étroitement délimités, et qui tous empruntent la plupart de leurs éléments à la grammaire objective en leur faisant subir telle ou telle modification spécifique. Qu'on songe par exemple à nos constructions interrogatives en français, ou aux ellipses de l'exclamation. Tous ces faits sont en eux-mêmes d'un haut intérêt, mais, dans le point de vue qui est le nôtre, ils s'effacent entièrement derrière ceux dont il a été parlé." It is clear from the last sentence that Sechehaye is aware of the interest of research into affective speech. Another quotation will make still clearer the essential community of views between the two scholars despite the difference in the fields they prefer to investigate : " A un certain point de vue tout ce qui dans la langue touche à la vie affective et aux mouvements de l'âme est d'un intérêt primordial et l'emporte sur tout le reste. S'il s'était agi de l'origine du langage ou des causes des évolutions linguistiques, si on avait voulu faire la psychologie de la parole et surprendre les secrets de l'expressivité et du style, ç'aurait été une grande erreur de négliger les divers modes du verbe et tout ce qui dans la grammaire est teinté de subjectivité " (*op. cit.*, p. 211). He has himself more than once touched upon stylistic matters, for instance, in the articles *La stylistique et la linguistique théorique* (in *Mélanges linguistiques offerts à M. Ferdinand de Saussure*, Paris, 1908), where, according to L. Havet, *Bull. Soc. Ling.*, XVI (1909–10), p. 11, he questions the possibility of an exclusively stylistic discipline, and *Les règles de la grammaire et la vie du langage* (*Germanisch-romanische Monatsschrift*, VI [1914], pp. 288 f. and 341 f.). The latter study is important, among other reasons, as attempting to reconcile the rigidity of the rules of grammar, which the linguistic system strictly enforces, with the need for a fresh and personal form of expression felt by the individual speaker. There exists, he tells us, a domain where ' grammar ', in the strict sense of the term, and ' stylistics ', or affective modes of speech, meet. To know this common ground, we must first have a clear view of the logical constituents of the language, which are more or less fixed and compulsory for all members of a linguistic community, and then proceed to what, in the actual practice of speech, is due to the workings of the individual sensibility. In other words : first ' grammar ' or ' la langue ', then ' stylistics ' or ' la parole '. This is the reverse of the procedure recommended by Vossler (see above, Chap. II, p. 88 f.). But Sechehaye recognizes that Vossler's method is right if it is the origin and development of a specific grammatical construction we wish to investigate, as only changing stylistic values will give us the key to these evolutionary changes. But when it is the system as a whole which is being examined, when we are pursuing synchronistic and not diachronistic linguistics, grammar must be our starting-point.

[1] A natural consequence of this difference is the sometimes excessive stress laid upon psychology in Sechehaye's work. In the book already quoted (p. 216), he gives certain reasons why this should be so : " Incapable de s'adapter défini-

It goes without saying that, as befits a true follower of Saussure, Sechehaye's linguistic work will be static, not historical or dia-chronistic.[1] Like Bally, who also studies ' la langue ', he takes his material from the common stock of accepted forms which ' la langue ' provides, not from the varieties offered by ' la parole ', but, unlike Bally, he is obliged by the nature of his studies to refer the uniformity and regularity of the written word to the vagaries of the more emotional spoken language. Like Bally again, Sechehaye has leanings towards the didactic. He, too, has chosen his own language, French, as his field of investigation, and is con-tinually preoccupied by matters of practice. Concerned as he is with a discipline which has long been an established branch of university study and not, like his colleague, with an entirely new departure, he would seem to have by far the easier task, but, in reality, the very fact that syntax is such a time-honoured subject of study makes the task of effecting any considerable change in the methods of teaching it much more difficult than would at first sight appear.

Sechehaye's list of published work is a long one. In addition to those already mentioned it contains : *Programme et Méthodes de la linguistique théorique. Psychologie du langage*, Paris–Leipzig–Geneva, 1908 ; *La méthode constructive en syntaxe* (in *Revue des langues romanes*, LIX [1916–17], p. 44 f.) ; *Les problèmes de la langue à la lumière d'une théorie nouvelle* (in *Revue philosophique de la France et de l'Etranger*, XLII (vol. 84) [1917], p. 1 f. ; *Les deux types de la phrase*[2] (in *Mélanges d'histoire littéraire et de philologie offerts à M. Bernard Bouvier*, Geneva, 1920) ; *Locutions et composés* (in *Journal de psychologie normale*

---

tivement aux exigences de la vie qui évolue et se renouvelle sans cesse, elle [la langue] reste toujours en conflit avec la psychologie spontanée de la parole et elle est toujours en voie de remaniement dans quelques-unes de ses parties ". " Sans confondre notre discipline avec la psychologie ou la logique, nous voyons par ces cadres et ces lois comment les principes de ces deux sciences s'appliquent dans un domaine spécial " (p. 217). Obviously, if he is investigating the relations between thought and expression, he is obliged to examine the psychological elements in language just as attentively as the purely linguistic.

[1] He began, however, with a study on historical syntax, his doctorate thesis, *L'imparfait du subjonctif et ses concurrents dans les hypothétiques normales en français, Romanische Forschungen*, XIX (1905–6), p. 321 f.

[2] The two kinds of sentence are : (*a*) simple sentences like *admirable, vains efforts*, etc., which give expression to one isolated idea : the ' sentences ' with which children begin to talk, and which were probably the first types of uttered judgments ; (*b*) propositions, like *le soleil brûle, cet homme est bon*, etc. Sechehaye calls the first ' *la phrase simple*', the second, ' *la phrase pensée* '. In Meillet's view (*v. Bull. Soc. Ling.*, XXII [1920-21], p. 172) this study of Sechehaye's is a fundamental contribution to the theory of the sentence.

et pathologique, XVIII [1921], p. 654 f.) ; *L'école genevoise de linguistique générale* (in *Indogermanische Forschungen*, XLIV [1926], p. 217 f.) ; *Les mirages linguistiques* (in *Journal de Psychologie* . . . , XXVII [1930], p. 337 f.) ; *La pensée et la langue, ou Comment concevoir le rapport organique de l'individuel et du social dans le langage* (*ibid.*, XXX, 1933, p. 57 f.) ; *Essai de classement des espèces de phrases et quelques observations sur les trois cas de l'hypothèse en latin*, in *Bull. Soc. Ling.*, XXXV (1934), p. 58 f.

Anything in the nature of a summary of these works is out of the question, nor is it really necessary, because whenever the author finds it desirable to justify his linguistic attitude, as he does sporadically throughout these studies, he does so in pronouncements which from the point of view of doctrine do not materially differ from those of the other representatives of the French school.[1] Moreover, any very revolutionary discoveries in such a well-worked claim as syntax were scarcely to be expected. As he himself says, in his *Essai sur la structure logique de la phrase*, p. 216 : " Rien de tout cela n'est bien nouveau. Sans y avoir mis aucun parti pris, nous nous trouvons même être très conservateur. Mais nous avons essayé de sonder les bases de principes déjà reconnus et de leur donner une systématisation solide." His principal innovations are to be found in points of detail and in terminology, and some of these we will enumerate.

The book *Programme et Méthodes* . . . contains, *inter alia*, a long and interesting discussion of Wundt's *Völkerpsychologie. I. Band : Die Sprache* (cp. above, Chap. II, p. 92), the main defect of which Sechehaye sums up as follows : " [Wundt] a été plus préoccupé de faire de la psychologie à propos du langage que la psychologie du langage à proprement parler " (p. 43). We should take into account on an equal footing both psychology and linguistics, that is to say, the mind of the individual and the laws to which he must conform when he speaks. Language proper consists of g r a m-m a t i c a l e l e m e n t s, which appertain to the domain of collective

---

[1] Sechehaye himself has contrasted his linguistic standpoint with that of Saussure in *Essai sur la structure logique de la phrase*, p. 219 : " Une différence essentielle entre la doctrine saussurienne et la nôtre, c'est que le *Cours de linguistique générale* ne tire de ses distinctions aucun principe de classement rigoureux et met plutôt en évidence les relations de réciprocité qui s'établissent entre les divers aspects du fait linguistique. Ainsi pour Ferdinand de Saussure la langue existe pour la parole, mais elle naît aussi de la parole ; elle en émane et elle la rend possible, et rien ne nous force à mettre l'une devant l'autre ou au-dessus de l'autre. C'est un complexe que seule l'abstraction analyse. Pour nous, au contraire, dans cette abstraction même nous apercevons un principe de subordination et de classement et nous mettons la parole, sous sa forme pré-grammaticale, avant la langue ".

psychology, and extra-grammatical elements which are matters of individual psychology. But inasmuch as there is no separating collective psychology from that of the individual, so the study of the grammatical and the extra-grammatical must go hand in hand. Under the latter heading is included the language of gesture, in the wide sense of the term, to which Sechehaye gives the name of pre-grammatical.[1] Grammar, he asserts, is " comme une déformation particulière du langage prégrammatical " (p. 71). Every form of grammar has an individual origin, and has its source in some pre-grammatical or extra-grammatical act which in process of time is transformed into grammar, just as inert matter when consumed by a living organism itself becomes alive. In language that is pre-grammatical the individual creates the signs he uses to express his psychical state ; in grammatical language he reproduces signs he has observed in others, or which exist in the current linguistic material. But in the latter case they are no longer signs in the strict sense of the word, but symbols, the mind having established a constant relationship between the sign and the idea. It is thus logic which constitutes the *ultima ratio* in the domain of grammar. In the expression of grammatical relationships there is nothing conventional like the arbitrary relationship between notion and name in words ; and when we speak we are compelled to respect the organization of the grammatical system, which is present in the minds of all of us.[2]

An important study from a methodological point of view is that entitled *La méthode constructive en syntaxe*,[3] in which Sechehaye endeavours to reconcile and associate two apparently conflicting kinds of syntactical enquiry, the one proceeding from form to content, the other following the reverse route.[4] " Le problème," he says, " est . . . le suivant : comment peut-on étudier une langue et plus spécialement un système syntaxique sans jamais quitter, ne fût-ce qu'un instant, le fait linguistique qui réside dans

[1] Sechehaye reverts to this term in his *Essai sur la structure logique de la phrase*, p. 219 f., where he considers the pre-grammatical as 'free and spontaneous expression,' anterior to any conventional linguistic organization. Linguistics should begin, he says, with the pre-grammatical and the grammatical, and proceed thence to organized speech, and finally to the evolution of the language system.

[2] Cp. Leo Jordan, *La logique et la linguistique*, in *La psychologie du langage* (= *Journal de psychologie*, XXX [1933]), p. 45 f., and *Schule der Abstraktion und der Dialektik*, Munich, 1932.

[3] Cp. Meillet's marginal commentary to this study under the heading ' Sur la méthode à employer en syntaxe,' *Bull. Soc. Ling.*, XX (1916), p. 133 f.

[4] The latter method has begun to be applied, particularly in recent years, as will be seen in the section on F. Brunot below.

l'union de ces facteurs hétérogènes ? " (*op. cit.*, p. 46). The way to achieve this end is pointed out in some detail with the help of numerous examples. We must start from the principal part of the proposition, which forms a nucleus round which are grouped all the determinants destined to elaborate the thought to its complete expression. As with a timepiece, " Il faut prendre chaque pièce l'une après l'autre avec sa forme et sa fonction, et la considérer à sa juste place dans l'ensemble entre le ressort qui donne le mouvement, le balancier qui le règle et les aiguilles qui marquent les heures. Or ceci ne peut pas se faire dans un ordre quelconque. Il y a des éléments essentiels, constitutifs, par lesquels il faut commencer ; il y en a d'autres, secondaires, qui n'existent que pour et par les premiers " (*ibid.*, pp. 47–8). The method must be therefore at once analytic and synthetic. " Cette construction se compose en réalité d'une série de petites syntaxes particulières, quelquefois juxtaposées, le plus souvent superposées et se portant les unes les autres comme les pierres de taille dans un mur. Un type syntaxique initial ou nouveau étant posé, il faut énoncer toutes les règles auxquelles il donne lieu, tout ce qui dans le jeu possible de cet organe syntaxique est incontestablement fait de langue, norme de construction dans la parole " (*ibid.*, p. 73). " L'esprit de la syntaxe, pour ainsi dire, doit être constructif et architectural. Ce que cette science demande, par sa nature même, ce n'est pas une énorme et savante compilation de faits superficiellement classés, mais un substantiel et lumineux raccourci de ces faits. Notre parole est faite, avec l'apport personnel que nous y ajoutons, d'un immense matériel d'unités significatives que la langue nous apporte rangées selon certains principes de construction et d'ordonnance qui sont comme le moule et la forme abstraite de toutes nos phrases. C'est de cette forme abstraite que la syntaxe doit nous rendre compte "[1] (*ibid.*, p. 76).

Sechehaye's most recent book on syntax is his *Essai sur la structure logique de la phrase*, Paris, 1926, from which we have already quoted a number of passages that throw light upon his doctrine. The leading idea of the work is one that recurs with some frequence in his writings, namely, that the grammatical form of the sentence is often in conflict with the movement of our thought. It thus may even come about that two absolutely

---

[1] The author has given practical application to the ideas contained in this article in a book entitled *Abrégé de grammaire française sur un plan constructif*, Zürich, 1926, for the use of French teachers in the schools of the canton of Zürich.

identical propositions can express entirely different things. Intonation and the arrangement of the sentence components come into play and produce these apparently strange results. The author's constant preoccupation with the relationship between thought and expression, a characteristic of Bally as we have seen, as well as of himself, is here again made manifest. So that although the *Essai . . .* is in reality an analytical study of the sentence from the point of view of logic and grammar, Sechehaye does not confine himself to the purely formal aspects of his problem, but explores its psychological implications as well, endeavouring to discover to what representational processes the traditional grammatical categories of substantive, verb, complement, predicate, etc. correspond.[1] Similarly, the pedagogical leanings of the author are displayed in the protests which, like Brunot (see below), he makes against the rigid and superficial methods which prevail in the teaching of grammar in educational establishments of every grade.[2]

With Sechehaye, as with Saussure, the term ' grammar ' has a very wide signification indeed : " La grammaire est pour nous tout ce qui concerne l'organisation de la langue, sons, lexique, syntaxe " (*Essai . . .* , p. 4). To the study of the combinations of linguistic signs, or, to use the accepted terminology, of syntactical constructions, he gives the name of syntagmatic grammar, while that of the signs considered alone he calls associative grammar, which reminds us of F. de Saussure's distinction between syntagmatic and associative relations between words (cp. p. 286 f., above). The nature and aims of these two kinds of grammar are defined by Sechehaye as follows : " En effet, le signe arbitraire et autonome est celui qui est significatif uniquement en vertu des différences de sens et de forme que l'on peut constater entre lui et les autres signes autonomes de la langue. Or, ces

---

[1] Cp. : " . . . le fait grammatical a cependant une valeur psychologique : il a été créé et il existe pour fournir une forme à un élément de pensée, et c'est dans la parole vivante que ces normes grammaticales sont nées " (*op. cit.*, p. 5).

[2] Sechehaye himself recognizes that this practical trend in his scientific activity, which, as we have seen, he shares with Bally, is characteristic of the Geneva school : " En conclusion, on peut dire que la caractéristique de l'école genevoise de linguistique, c'est l'union intime de deux tendances en apparence contradictoires : celle qui considère la linguistique comme une science aux principes abstraits dont l'intelligence demande un effort considérable et une initiation particulière, et celle qui vise à mettre cette science au service des fins les plus pratiques, d'en favoriser les applications à l'école et dans la vie journalière, de manière à en faire un véritable instrument de culture " (*Indogermanische Forschungen*, XLIV [1926], p. 239–40). One may be permitted to see in this tendency something of the practical rationalism characteristic of the French spirit.

signes n'ayant aucun contact nécessaire entre eux dans la phrase, ces différences ne se constatent que par l'association des idées. La valeur de *deux*, par exemple, repose sur une sorte de comparaison implicite que nous faisons spontanément avec *un*, *trois*, *quatre* et les signes des autres idées étroitement associées à celle de *deux*. A cette grammaire associative vient s'en ajouter une autre, la grammaire syntagmatique. Celle-ci a pour objet tout ce qui par opposition à sémantème on appelle des morphèmes.[1] Ce ne sont pas tous les syntagmes (toutes les successions de signes), mais tous les signes qui n'existent que par et pour les syntagmes " (*op. cit.*, pp. 220–1). The relations between associative and syntagmatic grammar are close. " Le procédé associatif se suffit à lui-même, et rien ne l'empêche, en théorie, de fonctionner seul. Le procédé syntagmatique, qui est une complication ajoutée au premier, présuppose toujours l'existence du procédé associatif, sans lequel il n'a pas de base dans la réalité " (*ibid.*, p. 222).

Sechehaye's works do not appear to have received much attention from reviewers in philological journals. Of the reviews known to the author, Meillet's comments upon *Programme et Méthodes* . . . , in *Bull. Soc. Ling.*, XV (1907–8), p. xxiii f., are of special interest, coming as they do from a representative of the same trend of linguistic thought. Meillet holds that it is impossible to separate static and evolutionary linguistics to the extent advocated by Sechehaye. Language, being spoken, is continually evolving. " En effet, on n'observe jamais une langue à l'état fixe ; une linguistique statique ne peut donc résulter de l'observation " (*loc. cit.*, p. xxiv). He also finds fault with Sechehaye for, like all psychological linguists, tending to consider solely the psychology of

---

[1] On the model of ' phoneme ', a term used by some phoneticians and roughly equivalent to ' sound ', the terms ' semanteme ', for the word or part of a word which conveys meaning in the strict sense, and ' morpheme ' for something that merely expresses a grammatical relationship, e.g. a flexion, have been coined. Sechehaye uses the latter term to include not only flexions, prepositions, conjunctions, suffixes, and the copula, but also the position of the words in the sentence and all forms of construction. On the ' phoneme ' cp. Al. Rosetti, *Curs de fonetică generală*, Bucharest, 1930, pp. 80, 81 and 98, and *Sur la ' morphonologie* ', in *Bulletin linguistique*, Bucharest, I (1933), p. 9 f. The term has been made much use of by the Prague group of linguists, whose publications (*Travaux du Cercle linguistique de Prague*, 1929–) contain a vast amount of material and numerous and lengthy disquisitions on this and allied topics. Though the whole matter of the ' phoneme ' may still be considered as *sub judice*, the work of the Prague group has, at least, considerably enlivened phonetic (and morphological) discussion. Reference may be made to an important article by N. Trubetzkoy, *La phonologie actuelle*, in *Journal de psychologie*, 1933, p. 227 f., and E. Sapir, *La réalité psychologique des phonèmes*, *ibid.*, p. 247 f.

the individual, and forgetting that language is a collective phenomenon.[1] Meillet also discusses in the same journal, vol. XXVII (1926–7), fasc. 2, p. 1 f., the *Essai sur la structure logique de la phrase*, whose conclusions he accepts as entirely reasonable, and capable of serving as a basis for the logical analysis of the sentence in any language. Others who have reviewed this book are Jules Bloch, *Revue critique d'histoire et de littérature*, vol. XCIV (1927), p. 346 f. ; G. Ipsen, *Indogermanische Forschungen*, XLVI (1928), p. 260 ; Elise Richter, *Die neueren Sprachen*, XXXVII (1929), p. 261 f. ; and N. Drǎganu, *Dacoromania*, V (1927–8), p. 706 f.[2]

★ ★ ★

Before turning to the next leading member of the French school, F. Brunot, two other scholars, who like Sechehaye have worked chiefly in the field of French syntax, should be mentioned, both of whose methods have a certain kinship with those of the Geneva group. The first of them, L u c i e n F o u l e t, is perhaps best known as the author of an excellent *Petite syntaxe de l'ancien français*, Paris, 1919 ; 2nd ed., 1923 ; 3rd, 1930, which was very favourably received by the critics.[3] In this work, although the author is dealing with the language of a past age and consequently might be expected, according to custom, to treat his subject histori- cally, he has preferred to give us a d e s c r i p t i v e syntax of the type advocated by Saussure and his followers. He states : " Nous avons poussé très loin notre détachement à l'égard des secours que

---

[1] Meillet is so insistent upon the collective character of language that he goes so far as to say in the same article (p. xxiv) : " L'innovation spontanée semble bien être, dès son principe et non par imitation, un fait collectif ", a rather surprising affirmation in view of the present trend of linguistic theory.

[2] Sechehaye has himself given an appreciation of his work in the article already quoted, *L'école genevoise de linguistique générale*, *Indogermanische Forschungen*, XLIV (1926), p. 234 f. Both his own and Bally's methods are discussed further by S. Eringa, in an article entitled *La méthode statique de l'école genevoise*, in *Neophilologus*, XVI (1930–1), p. 58 f. and 136 f. According to K. Lewent, *Neuphilologische Monatsschrift*, II (1931), p. 249, note 2, Eringa disapproves of the exclusively static method.

[3] Reviewed by : K. Sneyders de Vogel, *Neophilologus*, V (1920–1), p. 274 f. ; O. Bloch, *Bull. Soc. Ling.*, XXII (1920–1), p. 74 f. ; J. Vendryes, *Revue celtique*, XXXVIII (1920–1), p. 354 f. ; A. Meillet, *Bull. Soc. Ling.*, XXV (1924–5), fasc. 2, p. 94 f. ; H. Yvon, *Rev. de phil. française*, XLIII (1931), no. 1 ; A. Lombard, *Studia neophilologica*, III (1930–1), p. 92 f. ; A. Meillet, *Bull. Soc. Ling.*, XXXI (1931), p. 146 f. ; A. Dauzat, *Rev. des langues romanes*, LXVI (1929–32), p. 210 f. (The last four reviews are of the third edition.)

pouvait nous apporter l'histoire de la langue." " Au lieu de voir dans le vieux français un idiome instable et provisoire dont la fonction propre est de relier deux langues complètes et définitives, le latin et le français moderne, on en vient ainsi à s'arrêter avec complaisance devant des phénomènes linguistiques dont les contemporains n'ont nullement soupçonné le caractère transitoire " (p. v, 2nd ed.). The point of view of static as against evolutionary linguistics could scarcely be put more aptly or with more subtle irony. On the other hand, the author has not hesitated to compare the facts of Old French, more strictly speaking of thirteenth-century Old French (as most of his examples are of that period), with those of modern French, not only for the purpose of explanation but also, apparently, to show that if we do compare two linguistic states of different periods it is at least as profitable and as safe to work back from the present to the past as from the past to the present. That Foulet has no real aversion for the historical method is clear also from his interesting articles on syntax published in *Romania*, for example : *La disparition du prétérit*, XLVI (1920), p. 271 f. (cp. p. 307, above) ; *Comment ont évolué les formes de l'interrogation, ibid.*, XLVII (1921), p. 243 f. ; and *Le développement des formes surcomposées, ibid.*, LI (1925), p. 203 f.[1]

The second is the Dutch scholar, C. de Boer, who, after at first specialising in the field of Old French, has in recent years concentrated mainly upon syntax, and whose approach to the subject is so definitely anti-historical that he may fittingly be associated with the Geneva group as a convinced and occasionally combative advocate of the synchronistic as against the diachronistic method. From among de Boer's syntactical studies we may mention : *Essais de syntaxe française moderne*, Paris-Groningen, 1923 ; *Essai sur la syntaxe moderne de la préposition en français et en italien*, Paris, 1926 ; *Etudes de syntaxe française*, in *Revue de linguistique romane*, III (1927), p. 283 f., and IV (1928), p. 290 f. ; *L'évolution des formes de l'interrogation en français*, in *Romania*, LII (1926), p. 307 f. ; and *Introduction à l'étude de la syntaxe du français*, Groningen–Paris, 1933. In the study on the forms of the interrogative sentence in French we

---

[1] The growth of the ' super-compound ' forms (e.g. *j'ai eu dit, j'avais eu fait*, etc.) is in close relationship with the disuse of the preterite, and with the use of the perfect with purely aorist value, which has called for the creation of new perfects of the type *j'ai eu fait*. A similar phenomenon is observable in Rumanian where the preterite is in similar disuse. The Moldavian dialect, which lost its preterite earlier than other areas, has a super-compound form, e.g. *m'am fost dus* (= ' I have been gone '), which is current, particularly in the specifically Moldavian areas of the north of the province, with merely ' perfect ' meaning.

find an interesting linguistic point, namely a linking up of the question of word order with that of word and sentence rhythm. De Boer holds that the placing of the predicate at the end of the interrogative sentence is psychological in origin, and due to the desire to set the most important ingredient of the sentence in the strongest position. A similar order is observable in other languages, but has not become 'grammaticalized' as in French, where it fits in admirably with the prevailing tendency manifest in word and sentence stress, namely an ascendant rhythm throwing into relief final syllables and final words. Finally, on the terminological side, mention may be made of De Boer's distinction, in *Essais de syntaxe française*, p. 12, between 'syntaxe vivante' and 'syntaxe figée ou locutionnelle', meaning by the latter the petrified type of syntax which is no longer capable of analysis and which we find in words or locutions like *s'en aller, pour le coup, Le Hâvre*, etc.[1]

★

We have seen that one of the principal preoccupations of both Bally and Sechehaye is the relationship between thought and

Ferdinand Brunot

expression. A similar interest is manifest in the work of Ferdinand Brunot, a member of the Institut de France, and Honorary Dean and an Honorary Professor of the Faculty of Letters in Paris University. His name is familiar to all Romance scholars as the author of a monumental *Histoire de la langue française des origines à 1900*, Paris,

---

[1] Cp. also *Introduction à l'étude de la syntaxe du français*, p. 89 f. Sechehaye, in *Programme et Méthodes* . . ., makes a similar distinction between 'syntaxe' and 'symbolique', and in *Essai sur la structure logique de la phrase*, between 'grammaire syntagmatique' and 'grammaire associative', although the terms do not entirely cover those used by de Boer. The latter's articles in the *Revue de linguistique romane* are in part controversial ; cp. S. Eringa, *ibid.*, V (1929), p. 274 f. ; and E. Lerch, *ibid.*, VI (1930), p. 124.

On syntax in general, see K. v. Ettmayer, *Zu den Grundlinien der Entwicklungsgeschichte der Syntax*, in *Germ.-roman. Monatsschrift*, XX (1932), p. 208 f. ; and *Syntax, Psychologie, Philosophie*, in *Zeitschr. f. franz. Spr. u. Lit.*, LVI (1932-3), p. 21 f. Von Ettmayer is also the author of a comprehensive work in two volumes entitled *Analytische Syntax der französischen Sprache*, Halle a.S., 1930 and 1936. Ettmayer's work has been criticized by M. Regula in *Archivum Romanicum*, XV (1931), p. 47 f., and in *Zeitschr. f. franz. Spr. u. Lit.*, LVII (1933-4), p. 10 f. ; cp. also N. Drăganu, *Dacoromania*, VII (1931-3), p. 289 f. On other recent work in French syntax see G. Gougenheim, *La Syntaxe française*, in *Le français moderne*, II (1934), p. 33 f.

1905, and succeeding years, which is still in process of publication.[1] Although, by the nature of his ' diachronistic' investigations he differs from the majority of the representatives of the French group, he is none the less of the school of Saussure and Meillet by his sociological outlook upon language. He has even gone so far as to say : " Il m'apparaît aujourd'hui clairement que les divers faits de la vie des langues, même ceux de leur vie intérieure, s'expliquent par la vie des peuples, des groupes sociaux, des individus. . . .",[2] and the influence of social factors upon the growth and development of French is a dominating theme throughout this great historical work.

But the work of Brunot's with which we are more immediately concerned here is his book entitled *La pensée et la langue.*[3] *Méthode, principes et plan d'une théorie nouvelle du langage appliquée au français,*

---

[1] The following volumes have so far appeared : Tome I, *De l'époque latine à la Renaissance ;* T. II, *Le seizième siècle ;* T. III, *La formation de la langue classique* (in two vols.) ; T. IV, *La langue classique* (two vols.) ; T. V, *Le français en France et hors de France au XVIIᵉ siècle ;* T. VI, *Le dix-huitième siècle, Première partie :* Le mouvement des idées et les vocabulaires techniques (two fascicules), *Deuxième partie :* La langue postclassique (two fascicules) ; T. VII, *La propagation du français en France jusqu'à la fin de l'Ancien Régime ;* T. VIII, *Le français hors de France au XVIIIᵉ siècle, Première partie :* Le français dans les divers pays d'Europe (one vol.), *Deuxième et troisième parties :* L'universalité en Europe. Le français hors d'Europe (one vol.) ; T. IX, *La Révolution et l'Empire, Première partie:* Le français, langue nationale (one vol.), *Deuxième partie :* Les événements, les institutions et la langue (in the press, one vol.). The tenth and eleventh tomes are still on the stocks and are to be entitled, one, *La langue classique dans la tourmente,* the other, *La perte de l'hégémonie en Europe.* The author studies the development of the language from its earliest stages onwards, taking into account all the various influences which have conditioned its growth. He thus is concerned, to use the Saussurian terminology (cp. p. 284 above), with both internal and external linguistics. For any work at all comparable in extent and value upon the history of the French language we have to turn to the famous *Grammaire historique de la langue française* by the late K. Nyrop of Copenhagen, which, however, save for the early part of vol. I, is confined to the internal history of French. Nyrop's grammar comprises six volumes, allotted one each to Phonology, Morphology, Word-formation and Semantics and two to Syntax, and published at intervals from 1899 to 1930 in Paris and Copenhagen. Mention should be made here of F. Brunot's *Précis de Grammaire historique de la langue française,* a work originally published in 1887, and many times reprinted, until finally it was entirely rewritten by F. Brunot and Ch. Bruneau (see above, p. 205 f.). A second edition of the book in its new form bears the date 1937.

[2] Quoted in a review of vol. VII of the *Histoire de la langue française* in *Revue belge de philologie et d'histoire,* VI (1927), p. 327. Brunot is equally categorical in the following passage from *La pensée et la langue,* of which we are about to speak : " Tout le monde est d'accord, je crois, pour considérer le langage comme un fait sociologique, qui se produit, se développe, s'altère, se perfectionne en fonction de la société à laquelle il appartient, qui en reflète la pensée collective, avec les nuances que peuvent y apporter, consciemment ou inconsciemment, les groupes et les individus " (*op. cit.,* p. xxi).

[3] Not to be confused with *Le langage et la pensée* by H. Delacroix, Paris, 1924, 2nd ed., 1930, which we have frequently had occasion to quote. Delacroix' book was reviewed very favourably from the linguistic point of view by A. Meillet, in *Bull. Soc. Ling.,* XXV (1924-5), fasc. 2, p. 4 f., and the second edition *ibid.,*

Paris, 1922, 3rd ed., 1936, because on the one hand we have here a work of static or synchronistic linguistics, and, on the other, the whole problem of the relationship between thought and expression in French is here treated in extenso. In his introduction to this voluminous work Brunot makes clear at the outset that it is neither a psychological treatise, although it contains numerous psychological analyses which, given the nature and purpose of the book, must of necessity be somewhat superficial, nor a grammar in the usual sense of the word, although it will talk of verbs, substantives, etc., and of the grammatical rules. " Ce que j'ai voulu, c'est présenter un exposé méthodique des faits de pensée, considérés et classés par rapport au langage, et des moyens d'expression qui leur correspondent " (p. viii, 1st ed.).

Brunot's book was born of the practical observation, made by others as well as himself, that in French schools of all grades the mother tongue was taught in a most deplorable fashion.[1] Not only was teaching hampered by an antiquated system of spelling, but grammar had not advanced beyond the elucubrations of eighteenth-century logicians. We are not to imagine, however, that the remedy is to be found in historical grammar, whose remarkable development still impresses many scholars. Historical grammar has not brought forth the fruits which were expected of it some thirty or forty years ago, chiefly because it has been concerned overmuch with explaining archaisms, and has neglected the language as it exists to-day. It is with this present-day language that real grammar has to deal. It is true, of course, that the speech of to-day is a natural outcome of the speech of earlier times, but it does not follow that because a word or a construction has a certain specified origin present-day speakers are conscious of the fact. *Te voilà* contains the imperative of the verb[2] *voir*, but who is

XXXII (1931), fasc. 3, pp. 1-2. Cp. also, L. Weber, *Rev. de Métaphysique*, 1926, p. 93 f., and (2nd ed.) O. Densusianu, *Grai şi suflet*, V (1931-2), p. 364 f.

Another work with a similar title is *Des Mots à la Pensée. Essai de Grammaire de la Langue Française*, by J. Damourette and Ed. Pichon. This work, published in Paris, already runs to five thick volumes (1911-36), and a sixth and last is to appear shortly. It is a richly documented descriptive grammar of present-day French, novel both in treatment and terminology, and has won general admiration by the remarkable linguistic acumen which it displays.

[1] We thus find in Brunot, as in Bally and Sechehaye, a practical concern for pedagogics, very natural to him in view of the leading part he has played in all questions of educational reform in France during the last thirty or forty years. Another point to be remembered also is that the book is based on lectures actually delivered by the author at the Ecole normale de Sèvres, and is therefore didactic in its origin.

[2] More accurately, perhaps, the indicative present.

there to-day who feels it as the equivalent, semantically, of *regarde-toi là*? Similarly, in *vive la France*, no one feels *France* as the subject of the verb *vive*, as historically it is. So let neither the logician nor the etymologist be our master.

There is a further difficulty. The grammars are continually talking of ' parts of speech ', of substantives, adjectives, verbs, etc., as if they were entirely distinct categories, whereas, in reality, we see them continually mingling and overlapping, a substantive, for example, acting as an adverb, an adjective taking the place of a substantive, etc. etc., so that linguists are not yet agreed upon how to define them. Again, the language as it appears in grammatical treatises is fundamentally different from what it is in reality. Grammar presents it to us as something ordered and consistent, whereas everywhere in real speech there is complete disorder, that is to say, all the complexity and variety of life. The reason for this difference is that grammar neglects a good two-thirds of the language as it really is. Under the heading ' degrees of comparison,' for example, in most cases, only the adjective is mentioned, regardless of the fact that adverbs and adverbial phrases are also compared, and even certain substantives as well. Or again, under the imperative, it is quite forgotten that *silence !*, *dehors !*, *tenir debout !* are words of command, although they are not verbs, or, if they are verbs, are not in the imperative form.

How then are we to proceed ? How can we fit language into grammar ? Life with all its rich variety, with all its complexity, into rules and regulations ? There is only one thing to be done, to take the idea as our guide : " Entre les formes les plus diverses de l'expression, entre les signes les plus disparates, il y a un lien, c'est l'idée commune que ces signes contribuent à exprimer " (p. xviii). Proceeding thus, *quelques hommes* will no longer figure in the chapter on the indefinite pronoun, *des hommes* under the article, *une poignée d'hommes* under the noun, *vingt hommes* under the numerals, but they will all be listed together as terms expressing with greater or less precision one idea, that of quantity. This method has the advantage not only of avoiding the errors mentioned above, but also of being more in accord with the nature of speech ; when we talk, the idea comes first, and expression afterwards ; so in grammar we must begin with the content and then pass to the form.

The author foresees possible objections to this mode of procedure and endeavours to meet them at the outset. It might be said, for example, that the method he proposes would tend to revive the ideological conception of language of former days. He replies that linguistics is to-day a well-established positive science and that there is now no risk of grammatical studies taking this wrong direction. His ideas are thus in close relationship with those of Bally, who in an article entitled *Stylistique et linguistique générale*[1] urges the same procedure, namely, that of starting from the idea in order to determine first the relation between it and the corresponding expression, and then to show by what process the ' fait de pensée ' has become a ' fait d'expression '. It is the method which he has applied in his *Traité de stylistique française*. Similarly, Brunot declares (p. xx) : " Il faut se résoudre à dresser des méthodes de langage, où les faits ne soient plus rangés d'après l'ordre des signes, mais d'après l'ordre des idées." As for the arrangement of the ideas, this will be done in conformity with the purpose we have in view, that of discovering by what means the language expresses them. We shall thus neither transform grammar into a branch of philosophy nor trespass upon the preserves of the psychologist whose task is to classify notions in and for themselves.

Again, it might be objected that his method, by definition, excludes all reference to phonetic phenomena, seeing that, according to many linguists, the sounds of a language are entirely independent of the mind. Brunot retorts that the old method also left them out of account, but adds that phonetic research has proved on the contrary that many of the changes undergone by sounds are psychological in their origin. Nor must it be forgotten, further, that sound-changes are often hindered by a variety of causes that are likewise of a psychological order, those arising, as it used to be said, from analogy, but which now, thanks to Gilliéron's work in linguistic geography, are seen to be extremely varied and complicated, although always due to the need for preciseness and clarity felt by the speaking individual.

After this theoretical exordium the author passes to his main theme, ideas and their expression in French. We shall not attempt to summarize the work, but confine ourselves to giving a list of chapter headings which will suffice to convey a general idea of its contents. First of all ' generalities ' : (1) exclamations ; words ;

---

[1] Published in *Archiv f. d. Stud. der neueren Spr. u. Lit.*, CXXVIII (1912), p. 87 f., and reproduced in *Le langage et la vie*, 2nd ed., p. 97 f.

relations between words ;[1] (2) 'indications' (notices, signs, advertisements, titles of works, etc.) ; (3) 'presentations' of people, things, ideas, actions (the use of such words as *voici, voilà*) ; (4) 'enunciations' ; ideas and phrases ; (5) other forms of the phrase (referring not to a person or a thing but to a situation, e.g. expressions of the type : *il pleut, il y a urgence*, etc.) ; (6) reduced phrases (*à quoi bon ?, à la porte !* etc.) ; (7) 'formes à reprises' (e.g. *en voilà des affaires* !) ; (8) complex phrases ; (9) from the phrase to the sentence ; (10) the grouping of phrases ; (11) meaning and form of the sentence ; (12) the formation of the sentence in French. Part I : Persons, things, ideas and their names : (1) proper names ; (2) common names ; borrowings ; (3) adaptation of existing words ; (4) formation of new words ; composition ; (5) derivation ; (6) noun equivalents (words and expressions which function as substantives, e.g. cette sacoche est *à moi, à toi, à lui ; quelque chose* de bleu ; *rien* n'était petit ; *tout* dans *un ;* son *peu* d'ancienneté ; *ce qui* tombe est perdu) ; all of these tend to become real substantives, as is seen by such expressions as *un petit rien, un petit quelque chose*, and some have actually become substantives, for example, le *moi* est toujours haïssable ; (7) the various categories of nouns classified according to their meaning ; (8) the name as a sign, etc. etc.

It is clear from the foregoing that, despite its title, *La pensée et la langue* is in reality simply a grammar constructed on a psychological basis, as distinct from grammars of the usual type which, starting as they do from the form and not from the idea, may be called logical or formal grammars. Nor is Brunot's method as novel as might appear at first sight. As is shown by A. Sechehaye in his article, *La méthode constructive en syntaxe*, mentioned above (p. 331), the monk Girard, nearly a century ago, applied the same method in his *Enseignement régulier de la langue maternelle* (1844), and his *Cours éducatif* (1845), after having used it in a more summary form in his *Grammaire des campagnes* as early as 1821.[2]

★

[1] The author's close kinship with the other members of the French school is apparent in the following remark taken from this section of his book : " Le langage doit être considéré tel qu'il est dans le cerveau du sujet parlant à l'époque où il parle, sous peine des pires erreurs d'analyse " (p. 6). That is to say : synchronistic or static linguistics, as recommended by Saussure, and religiously observed by Bally and Sechehaye in particular.

[2] For further details see p. 45 and p. 48 f. of the article, where we learn also that Brunot had already voiced his ideas in earlier works, without, however, succeeding in applying them consistently in practice.

Brunot's work called forth a great number of reviews and articles, of which the following are known either at first hand or indirectly to the author of the present book : Ch. Bally, *La pensée et la langue*, in *Bulletin de la Société de linguistique de Paris*, XXIII (1922), fasc. 3, p. 117 f. ; A. Counson, *Grammaire, histoire et géographie d'après la linguistique française*, in *Revue belge de philologie et d'histoire*, I (1922), p. 527 f. (this also discusses certain of Gilliéron's works) ; A. Meillet, *Bull. Soc. Ling.*, XXIII (1922), fasc. 2, p. 12 f. ; A. Wallensköld, *Neuphilologische Mitteilungen*, XXIII (1922), p. 153 f. ; N. Drăganu, *Dacoromania*, III (1923), p. 942 f. ; E. Huguết, *Une nouvelle théorie du langage*, in *Journal des savants*, 1923, p. 201 f. ; G. Millardet, *Linguistique et dialectologie romanes*, p. 457 f. ; L. Spitzer, *Literaturblatt f. germ. u. rom. Philologie*, XLIV (1923), col. 316 f. ; Leo Jordan, *Archivum Romanicum*, IX (1925), p. 335 f. ; E. Lorck, *Jahrbuch für Philologie*, I (1925), p. 25 f. ; K. Sneyders de Vogel, *Neophilologus*, X (1924–5), p. 59 f. In general, the reviewers praise the intentions of the author in endeavouring to direct the study of grammar into new paths—although his aims are far from being as revolutionary as some would have us think—but express a certain dissatisfaction with the results achieved. In fact, Brunot makes use of the old terminology and quite frequently is indistinguishable from his predecessors even in his manner of conceiving the nature of grammar. His system thus becomes of necessity a mixture of the old and the new, which Millardet, for example, considers to be extremely dangerous, inasmuch as it substitutes a state of chaos for that coherence which, despite its shortcomings, the formal method at least possessed. Others have found fault with the title of the book as being entirely out of keeping with its contents. A title like ' Thought and Language ', it is said, raises hopes in the reader which remain unfulfilled. Such a title would only be justified if the author discussed fundamental problems like the nature of language, or the relations between language in general and *a* language, etc.

We would dwell for a moment on the review of the book by Bally, which seems to us important, not only by its extent and its philosophical treatment of the whole problem, but also as a pronouncement from one who is of the same school of linguistic thought as Brunot himself, the latter, as we have seen, having taken as a foundation of his system certain principles drawn from the doctrine of Saussure. From Bally's account, it would appear that Brunot is not exactly enlightened upon the problems of general linguistics, in particular upon the relations between thought and speech, although this is ultimately the real subject of his book. The reviewer thus feels constrained to clear up certain fundamental points. " La langue ", he says, " est donc un système de signes virtuels destinés à être actualisés, dans chaque circonstance, pour l'expression d'une pensée donnée ; le fonctionnement de la langue consiste à transformer le virtuel en actuel ; tout un ensemble de signes sont affectés à cet usage " (*loc. cit.*, p. 118, note). Thus : " *roi* est un signe virtuel ; au contraire ' le roi (est mort) ', ' mon roi,' ' un roi ', ' les rois ', ' deux rois ', ' quelques rois ', ' aucun roi ', ' le roi (est le père de ses sujets) ' sont des exemples d'une notion virtuelle actualisée, devenue élément d'une pensée réelle, et représentant, dans le cas particulier, un individu (déterminé ou non), une somme d'individus, une partie (déterminée ou non) de cette somme, enfin un genre " (p. 118, note). In other words, *king* (with no adjunct) is an element of ' la langue ' which exists as a system potentially in the mind of every speaker ; *the king*, or *a king*, etc., are elements of ' la parole ', of actualized language. From the point of view of grammar, the lexical sign *king* becomes a component of a sentence, capable of fulfilling a specific function, when once it has become clear what king is meant. Psychologically, *king* expresses a vague and indeterminate notion, calling up no definite image of anything known ; *the king is dead*, or *our king*, etc., actualizes the potential sign and calls to the mind the representation of a specific individual.

Further on Bally provides us with other interesting definitions of linguistic notions. " En effet, la syntaxe, dans le sens strict, peut être définie ' l'étude des combinaisons entre termes actualisés ' ; toutes les combinaisons entre signes virtuels ne sont plus de la syntaxe pure et se rapprochent, à des degrés infiniment variables, du vocabulaire, c'est-à-dire de ce qui est donné, imposé " (p. 126). (Cp. *Le ciel est bleu* and *ciel bleu*.) " En principe, toujours au point de vue des idées à exprimer, il n'y a pas de cloison étanche entre le vocabulaire et la grammaire ; on peut même dire qu'une idée grammaticale, localisée dans des tours syntaxiques, ne s'identifie que par des mots ; cf. ' je suis malade de froid ' et ' le froid est la cause de ma maladie ' ;[1] d'autre part il n'y a qu'un passage insensible de la grammaire aux mots : cf. *cause, à cause de, parce que, de*, etc." (p. 126).

Bally is not impressed by Brunot's declarations with regard to

---

[1] That is to say, the purely grammatical link *de* in the first sentence expresses the same relationship as the substantive *cause* in the second.

historical grammar which we have summarized above, and his abjuration of etymology. He asserts, on the contrary, that Brunot's attitude at every step is that of the historian : " l'axiome, ' le passé explique le présent ', a la vie dure," he says. In investigations of this kind the historical view is quite out of place inasmuch as it entirely falsifies our understanding of grammatical relationships. Just as the speaking individual takes no thought of previous linguistic states, so the linguist who studies the language of that individual should forget his history and ignore the origin of the phenomena he is investigating. Otherwise he will perforce add something of his own which is absent from the mind of the speaking individual, and consequently from his language. The grammarian is neither called upon nor competent to explain anything but what the speaker himself understands. When the latter cannot himself by analysis account for the linguistic signs he uses it follows that they have become completely synthetized. " Le degré d'incompréhension des faits linguistiques par les sujets est un critère négatif, mais essentiel, de la délimitation,[1] et c'est ce qui pousse à l'aigu le conflit entre la statique et l'histoire ; la méthode historique a pour effet de mettre partout plus d'analyse que n'en comporte le fonctionnement de la langue "[2] (p. 130).

★　　★　　★

[1] By ' délimitation ' is meant : the extent to which the speaker is conscious of the individuality and independent value of the several linguistic signs he uses.

[2] We have seen that Bally, Sechehaye, and Brunot are alike in their desire to see a radical change in the methods of teaching their mother tongue. We are far from disparaging this pedagogic bias, as some have done. Not only have these three scholars a scientific equipment which makes their didactic works as important as any study in pure linguistics, but their realization of the supreme importance of instruction in the mother tongue is worthy of our unreserved approval. It is our mother tongue which contributes in a large measure to the formation of our thought. Serving as it does as our means of expressing what we think and feel, it has a profound influence upon our minds, not only by what it brings to them from the immense store of its literary monuments, but also by the trend it gives to our thoughts, imposing upon them its own peculiar forms and obliging us to cast the products of our intellect in a mould which differs greatly from one nation to another. (Cp. H. Delacroix, *Le langage et la pensée*, 2nd ed., p. 416 f.)

The problem raised by these French linguists has attracted attention elsewhere, particularly in Germany. An important name in this connection is that of Leo Weisgerber, author of *Muttersprache und Geistesbildung*, Göttingen, 1929 ; ' *Neuromantik* ' *in der Sprachwissenschaft*, Germ.-rom. Monatsschrift, XVIII (1930), p. 241 f. ; *Die Stellung der Sprache im Aufbau der Gesamtkultur*, Wörter und Sachen,

Grammont, a professor in the University of Montpellier, and, like Meillet, and at about the same period, a pupil of Saussure's, stands somewhat apart from the other members of **Maurice Grammont** the French school, both by the nature of his investigations and by certain special interests. In the first place, he attaches unusual importance to phonetics, which he has made his peculiar province, and, secondly, he is deeply interested in the aesthetic aspects of language. Saussure, we have seen, placed phonetics, quite rightly, be it said, among the sciences ancillary to linguistics, excluding it from linguistics proper. Similarly, he showed complete unconcern for what constitutes, or may constitute, the artistic side of human language. The attitude of the other members of the French group is similar ; like Saussure himself, they study sounds only when engaged in ' diachronistic ' investigations, while with regard to the aesthetic elements in language, even Bally, the founder of ' la stylistique ', takes no heed of them in his earlier work, claiming that they do not occur in familiar speech. Yet Grammont belongs none the less to the French school, both by his sociological attitude to language and by his preference for the synchronistic as opposed to the diachronistic method. We are therefore justified in considering him here.

We have said that Grammont has made phonetics his special province, but some qualification of this statement is necessary. We do not mean that he has devoted himself to the study of what we may call the physiology of sounds, the description of their multitudinous varieties, and the physical phenomena of articulation and modification of utterance, nor do we mean the historical study of their development through process of time within a given

XV (1933), p. 134 f. and XVI (1934), p. 97 f. Weisgerber, like the French linguists, also stands for the sociological conception of language. But whereas the latter concern themselves chiefly with the influence of man's social life and environment upon his language, Weisgerber studies the influence of language upon other fields of intellectual activity, and upon individual and collective psychology. *Muttersprache und Geistesbildung* was reviewed by H. Güntert in *Wörter und Sachen*, XII (1929), p. 405 f., to whose article in the same volume, p. 393 f., we have referred above on p. 107, note 2. Both Weisgerber and Güntert, like certain members of the French school, are interested in ' meaning ' rather than ' form '. Meillet, however, in a review of Weisgerber's *Wörter und Sachen* article mentioned above, condemns him for attempting, as he says, to resuscitate the doctrine of von Humboldt (*v. Bull. Soc. Ling.*, XXXIV [1933], pp. 6–7). For reviews of Weisgerber's work see also H. Ammann, *Indogermanische Forschungen*, XLIX (1931), p. 59 f. (on *Muttersprache* . . .), and *Zeitschr. f. deutsches Altertum und deutsche Literatur*, LXXI (1934), nos. 1–2, and H. Teuchert, *Teuthonista*, X (1934), nos. 1–2.

language or languages. Grammont's field is ' general phonetics ' ;[1] just as other scholars pursue the study of general linguistics, he endeavours by investigating certain phenomena, like dissimilation, metathesis, and assimilation, in a great variety of languages, to arrive at general conclusions concerning the nature, extent, and causes of these phenomena, which will hold good for human speech as a whole.

We have already had occasion to make acquaintance with some of his ideas when discussing the question of the sound-laws (v. Chap. I, p. 40 f.), where we explained his use of the terms ' phonetic laws ' and ' phonetic formulae '. We saw that by the former he meant general tendencies of sound-change which exist potentially in all languages inasmuch as they originate from man's physical and mental constitution, which is everywhere more or less the same, whereas the latter are the particular manifestations of these tendencies within a given language, in other words, are identical with what is usually understood by sound-laws. This distinction reminds us not only of Saussure's differentiation between ' la langue ' and ' la parole ', but also, and more particularly, of Schuchardt's conception of the fundamental or ' elementary ' relationship between all languages (cp. Chap. I, p. 56 f.). For further details upon this topic we refer the reader to the chapter quoted, and now turn to a closer examination of some of Grammont's works.

His earliest study is entitled *La dissimilation consonantique dans les langues indo-européennes et dans les langues romanes*, and was published in 1895 at Dijon.[2] Though it has long been out of print and was not accessible to the present author, it is possible to give a satisfactory account of Grammont's theories upon the phenomenon of dissimilation from his important article in *Revue des langues romanes*, L (1907), p. 273 f., entitled, *A propos des ouvrages de M. A. Thomas. Notes sur la dissimilation*,[3] where he replies to Thomas' criticisms and makes some interesting counter-strictures upon Thomas'

---

[1] Not in the sense understood by Al. Rosetti, in *Curs de fonetică generală*, Bucharest, 1930, who uses the term as roughly equivalent to the physiology of sounds ; cp. by the same author, *Fonetică istorică, fonetică generală şi fonetică experimentală* in *Minerva* (Iaşi), II (1928), no. 1, p. 27 f.

[2] Reviewed by, *inter alios*, G. Paris, *Journal des savants*, February, 1898, and criticized on various occasions by A. Thomas in *Essais de philologie française*, Paris, 1897, *Mélanges d'étymologie française*, Paris, 1902 (2nd ed., 1927), and *Nouveaux essais de philologie française*, Paris, 1904. On assimilation and dissimilation, cp. Delacroix, *op. cit.*, pp. 165–6 ; cp. also A. Philippide, *Principii de istoria limbii*, p. 31 f., and Al. Rosetti, *Curs de fonetică generală*, p. 82 f.

[3] See now Grammont, *Traité de phonétique*, Paris, 1933, p. 269 f.

excessively neo-grammarian outlook. Dissimilation, to Grammont, is a 'phonetic law' (i.e. a general tendency of language, see above), quite distinctive in character, primarily because its causes are both physiological and psychological. "La dissimilation est régie par une loi unique : la loi du plus fort " (*La dissimilation*, p. 186). "Des deux phonèmes en jeu c'est le plus fort qui dissimile le plus faible " (*loc. cit.*, p. 296). "La dissimilation peut être normale ou renversée. Elle est normale quand aucune cause spéciale n'intervient pour fortifier le phonème qui est par sa position le plus faible ou pour affaiblir le plus fort " (*ibid.*, p. 296). In all, Grammont identifies twenty types of dissimilation, which he calls twenty 'laws', and which he groups and classifies according to the different conditions in which the phonetic change comes about. Thus, the first group, for instance, comprises those cases where the dissimilating phoneme owes its strength to the purely mechanical fact that it is under the stress. The following are some of the 'phonetic formulae' covered by this 'law' : (1) a stressed 'implosive' (i.e. the final consonant of a syllable) dissimilates an unstressed implosive, e.g. *golpil*>*gorpil*, *balbel*>*babel* ; (2) a stressed 'combined' consonant (i.e. one of a group in the same syllable) dissimilates an unstressed combined consonant e.g. Old Fr. *trastre*>*traste*, *flamble*>*flambe*. In another series the strength of the dissimilating consonant is due to its position in the syllable, again a purely mechanical phenomenon. 'Formulae' embodying this 'law' are : a supported consonant (i.e. one preceded by another belonging to the same syllable) dissimilates a consonant that stands between vowels, e.g. **courindrou*>Prov. *coulindrou*, 'gooseberry', or, again : when two consonants are separated by an occlusive the first is dissimilated, e.g. *partret*[1]>*paltret*, *portrait*>*poltrait*, etc. A third category is composed of cases in which the active phoneme is more powerful because of its position in the word ; here, it is claimed, psychological factors come into play. One 'formula' in this group runs as follows : of two intervocalic consonants the first is always dissimilated, e.g. Lombard *leveriçi* for Ital. *riverisco* (the first *r* being intervocalic when it is preceded by the pronoun subject), or *La Gaulteralière*> *La Gaultenallière*, *melancolie*>Old French *merancolie*, etc. etc.

All the formulae of normal dissimilation can be reversed, as we have seen, if some physical or psychological phenomenon inter-

---

[1] For *parteret*, ' pavier's hammer ' in the French of Blois.

venes to weaken the stronger phoneme or strengthen the weaker. In reality there is only one purely physical or mechanical disturbance of this kind, namely : a phoneme which is normally before a pause is pronounced weakly ; thus, *Brieure* becomes *Brieulle*, being a proper noun and generally pronounced in such groups as : *je suis de Brieure, je vais à Brieure*, or *j'habite Brieure*, etc., i.e. generally in final position, before a pause. The psychological causes of this inversion are two in number : (1) a ' normal ' dissimilation might have produced an unfamiliar sound sequence, e.g. Lat. *cerebrum* gives Ital. *celebro* because the group *bl* has disappeared from Italian, having given way centuries ago to *bi*, and thus **cereblo* is impossible ; similarly Tuscan *veladro* for Latin *veratrum* avoids the inacceptable groups *tl* or *dl* ; (2) a sound may escape dissimilation when it is known or felt to have some morphological value, or when it serves to link a word up with other words of the same family, e.g. *presseur* becomes *presseul* because the *r* of the initial group is fortified by the *r* of *presse, presser*, etc.

Another phonetic change which Grammont attributes to a general tendency of human speech is that of Assimilation, a phenomenon which in its results is exactly the reverse of dissimilation. Here again it is a case of the sound which has the greater strength, resistance, or stability, or which enjoys the greater favour, influencing a weaker sound. In other words, ' la loi du plus fort ', holds good for assimilation as for dissimilation. Grammont treated this phenomenon in a study entitled, *Notes de phonétique générale. VIII : L'assimilation*,[1] published in *Bulletin de la Société de linguistique de Paris*, XXIV (1923–24), fasc. 1, p. 1 f. He first of all defines assimilation as follows : " L'assimilation consiste dans l'extension d'un ou de plusieurs mouvements articulatoires au delà de leur domaine originaire. Ces mouvements articulatoires sont propres au phonème agissant ; le phonème agi, en se les appropriant aussi, devient plus semblable à l'autre, d'où le nom d'assimilation. Pour les raisons qui ont été données dans les *Mémoires Soc. Ling.*, t. XIX, p. 258,[2] ce nom sera réservé aux cas où les deux phonèmes en cause sont en contact l'un avec l'autre " (p. 1). The common

---

[1] The article formed the eighth of a series, earlier numbers of which appeared in the *Mémoires de la Société de linguistique de Paris*, vol. XIX (1914–16), p. 245 f., and XX (1916–18), p. 213 f., and treated of various phonetic phenomena occurring in the Eastern Indo-European languages. For Grammont's more recent discussion of Assimilation, see *Traité de phonétique*, p. 185 f.

[2] *v.* preceding note.

distinction between progressive, regressive, and reciprocal assimilation, he holds to be without importance. What we have to keep
continually in mind is merely the nature of the phenomenon as
set forth above. In each case the phonetician has to explain for
what reason such and such a sound is the stronger, and to retrace
the process of change, explaining if needs be, in particular instances,
why the ' law ' has failed to operate.

After these general remarks the author proceeds to group his
examples and to determine the conditions which govern the
phenomenon. The two sounds concerned may be either (a) two
consonants, (b) a consonant and a vowel, or (c) two vowels. With
regard to (a) the following ' formulae ' can be established : (1)
when both consonants are occlusives : theoretically, they are of
equal force, but in fact their position in the word is the decisive
factor, and in particular the occlusive supported by another sound
dominates the other; (2) occlusive and fricative ([s, z, ʃ, ʒ], etc.):
the latter very frequently wins, as having intrinsically the greater
resistance ; (3) occlusive and nasal or liquid : either of the latter
is stronger than the occlusive ; (4) occlusive and a consonantized
i or u : the occlusive frequently becomes affricated (ti becomes ts,
ci [tʃ], etc.); (5) neither consonant is a pure occlusive. Similarly,
under (b) there may also be a great variety of cases : (1) consonant
between two vowels : the vowels always predominate (intervocalic t changes to d, d to [ð], etc.);[1] (2) consonant group between
vowels : as for (1), save that there is occasionally some discrepancy
as the conditions are not entirely identical ; (3) a consonant
group belonging to different syllables, preceded and followed by
a vowel : here the first consonant is weak, the second strong ;
(4) l between a consonant and a vowel : it becomes a consonantal i,
e.g. Ital. chiave from Lat. clavem ; (5) assimilation of consonant to
vowel by shifting of point of articulation, e.g. c becoming ts or
[tʃ] before e or i; (6) assimilation of vowel to consonant, e.g.
Ital domandare from demandare. Under (c) we find two cases :

---

[1] This particular ' formula ' is of special importance for the Romance languages,
where t has become d, c changed to g, p to b, d to [ ], g to [ ], etc., in other words,
where voiceless plosives have become voiced, and voiced plosives have become
fricatives, frequently to disappear entirely. This last stage is well represented in
French where nothing remains of intervocalic t or d, and little of c or g, and where
p and b in the same position have been reduced to v. An earlier stage of development is to be found in Spanish, where the Latin intervocalic plosives appear as
voiced fricatives, and a still earlier stage in Provençal where the voiceless plosives
are voiced. In all these cases we have an assimilation of the consonant to the
vowel environment. Cp. Traité de phonétique, p. 162 f.

(1) monophthongisation : a diphthong[1] may be reduced to a single vowel, e.g. Lat. *au* to Romance *o*, Old Rumanian *ea* to Rum. *e*, etc. ; (2) contraction : two separate vowels coalesce into one, e.g. Old Fr. *traître* (three syllables) becomes *traître* (pron. *trètre*) through the intermediate phases **traetre* (*i* assimilated to the fuller sound *a*) and **treetre* (*a* assimilated to the stressed *e*).

Grammont has treated in similar fashion other 'phonetic laws', for example Metathesis, concerning which he has published the following studies : *La métathèse dans le parler de Bagnères de Luchon*, in *Mémoires de la Soc. de linguistique*, XIII (1903–5), p. 73 f. ; *La métathèse en arménien*, in *Mélanges linguistiques offerts à M. Ferdinand de Saussure*, Paris, 1908, p. 231 f. ; *Une loi phonétique générale*, in *Philologie et linguistique. Mélanges offerts à Louis Havet*, Paris, 1909, p. 179 f. ; *Sur la métathèse*, in *Miscelánea filológica dedicada a Don Antonio Ma. Alcover con motivo de la publicación del Diccionari català-valencià-balear*, Palma de Mallorca, 1932 ; and finally, *Traité de phonétique*, p. 339 f. We shall not dwell further upon these as the reader is now sufficiently informed upon Grammont's method of approach to questions of phonology. It should also be abundantly clear that the statement that Grammont has pursued the study of 'general phonetics' in a manner comparable to Schuchardt's or Saussure's study of 'general linguistics' is fully justified. He may even be considered as the founder of this exacting discipline which he has practised for some forty years with complete mastery. For work of this kind he had the necessary wide and varied equipment : a knowledge of both descriptive and experimental phonetics, a familiarity with a great number of languages and dialects,[2] both related and unrelated, particularly with regard to their sounds both present and past, and further the trained skill of the observer who can detect the characteristic features of linguistic phenomena and classify them accordingly.

Among Grammont's other writings upon phonetics we would

[1] Grammont's definition of a diphthong may be quoted : " Une diphtongue est une voyelle unique, généralement longue (il en est de brèves), qui change de timbre au cours de son émission, c'est-à-dire qu'à un certain point de sa durée, d'ordinaire vers la fin du deuxième tiers, les organes et en particulier la langue se déplacent et prennent une autre position articulatoire " (*loc. cit.*, p. 101). Cp. also, *Traité de phonétique*, 109–10, 223, and Al. Rosetti, *Remarques sur les diphtongues*, in *Bulletin linguistique* (Bucharest), II (1934), p. 21 f.

[2] Grammont has also published work upon dialects, which he has investigated on the spot ; cp., for example, *Le patois de la Franche-Montagne et en particulier de Damprichard (Franche-Comté)*, Paris, 1901, a reprint of various articles published in the *Mémoires de la Soc. de linguistique* from 1889 to 1900.

mention, in addition to his recent comprehensive survey of the whole field in *Traité de phonétique*, Paris, 1933,[1] his *Traité pratique de prononciation française*, Paris, 1914 (6th ed., 1928), and a study, *La psychologie et la phonétique*, Paris, 1930,[2] first published in *Journal de psychologie normale et pathologique*, XXVI (1929), p. 5 f., and XXVII (1930), pp. 31 f. and 544 f. The former of these, despite its entirely practical purpose of serving as an aid to foreigners and provincials desirous of acquiring a standard French pronunciation, is none the less of considerable scientific interest, and displays particularly a very penetrating knowledge on the part of the author of the errors peculiar to this or that type of foreigner in his pronunciation of French, as well as an awareness to minutiae of French pronunciation of which the educated native speaker himself is far from being always conscious. As for the second study, its main theme is that psychological factors come into play very frequently, in fact nearly always, but generally unconsciously, in combinative (but not in isolative), sound-change, and that among these factors are to be reckoned negligence and lack of attention, either intellectual or physiological.

We now turn to Grammont's investigations of the aesthetic side of language which distinguish him from so many of his compatriots, who, in conformity with the rationalistic French tradition, are prone to see in language nothing but a means of intellectual exchange between men. We must not imagine, however, that Grammont will align himself with Croce and Vossler and, like them, identify linguistics with aesthetics. He does no more than recognize that human speech has its artistic side which we are not entitled to neglect. His attitude is made plain to us, for example, in his review of Vendryes' *Le langage*, in *Revue des langues romanes*, LXI (1921-2), p. 369 f. Grammont here takes Vendryes to task for not only neglecting in practice all reference to the aesthetic element in language, but for actually denying its existence by maintaining that human speech has fully attained its aims, when those who make use of it succeed in understanding each other

---

[1] For reviews, see P. Fouché, *Revue des langues romanes*, LXVI (1929-32), p. 476 f. ; I. Iordan, *Buletinul Institutului de Filologie Romînă*, I (1934), p. 182 f. ; G. S. Colin, *Hespéris*, XVI (1933), p. 162 f. ; A. Meillet, *Bull. Soc. Ling.*, XXXIV (1933), fasc. 3, p. 2 f. ; E. W. Selmer, *Teuthonista*, IX (1933), p. 160 f. (under the title, *Phonologie und Phonetik*) ; O. Densusianu, *Grai și suflet*, VI (1933-4), p. 350 f.

[2] Reviewed by : A. Meillet, *Bull. Soc. Ling.*, XXXI (1931), fasc. 3, pp. 3-4 ; P. Fouché, *Rev. des langues romanes*, LXVI (1929-32), p. 233 f. ; A. Dauzat, *Rev. de philologie française*, XLIII (1931), p. 225 f.

without difficulty, and that when this is attained there is no choosing between one language and another.[1] Grammont refuses to accept this contention. His own attitude would appear to be similar to that of Schuchardt, who takes up a position half-way between Saussure and Vossler, when he declares : " Aus der Not entstanden, gipfelt die Sprache in der Kunst."

It should be made clear, however, that the artistic element in language as conceived by Grammont is confined to purely phonetic factors ; the harmony and expressiveness of a language, and its beauty, are in its sounds and rhythms. His aesthetic is consequently purely auditive. It is well known that various sounds awaken within us certain images, that they possess, in other words, psychological values, and can consequently convey certain well-defined psychical conditions.[2] With this and similar considerations as his starting-point, and backed up by his own phonetic investigations, Grammont set out to write his voluminous work upon French versification, which represented quite a new departure in this branch of study, *Le vers français. Ses moyens d'expression. Son harmonie*, Paris, 1904 (2nd, 3rd, and 4th eds., 1913, 1923, 1937).[3] His aims are set forth in the introduction to the work. After distinguishing between a line that is merely correct and a good line of poetry, he continues : " La correction c'est dans la forme du vers la partie

---

[1] Grammont's general linguistic standpoint is well illustrated by a further criticism. Vendryes, like Saussure, refuses to admit that there is any connection between the development of a language and the mentality of the people who speak it. Grammont opposes this view, reminding the author that a society creates progressively the type of language most suited to its peculiar spirit and way of life. He quotes the case of English and German. Although identical in origin, the former has become a commonplace idiom, ' plate et terre à terre ', while the latter is a language with a rich vocabulary, but lacking the finer shades, and full of useless complications. How else, he asks, are we to explain this phenomenon than by the mentality of the respective peoples !

[2] Cp. above, p. 55 f. Grammont himself has treated similar questions in his study, *Onomatopées et mots expressifs, Revue des langues romanes*, XLIV (1901), p. 97 f., where he shows that the domains of these two classes of words are much more extensive than is usually supposed and frequently overlap, some words being onomatopœic or merely expressive according to the intention of the speaker. On onomatopœia reference may be made to : S. Pușcariu, *Despre onomatopeie în limba romînă, Dacoromania*, I (1920-1), p. 75 f. ; F. Rauhut, *Probleme der onomatopöie, Volkstum und Kultur der Romanen*, I (1928), p. 113 f. ; K. Bühler, *L'Onomatopée et la fonction représentative du langage*, in *Psychologie du langage* (= *Journal de psychologie*, 1933), p. 101 f. ; A. Debrunner, *Indogerm. Forschungen*, LI (1933), p. 229 f. ; W. Oehl, *Das Lallwort in der Sprachschöpfung*, Freiburg (Switzerland), 1933 ; J. Marouzeau, *L'usure des onomatopées*, in *Le français moderne*, III (1935), p. 289 f.

[3] Published in the ' Collection linguistique' of the Société de Linguistique de Paris, a tribute to its strictly scientific character, which distinguishes it from many similar undertakings, and which, allied with the author's gifts of understanding and feeling, gives weight and reliability to his judgments.

23

mécanique, tandis que l'harmonie et l'expression représentent la partie artistique. C'est cette seconde partie que nous nous proposons d'étudier ici. Quels sont les moyens d'expression dont dispose la poésie française, quelle est la valeur sémantique des différents rythmes et celle des différents sons, telles sont les premières questions auxquelles nous essaierons de répondre. Puis passant à un autre ordre d'idées, nous rechercherons ce qui fait qu'un vers donné est ou n'est pas harmonieux, quels que puissent être d'ailleurs ses défauts ou ses qualités à d'autres points de vue " (p. 2). Further down (pp. 2–3) he tells us what his book is not : " Ce livre n'est donc pas un traité de versification française, quoiqu'on y trouve à l'occasion des préceptes ou, comme on dit couramment, des règles de facture. Ce n'est pas non plus une histoire du vers français et de son développement, bien qu'à différents endroits certaines phases de son évolution y soient exposées ou au moins indiquées." A characteristic feature of the work is that in order not to influence himself or his readers, the author has no recourse to actual verse in his theoretical discussion of the means of expression available for French poetry ; although an attractive example here and there might have been very persuasive, he resists the temptation and only uses verse to illustrate or substantiate his theory.

These means of expression are, according to Grammont, rhythm and sounds, the latter including not only consonants and vowels, but also hiatus and rime. Each of these he analyses minutely and precisely, enquiring in what exactly expressiveness consists, what sounds are more expressive than others, and why, etc. He then turns to the question of harmony in French verse, what it signifies, and how it may be secured. The results of his enquiry are widely different from those of his predecessors[1] in the field. It had been thought, for example, that rhythm was entirely a matter of intensity or stress, an alternation of strong and weak beats. Grammont proves that in the production of rhythm, stress, length, and pitch play equally important parts. Frequently, indeed, one of these qualities of sounds can take the place of another, by compensation. Stress, for instance, may be absent, and the rhythmic accents be provided by length or pitch. But though the nature of the rhythmic elements may vary, as we have seen, rhythm or measure, the basis of all

[1] Among these, one of the most noteworthy was Adolf Tobler, Morf's predecessor in the chair of Romance Philology in Berlin, whose *Vom französischen Versbau alter und neuer Zeit*, Leipzig, 1880, saw its sixth edition in 1921.

verse—for there can be no verse without symmetry, and symmetry is rhythm—remains unimpaired ; it continues to exist, although as we listen to the verse, we are unaware that the measure is now musical, now changed to stress, and so on.

Grammont, having based his investigations upon an enormous stock of examples, drawn from a great number of authors, feels constrained, again with a view to correcting certain deep-rooted opinions, to draw up a classification of some of the greatest French poets from the point of view of the harmony of their verse. Without dwelling upon the details of his analysis, we may quote, as a mere matter of interest, his order of merit : Racine, Hugo, Musset, Leconte de Lisle, Boileau, Lamartine (*op. cit.*, 3rd ed., p. 436).[1]

★ ★ ★

We announced at the beginning of this chapter that we would discuss the topic of slang or argot, or, more exactly, give some account of work published upon the subject.

Slang and Slang Studies Despite the great variety of views concerning the nature and significance of slang, all linguists are agreed in defining it as a special type of language, peculiar to a single and well-defined social group. We are therefore justified in discussing it in a chapter devoted to the French school, whose basic doctrine is that language is a social fact, existing in and through society, and continually modified and conditioned by the manner of life of the community. For argot is born and endures for similar reasons ; if smaller groups, with special interests and consequently a special mental attitude, did not come into being within the greater community argot would be inconceivable. Again, the synchronistic method favoured by the French school is, in the nature of things, particularly applicable, and indeed has generally been applied to the study of slangs. Finally, it so happens that the great majority of the works upon slang are either from French pens or relate to the argots of France, and that the pioneers

---

[1] The second edition of Grammont's book was reviewed in great detail by J. Acher, in *Revue des langues romanes*, LVII (1914), p. 374 f. Among reviews of the third edition we mention A. Meillet, *Bull. Soc. Ling.*, XXV (1924-5), fasc. 2, p. 104 f., and J. Ronjat, *Rev. des lang. rom.*, LXIII (1925), p. 144 f. Meillet declares (*loc. cit.*, p. 107) : " M. Grammont est le seul linguiste qui étudie à fond, et avec des principes assurés, l'emploi esthétique de la langue ".

in this field of linguistic enquiry were scholars who were in close relationship with the French group we have been here discussing.

The subject of slang has attracted a great deal of attention in recent years,[1] but to a non-specialist in the field the situation is still somewhat obscure. We shall therefore express no personal views but endeavour to satisfy the needs of students by drawing enlightenment from others more qualified to speak. But first let us enquire what is understood by ' argot ' or ' slang '. Both the French and the English term are used in a variety of ways : (1) to denote the special language of the criminal and vagrant class, of the underworld ; (2) to denote what is also and perhaps more fittingly called ' jargon ', namely, the peculiar speech of certain well-defined social groups, like soldiers, artisans, students, artists, schoolboys, etc. ; (3) to describe the more vulgar elements which find currency in familiar speech but which offend the more fastidious speaker. The French term, argot, is more widely used in the first sense, which is indeed its original meaning.

W. von Wartburg, in an article entitled *Vom Ursprung und Wesen des Argot*[2] (*Germanisch-romanische Monatsschrift*, XVIII [1930], p. 376 f.) gives us what may be called a summary of the present state of our knowledge with regard to the whole problem, and on this we propose to draw freely in the following pages. What is known in French as ' l'argot des malfaiteurs ' is a product of ' le milieu ', a term which is defined as " l'ensemble des individus qui n'exercent aucun métier avouable, vivent des subsides des filles soumises et des produits de vol de toutes catégories." It is in no sense a conventional, artificially constructed language,[3] nor

---

[1] A contribution to the bibliography of the subject will be found at the end of the present section, p. 374 f.

[2] Reviewed by Mario Roques, *Romania*, LVII (1931), pp. 287-8.

[3] Max Kuttner, *Von der Geltung des Argot, Festschrift für Eduard Wechssler*, p. 346 f., goes further and maintains that argot is a ' Natursprache ', as distinct from the language of literature, which is more or less an artificial product. Argot is thus much the same thing as popular speech, in the strict sense of the word. This view is opposed by Spitzer (see bibliography, p. 374), who, quoting assertions by French writers in support, alleges argot to be what he calls a ' Ziersprache ', ' display ' speech, with a definite purpose behind it ; the argot-speaker feels that he is not like other men, and his speech is at once a proof and a result of this feeling. Just as we all experience from time to time a need to escape, if but for a moment, from the common round of existence, so the speaker of argot finds satisfaction in replacing the everyday form of speech by another, which gives him, maybe for only a brief instant, that illusion of change which is so necessary to the human spirit. Thus it is that argot does not ' take on ' with everybody ; on the lips of children, of over-serious folk, and particularly of foreigners, it appears unnatural, because their peculiar position does not qualify them to adopt, with regard to the legalized norms of the common tongue, that attitude of independence

comparable with the attempts at a universal language, like Esperanto, but it has the following two essential characteristic features : (*a*) It belongs to a certain social category, comparatively circumscribed, which makes use of the common language as well as of argot, and (*b*) it is capable of being used in order to avoid being understood by the uninitiated (but this, it should be added, though the most important, is not the only purpose served by argot proper).[1]

But other social groups beside the criminal and vagrant classes, for example the various trades and professions, have their own special language. Here, in the majority of cases, it is merely a matter of special terms and expressions relating to a particular field of activity, and the desire to be understood only by the fraternity is generally absent. Not always, however : sometimes the technical vocabulary is used protectively, as when, for example, in a case of serious illness, two doctors may resort to medical terminology in order not to be understood by the patient. Typical of such ' special languages ' are : soldiers' slang, which, in countries where military service is compulsory and lasts over a

---

which such speech implies. Spitzer is thinking primarily of those who speak argot but do not belong to the social category mentioned above. His remarks apply, however, to a considerable degree also to those who are the originators or repositories of argot. They, too, are posing when they speak argot before others, but it is a pose that in their case is ' becoming '.

[1] This is the view now held by most linguists, whereas previously the desire for concealment was considered to be the sole source of argot. Hence, no doubt, the deeply-rooted belief that it was an artificial language, in the strict sense, a form of speech deliberately invented, a belief fostered by early works of a popular kind such as : " Pechon de ruby " (slang for ' enfant éveillé '), *La vie genereuse des Mercelots, Gueuz et Boesmiens* . . . , 1596, and [Olivier Chéreau], *Le Jargon ou Langage de l'Argot reformé* . . . , 1628. We append some judicious remarks from another source to supplement those set forth above. Marcel Cohen, *Note sur l'argot*, in *Bull. Soc. Ling.*, XXI (1918–19), p. 132 f., states, *inter alia :* " De tout ce qui précède il résulte que la notion : argot=instrument de défense du groupe, est une mauvaise explication finaliste. Nous y opposerons l'observation positive : l'argot est, comme est le compartimentage social " (*loc. cit.*, p. 140). " C'est que la société était autrefois plus compartimentée que maintenant : la caste faisait des hors-castes. Il suffit de rappeler que les comédiens étaient excommuniés en France, le catholicisme était religion d'Etat. Les ouvriers avaient, en face des castes privilégiées, leurs associations secrètes de compagnonnage. Sociétés secrètes, et rivales sans cause. N'était-il pas naturel que des compagnons du tour de France qui, ayant même profession et mêmes intérêts, engageaient un duel au bâton avec tout camarade rencontré qui n'était pas de la même secte compagnonne —ce qui est bien agir au rebours de l'utilité—aient aussi parlé entre eux sans utilité, des jargons spéciaux ?—Les argots de métiers ambulants qu'a réunis M. Dauzat [see below] sont sans doute liés à des compagnonnages restreints. Argots de petits gens (*sic*) ' en route ', il n'est pas étonnant qu'ils aient de multiples contacts avec les anciens argots des ' gens de la route ', mendiants, vagabonds et voleurs de grand chemin " (*ibid.*, pp. 140–1). After this sociological explanation of all types of slang, in the strict sense of the term, Cohen goes on to show how, with the breaking down of castes, the slang material naturally spread, as we shall see later, into current colloquial French.

long period, penetrates freely into current colloquial speech, and school and university slangs, which are less developed, particularly the latter, in France than in Germany, where students led, and still lead, a life more distinctive than that of the remainder of the population. The most appropriate term for these ' special languages ' is ' jargon ' ; ' argot ' is best reserved for the language of those various categories we may designate comprehensively as the under-world.[1]

★

Having thus described the, so to speak, outward characteristics of slang, let us now turn to its more purely linguistic features, confining our considerations as hitherto to French. From the point of view of sounds, morphology, and syntax, ' argot ' is in no wise different from the common tongue ; it too is French. Its distinctive quality lies in its vocabulary, in the special words it uses and the special meanings it gives to current words. In this, argot is distinguished from dialect, which, compared with standard speech, has not only its peculiarities of vocabulary, but also of sounds and grammar. Moreover, dialect can be, and constantly is, used exclusively by some speakers, whereas argot is confined to conversation between members of the same fraternity ; outside this restricted circle a wider medium of intercourse, either standard speech or, in some cases, a provincial dialect, will perforce be employed.

Most, though not all, slang expressions are of ' affective ' origin. The words of normal speech are replaced by others felt to be more adequate, more expressive ; and in circles where affective tendencies have full play, where a sense of responsibility is lacking, either through youth or delinquency, as, shall we say, among schoolboys or gangsters, there is a strong temptation to play fast and loose with the accepted linguistic norms. But this need for expressiveness is never fully satisfied ; there is an unceasing search for livelier forms, and consequently a continuous process of renewal, which is one of the characteristic features of slang. The most forceful

---

[1] As proposed by Spitzer, p. 207, note 2, of the article listed below, p. 374, following the practice of K. v. Ettmayer in *Über das Wesen der Dialektbildung* (cp. Chap. III, above, p. 239 f.).

expression grows weak with time, and very quickly indeed in the case of slang, and a fresh one takes its place, to weaken in its turn. The words that have lost their vigour are discarded or may survive in the common speech, particularly in its more popular forms. We may thus have, for certain notions, an extraordinary wealth of terms of slang origin, of greater or less vitality ; for example, von Wartburg has counted forty-one words, in French, for ' head ', thirty-six for ' to go away ', and eighty-one for ' foolish ' : a veritable lexical plethora,[1] as Gilliéron might have said. The commonest means of enriching the slang vocabulary is by what has been called synonymic derivation, a process first pointed out by Schwob and Guieysse (see below, p. 363). It may be described as follows : when a word has taken on some special metaphorical meaning, any synonym of the word, and many expressions that are merely allied to it, or commonly associated with it, can, in time, take on the same figurative meaning. For example, polir means ' to steal ', and, although etymologically a different word from polir, ' to polish ', it was felt to be the same ; as a consequence, verbs more or less synonymous with polir in the second sense, like fourbir, nettoyer, etc., also come to mean ' to steal '. Or again, for some reason or other, poire came to be used for ' head ' ; forthwith other names of fruit, like pêche, pomme, citron, etc., take on the same meaning.[2]

Argot, like French proper, can also increase its vocabulary by borrowing from its fellows in other lands, for all, or nearly all, the European countries have their own varieties of underworld speech : Germany its ' Rotwelsch ', Italy its ' gergo ' and its ' furbesco ' or ' lingua furbesca ', Spain its ' germanía ' and ' caló ', Portugal its ' calão ', England its ' cant ', etc. ; and just as the relations between the law-breaking fraternities of the several countries can be very close, so it is possible to discover common elements in their several slangs. This professional and linguistic internationalism among delinquents, of which it is no exaggeration to speak, is singularly fostered at the present day by the rapidity and frequency of our modern means of transport.

Similarly, argot, like the common tongue, can also borrow from

---

[1] One reason for this, no doubt, is the vital importance of quick wits and prompt departures in the life of the crook.

[2] The examples are taken from Dauzat, Les argots, p. 138, where this process, a common feature of colloquial speech, is discussed in detail.

dialect. A considerable number of French argot words come from this source. This is particularly true, however, of present-day soldiers' slang. Before the war, soldiers' slang contained few or no dialect elements. The recruits, coming in the majority of cases from small and quite unimportant localities, and being of tender years, were chary of using their local vernacular. But during the Great War conditions were different. Life in the trenches was easy-going and unrestrained, and the peasant soldiers of forty or over, of whom there were many, were both inveterate dialect speakers and, unlike the young conscript of earlier days, had no compunctions about using their local speech ; a great number of dialect words thus caught on and became current in army slang.

Another feature that argot has in common with standard French is that it may augment its vocabulary from within by the same processes of word-formation as are available to the latter. Derivation, by suffix and prefix, composition, and abbreviation, are all made use of by argot and standard alike ; but the former has a special preference for metathesis and what we may call anagrammatic changes. Thus *La Lorcefé* is argot for *La Force*, one of the Paris prisons, *lincepré* is for *prince*, etc. The butchers of La Villette speak, or spoke, a slang called *loucherbem*, or *largonji*, in which this process is systematically employed, *loucherbem* itself being the word ' boucher ' with the *b* transferred to the end and the syllable *em* added, an *l* taking the *b*'s place ; while *largonji* is the word *jargon* similarly dislocated and augmented. It is clear from these examples that the process has little in common with derivation proper as met with in ordinary speech, but is a deliberate modification of an existing word.

We have stated above that the majority of argot terms disappear, and that fairly rapidly, as they soon cease to satisfy the affective impulses constantly present in those who speak it. But a portion escape this fate through being adopted by current colloquial speech, where they gradually acquire full citizen rights and their origins are forgotten. Words of this type are naturally more numerous in the speech of the lower than of the higher classes of society, because of the closer contacts and affinities of the former with the various argot-speaking groups. But no clear line can be drawn in this respect, and a speaker of any class may have recourse to argot words and expressions when he is prompted to do so by his mood or his surroundings. In current colloquial French, words

like *se balader* ' se promener ', *balancer* ' jeter ', *balle* ' franc ', *galette*
' argent ', *dèche* ' misère ', etc., are in common use. Some of them
preserve a trace of their disreputable character and are used with
diffidence. But custom gradually obliterates the stain until finally
it disappears. In this manner argot escapes in some measure from
the complete oblivion with which it is inevitably faced. But it
depends entirely on the word itself, its qualities or perhaps its good
fortune, whether or not it will be adopted in common parlance
and thus survive.

But though, in the nature of things, an evanescent type of speech,
French argot is not without a history. As von Wartburg and others
have pointed out, a certain amount of argot material has come
down to us from the mediaeval period. In the *Jeu de St. Nicolas*,
by Jean Bodel, a play of the second half of the twelfth century,
there is a fair sprinkling of argot words throughout the text, which
renders many passages obscure. Later, in the fifteenth century,
there are some ten ballades by Villon in a jargon he calls ' jobelin '.[1]
Since then, argot of various types has made intermittent appear-
ances in literature ; for example, in a farce, probably of the late
fifteenth century, discovered at Fribourg, and published by P.
Aebischer in *Revue du XVIᵉ siècle*, 1924, p. 157 f., in the plays of
Vadé, in the eighteenth century (' la langue poissarde ' or ' fish-
wives' slang '), and, comparatively recently, in the argot poems
of Richepin and Rictus. But the most important historical
document on early slang is a glossary compiled in the fifteenth
century by a recording officer of the tribunal of Dijon. In 1455,
between the 3rd of October and the 5th of December, an extremely
arduous investigation was conducted into the malpractices of the
so-called ' coquillards ' or ' compagnons de la Coquille ', a band
of evil-doers whose members were extremely numerous and widely
spread throughout the whole of France. One of the fraternity
turned king's evidence and, thanks to him, this glossary of their
secret language, the first monument of the ' argot des malfaiteurs ',
was compiled actually at the trial. As there is contemporary
evidence that Villon had two ' coquillard ' associates, this may

---

[1] The following is a sample :

> A Parouart, la grand mathe gaudie,
> Ou accollez sont duppez et noirciz
> Et par anges suivant la paillardie
> Sont greffiz et prinz cinq ou six.
> (Ballade 1, ed. Schöne.)

account for the resemblances between the jargon of his ballads and that of this criminal society.[1]

★

Upon Romance slangs other than French, information is much scantier and of more recent date. For Italy we have the *Modo novo da intendere la lingua zerga cioè parlar furbesco*, Venice, 1549, the *Vocabolario della lengua zerga*, Venice, 1556, by Pietro and Giovanni Maria Sabio, and, by the same authors, the *Libro zergo da interpretare la lingua zerga*, Venice, 1575.[2] But earlier traces are to be found, according to Sainéan, *L'argot ancien*, p. 12, in a document of 1472 addressed by the poet Luigi Pulci to Lorenzo Magnifico and containing a list of ' furbesco ' words with their meanings. For Spain, according to the same authority (*loc. cit.*, p. 13), the evidence is later still. In 1609, at Barcelona, a book was published entitled, *Romances de germanía de varios autores* . . ., which contains a number of ballads in slang, and a glossary, and some further information is provided by such works as *Don Quixote*, or the numerous picaresque novels, of which the earliest, *Lazarillo de Tormes*, goes back to 1554. With regard to Rumanian slang, little is known to us at present. Sainéan (*loc. cit.*, pp. 14–15) names two authors who have recorded some of it : G. Baronzi, *Limba romînă şi tradiţiunile ei*, Brăila, 1872, pp. 149–51, and V. Scînteie, in the newspaper *Dimineaţa*, 21st November, 1906, under the heading *Şmechereasca*. To these should be added an article on gaol-bird and criminal slang in *Adevărul literar şi artistic*, seria III, anul III, nos. 107–10, and a similar article entitled *Am aruncat laba'n ploscă*, in *Dimineaţa*, 1st May, 1932, which contains fragments of conversation in convict slang, with explanations.[3]

★ ★ ★

[1] For further details on the early and recent history of French slang the reader is referred to the works of L. Sainéan mentioned below, p. 364.

[2] Cp. G. I. Ascoli, *Kritische Studien zur Sprachwissenschaft*, Weimar, 1878, p. 149. The forms *zergo* and *zerga* in the above titles are Venetian forms of Ital. *gergo*.

[3] Baronzi, in the book mentioned above, calls the Rumanian cant language ' limba cîrîitorilor ', i.e. ' chatterers' language '. Another name is ' limbă păsărească ', ' bird or sparrow talk '. It is possible that this is a case of ' synonymic derivation ' (see above, p. 359), as the gypsies, who form the majority of the vagrant and thieving population, are nicknamed *ciori*, ' crows ', and more

We turn now to the more conspicuous workers in the field of slang, and it must be said that there has been no dearth of interest in the subject. Up to the year 1901, and including such works as slang glossaries and word-lists, a total of 356 items had been recorded by a Paris bibliographer.[1] But with two exceptions, Fr. Michel's *Etudes de philologie comparée sur l'argot*,[2] Paris, 1856, and Marcel Schwob and Georges Guieysse, *Etude sur l'argot français*, in *Mémoires de la Société de linguistique de Paris*, vol. VII (1889–92), p. 33 f.,[3] the earlier studies there recorded are devoid of any scientific value. Of Michel's work, on the other hand, although it can scarcely be said to comply with all the requirements of modern scholarship, Sainéan has said (*L'argot ancien*, p. ii) that it is " jusqu'ici le seul qui considère l'argot dans son ensemble " and that it remains " le point de départ des études ultérieures." As for the study by Schwob and Guieysse, it may be affirmed that this is the first piece of strictly scientific investigation in the field. Among earlier studies concerning slang other than French, however, mention should be made of B. Biondelli's work upon ' furbesco ' : *Delle lingue furbesche*, in *Rivista europea*, Milan, 1846, p. 81 f., and *Studii sulle lingue furbesche*, Milan, 1846, reprinted in his *Studii linguistici*, Milan, 1856.

★

As we have pointed out, of all the Romance slangs, the French varieties have been the most thoroughly investigated and are the best known. Among the scholars who have con-
Lazare Sainéan tributed most to make this the case a pre-eminent place is due to the Rumanian, Lazăr Șăineanu, who, after publishing in his home country a number of works

euphemistically ' sparrows ', both of them typically loquacious types of birds. In any case, it is a fact that the gypsy elements in Rumanian cant are far more numerous than are the Romance, although Sainéan, *loc. cit.*, p. 154, says that he has found no gypsy words in the earlier slang and only very few in the modern variety. (Cp. A. Graur, *Les mots tsiganes en roumain*, in *Bulletin linguistique* (Bucharest), II (1934), p. 108 f.)

[1] R. Yve-Plessis, *Bibliographie raisonnée de l'argot et de la langue verte en France, du XVᵉ au XXᵉ siècles*, 1901. The book is prefaced by a dialogue, of which Gaston Esnault (see below) is the author ; the speakers are Jean and Hylas, the latter being Esnault's mouthpiece.

[2] Michel studies French argot in comparison with that of Italy and of Spain.

[3] In the same volume Schwob also published independently (pp. 168 f. and 296 f.) a study entitled *Le jargon des Coquillars*, which he states is a continuation of that undertaken in collaboration with Guieysse.

relating to Rumanian, settled in Paris some thirty odd years ago
and made the investigation of French argot and kindred forms of
speech his own particular province, for the author, Lazare Sainéan,
whom we have already had so often occasion to quote, and of whom
Dauzat, *Les argots*, p. 25, says that in argot studies " L'impulsion
décisive fut donnée par M. Lazare Sainéan, qui s'attacha d'abord
à l'ancien argot des malfaiteurs français (antérieur à 1850). Il
débrouilla la matière dans *l'Argot ancien*. . . ." is no other than
Lazăr Şăineanu, the author of *Istoria filologiei romîne*, of *Basmele
romîne*, of *Influenţa orientală asupra limbii şi culturii romîne*, and of other
similar works. In *L'Argot ancien*[1] Sainéan treats of slang of the period
between 1455, the date of the ' coquillard ' glossary mentioned
above (*v.* p. 361), and 1850. The author's own description of his
work is as follows (*loc. cit.*, p. iii) : " La présente étude est la première qui traite de l'argot dans son développement chronologique.
Chez Fr. Michel le passé et le présent se confondent ; les remarques
faites par Schwob s'appliquent exclusivement à la phase contemporaine de l'argot." And further on : " Mon travail est purement
linguistique ; j'ai délibérément laissé de côté les considérations
historiques et sociologiques." The body of the book contains
chapters like the following : Characterization of argot, its methods
of word-formation in their phonetic, morphological, and semantic
aspects, and the influence of argot. His second work, *Les sources
de l'argot ancien*, 2 vols., Paris, 1912,[2] can be considered as a continuation of the first. In order to facilitate further research, the
author provides the reader with a wealth of material, from the
earliest sources down to 1850, and almost half of the second volume,
some 200 pages in all, is made up of an etymological dictionary
of early slang.

In 1920, Sainéan published a further work, *Le langage parisien
au XIXe siècle*, which brings his investigation right up to the present
day. He had already asserted in his ' *Sources* ' (p. x) that nowadays
argot and ' langage populaire ' had come to be much the same
thing : " En réalité, c'est déjà dans la première moitié du XIX[-e]
siècle que se font jour les tendances nouvelles, et que l'argot
pénètre de plus en plus profondément dans les couches populaires,

---

[1] Full title : *L'Argot ancien* (1455–1850). *Ses éléments constitutifs, ses rapports
avec les langues secrètes de l'Europe méridionale et l'argot moderne. Avec un appendice
sur l'Argot jugé par Victor Hugo et Balzac.* See the reviews by P. Meyer, *Romania*,
XXXVII (1908), p. 465 f. ; O. Driesen, *Archiv f. d. St. der neueren Spr. u. Lit.*,
CXXIII (1909), p. 198 f. ; and A. Thomas, *Journal des Savants*, 1909, p. 437 f.
[2] Reviewed by Meillet, *Bull. Soc. Ling.*, XVIII (1912–13), p. ccxcii f.

invasion déjà constatée par Vidocq. Cependant, c'est seulement
dans la seconde moitié du XIXe siècle que s'opère à peu près
complètement la fusion du jargon des malfaiteurs avec le langage
populaire parisien, de sorte que l'apache de nos jours se sert essentiellement de la même langue que l'ouvrier, le soldat, la fille, le
voyou. Le bagne, la caserne et l'atelier ont apporté chacun leur
contingent au bas-langage existant depuis des siècles ; il en résulte
un mélange qu'on a improprement appelé argot et qui n'est
aujourd'hui que le parler des basses classes parisiennes."[1] *Le
langage parisien* is thus in the author's view a continuation of his
earlier work, and a study of the popular speech of Paris into which,
he maintains, the earlier argot, or what is left of it, has been
incorporated. Among the characteristics of this low-class Parisian,
which differs in pronunciation, grammar, and vocabulary very
markedly from the speech of educated people, two of the most
striking are its archaism, on the one hand, and its propensity to
change on the other.

During the war Sainéan interested himself in the slang of the
French soldiers. An article he published in *Le Temps*, 29th March
1915, having attracted the attention of people at the front, he
received a considerable amount of material direct from the trenches.
This, and information drawn from other competent sources, he
embodied in his book, *L'Argot des tranchées. D'après les lettres des
poilus et les journaux du front*, Paris, 1915,[2] which investigates only
" des vocables relativement récents ou des créations de la guerre
actuelle, produits immédiats de la vie des tranchées " (p. 31),
leaving aside, as already sufficiently well known, the purely
Parisian slang terms his informants had collected. The actual
study of the words, which, among other things, brings out the
interesting point that the war had put into general circulation a
number of terms previously confined to certain restricted circles,
is followed by a collection of ' pièces documentaires ', consisting of
soldiers' letters and front-line journals, and a short glossary.[3]

In close relation with Sainéan's investigations into slang is his

---

[1] Spitzer, in the article referred to on p. 374, opposes this identification of
argot and langage populaire, quoting at the same time a still more categorical
passage from Sainéan's *Le langage parisien*.

[2] Cp. M. Cohen, *Bull. Soc. Ling.*, XX (1916), p. 69 f., and R. Gauthiot, *ibid.*,
p. 75 f.

[3] Sainéan's material, together with other matter collected independently,
from journals and soldiers' songs, was worked up by Otto H. Brandt in an article
entitled *Von der Sprache des Poilus*, in *Neuphilologische Monatsschrift*, I (1930), p. 399 f.

work on the language of Rabelais. As is well known, Rabelais' writings, independently of their literary merits, are linguistic monuments of the first importance, and among the wealth of words which the author has accumulated, some of his own coining, and others drawn from the speech of every social category, argot expressions could not fail to be encountered. This slang material is studied in the second part of Sainéan's *La langue de Rabelais. I : La civilisation de la Renaissance ; II : Langue et vocabulaire*, 2 vols., Paris, 1922–3.[1]

Finally, we may mention under the present rubric, although they are not primarily concerned with slang, certain other works by Sainéan, some early, some late, but all of them showing that same interest in the linguistic manifestations of popular emotion and popular fancy which is characteristic of this productive scholar. They are : *La création métaphorique en français et en roman*, I, Halle a.S., 1905 ; II, *ibidem*, 1907,[2] in which he investigates the metaphorical names given to domestic animals (the reader will remember that metaphor is one of the most fertile sources of argot vocabulary), and the monumental work entitled : *Les sources indigènes de l'étymologie française*, in three volumes (Paris, 1925–30),[3] with a fourth entitled : *Autour des sources indigènes. Etudes d'étymologie française et romane*, Florence, 1935, *Biblioteca dell' Archivum Romanicum*, serie II, vol. 20. In these four books the author applies with insistence, and often successfully, a principle which he had already formulated in the earlier work, namely : " Faute d'une étymologie positive latine ou germanique, c'est dans les éléments originaux des langues romanes, dans leur activité créatrice ou simplement fécondante, qu'il faudra chercher la solution de la

---

[1] Undertaken at the instigation of the ' Société des études rabelaisiennes ' whose organ, *Revue des études rabelaisiennes*, was founded in 1903, to become later the *Revue du seizième siècle* under the direction of Jean Plattard. This review has now ceased publication, its place being taken, since 1934, by *Humanisme et Renaissance*. The society also undertook a critical edition of Rabelais' works, which is still unfinished. On Rabelais studies, see P. Rackow, *Der gegenwärtige Stand der Rabelais-Forschung*, in *Germ.-roman. Monatsschrift*, XVIII (1930), pp. 198 f. and 277 f. Among linguists mentioned in the present work who have concerned themselves with Rabelais, Spitzer calls for special mention ; he, in addition to the work mentioned above, p. 135, has published various notes in *Zeitschr. f. rom. Phil.*, XLIII (1923), p. 611 f., XLIV (1924), p. 101 f., and elsewhere.

[2] Cp. A. Thomas, *Romania*, XXXV (1906), p. 471 f., and E. Herzog, *Literaturblatt f. germ. u. rom. Phil.*, XXVIII (1908), col. 233 f.

[3] Reviews by L. Spitzer, *Literaturblatt f. germ. u. rom. Phil.*, XLVIII (1927), col. 27 f. ; Elise Richter, *Arch. f. d. Stud. d. neueren Spr. u. Lit.*, CLIV (1928), p. 107 f. ; G. Rohlfs, *ibid.*, CLIX (1931), p. 115 f.

plupart des problèmes qui ont résisté jusqu'ici à l'investigation étymologique " (*La création métaphorique*, II, p. vii).[1]

Next after Sainéan comes a scholar with whom we are already well acquainted, Albert Dauzat, who by the number and variety of his publications occupies a leading position in slang studies. First in chronological order was his book entitled *Les argots de métiers franco-provençaux*, Paris, 1917,[2] an investigation into the slangs of a number of trades from the Franco-Provençal area, that is to say, the French and Swiss territories in the Middle Rhone basin, though for reasons which he himself explains he occasionally trespasses outside this region. The word ' métier ' in the title has its literal meaning, for Dauzat has excluded all consideration of criminal slang, just as he has neglected trade language which is not strictly slang, like the so-called ' canut ' of the Lyonnese silk-weavers. In the first part of the book the author endeavours to elucidate the principles which govern the formation of these slangs. He notes, for example, the important fact that only a small portion of these types of speech is really slang. Unlike the slang of the delinquent classes, trade slangs preserve unchanged those elements which they share with the current language. But there are, none the less, features that are common to both varieties. It is a well-known fact that in France certain callings like that of the mason, the sweep, or the tinker are, or were, of the seasonal type and exercised by itinerant groups of workers. Workers of this type thus led, and still lead, to some extent, a life comparable to that of the vagrant criminal, who is frequently gregarious as well as migratory. This it is that has brought a strong admixture of strictly argot elements into the trade slangs in question. There is also a considerable purely popular element, which leads the author to suggest that a comparative study of these slangs should be conducted on the lines of linguistic geography, with due regard, of course, for the special character of the material. The second part of the book contains glossaries of the trade slangs arranged geographically.

Like Sainéan, Dauzat was attracted by the language of the soldiers in the trenches. To collect his material he went to the fountain head, and through correspondents at the front was able

[1] Other contemporary etymologists, in particular L. Spitzer, have adopted a similar attitude.

[2] Reviewed in the *Bulletin de la Société de linguistique de Paris*, XXI (1918–19), p. 254 f., by M. Cohen.

Albert Dauzat

to amass a considerable amount of information which he claims to be more reliable than that secured by Sainéan, whose material frequently came from printed sources that were often somewhat artificial and at times actually fictitious.[1] It is this first-hand information that Dauzat utilized in *L'Argot de la guerre. D'après une enquête auprès des officiers et soldats,* Paris, 1918, 2nd ed., 1919.[2] The question had been raised : had the war brought into being an entirely new slang, or had it merely given more vigorous development to that already existing in army circles (cp. above, p. 357) ? After discussing the matter in detail, Dauzat comes to the following conclusion : " Non ! l'argot de la guerre n'est pas un phénomène extraordinaire ni une langue créée de toutes pièces. C'est autre chose et c'est beaucoup mieux : c'est la transformation de l'argot de caserne, profondément modifié par la vie guerrière, enrichi par les apports de l'argot parisien, des provincialismes de bonne frappe et des mots exotiques que nos troupes ont empruntés aux contingents coloniaux et étrangers, ou aux populations indigènes avec lesquelles ils ont été en contact dans les expéditions lointaines " (*op. cit.,* 2nd ed., p. 27). This view is confirmed by the statistics on page 7 of the volume, where we see that of the, roughly, two thousand words or expressions investigated by the author, a third is made up of Parisian slang, a third of old military slang or provincialisms, and a third of new formations due to the war. The author examines in turn the older terms, and the recent innovations and borrowings, and then discusses the semantic and formal changes, many of them, particularly the former, being shown to be of a type analogous to those found in the argot of the underworld. Finally, he has something to say on what he calls ' special slangs ', bringing out the important fact that even a language like war slang, the product of quite special circumstances, had also its different varieties, determined by differing conditions of life, an instructive illustration of the truth of that dictum, " la langue est un fait social ", which is the corner-stone of the doctrine of the French school. Each arm, each branch of the service, had its own expressions, which were either lacking in the speech of other

---

[1] See *Revue de philologie française,* XXXIV (1922), p. 140, and *Les argots,* p. 50. Dauzat, in a letter to the present author, refers somewhat scathingly to the ' prétendues lettres de poilus ' which the newspapers published during the war and which Sainéan accepted at their face value. He admits on the other hand that Esnault's material in *Le poilu* (see below) is superior to his own, as it was collected on the spot.

[2] Reviews by M. Grammont, *Rev. des langues romanes,* LX (1918–20), p. 321 f., and A. Meillet, *Bull. Soc. Ling.,* XXI (1918–19), p. 93 f.

branches or, what is even more interesting, if used, had a different meaning. The word *billard*, for example, in hospital, meant the ' operating table ', while in the trenches it denoted the open space between the opposing front lines. We must not imagine, however, that such variations were either very numerous or very important. Generally speaking, war slang was uniform, and became increasingly so as time went on. In the preface to the second edition (p. 8), Dauzat quotes a correspondent, an ' agrégé de grammaire ', as having noted " la tendance très nette . . . à la constitution d'une langue commune sur tout le front et la fusion progressive des langages spéciaux." Another observation of some theoretical importance made by Dauzat is the following : " Le vocabulaire que nous avons recueilli donne le plus flagrant démenti aux théories trop absolues suivant lesquelles tout argot est un langage secret créé consciemment pour la défense du groupe. Ces théories, nous les avons toujours combattues, non qu'elles ne renferment pas une part de vérité,—la généralisation inverse serait également, quoiqu'à un degré moindre, inadéquate aux faits,—mais parce que l'argot, comme tout langage, est dans l'ensemble une formation collective, inconsciente dans ses moyens, soumise à divers facteurs psychologiques ou externes ne relevant pas de la volonté individuelle " (p. 221). A most convincing proof of this contention is that the slang of French war prisoners in Germany actually contained a considerable number of German words.

Dauzat's third work in the domain of slang is the book entitled, *Les argots. Caractères, évolution, influence*, Paris, 1929, which we have already had occasion to quote. Like *Les patois* by the same author (cp. Chap. III, p. 217, above), this work is of a semi-popular character, and discusses lucidly and precisely the various problems raised by slangs, both the argot of the criminal classes and the special slangs of the various trades. The chapter headings are as follows : the characteristics of slang, the various types of French slang[1] and their evolution, renewal of vocabulary (borrowing), changes in form (alteration and deformation), changes in meaning, the influence of argot proper upon standard French, upon the slangs

---

[1] The types he mentions are : (*a*) criminal slang (with the variants, jobelin, jargon, and largonji) ; (*b*) slangs of itinerant traders ; (*c*) other trade slangs, like the ' canut ' of Lyonese silk-workers, theatre slang, butchers' slang, etc. ; (*d*) school slangs, of which the two most important are those of the ' Ecole polytechnique ' and of Saint-Cyr ; (*e*) military slangs (barrack-room, war, and prisoner slangs) ; (*f*) sporting slang. On the latter cp. also *La vie du langage* by the same author, 4th edition, Paris, 1928, p. 287 f.

24

of trades, and upon popular speech. The author provides likewise a concise account of slang studies, and a fairly complete bibliography of the principal works on slang, both French and foreign. Despite the absence of any scientific apparatus of the abstruser kind, the book displays a complete familiarity with the subject matter, and even the specialist reader may turn to it with profit and complete confidence.

Dauzat, whose more specialized articles, *Les emprunts dans l'argot*, in *Revue de philologie française*, XXV (1911), fasc. 1 and 2, and XLIV (1932), p. 41 f., should also be recalled here, has concerned himself, finally, with war slangs other than French, having published in the *Revue des langues romanes*, LX (1918-20), p. 387 f., a study entitled, *Trois lexiques d'argot militaires romans recueillis pendant la guerre*, which contains lists of words from Belgian-French, Italian, and Portuguese sources.

A number of the enquiries into French slang have been conducted by men whose names are less familiar to Romance scholars, though **Other Investigators of Slang** this does not imply that their work is in any sense inferior. On the contrary, one of these investigators, Gaston Esnault to wit, who, as early as 1901, was responsible for the preface to Yve-Plessis's *Bibliographie* (see p. 363, note 1), may be considered to be the leading authority on matters concerned with French war slang. The reviews[1] which greeted his voluminous work, *Le poilu[2] tel qu'il se parle. Dictionnaire des termes populaires, récents et neufs, employés aux Armées en* 1914-1918, *étudiés dans leur étymologie, leur développement et leur usage*, Paris, 1919, 2nd ed., 1936, were most laudatory and enthusiastic, and the work received official commendation in the shape of the award of the ' prix Volney ', for 1920, by the Académie des Inscriptions et Belles Lettres. Esnault's advantage over Sainéan and Dauzat lies in the fact that his material is the result of direct personal observation, and that his book is the work of a soldier as well as a lexicographer. As

---

[1] The reader is referred particularly to the reviews by M. Cohen, *Bull. Soc. Ling.*, XXI (1918-19), p. 258 f., and by L. Spitzer, *Literaturblatt f. germ. u. rom. Phil.*, XLVI (1925), col. 104 f. Other reviews are listed by the author in *L'imagination populaire*, mentioned below.

[2] The term ' poilu ', as is convincingly shown by Dauzat, *L'argot de la guerre*, p. 48, is at least a hundred years old, and meant " l'homme qui a du poil au bon endroit—pas dans la main—symbole ancien de la virilité ". The war not only popularized the term, but gave it an added significance : " Car le civil, depuis 1914, a donné une nouvelle valeur au mot : le poilu est désormais le soldat-combattant (qui s'oppose à l' ' embusqué '), le héros qui défend notre sol " (*op. cit.*, pp. 51-2). *Le poilu*, as used in the above title, means of course ' la langue du poilu '.

Spitzer says in the review quoted in the note above, the life of the language investigated is felt on every page, as it was heard and felt by the author himself, not culled from books or newspapers. Esnault excels in what Spitzer terms ' microscopic etymology ' : he is not satisfied with merely determining an etymon, as is the usual practice, but examines in detail the various new meanings a word acquires, accounting as far as possible for them all.

Another work by Esnault in an allied field should also be mentioned here, namely, that entitled *L'imagination populaire. Métaphores occidentales. Essai sur les valeurs imaginatives concrètes du français parlé en Basse-Bretagne comparé avec les patois, parlers techniques et argots français*, Paris, 1925.[1] As is clear from the title, and from much of what has been said above in the present section, there are many features shared in common by popular speech and argot proper, one of which, the main theme of Esnault's work, is the enrichment of the vocabulary by metaphor. The book is therefore of considerable importance for the light it throws upon the creative methods applied in slang.

This relationship between popular speech and slang also justifies the inclusion in this section of a work by Henri Bauche, *Le langage populaire. Grammaire, syntaxe et dictionnaire du français tel qu'on le parle dans le peuple de Paris, avec tous les termes d'argot usuel*, Paris, 1920, 2nd edition, 1929,[2] the title of which, in this connection, is itself significant. Although the scientific equipment of the author leaves something to be desired, he has none the less provided us with a study of the phonetic, morphological, and syntactical features of popular Parisian, comparing them with those of standard speech, and accounting for differences. The vocabulary, which runs to over sixty two-column pages, is of particular interest, not only by reason of its amplitude, but also because among the words it registers we find a number that show striking resemblances to popular terms in other languages, allowing us to conclude that there is a class psychology that manifests itself in similar ways in different linguistic systems.

[1] Reviewed by Iorgu Iordan in *Arhiva*, XXXIII (1926), p. 283 f. ; G. Dottin, *Revue de philologie française et de littérature*, XXXVIII (1926), p. 161 f. ; A. Meillet, *Bull. Soc. Ling.*, XXVII (1926-7), fasc. 2, p. 110 f. ; and R. Riegler, *Archiv f. d. St. d. neueren Spr. u. Lit.*, CLII (1927), p. 144 f.

[2] The book was, in general, well received by critics and was awarded a prize by the French Academy. For reviews see : A. Meillet, *Bull. Soc. Ling.*, XXII (1920-1), p. 83 f., and (of the 2nd edition) A. Grégoire, *Rev. belge de philologie et d'histoire*, VII (1928), p. 1536 f. ; R. Olivier, *Archiv f. d. St. d. neueren Spr. u. Lit.*, CLV (1929), p. 291 f. ; J. A. Strausbaugh, *The Romanic Review*, XXIII (1932), p. 57 f. ; Iorgu Iordan, *Revista critică*, VI (1932), p. 159 f.

If further proof were needed of the keen interest at present being taken in colloquial and popular speech it would suffice to point to the fact that it has even become a subject for doctorate theses, witness the supplementary thesis sustained by G. Gougenheim in Sorbonne, entitled : *La langue populaire dans le premier quart du XIX-e siècle, d'après Le petit Dictionnaire du Peuple de J. C. L. P. Desgranges* (1821), Paris, 1929.[1]

★

With regard to Romance slangs other than French we must perforce refer the reader to the appended bibliography. These slangs having not, as yet, been investigated as comprehensively as French slang, there are no works of the type we have been describing for the latter, so that any general characterization of them is impossible. We shall confine ourselves to a brief mention of the work in this field of two of the most outstanding Romance scholars, Leo Spitzer and Max Leopold Wagner.

The former has always shown a keen interest in popular types of speech and a ready understanding of their peculiar characteristics. He is the author, for instance, of a work upon colloquial Italian, *Italienische Umgangssprache*, Bonn-Leipzig, 1922, and of two studies upon the speech of Italian prisoners of war in Austria. One of these has some analogies with certain sides of the work of Esnault upon metaphor in popular French, namely, *Die Umschreibungen des Begriffes " Hunger " im Italienischen. Stilistisch-onomasiologische Studie auf Grund von unveröffentlichtem Zensurmaterial*, Halle a.S., 1922. The book is based on material which passed through the author's hands in his capacity as censor of prisoners' letters. The prisoners, although they frequently suffered from extreme hunger, were forbidden to mention this fact in their letters home, but showed extreme ingenuity in inventing metaphors and periphrases in their endeavour to inform friends and relatives of their plight. This rather pathetic material throws up in sharp relief processes of popular nomenclature which are observable, though not so conspicuous, in the ordinary practice of speech. The second study, *Italienische Kriegsgefangenenbriefe. Materialien zu einer Charakteristik*

---

[1] Reviewed by : Ch. G.[uerlin de Guer?], *Rev. de phil. franç.*, XLII (1930), p. 232 f. ; A. Dauzat, *Rev. des langues romanes*, LXVI (1929–32), p. 101 f. ; E. Bourciez, *Revue critique*, yr. LXIV (1930), p. 89 f. ; A. Meillet, *Bull. Soc. Ling.*, XXX (1930), pp. 141–2.

der volkstümlichen italienischen Korrespondenz, Bonn, 1921, though drawing its material from the same source, is somewhat remote from the field of slang, and indeed scarcely of a linguistic character. Questions of language proper are discussed to some extent in the introduction, but the main purpose of the work is rather ' stylistic ' in the old sense, the author endeavouring to determine, on the basis of this humble epistolary literature, certain characteristic features of Italian popular mentality. An interesting feature, however, in the present connection, is the two letters in *tARÒM solandro*, slang of the valley of Sola, Trentino, which the volume contains.

Max Leopold Wagner, whose comprehensive linguistic equipment we have already remarked upon (*v. p.* 69 f.), has also evinced an interest in popular speech and slang, particularly in the Hispanic field. We owe to him two important studies : *Mexikanisches Rotwelsch*, in *Zeitschrift für romanische Philologie*, XXXIX (1919), p. 513 f., and *Notes linguistiques sur l'argot barcelonais*, Barcelona, 1924.[1] The former is an account of the present-day criminal slang of Mexico city, locally called *léperos*. It describes its constituent elements (Spanish, Romany, and English), and the methods it employs for increasing its vocabulary, and provides etymological explanations of a list of words recorded alphabetically. The latter is a thorough-going investigation of the components of Barcelona ' argot ', preceded by a theoretical introduction. From the latter we cull the following statement of the author's views on the difference between popular speech and slang : " Le langage populaire, tout en se servant de procédés semblables dans la création des mots, se distingue du véritable argot par l'absence de préméditation, c'est-à-dire l'intention d'envelopper les mots dans un voile épais de ténèbres " (p. 7). Among the ingredients of Barcelona slang, the numerous and most distinctive are those taken from gypsy speech : almost half of the vocabulary compiled by Wagner is from this source. It is of interest to note in this connection that the first documentary evidence of the presence of gypsies in Spain is with regard to Barcelona itself, and goes back to 1447. Gypsy influence in Spain is thus of long standing, and, as Wagner has pointed out elsewhere, *Volkstum und Kultur der Romanen*, III (1930), p. 114, is becoming increasingly marked in the language of the lower classes ; so that, in this particular argot, not only Romany words, but

---

[1] Reviewed by Bruno Migliorini, *Archivum Romanicum*, X (1926), p. 302 f., and by L. Spitzer, *Literaturblatt f. germ. u. rom. Phil.*, XLVIII (1927), col. 125 f. The latter proposes a number of alternative explanations to those given by Wagner.

Romany suffixes appended to Romance roots are to be found, and even semantic changes in native words provoked by contacts with Romany equivalents.[1] The remaining words are from a variety of sources, the majority coming from the vernaculars of the peninsula ; French words provide the next largest contingent, though these are remarkably few considering the nearness of France, and the remainder come from Italy and the Americas, and one even from Norwegian, which, to say nothing of the gypsy words, is enough of itself to disprove Sainéan's bold assertion that there are no non-Romance elements in Romance slangs. This study of Wagner's contains, further, a fairly extensive bibliography.[2]

★ ★ ★

[1] Thus Spanish *potro*, ' horse ', ' pony ', means, in Barcelona slang (where it is pronounced *potru*), ' fat ', because the gypsy word for ' horse ' also means ' fat '. On these ' calques linguistiques ', cp. Mirko Deanović, *Osservazioni sulle origini dei calchi linguistici*, *Archivum Romanicum*, XVIII (1934), p. 129 f. ; cp. also Th. Capidan, *Calques linguistiques*, *Dacoromania*, I (1920–1), p. 331 f.
As we have seen above, p. 362 f., gypsy words abound also in Rumanian slang. It is doubtless also through gypsy intermediaries that certain Rumanian words are to be found in Spanish slang.

[2] As some contribution to the bibliography of Romance slang studies generally we add the following items to the list of works mentioned in the text :
General works : A. Niceforo, *Le génie de l'argot*, 2nd ed., Paris, 1912 (in the author's own words : " . . . un essai sociologique, qui . . . étudie les lois qui règlent la naissance, la formation et le développement des langages spéciaux ") ; A. van Gennep, *Essai d'une théorie des langues spéciales*, in *Religion, mœurs et légendes*, II-e série, 1908 ; A. Niceforo, *Essai d'une théorie bio-sociologique sur la vie des langages spéciaux*, in *Anthropologie* (Prague), X (1932) ; cp. also Ch. Bally, *Traité de stylistique française*, I, 2nd ed., p. 242 f. ; J. Vendryes, *Le Langage*, p. 295 f. ; Albert J. Carnoy, *The Semasiology of American and other Slang*, in *Leuvensche Bijdragen*, 1921, p. 49 f. and p. 181 f. ; Fr. Schürr, *Sprachwissenschaft und Zeitgeist*, Marburg a.L., 1922, p. 61 f.
French slang (and *popular French*) : L. Ayne, *L'argot pittoresque*, Paris, 1930 ; E. Chautard, *La vie étrange de l'argot*, Paris, 1931 ; L. A. Fouret, *L'évolution du langage populaire*, in *Zeitschr. f. franz. u. englisch. Unterricht*, XXX, No. 8, Dec., 1931 ; G. Esnault, *Les lois de l'argot*, in *Rev. de phil. fr.*, XXVII (1913), p. 161 f., XXVIII (1914), p. 210 f., and XLI (1929), p. 118 f. ; Max Kuttner, *Von der Geltung des Argot*, in *Philologisch-philosophische Studien. Festschrift für Eduard Wechssler zum 19. Oktober 1929*, Jena–Leipzig, 1929, p. 346 f. ; idem, *Noch einmal Argot*, in *Neuphilologische Monatsschrift*, I (1930), p. 339 f. (in reply to L. Spitzer, *Zum Problem des französischen Argot, ibid.*, p. 205 f., where his previous study is criticized) ; M. Valkhoff, *Argot en bargoens*, Groningen–den Haag–Batavia, 1933 (a characterization of French argot and Dutch slang, ' bargoens ') ; N. E. Taube, *Etude sur l'emploi de l'argot des malfaiteurs chez les auteurs romantiques*, Uppsala, 1917 ; G. Rieder, *Probleme der Kriegsfranzösischen*, in *Hauptfragen der Romanistik. Festschrift für Philipp August Becker*, Heidelberg, 1922, p. 155 f. ; Curt Sigmar Gutkind, *Struktur der französischen Wirtschaftssprache*, in *Neuphilologische Monatsschrift*, II (1931), p. 385 f. (stock-exchange slang) ; P. Aebischer, *Un argot de malfaiteurs parlé dans le canton de Fribourg à la fin du XVII-e siècle*, in *Rev. de phil. franç.*, XLII (1930), p. 106 f. (from court records of a trial held at Fribourg in 1699 ; cp. *Romania*, LVIII, 1932, p. 145) ; W. Gottschalk, *Französische Schülersprache*, Heidelberg, 1931 (reviewed by O. Bloch, *Literaturblatt*, LIII [1932], col. 181 f. ; M. Kollmeyer,

To terminate this chapter it remains to say something of a line of enquiry which, as we stated at the beginning, has much in

Language Characteriza- tion

common with the methods and doctrine of the French school, and which has indeed been followed, as we shall see, by one of its most distinguished members, Ch. Bally. Every language has its own peculiar features, which distinguish it not only from languages with which it is unrelated, but also from members of the same linguistic family. These features have a variety of causes, some of them historical, such as contact with foreign peoples, special social conditions, and the like, while others, of a purely linguistic nature, are, so to speak, inherent in the particular system, and give rise to sounds, flexions, and syntactical devices which it would be impossible to parallel even in a kindred language. It is with attempts to specify these features characteristic of a given language that we propose at present to deal ; and here again, as with slang, it is with French

Die neueren Sprachen, XL [1932] No. 4; A. Lângfors, *Neuphilologische Mitteilungen*, XXXIII [1932], nos. 1–5 ; and M. Moser, *Zeitschr. f. frz. Spr. u. Lit.*, LVI [1932–3], nos. 5, 6) ; idem, *Die sprichwörtlichen Redensarten der französischen Sprache. Ein Beitrag zur französischen Stilistik, Kultur- und Wesenskunde*, 2 vols., Heidelberg, 1930 (reviewed by R. Olivier, *Zeitschr. f. rom. Phil.*, LIV [1934], p. 616 f.) ; M. Cohen, *Le Langage de l'Ecole polytechnique*, in *Mém. Soc. Ling.*, XV (1908), p. 170 f. (cp. also A. Lévy and G. Pinet, *L'Argot de l'X illustré par les X*, 1894, and R. Smet, *Le Nouvel argot de l'X*, 1936).

Italian : G. I. Ascoli, *Kritische Studien zur Sprachwissenschaft*, Weimar, 1878, p. 148 f. ; idem, *Studj orientali e linguistici*, fasc. 3, Gorizia, 1861, p. 379 f. (cp. also, idem, *Zigeunerisches*, Halle a.S., 1865) ; A. Rovinelli, *Il gergo*, Milan, 1905 ; R. Renier, *Cenno sull' antico gergo furbesco nella letteratura italiana*, in *Miscellanea di studi critici edita in onore di Arturo Graf*, Bergamo, 1903 ; A. Niceforo, *Il gergo nei normali, nei degenerati e nei criminali*, Turin, 1897 ; idem and E. Sighele, *La mala vita a Roma*, Turin, 1898 ; E. Mirabella, *Mala vita. Gergo, camorra e costumi degli affiliati, con 4500 voci della lingua furbesca . . .*, Naples, 1910 ; P. S. Pasquali, *Appunti lessicali furbeschi*, in *L'Italia dialettale*, VIII (1932), p. 254 f. (contains a bibliography of detailed studies on Italian slangs) ; Ugo Pellis, *Il gergo dei seggiolai di Gosaldo*, in *Archivio glottologico ital.*, XXII–XXIII (1929), p. 542 f. (bibliography) ; Gianfranco Contini, *Note sul gergo varzese*, in *L'Italia dialettale*, VIII (1932), p. 198 f. ; O. Keller, *Die Geheimsprache der wandernden Kesselflicker der Val Colla (Tessino)*, in *Volkstum u. Kultur der Rom.*, VII (1934), p. 55 f. ; G. M. Calvaruso, '*U Baccàgghiu. Dizionario comparativo etimologico del gergo parlato dai bassifondi palermitani*, Catania, 1929 (v. *Deutsche Literaturzeitung*, LIII [1932], col. 92 ; (reviewed by M. L. Wagner, *Volkstum u. Kultur der Rom.*, IV [1931], p. 181 f.) ; M. L. Wagner, *Über Geheimsprachen in Sardinien*, in *Volkstum und Kultur der Rom.*, I (1928), p. 69 (with fairly extensive bibliography) ; Ugo Pellis, *Note sul gergo sardo*, in *Bollettino dell'Atlante linguistico italiano*, I (1933), no. 1, p. 36 f. (cp. M. L. Wagner, *Volkst. u. Kult. d. Rom.*, VII [1934], p. 349 f.).

Spanish : W. Beinhauer, *Spanische Umgangssprache*, Berlin–Bonn, 1930 (see p. 140, note 5) ; L. Besses, *Diccionario de argot español, o lenguaje jergal, delincuente, profesional y popular*, Barcelona, 1931 ; J. Givanel i Mas, *Notes per a un vocabulari d'argot barceloní*, in *Butlletí de dialectologia catalana*, VII (1919), p. 11 f. (unconvincing etymologies, and largely drawn from printed sources ; consequently very incomplete).

that the few scholars who have pursued this line of investigation have been mainly concerned.

The method is essentially descriptive and synchronistic, that is to say, its purpose is to describe things as they are (or were) at a given time. In practice, however, the investigator will frequently be obliged to revert to the past to explain the present, particularly when characterizing a language by comparison with another, or others, belonging to the same linguistic group. The extent to which the strictly synchronistic method will be departed from will depend to some extent upon the circumstances of each particular case, but will as a rule be determined very largely by the training and outlook of the individual investigator. A scholar brought up in the traditional school will naturally tend to over-stress the evolutionary aspect of his phenomena, whereas a pure Saussurian will reduce historical considerations to a minimum, or even entirely eliminate them.

Although a trail had been blazed to some extent by earlier scholars, such as von Humboldt, and more recent linguists like G. von der Gabelentz, F. Misteli, and F. N. Finck, this type of investigation is still at its beginnings, and its methods are consequently somewhat uncertain. Thus one and the same language, French to wit, takes on quite a different aspect when ' characterized ' by Meyer-Lübke on the one hand or by E. Lewy (see below) on the other. This merely means that there is as yet no agreement on what exactly is to be considered as characteristic, and that no precise criteria of differentiation have so far been generally adopted. The difficulty of determining such criteria is not wholly of a subjective order, resulting, that is to say, from the varying outlook and training of individual investigators, but is really inherent in the linguistic situation. To a Frenchman sizing up another language, for example, those features will appear characteristic which his own language does not possess. Meyer-Lübke, in *Einführung in das Studium der romanischen Sprachwissenschaft*, 3rd ed., § 54 (p. 65 f.), has well pointed out some of the difficulties which beset this method of enquiry. Alluding to the French nasalized vowels, he asserts quite rightly that these will appear to be a special and charac-teristic feature of the French language to, say, a German, an Italian, or a Spaniard, in whose languages vowels of this type are not to be encountered, whereas to a Pole or a Portuguese they will appear wholly natural and familiar, and consequently entirely undistinctive. Much preliminary work is therefore still required before the method can yield the fruits which, theoretically at least, we are entitled to expect of it.

★

An excellent essay in language characterization is the one attempted by Meyer-Lübke himself, *op. cit.*, § 55 f. (p. 66 f.), where he describes the external characteristics of present-day French. From the phonetic point of view he notes : the ending of words by a stressed vowel, the great variety in vowel sounds (in addition to *a, e, i, o, u*, there are also [y] and [œ], and most of these can have various shades of ' timbre ', while *a, e, o*, and [œ] can be nasal as well as oral), the main stress on the final syllable, front articulation, an acoustic impression that is predominantly vocalic, clear-cut articulation of consonants, and consequent absence of glide sounds. With regard to flexion, the chief characteristic of French, according to Meyer-Lübke, is the tendency to express grammatical relationship by means of pre-posed particles (e.g. the proclitic articles before the substantives, the equally indispensable proclitic pronouns that mark the persons of the verb, and the proclitic auxiliaries), a feature which is in keeping with the final stressing of words, or the so-called ascendant or oxytonic rhythm of French. Even apparent exceptions confirm this tendency. Thus the second element of the negative, *pas, guère, point*, etc., follows the verb for the very reason that originally these were independent words, whose importance caused them to be stressed more strongly than the verb itself. To this day they carry the main stress, even when, as in such popular expressions as *je sais pas*, they function purely as negative particles. This tendency towards final stress has its effect even upon word order ; thus, qualifying words are thrown into relief by being set after the word qualified (cp. *la fille du roi*, as against Lat. *regis filia*, or Old Fr. *la roi fille*), the adjective, except when its function tends, so to speak, to be merely ornamental, generally following the noun, while demonstrative and possessive adjectives precede it.[1]

★

[1] In *cet homme, mon livre, cet* and *mon* are, so to speak, mere appendages of the noun ; to give them value we must say *cet homme-ci, mon livre à moi*, where the significant *ci* and *moi* receive the stress. With regard to the place of the adjective, cp. *un jeune homme* and *un homme jeune*, where in the first example we have almost a compound word, while in the second the adjective has its full descriptive value. As the most recent French grammar puts it : " En général, placée avant le nom, l'épithète a une valeur plus subjective ou sentimentale, et, placée après le nom, elle a une valeur plus objective : *un affreux spectacle, un spectacle affreux, un vulgaire coquin, un coquin vulgaire* " (*Grammaire Larousse du XX*ᵉ *siècle*, Paris, 1936, p. 226).

Another characterization of French is from the pen of Ernst Lewy,[1] and entitled *Zur Wesengestalt des Französischen, Zeitschrift für romanische Philologie*, XLII (1922), p. 71 f. Unlike Meyer-Lübke, Lewy analyses a single feature of French, namely, its clarity, or, what is to him the same thing, its abstract character. Numerous are the phenomena he interprets in this sense, for example, the analytic inflection of the nouns, i.e. by means of separate words instead of endings (e.g. *de la mère*, as compared with *matris*, or *aux hommes* beside *hominibus*, etc.), word-order (viz. subject—predicate—object, an order which may be departed from only in special cases like interrogative sentences), the repetition of the subject in such constructions as *ton père est-il venu ?*, etc. As evidence of the same tendency towards clarity, and as showing close observation and precise rendering of facts, he alleges, further, such points as the use of prepositions of place to express various forms of relationship (*de* for the genitive, *à* for the dative, etc.) and of formulae like *auprès de*, *à côté de*, where the place element has acquired a kind of substantival character, or again the building up of the demonstrative pronouns with the help of *ci* (e.g. *cet homme-ci*), and of subordinating conjunctions with the help of *que*, and so forth.

Clearly, as we have said, these two characterizations of one and the same language are far from being alike. The facts brought out by both scholars are accurate, and indeed sometimes the same points occur in both surveys. But the point of view in each case is different. Meyer-Lübke, as a Romanicist and a grammarian, is attracted by the outward and formal aspects of the language ; Lewy, on the contrary, a stranger to our branch of study, has dwelt upon a quality of French which is better known to the non-specialist, and which is generally considered as the distinguishing feature *par excellence* of all the products of the French spirit.

★

[1] Ex-Professor of Finno-Ugrian languages in Berlin University, and a pupil of F. N. Finck, whom we mentioned above as having been one of the precursors in this form of investigation. Finck is the author of *Die Haupttypen des menschlichen Sprachbaus*, Leipzig-Berlin, 1910 ('Sammlung Göschen'), where he endeavours to classify all the languages of the world into six main groups on the basis of their fundamental characteristics. The latter he brings out by examining in detail a text from the language most representative of each group. Lewy applies his master's method preferably to languages of the Finno-Ugrian group (cp. *Zum Bau des Erdsja-Morduinischen*, in *Heinrich Winkler zum 60. Geburtstage*, Mellrichstadt, 1920, p. 8 f., and *Kurze Betrachtung der ungarischen Sprache*, in *Ungarische Jahrbücher*, IV [1924], p. 41 f.), but also to others, witness the article under discussion and also *Betrachtung des Russischen*, in *Zeitschrift für slavische Philologie*, II (1925), p. 415 f.

A closer and more searching analysis of the distinctive characteristics of French is that provided by Ch. Bally (see p. 315 f.) in his *Linguistique générale et linguistique française*, Paris, 1932. The work, like much of Bally's research, is pedagogic in its origins, and represents a fusion of two aspects of his teaching, the purely linguistic, in his capacity as successor to Saussure, and the practical, as an instructor of ' alloglots ' in the use of French. As the title indicates, it falls into two parts. The first, though not strictly concerning us here, deserves description as an important contribution to linguistic theory, and is a penetrating analysis of the sentence, on logical and psychological lines. Every type of enunciation, including commands and questions, is reduced to a judgment, actualizing a representation of the mind by situating it in a subject. Every sentence, and every syntagma (see p. 286), is shown, logically, to be composed of a theme and a statement, or, in the case of the lesser syntagmas, of a ' déterminé ' and a ' déterminant ', and this binary structure is of the essence of every syntagma. After discussing ' agreement ' and ' government ', or the methods of expressing ' inherence ' on the one hand and ' relationship ' on the other, and distinguishing between ' actualization ' and mere ' characterization '—*le fils du fonctionnaire* as against *fils de fonctionnaire*—Bally proceeds to view the sentence in its genetic and psychological aspects, its development from the ' monorheme ' to the ' dirheme ' by a process of integration or ' condensation ' of two originally independent units (*canis+latrat>canis latrat*), and then to the more intricate patterns resulting from co-ordination, segmentation, and complete unification of compound sentences, incidentally insisting upon the grammatical and syntactical importance of intonation and rhythm. A second section treats of the manner in which these logical values, or ' signifiés ' are given expression, in the actual linguistic material, by the ' signifiants ' or signs, viewed as a system, and brings us an interesting definition of synthetic as opposed to analytic modes of expression : "La synthèse est l'ensemble des faits linguistiques contraires, dans le discours, à la linéarité,[1] et, dans la mémoire, à la monosémie" (*op. cit.*, p. 112).

We are thus led progressively to the second portion of the book, as these questions of greater or less synthesis in expression will be one of the main features upon which his characterization of French will turn. Non-linearity of structure is shown to be present when

[1] Cp. : " Les signes sont linéaires lorsqu'ils se suivent, sans se compénétrer, sur la ligne du discours " (*ibid.*).

a sign ' cumulates ' more than one function (*pire*, for example, as against *plus mauvais*, cumulates the notions of ' bad ' and ' more '), or when a single notion is expressed by several pseudo-independent signs (e.g. *tout-à-coup*), or when a notion is expressed twice, like that of plurality in *nous* aim*ons*, or has to be supplied implicitly, or when the sign is broken as in *ne . . . pas*, etc. ' Polysemia ', the other factor of synthesis, exists when a sign has several meanings, or when one meaning is shared by several signs. A clear case of the former is homonymy, which, however, is not confined to vocabulary : *in-* in *inconnu* and *insuffler* is a homonym ; *faites le voir* is a syntactical homonym, as it may mean ' make him see ' and ' make him be seen ', and we may even speak of phonetic homonyms (thus Fr. *la* may be *l'a* or *la*). The reverse phenomenon is seen in an acute form in *allons, irai, va*, where the notion ' going ' is conveyed by three entirely different symbols, but it is also present in *père—paternel*, where, as frequently happens in French, noun and kindred adjective are phonetically very far apart.

Synthesis in a language consists then in mingling things which are logically distinct, and in severing what should, in logic, be united, whether in the concrete components of speech, or in the associative activities of the mind. A synthetic mode of speech calls for an effort of ' delimitation ' on the part of the mind, particularly in the hearer, in order to re-establish the linear pattern, or of ' identification ', in order to attain a singleness of meaning.

The second part of the work sets out to discover how French looks when considered in the light of these general laws of enunciation and of the various forms of dystaxis and polysemia, in a word, to provide a thorough-going characterization of French as a system of expression. This is achieved in very telling fashion by comparing French at every step with German, and it would even appear that the characterization method finds its most valuable and convincing application when thus conducted comparatively. A preliminary survey of its most striking features shows French to be less synthetic than German by its fewer flexions, its affection for progressive as against anticipatory order of words, a greater ease in ' transposition ', whereby, for example, words may be switched from one grammatical category to another, or principal clauses may be made subordinate. The same trends are to be distinguished in the oxytonic rhythm of French, as against the anticipatory barytonic rhythm of German, and in the sound-system, the well-defined sounds of French, with its absence of diphthongs or complex phonemes, contrasting in a marked degree with the diphthongs and closely welded groups of consonants in German.

On the other hand, French reveals tendencies which make it less analytic than German : the word in French is less independent of its context, less autonomous than in German ; it lives enclosed in compact rhythmical groups with a single stress, the elements of which are blended closely together, often by elision and liaison ; and within the word itself the component elements are fused and less distinct ; the syllables are less individualized, and their boundaries frequently do not coincide with those of the sense elements. French is thus tending towards the simple and purely arbitrary linguistic sign, applied to design things and processes envisaged as accomplished facts, whereas the signs in German are complex and motivated, designing objects and processes by a kind of detailed analysis ; French, in a word, is static, German, dynamic. The remainder of the work is devoted to a close examination of three of these fundamental points : progressive sequence in word order, condensation of the linguistic sign, and the static tendency of French expression. We must perforce forgo a complete analysis of these chapters. The reader finds not only instruction from one whose occupation and linguistic acumen have brought him a peculiar insight into the nature of French, but also stimulus and food for thought, as Bally opens up new view-points upon attractive fields of future investigation. Of particular interest is the attention given to sounds, intonation, and rhythm, not viewed in themselves, but as highly significant and highly characteristic elements in the language system, of which they form an integral part, and one which the written word does not reveal but which must be taken into full account before any investigation of a language can claim to be complete. There is thus a vast difference between the purely formal phonetic characterization of a Meyer-Lübke and this organic and functional treatment of sound phenomena by Bally. Similarly, the whole problem of French ' clarity ' discussed by Lewy undergoes, in Bally's hands, a much more searching and fundamental investigation. If French is clear, says Bally, German is precise, because of its analysis of facts and phenomena. French is clear, because its words are, as it were, mere labels, while the German words define and describe ; and being mere arbitrary labels, the writer or speaker who uses them must be at pains to place them in their appropriate context, upon which they depend for their identification much more than do the motivated, self-explanatory signs of German. In other words the clarity of French is shown to be as much a necessity as a quality.[1]

[1] For reviews of this work of Bally's the reader is referred to : O. Bloch, *Rev. critique*, yr. LXVII (1933), pp. 178–9 ; A. Meillet, *Bull. Soc. Ling.*, XXXIV (1933), fasc. 3, p. 84 f. ; A. Dauzat, *Le français moderne*, I (1933), p. 160 f. ; Iorgu Iordan, *Buletinul Institutului de Filologie Romînă " Alexandru Philippide "*, I (1934), p. 206 f. ; E. Gamillscheg, *Deutsche Literaturzeitung*, LV (1934), col. 253 f. ; A. Zauner, *Zeitschr. f. franz. Spr. u. Lit.*, LVII (1933–4), p. 487 f. ; Leo Jordan, *Literaturblatt f. germ. u. rom. Phil.*, LVI (1935), col. 31 f. ; W. v. Wartburg, *Zeitschr. f. rom. Phil.*, LV (1935), p. 252 f. ; Leo Spitzer, *Indogermanische Forschungen*, LIII (1935), p. 207 f.

CONCLUSION

HAVING completed the enquiry which was the object of this book, it is appropriate that we should cast our gaze backwards, and survey the development of Romance linguistics during the hundred years or so of its existence as a really scientific discipline. The first feature that strikes us is the remarkable variety and productiveness of the work that has been and is still being conducted in this domain. Despite the multitude of names and references the reader has encountered in the preceding pages, the information he has received is still far from exhaustive ; to have made it so would have exceeded both the writer's intentions and his powers. Anyone who follows at all closely the periodical literature appertaining to our subject will readily realize that it is beyond the power of any scholar, even were he entirely free from other obligations, to have a first-hand knowledge of everything published in the Romance field. And when to current output is added the accumulated production of the now lengthy past the task becomes insuperable, particularly as there is no single library in the world sufficiently well equipped to provide all the material. But even had it been possible, it was no part of our programme to provide an exhaustive account or complete catalogue of Romance scholarship. In a work like the present, which aims at a general survey of progress over a long period, what matters most is to throw into relief, and to dwell upon at some length, those contributions to scholarship that have spelt a step forward, either in doctrine or in method. But even this more limited task is not without its perplexities. For we must pick and choose, and this is a delicate matter which may give rise to much discussion, interesting discussion no doubt, but of necessity somewhat unfruitful, inasmuch as in the last resort our choice will always be to some extent subjective and, despite all our care and watchfulness, coloured by our own particular leanings and predilections.

Thus, in the present book, the author has thought fitting to pass somewhat hastily over the work of the neo-grammarians, or as

Vossler calls them, the ' positivists ', his reason being that this school is one of some fifty years' standing, and professes doctrines which are in opposition with the newer trends in linguistic theory and method. This is not to say that the neo-grammarians are at present few in numbers. They still form an imposing majority when compared with the representatives of those three main modern schools of thought that we have analysed from Chapter II onwards. But, for the reasons shown, we have made no mention of the greater number of them ; neither with regard to the shaping of our discipline as a whole, nor even as upholders of a tradition, does their work, despite its intrinsic value, show up with any special prominence in this backward view. None the less, though our attitude may provoke, and has provoked, criticism, it should not be interpreted as showing either ignorance or disdain with regard to such a number of industrious and meritorious workers.[1]

[1] Cp. W. Meyer-Lübke, *Revue de linguistique romane*, I (1925), pp. 11–12, and E. Gamillscheg, *Festschrift zum 19. Neuphilologentag*, Berlin, 1924, p. 2, note (in off-print). Any suggestion of disdain on the part of the present author for the ' positivist ' school is all the more unfounded in that nearly all his linguistic writings have been along traditional lines. But this has not prevented him from recognizing and appreciating the good points in the newer methods and doctrines. ' Positivism ', as a method, still exists and must exist, because, among other reasons, there are certain fields to which it alone is applicable, for example, the study of place-names and the names of persons. A few bibliographical notes with regard to Romance toponymy and onomastics may perhaps be welcome in this connexion. Both topics are discussed from a general point of view by Meyer-Lübke, in *Einführung in das Studium der romanischen Sprachwissenschaft*, 3rd ed., p. 243 f., and (toponymy alone) in Ernest Muret, *Les noms de lieu dans les langues romanes*, Paris, 1930. A general survey of work in French toponymy and onomastics is provided by A. Dauzat, in *Le français moderne*, II (1934), p. 97 f. For France, cp. also A. Longnon, *Les noms de lieu de la France*, Paris, 1920–9, and Dauzat, *Les noms de lieux*. *Origine et évolution*, Paris, 1926 ; for Belgium : Auguste Vincent, *Les noms de lieux de la Belgique*, Bruxelles, 1927 ; Albert Carnoy, *Origine des noms de lieux des environs de Bruxelles*, Bruxelles (undated) ; for Italy : Silvio Pieri, *Toponomastica delle valli del Serchio e della Lima*, in *Supplementi periodici dell'Archivio glottologico italiano*, V (1898), pp. 1–242, and *Toponomastica della valle dell'Arno*, Roma, 1919 ; Dante Olivieri, *Saggio di una illustrazione generale della toponomastica veneta*, Città di Castello, 1915 ; Gino Bottiglioni, *Elementi prelatini nella toponomastica corsa*, Pisa, 1929 ; G. D. Serra, *Contributo toponomastico alla teoria della continuità nel Medioevo delle comunità rurali romane e preromane dell' Italia Superiore*, Cluj, 1931 ; C. Battisti, *I nomi locali dell' Alta Venosta*, pt. I, Florence, 1936 ; for the Iberian peninsula : Georg Sachs, *Die germanischen Ortsnamen in Spanien und Portugal*, Jena–Leipzig, 1932 ; Joseph M. Piel, *Os nomes germánicos na toponimia portuguesa*, in *Boletim de filologia*, II (1933–4), pp. 105 f., 224 f., 289 f., III (1934–5), pp. 37 f., 218 f., 367 f. (proceeding) ; H. Lautensach, *Die portuguiesischen Ortsnamen*, in *Volkstum u. Kult. d. Rom.*, VI (1933), p. 136 f. ; for Rumania : Iorgu Iordan, *Rumänische Toponomastik*, Bonn–Leipzig, 1924–6 ; Gustav Kisch, *Siebenbürgen im Lichte der Sprache*, in *Archiv des Vereines für siebenbürgische Landeskunde*, XLV (1929), pp. 33–328 ; N. Drăganu, *Romînii în veacurile IX–XIV pe baza toponimiei şi onomasticei*, Bucharest, 1933. Onomastic studies are less numerous, no doubt because person names throw less light upon the history of the Romance languages. We would mention, however : Meyer-Lübke, *Romanische Namenstudien*, in *Sitzungsberichte der Akademie der Wissenschaften in Wien*, 1904 and 1917 ; B. Migliorini, *Dal nome proprio*

Accompanying this variety and wealth of production, and in part accounting for it, is a remarkable widening of the linguistic horizon, which is a further characteristic of the progress of our studies, particularly during the last few decades. The Romanicist of the middle of last century and onwards was concerned almost exclusively with historical and comparative philology, that is to say, with the relationships between the Neo-Latin languages and Latin, or between the Neo-Latin languages themselves ; and even dialect studies were conducted on the same basis. To-day, the problems discussed by his successors are so numerous and varied that in no other allied discipline can it be said that such a distance separates the scholars of the present from those of yesterday. This breadth and variety of outlook has of necessity brought with it increasing variety of method : we have but to think of scholars like Jaberg, Wagner, Jud or Spitzer, and the great diversity of methods they employ, when occasion demands, in the solution of a single problem, irrespective of their own inherent differences of outlook. And this eclecticism is not confined to these more out-standing linguists, whom we quote merely as representative. There are hosts of others who possess an equal versatility of method, and know how to vary their technique according to the nature of their specific investigations ; whereas among the scholars of last century anything approaching such versatility is an exception, and to be found only in scholars like Schuchardt, whose innate gifts set him in a class by himself.

A further advance, and one of equal importance, is to be noted in the relative positions of Romance and other branches of linguistic study. Our discipline, as we have seen, came into being some hundred years ago, and was directly due to the impulsion provided by the foundation of Indo-European philology a few years previously. Its subsequent history, until comparatively recently, had been

al nome comune, Florence–Rome–Geneva, 1927 ; Albert Dauzat, Les noms de personnes. Origine et évolution, Paris, 1925 ; Paul Aebischer, Sur l'origine et la formation des noms de famille dans le Canton de Fribourg, in Biblioteca dell' Archivum Romanicum, serie II, Linguistica, vol. 6, Geneva, 1924 ; and L'anthroponymie wallone d'après quelques anciens cartulaires, in Bulletin du Dictionnaire Wallon, XIII, Liège, 1924, p. 73 f. ; G. D. Serra, Per la storia del cognome italiano, in Dacoromania, III (1923), p. 523 f., IV (1924–6), p. 517 f., and Revista filologică, I (1927), p. 85 f. ; Dante Olivieri, I cognomi della Venezia Euganea, in Bibl. dell' Archivum Romanicum, serie II, Linguistica, vol. 6, Geneva, 1924 ; P. Aebischer, Essai sur l'onomastique catalane du XIe au XIIe siècle, in Anuari de l'Oficina romànica, I (1928), p. 43 f. ; J. Clapés i Corbera, Els cognoms catalans, Barcelona, 1929 ; J. Leite de Vasconcellos, Antroponimia portuguesa, Lisbon, 1928 (v. Volkstum u. Kultur der Rom., II [1929], p. 104 f., and III [1930], p. 301) ; Şt. Paşca, Nume de persoane şi nume de animale în Ţara Oltului Bucharest, 1936.

25

determined entirely by the circumstances of its birth, and during the whole of the nineteenth century Romance philology submissively followed the lead of the older discipline along the paths of the historical and comparative method. But now, thanks to the outstanding genius of men like Gilliéron and Schuchardt, the position is reversed, and not only has her *status pupillaris* ceased, but she has definitely taken the lead and is at present an example to her sister disciplines. The methods tried out in the field of the Romance languages are now being successfully and fruitfully applied in kindred domains, and the whole science of language has received fresh enlightenment and a new outlook. If Romance linguistics now enjoys this privileged position, it is due, primarily, to that greatest of all its achievements, the foundation of linguistic geography and geology described in Chapter III, though we do not forget the aesthetic school founded by Vossler, or the stylistic work of Bally and of Spitzer, all three of whom, by concentrating more particularly on the expressive side of language, have given, directly or indirectly, a new stimulus to the investigation of language as the medium of literature, and helped to break down the wall between philology and literary history.

We have spoken above of fresh enlightenment and a new outlook. We refer first of all to the problem of the sound-laws. Nearly all the scholars we have discussed in the preceding pages have been opponents of the neo-grammarians, or, what is really the same, of the sound-laws, for, in general, it is the attitude of a linguist to this problem which stamps him as a traditionalist or the reverse. From the first, the neo-grammarians encountered hostility in various quarters, both Indo-European and Romance, but it was from the latter that they received the heaviest blows, and no scholars did more to shake belief in the infallibility of phonetic laws as conceived by the neo-grammarians than Schuchardt, who was their adversary from the beginning, and Gilliéron, whose close contact with the realities of language made of him their most formidable opponent. Freed from the shackles of the sound-laws, linguistics has moved onwards, its scope has widened, and understanding has deepened ; it works in a new atmosphere ; and this, in a large measure, is due to the efforts of Romance scholars.

But there are more positive and palpable results than this change of linguistic climate. To begin with, through the removal of the historical bias from linguistic enquiry, the whole study of language has been enriched, and the broad and fruitful domains of living speech have been thrown open for investigation. Partly through the influence of Indo-European philology, which has to deal in the majority of cases with the languages of the past, and partly also because of the historical outlook characteristic of the period, and prevailing in every branch of intellectual activity, Romance scholars in the nineteenth century concerned themselves almost exclusively with the earlier phases of the respective languages ; even when they chanced to turn their attention to living forms of speech, they applied the historical method, and viewed their material entirely from the historical angle. They were convinced that it is the past that enables us to understand the present, holding firmly to the belief, as many still do, that history is man's chief instructress. In reality, however, the only phenomena we can observe and study with all the completeness that science demands are those before our eyes, which means, in language, the speech, either standard or dialect, that is current at the present time. The results accruing from the close scrutiny of these present-day phenomena, after repeated verification under varying conditions, alone entitle us to draw general conclusions with regard to language as a whole ; and these we may use to throw light on the linguistic conditions of the past, on earlier stages of a language that are otherwise only accessible to us through the imperfect or distorted media of written documents. Here again linguistic geography has been a prime factor in securing general recognition of this important fact.

We pass to another important achievement to be set to the credit of Romance scholarship. Despite the great diversity, both in origin and tendencies, which mark off sharply the schools discussed above, from Chapter II onwards, there are certain features which they share in common. Among these, the recognition that the source of linguistic change is to be sought in the mind of the speaker is of quite outstanding significance. This conception is of course differently manifested in the works of the several scholars. The French group, Gilliéron as well as Saussure, tend to stress the rational element in language, its use as a means of communication between men, and the consequent striving for clarity ; the Germans, Vossler and his disciples, on the other hand, have a predilection for what is intuitive, expressive, artistic, and creative in speech. But, none the less, there is in both camps this common recognition of the importance of the human mind. Here again we have a reaction against the doctrine of the neo-grammarians. It is true that some of them, H. Paul, in particular, had asserted that language only existed in and through man, but, in practice, their conception of language was shown to be almost exclusively physiological. With the newer schools this assertion has ceased to be a mere theoretical proposition ; it has become something real, that we encounter on every page of their writings, deepening their understanding and adding substance to their work. This it is that has enabled linguistics to rank as a moral science, and has rid it of those materialistic and mechanical doctrines which it owed to its naturalist leanings and ambitions of earlier days. The study of language has thus gained greatly in depth. No longer may we be content with examining its purely formal elements, when seeking to account for linguistic change ; no longer is it enough to quote some convenient ' laws ', or to speak of this or that ' exception '. We are obliged to probe into the mind of the speaker, and to endeavour to discover and understand the psychical process behind our several phenomena. Linguistics, in a word, has thus found closer touch with reality. Having ceased to envisage language as an independent entity, as something, so to speak, apart from man, it has left for good that realm of abstraction where so many were content to dwell and has come to earth, and, characteristically enough, has even shown, in the case of some scholars of the last few decades, a predilection for the cruder forms of speech, the popular vernaculars, the colloquial language of the lower orders, and slang.[1]

To attach due importance to the mind is at the same time to attach due importance to the individual, and this again is one of the conspicuous achievements of Romance linguistics, and is manifest in the present attitude of the majority of its representatives with regard to the problem of the creation and adoption of linguistic changes. It is now almost universally admitted that these are individual in their origin ; a change takes place in the speech of a single person and then, if circumstances are favourable, that is, if the change is felt to be in conformity with the linguistic sense of the community, it catches on, and spreads progressively to every member. In this regard, as we have seen, there is little difference between the respective schools. Their terminology may vary, and

---

[1] Cp. the opinion expressed by L. Weisgerber, in *Wörter und Sachen*, XV (1934), p. 134, where he states that the greatest achievement made by linguists in the nineteenth century was to have moved from a grammatical to a linguistic conception of language.

some will talk of ' the linguistic system ' and others of ' the general tendencies of the language ', but it is much the same thing that is meant. Indeed, the idea is of long standing, and is to be found, sixty or seventy years ago, in the works of scholars like J. Schmidt and Schuchardt (*v.* Chap. I, p. 52, n.) as ' the wave theory ' ; but it took time, and particularly sound documentary proof, to win it acceptance. It gained substantial support through Saussure, with his distinction between ' la langue ' and ' la parole ' ; it is in ' la parole ' that linguistic changes take place, and from ' la parole ' they make their way into ' la langue ' ; not all of them, of course, but only such as are in conformity with the ' spirit of the language '. Hence it is that of all the numerous and varied individual innovations only a mere fraction succeed in becoming general.

As a result of the achievements we have enumerated, it can be confidently asserted that the whole conception of language, and of the problems attaching to language, is sounder than in the past. The close observation of living forms of speech, and the effort to reach down to the underlying psychical phenomena have sharpened our understanding of this the most characteristic of man's activities. The nature and life of language, all the modifying influences which unceasingly play upon it, its origin even, these are questions, to say nothing of less fundamental problems, on which to-day a clearer light has been thrown, and towards which the attitude of scholars, in the main, is nearer to the truth than formerly. It is thus characteristic of our times that there is a liking, not to say a weakness, for problems of general linguistics.[1] Much, overmuch perhaps, is being written in this domain, which would appear to be so easy of access, but which is far from being so in reality. Yet, despite the meagre contributions to knowledge which some of our present-day writers bring, this should not imply that, on principle (cp.

---

[1] Of this the reader has already had ample evidence in the preceding pages. If further confirmation were necessary it would be sufficient to point to three characteristic compilations of recent years. In 1922 a presentation volume in honour of Vossler bore the title *Idealistische Neuphilologie,* the name of the doctrine of the recipient himself, and aimed at a comprehensive and unified survey of the main achievements of a whole school of linguistic thought. Similarly, in 1921, the *Journal de psychologie normale et pathologique* published a special number containing a collection of articles on the psychology of language, most of them inspired by the doctrines of Saussure. Again, in 1933, the same journal appeared in volume form, with the title *Psychologie du langage.* This volume, which we have frequently had occasion to quote, contained six sections entitled : I, Théorie du langage ; II, Linguistique générale ; III, Système matériel du langage ; IV, Système formel du langage ; V, Acquisition du langage ; VI, Pathologie du langage.

p. 22 f., above), we should be suspicious or neglectful of problems of linguistic theory. We ought only to demand that studies in this field should be based on the fullest possible documentation, if any credence is to be given to the opinions advanced by their authors. In other words, let ' positivism ', that is to say, a thorough and secure knowledge of the facts, be our starting-point, and ' idealism ', in its etymological sense of general conceptions, leading up to the philosophy of language, be our goal. It is thus that we may seek to reconcile the old and the new methods, and achieve results that will be of permanent value and accepted by all ; let ' positivism ' be quickened by the newer outlook, and let the newer doctrines receive the secure foundation of which they stand in need by a substantial accumulation of precise facts. Linguistics, like the material it studies, must march with the times, and though, to quote Fr. Schürr, *Sprachwissenschaft und Zeitgeist*, p. 78, we do not mean to imply that the old school is bankrupt, we would wish to see it infused with a new life.

To sum up, to speak of the present ' state ' of Romance linguistics would be 'a misnomer, if ' state ' were to imply ' static ', for its condition is very definitely one of motion. At no time have more plentiful or more important problems been ventilated than now. There is no question of standing still ; the unceasing quest for truth goes on, a truth which, though essentially the same, is for ever changing, inasmuch as it is conditioned by continually changing methods and conceptions. To quote Schuchardt's happy phrase : " There is talk at present of a ' crisis ' in linguistics ; that's the word one likes to hear."[1]

---

[1] " Man hört jetzt : in der Sprachwissenschaft kriselt es ; das ist ein gutes Wort " (*Hvgo Schuchardt-Brevier*, 2nd ed., p. 451).

THIRTY YEARS ON

A SUPPLEMENT

by

R. POSNER
Reader in Language, University of York

BASIL BLACKWELL
OXFORD

PREFACE

In writing this supplement I was immeasurably helped by the large number of scholars who gave me off-prints, information and advice: among these I should especially like to thank Yakov Malkiel, André Martinet, Robert A. Hall, Jr., Knud Togeby, Bernard Pottier, and Pierre Guiraud. To Stephen Ullmann, editor of the series, I owe a special word of thanks, for his numerous and detailed suggestions and for his kindly encouragement. I am also particularly grateful to John N. Green, one of my colleagues at York, for his unstinting aid especially with the bibliography and the index. The tolerance of Henry Schollick, of Blackwell's, and of my family deserves recognition: I am especially grateful that my two infant children, Christopher and Barbara, did not prove as much of a hindrance as they might have been.

Needless to say, the errors in this supplement are all my own.

University of York   REBECCA POSNER
May, 1969

NOTE

The phonetic symbols used are those of the International Phonetic Association.

> Square brackets are used for phonetic transcription: thus [Roma]
> Slant lines are used for phonemic transcription: thus /roma/
> Braces are used for morphemic transcription: thus {Roma}
> Italics are used for foreign words in their usual spelling: thus *Roma*
> Capitals and small capitals are used for Latin words: thus ROMA
>   > indicates "goes to", or "becomes"
>   < indicates "comes from"
>   / = coexistent in the same dialect: thus *bon/bonne*
>   ~ = different forms of the same item: thus /bonə/~/bon/
>   * indicates that an item or sequence is unattested or ungrammatical.

Periodical articles are cited in the text and footnotes but not in the Bibliography: where the periodical is frequently cited an abbreviation is used (see the List of Abbreviations, p. 544). Books are referred to in the text and footnotes by the heading used in the Bibliography (p. 548). The 'heading' normally used consists of the author's name and the date of publication, though in some cases an abbreviation is used. In most cases the date used in the 'heading' refers to the first edition, but sometimes for special reasons another edition is referred to. Where a reference is made to an edition other than that cited in the 'heading', the date of the relevant edition is enclosed in brackets: thus

K. Togeby 1951 (1965) or
W. von Wartburg 1943 (French transl. 1963).

The Bibliography covers only books mentioned in the supplement: the original gives bibliographical references in text and footnotes. It was felt, however, that, for ease of reference, a separate bibliography for the supplement was desirable.

The Index of Proper Names refers to both the original and the supplement; the Word and Subject Indexes, to the original alone.

CONTENTS

A. INTRODUCTION

To attempt a survey of developments in Romance linguistics in the last thirty years requires, as one distinguished colleague remarked, both 'nerve and verve'. 'Nerve' enough to brave the disapproval of those who feel I misrepresent, or underrepresent, the work of some scholars; 'verve' to overcome the turgidity consequent on trying to cover such a vast field. Limitations will inevitably be imposed by my own ignorance of, and lack of interest in, some developments: for these I can only apologize. But the principal danger, as I see it, is that of submerging the reader in too much bibliographical detail without bringing into relief the methodological trends that have prevailed in the last three decades. Bibliographical surveys for the use of students of Romance languages are amply available[1] (though alas, in these days of copious publication,[2] rapidly out-dated) and some of them have been accused of lack of selectiveness. I shall make no attempt at duplication or

Apologia

---

[1] Bibliographical guides to Romance linguistics include M. de Paiva Boléo ed. 1951, W. Bahner 1962, and T. R. Palfrey *et al.* 1963. Most introductory books on Romance philology and linguistics include selected bibliographies, but especially useful are G. Rohlfs 1950–51 and W. Bal 1966. Among bibliographies for the individual languages we have especially R. A. Hall, Jr. 1958, for Italian; R-L. Wagner 1955, for French; H. Serís 1964, for Spanish; M. T. Atzori 1953 and 1961, for Sardinian; A. Griera 1947, for Catalan; *BFP* (1945–   ), G. Manuppella 1950 and M. J. de Moura Santos 1966 for Portuguese; M. F. Maxfield 1941 and *Bibl. bünd.-rom.* 1956, for Rhetian. Running bibliographies are to be found especially in *ZRP* Supplements—the most recent to date (1967–68) covers the years 1963–64 (cf. G. Ineichen and K. Reichenberger 1967–68)—and there is a yearly survey of work both in Romance linguistics and for each of the individual languages in *YWML*. Each year in the May issue of *PMLA* a current bibliography is to be found: before 1956 this was limited to American authors but it is now international in its coverage.

More general linguistic bibliographies abound. A handy recent one is F. Rice and A. Guss 1965. Also useful is the C.U.P. *Language-Teaching Bibliography*. A complete running bibliography is published by the Comité International Permanent des Linguistes *Bibl. Ling.* (1949–   ): Vols. i–ii cover the years 1939–47, thereafter there is a separate volume every year. Among volumes of abstracts published periodically particularly useful are *Language-Teaching Abstracts* (1968–   ) and *Bull. sig.*—section 21 (1961–   ).

[2] As an example, see the list of relevant periodicals that have begun publication since 1938 (Appendix pp. 541–3).

exhaustive supplementation of such surveys, though I shall pick out those works that seem to me, personally, important, and indicate, for those who wish to pursue any subject in more depth, sources of bibliographical information.

The style of presentation I have adopted is largely dictated by the original text which I have the honour of supplementing. I shall try to retain some of the liveliness and originality of Iordan and Orr's survey, by deliberately selecting some 'schools and scholars', at the risk of offending worthy workers in the field who may be passed over quickly or in silence. My feeling is that the partisan spirit of *Iordan–Orr* partly accounts for its continuing appeal to students: I too shall show, if not partisan spirit, at any rate preference, in that I shall attempt to highlight controversial and personal views rather than to iron out differences to a flat, featureless set of compromises. I am bound thus to appear unfair to some, even though I should disclaim any intention of denigrating the competence or integrity of any. The scholarly world is no stranger to bitter controversy, and its linguistic community often appears to have more than its fair share. Even though disagreement is often nowadays, especially in America, expressed in immoderate terms, it is, I feel, a sign of life, and we should view with alarm any signs of a move towards greater conformity among linguists, especially as a complex reality like language can be observed from many angles each of which will reveal it in a new and valuable light.

In recent years the revolutions and counter-revolutions within linguistics have forced on us an interest in the 'history of the science'. The needs of students, bewildered by the conflicting aims, views, methods and, especially, terminology of rival theorists have dictated the publication of a number of excellent works on 'trends in linguistics', which fill in the gaps left by *Iordan–Orr*, both by tracing back currents of linguistic thought to ancient times and, more often, by describing developments from the 'thirties to the present day. To a large extent my essay overlaps with such works, especially in discussion of those ideas which were not developed primarily by Romanists. A criticism I am bound to meet is that I devote too much space to the work of non-Romanists: this I fear is inevitable in an era in which Romance Linguistics is no longer in the forefront of General Linguistics. But I do attempt in every case to discuss the work of Romanists within the framework of a more general theory. In this I supplement other general surveys of linguistic trends, which I shall introduce briefly to the reader in the following paragraphs.

Perhaps the most significant volumes surveying recent 'trends' in linguistics are those published on the occasion of the 9th International **Histories of** Congress of Linguists.[1] They bring together essays **linguistic** on various aspects of linguistics, and on the activities **thought** of linguists of different nations, written by distinguished scholars. The contributions are uneven in quality, and the second volume is rather a rag-bag which inadequately fills the lacunae left by the first. Some of the essays are, however, indispensable guides to aspects of linguistics and I shall have occasion to refer to them again and again. Another valuable work by a Romanist, B. Malmberg,[2] gives an excellent survey of modern trends, though it is rather unsympathetic to American schools. L. Kukenheim 1966 examines the history of French linguistics within the framework of General and Romance Linguistics, and as such is invaluable to Romanists. M. Leroy 1966 is less comprehensive, but can serve as a comparatively superficial introduction.[3] We should mention too M. Ivić 1965 which devotes a good deal of attention to work of Romance scholars, overlapping with *Iordan–Orr* to some extent, but covering also more modern schools. Mostly concerned with modern linguistics is G. C. Lepschy's Italian paperback[4] which gives an excellent picture of current modes of thought. Although in the form of an introductory text-book, F. P. Dineen 1967 is more useful as a survey of recent ideas on linguistics than as a student's handbook: giving as it does potted versions of a number of scholars' views (Saussure, Sapir, Bloomfield, Firth, Hjelmslev, and Chomsky) it enjoys a certain popularity among linguistic neophytes.

Shorter essayistic surveys of the contemporary scene include E. Haugen, "Directions in Modern Linguistics", *L* xxvii (1951), pp. 211–22; A. Martinet, "Structural Linguistics", in A. Kroeber

---

[1] *Trends i* (1961) and *Trends ii* (1963). The new editions and translations of Iordan's original work will be discussed below. The projected series of twelve weighty volumes entitled *Current Trends in Linguistics* is of quite different character, aiming at much more complete coverage and at encouraging original research contributions in the subjects discussed. Essays contained in the "Theoretical Foundations" volume (T. A. Sebeok (ed.) 1966*a*) are based on a series of special lectures given at the American Linguistic Society Summer Institute; the other volumes are independent surveys of research in various areas (cf. e.g. P. L. Garvin *et al.* (eds.) 1963; R. Lado *et al.* (eds.) (forthcoming); E. Haugen and W. Winter (eds.) (forthcoming)).

[2] B. Malmberg 1964. The work was originally destined for Swedish readers, however, so Romance examples are few: in the French translation some French illustrations have been added. For other work by Malmberg cf. pp. 538.

[3] We look forward to the publication of G. Mounin (forthcoming), which promises to be useful for students of Romance.

[4] G. C. Lepschy 1966. In Portuguese we also have S. Elia 1955, and in Spanish A. M. Badía Margarit and J. Roca Pons 1958.

(ed.) 1953 pp. 574–86, comparing American and European thought;[1] E. Benveniste, "Tendances récentes en linguistique générale", in E. Benveniste 1966, a masterly *tour d'horizon*; and N. Ruwet, "La linguistique générale aujourd'hui", in *ArES* v (1964), pp. 277–310.[2] R. A. Hall's surveys of the American linguistic scene (cf. p. 510) are mentioned in the section on the American school. His most recent survey, however, discussing as it does Chomskyan ideas, more properly deserves mention here: "Some recent developments in American linguistics", in *NMi* lxx (1969) pp. 192–227.

In a rather different category are those works which seek to describe the scope of linguistics today: designed principally for the British undergraduate-to-be we have D. Crystal's little book *What is linguistics?*[3] while a wider audience is envisaged in a number of inaugural lectures given at British universities.[4] Here too we should mention the more essayistic discursions on language and linguistics that have been prompted by recent controversies in the discipline— like those of N. A. Chomsky, *Cartesian Linguistics* and *Language and Mind*,[5] R. A. Hall, Jr., *An Essay on Language*,[6] C. F. Hockett, *The State of the Art*[7] and E. Pulgram's "Science, Humanities and the Place of Linguistics".[8]

Most surveys of contemporary thought look back, as does *Iordan–Orr*, to earlier linguistic ideas, in an attempt to put present trends in proper perspective. Recently, study of the history of linguistic thought has become popular and a number of works are now available to the student. The nineteenth century—during which linguistics came to be regarded as a science—often receives most attention: the classic (1924) work by H. Pedersen has recently been re-issued

---

[1] Cf. also R. d'Avinos's survey "Strutturalismo", in *Enciclopedia Italiana 1949–1960*, and H. H. Christmann, "Strukturelle Sprachwissenschaft", in *RJ* ix (1958) pp. 17–40 and xii (1961) pp. 23–50.

[2] The other work of A. Martinet is discussed pp. 491–92; that of the younger Belgian scholar, N. Ruwet, is mentioned in my discussion of Chomskyan theory (pp. 519–23). Emile Benveniste, however, is not separately discussed as he is not primarily a Romanist, though he is a highly distinguished general linguist and Indo-Europeanist. Born in 1902, he has taught at the Ecole des Hautes Etudes since 1927 and at the Collège de France since 1937, and has profoundly influenced many Romance linguists.

[3] D. Crystal 1968.

[4] Cf. P. Strevens (ed.) 1966, especially W. S. Allen, "On the Linguistic Study of Languages" (also published separately by Cambridge U.P., 1957); T. F. Mitchell 1965; and J. Lyons 1967.

[5] N. A. Chomsky 1966 and 1968.

[6] R. A. Hall, Jr. 1968.

[7] C. F. Hockett 1968.

[8] In D. E. Thackray (ed.) 1967, pp. 67–95.

and revised;[1] J. Waterman 1963 shows how American structuralism has its roots in neo-grammarian thought; and other works give pride of place to the nineteenth and twentieth centuries.[2] The growth of influence of the Chomskyan school has, however, led to a revival of interest in seventeenth- and eighteenth-century ideas;[3] R. H. Robins 1967 also devotes a relatively large amount of space to ancient and medieval theories, as well as to non-European ideas.[4] Besides narrative accounts, we now also have collections of readings illustrating changing tendencies: most interesting perhaps is T. A. Sebeok's *Portraits of Linguists*,[5] which reproduces ninety obituary and memorial notices of seventy-three linguists born before the twentieth century, including a fair number of Romanists; other useful source-books include V. A. Zvegincev 1964, T. Bolelli 1965, W. P. Lehmann (ed.) 1967, D. E. Hayden *et al.* (eds.) 1968 and A. Jacob (forthcoming). M. Joos (ed.) 1957 (1966) though when it first appeared in 1957 apparently an illustration of accepted twentieth-century American linguistic thought, now can be considered as a historical source-book, and is now supplemented by a second volume,[6] which covers the much less homogeneous European thought of a similar period. J. A. Fodor and J. J. Katz (eds.) 1964 performs the same function for linguistic ideas along Chomskyan lines.[7]

The growth in popularity of linguistics as an undergraduate subject has led also to a spate of general and introductory books on language,[8] many of which have a definite methodological slant;

---

[1] H. Pedersen 1962.

[2] E.g. C. Tagliavini 1963; A. Graur and L. Wald 1965; G. Mounin 1967, to be supplemented by a twentieth-century volume; and M. Lema Mourelle 1968. Also *AnL* v, 1 (1963), a volume devoted to the history of linguistics, with articles by a number of distinguished linguists. In Spanish we also have M. Alvar 1951 and A. Llorente 1967, in Portuguese J. P. Machado 1942, and in Italian, on Romance studies, A. Viscardi *et al.* 1955.

[3] Besides N. A. Chomsky 1966, we should mention R. A. Donzé 1967 and the articles shortly to appear in *Gl*, L. Benoit, "Cartesian linguistics: a rebuttal", and R. Predovich, "A critique of Chomsky's *Cartesian Linguistics*". For Spanish linguistic thought at the same period, see W. Bahner 1956 and F. Lázaro Carreter 1949. On linguistic thought in Romania at even earlier periods cf. R-L. Wagner, "Contribution à la préhistoire du romanisme", *Conférences de l'Institut de Linguistique de Paris* x (1950–51) pp. 101–24.

[4] As yet unpublished, the proceedings of a symposium on "Revolution vs. Continuity in the Study of Language" held under the auspices of the Wenner-Gren Foundation for Anthropological Research in August, 1964, provide a particularly stimulating account of the history of linguistics. Among those invited were the Romanists Y. Malkiel, P. Guiraud and A. J. Greimas.

[5] T. A. Sebeok (ed.) 1966*b*.

[6] E. P. Hamp *et al.* (eds.) 1966.

[7] For a collection of 'readings' within the field of Romance linguistics cf. J. M. Anderson (forthcoming).

[8] E.g. from Romanists and Romance-speaking scholars: B. Terracini 1942; B. Migliorini 1946; M. Cohen 1950*a*; J. Vendryes 1950; C. Tagliavini 1950;

some of these will be mentioned later as representing a particular school of thought but in general neither such works nor glossaries of linguistic terminology[1] fall within the scope of this essay.

Iorgu Iordan's original work on Romance linguistics[2] was an early example of the now popular *genre* of 'history of the science' and **Iordan–Orr: history of the text** 'state of the art'. Its reception[3] was mixed, though on the whole favourable: complaints were made about lacunae[4] and biased judgements,[5] about the misleading title,[6] about its theoretical, rather than practical, slant.[7] But some scholars were enthusiastic.[8] Sneyders de Vogel's comments are worth quoting here (if only as some sort of vindication for the present exercise):

C'est un livre très bien fait et je n'hésite pas à le recommander chaudement aux étudiants et à tous ceux qui veulent se tenir au courant des grandes

M. A. Pei 1952; J. Perrot 1953; A. Graur 1958; J. M. Câmara, Jr. 1959; A. Martinet 1960; C. Schick 1960; S. da Silva Neto 1960; W. von Wartburg 1963; R. A. Hall, Jr. 1964; J. G. C. Herculano de Carvalho 1967; D. Bolinger 1968; G. Mounin 1968; R. W. Langacker 1968. See also the translations of E. Sapir 1921. Among works written by non-Romanists especially to be recommended are: C. F. Hockett 1958; R. H. Robins 1964; J. Lyons 1968. Purely on descriptive linguistics of the American type we should mention: Z. S. Harris 1951; A. A. Hill 1958 and H. A. Gleason 1961; and on historical linguistics, B. Terracini 1949; G. Devoto 1951; H. Hoenigswald 1960 and W. P. Lehmann 1962. T. B. W. Reid's inaugural lecture at Oxford (T. B. W. Reid 1960) also deserves mention here.
[1] E.g. of more general scope: F. Lázaro Carreter 1962, M. A. Pei 1966, D. Steible 1967, R. Nash 1968, M. A. Pei and F. Gaynor 1968; and concerned with the terminology of particular schools of thought: E. de Felice 1954, for the school of Ascoli; J. Vachek 1960, for the Prague school; E. P. Hamp 1963, for American usage; and R. Engler 1968, for Saussurean usage.
[2] Iordan 1932. An article in W. Streitberg 1924 (fest.) ("Der heutige Stand der romanischen Sprachwissenschaft", pp. 585–621) preceded the book, and aroused the wrath of the master, Meyer-Lübke himself, who objected to Iordan's 'antipositivist' position (cf. "Die romanische Sprachwissenschaft der letzen zwölf jahre", *RLiR* i (1925) pp. 11–12).
[3] Cf. for reviews O. Densusianu, *Grai şi suflet* (1931) pp. 390–2; P. Fouché, *RLaR* lxvi (1932) pp. 474–56; A. Långfors, *NMi* xxiv (1933) p. 203. A. Graur, *BSLP* xxiv (1933) pp. 78–80; W. J. Entwistle, *MLR* xxix (1934) pp. 212–15; S. Puşcariu, *Dacorumania* vii (1934) pp. 474–4; W. Giese, *ZRP* xiv(1935) pp. 215–16; V. Buben, *ČMF* xxv (1938–39) pp. 213–14.
[4] By M. Valkhoff, for instance, and R. C. Johnston, in their reviews of *Iordan–Orr* (cf. below, p. 405 n. 1). Johnston complains especially about the lack of attention paid to phoneticians and Latinists.
[5] E.g. by P. Fouché. Jud, in his review of *Iordan–Orr* (below, p. 405, n. 1), complained of its unsympathetic treatment of toponymical studies, while Wartburg thought it too pro-Vossler.
[6] E.g. P. Fouché and A. Graur.
[7] E.g. A. Graur.
[8] E.g. W. Giese, and A. Långfors ("Ce livre, qui est matériellement d'une rare exactitude, est, avec sa richesse de détails de toute sorte, un très précieux instrument de travail.").

questions discutées et des beaux résultats acquis par la science actuelle. Le malheur est que les livres de ce genre vieillissent vite . . . A cet inconvénient pourra seule remédier une suite de rééditions toujours mises à jour, succès que nous souhaitons vivement à ce beau livre.

The first of the re-editions was the translation and reworking of Iordan's text by John Orr, published in 1937, and here reprinted with only a few minor corrections. The almost universal acclaim[1] that greeted this version in itself justifies a re-issue, for it has become a source document of great importance shaping the theoretical attitudes of a generation of Romance linguists.[2] As an undergraduate in the early 'fifties, I myself turned with joy to its lucidity and attractiveness (of style, presentation, and typography), after the worthy, but, for the young, arid and indigestible (not to say musty) volumes that were the everyday fare of budding Romance linguists. Even at that time the book was virtually unobtainable and was treasured as providing a methodological guide to the work of scholars whose austerity often led them to eschew all but hard facts and rigorous reasoning. Moreover, and even more important, *Iordan–Orr* provided the bridge between our philological studies and our practical language and literary programmes, illuminating for us the relevance of a scientific study of language *per se*, to the rather different disciplines united with it in the traditional language and literature course.

Other versions of Iordan's work have since appeared: in 1962 a new, refurbished Rumanian edition was published, at the same time as its translation into German, which was supplemented by a brief review of structuralist trends in linguistics by the translator, the East German scholar, W. Bahner:[3] not unnaturally his sympathy appeared to lie more with modern German thought (especially the

---

[1] For reviews, cf. M. R.(oques), *R* lxiv (1938) p. 142; J. Jud, *VR* iii (1936) pp. 392–32; W. von Wartburg, *ZRP* lix (1939) pp. 108–9; R. C. Johnston, *MLR* xxxiv (1939) pp. 101–2; E. Lerch, *RF* liii (1939) pp. 356–8; M. Valkhoff, *Museum* xlvii (1940) pp. 114–15; K. Sneyders de Vogel, *N* xxvi (1941) p. 61. M. de Paiva Boléo, *Biblos* xix (1943) pp. 574–8.

[2] See the comment of Y. Malkiel (*RPh* xvii (1964) p. 827) ". . . the superbly printed English version of the book acquired real importance". R. A. Hall, Jr. 1963 perhaps even exaggerates the influence that the book has had—to his mind an evil influence: (p. 84) "That Romance linguistics is still plagued with a division into "schools" and with sterile debates between the adherents of one "leader" and those of another, is due in large part to the influence of Iordan and Orr. The *Introduction* has been used to give many neophytes their first acquaintance with the field of Romance linguistics, being used (as it should not have been) in substitution for a true elementary manual, and determining attitudes in advance of factual knowledge rather than presenting data first." Cf. also p. 451 for Hall's criticisms of *Iordan–Orr*.

[3] I. Iordan 1962 and *Iordan–Bahner* 1962. A short introduction on the 'pre-history of Romance Linguistics', by Bahner, is also included in the German edition.

Trier-type 'semantic field' approach) than with more influential American ideas. It is the 1962 Rumanian version, too, that was translated into Spanish and partly reworked by Manuel Alvar for publication in 1967:[1] Alvar's supplementations are slotted into the original text and concern mainly Spanish and Portuguese contributions, especially in dialectology and stylistics.

My own efforts at supplementation do in some ways overlap with Iordan's own revisions and additions in his 1962 text. However, I have tried to retain more the 'theoretical bias' and 'eclecticism' of the 1937 text, and have paid most attention to those schools of thought which have, I believe, changed the direction of linguistic studies in the last thirty years, and for which Iordan as an octogenarian (albeit a sprightly one) can hardly be expected to have much sympathy.

In 1968 Iordan was eighty years old, an eighty years in which his homeland, Rumania, has undergone many tribulations; yet nonetheless his contributions to language studies **Iorgu Iordan (1888–).** have been copious.[2] To most Romanists Iordan is known as the theoretician of Romance linguistics,[3] but most of his work has been concerned with the Rumanian language, especially dialectology and stylistics. His initial training, however, was in German, and after taking his first degree in 1911 he taught in secondary schools, taking his doctorate in Modern Philology in 1919. The years 1921 to 1926 were spent abroad, first in Germany (Bonn and Berlin) and then in Paris; he returned to Rumania to teach at Jassy University until 1946, becoming a corresponding member of the Academy in 1934. After the war he became Professor at Bucharest University (taking leave to serve as ambassador to the USSR in 1945–47), and he was its Rector from 1957 to 1958. In 1963 he "retired" to the post of "Consultant Professor". He became a full Academician in 1945 and was Vice President of the Academy in 1966. He was director of the Academy's Institute of Linguistics from 1949 to 1952, and again from 1958 onwards. He is an honorary president of the Société de Linguistique Romane.

[1] *Iordan–Alvar* 1967. A notable gap in Iordan's survey was the comparative lack of attention paid to Spanish linguists.

[2] For bibliographies cf. especially Iordan's 70th birthday presentation volume: I. Iordan 1958 (fest.): and in the article in homage to him on his 80th birthday, in *RRL* xiii (1968) pp. 388–96.

[3] Cf., for instance, besides his books, "Lucrări recente de lingvistica romanică generală", *RFRG* vii (1963) pp. 121–6 (also in French in *RRL* viii, pp. 285–91) and "Problèmes généraux de la linguistique romane", in *Actes 11ᵉ Cong. (Madrid) 1965* pp. 103–16.

Iordan's views are those that come over clearly in the Introduction—his sympathy with Idealist thought is tempered by his own honest-to-goodness empiricism. He believes that dialectological studies are of particular importance in reminding us that language is spoken by *people*. Thus his own humanist and sociological interests can embrace such apparently widely different studies as literary style or slang and popular speech.

In John Orr, Iordan found a translator who was not only virtually an age peer but also in some ways a kindred spirit.[1] They worked

John Orr (1885–1966)[2] for the most part, however, in different fields within Romance linguistics—Orr being a French specialist with a particular interest in etymology.[3]

Indeed, it seems rather odd that Orr's first really major publication (apart from work on medieval French texts) should have been one with a methodological and theoretical slant, for interest in 'meta-language-study' seemed to go against the grain for Orr. It may be that it was because the Iordan original did unite humanistic bias with interest in method that Orr was attracted by it.

His own attitude to language is summed up in his preface to a collection of his essays published in 1953, under the title *Words and Sounds in English and French*[4] and dedicated to the memory of Jules Gilliéron. Referring to his own writings he says:

... they are as far removed from the pseudo-science of the neogrammarians as from the pseudo-mathematics of the Structuralists and 'Linguisticians'. They are, in fact, completely out-of-date, no less those written yesterday than those composed some twenty years ago. Secondly, and more positively, they attempt to mitigate as far as possible the unavoidable danger that besets all study of language, namely, that of doing violence to, if not destroying, the very object of study by isolating its closely integrated elements, sound and sense, form and content. Finally, they attempt to view language as an essentially human activity, complex, purposeful and gratuitous, fumbling and ingenious, practical and playful, serious and whimsical.

Although born in Cumberland, Orr spent his childhood in Tasmania, taking his first degree, in classics, at Hobart University

---

[1] An obituary of Orr by Iordan appeared in *SCL* xviii (1967) pp. 365–6.

[2] Among obituaries we should mention T. B. W. Reid's in *MLR* lxii (1967) pp. 190–1, A. Ewert's in the *Proceedings of the British Academy* lii (1966) pp. 323–31, and those by P. Gardette and G. Straka and by A. Gill in *RLiR* xxxi (1967) pp. 1–10. An earlier account of his work, by D. Legge, appeared in *O* i (1952) pp. 278–81.

[3] Bibliographies of his work appeared in the presentation volume J. Orr, 1953 (fest.) and in *RLiR* xxxi (1967) pp. 11–15.

[4] J. Orr 1953. Cf. also J. Orr 1963: "Il est certes légitime, et sans doute profitable d'examiner sous le microscope une abeille morte ou vivante mais le naturaliste qui se livre à cet examen, quels renseignements en tire-t-il sur l'activité prodigieuse de la ruche?"

(1903–5). As a Rhodes Scholar at Balliol College, Oxford, he read for Honour Mods (in classics), followed by Schools in Jurisprudence (1909). As an undergraduate he made his mark in Balliol, being President of the Arnold Society and rowing in the college eight. In 1910 he went to France to prepare a B.Litt. degree on Guiot de Provins, and married, during his stay, a Frenchwoman from St. Petersburg (who died in 1961). It was during this period, under the guidance of Gilliéron, Bédier, A. Thomas, A. Jeanroy and M. Roques, that he must have developed the linguistic tastes that afterwards characterized him. When an Assistant Lecturer at Manchester, his career was interrupted by the Great War: from 1915 he served in the army.[1] After the war he went to a Chair at Manchester (1919), and thence, in 1933, to the Chair of French Language and Romance Linguistics at Edinburgh where he lived till his death, after retiring from his post in 1955. He was in the same year made Commandeur de la Légion d'Honneur. After playing a leading rôle in the reconstitution of the Société de Linguistique Romane in 1953, he was active in the society until his death. He stood aside from nomination as president in favour first of Mario Roques and then of Walther von Wartburg, so that when he did eventually accept the presidency, in 1965, it was to be only for a short time. In 1964 he was also elected president of the Fédération Internationale des Langues et Littératures Modernes, but his death occurred shortly before the 1966 Strasbourg Congress that he was to preside over.

Given the personalities and preferences of the authors, the outstanding features of *Iordan–Orr* are predictable: its 'humanistic' rather than 'scientific' bias, for instance, and its

Iordan–Orr's approach

rejection of language study divorced from the study of man. In contrast to most of the Romanist works of the preceding generation, it emphasized the living, lively, 'open-air' quality of the discipline,—the field-worker cycling around to chat with peasants, rather than the philologist poring over the dusty manuscripts of the medieval clerk. It stressed too the importance of study of the present-day languages, whereas previously more attention had been paid to Late Latin and Medieval Romance. Moreover, it was ready to recognize the vital contribution to linguistic development made by creative users of the language, so that texts of literary merit are thought particularly worthy of linguistic study.

---

[1] We might mention here his grievous loss in the second World War when, in 1944, his only son was shot down on an R.A.F. mission.

Other qualities (or, for some critics, 'defects') of the book stem
from its purpose as an introductory work. Its emphasis on differences
in methodological approach is connected with its view of Romance
linguistics as a living subject: the student learns how to *do* it, rather
than merely memorizes 'established' facts. If vigour appears sometimes to take precedence over rigour in *Iordan-Orr*, this is all in
keeping with its aim actively to involve its readers in the burning
issues of the discipline. The book's eclecticism too is an essential part
of its liveliness, for the authors, being only human, could not be
equally as enthusiastic or knowledgeable about all work in the field.

Romance linguistics for *Iordan-Orr* was still primarily a historical
study—even though, after Saussure, interest was beginning to turn
to linguistic description. Where descriptive work is discussed (as
in dialectological or 'popular language' studies) it is usually seen in a
dynamic perspective. More static descriptivism has tended to
'balkanize' Romance linguistics—in that each of the individual
Romance languages may seem to share few synchronic features with
its fellows, and so a comparative approach appears to yield only
scant results. The 'crisis' of Romance linguistics dates from after
Iordan-Orr and must be viewed in relation to developments in the
field of General linguistics since 1937.

Perhaps the single most significant 'external' factor occasioning
change in the linguistic scene since just before the war has been the
Changes in shift of the scholarly 'centre of gravity' across the
linguistics Atlantic. Fascism in Europe led to the migration of
since Iordan- many European scholars to America; then the war
Orr and its economic aftermath left European universities in a weak state, while the American postwar boom financed an
unprecedented expansion of all education and research activities.
The 'brain drain' of European scholars of all grades of seniority
continues—though, in linguistics, it is more often the younger
researchers who seek in USA Graduate Schools, not their fortune,
but a degree of technical training not catered for in the European
university system.

One corollary of the American predominance in linguistics has
been that German traditions of scholarship have been preferred to
those of the Romance world.[1] In graduate schools, in particular,

[1] On the state of Romance linguistics in America until recently, see especially

technical know-how has taken precedence over intuition; moreover, the structure of their courses has favoured a separation of linguistic from literary programmes. Physical distance, if nothing else, has rendered Americans less interested in European linguistic problems: the rich 'native American' (Indian) linguistic material close at hand has often held more attraction. Of less general significance but still important, is the fact that the learning of French—the Romance language most copiously supplied with linguistic commentaries—is comparatively little favoured in the US.

Among 'internal' linguistic developments the most important has been the growing emphasis on 'scientific' approaches to language. 'Scientific' in this context is not always synonymous with 'empirical', but does entail concern with definitions, procedures and general theories, an interest in methodology and pursuit of knowledge at a high level of abstraction. Links between linguistics and such disciplines as mathematics and cybernetics have flourished, and often the old-fashioned humanist linguist finds himself at sea among modern 'linguisticians'.

The scientific bias of modern linguistics is obviously connected with American dominance of the field. The same is true too of the way in which practical 'applied' linguistics has assumed importance in the last three decades—problems of language teaching, of machine translation and so on are not, of course, exclusively studied by Americans, but it is probably fair to say that the impetus has come principally from America.

The shift of interest from linguistic history to linguistic description is certainly not exclusively American in origin, though Americans have sometimes been more vehement in their rejection of the dynamic perspective than Europeans. Patently, concern with abstract structures, with languages of non-literate societies, or with practical language problems, all in their different ways point to the need for developing techniques of language description. But more probably, the fading out of historical linguistics of late has been due to a feeling that the nineteenth-century masters had overcome the problems and formulated the relevant technical procedures, so that adventurous spirits have preferred to turn to the comparatively unexplored field of linguistic description. The temporary[1] eclipse

Y. Malkiel's comment in *RPh* xxi (1968) p. 366: "For a dreary stretch of thirty or forty years practitioners of Romance linguistics in this country had found it hard to walk with heads erect—such was their acute awareness, and so frequent were the painful reminders, of the relative weakness of their discipline in comparison to its rivals, of far more obvious appeal."

[1] A new renaissance in historical linguistics may now be expected: Cf. especially W. P. Lehmann and Y. Malkiel (eds.) 1968.

of historical linguistics has been bound to bring with it a neglect of the study of language families: Romance linguistics has perhaps suffered most. This is not to say that work in the field has become less abundant, but it does mean that Romanists are rarely any longer in the forefront of linguistic progress.

The picture of the Romance linguistic scene, as painted by *Iordan–Orr*, has changed for the worse in the last thirty years: for

The crisis in Romance linguistics

one thing, as was only to be expected, many of the brilliant figures featured there have disappeared.[1] But the change has been more radical than that, so much so that Romanists unite to bewail the crisis that their discipline is passing through.[2] The symptoms are not hard to see: the prestige that once attached to Romance linguists is lost, and now

[1] The toll has been heavy, even though many of the Romanists mentioned in *Iordan–Orr* have lived to a ripe old age (for *Festschriften* and memorial volumes see the Bibliography). It is painful to record that nearly every year has seen the death of at least one 'grand master'.

1938	F. Brunot, Densusianu, Ettmayer, Trubetzkoy.
1939	Grandgent, Pichon, Sapir.
1940	Passy.
1942	Bertoni, Brøndal, Gauchat, Sandfeld, Wilmotte.
1943	Damourette.
1945	van Ginneken, O. Keller.
1946	Bàrtoli, Bourciez, Grammont, Haust, Henríquez Ureña, Sechehaye.
1947	Bally, de Boer, Melander.
1948	Puşcariu.
1949	Bloomfield, Vossler.
1950	Ostermann.
1952	Amado Alonso, Croce, Jud, Lerch.
1953	Millardet.
1954	Tesnière.
1955	Dauzat, Terracher.
1956	Duraffour, Grégoire.
1957	E. Auerbach.
1958	L. Foulet, Jaberg, A. Långfors, Sneyders de Vogel.
1959	da Silva Neto.
1960	Elcock, Gustave Guillaume, Merlo, Muller, Spitzer, Vendryes.
1961	M. Roques, S. Pop.
1962	K Michaëlsson.
1963	M L. Wagner.
1965	A. Sommerfelt.
1966	J. Orr, Hubschmied.
1967	P Fouché
1968	R. Menéndez Pidal, E. Petrovici, B. Terracini.

However, among those mentioned by *Iordan–Orr*, we are glad still to have with us (early in 1969) as senior representatives of Romance linguistics, such distinguished scholars as C. Bruneau, Marcel Cohen, A. Ewert, E. Gamillscheg, G. Gougenheim, A. Graur, A. Griera, H. Kahane, B. Migliorini, T. Navarro, G. Rohlfs, A. Rosetti, F. Schürr, B. E. Vidos, and W. von Wartburg. Other names have also come into prominence, and we shall have occasion to refer to them in the course of this essay. P.S. It is with great sorrow that I learn the death of Alfred Ewert (Oct. 1969).

[2] Cf. Iordan's triennial reports to the Romance linguistics congresses (e.g. to the 10th Congress, where he regretfully admits that "les progrès accomplis sont plutôt quantitatifs que qualitatifs").

accrues to the more theoretically minded 'scientific' linguists, who often rise meteorically to university's posts of eminence that their elders toiled for long years to attain. Both dusty manuscripts and open-air field-work are replaced by armchair speculation, and the silence of individual worrying out of problems by the garrulity of group discussion and oral interchange of ideas. The Romanist, in objecting to new trends, is often put in the position of the testy old man who cannot keep up with activities of nimbler youth. In short, Romance linguistics often appears old-fashioned,[1] a refuge for the slower-witted but conscientious academic 'swot'.

In that apprentices in the Romance field have to become acquainted with a vast amount of work done by their predecessors, it is true that they have to be 'swots': many younger linguists today are only too eager to believe that anything written more than a few years ago is not worth reading, but all too often scorn for their elders is only a cloak for their own indolence. It is true too that the Romance languages present such a plethora of material that those who seek to draw up neat and elegant schemata are daunted by them. More important, perhaps, the most outstanding problems of Romance linguistics appear to be solved, or insoluble, while more readily accessible problems in other fields remain untouched: the young scholar is spurred on by the hope that he will make a momentous contribution to knowledge and fears that Romance linguistics offers no scope for his ambition.

Our diagnosis of the complaint will necessarily influence the remedy we propose (if we are not merely to let the patient die quietly). Iordan[2] is not prepared to accept modernist theories, but feels that Romanists should make an effort to master them, if only to refute them. A. Roncaglia,[3] on the other hand, thinks they should turn towards a study of Western European civilization, broadening the scope of their interests. R. A. Hall, Jr.,[4] believes that a return to

---

[1] As S. Ullmann mildly puts it, in his comments on the 10th Congress (1962): "On the whole, however, one came away with the feeling that Romance scholarship is somewhat outside the mainstream of developments in contemporary linguistic theory . . ." *FS* xx (1966), pp. 435–6.

[2] "L'état actuel de la linguistique romane et ses perspectives de développement", *Actes 10e Cong. (Strasbourg) 1962*, pp. 71–84.

[3] "Prospettive della filologia romanza", *CN* xvi (1956) pp. 95–107.

[4] R. A. Hall, Jr. 1963 p. 19. "There should be going on in the Romance field—should have been ever since Meyer-Lübke's time—an intense activity in the reconstruction of Proto-Romance and intermediate proto-stages, and in the testing and refining of already proven procedures. Yet no such activity is going on; on the contrary, it is neglected or opposed. Romance linguistics are now, as a group, over half a century behind the times in their general refusal to accept modern developments in structural linguistics, in their refusal to advance beyond the level reached

by Jules Gilliéron (1854–1926) in linguistic geography, and in their continued opposition to historical reconstruction. This backwardness is due to two chief influences: the continuing dead hand of Schuchardtian attitudes, and the principles of idealism developed in the first third of the twentieth century."

I hope I may be forgiven if I quote from my own reply to Hall on the value of reconstruction ("Positivism in Historical Linguistics", *RPh* xx pp. 327–30):

"The utility of reconstruction as a way of stating concisely the highest common factor of forms obviously related in form and meaning is evident. The starred forms produced by our reconstructive exercise can easily be matched against any new sets of data that may emerge, providing a valuable check on the method. In some cases, as in the reconstruction of, say, Proto-Negro-African, the chances of finding corroborating documentary evidence are slim: the methods used must be modelled on those carefully worked out in a data-rich field like Romance. In Romance the match between our reconstruction and the data provided by Latin texts is amazingly good (of course, the fact that we knew Latin BEFORE we embarked on reconstruction kept us on the right tack). Still, the match is not perfect, and much of the research done in Romance linguistics aims at accounting for the discrepancies between our Proto-forms and their attested counterparts . . .

"The concept of the 'ancestral language' as a way of explaining certain types of similarity between languages presumably grew from the known historical facts in Romance, coupled with the assumption that certain items of the language— grammatical morphemes, basic lexicon—tend to be transmitted from generation to generation, not being subject to loss and substitution at the same rate as other parts of the language . . . Another observed fact that led to the 'ancestral language' hypothesis was, no doubt, that 'older stages' of related languages are, in general, more similar than 'later stages' (though the absorption of lexical and syntactic Latinisms has, to some extent, counter-balanced this trend in Romance). Where we have diverging lines, it is tempting to produce them until they converge on a point, thus:

"Certain conceptual difficulties arise in performing this 'triangulation' exercise, however. One, most important, is to know how far A is linearly descended from Old A, i.e., how far there has been continuity in the use of Old A to the present day. It is possible that the sample of Old A available to us for study is an unrepresentative one—the very fact that texts survive suggests that they may have been particularly treasured, in some cases for material reasons (e.g., legal documents), in others for 'higher' motives (e.g., literary works). In any case, their 'register' is likely to be 'non-casual', and we rarely have evidence of the spoken norm against which to measure them. Besides, the language process must imply some creativity, and a constant dialectic opposition between social continuity and individual discontinuity. Hence some modern historical linguists prefer to think in terms of 'replacement'—a discontinuous process—rather than of 'change'—implying linear progression. . . ."

Hall may be pleased to find that a representative of another 'enemy' camp, the Chomskyan, uses what are virtually reconstructionist techniques in what purports to be a linguistic description. S. A. Schane 1968 constructs as the 'underlying form' of French something that could pass as Proto-Romance: in fact his method, of seeking to resolve morphophonemic anomalies by reference to an underlying regular form is virtually identical with that of 'internal reconstruction': cf. H. Hoenigswald, "Sound Change and Linguistic Structure", in M. Joos (ed.) 1957 (1966) pp. 139–41.

neogrammarian reconstructionist methods is the only solution for Romance linguistics, which has been intolerably perverted by Idealist notions. Y. Malkiel[1] feels that Romance linguistics has developed a 'style' of its own, and has an important contribution to make to linguistics as 'a highly atypical subdiscipline'.

Perhaps, however, in recognizing his malady, our patient is recovering himself: papers presented at the 1968 Bucharest Congress show more awareness of modern linguistic ideas, and the number of Romance linguists is growing yearly. Certainly, the number of general and introductory books has increased by leaps and bounds— an indication that the general public think there is life yet in Romance linguistics.

General and introductory works in Romance linguistics can take many forms. The comparative historical grammar[2]—on the Diez and Meyer-Lübke pattern—is not now common, but H. Lausberg 1956–62[3] is an excellent example. More often the pattern that is followed is that of the Bourciez manual,[4] discussing each language in turn, after a survey of the common source in Latin—W. D. Elcock 1960[5] is a good example of this type, and so is, for the earlier periods, the more detailed C. Tagliavini 1959.[6] Some valuable works are more

General books on the Romance languages

[1] Cf. especially "Three Definitions of Romance Linguistics", *RPh* xv (1961) pp. 1–7, and "Distinctive Traits of Romance Linguistics", in D. Hymes (ed.) 1964 pp. 671–88: "Easily the most precious gifts that Romance linguistics has so far tendered to general linguistics include an almost oversubtle approach to dialect geography, a firm grasp of the osmosis between literary languages and the corresponding gamut of vernaculars, and a vast reservoir of practice in etymology, with a record of meticulous, zestfully conducted monographic researches not yet welded into a single thoroughly integrated discipline."
[2] Cf. especially Y. Malkiel, "A tentative typology of Romance historical grammars", *Li* ix (1960) pp. 321–416, reprinted with slight modifications in Y. Malkiel 1968.
[3] Though the four pocket-size volumes do not compare, in physical weight, with the older models. Lausberg's work is a replacement for A. Zauner 1900, and shows marks of his 'diachronic structuralist' approach (cf. p. 494). Born in 1912, Lausberg worked from 1937 to 1941 with Wartburg on his French etymological dictionary and became, after the war, professor at Münster.
[4] Recent editions of this work (e.g. E. Bourciez 1967) owe much to Edouard's son, Jean Bourciez (born 1894, professor at Montpellier).
[5] For Elcock cf. p. 470. His book *The Romance Languages* (1960) was the first truly 'introductory' text-book on the subject. Besides accounts of the "Latin Foundation" and the creation of each of the Romance standard languages, it includes discussion of early non-Latin influences, both substratal and superstratal, as well as of medieval Latin and its inter-relationship with the Romance vernaculars.
[6] Tagliavini, professor at Padua, was born in Bologna in 1903, and spent some time in Holland, at Nijmegen (1927–28), and in Hungary, at Budapest (1929–35).

in the nature of bibliographical guides to the problems of Romance linguistics and literatures—the best of this type is perhaps G. Rohlfs 1950–52 and 1966, and A. Kuhn 1951[1] is also to be recommended.[2] E. Auerbach 1949 provides a more readable introduction to languages and literatures.

General methodological surveys, in both cases rather anodyne, are to be found in B. E. Vidos 1956[3] and W. Bal 1966.[4] In Vidos, there follows a Bourciez-type survey, while Bal omits linguistic discussion of the individual languages, substituting demographic and geographical information. I. Iordan and Maria Manoliu 1965 is an excellent introduction, with Iordan providing an account of 'external' history and Maria Manoliu a succinct comparative historical grammar. R. Posner 1966 is meant for the general reader and is accused of being rather chatty: it examines such questions as 'In what sense are the Romance languages derived from the same source?' and 'How did they differentiate?' and makes a point-by-point comparison of all the languages, literary and non-literary.[5]

One of the most important problems for comparative Romance linguistics concerns the status of 'Vulgar Latin' or 'Proto-Romance' —either as a form of popular Latin or a theoretical construct.[6]

His linguistic interests cover Hungarian and Albanian, as well as Romance. C. Tagliavini 1959 contains a brief survey of developments in Romance linguistics, and lists outstanding scholars.

[1] A. Kuhn (1902–68) was from 1940 to 1952 professor at Marburg, and then, till his death, at Innsbruck. Cf. A. Kuhn 1963 (fest.).

[2] Less useful, being rather sketchy, is R. Rohr 1964.

[3] Vidos's survey is a paler version of *Iordan–Orr*, brought up-to-date with a rather unsympathetic review of modern trends. Vidos, professor at Nijmegen since 1946, was born in Budapest in 1902, taking his doctorate there in 1928; after stays in Italy and France, he took up residence in Holland in 1932. His linguistic interests are mainly lexicological.

[4] W. Bal, a Belgian, wrote the work keeping in mind the needs of his students at Lovanium University in the Congo. He has now returned to its *alma mater*, the Catholic University of Louvain.

[5] Other works that deserve mention are P. Skok 1940, S. Battaglia 1946, A. Monteverdi 1952, M. V. Sergievski 1952, P. Bec (forthcoming), J. Cremona (forthcoming). Collections of texts: I. Iordan (ed.) 1962–68, which includes dialect material, and B. Pottier 1964.

[6] Works on Latin that are of particular interest to the Romanist include G. Devoto 1940, J. Marouzeau 1954, L. R. Palmer 1955 (which devotes considerable attention to popular Latin and Christian Latin), W. S. Allen 1965 (which uses Romance evidence to discover how Latin was pronounced), E. Löfstedt 1959 (on Late Latin) and J. B. Hofmann 1951 (on colloquial Latin). E. Pulgram 1958 is more a history of man in Italy following him through from prehistory to modern times. Most introductory books on Vulgar Latin are concerned with defining the scope of the term: cf. for instance C. Battisti 1949, K. Vossler 1954, E. Coseriu 1954*b*, C. Mohrmann 1955, T. H. Maurer 1962, C. H. Grandgent 1962, V. Väänänen 1963, J. Sofer 1963, R. A. Haadsma and J. Nuchelmans 1963, J. Herman 1967. On particular aspects of Vulgar Latin recent works include V. Väänänen 1966, H. Mihăescu 1960, S. Stati 1961, A. Stefenelli 1962. Selections of texts

Another burning question concerns the way the different languages split off from the common source.[1] Beyond the early periods of the languages, the advantages of comparison are less obvious, and individual languages are most often treated separately.[2] Comparative Romance studies in phonology,[3] morphology[4] and lexicology[5] are not infrequent, but in syntax they are rare.

Though the written word remains the main means of communication in Romance linguistics, a triennial international Congress gathers many of them together for interchange of opinions. An account of the Société de Linguistique Romane might not therefore be out of place here.

After the Congress at Nice in 1937, the war and its aftermath put paid to many of the activities of the Société de Linguistique Romane:

The Société de Linguistique Romane (1924–) and its Congresses (1928–) the *RLiR* issue of 1939 was followed at a long interval by that of 1946 which was completely taken up by the (unfinished) thesis on Racine by J. G. Cahen, shot without trial by the Gestapo in 1944. The next issue appeared in 1950 and contained surveys (by

include G. Rohlfs 1951 and M. C. Díaz y Díaz 1960. On medieval Latin we should mention K. Strecker 1948 and G. Cremaschi 1959.

[1] E.g. W. von Wartburg 1938 and 1950, H. Meier 1941, M. Křepinsky 1951 and 1958, G. Reichenkron 1965–.

[2] Here we might mention O. W. Heatwole 1949 and the descriptions of Romance languages by C. F. and F. M. Voegelin in *AnL* vii (1965) part I. Among works on individual Romance languages we might mention here:

For French (description) G. Gougenheim 1939, K. Togeby 1951, Gram.Lar. 1964, J. Dubois 1965, 1967 and 1969, R. L. Wagner 1968, G. Galichet 1967; (history) W. von Wartburg 1934, M. Cohen 1967, A. Ewert 1933, M. K. Pope 1934, J. Fox and R. Wood 1968.

For Spanish (general) M. Criado de Val (1954), M. Alvar *et al* (eds.) 1960–, *Pres y fut. español* 1964; (history) R. Menéndez Pidal 1904 and 1926, W. Entwistle 1936, R. Lapesa 1942, R. K. Spaulding 1943, G. B. Pellegrini 1950, V. García de Diego 1951a, J. B. Trend 1953, G. Rohlfs 1957.

For Italian (general) M. A. Pei 1941; (descriptive) M. Regula and J. Jernej 1965; (history) B. Migliorini 1960.

For Sardinian M. L. Wagner 1941, 1951 and 1952.

For Portuguese (history) E. B. Williams 1938, M. de Paiva Boléo 1946, S. da Silva Neto 1952 and 1957.

For Catalan (description) F. de B. Moll 1968; (history) A. M. Badía Margarit 1951, F. de B. Moll 1952.

For Rumanian (description) I. Iordan 1937, 1943, 1954; (history) A. Rosetti 1938–46, A. Rosetti and B. Cazacu 1961–.

[3] Cf. e.g. F. Schürr, "La diphtongaison romane", in *RLiR* xx (1956) pp. 107–44, H. Lüdtke 1956, H. Weinrich 1958, R. Posner 1961, A. Galmés de Fuentes 1962, U. L. Figge 1966, L. Romeo 1968.

[4] E.g. H. Schmid 1949, W. Roth 1965, R. de Dardel 1962 and 1965, J. Herman 1963, R. Posner, "The Imperfect Endings in Romance", *TPS* 1961 pp. 17–56.

[5] Cf. e.g. R. Chatton 1953, F. Schalk 1955, J. Renson 1962.

Togeby and Edgren) of Romance linguistics in Denmark and Sweden during the war years. A year later, at the Congress at Liège,[1] on the instigation of John Orr, a resolution was passed "que la Société reprenne son activité et publie regulièrement sa revue" and a committee, under the chairmanship of John Orr, was elected to reconstitute the 'Bureau'. After the 1953 Barcelona Congress,[2] *RLiR* began publication again in 1954: the *Société* membership was extended (to number, in 1954, 305 members compared with 118 at its inception in 1924) and application was made for affiliation to Unesco. The next congress took place in Florence in 1956[3] and the 9th Congress in Lisbon in 1959.[4] The 10th Congress in 1962 was at Strasbourg,[5] the 11th (1965) in Madrid[6] and the 12th (1968) in Bucharest.[7]

Two possible 'definitions' of Romance linguistics cover work done by Romance-speaking linguists and work done on the Romance languages. We may well expect that, where these **National Trends** two strands cross, Romance linguistics will be strongest. However, even within Romania, linguistic approaches differ—a variation often dependent on cultural tradition, on university organization, or on the impact of charismatic personalities. I shall briefly survey the state of Romance linguistics in each of the Romance speaking nations, attempting to underline the salient national trends in each case. Here my 'typological classification' of Romanists will cut across the one made later in this essay, into 'schools of thought': each of the classifications is, of course, too simplistic, but taken together they may help the reader to sort out the different strands of work in Romance linguistics.

National Trends Within Romania

In France,[8] Romance linguistics as such has comparatively little

---

[1] *Actes 6ᵉ Cong. (Liège) 1951.*   [2] *Actes 7ᵉ Cong. (Barcelona) 1953.*
[3] *Actes 8ᵉ Cong. (Florence) 1956.*
[4] Vols. xviii–xx of *BF* (1961–62) are devoted to the Lisbon congress. Membership had now risen to 522. Mario Roques was elected president, with John Orr and Walther von Wartburg vice-presidents. Pierre Gardette continued as secretary.
[5] *Actes 10ᵉ Cong. (Strasbourg) 1962.* W. von Wartburg was elected president.
[6] *Actes 11ᵉ cong. (Madrid) 1965.* Participants at the Congress now numbered 420: membership of the Society now stood at 606. John Orr was elected president.
[7] By now membership of the society had reached 723. A. Badía Margarit was elected president and I. Iordan, honorary president.
[8] Cf. G. Gougenheim, "Les travaux français relatifs à la linguistique romane de

following, but the vitality of General linguistics and of the linguistics
France   of French has not wavered in the last three decades, in spite of lack of institutional encouragement. The 'French School'[1] of sociological linguistics has had an enduring influence on linguistic attitudes: M. Cohen[2] is perhaps the most direct descendant of the Meillet–Vendryes line, but lexicological (G. Matoré)[3] and semiological (R. Barthes)[4] trends also owe much to 'French school' traditions. The most powerful influence on French linguistic attitudes in the last three decades has probably been exercised by A. Martinet[5] and by G. Guillaume.[6] Saussurean-type structuralism is almost universally accepted. Dialect studies have not meanwhile diminished in quantity or quality.[7] Centres of linguistic study include the Sorbonne, (under Martinet), Nanterre (under Pottier), Besançon (under Quemada) and, now, Vincennes (under gross), but probably the most important focus of activity in Romance linguistics is in Strasbourg, at the Centre de Philologie et de Littératures Romanes, under the direction of G. Straka.[8] Other contemporary linguists of note are P. Guiraud,[9] G. Mounin,[10] G. Gougenheim[11] and J. Dubois,[12] as well as the dialectologists P. Gardette (born 1906) and J. Séguy (born 1914).

It is not surprising that Swiss linguists[13] should show so much interest in dialectology, given the bewildering variety of languages
Switzerland   to be found in such a small land. But, on the theoretical side, Switzerland can also boast of its son—perhaps the greatest linguist of all—Ferdinand de Saussure. In the past thirty years Swiss linguistics has continued along the

---

1939 à 1947", in M. de Paiva Boléo (ed.) 1951 pp. 105–46; A. Dauzat and C. Bruneau 1949; L. Kukenheim 1966; and R. Levy, "Background and Trends in French Linguistics", in M. Delbouille 1964 (fest.) pp. 395 ff.

[1] Cf. A. Sommerfelt, "The French School of Linguistics", in *Trends i* 1961 pp. 283–93.

[2] Cf. especially M. Cohen 1955.   [3] Cf. p. 464.

[4] Cf. p. 464, n.2.

[5] Cf. pp. 486–91.

[6] Cf. pp. 496–502.

[7] Cf. pp. 467–70.

[8] Cf. G. Straka and P. Simon, "Quarante ans d'études de linguistique et de philologie à l'Université de Strasbourg (1919–1959)" in *O* ix (1960) pp. 495–555, and the annual *Brochure-Programme* of the *Centre* (1955–). Its publications include the series *Bibliothèque française et romane* (Paris, Klincksieck, 1966–), and the periodicals *TLLS* 1963–, and *Bulletin des Jeunes Romanistes* 1960–.

[9] Professor at Nice. Cf. pp. 447–51.

[10] Professor at Aix.

[11] Professor at Paris, now retired. Cf. p. 531. See, for French work in Phonetics, pp. 536–7; in Applied Linguistics, pp. 531–2; in Mathematical and Statistical Linguistics pp. 533–5; and for Lucien Tesnière, pp. 525–7.

[12] Professor at Nanterre.

[13] Cf. H. Schmid, "Chronique des travaux de linguistique romane publiés en Suisse de 1939 à 1947", in M. de Paiva Boléo (ed.) 1951 pp. 63–104.

same lines as before the war—dialect studies and Saussurean exegesis.[1] Some of the outstanding personalities have died: Jaberg and Jud, Bally, Hubschmied,[2] Gauchat: but happily H. Frei and Walther von Wartburg,[3] now an octogenarian, are still with us. Among names that have become known more recently we should mention C-T. Gossen,[4] R. de Dardel, R. Godel, and H. Lüdtke, as well as P. Zumthor, now in Holland, and K. Baldinger (born 1919) at present Rector of Heidelberg University, a Vice-President of the Société de Linguistique Romane, editor of *ZRP*, and one of the most influential among Romanists.

Walloon Romanists[5] lost M. Wilmotte in 1942 and J. Haust in 1946. Besides dialectology, one of their main interests has been, with M. Grevisse, in preserving "Le bon usage"—as **Belgium** peripheral users of French they are more than conscious of regional differences in their language, and, locked as they are in an ethno-linguistic struggle with their Flemish co-citizens, they fear to lose grip on their linguistic standards. From a methodological point of view, they tend to be traditionalist.[6] Among outstanding personalities, we should mention first the veteran philologist, socialist, senator, and academician Maurice Delbouille,[7] followed closely by such others as G. de Poerck (born 1910), A. Henry, L. Remacle (born 1920), Rita Lejeune, W. Bal, and J. Renson.

Any account of Spanish linguistics[8] in the last half-century must centre around the person of Ramón Menéndez Pidal (1869-1968), **Spain** whose influence on the development of the discipline was paramount.[9] Among those scholars who have

---

[1] Cf. R. Godel 1957 and F. de Saussure 1916 (1967).

[2] Survived by his son who adopted the spelling of his name without an *e*, Professor at Berne. [3] Cf. p. 469.

[4] Professor at Bâle and editor of *VR*.

[5] Cf. L. Warnant, "La linguistique romane en Belgique", in M. de Paiva Boléo (ed.) 1951 pp. 175-202. M. Delcourt and M. Derwa, "Les débuts de la philologie romane", *MRo* xviii (1968) pp. 3-12, give an account of Romance studies at Liège.

[6] Cf. R. Posner, "Modernists Versus Traditionalists: A Confrontation in Continental Europe" (rev. art of P. Delbouille *et al.* (eds.) 1966) in *RPh* xxi (1968) pp. 544-58.

[7] Born 1903; his scholarly traditions are carried on by his son Paul (cf. P. Delbouille 1961).

[8] Cf. A. Zamora Vicente, "Bibliografía Lingüística Española, (1939-1947)", in M. de Paiva Boléo (ed.) 1951 pp. 203 ff, and D. Catalán 1955. Particularly valuable are Y. Malkiel's surveys "Old and New Trends in Spanish Linguistics", in *SP* xlix (1952) pp. 437-58, and "La filología española y la lingüística general", in *Actas i Cong. Int. Hisp. 1962* pp. 1-20. Among Spanish periodicals we should mention *RFE* and *RDTP*, edited by V. García de Diego.

[9] To quote from Malkiel, *SP* xlix (1952) p. 444: "Menéndez Pidal's undisputed position of eminence among Spanish scholars, over a period of half a century, has

worked under his spell we might make special mention of two more junior members of his family—A. Galmés de Fuentes and D. Catalán. But in the broader sense all recent Spanish linguists have been part of Menéndez Pidal's family and have maintained traditional linguistic interests—in medieval language, for instance, in dialectology and in literary–linguistic history: let us mention, among a host of others, M. Alvar,[1] A. M. Badía Margarit,[2] J. Corominas,[3] V. García de Diego,[4] S. Gili y Gaya, R. Lapesa,[5] A. Llorente, L. Rodríguez Castellano, and A. Zamora Vicente,[6] as well as the Catalan 'grand masters', A. Griera (born 1887) and F. de B. Moll (born 1903).

Amado Alonso[7] and the phonetician T. Navarro Tomás[8] spent much of their lives in the New World, but still did not lose the 'Spanish' tinge to their linguistic thought. Where influence from outside has been most strongly felt, in the work of D. Catalán and E. Alarcos Llorach,[9] it has been from Martinet and the Prague School.

In Spanish America[10] special mention should be made of the Argentine: Amado Alonso spent some time as director of the Instituto de Filología at Buenos Aires,[11] and F. Krüger (born 1889) is still at Mendoza, while for a short period J. Corominas was also at the Cuyo Instituto de Lingüística (which since 1941 publishes its *Anales*); B. Terracini found refuge from Mussolini in Tucumán before return-

Spanish America

been one potent reason for the peculiar course which Hispanic studies took in his own country until the outbreak of the Civil War. The separation of the mainstream of philology into the more narrowly specialized branches of general culture history, historical linguistics, textual criticism beside palaeography, and history of literature, which marks such a sharp line of cleavage between the generations of Tobler and Meyer-Lübke in Germany and of Paris and Thomas in France, has at no time tended to repeat itself in Spain, possibly in harmony with the prevailing integralismo, to quote Castro's felicitous term."

Equally important in a different way, is Dámaso Alonso, writer and poet, born 1898, and professor at Madrid since 1939; cf. D. Alonso 1960–63 (fest.).

[1] Born 1923, professor at Granada.

[2] Born 1920, professor at Barcelona; President of the Société de Linguistique Romane.

[3] Born 1905, now at Chicago.

[4] Born 1878, professor at Burgos, editor of *RFE* and *RDTP*.

[5] Born 1908, professor at Madrid.

[6] Born 1916, professor at Madrid.

[7] Cf. p. 430.

[8] Cf. p. 537.

[9] Cf. p. 482.

[10] Cf. A. M. Barrenechea and N. B. Costas, "Bibliografía Lingüística Argentina (1939–1947)", pp. 147–74, and M. L. Wagner "Crónica bibliográfica hispano-americana", in M. de Paiva Boléo (ed.) 1951 pp. 369–98; also R. Lado *et al.* (eds.) (forthcoming).

[11] *BDH* is published in Buenos Aires; so was *RFH* (1939–46).

ing to his native Italy after the war. Among native Argentinians, we should mention P. Henriquez Ureña (1884–1946) and R. Lida (as well as his sister, late wife of Yakov Malkiel, María Rosa Lida de Malkiel). South America offered shelter too to E. Coseriu who spent some time in Montevideo[1] before going to his present post in Tübingen. The work of the Instituto Caro y Cuervo at Bogotá,[2] also merits attention: L. Florez is among its important figures. We also note the work of A. Rosenblat in Venezuela, R. Oroz in Chile and J. Lope Blanch in Mexico.[3]

Portugal In Portugal[4] only two Universities—Lisbon and Coimbra—are concerned with the teaching of Romance linguistics. M. de Paiva Boléo (born 1904) and J. G. C. Herculano de Carvalho are professors at Coimbra where *RPF* is edited.[5] Most linguistic work in Portugal is concerned with the Portuguese language.

Brazil The same is broadly true of Brazilian linguistics:[6] outstanding names are S. da Silva Neto (died 1959), F. da Silveira Bueno, and J. Mattoso Câmara, Jr.

Italy In Italian universities expertise in Romance linguistics often goes hand in hand with specialized knowledge of Latin and pre-Latin substrata. Special attention is given too to dialectology, as well as to socio-cultural aspects of language.[7] In some ways, then, Italian linguistics is *sui generis*, comparatively little influenced from outside.[8] The names that have resounded in the Italian linguistic world during the last three decades have nearly all been to some extent associated with 'Idealist' trends:[9] Bertoni, Bertoldi, Bàrtoli, Terracini, Migliorini, Tagliavini, Pisani, and Devoto—though, admittedly, a few retained a neo-grammarian position—Goidànich (1868–1953), and Merlo (1879–1960). Outstanding new names are few—G. C. Lepschy,

[1] Cf. pp. 454–5.

[2] Its *Boletín* . . . (1945–) has borne the name *Thesaurus* from vol. vii onwards.

[3] *NRFH* (1947–) is published in Mexico.

[4] Cf. M. J. de Moura Santos 1960, and H. Meier, "Um século de lingüística românica", *RP* xi (1947) pp. 3–14.

[5] Other relevant Portuguese periodicals are *BF* and *RP*.

[6] S. da Silva Neto, "A Filologia portuguesa no Brasil (1939–1948)", in M. de Paiva Boléo (ed.) 1951, pp. 340–68.

[7] Cf. C. Battisti, "Orientamenti generali della linguistica in Italia 1930–1960", in *Trends i* pp. 240–82 and R. M. Ruggieri, "I lavori di linguistica romanza in Italia dal 1939 al 1948", in M. de Paiva Boléo (ed.) 1951. Periodicals include *CN, SRo, LN, AGI, ID*.

[8] Cf. C. Battisti, *Trends i* p. 240: "In genere la linguistica in Italia non si chiude alle innovazioni di metodo che giungono dall'estero; è però restía dall'accettarle senza elaborazione."

[9] Cf. pp. 451–3.

now in Britain, G. Contini, Norma Costabile, and U. Eco deserve special mention.

Perhaps because of its geographical position as the only Romance-speaking country in the Balkans, Rumania[1] has maintained an active tradition of Romance linguistics. To counter-**Rumania** act the natural tendency to isolation that must beset such a peripheral part of *Romania* great efforts have been made of late to encourage contact between Rumanians and other Romance linguists: an annual Summer School is organized by the University of Bucharest, and International Congresses of Linguists (1967) and of Romance Linguistics (1968) have been held in Bucharest.

Several periodicals, published in Rumanian or French, devote space to Romance linguistic problems[2] and a very active Société Roumaine de Linguistique Romane founded in 1964 (President: I. Iordan) publishes a regular bulletin. The two principal centres of Romance studies are Bucharest and Cluj (where E. Petrovici, who died in 1968, was professor).

The 'grand masters' of Rumanian linguistics remain I. Iordan, A. Graur, and A. Rosetti, but also outstanding in the last three decades have been B. Cazacu,[3] and I. Coteanie. Other new names are too numerous to mention:[4] they include Andrei and Mioara Avram, D. Copceag, Alexandru and Florica Niculescu, Sanda Golopenţia-Eretescu, Valeria Gutu-Romalo, Maria Iliescu, D. Macrea, H. Mihăescu, Maria Manoliu, Alexandra Roceric-Alexandrescu, M. Sala, S. Stati, and E. Vasiliu. The principal field of study is, naturally enough, the Rumanian language, and its relationship to other Romance languages. Dialectology[5] and stylistics[6] receive particular attention, but the more technical aspects of linguistics, like mathematical and statistical[7] or phonetic[8] studies are far from neglected.

National Trends Outside Romania

Outside the Romance-speaking countries, it is the Germanic nations that show most interest in Romance linguistics. Perhaps

---

[1] Cf. especially I. Popinceanu and T. Onciulescu, "Les études de linguistique roumaine de 1939–1959", *RPF* suppl. bibl. ii (1953) pp. 137–224, and I. Ghetie and I. Rădulescu, "Où en sont les études de linguistique roumaine en Roumanie?" *RLiR* xxxii (1968) pp. 362–79. Also D. Macrea 1959.

[2] *LiR, CLin, SCL, RRL, RFRG.*

[3] For his wife, the psycholinguist, Tatiana Slama-Cazacu, cf. p. 532.

[4] A collection of articles that deserves mention is *Rec. d'et. rom.* 1959.

[5] Cf. p. 467.

[6] Cf. p. 461.

[7] Cf. p. 535.

[8] Cf. p. 537.

because national pride is not bound up with the study of neo-Latin tongues, the popular appeal of Romance linguistics is less. In Britain interest has appeared to decline in the last half-century, but in Germany and Scandinavia Romance studies are still going strong. In the USA it is perhaps significant that California, with its Mediterranean climate, and cosmopolitan cultural atmosphere, is becoming the cradle of the reborn interest in Romance. In the following paragraphs, I shall briefly survey the state of Romance linguistics in a number of non-Romance countries: omissions are inevitable and wholly due to my own ignorance, but I feel nevertheless that some such survey is of interest to readers.

Romance linguistics has had a poor showing in Britain in the last 30 years;[1] indeed it is hardly recognized institutionally at all.

Britain University posts in the philology[2] of individual languages are nearly always linked with medieval literature, and often they are held by professional medievalists with only an indirect interest in modern linguistics. The Oxford Chair of the Romance Languages has been occupied during this period by two French medievalists—A. Ewert and T. B. W. Reid; however, the advent in 1968 of Stephen Ullmann, whose interests are more avowedly linguistic, and modernist, might change the tradition. To the Edinburgh Chair of French and Romance Philology, John Orr was succeeded by D. MacMillan, who has shown comparatively little interest in modern linguistics. On W. D. Elcock's death in 1960, his Chair at Westfield College, London, went to R. C. Johnston, previously Professor of French at St. Andrews, who is principally known as a medievalist. To the Chair of Leeds in French Language and Romance Philology, previously occupied by Ullman, has now been elected T. E. Hope, who immediately previously was at Manchester.[3] On the retirement of Lewis

---

[1] W. D. Elcock, "The Contribution of English Scholars to Romance Linguistics 1939–1948", in M. de Paiva Boléo (ed.) 1951 concludes (p. 62): "Such, briefly, is the harvest of the past ten years: rather a thin one, but the years were lean." Since then one Chair of Romance has been lost—at Manchester, after T. B. W. Reid went to Oxford, it was converted to a Chair in French Language, though a senior post in Romance still exists.

[2] In British usage this term indicates mainly what is called elsewhere 'historical linguistics'.

[3] His interests lie mainly in the interaction of French and Italian: cf. "The process of neologism reconsidered with reference to lexical borrowing in Romance", *TPS* 1964 pp. 46–84 and T. E. Hope (forthcoming).

Harmer, the Draper Chair of French Language and Literature at Cambridge went to a literary specialist. The Cambridge lectureship in Romance Philology, held by J. Cremona, Fellow of Trinity Hall,[1] omits French from its orbit: French historical linguistics is covered by P. Rickard, Fellow of Emmanuel, whose interests lie mainly in medieval and sixteenth-century French. At Oxford a number of non-cathedratic posts cover aspects of Romance linguistics: we should here mention C. A. Robson (Fellow of Merton), whose work has been partly concerned with Old French dialects, Mrs. D. R. Sutherland (Fellow of Lady Margaret Hall) principally a Provençalist, and F. J. Barnett (Fellow of Trinity) whose interests cover French and Rumanian.[2]

Elsewhere we might pick out Bedford College, London, where N. C. W. Spence[3] is Reader in French Linguistics, as well as Manchester and Stirling where W. Rothwell and G. Price are Professors of French; H. Ramsden, too, Professor of Spanish at Manchester, has done work on historical Romance linguistics,[4] and K. A. Whinnom, Professor of Spanish at Exeter, has made contributions to the study of creole languages.[5]

Outside the sphere of 'Modern and Medieval Languages and Literatures' Departments, there has been sparse development of Romance linguistics: in those universities that have developed Linguistics Departments, English and non-European language specialists usually predominate.[6] I believe York is the only University that unites teaching of Romance language skills (French and Spanish) and of linguistics within the same department, though some other universities offer degrees that combine courses given in Modern Language Departments and Linguistics Departments.[7] The prospects for the future development of Romance linguistics in Britain are therefore dim, unless there is some change of heart among University governing bodies.

---

[1] Maltese by origin, Dr.Cremona spent his childhood in Italy. He took up his post in Cambridge after working with Elcock in London mainly on dialectology.

[2] Cf. especially "The origins of the *lui-lei* forms in Romance", *TPS* 1965 pp. 97–104.

[3] His doctorate thesis was a glossary of Jersey French, and he has since shown interest in linguistic questions, cf. p. 454.

[4] Cf. H. Ramsden 1963.

[5] Cf. K. A. Whinnom 1956 and p. 471.

[6] Even when linguistics specialists received their early training in Romance, they often leave it aside to work on English: I think here of P. H. Matthews (Reading), and R. C. Huddleston (University College, London)—but cf. p. 529. Curiously enough, too, G. C. Lepschy, the Italian linguist, is in the Italian Department at Reading and not the Linguistics Department.

[7] E.g. Edinburgh, London, Reading, Stirling.

In 1948 when E. B. Williams[1] wrote his survey of a decade of Romance linguistics in the USA, the discipline was still in the doldrums.[2] Since then, however, Romanists have **USA** sometimes been permitted to take their place in the intellectually active Linguistics departments, rather than in the overworked Language departments, and so have been able to make more of a mark. Although the influence of Muller[3] and Spitzer[4] has begun to fade, other masters have come to the fore. Romance applied linguistics has leaped ahead;[5] S. Saporta at Seattle has gathered around him some young transformationalists[6] for whom the future looks bright; R. A. Hall, Jr.,[7] at Cornell, has a following among historical reconstructionists. The most active school of Romance linguistics in the USA is, however, undoubtedly situated in Berkeley, California, centred around the person of Y. Malkiel,[8] and with as its organ, the journal *Romance Philology* (*RPh*). In all probability, this school will continue to flourish, and lost ground will quickly be regained.

Such a small country as Holland[9] can hardly support many Romance linguists:[10] it has, however, welcomed foreign Romanists **The** to its university posts (e.g. the Hungarian B. E. **Netherlands** Vidos,[11] the Italian G. Francescato, the Swiss P. Zumthor, and the Frenchman P. Guiraud). Several of its native-born distinguished personalities have died within the last thirty years (Sneyders de Vogel, A. W. de Groot, and C. de Boer): L. Kukenheim,[12] and L. Geschiere[13] are perhaps the most outstanding French linguists in present-day Holland. Mention should also be made of H. Schogt,[14] a pupil of Martinet's, who is at

---

[1] "Romance Philology in the United States since 1939", in M. de Paiva Boléo (ed.) 1951 pp. 275–84. See, for American 'structuralism' pp. 507–19; for transformational-generative grammar pp. 519–23; for phonetics, pp. 535–6; for mathematical and statistical linguistics pp. 533–5.

[2] Cf. p. 410.

[3] Cf. p. 453.

[4] Cf. p. 453.

[5] Cf. pp. 530–2.

[6] Cf. J. E. Lackstrom 1968; P. W. Klein 1968; J. S. Falk 1968. San Diego, California, too, appears to be a centre of Romanist transformationalists—e.g. S. A. Schane and R. W. Langacker.

[7] Cf. pp. 515–9.

[8] Cf. pp. 434–47.

[9] Cf. E. C. van Bellen, "La philologie romane en Hollande depuis 1939", in M. de Paiva Boléo (ed.) 1951 pp. 285–302.

[10] It does support three important linguistic journals: *N, Li, Lis*, and the prolific linguistic publications of Mouton & Co., The Hague.

[11] Cf. p. 415.

[12] Born in Amsterdam 1905, Professor at Leiden since 1951.

[13] Professor at Amsterdam.   [14] Cf. p. 480.

present in Canada, at the University of Toronto, of M. Valkhoff (born 1905) who is now in South Africa and of Q.I.M. Mok (Amsterdam).

Romance linguistics has long flourished in Germany—partly, I am told, as a result of Humboldt's political influence which led to the creation of a number of university posts in linguistics. Be that as it may, the number of outstanding German-speaking Romanists is too long to cite here:[1] although some, like Vossler and Lerch, have died since *Iordan-Orr*, others have reached a ripe old age, like Rohlfs[2] and Gamillscheg.[3] If German-speaking Romanists display any particular preferences within the field of linguistics, it is probably to lexicological and etymological studies (W. T. Elwert,[4] E. Gamillscheg, K. Heger,[5] M. Regula,[6] H. Meier,[7] and K. Baldinger[8]) though they are equally at home in dialect studies (G. Rohlfs and F. Schürr[9]) and structuralist historical grammar (H. Lausberg and H. Weinrich[10]). Of the numerous others who should be mentioned let us cite F. Schalk[11] and M. Wandruszka.[12] Certainly there is no sign of faltering in the growth of German Romance linguistics.

Germany and Austria

At Copenhagen[13] there are two chairs of Romance languages, both of which became vacant in 1942 with the deaths of K. Sandfeld and V. Brøndal (who succeeded K. Nyrop). B. Hasselrot (a Swede) and H. Sten[14] were elected in their place but Hasselrot returned to Sweden in 1959; K. Togeby[15] became professor in 1955.

Denmark

At Aarhus another chair of the Romance languages has been occupied by A. Blinkenberg[16] since 1934: he was rector of the university from 1937–40. Mention should be made too of P. Høybye,[17]

---

[1] Cf. A. Kuhn, "A lingüística românica na Alemanha no decénio de 1939–1948", in M. de Paiva Boléo (ed.) 1951 pp. 303–39, and H. Flasche 1958.

[2] Cf. p. 468.

[3] Cf. p. 469.

[4] Born 1906, professor at Mainz.

[5] Professor at Kiel.

[6] Now retired from his post at Graz.

[7] Professor at Bonn, editor of *ASNS*.

[8] A Swiss by origin, professor at Berlin 1948–57, and, since 1957, at Heidelberg, where he is now Rector. Cf. p. 419.

[9] Now retired from his post at Freiburg.

[10] Cf. p. 494.

[11] Professor at Cologne.

[12] Professor at Tübingen.

[13] P. Høybye, "Les études de linguistique romane au Danemark 1939–48", in M. de Paiva Boléo (ed.) 1951 pp. 33 ff. Cf. also *The Copenhagen School* pp. 472–80. Periodicals published in Denmark include *AL, RRom, and TCLC*.

[14] Born 1907.   [15] Cf. pp. 476–80.

[16] Born 1893. Cf. p. 524, and A. Blinkenberg 1963 (fest.).

[17] Born 1903, since 1955 Professor of French at the Handelshøjskolen.

who, like most of the other Danish Romanists cited here, is mainly concerned with the French language. Among younger Danish Romance scholars special mention might be made of E. Spang-Hanssen.

Sweden

In Sweden[1] too particular attention is paid to French linguistics: Gothenburg, Lund and Uppsala all have Chairs of Romance Languages, often occupied by a French specialist. K. Michaëlsson was professor at Gothenburg till his death in 1962. Since 1938, Alf Lombard[2] has been professor at Lund; since 1957 H. Nilsson-Ehle[3] has also held a Chair at Lund and B. Hasselrot,[4] who was from 1945 to 1959 professor at Copenhagen, is now at Uppsala. G. Tilander[5] was professor at Stockholm from 1937 to 1960. For the Romance phoneticians B. Malmberg (Lund) and G. Hammarström (Uppsala till 1965, but now in Australia) see p. 537.

Other countries

Romance linguistics enjoys comparatively little popularity in other countries: in the USSR[6] it is geared mainly to language teaching needs; in Finland[7] Vulgar Latin especially attracts most attention; in Jugoslavia[8] the only active centre is Zagreb, where the linguistic geographer M. Deanović[9] was professor; in Hungary[10] we should mention the work of J. Herman; in Czechoslavakia,[11] of Křepinsky (born 1875) and Ducháček, especially; in Poland, of H. Lewicka, editor of *Kwartalnik Neofilologiczny*.

---

[1] L. Wiberg, "La philologie romane en suède depuis 1939", M. de Paiva Boléo (ed.) 1951 pp. 1–32. Periodicals published in Sweden include *SL* and *SN*.
[2] Born 1902.
[3] Born 1910.
[4] Born 1910.
[5] Born 1894.
[6] Cf. the periodical *Romanskaia Filologiia* (Leningrad). Mention should be made of R. A. Budagov (comparative Romance semantics) and R. G. Piotrovskij (stylistics).
[7] Cf. the work of Väänänen (born 1905), and e.g. R. Hakamies 1951 and L. Löfstedt 1966. Also B. Hasselrot, "La linguistique romane en Finlande (1939–1951)", *RLiR* xviii (1954) pp. 117–27. *NMi* is published in Finland.
[8] Z. Muljacic, "Gli studi di linguistica romanza in Iugoslavia 1964–1966", in *RLaR* lxxvii (1967) pp. 187–201. P. Skok (1881–1956) was an outstanding Jugoslav Romanist.
[9] Born 1890. Cf. p. 468 and the article in honour of his 70th birthday by J. Gorup in *O* ix (1960) pp. 222–31. P. Guberina is another Jugoslav Romanist who was at Zagreb: he is especially known for his work in CREDIF; cf. p. 531. Also at Zagreb, J. Jernej should be mentioned. The periodical *SRAZ* is published in Zagreb.
[10] Among emigré Hungarians we should mention S. Ullmann and B. E. Vidos.
[11] Cf. the periodical *ERB*.

'Schools and scholars'

In adopting Orr's sub-title, I am aware that such labels as are implied by the term 'Schools' are unpopular, and I do recognize the essential originality and individuality of the outstanding personalities in the field. Yet (to borrow a technique from Prague-school phonology) I believe a distinctive, if not a substantial, classification of Romance scholars is possible, even though some will fall into several classes. True, the 'paradigms' of principles with which they work are often developed in other linguistic domains and applied by individual scholars to Romance problems (and thereby adapted). But I think we *can* ask what problems interest which scholars and what factors (training, experience, personality, etc.) influence their choice of method or sub-discipline. I shall try to define in broad terms each method and the scope of each sub-discipline, and, as far as possible, to clothe bare theoretical bones with the flesh and blood of real Romance scholars, whose individual and unique trajectories through the realms of scholarship might exemplify the preoccupations and motivations of their fellows.

My survey is composed of thirteen sections, ten of which cover different methods of approach to language—'schools' properly so-called—while the other three cover less homogeneous methodological approaches, but more narrowly technical subject-matter —Phonetics, Applied Linguistics, Mathematical and Statistical Linguistics. Influential scholars who do not work in the Romance field will of course be discussed, but I shall try as far as possible to concentrate attention on their colleagues who applied their general principles to the Romance languages.

B. SCHOOLS AND SCHOLARS

1. *Traditional*

It may well be foolhardy of me to begin my discussion of 'schools and scholars' in Romance linguistics over the last thirty years with the heterogeneous, and possibly non-existent, category of 'traditionalists'. It is true that the 'traditional' Romance linguist is individualist and eclectic in scholarly attitudes: what I seek to emphasize by devoting a brief section to him is just what he is *not*, in any overwhelming degree at any rate—neither idealist, nor structuralist nor, indeed, wed to any particular school of theoretical reasoning. However, through all the vicissitudes of linguistic fashions, 'traditional' scholars appear numerically preponderant in the Romance field and so some discussion of their shared attitudes is called for here.

The traditional philologist is often a butt of satire (witness, for instance the caricatural figures in Eugène Ionesco's *La Leçon* and in **Philology** Elias Canetti's *Auto da Fé*)[1] in his remoteness from **and** modern life and absorption in dusty manuscripts: **Linguistics** the story told by Schuchardt and quoted in footnote 1 on p. 6 of *Iordan–Orr* is only one of a whole canon of comic anecdotes to this effect. In his own view, however, the philologist is a man of broad interests and humanist leanings: to quote the 1911 edition of the *Encyclopaedia Britannica*, philology "designates that branch of knowledge which deals with human speech and with all that speech discloses as to the nature and history of man". In British usage the

---

[1] If I may be excused a moment of frivolity, I should like to quote, from the Oxford don detective novelist Michael Innes, this portrait of a Romance philologist (from *The Weight of the Evidence*): "Professor Prisk held the chair of Romance Languages. But why, Appleby speculated, do professors have chairs? Why not desks? Or even boxes or bags? What Prisk ought really to have was a bag. He was using a sort of invisible bag now. It held what our Saxon forebears would have called his word-hoard. Prisk dipped into his invisible bag, drew out a word apparently at random, fingered it jealously for some minutes, returned it, and brought out another word. He was wholly absorbed in the contents of his invisible bag, so that Appleby thought he was rather like an ingeniously conceived allegory of miserliness."

'philologist's' interests are mainly linguistic (concerned principally with language history), though older established university posts in Romance Philology are firmly linked with the teaching of medieval literature.[1] Elsewhere (especially in Germany, and hence America) 'philology' is concerned as much with literature and civilization as with the language as such: even in this era of specialization, senior, distinguished Romance linguists, especially in Scandinavia and Germany, devote a good proportion of their time to literary studies. Certainly one of the main activities of traditional Romance linguists everywhere remains the meticulous editing of texts, especially medieval texts, and the description of the language of such texts is still a common choice of topic for doctoral degrees. It is hard to achieve distinction in such studies before full maturity of age, so not surprisingly many of the outstanding figures of the last three decades were already mentioned by *Iordan–Orr*.[2] The work of such scholars is usually, by its nature, of local interest, concerned with a single Romance language and only indirectly with Romance linguistics in general. In Italy, traditional linguistic scholarship has a slightly different orientation, partly perhaps because chairs of *glottologia* link Romance linguistics with classical and Indo-European studies: certainly few Italian linguists have not been influenced by 'idealism' or, at any rate, by 'linguistic geography'.[3]

Of recent years 'traditionalist' preoccupations have included especially pre-Romance substratum studies and hence a particular interest in place-names (as well as onomastics in **Substratum studies** general). Outstanding in this field is the Swiss J. Hubschmid who carries on the work of his father, J. U. Hubschmied (d. 1966), discussed by *Iordan–Orr* (pp. 229–30).[4] Such studies tend to value documentation for its own sake and so

---

[1] Among such scholars one could mention two successive Professors of the Romance languages at Oxford—A. Ewert (b. 1891) and T. B. W. Reid (b. 1901). In France Mario Roques (1875–1961) was an outstanding figure. The most towering personality of all was probably Ramón Menéndez Pidal (1869–1968, professor at Madrid since 1925) whose influence on Spanish linguistics has been paramount for well over half a century and who represents all that is good in traditional philological scholarship, (cf. p. 419). Perhaps the greatest of his pupils was Amado Alonso (1896–1952). The weightiest of this scholar's purely linguistic works was probably A. Alonso 1955. A memorial volume *Miscelánea filológica en memoria de Amado Alonso* appeared in *Arch.* iv (1954). Cf. also p. 420.

[2] Cf. p. 411, n. 1.

[3] Cf. pp. 451–3.

[4] Hubschmid adopted the older spelling of his father's name in 1946. His voluminous and astonishingly erudite work includes the following monographs in the *RH* series: J. Hubschmid 1949, 1955, 1960 *a* & *b*, 1965. For a searching examination of Hubschmid's work and of substratal studies in general cf. Y. Malkiel in *L* xxxviii (1962) pp. 149–85.

are trying for the reader, however fascinating for the writer. They often combine meticulous examination of data with bold conjecture about little-known pre-Romance tongues, but contribute little to linguistic theory and methodology and so are hardly appreciated outside their specialist field.

Confrontation between 'traditionalists' and 'modernists' is rarely risked, each type of linguistic scholar cautiously avoiding the other. When a meeting does take place—as at a Liège colloquium in 1964,[1] collaboration is often revealed to be almost unattainable, owing to the different tastes, aims, and methods of the groups. At Liège, those who rallied to the 'traditional' banner saw themselves as essentially positivist, concerned with 'petits faits vrais' as distinct from the abstract schemata of the structuralists[2] (and before them, in the same line of development, the neogrammarians). By the same token, they also regard themselves as 'humanist', fascinated by the immense variety of linguistic behaviour, reflecting the multiple facets of human nature and society. On a less fundamental level, traditionalists have a distaste for abstract—nay 'abstruse'—exposition and terminology, preferring discursive and anecdotal style and even daring to appear frivolous in face of the severity of much modern linguistic writing. They do, however, show more tolerance for others' views than most modernists, ready to accept that truth has many aspects each to be approached from a different angle.

Traditional versus modern

The traditionalists' opponents condemn their lack of interest in methodology and their dislike of generalization and abstraction, regarding their ad hoc empiricism as indicative of a clinging to outmoded scientific method. Thus, in this technocratic age, for all their meticulous integrity, they are often regarded as 'unprofessional', preferring genteel games to the austere and rigorous pursuit of abstract truth.

One American caricature—Eugene Nida's Dr. Zilch[3]—comically portrays the 'traditionalist' bugbear of linguists of the Bloomfieldian era, who sneers at the structuralists' interest in 'illiterate' languages, which as objects of study can never rival the glories of Greek and

[1] The proceedings of the colloquium are published as *Méthodes de la grammaire* (P. Delbouille *et al.* (eds.) 1966); cf. R. Posner "Modernists Versus Traditionalists: a confrontation in Continental Europe", *RPh* xxi (1968) pp. 544–58.

[2] Oddly enough, in America it is the Bloomfieldian structuralists who are now dismissed as positivist (or more exactly 'Baconian') by the Chomskyist 'Keplerians' who see themselves the guardians of scientific method: cf. E. Bach, "Linguistique structurelle et philosophie des sciences", in *Problèmes du langage* 1966, pp. 117–37.

[3] In E. Nida 1947.

Latin. Furthermore he maintains a 'purist' attitude to correctness in language, blindly equating socially unacceptable native usage with non-native and ungrammatical linguistic constructions. His dislike of novel methods and fresh approaches to the study of language is symbolized by his rejection of exact terminology in favour of time-honoured vagueness.

Needless to say, the upholders of linguistic tradition protest against such cartoon Aunt Sallies. With some justification, they do admit suspicion of linguistic methods exemplified mainly in description of exotic, unwritten languages, but this is partly because the end results are not easily verifiable. Where they appear 'purist' in linguistic orientation they often point to the complexity of social attitudes to language in the highly developed cultures with which they are concerned, as distinct from the 'primitive' social and economic organisms of non-literate societies. Moreover they often suspect that the modern delight in the creation of new terminology betokens a desire for mystification and an impatient rejection of the fruits of centuries of scholarship.

Self-styled traditional linguistic scholars are by no means only medieval or classical in their orientation. A long tradition of empiricist linguistic description serves the needs of **Traditionalist studies of contemporary languages** language teaching and there is today no shortage of scholars to carry on the tradition. In this respect, French is the best served of the Romance languages, perhaps because the most widely taught. Apart from native French speakers,[1] Scandinavian linguists[2] most often engage in careful description of the French language. The material for such descriptions is provided primarily by the written language, as used by the 'best authors'. The linguistic value-judgement implied in the choice of such material is anathema to some 'modern', especially American, schools of thought, but the basis for protest is possibly more socio-cultural than linguistic. Sometimes, of course, purist outbursts are so flamboyant as to capture popular imagination and hit the headlines: Etiemble's condemnation of 'franglais' is the supreme example. But such outbursts do not represent serious linguistic scholarship though they may be revelatory of tensions that lie below the placid traditionalist surface.

[1] Cf. p. 418. Let us mention, for instance, P. Imbs (b. 1908), ex-Rector of Nancy (cf. P. Imbs 1953 and 1960). He shows the influence of G. Guillaume, as does another important French 'traditionalist', R-L. Wagner (b. 1905, professor at Caen 1934–46, and at Paris since 1947).

[2] Cf. pp. 426–7. One example in A. Blinkenberg (b. 1893), Professor at Aarhus, Denmark (cf. A. Blinkenberg 1929–33 and 1960).

In linguistics as elsewhere it may be true that 'tradition is digested experience'—certainly traditional Romanists absorb eclectically features of all established schools of thought while resisting anything that savours of charlatanism or humbug. Today they owe most to empiricism and to sociological thought in the French tradition, but they have also adopted some of the less extreme contributions of idealist linguistics and of linguistic geography. They still resist post-Saussurean structuralism and are particularly hostile to quasi-mathematical formalism. Their works rarely lack integrity and honesty, but they show little sign of excitement for the experimentation and controversy that have made linguistics so enthralling a discipline in the last few decades.

Work on the Romance languages is still predominantly traditional in its methodological orientation: a catalogue of worthy linguists following the tradition would be superfluous here. We have only to look at the papers given at recent Congresses of Romance Linguists to see that solid empirical work is more in evidence than sparkling theoretical innovation. It may even be that the Romanist's unwillingness to depart from well-worn paths—partly for institutional reasons and partly perhaps because of the nature of the material he handles—is one of the causes of his sub-discipline's falling out from the forefront of linguistic science.

2. *Neo-Traditional*

Scholars are rare who can combine the 'digested experience' of tradition with the breadth of vision that engenders methodological innovation, bridging the gaps between 'outworn' positivism and 'new-fangled' formalism. For one thing, the physical and mental effort of mastering different linguistic techniques and absorbing, without confusion, the prolific and heterogeneous literature of a century and a half of linguistic scholarship is beyond the capacities of most. Too often scholars make the choice either of ignoring work in a contemporary vein, or of not exploring, for the nuggets of truth it may contain, past work whose methodological framework may be out-moded.

Scholars who do perform the arduous feat of 'bridge building' can hardly expect a large following of disciples, but do, I think, deserve special attention and admiration. My title 'neo-traditional' attempts to group together two such Romance scholars—who have otherwise little in common—Yakov Malkiel and Pierre Guiraud.[1] They both share an interest in 'traditional' problems (especially etymology and word formation) and a mastery of 'positivist' methods (meticulous attention to detail and accurate consideration of data) coupled with an appreciation of methodology and a gift for an innovatory thought. Guiraud differs from Malkiel especially in his statistico-mathematical orientation; Malkiel is perhaps unique in his combination of 'flair' with rigorous methodology and theory and scrupulous collection of data.

Malkiel was born in Kiev in 1914 and took his Ph.D in Berlin in 1938. Nazi oppression occasioned his emigration to the USA, where he has graced the Californian campus of Berkeley since 1942. His doctoral thesis *Das substantivierte Adjectiv in Französischen* was hailed in reviews[2] as representative of the best traditions of European scholarship and was to herald a prolific production of monographs and articles, at first mainly on Hispanic themes. In Malkiel's early years in America a certain lack of familiarity with his academic surroundings, as well as some unsureness in his use of the English language, led to his writing meticulous and detailed work of a more distinctly traditional flavour. In his prime, however, his methods became more daring without ever slipping from scrupulous integrity, and he also became the most articulate of Romance methodologists, exposing with clarity and coherence the often unformulated principles and techniques that underlie Romance linguistic scholarship. In the academic atmosphere of the 'fifties his was often a voice in the wilderness, but the greater tolerance of the 'sixties has brought him into his own—and indeed he was in 1965 President of the Linguistic Society of America, a much coveted honour. The quick brilliance and wit of his thought, coupled with the breadth and depth of his knowledge, bear the mark of central European education 'de

Yakov
Malkiel

---

[1] The title has previously been applied to Ramón Menéndez Pidal, by my lights a 'traditionalist'; it is perhaps a more apt description of two more junior members of the Menéndez Pidal family—Diego Catalán and Alvaro Galmés de Fuentes.

[2] By U. T. Holmes, Jr. in *L* xv (1939) pp. 205–17; by L. Spitzer in *MLN* liv (1939) pp. 148–59; and by E. Lerch in *ZRP* lx (1940) pp. 286–90.

l'époque': today his English style has acquired a sparkle only found among those who came late to the language. Peculiarly enough then, although often his subject-matter might appear in other hands turgid and unwieldy, his treatment of it has on one occasion been passed over as 'fun'—though never as 'lightweight'.

Perhaps from modesty, Malkiel has not yet published a 'hard cover' book-length continuous work, though one volume of collected essays has now been published and another is in the press.[1] It may be that he remains 'traditional' enough to prefer to leave aside his 'great work of synthesis' for full maturity: haste to get into print is one of the more distasteful aspects of the modern academic scene! He himself foresees that he will continue to alternate monographic and theoretical probings, for, he says, "pure theory happens not to satisfy me".

Apart from his great, indeed unique, contribution to Romance linguistics in his essays and monographs, Malkiel's work as editor of **"Romance Philology"** *Romance Philology* calls for special note here. Founded in 1946, when the end of the war brought a spate of new linguistic periodicals, it is published by the University of California Press and, even though geographically located far from Romance cultural centres, it has become one of the most prestigious periodicals in its field, with a circulation of more than eleven hundred. Its 'traditional' name reflects its comparative friendliness towards both literary and linguistic studies of the Romance languages; unlike some other periodicals it has always been marked by tolerance in theoretical attitudes. Any contributor will bear witness to the amount of labour and care Malkiel and his assistants lavish on the pieces submitted to them: moreover, to retain balance and interest Malkiel often solicits articles, paying particular attention to provoking lively discussion in the important review article section. In a field like Romance philology where today scholarly work sometimes passes nearly unnoticed and rarely awakens echoes in wider realms, Malkiel's efforts to provoke and maintain exchange of opinion are of prime importance and, if there *is* to be a 'renaissance' of Romance linguistics, he will probably be its leader.

Malkiel's linguistic interests are predominantly, though not exclusively, historical and his special competence is in the Hispanic languages.[2] His Argentinian wife, María Rosa Lida, who tragically

---

[1] Y. Malkiel 1968 and (forthcoming).
[2] For general appreciation of Malkiel's works by one of his pupils, cf. K. D.

died in 1962, was a Hispanic and classical philologist of traditional leanings,[1] who may have inspired him to retain his respect for the more unfashionable type of scholarship amid the alien atmosphere of post-war America.

The historical problems that have been Malkiel's continuing preoccupation concern especially the lexical aspects of language—in particular etymology and word formation—though he has made original and inspired contributions to the study of historical morphology and phonology. His particular talent lies in his ability deftly to interweave the strands of lexical, morphological, and phonological data into a tapestry that displays the structural development of a language: what might in other hands appear a confused and tangled mass of unrelated *faits divers* is carefully sorted out into meaningful order. His versatility and his penchant for theoretical generalization, help to account for the leading position he occupies in Romance linguistics today. I hope I owe no apology for allotting him space almost proportionate to his stature.

In sheer bulk etymological studies are very important especially in Malkiel's earlier work: etymology has been a continuing interest

Etymology

for him, but it has been supplemented particularly in the last decade by a growing mass of studies on historical phonology and morphology (especially verbal inflection) as well as more and more theoretical and methodological essays principally concerned with the scientific status of historical linguistics.

A traditional form taken by etymological studies is that of the succinct note discussing the origins and history of a single word: it is this sort of etymological scholarship that is often derided as trivial and dilettante, especially when the words studied are chosen for their titillating semantic characteristics (scatological or obscene items are of special appeal to some etymologists!). Short etymological notes are to be found in Malkiel's work,[2] but even then they include

Uitti, "Problems in Hispanic and Romance Linguistics (Selected Writings of Yakov Malkiel)", in *HR* xxxiv (1966) pp. 242–55.

[1] For obituary and other appreciations cf. especially *RPh* xvii (1963). María Rosa Lida was 'traditional' only by Anglo-Saxon standards: she was by all accounts 'farouchement indépendante'. Professor Malkiel writes "She never interfered with my editorial decisions and at no time tried to influence my own research."

[2] E.g. "Old Judaeo-Spanish *yegüeria* 'mess, dish', in *L* xxi (1945) pp. 264–5; "The Etymology of OSp *apesgar*", in *MLQ* vi (1945) pp. 149–60 (taken up again, corrected and revised as "Latin PEDICA, *PENSUM and PERTIGA in Hispano-Romance", in A. Lombard 1968 (fest.); "The Etymology of Old Spanish *calano*", in *PQ* xxvii (1948) pp. 112–22; "The Etymology of Spanish *asperiega, esperiega*", in *PQ* xxviii (1949) pp. 294–311; "The Etymology of Hispanic *terco*", in *PMLA*

references to the "word families" to which his chosen items belong. Most of Malkiel's etymological studies are concerned with such word families—grouped onomasiologically,[1] etymologically,[2] morphologically,[3] phonologically,[4] as well as semantically and derivationally.[5] Malkiel's concern principally with the 'families' or 'fields' is essentially structural in its theoretical base, but always dynamic rather than static: he is always at pains to demonstrate the interaction and interpenetration of members of the same family, introducing a complexity of development not easily summed up in abstract formulae. He himself admits a fascination which springs from the very intractability of the material he juggles with, and he refuses to take the easy way out. A recent work of synthesis[6] describes his attitude, emphasizing that—attractive though etymological explanations that rely on semantic association might be—the real test, rigid though negative, must be that of form, leading to elegant and adequate solutions in which "the grammatical jig-saw puzzle has been neatly solved and the semantic fitting into a cultural context has become perfectly smooth" (p. 183).

lxiv (1949) pp. 570–84; "Cundir. Historia de una palabra y un problema etimológico", in R. Oroz 1954–5 (fest.) pp. 249–66; "Antiguo español y gallegoportugés *trocir* 'pasar'," in *NRFH* x (1956) pp. 385–95.

[1] "Studies in Hispano-Latin Homonymics: PASSULUS, PACTUS, PECTUS, DESPECTUS, SUSPECTUS, FISTULA in Ibero-Romance", in *L* xxviii (1952) pp. 299–338; "Studies in Spanish and Portuguese Animal Names", in *HR* xxiv (1956), pp. 115–43 and 207–31.

[2] "Italian *ciarlatano* and its Romance offshoots", in *RPh* ii (1949) pp. 317–26; "From 'bay-coloured' to 'spleen': the Romance phase of Latin BADIUS", in *AGI* xxxix (1954); pp. 166–87. "The Luso-Hispanic Descendants of POTIO", in I. González Llubera 1959 (fest.) pp. 193–210.

[3] "Hispanic *algu(i)en* and related formations. A Study of the Stratification of the Romance Lexicon in the Iberian Peninsula", in *UCPL* i (1948) pp. 357–442. The companion piece is "Old Spanish *nadi(e)*, *otri(e)*", *HR* xiii (1945) pp. 204–30.

[4] "La derivación de *rebelde*, *rebeldía* y las fuentes del grupo de consonantes -ld- en iberorrománico", in R. Menéndez Pidal 1950 (fest.) pp. 91–124; "Etimología y cambio fonético débil (Trayectoria ibero-románica de MEDICUS, MEDICAMEN, MEDICINA)", *Ib* (1961) [June, 1963] pp. 127–71.

[5] "*Atristar–entristecer.* Adjectival Verbs in Spanish, Portuguese and Catalan", *SP* xxxviii (1941) pp. 429–61; "The Word-Family of Spanish *desmoronar*, Portuguese *esb(o)roar* 'crumble' ", in *PMLA* lxiii (1948) pp. 785–802; "The Etymology of Hispanic *restolho*, *rastrojo*, *rostoll*", in *RPh* i (1947–48) pp. 209–34; "The Ancient Hispanic Verbs *posfaçar*, *porfacar*, *profaçar*. A Study in Etymology and Word-Formation", in *RPh* iii (1949–50) pp. 27–72; "Old Spanish *paladino*, *palaciano*, *palanciano*, *palaciego*", in *PMLA* lxv (1950) pp. 944–74; "Spanish *duende* and *duendo*, Portuguese-Galician-Asturian *dondo*, Leonese *dondio*, Central American *dundo*", in A. M. Huntington 1952 (fest.) pp. 361–92; "Español 'negrestino' y 'blanquecino'", in *Quaderni Ibero-Americani* (Turin) xviii (1956) pp. 89–92; "Español antiguo 'cuer' y 'coracón'", in *BH* lx (1958) pp. 180–363 and 327–63; "Sobre el núcleo etimológico de esp. ant. 'desman(d) ar', 'desman(o)', Lat DE-, DI- MANARE", in *Fi* viii (1962) [1964] pp. 185–211.

[6] "Form versus Meaning in Etymological Analysis: Old Spanish "auze" 'luck'," in J. H. Merriott 1966 (fest.) pp. 167–83.

Malkiel's etymological theories are aptly summed up in his 1962 essay "Etymology and General Linguistics".[1] Here he claims some degree of autonymy for etymology, within the realm of lexicology, setting out four reasons for such a claim (pp. 100–1). He outlines a programme for the encouragement of etymological studies, including some suggestions for refinement of technique. Malkiel is, however, perhaps too optimistic about the possibility of the establishment of etymology as a discipline with substantial following: he himself admits (p. 219)

Methodology in etymology

> Only at rare intervals do etymological cruxes qualify as thesis subjects, since they present an uncomfortably high concentration of difficulties and presuppose such balanced perspective as can be slowly gained from experience alone.

The flash of inspiration and enlightenment that is part of the etymologist's special gift is recognized as essential by Malkiel, though he casts some doubt on Spitzer's dictum "Such' keine Etymologien; finde sie!" The flash, he claims, has to be preceded by careful and rigorous ordering of material. In today's restless academic atmosphere young scholars are more often attracted by the broad sweep of abstract theory than by painstaking accumulation of data: etymology will in all probability remain a domain of the gifted and the experienced.

Malkiel's interest in the development of 'word families' has its morphological corollary in his work on word formation and derivation. Although numerically his monographs in the more specialized field are less numerous than in etymology,[2] it is here perhaps

Word formation

---

[1] In *Wd* xviii (1962) pp. 198–219; cf. also "The Uniqueness and Complexity of Etymological Solutions", in *Li* v (1956) pp. 225–52. Both articles, slightly retouched, are included in Y. Malkiel (1968) pp. 175–98 and 229–58. We might mention here the pronouncements of other scholars on method in etymology: K. Baldinger, "L'étymologie hier et aujourd'hui", in *CAIEF* xi (1959) pp. 233–64; and H. Meier, "Zur Geschichte der romanischen Etymologie", in *ASNS* xxi (1964) pp. 89–109.

[2] "The Development of *iuu* in Latin and Romance", in *L* xvii (1941) pp. 99–118; the counterpart "Zur Substantivierung der Adjektiva im Romanischen: über den Ursprung des Typus ATTRACTĪUU, INITIĀTĪUA", appeared in occupied Copenhagen in 1943 in *Classica et Medievalia* v (1943) pp. 238–56; "Three Old French Sources of the English 'arrival', 'withdraw-al' type", in *Journal of English and German Philology* xliii (1944) pp. 80–7; "The Derivation of Hispanic *fealdad(e)*, *fialdad(e)* and *frialdad(e)*", in *UCPL* i (1945) pp. 189–214; "The Latin Background of the Spanish Suffix *-uno*. Studies in the Genesis of a Romance Formative", in *RPh* iv (1950) pp. 17–45; "Los interfijos hispánicos. Problema de lingüística histórica y estructural", in A. Martinet 1957–62 (fest.) ii, pp. 107–99; "The Two Sources of the Hispanic Suffix *-azo*, *-aço*", in *L* xxv (1959) pp. 193–258; "Nuevas Aportaciones para el estudio del Sufijo *-uno*", in *NRFH* xii (1959) pp. 241–90; (with K. D. Uitti) "L'ancien français *gab-ois*, *ir-ois*, *jargon-ois*, et leurs contreparties

that Malkiel has exerted most influence on young scholars.[1] We are lucky enough, to have, from Malkiel's own pen, a masterly and scintillating synthesis of a quarter of a century's work and thought on the subject—a series of talks given by special invitation at the Linguistic Institute of America in 1964, published under the title *Genetic Analysis of Word Formation*.[2] Here Malkiel explains his choice of a field of scholarly endeavour which seems to some unattractive and unrewarding (p. 307):

> I believe in retrospect that I have, over the years, been greatly disturbed by two mutually exclusive currents of linguistic thought and practice by which it has been my fate to be caught in different climates and that research in derivation and composition has offered me, on both occasions, some kind of powerful anti-toxin. I shall call these two currents lexicalization as against grammaticalization of linguistic thought.

Lexicalization is the term Malkiel applies to atomistic anti-abstract attitude to language study that was fashionable in pre-war Europe (and of which incidentally *Iordan–Orr* was the most influential mouthpiece). Linguistic geography, especially in its Word-and-Thing branch, and 'idealistic' linguistics concentrated most on multifarious lexical aspects of language. *Grammaticalization* is Malkiel's term for the post-war American fad for abstract structural

dans l'anglais d'Amérique", in *RLiR* xxxii (1968) pp. 126–74. Cf. also "Studies in Irreversible Binominals" in *Li* viii (1959) pp. 113–60, also Y. Malkiel 1968 pp. 311–55 (concerned with such 'set-phrases' as 'odds and ends' etc.) and also, less directly, "Secondary Uses of Letters in Language" in *RPh* xix (1965–66) pp. 1–27 (revised and much expanded in Y. Malkiel 1968 pp. 357–98). An important detailed study, "Patterns of Derivational Suffixation in the Cabraniego Dialect of East-Central Asturian", is also due to appear shortly in M. R. Haas (forthcoming) (fest.).

[1] Some works on word-formation that bear Malkiel's distinctive marke are: J. R. Craddock and E. S. Georges "The Hispanic Sound-Suffix *-ido*", in *RPh* xvii (1963–64) pp. 87–107; J. R. Craddock, "A Critique of Recent Studies in Romance Diminutives", in *RPh* xix (1965–66) pp. 286–325; W. E. Geiger, "'Fruit', 'Fruit Tree' and 'Grove' in Spanish: a Study in Derivational Patterning", in *RPh* xx (1966–67) pp. 176–86; Anita K. Levy, "Contrastive Development in Hispano-Romance of Borrowed Gallo-Romance Suffixes", in *RPh* xviii (1965–66) pp. 399–429, xx (1966–67) pp. 296–320; P. M. Lloyd "An Analytical Survey of Studies in Romance Word-Formation", in *RPh* xvii (1963–64) pp. 736–70; Margaret Hoffman, "A General Linguist's View of Word Formation in Middle French", in *RPh* xviii (1964–65) pp. 54–63. J. R. Craddock's doctoral thesis has been accepted for publication: J. R. Craddock (forthcoming): while his shorter companion piece: "Latin Diminutive Versus Latin-'Mediterranean' Hybrid: On Proparoxytonic Derivatives of GALLA in Hispano-Romance and Sardinian", has appeared in *RPh* xxi (1968) "Emmanuel S. Georges Memorial" (pp. 436–49), which likewise includes a major chunk, meticulously revised by his executors, of Georges' own thesis: "Past-Participal Nouns: Their Development from Latin to Romance", pp. 368–91. Finally, there has appeared P. M. Lloyd 1968, his first post-doctoral book-length study.

[2] T. A. Sebeok (ed.) 1966*a*, pp. 305–64.

model building, in which the less tidy lexicon was neglected in favour of the 'closed systems' of grammar and phonology, which lend themselves to elegant and economical description.

For Malkiel the special fascination of a study of word formation, and especially of affixal derivation, is that it necessitates a dialectic between the two modes of thought: parts of the apparently amorphous lexicon are morphologically structured, though not with the tightness of, for instance, inflectional paradigms. Loose, uneconomical structures are less likely to be stable than more tightly-knit ones, consequently dynamics of word formation appear more kaleidoscopic and less easily formulable into static algorithms. Malkiel's talents, as we have seen, are better displayed to advantage in the piecing together of mosaics than in the manipulation of Saussurean chessmen or digital computers, and yet he is quick to detect the triviality of atomistic studies: hence his predilection for a no-man's-land so often deserted by both 'humanists' and 'scientific' linguists.

In his potentially seminal synthesis, Malkiel constructs an explicatory model for the description of affixal derivation, attaining all the rigour, though none of the aridity, of modern linguistic practice; at every stage he aptly illustrates, especially from Romance languages (indeed he would be quick to point out that he does not use data to illustrate abstract features, but constructs his model on the basis of generalization from data). At one point (p. 338) he gives an invaluable outline of the canon of operations by which to seek an explanation of a derivational suffix in any language: first, sifting the suffixal material into lexical strata (semantic, morphological, and chronological); secondly, examining it in relation to its potential rivals among other suffixes in the language; and lastly, focusing attention on the various pressures that can bring it to prominence within its structure. One language item is thus examined within the framework of the whole economy of the language, which in its turn is firmly placed in its socio-cultural and chronological setting.

For the complexity of his model Malkiel makes no apology, eschewing the (p. 364) "temptation to sweep under the rug whatever pieces do not fit into . . . rigid pigeon-holes". Indeed, he "treasures anomalies since they may serve as priceless clues to past stages, buried under later deposits and equally important to future phases not yet clearly outlined". Nevertheless anyone who is familiar with the chaotic character of the raw material that can so easily overwhelm the unskilled, will marvel at the economy and elegance of Malkiel's exposition, never deteriorating into dull cataloguing and yet retaining the rigour demanded by modern linguistics.

Malkiel's third specialist interest lies in the processes of change within the more tightly structured aspects of language. Again his

Historical phonology and morphology
aim is explanation, rather than merely description and he tends to stress interaction of linguistic levels rather than separation of levels. On the phonological level, Malkiel is far from denying the utility of sound laws, but he does emphasize that their scope is limited and that the data on which they are constructed should be carefully sifted to exclude the effect of extraneous influences (morphological, lexical, cultural, and so on). His purely phonological writings[1] are concerned primarily with a more rigorous definition of the environmental conditioning of 'regular' sound change.[2] More often, however, Malkiel is at pains to point out the complex interlocking of different types of sound change, conditioned by the needs of all the complementary aspects of language structure.[3] The novelty of Malkiel's approach is summed up:[4]

> Whereas the older historical grammar operated chiefly with alternatives (e.g. substratum influence vs. internal sound change) the explicative grammar of the future after carefully isoalting and defining each force that can possibly have been involved, will start from the assumption that in the overwhelming majority of observable situations there have been at work configurations of contributing forces. The highest attainable level of analysis will then be a systematic enquiry into the tendential complementarity, i.e. co-efficiency, or mutual exclusion, of such isolable agencies.

Malkiel pays special attention to the classic category occasioning 'disturbance' of regular phonological processes which is often known

---

[1] E.g. "Towards a Unified System of Classification of Latin-Spanish Vowel Correspondences", in *RPh* xvi (1962–63) pp. 153–69; "Quelques fausses applications de la "Loi de Verner" aux faits romans", in *CFS* xxiii (1966) pp. 75–87 ("Mélanges A. Burger").

[2] The following articles on Hispanic phonological themes by C. Blaylock owe much to Malkiel's influence: "The Monophthongization of Latin AE in Spanish", in *RPh* xviii (1964) pp. 16–24: "Hispanic Metaphony", in *RPh* xviii (1965) pp. 253–71; "Assimilation of Stops to Preceding Resonants in Ibero-Romance", in *RPh* xix (1966) pp. 418–34; "Latin L-, LL- in the Hispanic Dialects; Retroflexion and Lenition", *RPh* xxi (1968) pp. 368–91. These four pieces jointly form a distillation of the author's Berkeley thesis (1964), *Studies in Possible Osco-Umbrian Influence on Hispano-Romance Phonology*.

[3] E.g. "Weak Phonetic Change, Spontaneous Sound-Shift, Lexical Contamination", in *Li* xi (1962) pp. 263–75; "Economie phonologique et perte lexicale", in M. Delbouille 1964 (fest.) i, pp. 409–16; and the monograph-length "The Interlocking of Narrow Sound Change, Broad Phonological Pattern, Level of Transmission, Areal Configuration, Sound Symbolism", in *ArL* xv (1965) pp. 144–73, xvi (1966) pp. 1–33. (Cf. T. Montgomery's detailed critique in *HR* xxxvi (1968) pp. 54–9.)

[4] *Li* xi (1962) p. 275.

as 'analogical levelling'.[1] It has long been recognized that the morphological paradigms partake in idiosyncratic diachronic processes, but the mechanism of 'analogical levelling' is not satisfactorily understood.[2] Taking into the account the interlocking structural levels, Malkiel has concerned himself particularly with the development of Hispanic verbal paradigms. His earliest ventures in this field[3] were of particular moment to me personally, as they opened my eyes to a way of solving an intractable problem I was tussling with in my early post-doctoral days—the 'irregular' phonological development of the Romance verb imperfect endings.[4] Later, more extended monographs have developed and perfected Malkiel's ideas, especially on means by which sound change is occasionally conditioned by the demands of morphological economy.[5] A very recent essay[6] shows that Malkiel has not meanwhile abandoned the line of thought of his 1959 article, that I had found so inspiring—that of a dynamic structuralist approach to morphology tracing the interaction of syntactically related forms, as well as their mutual repulsion when pathological homonymy threatens. A quotation[7] aptly underlines one of the original features of this approach which seeks to explain

[1] Cf. *Iordan–Orr*, p. 14, etc.

[2] Recent work on analogical levelling includes several articles by W. Mańczak: cf. especially "Tendances générales des changements analogiques", *Li* vii (1959) pp. 298–325 and 387–420; "Tendances générales du développement morphologique", *Li* xii (1963) pp. 19–38; "Sur quelques regularités dans le développement de la conjugaison espagnole", *RLiR* xxvii (1963) pp. 436–9; "Développement phonétique irrégulier et fréquence d'emploi", *Actes 10ᵉ Cong. (Strasbourg) 1962* vol. iii, pp. 911–24; and "A propos de l'analogie progressive; *Lis* xxxiii (1967) pp. 82–7. Cf. also K. Baldinger, "Die progressive Analogie (Am Beispiel von *vuelent, puelent, sielent, chielent)*", in M. Delbouille 1964 (fest.) pp. 65–82.

[3] "The Contrast *tomáis ~ tomávades, queréis ~ queríades* in Classical Spanish", in *HR* xvii (1949) pp. 159–65; "Towards a Reconsideration of the Old Spanish Imperfect in *-ia ~ -ie*", in *HR* xxvii (1959) pp. 435–81.

[4] Cf. R. Posner, "The Imperfect Endings in Romance", *TPS* 1961 pp. 17–55; other studies by me on verbal inflection that owe much to Malkiel's indirect influence are "Phonology and Analogy in the Romance Perfect", in *RPh* xvii (1963–64) pp. 419–31, and "The Romance Imperfect and Conditional Endings—a Further Contribution", in *SN* xxxvii (1965) pp. 3–10.

[5] "Paradigmatic Resistance to Sound Change. The Old Spanish Preterite Forms *vide, vido* against the background of the Recession of primary *-d-*", in *L* xxxvi (1960) pp. 281–345; "Diphthongization, monophthongization, metaphony. Studies in their Interaction in the Paradigm of the Old Spanish *-ir* Verbs", in *L* xlii (1966) pp. 430–72; "The Inflectional Paradigm as an Occasional Determinant of Sound Change"—paper given to a symposium on historical linguistics in Austin, Texas, 1966, and printed in W. P. Lehmann and Y. Malkiel (eds.) 1968 pp. 21–64.

[6] "Le nivellement morphologique comme point de départ d'une 'loi phonétique'. La monophtongaison occasionnelle de *ie* et *ue* en ancien espagnol", to appear in J. Frappier (forthcoming) (fest.). Cf. also a new "Deux problèmes de linguistique générale illustrés par le parfait fort de l'ancien hispano-roman", in R. Lejeune 1968 (fest.) pp. 587–99.

[7] From *HR* xvii (1949) p. 165.

an existing anomalous situation by going on to reconstruct the (non-existent) state of affairs that one would have expected to have prevailed under normal circumstances and subsequently by attempting to determine the specific inconveniences which, in the given case, appear to have deterred a group of speakers for quite some while from accepting that norm.

Explanation of morphological change as influenced by structures of homonymy ("certaines symétries structurales gravement compromises") is heralded in Malkiel's recent essay as "une nouvelle brèche faite à la théorie des soi-disant forces aveugles, qui sont censées opérer au hasard". Here, as elsewhere, Malkiel has sought by dint of careful scholarship and rigorous reasoning to reduce to a minimum the appeal in language history to mysterious and irrational forces.

One of the original—almost idiosyncratic—contributions made by Malkiel to scholarship is to be found in his typological classifications of linguistic studies. In a way, these may be regarded **Typological** as extremely sophisticated bibliographies, classified **studies** in a way that contrasts and compares its items, exposing lacunae as well as underlining positive features. Three such classifications have so far been published—one of etymological studies[1] is little more than a sketch, but the others of Romance historical grammars[2] and of Spanish dictionaries[3] are full-scale wholly original and successful surveys of the field chosen, that reveal an inimitable grasp of bibliographical detail combined with a breathtaking breadth of vision. To avoid, on the one hand, the tedium of the catalogue, and, on the other, slap-dash superficiality in such work requires a touch of a master with great originality of conception. Malkiel chooses to classify his material on the basis of 'distinctive features', operating[4] "on a theory that a monograph or handbook is analysable as a bundle of characteristic traits that can be re-assembled, as it were, in miscellaneous arrangements". Thus he is able to pinpoint the salient features of works he mentions. No

---

[1] "A tentative typology of etymological studies", in *IJAL* xxiii (1957) 1–17, reprinted, with its bibliographic supplement brought up-to-date, in Y. Malkiel 1968 pp. 199–227.
[2] "A tentative typology of Romance Historical Grammars", in *Li* ix (1960) pp. 321–416. Reprinted with revised and expanded bibliographic supplement, in Y. Malkiel 1968 pp. 71–164.
[3] "Distinctive Features in Lexicography. A Typological Approach to Dictionaries Exemplified with Spanish", in *RPh* xii (1950) pp. 366–99, xiii (1959) pp. 111–55. A condensed and modified version appeared (pp. 3–24) in the *IJAL* volume xxviii:2 (1962) Part iv (also F. W. Householder and S. Saporta (eds.) 1962) under the title "A Typological Classification of Dictionaries on the Basis of Distinctive Features" (reprinted in Y. Malkiel 1968 pp. 247–79).
[4] *Li* ix (1960) p. 322.

serious student of Romance linguistics can afford to ignore, in particular, Malkiel's indispensable guide to the classics of Romance historical grammar, covering substantially more than two hundred works: their scope, presentation, theoretical framework, and so on, are subject to a searching scrutiny that cannot fail to bring illumination to potential readers. As we have come to expect from him, Malkiel ends on a programmatic note which foresees a renaissance of historical grammar in new forms, with less concentration on "clogging detail" and more "coherent integration of the whole" (p. 100).

It is not surprising that someone like Malkiel, who has such a profound knowledge of the relevant literature and a zest for theoretical speculation, should show interest in the 'history of the science' aspect of his subject. Linguistics today has reached a point in its development from which it is possible to look back and assess the achievements, as well as evaluate the prejudices, of our predecessors: hence the popularity of surveys of 'trends' that I have already mentioned (pp. 401-2). Malkiel's contributions have characteristically been subtle and discerning appreciations of the 'whole man' who produced the linguistic works, rather than impersonal and skeletal accounts of trends and schools. His obituaries are works of art which bring alive again the scholarly preoccupations of their subjects.[1] Apart from his discussions, already mentioned,[2] of the rôle of Romance linguistics within the discipline as a whole, Malkiel's most important essayistic venture in this domain is entitled "Each word has a history of its own",[3] where he pithily underlines the fundamental

History of the science

---

[1] Cf. especially obituaries in *RPh* of A. Dauzat (ix, 1955-56, p. 402), E. Auerbach (xi, 1957-58 p. 1962), K. Jaberg (xii, 1958-59 pp. 258-61), J. Vendryes (xiv, 1960-61 p. 27), H-F. Muller (xiv, 1960-61 p. 188); L. Spitzer (xiv, 1960-61 pp. 285 ff), M. L. Wagner (xvi, 1962-63 pp. 281-9), A. Steiger (xviii, 1964-65 pp. 284-96), J. Orr (xx, 1966-67 p. 191). The important obituaries of Jaberg, Spitzer and M. L. Wagner are reprinted in T. A. Sebeok (ed.) 1966*b*. Cf. also the obituary of U. Weinreich in *L* xliii (1967) pp. 605-10. Sketches of other linguists, for the *Encyclopaedia Britannica*, include Amado Alonso, and Meyer-Lübke (in the 1964 edition) and Jakob Jud and Menéndez Pidal (yet to appear). Cf. also "Leonard Bloomfield in Retrospect", in Y. Malkiel 1968 pp. 165-74.

[2] Cf. p. 414.

[3] A paper originally presented to a 1964 symposium of the Wenner-Gren Foundation for Anthropologial Research on "Revolution vs. Continuity in the Study of Language" (Cf. p. 403 n. 4) and published in *Gl* i (1967) pp. 137-49. Another, as yet unpublished, paper presented to a Chicago symposium on the "History of Linguistics" in 1968 deserves mention here. Under the title "Theory versus Practice as a Starting Point for Discoveries in Linguistic Research", Malkiel points out that the current taste for logico-mathematical theoretical models might lead to the ignoring of certain complexities that force themselves on the attention of the data-oriented linguist; he illustrates his argument from the work of Romance linguists.

antagonism between 'neo-grammarian' and 'linguistic geography' theories and practice.

It is only to be expected that Malkiel, for all his capacity for self-effacement and self-criticism, should, in his prime of life, be ready to risk general theoretical statements, synthesizing **Genetic linguistics** the experience of decades of detailed scholarship. The last few years have seen the publication of a number of theoretical essays and mark him out as a leading figure of historical linguistics.

Of these the most important is the pyrotechnical performance, for the benefit of other experts, of his presidential address delivered to the Linguistic Society of America in December 1965;[1] less taxing for the inexpert is the more popularizing synthesis "Genetic Linguistics".[2] Malkiel launches the term 'genetic linguistics' or 'glotto-dynamics' to replace the traditional 'historical linguistics' which has acquired connotations not wholly compatible with modern approaches to language study: one of the aims of the discipline he envisages is

to isolate a core of theory and exemplification—if necessary, at the cost of studied restraint and even of painful surgery—and establish a discipline concerned with the universals, as against the particulars, of change.[3]

He even goes further and abjures the traditional academic divorce from 'real life' problems suggesting that the linguist might be permitted,

if circumstances so warrant, even to throw his weight behind shifts and movements deemed desirable—if not qua linguist stricto sensu, at least qua linguistically enlightened and chaste layman.

Malkiel's own work in historical linguistics would lead one to expect that he would eschew over-simplified analysis and seek always explanation rather than mere description. His more theoretical works underline his preferences: in "Multiple vs. Simple Causation in Linguistic Change",[4] Malkiel points out the folly of using Occam's razor to get rid of 'redundancy' in causal explanation of many changes—where a single conditioning factor may not be sufficient to spark off a change (especially one traditionally labelled 'sporadic'),

---

[1] Published substantially unaltered under the title "Linguistics as a Genetic Science", in *L* xliii (1967) pp. 223–45.

[2] To be found in Y. Malkiel 1968 pp. 1–18, and in the *International Encyclopaedia of Social Sciences* ix (1968) pp. 371–80 under the original title "Historical Linguistics".

[3] *L* xliii (1967) p. 225.

[4] In R. Jakobson 1967 (fest.), vol. ii, pp. 1228–46.

a combination of causes may do the trick.[1] As a result of eschewing the exclusive pursuit of 'economy' in causal explanation, Malkiel is able to isolate hitherto unrecognized forces for change, often overlaid by other more familiar factors—among these are 'weak' sound changes, tendency to morphological 'hyper-characterization' and lexical and morphological pressures.

Another complexity of historical linguistics that Malkiel underlines is concerned with the difficulty of tracing a straight line of development for any linguistic item, especially when documentary evidence reveals an oscillation between a number of different forms. In "Initial Points vs. Initial Segments of Linguistic Trajectories",[2] he shows that the oldest recorded form—"the initial point"—may be a misleading place from which to trace a historical trajectory, as it may represent a wild swing in the oscillation of forms:

> A generously carved out initial segment, extending preferably over several centuries, is needed to help us discriminate between the principal line of advance and some temporary disturbance eventually overcome and conspicuous mainly because, through the caprice of our fragmentary records, the distortion it was causing coincided with the earliest tangible traces of given development (p. 403).

In a recent essay "Range of Variation as a Clue to Dating"[3] Malkiel makes original use of oscillation of forms in documentary evidence to outline a new method of dating of linguistic change that can supplement established methods. Presuming that proliferation of variants is likely to result from dialect mixture, or from internal linguistic tendencies like analogical innovation, or as an "uncoordinated set of reactions" to some cataclysmic linguistic change, he seeks to isolate the conditions in which oscillation is found and, where relevant, to assign a chronology to the changes involved. Examining as an example the wide variation in medieval Hispanic preterite forms of Latin *trahere*, he sees therein a rebellion against the 'unwanted' type *tre(i)x-*, alternating with *trax-*, which would have regularly resulted from phonetic changes. The chronology of the variation points to a 'cataclysm' in the early medieval era—a

---

[1] I am honoured that Malkiel should have chosen as one of his illustrations for his thesis, my own work on *Consonantal Dissimilation* (cf. R. Posner 1961 and pp. 493-4) in which I argue for multiple causation of sporadic sound-change, and which flatteringly provoked a lengthy review article by K. Togeby, "Qu'est-ce que la dissimilation?" in *RPh* xvii (1963-64) pp. 642-67 (also in K. Togeby 1968 pp. 96-121) which argues the dispensability of some of the posited conditioning factors and consequently 'balkanizes' developments that appear to hang together.

[2] In the *P9th ICL* 1964 pp. 402-5.

[3] The first part has appeared in *RPh* xxi (1967-68) pp. 463-501.

dating which harmonizes with that presumed for the regular sound-changes concerned.

Yet another and quite different way in which Malkiel has made a theoretical contribution to historical linguistics is illustrated in his paper "Some Diachronic Implications of Fluid Speech Communities".[1] Here he indulges in the fashionable game of model building but using a geometric rather than an algebraic technique. Instead of the familiar 'reconstructional' model of comparative linguistics, Malkiel experiments with a simplified socio-geographical model, postulating the occurrence of various types of socio-cultural developments, and examining the potential linguistic results. His model is obviously based on the reality of the Iberian peninsula, but it makes clear certain lines of development that become obscured in a short-sighted examination of data. Malkiel's willingness to experiment with schematic models demonstrates once more how far he marries successfully modern and traditional linguistic skills. It is fitting to end this assessment of his work by quoting the paper's concluding paragraph in which he skilfully balances the advantages of both approaches:

The working with models temporarily relieves the explorer of certain onerous obligations (e.g. of the need to pay constant attention to distracting details characteristic of societies in flux or to engage in time-consuming bibliographic research): for a while it frees his mind and channels his cognition in the direction of, dynamically speaking, essentials. In this manner, hidden possibilities of interaction between discrete forces can sometimes be visualized for the first time. At a later date the wisdom of such assumptions can be tested by application of the schema to ensembles of interlocking circumstances operative in actual linguistic change, i.e. to a set of situations necessarily far more complex than are the initial schemata.

Pierre Guiraud needs little introduction to students of French, who will already treasure the dozen invaluable little books he has written for the *Que Sais-Je?* series.[2] These are models of the
Pierre Guiraud popularizing art, always original in conception as well as lucid in exposition, and never descending to the level of merely attractively re-hashing the ideas of others.

Although he is a few years senior to Malkiel,[3] Guiraud's interests

[1] In *AmA* xlvi (1964) pp. 177–86; reprinted in Y. Malkiel 1968 pp. 19–31.
[2] In the realm of lexicology: P. Guiraud 1955, 1956, 1961, 1964a & b, 1968b; on French 1960, 1962, 1963a & b, 1965, 1968a; on style, 1954b.
[3] Guiraud completed his Paris doctorate in 1951–52. After a short spell at the

have not developed as widely; I venture to group him under the
same heading because of his ability to combine an interest in the
'traditional' problems—principally lexicological and stylistic—with
modern techniques (here statistico-mathematical). Guiraud's
interests are, however, more geographically localized than Malkiel's
and his empirical works are concerned wholly with French and
dialects spoken in France.

Guiraud's Parisian doctoral thesis[1] attempts to define, with the
help of statistics, some of the elusive characteristics of poetic dis-

Stylistic statistics
course, with special consideration of Valéry (chosen
no doubt because this poet's quintessentiality
presents a particular challenge to the analyst).
Guiraud's study covers the phonetic, lexical and syntactic aspects
of his subject, as well as use of the imagery, paying particular
attention to rhythmic and harmonic factors. His findings are varied
and valuable: on the phonological level, for instance, we read that
Valéry's verse uses an abnormally high proportion of mute e's and of
long vowels and syllables; on the level of imagery, we discern a
reaction against the Baudelairean type of metaphor, towards more
audacious syntactic constructions; on the lexical level, we recognise
Valéry's recurrent poetic preoccupations via the two hundred
mots thèmes which occupy half of the text.

Guiraud's supplementary thesis[2] is a more purely methodological
consideration of statistical approaches to vocabulary study.[3]

Lexical statistics
Examining the classic rank-frequency model of
vocabulary distribution in a text, devised by Zipf,[4]
Guiraud suggest certain modifications on the basis of
empirical data. He goes on to propose a measure of vocabulary
distribution—'concentration', 'richness', 'extension'—that can be
used in stylistic comparison between authors. Other measures he
proposes concern the relative frequency of parts of speech and the
statistical isolation of *mots-thèmes* and *mots-clés* (categories familiar
from Matoré's *Lexicologie*[5]). Guiraud's illustrations illuminatingly
compare the vocabulary of French symbolist poets.

University College of Swansea, he became Professor of Romance Languages at
Groningen, before taking up his present post at Nice.
[1] P. Guiraud 1952.
[2] P. Guiraud 1954a.
[3] For a general discussion of work on stylostatistics, including the contribution of
Guiraud, cf. R. Posner, "The Use and Abuse of Stylostatistics", in *ArL* xv (1963)
pp. 111–39. See also pp. 461 and 533.
[4] Cf. especially G. K. Zipf 1949.
[5] Cf. p. 464 for more on Matoré's work.

Much of Guiraud's later work concerns linguistic statistics in general:[1] his lucid synthesis *Problèmes et Méthodes de la Statistique Linguistique*,[2] exemplifying statistical approaches to lexicological, stylistic, and phonological problems, deserves special mention. More and more, however, his attention has been turned to the lexicon (computer-aided indices of literary vocabulary figure large in his work[3]) and especially to structural etymology.[4] His work in this latter field, which he feels best expresses his own talents and predilections, is synthesized in his book *Les Structures Etymologiques du Français*.[5] Here the affinity of Guiraud's and Malkiel's work is most obvious: although Guiraud constructs a statistical model (pp. 180–8) on the basis of his work it is *post hoc* and does no more than confirm what "une analyse purement qualitative et, jusqu'ici, intuitive nous a amené à imaginer" (p. 180). He admits at one point that experience has taught him that modern 'formal' analysis cannot replace more traditional methods (p. 127):

Linguistic statistics

Structural etymology

> Il n'est pas douteux, qu'au départ, nous avons surestimé la valeur de l'analyse formelle aux dépens des coordonnées historiques, nous sommes revenus en arrière depuis et avons constamment insisté—dans la théorie et la pratique-sur l'importance de l'analyse externe, montrant que les deux approches étaient complémentaires.

Guiraud seeks the etymology of his chosen items (often plant or animal names) in the 'structures' to which they belong, tracing skilfully the interaction of all members of the structures. Like Malkiel he does not reject the possibility of 'multiple causation', and he is ready to accept that one and the same item may have a double etymology (p. 59):

> Et ceci vérifie une nouvelle fois ce qui est le postulat fondamental de la méthode, la convergence des motivations internes et externes: il y a eu

---

[1] Cf. P. Guiraud 1954*c*.
[2] P. Guiraud 1960*b*.
[3] P. Guiraud 1953–54 and 1953–57.
[4] Cf. "Le champ morpho-sémantique de *chat*", *Actes 8e Cong. (Florence) 1956* pp. 549–54; "Les champs morpho-sémantiques (critères internes et critères externes en étymologie)", in *BSLP* li (1956) pp. 265–88; "Des chevaux et des femmes", in *FM* xxiv (1956) pp. 216–20; "Une forme de la fausse étymologie: la contamination tautologique", in *N* xl (1956) pp. 229–32; "Le champ morpho-sémantique du verbe *chiquer* (étude sur les radicaux onomatopéiques)", in *BSLP* lvi (1960) pp. 135–54; "Le champ morpho-sémantique des composés tautologiques", in *ZRP* lxxvii (1961) pp. 444–69; "Le champ morpho-sémantique de la racine T. K.", in *BSLP* lvii (1962) pp. 103–25; "De la grive au maquereau—le champ morpho-sémantique des animaux tâchetés", in *FM* xxxiv (1966) pp. 280–308; "Le champ morpho-sémantique des noms de matou", in *BSLP* lxi (1966) pp. 128–45.
[5] P. Guiraud 1967.

emprunt, il y a eu métaphore, il y a peut-être même eu coquille dans la mesure où tous ces phénomènes sont venus se greffer sur la matrice dont ils actualisaient le sémantisme virtuel.

For Guiraud lexical structures can be defined in the following ways: 1° morphologically—items with the same formal make-up; 2° semantically—as when for instance spotted creatures are given related names; 3° onomatopoeically—as when words with the same sound symbolism form a semantic content field; 4° paronymically— a category into which Guiraud groups 'pseudo-suffixation' when formally related items have differing semantic content, and 'onomastic metonymy', by which proper names are used for objects or animals; 5° morpho-semantically—when formally related items acquire by mutual attraction similar semantic content; 6° semically —when formal linguistic items can be regarded as covering configurations of 'semes' or 'semantic components'.

Guiraud's most original contributions lie in his studies of morphosemantic structures, where his method enables him to detect previously unsuspected influences and etymologies. He accepts the postulate, advanced by Hjelmslev and recently developed in independent ways by Greimas and the Chomskyist semanticists Katz and Fodor,[1] that a structured grouping of units of content—'semes'—can be mapped on to each unit of expression. Thus content structures can be analysed as consisting of morphemes sharing the same semes.

Morpho-semantic structures

Guiraud's theoretical framework, however, owes most to Saussure: the duality of the linguistic sign is basic to his thought, which envisages a dynamic interaction between *signifié* and *signifiant*.[2] He quotes with approval some of the ideas of Guillaume,[3] and his search for the *macro-signe*, or 'semiological category' which in its abstraction over-rides the sporadicity and contingency of the 'micro'-data is reminiscent of Guillaume's *psycho-systématique*. To quote his own words (p. 202):

De ce procès Guillaume a donné des exemples grammaticaux tout en reculant devant le lexique qu'il jugeait trop engagé dans l'événement pour qu'on pût le reduire à une structure abstraite, nous avons essayé de montrer que toute création lexicale est bien contingente, mais en partie seulement et dans les limites d'un certain nombre de conditions nécessaires: *le discours*

[1] Cf. esp. A. J. Greimas 1966 and especially J. A. Fodor and, "The Structure of a Semantic Theory" in their selection of readings (1964); also p. 521.

[2] In this particular, Guiraud's historical semantic outlook resembles that of Ullmann (cf. p. 458). His impatience with bibliographical detail, however, prevents one from tracing accurately the sources of his thought.

[3] For a more general discussion of Guillaume cf. pp. 496–501.

crée de nouveaux mots au moyen des matériaux qui lui sont fournis par l'histoire et qu'il utilise en raison de besoins accidentels, mais conformément à un système de matrices lexicales.

It can be seen then that Guiraud, though working in a different theoretical climate from Malkiel, has also come to apply structural methods to the apparently chaotic domains of word formation and etymology, thereby gaining new and fascinating insights into language dynamics.

3. *Idealism (or Humanism)*

The group of scholars who called themselves, perhaps unfortunately, 'idealists' received ample discussion in *Iordan–Orr*, because they represent a twentieth-century revolt against neo-grammarian and positivist linguistics. Their main tenet was humanistic—language is essentially used by people, not only for communication but for creative expression; therefore abstract, immanent methods are unsuitable for its study. 'Tigers of wrath' rather than 'horses of instruction', they insisted on the need for flair and intuitive sensitivity in linguistic investigation rather than on plodding logic, careful analysis and abstract schematization. Naturally enough their interests were more semantic and stylistic than grammatical, and the linguistic material they studied would be most often the considered, and unique, production of the creatively gifted—the 'best authors'. Inevitably, theirs was a historical approach—for the authors live in time—but one essentially different from that of the reconstructive and regularist neogrammarians.

Any account of idealist linguistics in 1968 will necessarily depict a Götterdämmerung[1]—a summary of work by now deceased or ageing figures. Yet some account, however brief, is **Hall's criticisms** necessary, in view of R. A. Hall's[2] contention that this school has exerted a nefarious and permanent effect on Romance linguistics (p. 3):

[1] Cf. Y. Malkiel, *RPh* xvii (1964) p. 828, who suggests that some might prefer, with Nietzsche, to label it a *Götzendämmerung*.
[2] R. A. Hall, Jr. 1963, which represents a reworking of articles appearing from 1941 onwards. Other recent studies of 'Idealism' include S. Cavaciuti 1959 and J. L. Varela 1954.

It has constituted, within modern linguistics, an antiscientific element which has been at work undermining the essential base of linguistics itself. Linguistic studies based on idealistic principles have thereby been deprived of their necessary scientific foundation, and much work—especially in linguistic geography—which might otherwise have been of major worth, has been rendered less valuable by the presence of unscientific procedures and hence of faulty conclusions. Even worse, idealistic preconceptions have kept the minds of many (perhaps even most) Romance scholars closed against the merits of a scientific approach, both in structural analysis on the descriptive plane and in comparative reconstruction in the historical plane. As a result, from the methodological point of view, Romance linguistics has taken as a whole, fallen badly behind other fields in the development and adaptation of modern techniques of analysis and statement.[1]

Unfairly, considering *Iordan–Orr's* cogent criticisms of the idealists, Hall blames their book for the decadence of Romance linguistics (p. 84):

The Iordan–Orr *Introduction* has done a major disservice to Romance linguistics in three ways: (1) it has persuaded many younger scholars to take the idealists at their own valuation . . .; (2) it has perpetuated the organization of Romance scholarship into divisive schools;[2] and (3) largely through its misleading title it took the place of and delayed the production of up-to-date manuals of Romance linguistics for nearly twenty years.

Hall is perhaps hitting under the belt when he points out links between Italian idealism and fascism, though admittedly they should not be concealed: still, some of the scholars who may be implied to be 'guilty by association' led a long fight against fascism in the dark interwar years (like Iordan who could almost be called a 'premature anti-fascist'!) and some were unhappy victims of fascist prejudices (like Spitzer who fled to Istanbul in 1933, before settling in America in 1936, and Terracini,[3] exiled in Argentina from 1941 to 1946).

Strangely enough, Hall's fears have nevertheless nearly been realized, for recent American linguistics—probably quite independently of European idealism, though certainly influenced, via Roman Jakobson, by Prague structuralism—has taken on an anti-positivist tinge: the Chomkyist distinction between 'surface structure' and 'deep structure' is especially reminiscent of Humboldt (see *Iordan–Orr*, pp. 111–15).

Of the Idealist Divines whose twilight years we should mention,

---

[1] For a different point of view cf. R. Posner "Positivism in Historical Linguistics", *RPh* xx (1967) pp. 321–30.

[2] I fear I must brave Hall's wrath for perpetuating the *Iordan–Orr* crime.

[3] 1886–1968, professor at Turin; cf. especially B. Terracini 1957, a collection of his essays in honour of his 70th birthday, and, in honour of his 80th birthday, also B. Terracini 1968 (fest.) which coincided by unhappy accident with his death.

the most god-like was Leo Spitzer (1887–1960), who became more
extreme and irascible in post-war America, where
Leo Spitzer he felt constantly on the defensive;[1] nevertheless
much of his work still displayed the fine sensibility
towards linguistic and literary nuances of his earlier years.[2] Such
a charismatic personality could not fail to attract followers, though
these have often made more of a mark in literary than linguistic
studies.[3] Another idealist who deserves mention is Giulio Bertoni
(1878–1942), who completed in 1939[4] the trilogy mentioned by
Iordan-Orr (p. 143, n. 1). Of his disciples the most outstanding is
Giuliano Bonfante who became the champion of 'neolinguistics'
against American attackers.[5]

In general, the aftermath left by the Idealists was not so much a
faith in their dogma, but more an appreciation of the influence of
social and cultural trends on language history. An
H.-F. Muller important representative of this more 'humanist'
approach was Henri-François Muller (1879–1960)
who placed the emergence of Romance from Latin at a much later
date than traditionally supposed,[6] attributing to the spread of
Christianity, and to its different social manifestations, major
linguistic repercussions.[7] Although his views did not gain widespread currency, he did for many years influence a number of
students at Columbia who served their apprenticeship with doctoral
theses on Dark Age Latin—notable among these are Mario Pei[8] and
R. L. Politzer.[9] Immediately after the war, he was the figurehead of

---

[1] Cf. especially the obituary by Y. Malkiel reprinted in T. A. Sebeok (ed.)
1966b pp. 522–6.
[2] Especially L. Spitzer, 1948a and b, 1949, 1954, 1956 and 1958 (fest.).
[3] Cf. especially the numerous works mentioned in H. A. Hatzfeld 1953 and 1966,
and H. A. Hatzfeld and Y. Le Hir 1961. Helmut Hatzfeld (b. 1892) was a pupil
of Vossler, and has been spoken of as forming a Trinity with Spitzer and Vossler.
His work has been even more biased towards literature and art than Spitzer's,
though he retains an interest especially in semantics: cf. H. A. Hatzfeld 1964
(fest.).
[4] G. Bertoni 1939.
[5] Especially in "The neolinguistic position", *L* xxiii (1947) pp. 344–75, in which
Bonfante emphasizes "Every problem is unique, produced under unique conditions."
[6] H.-F. Muller 1929.   [7] H.-F. Muller 1945.
[8] Born in Rome 1901, professor at Columbia from 1952, Ph.D. (Columbia)
1932, on *The Language of the Eighth Century Texts in Northern France*, Pei is known
especially for his works of linguistic popularization which, though often severely
criticized by professional linguists, do enjoy great favour among the lay public. See
the Bibliography for some of his works.
[9] Born in Vienna in 1921, Ph.D (Columbia) 1947 on *A Study of the Language of
8th century Lombardic Documents* (publ. 1949), Politzer's more recent work has been
concerned largely with applied linguistics, especially language teaching (cf. p.
531). For some of his works see the Bibliography.

a new wave in American linguistics that was more European than Bloomfieldian, the mouthpiece of which was the periodical *Word*. To quote Muller's preface to the first volume in 1945:

With the title WORD we intend to emphasize the multiform natural structure of linguistic reality and the necessity for studying language in all the fullness of its various functions and relations.

As I have already pointed out (p. 433) 'traditionalist' linguists have adopted some of the less extreme, more humanist, attitudes of the idealists as their own. Such attitudes are evident, for instance, in Wartburg's *Problèmes et Méthodes* ... (1943) and in the work of Ramón Menéndez Pidal (cf. p. 430, n. 1). An account of Spanish attitudes, deriving largely from the work of this great scholar, and set in a fundamentally humanistic, or even idealist, framework, comes from the pen of his grandson Diego Catalán (Menéndez Pidal): *La escuela lingüística española y su concepción del lenguaje* (1955). The title of the work is misleading, as it is much less a survey of Spanish linguistics than a general linguistic work, with copious illustrations from Spanish. Diego Catalán insists on the role of individual creation in linguistic history, as well as on the expressive function of language; true to his grandfather's principles, however, he does not neglect the value of extensive documentation in the study of the history of language.

A modern representative of an 'Idealist' approach to linguistics is Eugenio Coseriu,[1] Rumanian by origin, who after many years in Montevideo, is now Professor at Tübingen. Coseriu **Eugenio** has, rather optimistically, been hailed as uniting **Coseriu** idealist and structuralist linguistic thought in a 'new synthesis':[2] however, there is no mistaking his decidedly 'idealist' bias that leads him to give precedence to the individual act of linguistic creation (though 'linguistic change' properly speaking, is regarded as the diffusion or generalization of such innovation). For Coseriu, intuition is the basic source of knowledge about man, and hence about language —"el hombre es objeto de un saber anterior a toda ciencia por la conciencia que tiene de sí mismo",[3]— so that so-called 'objective' methods are inappropriate to language. Needless to say, then, Coseriu's 'structuralism' is not Bloomfieldian, but Saussurean, and much of his discussion is concerned with the

---

[1] For some of his works, see the Bibliography.
[2] N. C. W. Spence, "Towards a New Synthesis in Linguistics: the Work of Eugenio Coseriu", *ArL* xii (1960) pp. 1-34.
[3] E. Coseriu 1954*a*, p. 7.

Coseriu and Saussure classic dichotomies, synchrony/diachrony and *langue/parole*. Coseriu sees no contradiction between synchronic description and diachronic study except in their methods of investigation. He does, however, reject Prague-type diachronic structuralism which, he thinks, confuses 'cause' and 'condition', and which treats language as an extra-individual structure: for Coseriu language, though a social institution, is essentially inter-individual, a "ser con otros". Thus *langue* is a sort of "sistema de isoglosas" which can be abstracted by the linguist:

> Desde el punto de vista diacrónico es un conjunto de modos lingüísticos tradicionales ('que se transmiten'); y desde el punto de vista sincrónico es un conjunto de modos comunes 'actuales' (en el momento considerado) que, sin embargo, no dejan por ello de ser tradicionales.

A link between the system—*la langue*—and *el habla—la parole*—is to be found in *la norma*:

> El sistema es 'sistema de posibilidades, de coordenadas que indican los caminos abiertos y los caminos cerrados' de un hablar 'comprensible' en una comunidad; la norma, en cambio, es un sistema de realizaciones obligadas . . ., consagradas social y culturalmente: no corresponde a lo que 'puede decirse' sino a lo que 'se ha dicho' y tradicionalmente 'se dice' en la comunidad considerada.[1]

Thus the inflexible 'norm' is underpinned by a more flexible 'system', allowing, within certain degrees of tolerance, scope for individual liberty. The introduction of a third term between *langue* and *parole* (similar to Hjelmslev's *usage*)[2] cuts the Gordian knot of how to discuss 'change' in terms of 'structure', allowing change to be described in 'more-or-less' terms rather than 'either-or', and most of all not losing sight of the speakers' rôle in language history.

Undoubtedly, then, 'idealistic' habits of thought still have some currency in Romance linguistics, but it can hardly be maintained that they are widespread, except in an attenuated form that emphasizes the 'humanist' side of language study as well as the 'scientific'.

---

[1] E. Coseriu 1958 pp. 28 and 31.
[2] L. Hjelmslev, "Langue et Parole", *CFS* ii (1942) pp. 29–44. For Hjelmslev *la langue* can be subdivided into three: *forme pure* or 'schéma'; *forme matérielle* or 'norme'; and *ensemble des habitudes* or 'usage'. The 'schéma' is "un jeu et rien de plus" and forms the framework of the *langue*, whereas "l'usage ne saurait être qu'un ensemble de possibilités entre lesquelles tout acte aurait libre choix". The 'norme' is for Hjelmslev superfluous, being a fictional organization of material substance. Thus Hjelmslev's 'schéma' and 'usage' correspond in some ways to Coseriu's 'sistema' and 'norma', while *acte* = *habla*.

4. Neo-Humanism—Linguistic Approaches to Semantics and Style

As we have already seen, two strands running through nineteenth- and twentieth-century linguistics might conveniently be labelled 'scientific' and 'humanist': the 'scientifically' inclined linguists emphasize more the autonomy of their discipline and concentrate on the more tightly structured realms of phonology and grammar; 'humanists' are more interested in the aspects of language that appear more complex and variegated and that can be studied profitably using interdisciplinary insights. For the humanist, the 'meaningful' character of language will hold more fascination than its formal structure, and his attention will turn more to the lexicon and to style. Modern linguistics has tended to value highly the more novel scientific approach which has made rapid progress, but which has also provoked violent reactions both among linguists (especially the 'idealists') and among literary scholars.

Under my general heading of 'neo-humanism' I group those linguists who interweave the two strands, by applying 'scientific' methods to the solution of 'humanist' problems, and who, in particular, try to bring to semantic and stylistic studies the 'structural' attitudes more easily developed in the examination of phonology and grammar.

The Romanist who most readily fits into this category is Stephen Ullmann,[1] whose attention has been mainly devoted to semantics and stylistics as well as to the interrelationship between the two fields of study. Born in 1914, in Budapest, where he took his Ph.D in 1936, Ullmann served at the B.B.C. during the war, before going to Glasgow University in 1946. From 1953 he was Professor at Leeds until he took up the Chair of the Romance Languages at Oxford in 1968. A well-known figure in Romanist circles, both linguistic and literary, Ullmann was co-editor of the journal *Archivum Linguisticum* (*ArL*) from its inception in 1949 till 1964. Much of Ullmann's work,

Stephen Ullmann

---

[1] Other outstanding representatives of this tradition include M. Regula and E. Gamillscheg (b. 1887, professor at Tübingen), both already mentioned by *Iordan–Orr.* L. C. Harmer (b. 1902, professor at Cambridge 1951–67) might also be included in this category; for K. Baldinger, who might fall into either the 'neo-traditional' or the 'neo-humanist' category ("Structures et systèmes linguistiques", *TLLS* v (1967) pp. 7–60, gives an account of his 'neutralist' position) cf. p. 419.

especially in stylistics, has been concerned with modern French: his studies in semantics have wider application and are among the most influential in the field.

Ullmann's breadth of interest and knowledge is what we have come to expect from educated Central Europeans of his generation; it is not surprising to find someone of his background less addicted to arid 'scientism' and formal statement than many younger scholars. Indeed it is perhaps fair to say that his work is better appreciated by his literary colleagues than by many linguists who find there little reflection of their own preoccupations: Ullmann's writings are often not primarily addressed to professional linguists, but to those whose interest in language has been aroused through more general cultural studies. For such readers, Ullmann filters out, from his own vast bibliographical experience, the essential insights that modern linguistic theory can provide, always with a degree of tolerance and kindly understanding that is only too rare in linguistic controversy today. In this way, he serves the function of intermediary between literary and linguistic scholars, whose antagonisms often preclude profitable cooperation.

Ullmann's own theoretical predilections are within the Saussurean tradition[1] and appear to be independent of American trends, with which, however, he is fully conversant. The post-Saussurean 'style' which most closely resembles his is that developed by Bally— described by *Iordan–Orr*, with evident admiration, as belonging to the 'French school' with its broad, socio-culturally oriented interests. It would appear, too, that Ullmann's semantic theories were profoundly influenced by his master at Budapest, Z. Gombocz (1877–1953).[2]

The 'scientific' strand in Ullmann's thought is to be traced in his interest in methodology, in formulation of generalizations and abstraction of principles. Here he is able, in semantics, to provide the link between philosophers and more pragmatic linguists, and, in stylistics, to demonstrate to his literary colleagues the utility of linguistic classifications. By viewing language as a structured whole, he is able to avoid the atomism of much traditional lexical and stylistic commentary. The 'scientific' features of modern linguistics that appear not to be to Ullmann's taste include the fashion for formal statement (he habitually uses elegant and lucid prose!) and

[1] Cf. especially Ullmann's contributions to the 1963 edition of W. von Wartburg 1943.
[2] For a discussion of Gombocz's theories cf. especially L. Rosiello's introduction to the Italian edition of S. Ullmann 1962.

the interest in discovery procedures (his methods often are impressionistic, placing reliance on his own sensitivity to features of importance). In these last two respects, as well as in his concentration on 'fringe' questions, rather than on the tightly structured aspects of language that can be treated within an autonomous linguistic discipline, Ullmann clings fast to the humanist tradition of language study. His continuing interest in historical problems, exemplified too by the historical orientation of some of his descriptive stylistic studies, also demonstrates his faithful attachment to more traditional standards.

Ullmann is probably best known to students through his works on semantics: his latest introductory book *Semantics: an Introduction to the Study of Meaning* (1962) fills a widely felt need for **Semantics** a clear, level-headed survey of the field, which takes into account the vast and variegated literature on the subject without wandering too deep into the maze of conflicting theories. His earlier full-length semantic works are *Principles of Semantics. A Linguistic Approach to Meaning* (1951, 2nd ed. 1959)—mainly methodological in orientation and particularly valuable in marrying philosophical and linguistic views of meaning—and *Précis de sémantique française* (1952, 2nd ed. 1959) which applies his methods to traditional problems of change in meaning. In both, he uses, in one of his illustrations, data derived from a detailed study on synaesthetic imagery, which ties up with his other work on imagery and stylistic devices in general.

Ullmann's *Principles* not only lucidly expounds the views of other scholars, but also fully explains his own answers to the philosopher's question 'What sort of thing is meaning?' Following in the footsteps of Saussure and of Ogden and Richards (1923), he makes use of a diagrammatic triangle to illustrate his ideas:

The name-thing (referential) relationship Ullmann, like Saussure, regards as arbitrary-conventional and outside the scope of linguistic semantics: 'meaning', its object of study, is the relationship between 'sense' and 'name', both non-concrete entities belonging to the abstract *langue* which is the collective possession of a linguistic community. This he views as a system of 'engrams' stored in the minds of speakers—where 'engrams' are "residual traces of an adaptation made by the organism to a stimulus". Thus Ullmann, while recognizing the cogency of the Bloomfieldian 'stimulus–response' theory of linguistic meaning, shrinks from the 'idiolectal', individualistic approach of a Robert A. Hall, Jr. Similarly, he is appreciative of the 'contextual' approaches to meaning advocated by some philosophers ("the meaning of a word is its use" of Wittgenstein), but insists too on the paradigmatic reality of word-meanings, as shared by speakers of the same languages, which can be described, however inadequately, in dictionaries.

While treating fully the philosopher's problem concerning the *nature* of meaning, Ullmann pays less attention to the questions that loom large in modern linguistics: 'what linguistic units have meaning?' and 'how do we discover, and describe, meaning?' The first question is avoided by a deliberate concentration on *lexical* meaning, with the 'word' treated as the basic meaningful unit: while discussing fully different definitions of the word, Ullmann inclines to the common-sense view that, for his purposes and in the 'civilized' languages with which he is concerned, the traditional delimitations of the word are good enough.

The second question is handled in a broadly 'humanist' manner: we have to have knowledge and experience of a language to know what is meant by any stretch of discourse, and a sensitive appreciation of nuances will help in its description. Beyond this, however, Ullmann does bring into play a Saussurean attitude to a lexical structure, by which individual words are members of paradigms of different sorts—morpholexical, syntactic, referential,—which determine their distinctive semantic 'value'. In this comparatively loosely structured part of the language, 'distinctiveness' is far from complete and a good deal of overlapping of unit-values is to be expected. Yet groups of so-called 'synonyms' can be differentiated in terms not only of the syntagmatic relations into which they enter, but also by their complex paradigmatic inter-relationships.

In this respect, Ullmann makes a valuable methodological contribution to semantics in his classification of paradigmatic lexico-semantic relationships in terms of the 'name-sense' dichotomy, distinguishing 'similarity' and 'contiguity' within each of the poles.

Ullmann's 'name-sense/similarity-contiguity' classificatory schema is, however, little used for descriptive purposes, for his interest is more turned to the traditional question—'how does meaning change?' Using his schema he is able to show how transfers of different sorts can account for the types of change of meaning that in more traditional works are classified as 'tropes' (or 'figures-of-speech'). In his *Précis* many of the examples familiar from Bréal, Darmesteter and Nyrop receive fresh elucidation. Ullmann is also able to use his schema to demonstrate universal characteristics of semantic structure and change,[1] thus pointing the way to speculation about human psychology in general.

Ullmann's interest in change of meaning is connected with his studies of literary imagery,[2] often there are similar mechanisms at work, even though individual creation, not collective acceptance, is more important in stylistic, as compared with semantic, phenomena.

Much of Ullmann's more recent work is concerned with the study of style in modern French literature.[3] Here his methods are

Style

similar to those of Bally, regarding stylistic devices as representing 'deviations from a linguistic norm' and originating in some element of choice on the part of the author. Thus a linguistic study of style can start from an account of the repertoire of 'choices' available in the language—*stylistique de langue*—and proceed to the use individual authors make of such 'choices'. In this way, Ullmann traces the use of the *style indirect libre* by Flaubert, 'nominal style' by the Goncourts, or the ways in which deviant word-order is utilized for stylistic effect in modern French literary works. His approach is historical rather than method-ological, and he relies, for the recognition of the significance of the phenomena he studies, on his own sensitive perception and ex-perience. Thus Ullmann's stylistic studies can be seen as adding a new dimension to literary criticism rather than as a contribution to linguistics as such.

Other Romance stylistic studies[4] in the last three decades have

[1] Cf. his contribution on "Semantic Universals", in J. H. Greenberg (ed.) 1963 pp. 217–63; also "Où en sont les études de sémantique historique", *Actes 10e Cong. FILLM 1966* pp. 105–22.

[2] Cf. S. Ullmann 1960.

[3] Cf. especially S. Ullmann 1957 and 1964, and recent articles: "Sémantique et stylistique", in M. Delbouille 1964 (fest.) pp. 635–52; "Images of Time and Memory in 'Jean Santeuil'", in G. T. Clapton 1966 (mem.) pp. 209–26; "Style and ex-pressivité", in *CAIEF* xvi (1964) pp. 97–108; "Style and Personality", in *A Review of English Literature*, vi. 2 (1965) pp. 21–32; "Les idées linguistiques de Proust dans Jean Santeuil", *RLiR* xxxi (1967) pp. 134–46; "L'esthétique de l'image dans *Contre Sainte-Beuve* de Marcel Proust", in W. von Wartburg 1968 (fest.) pp. 267–78.

[4] For a survey of recent work cf. especially R. Posner, "Linguistique et littéra-

tended to fall between the two stools of literary criticism and linguis-

Other stylistic studies tic description, and have often been unpopular in both camps. Apart from the 'idealist'-type 'New Stylistics' of Spitzer and his like (cf. p. 453), linguistic studies of style often concentrate on the language used by a single author and so tend to differ from ordinary language descriptions only in their emphasis and choice of examples. Sometimes, the aim is attribution of an unsigned text to its author on the basis of style.[1] In this, as in other types of stylistic study, quantitative methods are sometimes used, though these are often unsympathetically received.[2]

Often even professional linguists, like for instance Togeby, will deny the applicability of linguistic methods to the study of literature. Bloomfieldians often prefer, in their linguistic descriptions, to leave out of account the 'deviations' of literary usage, which would be assigned to peripheral, 'idiolectal' grammars.

Chomskyist transformational-generative grammar, with its insistence on 'creativity' in language usage and the 'infinity' of possible constructions within the language, has brought a change in the attitude of linguists to literary language. Its 'deviations' from the linguistic norm can be viewed as permissible degrees of ungrammaticality and studied in the same way as other aberrant sentences of linguistic 'performance', as measured against the requirements of 'competence'.

Needless to say, however, the literary merit of the deviations can hardly be discerned merely by application of the linguistic method, which is equally as utilizable for other types of deviation, including those used in advertising.[3]

So far, little work in this tradition has been done on Romance problems, though, with the growing popularity of Chomskyist methods in France, we may well expect a development of the trend.

---

ture", *MRo* xiii (1963) pp. 1–19; also P. Guiraud 1954*b* and R. Fernando Retamar 1958. Special mention might be made of J. Marouzeau 1950; G. Devoto 1950; M. Rodrigues Lapa 1945; I. Iordan 1944; A. Alonso and R. Lida 1942, and T. Vianu 1957. A Russian work that deserves note is R. G. Piotrovskij 1960. The work of both Alonsos, Amado and Dámaso, receives special attention in *Iordan-Alvar*, pp. 238–43, 579–80, and 582–3.

[1] Cf. e.g. M. Criado de Val 1953, H. Dieckmann 1948.

[2] Cf. especially P. Guiraud's work and p. 448; among critics, C. Stutterheim, "Modern Stylistics", *Li* iii (1952) pp. 52–68. However, even 'idealistically' inclined scholars sometimes use rough-and-ready counting techniques: e.g. D. Alonso 1950. For a survey of the use of statistics in the study of style cf. R. Posner, "The Use and Abuse of Stylostatistics", *ArL* xv (1963) pp. 111–39; also p. 533.

[3] Cf. in particular, S. R. Levin 1962; also papers in T. A. Sebeok (ed.) 1960.

Among Romanist studies of style of the younger generation, special mention should be made of Michel Riffaterre, born in France in 1924, but going to America in 1953 to study and then teach at Columbia. His book on Gobineau's style (1957) is lively and interesting but his most significant contributions to stylistics are methodological.[1] Questioning the now-classic 'norm-deviation' approach he insists that each reader will have his own norm—what he would have said himself—and that no absolute norm can exist. Stylistic effect, he thinks, is achieved by the element of surprise—the appearance of a turn-of-phrase in an unexpected context. The 'stylistic device' thus is not to be found only in the deviant form but in the combination of this form and its context. Riffaterre is careful to distinguish two types of relevant context—besides the syntagmatic environment, called by him the 'macro-context', he points to the importance of a paradigmatic 'micro-context', which imposes strict limits on the probability of occurrence of items. Thus even a short phrase, like Corneille's *obscure clarté*, can have stylistic impact, because the probability of *obscure* filling the adjectival slot before *clarté* is extremely small.

Although information theory might aid the stylistic analyst to estimate the probability of occurrence of certain items, Riffaterre insists that identification of a stylistic device can depend only on the effect it has on the reader. Seeking to avoid the introspective methods usually employed by students of style, he advocates the use of a 'jury' method, noting the reactions of a group of informants—collectively known as the 'average reader' (AR)—to the stimulus of style. The fact that the 'jury' is rarely contemporary with the literary works presented to it is not, for Riffaterre, of great importance, for he believes that one of the dimensions of literary style is its permanence, its extension through time.

Overlap between semantics[2] and stylistics is inevitable, especially where, as so often happens, stylistic effect is achieved by some seman-

[1] "Criteria for Style Analysis", *Wd* xv (1960) pp. 154–64; "Stylistic Context", *Wd* xvi (1959) pp. 154–74.

[2] I shall not attempt a general and bibliographic survey of semantics as this is adequately done elsewhere, particularly in Ullmann 1962, though mention should be made of E. Gamillscheg 1951, and K. Baldinger 1957. Cf. also, for developments in the field, P. Guiraud 1955, B. Malmberg 1964 (chapter on "Semantics", pp. 123–39), and, with more emphasis on the philosophical aspects of the problem, P. Ziff 1960, A. Schaff 1962 and F. H. George 1964. We should also mention the

tic deviation or ambiguity. Indeed, Riffaterre's
Semantic
studies   friend and colleague at Columbia, Uriel Weinreich, attempted to incorporate into a Chomskyist-
type model of semantic description an account of deviations of this
type.[1] Similarly, poetic metaphor and other striking transfers of
meaning between linguistic elements can usefully be treated within
the general framework of a semantic theory. 'Componential'
analysis of lexemic units (usually 'words') into hierarchical configurations of 'semes' (basic units of experience) is particularly
suited for the description of stylistic meaning transfers: the poet
may deliberately emphasize a seme that has minor importance
in normal discourse—so that, for instance, Valéry's *ce toit tranquille*
used to refer to the sea, conjures up a picture of gentle undula-
tion, rather than of the quality of keeping out the rain! A. J.
Greimas, in his *Sémantique Structurale*,[2] using a 'semic' or 'componential' method, is partly concerned with literary devices of this kind,
as well as with even more 'stylistic' problems, like the 'meaning' of
a literary work as a whole, though his general concern is with semiological methodology.

For Greimas, it appears, the term 'structural', applied to semantics, refers to the semic structure of lexemes— the way in which
components hang together to make up the 'meaning'
Structural
semantics   of the linguistic unit.[3] Others use the term 'structural semantics' in different ways: J. Lyons 1963, for
instance, is concerned with classifying lexemes according to their
semantic, or logical, relationships with other lexemes in the language
(synonyms, antonyms, hyponyms, etc.), and especially in terms of
their potentiality of being used in sets of sentences that are trans-
formationally related. Other 'structuralists' in the field of semantics
are more Saussurean in their approach, and often historically

---

important volume *Probleme der Semantik* (W. T. Elwert (ed.) 1968), the proceedings of
a colloquium held in Mainz in Dec. 1966, under the chairmanship of W. T.
Elwert, with papers by Baldinger, Coseriu, Ducháček, Heger, Pottier, and
Ullmann.

[1] "Explorations in Semantic Theory", in T. A. Sebeok (ed.) 1966*a* pp. 395–478.
Cf. also J. J. Katz, "Recent Issues in Semantic Theory", *FoL* iii (1967) pp. 124–95.
[2] A. J. Greimas 1966. Cf. also J. Cohen 1966 and L. J. Prieto 1967.
[3] 'Componential' analysis is especially useful in the description of watertight
socio-semantic systems like that of kinship: cf. especially F. G. Lounsbury, "The
Structural Analysis of Kinship Semantics" *P9th ICL* pp. 1073–93, and E. A.
Hammel (ed.). Extension of this method to the whole of the vocabulary is found in
Chomskyist semantics—cf. esp. J. A. Fodor and J. J. Katz, "The Structure of a
Semantic Theory", *L* xxxix (1963) pp. 170–210 (reprinted in J. A. Fodor and
J. J. Katz (eds.) 1964; cf. also p. 521); and J. J. Katz and P. Postal 1964. V.
Ikegami, "Structural Semantics", *Lis* xxxiii (1967) pp. 49–68 gives a useful survey.

oriented: special mention should here be made of the neo-Humboldtian 'semantic field' theorists, centred round J. Trier and L.
Weisgerber,[1] whose prime interest is the study of how language
patterns reality (to put it in Whorfian terms), and especially of how
changes in social attitudes are reflected by changes in semantic
relationships between words of similar referential value.[2]

Within the domain of Romance lexicon, the most important
'structuralist' school is hardly concerned with semantic meaning at
all, but much more with the structuring of vocabulary items.
Carrying on the French sociological tradition, Georges Matoré's
lexicologie aims at the study of society and its history through its
vocabulary, rather than at intra-linguistic description. Matoré,
born in 1908, Professor at Besançon from 1947, and at Paris since
1952, has exerted enormous influence on French lexical studies, and
has inspired numerous detailed investigations into the vocabulary
used within certain narrowly defined fields.[3]

His most important work is the slim hand-book *La méthode en
lexicologie* (1953) which serves as a guide to research. For each stage
of society, Matoré seeks the *mots-témoins*, around
**Georges
Matoré** which the hierarchy of the vocabulary is structured,
and the *mots-clés*, which represents the 'ideal' of the
socially most prestigious groups (like the seventeenth-century
honnête homme). Such words cannot be recognized by rule-of-thumb

---

[1] For bibliographical details cf. especially Ullmann 1962. Also *Iordan–Bahner*
1962 pp. 466–82; S. Ohmann, "Theories of the 'Linguistic Field'", *Wd* ix (1953)
pp. 123–34; N. C. W. Spence, "Linguistic fields, conceptual systems and the
Weltbild," *TPS* 1961 pp. 87–106; H. Basilius, "Neo-Humboldtian Ethnolinguis-
tics", *Wd* viii (1952) pp. 95–105; L. Seiffert, "Neo-Humboldtian Semantics in
Perspective", *JL* iv (1968) pp. 93–109; O. Ducháček 1960. For a survey of
onomasiological work cf. especially K. Baldinger, "Problèmes fondamentaux
de l'onomasiologie", *Actes 11ᵉ Cong. (Madrid) 1965* pp. 175–213, and "Sémasiologie
et onomasiologie", *RLiR* xxviii (1964) pp. 249–72; also K. Heger, "Les bases
méthodologiques de l'onomasiologie et du classement par concepts", *TLLS* iii
(1965) pp. 7–32. Cf. also R. Hallig and W. von Wartburg 1952.
[2] A line should perhaps be drawn between the neo-Humboldtians who espouse
what is often called the 'Whorf hypothesis'—that a language reflects the world-view
of its speakers—and the theses of 'General Semantics'. This latter is more psycho-
therapeutic than linguistic and maintains that many of the ills of the world spring
from misuse of language, and especially over-rigid categorization of semantic
concepts, cf. e.g. S. Chase 1938 and 1954; S. I. Hayakawa 1941; A. Korzybski
1948. Among theorists who suggest that vocabulary structure fashions modes
of thought (especially in these days of mass media and high-pressure salesmanship)
we might mention R. Barthes, e.g. 1967 (cf. also p. 532).
[3] Besides Matoré's own work (1951, 1953 and 1962) we should mention especially
A. J. Greimas 1948; B. Quemada 1955*a* and *b*; P. J. Wexler 1955 and J. Dubois
1962*a*. For a different approach to lexical structure, cf. E. Coseriu, "Pour une
sémantique diachronique structurale", *TLLS* ii (1964) 1 pp. 139–86 and "Lexical
structure and the teaching of vocabulary", in *Linguistic Theories and their application*
(1967).

criteria, like statistical frequency, but the percipient scholar must pick them out by discerning the importance of their rôle within the vocabulary as a whole. Neologism and changes in frequency of use of already existing items, can often be significant of shifts in social attitudes: Matoré illustrates his thesis by a survey of vocabulary used to refer to art and the artist in 18th- and 19th-century France, graphically tracing changes of fashion in aesthetic appreciation. Recently there has, I think, been some waning in the initial enthusiasm aroused by Matoré's *lexicologie*, perhaps because detailed works have not led directly to the 'synthesis', explaining causes of change, that Matoré predicted. Nevertheless French lexicographical work has certainly benefited from the insights and inspiration generated by Matoré.[1]

5. *Dialectology*

The section on linguistic geography in *Iordan–Orr* is the longest in the work[2]— a mark of what important innovations this type of study brought to Romance linguistics in the first quarter of this century. Inevitably some of the 'great men' featured there have since died: Jud, for instance, in 1952,[3] and Jaberg in 1958.[4] Again M. L. Wagner died in 1963, continuing until the last his interest in varied,

---

[1] Cf. e.g. P. Imbs (ed.) 1961, the record of a colloquium held in 1957 at Strasbourg; R. L. Wagner 1967; G. Mounin 1968; and B. Quemada 1968. Mention should be made here of Quemada's *Centre d'Étude du Vocabulaire Français* at Besançon, which is also discussed pp. 532–3.

[2] New editions of Iordan's work have devoted even more space to this aspect: *Iordan–Alvar* in particular pays special attention to linguistic geography in the Iberian peninsula (pp. 400–7 and 474–83). Other works that should be noted are E. Coseriu 1955, R. I. Avanesov and S. B. Bernštein 1958 and J. G. C. Herculano de Carvalho, "Coisas y palavras. Alguns problemas etnográficos e lingüísticos relacionados com os primitivos sistemas de debulha na Península Ibérica", *Bib* xxix (1953) pp. 1–365. On the work of Fritz Krüger we now have G. Moldenauer 1952; cf. also F. Krüger 1952 (fest.), and, in the 'Gegenstandkultur' tradition, W. Giese 1962. A survey of work is to be found in A. Kuhn, "Sechzig Jahre Sprachgeographie in der Romania", *RJ* i (1947–48) pp. 25–63, and in G. Bottiglioni "La geografia linguistica (realizzazioni, metodi et orientamenti)", in *RLiR* xviii (1954) pp. 143–60 (also in English, *Wd* x (1954) pp. 375–87).

[3] Cf. his 60th Festschrift, J. Jud 1943 (fest.).

[4] Jaberg continued his Word-and-Thing studies till the last: cf. "The Birthmark in Folk Belief, Language and Literature", *RPh* x (1957) pp. 307 ff. Cf. also J. Jaberg 1959.

if sometimes peripheral, Romance languages, especially Sardinian[1] and Latin American dialects.[2]

A name that did not figure so prominently in *Iordan–Orr* was that of Sever Pop (1901–61), who came to be a leading international figure in general dialectology, founding in 1952 the periodical *Orbis* as the mouthpiece of dialectologists, and initiating the first international Congress of the subject at Louvain and Brussels in 1960.[3] By origin a Rumanian, Pop was a leading light of the pre-war Rumanian Linguistic Atlases. In exile (at first in Rome, 1941–48) he established himself at the Catholic University of Louvain which thus became the world centre of dialect studies. His monumental work *La Dialectologie* (1950) gives a complete survey of work done up to that time and his *Bibliographie des questionnaires linguistiques* (1955) lists chronologically and comments on all such investigations from 1394 to 1954. Pop's interests appear to centre more round the techniques used in dialect studies than in their general methodological and linguistic significance.[4]

Sever Pop

A rather more methodologically oriented survey of recent Romance linguistic geography is to be found in M. Alvar (López) 1960, an expansion of a paper given in 1959 to a Bucharest colloquium. Though Alvar is still very much concerned with techniques—composition of questionnaires, choice of investigators and informants, etc.—he also notes problems raised by differences of phonological systems between neighbouring dialects, and, rather adventurously, suggests that linguistic geography should unite with sociolinguistics by investigating social penetration of dialects in the town, as well as their survival in the countryside.[5]

Manuel Alvar

On the whole, Romance linguistic geography has remained Word-and-Thing biased, interested as much in folk culture as in language as such: the motivation for continued activity in this field has been mainly antiquarian, feverishly attempting to collect information about

Word and Thing

---

[1] M. L. Wagner 1941, 1951, and 1952.

[2] M. L. Wagner 1949. A penetrating review of Wagner's life work is to be found in an obituary by Malkiel, *RPh* xvi (1963) pp. 281–9, and bibliographies of his works are to be found in *BF* xv (1954–55) pp. 39–124 (by G. Manuppella), and *RPh* xxi (1968) pp. 533–6 (by J. L. Butler).

[3] Cf. *Cong. Int. Dial. Gén. 1960*. The 2nd Congress took place in Marburg in 1965.

[4] Cf. also the posthumous collection of studies, S. Pop 1966.

[5] Other methodological discussions include G. Tuaillon, "Exigences théoriques et possibilités réelles des enquêtes dialectologiques", *RLiR* xxii (1958) pp. 293–316; W. Doroszewski, "Le structuralisme linguistique et les études de géographie dialectale", *P8thICL 1957*, pp. 230–52; M. Companys, "Les nouvelles méthodes

fast-dying cultures and languages. Hence such investigations remain largely lexical and often emphasize distinctive features of their regions.

The *Nouvel Atlas Linguistique de la France par régions*, launched by A. Dauzat in 1942, was intended not only to preserve the remains of obsolescent dialects, but also to improve on the **Linguistic atlases** original *ALF* and to enable linguists to trace dialect evolution since Gilliéron's day. Obviously, a common design for investigation was desirable and to some extent this was accepted. However, the first of the regional atlases to appear, P. Gardette's *Atlas linguistique et ethnographique du Lyonnais* (1950–56), used its own idiosyncratic questionnaire, in order to remain in touch with the preoccupations of the Lyonnais peasant (including, for instance, nine questions on the flail). The folklore orientation of such work, although valuable in itself, perhaps reduces its utility for linguistic comparison. Several other of the French regional atlases have since appeared, in part or complete, each with its own idiosyncrasies.[1]

Other Romance linguistic atlases to appear since the war include those from Rumania[2] and Andalucia.[3] Griera's *Atlas lingüístic de Catalunya*[4] which was cut short at volume 5 for many years, began publication again in 1962, under the direction of one of Griera's pupils, but the original projected Spanish Linguistic Atlas was stillborn after T. Navarro (Tomás) went into exile at the time of the Civil War.[5] The first volume of a new *Atlas Lingüístico de la Península Ibérica* appeared in 1962.[6]

Preparation and publication of a linguistic atlas is a lengthy and

d'enquête linguistique", *Via Domitia* iii (1956) pp. 89–146, v (1958) pp. 49–169; and C. Schick, "La geografia linguistica", *Paideia* ix (1954) pp. 241 ff. A dispute about Alvar's own methods (à propos of a study in the Canary Islands) appeared in *ZRP* lxxxii (1966): D. Catalán, in "El español en Tenerife—Problemas metodológicos", pp. 467–506, criticized Alvar's investigations in the Canary Islands, and Alvar replied pp. 507–48.

[1] J. Haust and L. Remacle 1953–55; J. Séguy 1954–66; P. Nauton 1957–; H. Guiter 1966–; H. Bourcelot 1966–.
[2] E. Petrovici *et al.* 1940–42; B. Cazacu *et al.* 1967–; cf. A. Rosetti, "*Le nouvel Atlas linguistique roumain* et le *Traité d'Histoire de la langue roumaine*", *Actes 10ᵉ Cong.* (*Strasbourg*) *1962* pp. 853–7. [3] M. Alvar 1961–65.
[4] A. Griera 1942–68; cf. also A. Griera 1949 and 1955–60 (fest.).
[5] Navarro himself produced a small-scale atlas of Puerto Rico: T. Navarro Tomás 1948.
[6] Cf. M. Sanchis Guarner 1953; For a report (1962) on progress on a new Italian atlas cf. C. Grassi, "Lo stato attuale dei lavori dell'Atlante Linguistico Italiano", *Actes 10ᵉ Cong.* (*Strasbourg*) *1962* pp. 841–5.

expensive task, yet all over the Romance world (not to mention elsewhere) such atlases are in progress, their justification often lying more in national or cultural pride than in purely linguistic utility. One project in particular, M. Deanović's *Atlante Linguistico Mediterraneo*,[1] can have comparatively little linguistic interest, covering as it does diversified language areas, although it may be able to trace common cultural trends in the Mediterranean basin.

The linguistic atlas is, however, far from being the only type of dialect investigation: other studies—dictionaries, descriptions of **Other** individual dialects, etc.—continue unabated and **dialect** remain favourite forms of research. I cannot **studies** attempt to provide an adequate coverage of the vast number of studies in this field—indeed, as they are often of local and not Pan-Romance interest such an account would be out of place here.[2] This is, however, I think, the place to mention the work of two outstanding figures of 'classic' dialectology, both of whom were already of an age to receive ample mention by *Iordan–Orr* in 1937— Gerhard Rohlfs and Walther von Wartburg.

Rohlfs (b. 1892 in Berlin) succeeded Vossler as Professor at Munich in 1934, where he served until his retirement in 1957 (for a time during the war he was, however, suspended by **Gerhard** the Nazi régime). His work on Italian and Gascon **Rohlfs** dialects cultivated in him a strongly positivist academic outlook, taking up cudgels against 'idealism' as early as 1926.[3] From 1931 to 1954 he was editor of the *Archiv für das Studium der neueren Sprachen*, thus exerting considerable influence.[4] In recent years, apart from his indispensable Italian historical grammar,[5] much of his work has been concerned with synthesis within the Romance field.[6] Rohlfs's lexical and onomastic interests are especially evident in his *Die lexikalische Differenzierung der romanischen Sprachen: Versuch einer romanischen Wortgeographie* (1954),[7] and in his collected *Studien zur romanischen Namenkunde* (1956).

[1] Cf. M. Deanović's report "Due Atlanti Plurilingui e la linguistica romanza", *Actes 10ᵉ Cong. (Strasbourg) 1962* pp. 847–51, in which he discusses the Mediterranean atlas (projected in 1937 and begun in 1956) and the *Atlas linguistique balkanique*, begun in 1959 (cf. also his article in *RLiR* xxv (1961) pp. 264–67, "Il progettato Atlante Linguistico Balcanico e la linguistica romanza").
[2] Introductory works on dialects of individual Romance countries include, notably, A. Zamora Vicente 1967, M. Alvar 1962, and P. Guiraud 1968a.
[3] Cf. "Idealistische Neuphilologie", in *ZFSL* xlviii (1926) pp. 121–36, and H. Weinrich's account of Rohlfs in *O* viii (1959) pp. 257–65.
[4] Cf. H. Lausberg, "Gerhard Rohlfs als Redaktor des Archivs", *ASNS* cxci (1955) pp. 1 ff.   [5] G. Rohlfs 1949–54.
[6] Cf. G. Rohlfs 1950–51, 1952 (a collection of his essays published on the occasion of his 60th birthday), 1958 (fest.), and 1968 (fest.).   [7] Cf. also G. Rohlfs 1952.

Rohlfs's experience in dialectology during his formative years predisposes him to see interaction between languages as a prime cause of linguistic change. The most important **Walther von Wartburg** advocate of this view in Romance is also primarily a dialectologist—Wartburg (b. 1888, Professor at Leipzig 1935–9, and then at Bâle)[1] whose monumental *Französisches etymologisches Wörterbuch*, begun in 1922, is now completed. No Romanist can be ignorant of Wartburg's epoch-making *Die Ausgliederung der romanischen Sprachräume* (1950.)[2] Here Wartburg traces the course by which common Romance (Vulgar Latin) split into different languages, a process preceded by an early dialect division between East and West, occasioned by different social tendencies and manifested by the different treatment of final -*s* and of intervocalic surds. He also assumes that the pre-Latin language—the *substratum*—of each part of the Empire exerted an influence on the Latin spoken there, and investigates signs of such influence. A further differentiating factor which he discerns— and herein lies his most original contribution—is the influence exerted by the languages of the barbarian invaders of the late Empire, the *superstratum* languages. Thus, for instance, many of the features that early differentiated French from the other Romance languages derive from Frankish influence. Wartburg's views have been hotly debated and frequently rejected on chronological or historical grounds,[3] but, whatever their intrinsic merit, they must always serve as a foundation on which to base any discussion of Romance differentiation.

Wartburg's interest in population mixture as a factor in language formation is also evident in some of his other works[4] including his important general work on linguistic methodology *Einführung in die Problematik und Methodik der Sprachwissenschaft* (1943) which reveals his own humanistic and dialectological bias and, although readable and attractive, is far from an introduction to modern linguistics.[5]

The field of dialectology is still amply peopled with distinguished

[1] Cf. his 70th and 80th Festschriften, W. von Wartburg 1958 (fest.) and 1968 (fest.).
[2] An initial sketch of his hypothesis appeared in *ZRP* lvi (1936) pp. 1–48.
[3] For a quite different point of view cf. especially H.-F. Muller 1945.
[4] E.g. W. von Wartburg 1939.
[5] The 1963 French translation, with additional chapters by S. Ullmann, fulfills better the promise of the title. Wartburg is comparatively uninterested in linguistic description, though the *Précis de syntaxe du français contemporain* (W. von Wartburg and P. Zumthor 1947) is a model of its kind. Most students will know Wartburg primarily from his immensely popular *Evolution et Structure de la Langue Française* (1934).

elderly scholars,[1] and with their juniors who have seen no need for radical change of method.[2] Indeed, in this domain, collection of data for their own sake is a worthwhile activity and Romance scholars who wish to formulate general hypotheses are grateful for the wealth of documentation provided by field-work. However, micro-dialectology may blinker some workers to the wider aspects of linguistics, rendering their contribution less valuable to their fellows. Often they will present their data in a framework that is purely historical, or merely pinpoint ways in which the dialect examined differs from the national standard. It is still quite rare for

Structural dialectology
Romance dialectologists to employ the descriptive techniques that have been developed especially for more exotic languages,[3] partly perhaps because they cannot hope to uncover the sort of novel structural features that will contribute to the elaboration of hypotheses about language universals. One notable exception is A. Martinet's *La description phonologique avec application au parler franco-provençal d'Hauteville (Savoie)* (1956),[4] which is as much about the methodology of such descriptions as about the dialect itself.

Other modern approaches to dialectology are concerned primarily with measurement of relationship between dialects—a

Linguistic relationship
relatively simple matter when traditional substantial (especially lexicophonetic) classification is used, but which presents particular problems for structuralists who need to formulate some criteria for recognition of 'partial similarity'. Phonological structures have received most attention, mainly via methods elaborated from suggestions made by Uriel Weinreich.[5] The clearest exposition of developments along these lines is that of E. Pulgram,[6] who critically examines the status of the 'diasystem'—a system abstracted from comparison of a number of different but similar systems, which can summarize the common structural features of related dialects. Pulgram equates such a

---

[1] Among numerous others one can cite A. Griera (b. 1887), Ch. Bruneau (b. 1883), E. Gamillscheg (b. 1887).

[2] E.g. A. M. Badía Margarit, professor at Barcelona (b. 1920). Mention might also be made of W. D. Elcock (1910–60), professor at Westfield College, London, who made a significant contribution to the study of Bearnese-Aragonese dialects (W. D. Elcock 1938).

[3] The techniques used in such investigations have recently been surveyed in a useful handbook: W. J. Samarin 1967. Cf. also M. Cohen 1950*b*.

[4] A revision of an article originally published in *RLiR* xv (1939) [actually appearing in 1945].

[5] "Is structural dialectology possible?", *Wd* x (1954) pp. 385–400.

[6] "Structural Comparison, Diasystems and Dialectology", *Lis* iv (1964) pp. 66–83.

diasystem with 'language' as the term is often used in non-technical contexts (as grouping within it a number of dialects), and even shows that reconstructed Proto-Romance[1] can be described as a diasystem at a relatively high level of abstraction. Another Romanist who makes use of the diasystem idea in his dialect studies is G. Francescato, a specialist in Friulan dialects. In his reply to Pulgram's hypotheses,[2] he is nevertheless sceptical of too sweeping a reliance on abstract construction.

A different attitude to the measurement of dialect similarity can be found among Chomskyist generative grammarians, who seek to **Chomskyist dialectology** derive dialect grammars from a basal grammar (whether an abstraction or an actual grammar of a real dialect) by ordering rewrite rules in such a way that dialect variations appear as peripheral additions to the main set of rules. This procedure may sometimes have the appearance of reconstructing historical processes, in that chronological sequence of change may be reproduced in the logical ordering of grammatical rules. This seems particularly evident in an account of Spanish dialect phonology by S. Saporta.[3] A recent general survey of this type of approach is to be found in A. R. Thomas's "Generative Phonology in Dialectology".[4]

I cannot close this section on dialectology without some mention of recent burst of activity in the study of extra-European Romance **Pidgins and creoles** dialects, especially of pidgins and creoles. Although methodologically they differ little from metropolitan dialect studies, they do have great significance for considerations of factors influencing linguistic change and of social language variation. When racial and linguistic admixture is present, as in creole situations, linguists vary widely in their attitudes as to what processes have been involved in change: some (like R. A. Hall, Jr.) think that, although change has been more rapid than in other instances, the types of process are those already familiar in classic historical linguistics; others believe that a radical mixing of languages has taken place; yet others (like K. A. Whinnom) think that most creoles are based on one and the same 'simplified' language—a sailor's *sabir* or a slaver's pidgin—with lexical items

---

[1] "Proto Languages as Proto-Diasystems: Proto-Romance", *Wd* xx (1964) pp. 373–83.
[2] "Structural comparison, diasystems and dialectology", *ZRP* lxxxi (1965) pp. 484–91. Cf. also "Struttura linguistica e dialetto", in *Actes 10ᵉ Cong. (Strasbourg) 1962* pp. 1011–18.
[3] "Ordered rules, dialect differences and historical processes", *L* xli (1965) pp. 218–24.   [4] *TPS* 1967 pp. 179–203.

taken wholesale from metropolitan standards. I shall not attempt to survey works in this field, but should mention two recent contributions of more general import, made by Romanists: R. A. Hall, Jr., *Pidgins and Creoles* (1966) and M. F. Goodman, *A comparative study of Creole French dialects* (1964).[1]

6. *The Copenhagen School*

Turning now to more cohesive 'schools' in modern linguistic thought, we shall first discuss a particularly active, if somewhat geographically isolated, group of linguists, deriving inspiration from Saussure, which was formed in Denmark in the early 1930s. Its leader was undoubtedly Louis Hjelmslev (1899–1965), who was one of the founders of the Cercle Linguistique de Copenhague in 1931 and succeeded Pedersen as Professor at Copenhagen in 1937. It did, however, unite many outstanding scholars of rather different outlook,[2] including notably the 'phenomenologically' inclined Romanist, Viggo Brøndal, who was with Hjelmslev co-editor of *Acta linguistica (Hafniensia)* from its foundations in 1939 till his death in 1942.[3]

Hjelmslev's theories had at first little repercussion outside Denmark, not only because they were sometimes written in a relatively inaccessible language,[4] but also perhaps

Louis Hjelmslev because the unfamiliarity of his approach repelled many linguists who waited in vain for a complete and

[1] A survey of recent theories, with particular reference to French creoles, is to be found in I. Vintilă-Rădulescu, "Remarques sur les idiomes créoles", *RRL* xii (1967) pp. 227–43, and "Les idiomes créoles et la linguistique romane", *RRL* xiii (1968) pp. 523–7. Cf. also M. C. Alleyne, "La nature du changement phonétique à la lumière du créole français d'Haïti", *RLiR* xxx (1967) pp. 279–303; K. A. Whinnom 1956, and "The origin of the European-based creoles and pidgins", *O* xiv (1965) pp. 509–27; and M. Valkhoff 1966.

[2] Cf. especially K. Togeby's survey, "Linguistics in Denmark, 1940–48", in *S* iii (1949) pp. 226–37, which compares Danish and American linguistic trends; and more recently the issue of *Ls* vi (1967), edited by Togeby and entitled *La glossématique, l'héritage de Hjelmslev au Danemark*, with contributions by a number of Danish scholars.

[3] Cf. especially his monographs which appeared posthumously in French translation: V. Brøndal 1948 and 1950. Brøndal was a friend of Trubetzkoy and Jakobson (cf. pp. 483–4) and exercised great influence during the 'thirties. Among present-day linguists who appear to have derived inspiration from Brøndal one should mention especially A. J. Greimas the semanticist (cf. also p. 463).

[4] Important works that have been translated from the Danish include L. Hjelmslev 1943 and 1963. Cf. also L. Hjelmslev 1959, a collection of his essays.

coherent exposition of his position.[1] In more recent times, Hjelmslev's general aims have met with more sympathy among linguists, for whom theoretical abstraction is now fashionable: some[2] even suggest that Hjelmslev was the initiator of the current fashion in linguistics, though it is more probably merely a manifestation of the general trend in scientific thought.

Hjelmslev's father was a distinguished mathematician but Hjelmslev always strenuously denied being influenced by his father's thought which he called essentially inductive—however, no doubt he acquired from his background a certain ease in the manipulation of abstract entities. Perhaps because of his taste for abstraction, his first work, *Principes de Grammaire Générale* (1928),[3] was considered as unsuitable for a doctoral thesis, so he presented instead a more traditional comparative *Etudes Baltiques* (1932). Indeed his thinking in historical and comparative linguistics was always firmly cemented in the neogrammarian tradition,[4] even though his synchronic linguistic thought was original and revolutionary.

Hjelmslev seized particularly on one aspect of Saussurean thought,

---

[1] Commentaries on Hjelmslev's work abound, although he himself never completed his long-promised treatise, originally planned with H. J. Uldall whose own contribution eventually appeared in 1957 (H. J. Uldall 1957). The most complete commentary available is B. Siertsema 1955. Mrs. Siertsema's book, though not wholly sympathetic to Hjelmslev, is an indispensable guide for the student who ventures to read his original works and who will certainly be bewildered by the variety, and oscillating usage, of Hjelmslev's terminology. Excellent brief surveys of glossematics are to be found in B. Malmberg 1964, pp. 140–57; by H. Spang-Hanssen, in *Trends i* pp. 128–64 (also H. Spang-Hanssen 1954); and in Greimas's introduction to L. Hjelmslev 1963 (French tr. 1966). The chapter on Hjelmslev in F. P. Dinneen 1967, pp. 326–54, is little more than a (rather inaccurate) potted digest of the 1961 English translation of L. Hjelmslev 1943: more satisfactory discussions of this important treatise are A. Martinet's "Au sujet des *Fondements de la Théorie Linguistique* de Louis Hjelmslev", in *BSLP* xliii (1942–45) pp. 19–42, and especially S. Lamb's "Epilegomena to a Theory of Language", in *RPh* xix (1966), pp. 521–73, which looks back at Hjelmslev with hindsight gained from a further 20 years' development of linguistic theory. Also worthy of note is W. Haas, "Concerning Glossematics", *ArL* viii (1956) pp. 106–10; and E. Haugen, "Directions in Modern Linguistics", *L* xxvii (1951) pp. 211–22, which compares glossematics with American schools of thought. Of especial interest to Romanists for its illustrations (even though it is a rather uncritical rehash of glossematic ideas), E. Alarcos Llorach 1951. Cf. also the survey in Italian by R. d'Avinos in *Enciclopedia Italiana 1949–1960*.

[2] Cf. A. J. Greimas in L. Hjelmslev 1963 (1966) p. 12.

[3] Cf. also A. Llorente [Maldonado de Guevara] 1953.

[4] Cf. the views expressed in L. Hjelmslev 1963; he also was an admirer of Rasmus Rask, editing his selected works in 1932, and his correspondence in 1941. Professor Togeby kindly points out (private communication) that Hjelmslev always tried to treat diachrony as a series of synchronic states. My judgment is based on Hjelmslev's view of traditional comparative linguistics as being concerned mainly with elements of substance; therefore, while quite legitimate in itself, it is less relevant to glossematics than typological comparison which operates with elements of form.

taking to its extreme consequences the dictum "la langue est une forme, non pas une substance": he meanwhile neglected certain other aspects of Saussure's ideas, especially those emphasized by the Prague school (for instance the social content of language and the distinctive substance of its elements), so that it is difficult to go all the way with Greimas[1] when he calls Hjelmslev "le véritable et peut-être le seul continuateur de Saussure". Assuming that a system must underlie all processes, including language activity, Hjelmslev advocated description of the language system in the form of an algebraic model applicable to all languages, and 'generative' in the sense that it should predict any possible text in any language: here he did not go so far as Chomsky in requiring explicitly that the model should enable rejection of *impossible* texts.

'Copenhagen' and Saussure

Mere descriptive praxis was by no means Hjelmslev's aim; for him the task of linguistics was to formulate a theory—to establish "a science of the expression and a science of the content on an internal and functional basis".[2] His method excluded consideration of non-linguistic 'substance', basing itself on language in and for itself: this is what he meant by 'immanent'. The originality of his approach compared with previous linguistic attitudes was underlined by its distinctive name—'glossematics'. One of the distinguishing marks of 'glossematics' is what Hjelmslev curiously calls the 'empirical principle', which requires that description should be self-consistent, exhaustive and simple (in that order of priority). Another essential feature of glossematic method is that it is 'deductive' not 'inductive'—terms that Hjelmslev also uses in rather a quaint way (and far from consistently). Deductive procedure, he says,

Glossematic Theory

may therefore be defined briefly as a progression from class to component, not from component to class, as an analytic and specifying, not a synthetic and generalizing, movement".[3]

In practice, this means that glossematicians begin with larger syntagmatic units (initially the 'text') and work down to the smallest units, whereas many other linguists operate primarily with minimal units (often segments) and proceed to build larger units therefrom.

As I have already mentioned, glossematics is concerned only with linguistic form and not with amorphous substance—whether

[1] L. Hjelmslev 1963 (1966) p. 13.
[2] L. Hjelmslev 1943 (Eng. tr. 1963) p. 79.
[3] *Ibid.* p. 13.

Linguistic form

semantic (content-substance) or phonetic (expression-substance). Linguistic form is to be studied on two inter-related but autonomous planes—of content and expression. The realm of 'content-form' is roughly that of American-type morphology—the preferred field of glossematic study—while that of 'expression-form' comprises phonology or phonemics. As substance is to be left completely out of consideration, form is described in terms of relationships: the 'objects' of linguistics, as of any other science, are seen to be intersections of relations, or 'dependences', and not substantial items. The possible types of dependence are basically three: *interdependence* or reciprocal presupposition; *determination* where one term determines the other but not *vice versa*; and *constellation* where terms are compatible but neither presupposes the other.

Process and System

Apart from 'content/expression', the most fundamental of Hjelmslev's dichotomies is that of 'process'/'system'[1] demanding analysis on two axes—the syntagmatic (both-and) and the paradigmatic (either-or). Each sort of 'dependence' can operate on either axis, that of the process or that of the system, so that, for instance, interdependence between syntagmatic terms is given one name, *solidarity*, whereas between paradigmatic terms it is called *complementarity*. An account of glossematic terminology would be otiose here (the *Prolegomena* contains no less than 108 definitions); however, the use made of the word 'function' does call for some comment because

Function

of the confusion it may cause to those familiar with Prague school 'functional analysis' (cf. pp. 480–1). For Hjelmslev, function has a logico-mathematical sense as a relationship between the two terminals (so that, for instance, interdependence is a function between two constants) though he does not exclude the etymological sense implying that elements play a definite rôle. Elements in a language will be defined in terms of their 'functions'.

Figurae

Although for glossematics language is a special case of a sign system, its ultimate elements are not signs but constituents of signs, *figurae*; these can be, for instance, phonemes (on the expression plane), or semantic components (on

---

[1] *Ibid*. p. 9 "*A priori* it would seem to be a generally valid thesis that for every *process* there is a corresponding *system*, by which the process can be analyzed and described by means of a limited number of premisses."
Also p. 39 "When it is a question of language (in the ordinary sense of the word) ... we can also use simpler designations: the process can here be called a *text*, and the system a *language*."

the content plane). Concerned as he is with theory and not praxis, Hjelmslev gives little guidance about how to isolate such elements (although in practice his 'commutation' seems very similar to American substitution procedures used on the syntagmatic expression plane). Glossematicians indeed rarely tackle previously unanalysed languages and it seems that their techniques are designed to be used only with languages they already know.

Much of other linguists' dissatisfaction with glossematics stems from the difficulty they experience in applying the theory to linguistic facts. Indeed it is not meant to be a system of **Glossematic** verifiable hypotheses but a model, formulated of **Practice** course on the basis of examination of data, but which can be tested only for appropriateness and not for validity. Most practical linguists feel uncomfortable in such a rarified atmosphere and will judge the theory only by the light it throws on real languages. The most important description of a real language in glossematic terms is *Structure immanente de la langue française*[1] by a Romanist, Knud Togeby;[2] it is mainly as an introduction to his work that discussion of glossematic theory can be justified here.

Togeby (b. 1918, Professor of Romance Languages and Literature at Copenhagen since 1955) was a pupil of Kristian Sandfeld and **Knud** Viggo Brøndal,[3] as a student of French at Copen- **Togeby** hagen from 1936 to 1942; during this time he spent a year in France, at Caen (under R.-L. Wagner) and at Paris (where Mario Roques influenced his thinking). During the war years he began to be influenced by Hjelmslev, and his thesis first appeared while he was a *lecteur* in Danish at the Sorbonne, in 1951, as a publication of the Copenhagen Linguistic Circle. It was

[1] K. Togeby 1951. Quotations are taken from the second revised edition (1965). A valuable comparison of the work with other recent French grammatical treatises is to be found in *Ls* vii (1967) pp. 34–57: M. Arrivé, "De F. Brunot à K. Togeby: regards sur quelques grammaires." Professor Togeby very modestly disclaims the position I have reserved for him here, pointing to the work of his colleagues H. Sten and P. Høybe, as well as of younger scholars like E. Spang-Hanssen. I nevertheless feel that I am justified as presenting him as the leading 'Copenhagen' figure among Romanists.

[2] A testimonial volume of some of Togeby's collected essays, for his fiftieth birthday, has appeared as a special number of *RRom* (1968) under the title *Immanence et Structure* (K. Togeby 1968). It contains a bibliography of his works.

[3] Cf. Togeby's "Viggo Brøndals sprogvidenskabelige Indsats", *Tr* 1944 pp. 17–23.

immediately hailed as the first coherent practical study of a language using glossematic methods.[1] In fact, Togeby is far from toeing any party line in his thesis, though he does espouse the fundamental Hjelmslevian principles. In a way, his work is less satisfactory as a study of French than as a comparative and contrastive discussion of different linguistic methods, using illustrations from French; even then many of his illustrations are drawn from other languages, especially English, so that one is left with the impression that actual analysis of French data occupies a relatively small part of the whole. Each stage of the analysis is preceded by a lucid exposition of the solutions that might plausibly be suggested by different linguistic schools, particularly the American and the Prague schools; usually, though not always, he finds himself in agreement with Hjelmslev, though he sometimes shows that the master does not always consistently follow his own principles.

The 'French' that Togeby seeks to describe is "la langue française nationale dans son ensemble", without reference to social or other variation. The delimitation of scope, together with the axiomatic exclusion of substance from analysis, makes the work less acceptable to some French linguists, in particular, who object that it is a 'classroom', written language that is being described rather than the living spoken language.[2] This certainly seems to be the case when we are told (p. 40):

"Structure immanente de la langue française"

> Les oppositions citées par la phonologie de Prague comme [bɔ̃]/[bɔn] ne sont que des transcriptions phonétiques de formes fonctionnelles qui se distinguent autrement: /bon/-/bonə/,

so that French nasal vowel phonemes can be conjured away and seen as a combination of oral vowel and nasal consonant. Although in some cases Togeby appears to be relying heavily on graphy (cf. p. 16):

> Si, par exemple, *petite* se distingue de *petit* par l'addition d'un *e* féminin (qui se prononce sous certaines conditions) *nue* se distingue de *nu* de la même manière, même si la plupart des Français n'entendent pas cette différence)

[1] Cf. e.g. reviews by A. G. Juilland in *RPh* (1953–54) pp. 354–60; and by A. Martinet in *Wd* ix (1953) pp. 78–82 (which contrasts sharply in tone with his earlier sympathetic article on Hjelmslev).

[2] This is not, however, to say that Togeby sets out to analyse the written language. As he himself points out (private communication) ". . . par opposition à Hjelmslev, j'ai toujours soutenu que la langue écrite est quelque chose de secondaire et de dérivé par rapport à la langue parlée. Je ne reconnais donc, dans mes analyses, et cela est d'une importance primordiale, lorsqu'il s'agit d'une langue telle que le français, que les différences audibles, et non pas les différences qui ne sont enregistrées que par l'écriture".

this is by no means wholly so—the *e féminin* is for instance presumed to be present in *cap* /ka-pə/, as well as in *cape* (p. 36). The striving for analytic simplicity is Togeby's justification for this type of juggling, and he makes extensive use of the useful *e féminin* element in other contexts: for instance long vowels are decomposed into short-vowel+ə: [mɛ-trə] *mettre*/[mɛə-trə] *maître*; [ʒø-nə] *jeune*/ [ʒøə-nə] *jeûne* etc. (p. 44).

In many cases the basis of Togeby's classification is unclear: sometimes he seems to admit that it is logical (cf. p. 75 for subject+ predicate), or semantic (p. 149 for modal verbs) but at other times he does not explain his criteria (cf. p. 111: "En français, les flexifs verbaux sont le mode, le temps et l'aspect"). Most often his morphological classes are those of traditional grammar: indeed one detects a great reluctance on his part to depart from tradition in his treatment of 'content-form', compared with his more revolutionary attitude to 'expression-form'. All in all, Togeby's *Structure immanente* does not fill the need for a scientific description of French, but it remains an invaluable work for its clear discussion of different linguistic approaches to detailed analytic problems. The French language presents particularly frightening problems to prospective analysts so that we must treasure the few coherent attempts at complete description that have been made: Togeby's is probably the most accessible of these, and, for all its conceptual difficulty, the most lucid and readable.

Togeby's later works appear to owe less and less to glossematics although he always retains methodical rigour and clarity of exposi-

Recent work

tion. His morphological analyses often appear as relatively short articles, and concern several other Romance languages—Rumanian,[1] Portuguese[2] as well as French.[3] His methods seem to have tended towards the distributionalist techniques of the Bloomfieldians, concentrating more on the plane of expression and on the syntagmatic axis,

---

[1] Cf. articles in *CSP*, "Le problème de l'article en roumain", (i, 1952, pp. 111–19); "Le problème du neutre en roumain", (i, 1952, pp. 265–8); "Déclinaison romane et déclinaison roumaine", (ii, 1953, pp. 35–43, also in K. Togeby 1968 pp. 139–49); "Le neutre en roumain et en albanais", (ii, 1953, pp. 121–31, also in K. Togeby 1968 pp. 195–201).

[2] "L'énigmatique infinitif personnel en portugais", *SN* xxvii (1955) pp. 211–18 (also in K. Togeby 1968 pp. 131–8).

[3] "La concordance des temps en français", *SN* xxvi (1954) pp. 143–56; "Les temps du français", *Li* iv (1955) pp. 379–93; "De+infinitif, successeur de l'infinitif substantivé", *FM* xxv (1957) pp. 1–5; "L'unicité de dont", *FM* xxxiv (1966) pp. 81–6; "Les pronoms interrogatifs-relatifs et les conjonctions de subordination", in P. Delbouille *et al.* (eds.) 1966 pp. 131–9; "La place de l'adjectif par rapport au groupe nom+de+nom", *RPh* xx (1967) pp. 331–8.

though he seeks unifying factors in the plane of content and in the system.

Since *Structure immanente* his only full-length linguistic work has been *Mode, aspect et temps en espagnol* (1953). In this he seeks to define the verbal categories in question in terms of their compatibility with certain non-verbal elements (especially adverbs).[1] Treating the non-verbal elements as invariant, the verbal class can be described in rules of this type:

La règle la plus caractéristique de la syntaxe modale espagnole en proposition principale est que la négation *no* est incompatible avec l'impératif.

Thus Togeby defines tense in terms of compatibility with such expressions as *ayer* or *mañana*; mood, with, for instance, *tal vez*; and aspect by compatibility or no with "les compléments adverbiaux désignant une limitation temporelle" (p. 60).

This definition of paradigmatic classes in terms of syntagmatic taxonomy seems much closer to Bloomfieldian practice than to Hjelmslevian and demonstrates Togeby's independence of the Copenhagen school.

Togeby has also made contributions to the historical study of the Romance languages—mainly in short articles and reviews.[2] Here he appears to be almost purely traditional, with the same neogrammarian background as Hjelmslev himself, regarding historical linguistics as concerned with process and expression, rather than with the more structured aspects of language. He seems somewhat antipathetic to Prague school diachronic structuralism,[3] believing that phonological change is occasioned by external factors—language

---

[1] Cf. also A. Klum 1961 for a rather different approach to a similar problem.

[2] E.g., "Qu'est-ce que la dissimilation?" *RPh* xvii (1964) pp. 642–67 (also in K. Togeby 1968 pp. 96–121); "Les désinences de l'imparfait (et du parfait) dans les langues romanes", *SN* xxxvi (1964) pp. 3–8; "Le sort du plus-que-parfait latin dans les langues romanes", *CFS*, xxiii (1966) pp. 175–84.

[3] E.g. review of Haudricourt & Juilland in *AL* vii (1952) pp. 87–91; "Désorganisation et réorganisation dans l'histoire des langues romanes", in A. Martinet 1958 (fest.) i, pp. 277–87; (also in K. Togeby 1968 pp. 71–82); "Les explications phonologiques historiques sont-elles possibles?", *RPh* xiii (1959–60) pp. 401–13 (also in K. Togeby 1968 pp. 83–95). Togeby is prepared to accept a Gilliéron-type attitude to 'linguistic pathology', but draws the line at such an approach in the phonological sphere: "Les collisions des phonèmes doivent avoir des causes extérieures, mais elles sont elles-mêmes les causes de presque toutes les réactions morphologiques et syntaxiques, de même qu'elles jouent un rôle prépondérant dans l'histoire du vocabulaire, comme l'a prouvé Gilliéron", *RPh* xiv (1960) p. 161. An example of Togeby's treatment of morphological change as structurally determined is to be found in his recent article, "suus et illorum dans les langues romanes", *RRom* iii (1968) pp. 66–71.

mixture, social upheaval etc.—and not by internal structural pressures.

Most of Togeby's work, especially in recent years, has been on literary, rather than linguistic themes.[1] He seems to believe that linguistics as such has comparatively little to contribute to literary analysis: indeed, one gains the impression, from a survey of the work of such a versatile and data-oriented scholar as Togeby, that the glossematic approach to language is so limited in its scope that it can cast little light on many aspects of linguistics, so that the glossematician must rely on other methods if he wishes to turn his attention to anything but pure theory. Perhaps this is why glossematics appears, today, to have led into a dead end, even though it introduced fruitful and revolutionary ideas at its inception.

7. *The Prague School*

The so-called Prague School of structuralism represents the modern linguistic trend that has made most impact on Romance linguistics— perhaps because it allows scope for diachronic investigation as well as synchronic description. Deriving their inspiration primarily from Saussure (though its Eastern European founders also looked back to Baudouin de Courtenay), 'Prague' linguists have neverthe-

'Prague' vs. 'Copenhagen' less emphasized rather different elements of Saussurean thought from their Copenhagen brethren (cf. pp. 472–80): they insist on the social function of language (while retaining intra-linguistic methods of study) and on distinctive substance in language. Their concern with substance and with distinctiveness is most evident in their preferred field of study, phonology[2] (whereas Copenhagen linguists are more morphologically inclined, reflecting their preoccupation with form—i.e. interrelationships—and with content). This is not to say that 'Prague' linguists study 'expression-substance' (i.e. phonetics)—on

---

[1] E.g. K. Togeby 1954, 1957a & b, 1960, and numerous articles. Togeby has, however, also written in Danish a lengthy grammar of French, which we are happy to learn, he is now translating into French.

[2] An important application of Prague methods to the description of the grammar of a Romance language as a whole is G. Gougenheim 1939. Another work in the same tradition that deserves mention is H. G. Schogt 1968.

the contrary, they concentrate on the paradigmatic aspects of sound-systems and neglect all but the 'distinctive' or 'pertinent' sound-features of phonetic substance. 'Syntagmatic' structuralism—characteristic of the Bloomfieldian approach—is foreign to Prague thought, which does not accept the single-standard methodology of distributional analysis, insisting always that language has two faces—both expression and function. Thus this approach is often called 'functional'—though the term is employed with quite a

Function different meaning from Hjelmslevian usage. 'Function' for Prague linguists has the everyday implication of 'language as a tool', though formal descriptions of the 'functionalist approach' differ somewhat in their emphasis. J. Vachek,[1] for instance, insists that "any item of language (sentence, word, morpheme, phoneme, etc.) exists solely because it serves some purpose, because it has some function (mostly that of communicating) to fulfill". André Martinet[2] in defining the functional attitude to structure is more explicit; a functional unit is "whatever in the substance is found to exert a communicative function in the ordinary meaning of the term. Units which are found to exert the same type of function are classified according to the substantial nature of their linguistically relevant features. Structure results from the various combinations of these features."

Thus Prague practitioners retain the Saussurean *signifiant/signifié* dichotomy. That of *langue/parole* is also accepted by them—

'Prague' and Saussure and here they differ radically from the Bloomfieldians[3]—with the proviso that *la parole* is not an abstract structure, but merely a set of concrete utterances implementing *la langue*. A Saussurean dichotomy they are not prepared to accept at its face value is that of *diachrony/synchrony*, for, unlike the Hjelmslevians, they envisage structure dynamically not statically, leaving room for the possibility of a 'diachronic structural' approach, which has in fact developed most fruitfully within their framework of thought.

The linguistic material studied by Prague linguists is most often taken from 'cultured' languages. Perhaps for this reason they are

Which 'langue'? particularly conscious of certain aspects of language that tend to be neglected by Bloomfieldians in their linguistic studies of less complex societies. Such

---

[1] J. Vachek 1966 p. 7.
[2] A. Martinet, "Structural Linguistics", in A. Kroeber (ed.) 1953 p. 583.
[3] E.g. Z. S. Harris reviewing Trubetzkoy (*L* xvii (1941) pp. 345 ff.) where he insists that the *Sprachgebilde* is merely a scientific arrangement of the *Sprechakt*.

aspects include the aesthetic functions of language and the co-existence of 'functional dialects' or styles (especially of written versus spoken style). Most especially, they recognize the 'structural defectiveness' of language that makes elegant simplicity of description less than realistic: the existence of minor sub-structures within one language may result from historical inertia or from dialect mixture, but its effect is to give language an instability which makes a dynamic approach imperative. 'Structure' for Prague linguists is based on 'tensions' which keep elements in their **Structure** place, but which may easily unbalance, leading to a collapse of one system that will then be replaced by another. This idea of 'structure' is often depicted spatially in diagrammatic form: imbalance will then be shown by gaps—*cases vides* or 'holes in the system'.

Bloomfieldians often find the Prague attitude to structure, as symbolized by their spatial analogies, 'mystical', and especially condemn their 'teleological' approach. Some **Teleology** Prague linguists do not conceal their teleological bias, however, for it springs from their functional approach. Roman Jakobson puts this point succinctly and lucidly in his essay "Efforts towards a means-end model of language in interwar continental linguistics":[1] after listing some of the various personalities[2] who can be said to subscribe to Prague principles, he says,

it would be easy to find individual features specifying the contribution of each of these outstanding innovators but we could hardly find a unifying

---

[1] In *Trends ii* p. 105. This short (4½ page) account of Prague linguistics is the most brilliant and incisive thing written on the subject. A more complete introduction is to be found in J. Vachek (1964 and 1966) though his approach is more nationalistic than is warranted in an account of a school whose greatest representatives were not Czech. A full and sympathetic account of Prague phonology is to be found in B. Malmberg 1964 pp. 74–98. Another valuable introduction, using Spanish material, is to be found in E. Alarcos Llorach 1950; the 2nd revised edition of this work omits the reference to the Prague school from its title, and indeed does rather extend its theoretical coverage, while nevertheless retaining a Prague-school bias, and expanding especially on diachronic phonology.

[2] These include, in the Romance sphere, such outstanding figures as E. Benveniste (France) (see p. 402 n. 2) and A. Rosetti (Rumania).

A. Rosetti was born in 1895 in Bucharest where he has studied and taught at the University, except for a period (1920–28) which he spent in Paris studying under Meillet, Roques, Rousselot, and Gilliéron. In 1938 he succeeded O. Densusianu to the Chair of the Rumanian Language at Bucharest, and in 1948 he became an Academician. A bibliography of his works up to 1965 is to be found in A. Rosetti 1965 (fest.). Collections of articles are A. Rosetti 1947 and 1967.

To Jakobson's list one might add other Romanists—besides A. Martinet who shall be discussed at length, the Spaniards, T. Navarro, A. Alonso, E. Alarcos Llorach; Italians, G. Contini, C. Segre, V. Belardi; Germans, H. Lausberg, H. Weinrich; in Sweden, B. Malmberg; in Switzerland, H. Lüdtke; and in France, G. Gougenheim; to name but a few.

pattern for the Prague group which would distinguish it from the other scholars mentioned above. At the same time, there is a typical drift which ties the work of all these investigators and strictly distinguishes them from older tradition and from some different doctrines which found their out-spoken expression likewise in the '30's.

The title of this paper defines this common drift as aiming toward a means-ends model of language. These efforts proceed from a universally recognized view of language as a tool of communication. Statements about language as a tool, instrument, vehicle, etc. can be found in any textbook, but, strange as it seems, the apparently self-evident inference from this truism was not drawn in the linguistic tradition of the past century. Thus the elemental request to analyse all the instrumentalities of language from the angle of the tasks they perform emerged as a daring innovation. The pro-longed neglect of any inquiry into the means-ends relationship in language —a neglect which still survives in some academic biases—finds its historical explanation in the inveterate fear of problems connected with goal-directed-ness. Therefore questions of genesis outweighed those of orientation, search for prerequisites supplanted the examination of aims.

Roman Jakobson is himself the most distinguished living repre-sentative of the Prague school, though the great classic work on
Roman Jakobson
Prague phonology is from the pen of Russian-born Prince Trubetzkoy (1890–1938).[1] Jakobson too is Russian by origin (born 1896 in Moscow), but in 1920 he went to Prague where he took his Ph.D in 1930, serving as professor in Brno from 1933 to 1939. Nazi occupation drove him from his second homeland and, after two years in Scandinavia he settled in America, at first in New York at the *Ecole libre des Hautes Etudes* (1942–46) and then at Columbia (1946–49). In 1949 he went to Harvard and since 1957 travels the 'longest mile in the world', serving both at Harvard and M.I.T. His influence has been enor-mous[2]—not the least being that exercised on Chomsky, who might be said to be 'out of Jakobson, by Z. S. Harris'.[3] Jakobson's versatility is proverbial—his first interest, retained throughout, was in Slavic literature and in poetics, but his phonological writings[4]

[1] Trubetzkoy (variously transliterated Troubetskoj, Trubetzkoj, etc.) was born in Moscow, fleeing after the Revolution to Sofia and settling in 1923 in Vienna. His *Grundzüge der Phonologie* was published posthumously in 1939; a French translation by Cantineau appeared in 1949. Trubetzkoy is mentioned in passing by *Iordan–Orr*.

[2] Two Festschriften pay tribute to him: R. Jakobson 1956 (fest.) and 1967 (fest.).

[3] In his early American years Jakobson was, however, sometimes on the defen-sive: see his reply to a 1950 review of a pupil's work by R. A. Hall, Jr.—which Jakobson has bothered to reprint in his *Selected Writings* (i (1962) pp. 435–42)—in which he defends himself against possible accusations of 'unAmerican' attitudes, humourously comparing them with attacks against Trubetzkoy and himself, from other political quarters, which taxed them with 'rootless cosmopolitanism'.

[4] Cf. especially R. Jakobson 1962 and 1963; R. Jakobson, G. Fant, and M. Halle 1952; R. Jakobson and M. Halle 1956.

are of more relevance in the present context. Such subjects as aphasia and child language early occupied him;[1] and more recently, in the M.I.T. context, he has taken an interest in information theory and mathematical linguistics.[2]

As I have already said, Prague theory is most highly developed in the phonological sphere: I think therefore that a brief delineation of Prague-type phonology is called for here.[3] Its first **Phonology** aim is the establishment of an inventory of paradigmatic functional sound-units—phonemes; the basic procedural tool used is that of commutation of minimal sound-segments, in such a way that, when the meaning of a stretch of speech (typically, a word) is changed by commutation, then the minimal segments are recognized as having different phonemic status (thus, for instance, /s/ is seen to be a different phoneme from /p/, because /sɪt/ has a different meaning from /pɪt/). This 'minimal pair' procedure is, of course, used by all phonemicists, but for the Bloomfieldians it is merely a heuristic device and not scientifically valid, based as it is on recognition of difference in meaning as well as in form: they therefore prefer to base their definition of the phoneme on distributional criteria. Prague phonologists have no such scruples, however, for they see the coexistence of form and meaning as an essential feature of language.

They do however, on the whole, prefer not to use, for classification of sound-segments into phonemes, the criterion of common phonetic substance; for them, as for Saussure, linguistic classes are 'distinctive' rather than 'substantial', recognized not so much by their positive characteristics as by the features that differentiate them from their neighbours. In this, Prague phonology differs from phonetically based phonemic theory such as that of Daniel Jones.[4]

It does share with Jonesian phonemics, however, its use of 'words' —independent meaningful units—as material for segmentation and commutation. For Bloomfieldians such pre-selection of short stretches of speech prejudges some of the issues and they prefer to utilize 'utterances' that have not been previously analysed in grammatical or semantic units: 'separation of levels' is a procedural

---

[1] Cf. especially R. Jakobson 1941.
[2] Cf. especially R. Jakobson (ed.) 1960 which includes his own paper on "Linguistics and Communication Theory".
[3] Cf. also J. W. Mulder 1968.
[4] Cf. D. Jones 1950: Jones defines the phoneme by both phonetic and distributional criteria—while using meaning-differentiation heuristically—"a family of phonetically related sounds, such that no member occurs in the same phonetic environment as any other member".

axiom. Prague linguists claim that different linguistic levels—the phonological and the grammatical, for instance,—are interdependent, and that language is a 'system of systems' and not merely a set of stratifications.

A frequent corollary of the Prague use of words as data in phonemic discovery procedure is the relegation to second place of suprasegmental (or prosodic) features, like intonation. Phonologists who use complete utterances as their raw data often assign more importance to such features.

The most outstanding characteristic of Prague phonology is its recognition of sub-phonemic entities— 'distinctive features' (or, in American terminology, 'phonological components').

Distinctive features Indeed the Trubetzkoyan definition of the phoneme characterizes it as "a bundle of phonologically relevant features".[1] Such features for Trubetzkoy were given articulatory labels—'labial', 'plosive', etc.; Jakobson, on the basis of the findings of acoustic phonetics especially since the invention of the spectrograph, has substituted acoustic labels—like 'grave/acute', 'tense/lax', etc. Moreover, correlations between phonemes which for Trubetzkoy could be multidimensional as well as unidimensional, are reduced by Jakobson to binary form—so that each phoneme will contain either plus or minus features. Although binarism has always been a feature of Jakobson's thought, the influence of M.I.T. computers is not far to seek in its more recent developments: the great achievement of his work in this field is that he has been able to postulate a small number of distinctive acoustic features (12 binary distinctions) that underlie the phonological systems of all known languages. Jakobson's collaborator Halle[2] has taken a step even further and has, within the framework of Chomskyist grammar, denied the need for 'phonemic' analysis altogether —passing straight from 'systematic phonemics' (i.e. morphophonemics—concerned with the phonemic shape of paradigmatic grammatical units) to 'systematic phonetics' (or distinctive feature analysis) without pausing at a stage of segmental phonemes.

Prague phonology is also distinguished by its use of the idea of

[1] The Cantineau version: "Le phonème est la somme des particularités phonologiquement pertinentes que comporte une image phonique" (*Principes*, p. 40) is somewhat misleading, as "image phonique" might imply some mystical entity. The original German is not wholly clear: "das Phonem die Gesamtheit der phonologisch relevanten Eigenschaften eines Lautgebildes ist" (*Grundzüge*, p. 35).

[2] M. Halle, "On the Bases of Phonology", and "Phonology in Generative Grammar", periodical articles reprinted in J. A. Fodor and J. J. Katz (eds.) 1964. A French version of the second article also appears in *Ls* viii (1967) pp. 13–36.

phonological 'neutralization' and the 'archiphoneme', first advanced by Jakobson in 1929. When phonemes are distinguished in some positions only, the distinction between them is said to be 'neutralized' in the others: rather than assign the segments occurring in these positions arbitrarily to one phoneme or another, Prague theorists prefer to speak of an 'archiphoneme'—in Trubetzkoy's definition, "the sum of distinctive qualities which are common to two terms of a neutralizable phonological opposition". Thus, for instance, French *é* and *è* tend to be neutralized in non-final position, where archiphoneme E can be said to occur, with its phonetic realization (beyond the features common to both *é* and *è*) determined by phonological environment. An advantage of the 'archiphoneme' concept is that it pinpoints one kind of 'structural defectiveness'—here, limited syntagmatic distribution of phonic units—and might help in study of language dynamics.

Neutralization

Another Prague concept that is of utility in dynamic linguistic investigation is that of 'functional load' (*rendement fonctionnel*)—a term used to designate the degree of utilization of a phonological opposition for differentiation of meaning. Where a large number of words are distinguished by the difference between a phoneme and its partner, we can assume that the phonological opposition is firmly rooted in the structure ('carries a large functional load'); when, however, an opposition serves to distinguish only very few forms (as for instance French /œ/ and /ø/, assigned phonemic status because of their rôle in the minimal pair *jeune/jeûne*) we may be able to predict eventual loss of the opposition altogether.

Functional load

The most outstanding representative of Prague-type linguistics in the Romance field is, without a shadow of a doubt, André Martinet, whose thought has developed along different lines from that of Jakobson and who has exercised enormous influence on young Romanists in the last twenty years. Martinet was born in 1908 in Savoie and lectured at the Paris Ecole des Hautes Etudes from 1938 to 1946 (with two years' interruption, some of which he was obliged to spend in a prisoner-of-war camp where he occupied himself by conducting a survey of

André Martinet

contemporary French speech habits[1]). In his lectures on historical phonology at the Hautes Etudes he developed ideas which were later to be elaborated by A. G. Haudricourt and A. G. Juilland in their *Essai pour une histoire structurale du phonétisme français* (1949)[2] and which appeared in definitive form in his epoch-making *Economie des changements phonétiques, Traité de phonologie diachronique* (1955). After the war Martinet went to New York where he worked for the Auxiliary Language Association before being appointed Professor of General and Comparative Linguistics at Columbia, where he served till 1955. During this time he was editor of *Word* (cf. p. 454), in partnership successively with Maurice Swadesh,[3] Joseph Greenberg,[4] and Uriel Weinreich.[5] In 1955 he returned to the Sorbonne[6] as Professor of General Linguistics: since then, his teaching and research has, of necessity, been concerned mainly with more descriptive and general linguistic problems but he has maintained his interest in Romance diachronic linguistics and, in spite of difficulties, has stimulated such interest in his pupils. In 1965 Martinet founded a new periodical *La Linguistique*[7] as a vehicle for "des travaux qui s'inspirent des mêmes convictions quant à la façon de concevoir et de poursuivre les recherches linguististiques" (*Avant-Propos*, pp. v–vi). These convictions are perhaps best expressed by his promise that

rien de ce qui touche aux langages et aux langues dans leur fonctionnement comme instrument de communication et d'expression, dans leurs variations dans l'espace et le temps, et dans leurs interférences mutuelles, n'est jamais exclu de ses pages (Avant-Propos, v).

[1] Published in 1945 (A. Martinet 1945).

[2] By all accounts, Haudricourt was an assiduous attender at Martinet's lectures and communicated their purport to Juilland, who prepared the monograph while Haudricourt was in Indo-China: it is a shame that such a seminal work should have been left in a rather rough state, but its main tenets have been further developed by Martinet, who wrote its preface, and now a revised edition is in preparation.

[3] Swadesh (1909–67) was best known for his glottochronological theories (cf. p. 534), but he was, before the American cold-war political atmosphere led him to take up residence in Mexico, one of the most promising of young general linguists. Although American Indian languages have undoubtedly benefited, perhaps General Linguistics has lost, as a result of his consequent isolation from current trends.

[4] Much of Greenberg's work is in African linguistics, but his recent publications on "Language Universals" (especially his contribution to T. A. Sebeok (ed.) 1966a) show the unmistakable influence of Prague-type thought.

[5] U. Weinreich 1953 is a short version of a thesis prepared under Martinet's guidance: this Polish-born American (1926–67) was a foremost expert on bilingualism, with a Prague-type interest in linguistic variation. Of more recent years, Weinreich's interests turned to semantics with, at the last, a Chomskyist twist (cf. his contribution to T. A. Sebeok (ed.) 1966a pp. 395–478).

[6] I had the privilege of attending Martinet's seminars soon after his return. It is to him I owe the main inspiration of parts of R. Posner 1961 (cf. p. 493).

[7] *LaL*, with a concurrent series of publications *Le Linguiste* (Paris, P.U.F.).

In general Martinet's views on linguistics are delineated in his own words (private communication):

> Je reste convaincu que le point de vue fonctionaliste est celui qui aboutit à donner, des réalites linguistiques statiques ou dynamiques, les représentations les plus exactes. Je reste également opposé au structuralisme bloomfieldien, trop simpliste, et au confusionisme idéaliste des guillaumistes et au mentalisme et à l'apriorisme chomskien.[1]

Martinet's contributions to linguistics may be discussed under two heads—synchronic and diachronic. It is in the latter field that he has made most impact on Romance linguistics, but his more general theories, and their application to French, merit discussion here.

Although we are most concerned with Martinet as a Romanist we should remember that he was by training a Germanist[2] and that he has always contributed towards more general linguistics (including Indo-European).

His most noteworthy publications in this sphere are: *Phonology as Functional Phonetics* (1949); *Eléments de Linguistique Générale* (1960); *A Functional View of Language* (1962); and the collection of essays *La Linguistique synchronique* (1966). The
Linguistic theory
first consists of three lectures delivered at the University of London in 1946, and represents a lucid popularization of Prague phonology—in an attempt to bridge the gulfs left by wartime separation—together with an application of the theories to the description of French. *A Functional View* . . . is also an expanded version of lectures before an English audience—this time the six Waynflete Lectures at Magdalen College, Oxford, in 1961. It is an elegant and attractive exposition of Martinet's views, most of which are expressed elsewhere, providing the ideal introduction for a student and illustrating the refreshing 'realism' of his linguistic approach. His *Eléments* . . . , though designed as an introductory text, is perhaps less successful as such, in that it is somewhat uneven in its coverage, as he himself admits (*Avant-Propos*, p. 7):

> Les différentes parties de cet ouvrage reflètent toutes, sans doute, les préférences et la personnalité de son auteur, mais à des degrés très divers: les principes de l'analyse phonologique sont, depuis longtemps, tombés dans le domaine public. Au contraire, ce qui est dit au chapitre 4 de la

---

[1] Martinet's surveys of different linguistic approaches are to be recommended: especially "Structural Linguistics", in A. Kroeber (ed.) 1953 pp. 574–86, and "The Unity of Linguistics", in *Wd* x (1954) pp. 121–5. Cf. also A. Martinet (ed.) 1968.

[2] A. Martinet 1937*a* & *b*, 1947.

syntaxe est neuf, trop neuf pour un manuel comme celui-ci; la nécessité de présenter une méthode de description couvrant, de façon cohérente, l'ensemble des faits de langue, nous a contraint de devancer l'aboutissement d'un effort collectif, encore que mal coordonné, qui tendait à dégager, pour les unités signifiantes, ce que représente la phonologie pour les unités distinctives. Ce qui est dit, aux chapitres 5 et 6, de la variété des usages et de la dynamique des langues est certainement moins original; tout cela a été, sous une forme ou sous une autre, explicité antérieurement; mais il s'en faut que ce qu'on y trouve soit universellement admis.

Here, as elsewhere, Martinet affirms his anti-formalism, insisting on the dual aspect of language as physical phonic reality and expression of experience. Linguistic structure, for him, is not merely an analytic convenience but a reality, and he is ready to accept complexity and co-existence of different systems as characteristic of reality. Unlike Bloomfieldians Martinet is not concerned with 'discovery procedures': as one reviewer remarks,[1] "the method is the traditional one: trial and error, inspiration and despair". In his attitude to phonology and to linguistic variety, Martinet shares the Prague outlook; his 'functional syntax' is much more his own original invention and has been developed, in recent years, through a series of articles.[2] He scorns the practice of using, at the morphological and syntactic levels, procedures developed for phonology and prefers, to the use of a formal segmental 'morpheme', a unit belonging to the plane of both expression and content, like the Saussurean 'sign'—the 'moneme'. Monemes (and *syntagmes* and *synthèmes*) are classified according to their syntactic autonomy: *autonomous* units carry within themselves the indication of their own function, like *hier*, or verbal elements (envisaged as independent basic elements around which every other member of the string must be ordered); *functional* units indicate the functions of units to which they are subjoined, bestowing on the *syntagme* as a whole syntactic autonomy (for instance, *à* signals the function of *Jean* in *il a donné le livre à Jean*); *dependent* units have syntactic function only by virtue of their position in the chain, or by addition of a functional moneme (thus a nominal element may be dependent on a verb—as its subject or object—and the definite article *le* hinges on a nominal element to which it is subjoined and without which it lacks any reference). The aim underlying Martinet's syntactic theories is to discover how a linear string of discontinuous elements can serve as a vehicle for global experience. Autonomous units would

[1] W. Diver in *Wd* xix (1963) p. 419.
[2] Cf. especially "L'autonomie syntaxique", in P. Delbouille *et al.* (eds.) 1966 pp. 49–64, and "Syntagme et synthème", in *LaL* 1967, 2 pp. 1–14.

convey in themselves a discrete segment of experience: for a language to use only autononous elements, however, would offend the demands of linguistic economy.

Martinet's studies of French linguistic problems[1] have always taken full account of degrees of tolerance allowed by social and regional variation, thus rendering them more valuable accounts of linguistic reality: we can only regret that he has not been able to devote more of his time to this side of his work.[2]

I have already mentioned the importance of Martinet's contribution to historical phonology.[3] This is not to say that he was the initiator of 'diachronic structuralism', which was

Historical phonology

first adumbrated by Jakobson.[4] However, Martinet developed the method along rather different lines, substituting for the idea of a vague 'systemic drift' a more positive motivation in language change—a striving for linguistic economy. In this he may have derived his initial inspiration from G. Zipf,[5] but in his modifications and elaborations the original model is hardly discernible. Martinet's view is that:

il y a conflit permanent entre la tendance de l'individu à restreindre sa dépense d'énergie et les besoins de la communauté qui réclament le maintien de distinctions jugées nécessaires par l'ensemble des usagers de la langue. C'est ce conflit que résume la théorie du moindre effort qu'on désigne également comme le principe d'économie.[6]

In ideal circumstances phonemic contrasts would be maintained by the tensions of the system, although zones of latitude would be allowed in phonetic realization. But

---

[1] Cf. especially "C'est jeuli, le Mareuc!" *RPh* xi (1958) pp. 345–55 and "De l'économie des formes du verbe en français parlé", in L. Spitzer 1958 (fest.) pp. 309–26 now both reprinted in A. Martinet 1969, which also includes a previously unpublished "Qu'est-ce-que le '*e* muet'"?

[2] There are signs, however, that he is influencing others in the right direction, cf. for instance, G. Deyhime, "Enquête sur la phonologie du français contemporain", in *LaL* 1967, 1 pp. 97–108, 2 pp. 57–84, which takes up the problems of Martinet's prisoner-of-war camp investigations (cf. p. 487, n. 1). Martinet himself discusses recent work on these lines in "L'évolution contemporaine du système phonologique français", in A. Martinet 1969.

[3] Apart from his *Economie* (1955) we should mention more recent articles: "Les problèmes de la phonétique évolutive" (*Proceedings of the 5th International Congress of Phonetic Sciences*, pp. 82–104)—an excellent exposition from which I shall quote (abbrev. *PPE*); "La phonologie synchronique et diachronique", in J. Hamm (ed.) 1967 pp. 64–78: and, on the more general problem of the relationship between linguistic variation in time and space, "Structural variation in language", *P9th ICL* pp. 521–32.

[4] Cf. especially R. Jakobson 1929 and "Prinzipien der historischen Phonologie", *TCLP* iv (1931) pp. 247–67. Cf. also A. G. Juilland, "A Bibliography of Diachronic Phonemics", *Wd* ix (1953) pp. 198–208.

[5] Cf. especially G. Zipf 1935.

[6] *PPE* p. 86.

même si les pressions de langue à langue ou de dialecte à dialecte était
supposés immuables, il resterait, dans l'asymétrie même des organes de la
parole, une source d'instabilité. L'expérience montre que certaines langues
conservent de larges pans de leur structure phonologique sans y rien changer
pendant les siècles, mais aussi que toutes celles qui restent des moyens
normaux de communication orale présentent immanquablement une
phonie en voie d'évolution sur quelque point.[1]

Thus phonological systems are often unstable, partly for physiological reasons (the back of the mouth being narrower than the front
leads to imbalance in the distribution of phonemic 'zones'), partly
for social reasons (existence of linguistic variation) and partly
because of the changing needs of the community. Sometimes two
phonemes will be used where before there was only one—when, for
instance, borrowed words introduce new sounds, or where contextual variants are left high and dry by the loss of the determining
contexts (thus /ati/ might be pronounced [at'i] but loss of [-i] might
lead to a phonemic distinction between /at/ and /at'/). Sometimes,
too, a phonemic merger might take place "lorsque la confusion des
deux phonèmes ne peut plus affecter très sérieusement la compré-
hension de ce qui est dit"[2]—that is, when the functional load carried
by the distinction between the two phonemes was small. Each
phonemic change, however, will inevitably lead to a shift of the
whole system to attain a new (if unstable) equilibrium.

Martinet does not think that in tracing the action of paradigmatic
sound-change he has found a unique answer to all diachronic phonological problems. As one would expect, he does not shrink from
the complexity of real phenomena: he does, however, delight in
thus being able to *explain*, in some sense, the hitherto 'blind' laws of
the neo-grammarians.

We must be grateful to Martinet for having, in part, illustrated his
theories with detailed Romance studies,[3] though these are not as
numerous as we would wish. Other Romanists have,
Martinet's
influence
however, been inspired by his work, directly or
indirectly: the 3-volume testimonial *Miscelánea
Homenaje a André Martinet*, "*Estructuralismo e historia*" (1957–62, ed.
D. Catalán) with its dedication to the "maestro y guía de una nueva
generación de linguistas", is ample testimony of that.

[1] *PPE* p. 93.   [2] *PPE* pp. 95–6.
[3] Reprinted in A. Martinet 1955 we have "La lénition en celtique et les consonnes du roman occidental", and "Structures en contact: le dévoisement des
sifflantes en espagnol"; and, more recently, "R du latin au français d'aujourd'hui",
in *Phon* viii (1962) pp. 193–202, and "Les voyelles nasales du français", in *LaL*
1965, 2 pp. 117–22, both now reprinted in A. Martinet 1969.

The first of the phonological studies written directly under Martinet's influence has already been mentioned: Haudricourt and Juilland's[1] lithographed "*Essai . . .*" (1949) (cf.

A. G. Haudricourt and A. G. Juilland

p. 487). Here the authors insist that their approach is complementary to those of traditional historical phonology and not meant to be a substitute for time-tested methods (p. 13):

En somme, notre façon de considérer les faits de langue laisse intactes les méthodes traditionnelles de la linguistique, l'histoire et le comparatisme. Il s'agit uniquement de les appliquer dans un esprit nouveau, celui qui anime la science moderne, le structuralisme. Au lieu de faire l'histoire de phonèmes isolés, nous nous sommes proposé de faire l'histoire des systèmes phonologiques: au lieu de comparer des phonèmes particuliers pris à des langues différentes, nous nous sommes proposé de comparer des structures linguistiques.

Two problems are studied: the disappearance of Latin quantity (vocalic and consonantal) and its consequences in Gallo-Roman; and Romance palatalizations (of occlusives and of Latin ū to [y] in Gallo-Roman).

In the first study, the authors see the loss of Latin phonological length as originating from a vulgar change in the prosodic system in about the 3rd century A.D., which spread unevenly through the Empire (being effected first in Sardinia and Corsica and then in Eastern regions, before passing to the more 'urban', *soigné* Western Empire). The treatment of the Latin diphthong AU is the test-case in the various regions: in the West it was retained late and, if incorporated into the simple vowel system, led to an upheaval in the whole system, which in some cases occasioned a new spurt of diphthongization. In a similar way, the notorious 'Western' voicing of intervocalic Latin surds is seen as a reaction against the loss of consonantal length (i.e. phonological double consonants). In the second study palatalizing processes in Romance are seen as deriving originally from the action of Vulgar Latin jod (which again owes its existence to a change in the accentuation system). In the East the syntagmatic changes occasioned by the new palatal phoneme take their course more unchecked than in the urbane West. The

[1] Alphonse Juilland, now at Stanford, is the head of a vast project designed to present *The Romance Languages and their Structures* (Series i, *Scholarly Works*; Series ii, *Practical and Applied Studies*) in which mechanical methods are being used to prepare frequency dictionaries for the five major Romance languages and for Latin: the Spanish and Rumanian dictionaries appeared in 1965. In A. Juilland 1961, he presents his analytic criteria, which appear to be broadly Prague-type, of a Jakobsonian kind.

North French palatalization of Latin C^{+A} is seen as connected with the phonological loss of [kw] ǫu and with the late levelling of au to o (leading to the need for a distinction between palatalized /k'o/ <cau and unpalatalized /ko/<co). Gallo-Roman palatalization of u>[y] is also seen as due to structural pressures after the passage of o>u: the asymmetry of speech organs determined the pushing forward of the displaced phoneme.

The fundamental causes of the structurally conditioned changes described are seen by Haudricourt and Juilland as social (the 'quality' of the Latin diffused to the different regions) and as occasioned by interaction of Latin with other languages (substratal and superstratal). Their general conclusions are thus similar to those of Wartburg, though their methods are very different.

Another work written directly under Martinet's influence is F. H. Jungemann's *La Teoría del substrato y los dialectos hispano-romances y gascones* (1955). Here Jungemann examines thoroughly Hispano-Romance phonological developments that have traditionally been thought to derive from substratal influence, cogently suggesting in each case alternative 'structural' explanations. His individual studies vary in length and depth, but are always excellently argued and documented. They include a discussion of Hispanic apical s, which Jungemann believes continues original Latin pronunciation, changed in other Romance languages under the pressure of phonemicization of /ʃ/. Hispanic palatalization of liquids and nasals also receive special tatention, as do the passage of f to h, the growth of the Castilian five-vowel system, confusion of b and u̯, voicing of intervocalic surds and Portuguese nasalization.

Less directly influenced by Martinet, but deriving inspiration from his work, we should mention R. Posner, *Consonantal Dissimilation in the Romance Languages* (1961), a condensation of an Oxford doctoral thesis. Taking up again the theme of M. Grammont's masterly 1895 thesis,[1] I redefine his *loi du plus fort* in structural terms—the 'stronger' phoneme being the one which serves a more important functional purpose. Where the functional load borne by the distinctive features that differentiate one phoneme from another, is heavy, those features are unlikely to be lost by 'sporadic' syntagmatic action, like that of dissimilation. Making use of a suggestion by W. Diver,[2] I roughly estimate the

[1] M. Grammont 1895, reworked in M. Grammont 1936.
[2] In *Wd* xi (1955) pp. 233–6.

functional importance of a phoneme in a language by means of its relative frequency in continuous texts. The less frequent phoneme will tend to be replaced, under dissimilatory influence, by its more frequent partner (sharing with the original some of its distinctive features, but often less 'complex' than the original). Use is made also of the concepts of neutralization and of phonemic repulsion[1] (which results in the selection by the speaker of allophonic variants that offer less overlapping and so tends to increase the distance between the phonemes, rather than to lessen or eradicate it). On the basis of the examination of a very large amount of Romance data, I suggest that 'sporadic' ('conditioned' or 'syntagmatic') sound-change may not result from completely different conditions from 'regular' ('unconditioned' or 'paradigmatic') change: in some cases, examples may represent a sort of 'mini-regularity', by which unstable positional variants of phonemes are affected, but which, for some reason or other (therapeutical phonemic reaction or conservative influence, for instance), does not spread to affect the whole phonemic system. Such mini-regularities are masked by the fact that individual examples can be explained away in many different ways, so that the pattern as a whole is not readily discernible.[2]

A group of German Romanists, centred round H. Lausberg[3] have also worked along the same lines as Martinet, though not

H. Lausberg, H. Weinrich, H. Lüdtke   directly under his influence. Notable among these are H. Weinrich[4] and H. Lüdtke[5] both of whom have been concerned with structural pressures for sound-change in Romance, but with a slightly more 'idealist' bias than Martinet,[6] putting more weight on the action of "la conscience linguistique" of speakers. The prime cause of Romance

---

[1] Cf. A. A. Hill, "Phonetic and Phonemic Change", in *L* xii (1936) pp. 15–22.

[2] Cf. also Y. Malkiel on "Multiple Causation . . .", (p. 445–6).

[3] Born 1912, among his publications we note especially "Zum romanischen Vokalismus", *RF* lx (1947) pp. 295–307; "Zum französischen Vokalismus", *Ibid.* pp. 308–15; "Beiträge zur italienischen Lautlehre", *RF* lxi (1948) pp. 300–23, and H. Lausberg 1956–62.

[4] Born 1927, professor at Kiel and then at Cologne: cf. H. Weinrich 1958. Weinrich's more recent works have been more literary and philosophical than linguistic. H. Weinrich 1964 and 1966 belong, perhaps, more to the neo-humanist than the Prague tradition.

[5] Born 1925, professor at Freiburg. Cf. especially H. Lüdtke 1956.

[6] Cf. R. A. Hall's slashing review of Lüdtke in *L* xxxiv (1958) pp. 420–3: "Such a mixture of out-of-date structuralism with misunderstood linguistic geography, distorted and falsified by idealistic philosophy, can only confirm the suspicions of those conservatives (unfortunately still in the majority in the Romance field) who consider structural analysis a valueless addition to an already perfected discipline."

vocalic changes appear to be, for Weinrich, with the Vulgar Latin change from a quantitative to a qualitative system; and, for Lüdtke, with change in the accentuation system.[1]

The most recent Romance work along lines initiated by Martinet (though perhaps not necessarily to the master's tastes) is also about early vocalic changes, by Luigi Romeo, *The Economy of Diphthongization in Early Romance* (1968).[2]

After a brief survey of earlier views on Romance diphthongization and on phonetic aspects of diphthongs, Romeo proceeds to **L. Romeo** construct a theoretical model, based on a 'master phonemic diagram'. He then sketchily matches Romance data against his model, contrasting Early Romance six-vowel (3-degree) systems—where diphthongization did not take place—and eight-vowel systems (4-degree)—where diphthongization of mid-vowels is conditioned by the inter-play of narrower zones of possible allophonic variation within the systems, so that the incorporation of Latin AU into the system tends to exert more pressure. Romeo concludes (p. 108): "Paradigmatic diphthongization, as a phonic change, is primarily due to *internal* factors operating on the system throughout Roumania [*sic*, but surely *Romania* is meant[3]], and not to *external* factors, such as substratum, adstratum, chronological differences, or geographical boundaries." By the same token, Romeo rejects the Wartburgian cleavage between East and West Romania, arguing that Early Daco-Rumanian knew extensive paradigmatic diphthongization.

I cannot help but feel that a 'realist' like Martinet might shrink from the extremism of a Romeo, who follows the current American fashion for abstraction and scorns obsession with data. However, Romeo undoubtedly treads the Prague path, even if into a dead end.

In general, I hope to have shown the importance of Prague-type thought, both in Romance and General Linguistics today, and therefore plead justification for the length of this section.

[1] Cf. the comparison of the two works by N. C. W. Spence in "Quantity and quality in the vowel system of Vulgar Latin", *Wd* xxi (1965) pp. 1–18.

[2] An almost unaltered 1960 doctoral thesis at the University of Washington, of which the most substantial section was published in *Wd* xix (1963) pp. 1–19, as "Structural Pressures and Paradigmatic Diphthongization in East Romance": cf. R. Posner, "Rumanian and Romance Phonology", *RPh* xix (1966) pp. 450–9. Romeo refers extensively to E. Dorfman's unpublished lectures at Seattle but the only published work by Dorfman that he quotes is the bibliography (prepared jointly with S. Lampach) of Martinet's writings, in A. Martinet 1957–62 (fest.).

[3] Romeo earlier makes a point of distinguishing the country, Rumania (as 'Roumania') from the Romance area (as 'Romania').

8. Guillaumians

It can only be with fear and trembling that one of the uninitiated dares to attempt a summary of the ideas of Gustave Guillaume (1883–1960). Most commentators pass swiftly over **Gustave Guillaume** his work, with either a sneer or puzzled admiration: reviewers (especially in America) often display irritation at being forced to rack their brains over what may well appear pretentious nonsense. And yet Guillaume's disciples are loyal and fierce in his defence: indeed much of the linguistic work on French of the last few decades has been written under his influence;[1] so much so that we sometimes hear talk of a Guillaumian 'cult'. It has been claimed that only those who were privileged to attend assiduously Guillaume's lectures at the Paris Ecole des Hautes Etudes in the period 1938–60 could hope adequately to penetrate his thought. True, his authoritative writings are few and, until recently,[2] were fairly inaccessible: however it appears that today a 'second generation' of Guillaumians who never heard the master[3] is appearing, so we certainly cannot afford to neglect such a potent influence within the field of Romance linguistics.

As may already have been gathered, Guillaume's linguistic theories are extremely difficult to understand—partly because of the abstraction of his thought[4] and the abstruseness of his terminology, but also because his preoccupations are so different from those of other linguistic schools. The result is that anyone working in other linguistic spheres will find that each time he approaches a Guillaumian work, he has to start again at the beginning, trying to reconstruct anew the fundamentals of the Guillaumian theory. Small wonder then that many linguists prefer to ignore Guillaumian

[1] Cf. in particular G. Moignet's "Bibliographie des travaux de linguistique française d'inspiration guillaumienne", in Ls vii (1967) pp. 101–4. Guillaume's three book-length works were published in 1919, 1929, and 1945.

[2] A posthumous collection of articles, some of which were previously unpublished, appeared under the title Langage et Science du Langage (G. Guillaume 1962). In his introduction (p. 20) R. Valin mentions the voluminous lecture-notes Guillaume left, but no one has yet done, for Guillaume, what Bally and Sechehaye performed for Saussure in publishing their own version of his lectures.

[3] R. Martin's thesis, Le mot 'rien' et ses concurrents en français (du XIVe s. à l'époque contemporaine) (1966) is unmistakably Guillaumian, and A. Jacob in his thesis Temps et langage (1967) does not disguise his admiration for 'chronogenetic' theory.

[4] Guillaume's own master, Meillet, is reported to have claimed that Guillaume was too clever to be appreciated by the linguists of his day. Certainly, he met with little recognition until fairly late in life and always encountered hostility. His own ill-health, which prevented him from frequenting conferences and so on, may have helped to confine his influence mainly to his pupils.

works altogether (with some grave consequences for the progress of French linguistics). Commentaries on the master's theories are, however, not lacking: Professor Roch Valin of Laval University, Quebec, is their most indefatigable popularizer,[1] but an authoritative comparison of Guillaume's work with that of other linguists has still to be written.

Guillaume derives his approach from Saussure, but places virtually no emphasis on the *social* aspects of language, being more
Guillaume and Saussure concerned with man's attitude to the Universe and how language helps him to master the amorphous mass of experience. Thus he is interested primarily in the processes that precede articulate expression—with, in Hjelmslevian terms, 'content-form'—and how this form is carved out of outside experience. The structure (*langue*) that results from this struggle of thought with disorganized substance is a 'psycho-system', and its study is 'psychosystématique' or 'psychomécanique du langage'. *Discours* (the term Guillaume substitutes for Saussure's *parole*) is a momentaneous realization of the potentialities that exist in *langue* (often entailing some selection of virtual features), and the *acte de langage* is the activity that connects the two (a *cinétisme* between two *statismes*). *Langue* is consequently an arcane, abstract entity, which cannot be observed directly: it is not, however, merely the linguist's organization of the facts observed in *discours*—it is presumed to be anterior to *discours*, as individuals do not invent language anew at each utterance. Thus it must be a set of habits developed by the linguistic community in its confrontation with the universe.

The Saussurean dichotomy of diachrony/synchrony loses much of its force in this context: for although *langue* is a *statisme*, any actualization is always a unique event involving a dynamic act: 'changes' can result from different virtualities being realized in different situations. Thus Guillaumian studies (concerned almost wholly with the semantic content of grammatical classes) use both diachronic and synchronic evidence to construct psychosystematic models.

The Saussurean *signifié/signifiant* dichotomy is accepted by Guillaume, though it would appear that for him *signifiant* represents more

---

[1] The *Cahiers de Linguistique Structurale* (*CaLS*) published by the Presses Universitaires Laval, are a series of Guillaumian monographs. Most important is R. Valin 1955, his own account of Guillaume's position. *Ls* vii (1967) includes two articles surveying Guillaumian work: J. Stéfanini, "Approche du Guillaumisme", pp. 74–92; and M. Toussaint, "Gustave Guillaume et L'Actualité Linguistique", pp. 93–100, which links Guillaume's thought with that of Chomsky. Cf. also H. Bonnard, "Guillaume, il y a vingt ans", in *LaF* ("La syntaxe") i (1969) pp. 21–35.

the relationship between the *signe* and the *signifié* than the more positive 'expression-form' implied in Saussure. For Guillaume, only the *signifié* is worthy of study (indeed the 'system' *can* have no *signifiant*). However, he does believe that some expression patterns can hint at a hidden form pattern. Indeed, his whole procedure, scorning positivist data-obsession, depends on intuitional perception of structure via clues—*faits révélateurs*—to be discerned in *signes* themselves. Thus, for instance, in his discussion of auxiliary verbs,[1] he claims that certain verbs have a particular 'vocation' for the auxiliary role, by virtue of their semantic *subductivité*:

ils descendent dans la pensée au-dessous des autres verbes, auxquels ils apparaissent idéellement préexistants . . . La subductivité est au maximum dans les verbes exprimant les idées fondamentales de genèse, d'existence, de possession (aperçue dans sa corrélation la plus étroite avec l'idée d'existence) et elle avoisine ce maximum, ou du moins s'en écarte peu, dans les verbes exprimant, sous une interprétation fort subtile, la puissance, la volition, l'aptitude, l'accession, l'adhésion, la préhension, etc. etc.

Marks of this *subductivité* may well appear, even though sporadically, in the expression—thus, in French, these verbs use a subjunctive form in the imperative (*aie, sois, veuille, sache*). Guillaume goes on to underline a major procedural principle:

Les menus faits de ce genre, nombreux dans toutes les langues, et d'apparence fort diverse, ont une haute valeur d'indice et méritent à ce titre plus d'attention qu'on ne leur en accorde d'ordinaire. Scrutés avec rigueur, ils révèlent dans maints cas des procès psychiques secrets, d'une importance extrême dans la construction des langues.

Much of the irritation that Guillaume provokes is connected with his contempt for data[2] coupled with his reliance on odd clues which trigger off his intuition. Often his conclusions will appear arbitrary and unsound, if rather clever-clever. Yet none can fail to be impressed by his flashes of insight, buried though they often are in his spatial diagrammaticization and abstruse terminology.

His first published work[3]—his doctoral thesis on the article (1919)—is more easily stomached by other linguists by virtue of its greater concern with linguistic data; it already **The definite article** reveals the basic elements of his thought, even though he virtually renounced the work later in life. In it he shows his preoccupation with the search for a semantic

---

[1] "Théorie des auxiliaires et examen des faits connexes", (*BSLP* 1938), reprinted in G. Guillaume 1962 pp. 73–86.

[2] G. Guillaume 1945 contains no examples.

[3] Cf. G. Guillaume 1919; also Gabriel Guillaume, "Echos d'un message linguistique: œuvres et leçons de Gustave Guillaume", *RLiR* xxix (1965) pp. 295–313.

constant in a grammatical class: when the class is semantically so amorphous and inconsistent as the Romance article the search must obviously be conducted at a high level of abstraction.

Guillaume sees the rôle of the article as limiting in *discours* the extension of the noun which has a wide virtual extension in *langue*:

> Le fait que l'article est senti moins nécessaire lorsque la différence entre le nom dans la langue et le nom dans le discours devient petite [e.g. when the noun is a proper name and therefore has a similar extension in *langue* and *discours*], est de nature à suggérer l'idée que l'article exprime cette différence (p. 21).

Already we can perceive Guillaume's tendency to spatializing analogy, conceiving of *discours* as effecting momentary *saisies* along the line of *langue*. The idea, too, of an oscillating movement between universal and particular, which was to be such a recurrent feature in Guillaume's thought, is also present—though not developed to the extent that we find later in the 1944 article "Particularisation et généralisation dans le système des articles français":[1]

> L'article *un*, porteur d'un mouvement se développant de l'universel au singulier, est la projection dans l'abstrait de la puissance que possède l'esprit de particulariser. Au terme de sa course, l'article *un*, qui déclare là sa valeur essentielle (finale), est un article de particularisation. L'article *le*, porteur d'un mouvement se développant, à l'inverse, du singulier à l'universel, est la projection dans l'abstrait de la puissance que l'esprit possède de généraliser. Au terme de sa course, l'article *le* qui, de même que l'article *un*, déclare là sa valeur essentielle (finale), est un article de généralisation.
>
> L'image que les deux articles suscitent du mouvement dont ils sont chacun porteurs est dans la langue celle d'un *entier* saisi en puissance, avant réalisation: c'est-à-dire avant dépense aucune du mouvement virtuellement évoqué. A cet état d'entier virtuel, le discours, qui survient ensuite, substitue celui de partie effective plus ou moins distante, par son degré de réalisation, de l'état d'entier virtuel dépassé.

The idea of movement between general and particular along a time–space axis is symbolized in Guillaume's ubiquitous diagram which represents the form taken by the *acte de langage*. The dotted

[1] *FM* 1944, reprinted in G. Guillaume 1962 pp. 143–56.

line marked X̄ marks the threshold of the passage from *langue* to *discours*. A dialectic swinging back and forth between infinity and zero is for Guillaume an essential feature of man's grasp of reality. That this process takes place linearly in time also appears to be essential to Guillaume's theory. His 'chronogenetic' approach was not, however, explicit in his doctoral thesis; it was only in *Temps et Verbe*[1] (1929) that some of his most idiosyncratic ideas were first formulated. For those readers who are inclined to ask, with W. G. Moulton,[2] "How did he [Guillaume] ever arrive at his systematic analysis in the first place?", Roch Valin's anecdote,[3] relating to Guillaume's experience in 1927, might be enlightening:

"Temps et Verbe"

> Depuis des années—porté en cela par le pressentiment que la catégorie grammaticale du verbe recélait en elle des secrets dont la pénétration permettrait de faire un pas important dans la connaissance de la nature du langage—M. Guillaume réfléchissait à ce que pouvait bien être dans la pensée un système verbal. Or un jour que, dans la rue, il méditait sur ce problème, voilà qu'un emploi singulier et en apparence aberrant des modes indicatif et subjonctif le frappe. L'exemple était celui-là même qui figure, page 49, dans *Temps et Verbe:*

> 'Si vous le faites et QU'il s'ensuive un accident, on vous en tiendra rigueur'.

> D'où vient, se demanda M. Guillaume, que, dans cette phrase et dans beaucoup d'autres semblables, la substitution de QUE à SI suffise à susciter l'apparition du subjonctif et qu'en tout état de cause le syntagme *que + subjonctif* s'équipolle, pour ce qui est du sens, au syntagme *si + indicatif*? Et soudain la lumière se fit dans son esprit: il comprit d'un coup que la fonction ordinaire de *si* étant—quel que soit le mode du verbe—de *supposer* 'existence des choses et celle de *que*, accompagné de l'indicatif, de *poser* les choses dans l'existence, le passage de l'indicatif au subjonctif avait pour effet de ramener le procès dans le champ de l'hypothèse et par conséquent s'accompagnait d'une remontée de *l'actuel* au *virtuel*, ce qui impliquait qu'en pensée le mode subjonctif occupait une position antérieure à celle occupée par l'indicatif et qu'à côté de la chronologie d'époque (passé, présent, futur) il existe une chronologie modale au sein de laquelle le subjonctif est vu comme un *avant*, un *passé* de l'indicatif. En d'autres termes, ce dont M. Guillaume eut alors l'intuition, c'est que la réalité mentale recouverte par le mot *si* est à celle que recouvre le mot *que* ce que, sous un certain rapport, la réalité mentale recouverte par le subjonctif est à celle que recouvre l'indicatif, et que ce certain rapport, c'est celui du virtuel à

[1] Cf. also H. G. Schogt, "*Temps et Verbe* de Gustave Guillaume trente-cinq ans après sa parution", *LaL* 1965, 1 pp. 55–74.

[2] In *RPh* xi (1957) p. 47.

[3] Cf. G. Guillaume 1962 pp. 12–13.

l'actuel, lequel est à son tour reductible au rapport ultime—mécanique—
d'un *avant* et d'un *après*.

This spatio-temporal model ('before-after') of the mental process
of representation of reality is often called *linguistique de position*,
perhaps because it assigns relative positions along the linear time
axis to different forms. Central to Guillaume's thought is the idea
that the process itself takes time (however infinitesimal)—le *temps
opératif*—and that different images of external reality will result from
interception at different points in the *temps opératif*. In the case of
the French verb system, interruption at an early point along the
horizontal axis will yield quasi-nominal, non-temporal forms like the
infinitive and participles (representing *temps in posse*); further along,
we find the *temps in fieri* of the subjunctive with a stunted tense
coverage; while at the furthest extreme, the indicative, the truly
temporal mood (*temps in esse*), is to be found. The tense system itself
is oriented round the present indicative with past and future on a
horizontal axis, while, in French, a vertical axis ranges between
incident (indicating *accomplissement* of an event, a point on the line of
time) and *décadent* referring to an event which is already partly
accompli and which therefore lies above, or along, the line of time).
Here again, we can perceive formal clues to the underlying system:
so that the *décadent* in both past (*imparfait*) and future (*conditionnel*)
share endings in *-ais, -ait, -aient*, while the *incident* counterparts
(*passé simple* and *futur*) have *-ai, -as, -a* in common. It is presumably
irrelevant to object that these formal parallels are not carried right
through the paradigms (e.g. *-âmes, -èrent* vs. *-ons, -ont*), as we are
concerned only with *faits révélateurs*, and not with systematic study
of forms.

After *Temps et Verbe* Guillaume's work became more and more
theoretical, often reworking the same themes (tense systems in
particular) at a more and more abstract level. It was
Guillaume's influence principally through his lectures, from 1938 on, that
he exercised his influence—outstanding among his
followers is to be noted G. Moignet,[1] but there are others who are
less extreme in their loyalty to Guillaumian methods but who
nevertheless do have some of the same preoccupations (though

---

[1] Cf. esp. G. Moignet 1959, 1961, 1965; "La forme en RE(T) dans le système
verbal du plus ancien français", *RLaR* lxxiii (1958-59) pp. 1-65; "La suppléance
du verbe en français", *FM* xxviii (1960) pp. 13-24 and 107-24. "L'opposition
NON/NE en ancien français", *TLLS* iii (1966) pp. 45-66; "Esquisse d'une théorie
psychomécanique de la phrase interrogative", *Ls* iii (1966) pp. 49-66.

tempered by traditionalist common-sense)—like P. Imbs and R-L. Wagner.[1]

Most Guillaumians work exclusively on French: a special place should be reserved here for the Romanist Bernard Pottier who is far

Bernard Pottier

from a party-line Guillaumian (he is "contre l'esprit de chapelle" as he himself puts it) but who undoubtedly shows all the marks of Guillaume's influence. Born in 1924, Pottier's initial training was in Spanish and phonetics, and he has worked in the Hispanic field throughout his career.[2] His teachers included Guillaume, Martinet, R-L. Wagner and P. Fouché, so that his Guillaumian tendencies were always tempered by other influences. His doctoral thesis (1955),[3] *Systématique des éléments de rélation. Etude de morphosyntaxe structurale romane*, is largely theoretical in orientation, with illustrations mainly from French, but including also comparative Latin and Romance data. In it, Pottier reviews (though somewhat perfunctorily) other linguistic schools, with a particular aggressivity towards American structuralism (to which he refuses the structuralist title, preferring to call it 'fonctionaliste'). His main bugbear is the 'commutation' method of identifying and classifying grammatical units, preferring, as he does, semantic criteria. Like Guillaume he believes that the study of concrete speech acts is anti-scientific, and he seeks the secret reality hidden beneath the surface. Moreover he feels that the American desire for simplicity and exhaustiveness in analysis tends to mask the complex 'tendencies' of linguistic reality: speaking, for instance, of the morphophonological description of gender variation in French adjectives he says:

> Pour la simplicité de la description, quelques linguistes considèrent l'adjectif français sous sa forme féminine, et en tirent le masculin par suppression de la consonne finale: [plat]→[pla], [grãd]→[grã]. La description se trouve énormément simplifiée, mais le mécanisme de l'opposition de genre en langue est détruit (p. 88).

[1] Although not a Guillaumian in any sense, deriving more from traditions represented by Brunot and Damourette and Pichon (cf. *Iordan–Orr* p. 338) we should also mention the 'psychological' grammar of G. Galichet (esp. 1967).

[2] Cf. B. Pottier 1947, 1957–1958, 1968 and forthcoming, and numerous articles (B. Pottier 1968 is a collection of 23 articles). For a complete bibliography of Pottier's work up to 1964, cf. *Centre de Philologie et de Littératures Romanes (Université de Strasbourg), Brochure-Programme*, Fasc. 9 (1964). In more recent years we note his work on Spanish lexicology including B. Pottier 1966 and "Le développement du vocabulaire des chemins de fer", in J. Sarrailh 1966 (mem.) pp. 261–3.

[3] B. Pottier 1962b. Cf. the review by R. Posner in *JLi* i (1965) pp. 76–82.

Like Guillaume, too, Pottier attempts to discover the system of 'values' (in the Saussurean sense) of elements of *langue*: the *valeur essentielle*, or *représentation*, of such an element covers all possible values it may have in discourse. He is quick, however, to disassociate himself from the 'traditionalist' quest for general meaning in linguistic elements, trying rather to define the distinctive features that characterize elements:

Nous partons à la recherche d'une représentation, d'un ensemble de traits pertinents différenciateurs, et non d'une signification de base, comme on le voit faire souvent (p. 126).

Pottier's ostensible object of study in his thesis are 'relational elements', which are to be distinguished from 'syntagmatic elements'
Relational elements —these latter are further subdivided into parts of speech on the basis of their 'incidence' ('incident' here = 'subordinate to, supporting'). Thus 'nouns' have substance incidental to itself; 'verbs' are incident to the person of the noun; 'adjectives' are incident to the noun (traditional adjective) or to the verb (traditional adverb), while 'adverbs' are incident to the incidence of adjective to noun (traditional fortifying adverb, e.g. "le chat *très* blanc"). Other traditional parts of speech may be 'syntactic variants' (e.g. the traditional pronoun which can replace a noun) or 'lexical substitutes' (in which one item replaces an 'analytic construction', as when *ici* is used in the same context as *à cet endroit-ci*). Substitution and variance are types of grammaticalization—replacement of *mots à lexème* by *mots sans lexème* (where a *lexème* is a member of an open-ended morpheme class distinct from the closed grammatical corpus of *formants*). The grammaticalization process is described in Guillaumian terms,[1] with reference to the notion of oscillatory movement of thought between universal and particular, abstract and concrete. As the neutral position—*lieu-zéro* or *temps-zéro*—is approached a grammatical element (e.g. *ici*) replaces a lexical element (e.g. *Paris*).

The general category of *formants* includes those (*flexifs*) which do not fall into Pottier's chosen class of relational elements. *Flexifs* include 'categorizers' which assign lexemes to a syntactic class, and 'agreement formants', which show the relationships between words in a syntagm. Prefixes, infixes and suffixes occupy more of Pottier's attention: unlike lexemes they have no predicative substance

---

[1] Cf. Guillaume's "Comment se fait un système grammatical", lecture at l'Institut de Linguistique de l'Université de Paris, 1939, reprinted in G. Guillaume 1962 pp. 108–19.

("*apport* de substance sémantique") but they have 'substance sémantique réelle' which modifies the predicative substance of the lexeme. These affixes are 'éléments de relation', where *relation* refers to "la prise de position exprimée par un élément relativement à la substance prédicative d'un ou plusieurs lexèmes" (p. 113), and not to syntagmatic relationship. Other members of the 'relational' category include articles, quantitatives, prepositions, conjunctions, comparative and superlative morphemes and case-endings: however different their syntactic use, we are urged to accept that they have similar psychological functions—"idéation notionnelle modificatrice" (p. 112). This description of their function echoes Guillaume's own words:

> Les petits mots grammaticaux du langage, et plus généralement les éléments formateurs particulaires du langage, sont universellement de puissants collecteurs, condenseurs et réducteurs d'impressions.[1]

The 'modification' contributed by any element is described by Pottier in Guillaumian spatio-temporal terms, where the model

$$(O) \longrightarrow (P)$$

showing a notion which "se développe à partir d'une origine (O) jusqu' à un point correspondant à la plénitude de substance, que nous désignerons par (P)" (p. 134), can incorporate an interception, representing a displacement of the *point de saisie*. Thus *peu* in *peu aimable* prevents *aimable* from attaining its full notional substance:

(O) peu aimable (P)   (O) aimable (P)

Similarly, different co-ordinating conjunctions represent different *points de saisie* on the familiar Guillaumian schema (p. 146).

Tension I   Tension II

∞ et   ou   ......O mais   ou   et   ∞

[1] G. Guillaume 1962 p. 43.

By the use of such reasoning, Pottier is able to 'explain' some otherwise puzzling facts. For instance, in discussing the "relation de soustraction" expressed by *mais* (pp. 142–3), he wonders why it can be used between verbs and adjectives:

> Pierre dort bien mais se couche tard;
> Pierre est aimable mais coléreux:

but not between nouns except when one term is negative:

> Je te donne non le livre mais le cahier.

This limitation, we learn, is due to the fact that the noun represents a *vision discontinue* (on the schema, Tension I, in which experience is enclosed within definite bounds, and from which a part cannot be subtracted), whereas verbal or adjectival form expresses an unbounded *vision continue* (Tension II) which allows 'more-or-less' representation.

Throughout Pottier represents the *valeur* of his chosen elements in spatial diagrams which, like Guillaume, he considers reflect linguistic reality. In, for instance, his discussion of *devant* and *avant* (pp. 227–8) he compares "Pierre est *devant* Jean" with "Pierre est *avant* Jean"

o ➡ O ➡ ESPACE   o ⬅ O ⬅ TEMPS

Jean   Pierre   Jean   Pierre

and argues for the *reality* of the directional movement of his arrows:

> Ces deux movements *sont inverses*. Le temps s'écoule continuellement; l'espace est à conquérir. Ce n'est pas de la philosophie, mais de la constatation banale qui ne peut laisser la langue indifférente.

Sometimes even Pottier admits himself baffled by his data: thus in discussing *par* and *pour* (p. 221), he confesses:

> Le groupe formé par *par* et *pour* est celui qui est le plus instable dans le français actuel. Les positions ne sont pas nettement fixées et nous sommes en ce moment à une mauvaise période de l'évolution de ce petit système pour l'étudier.

Although he suggests that *par* represents a completed movement between two limits:

O ➡ •

while *pour* never reaches the limit aimed at:

O ➡

he detects some contamination of the two, which leads to homonymy of *pour ce que* and *par ce que* (p. 225).

However difficult it may be to follow, Pottier's thesis certainly casts light, even though interspersed with shadows, on some sticky problems of Romance morphosyntax. We must, as Romanists, regret that more recently comparative little of his time has been given over to specifically Romance linguistics. After his move from Bordeaux to Strasbourg in 1958, Pottier's interests **Machine translation** began to centre around mechanical translation, being a member of the M.T. study group based at Nancy from 1960 on. In connection with this work, he was concerned with the formal analysis of French sentences,[1] but also developed further his interest in semantics. At the same time, Pottier pursued the study of American-Indian languages, as illustrative of general linguistic principles.[2] Since 1964, when he took up his chair at Nanterre, Pottier has been occupied more and more with **Linguistic theory** linguistic theory. His writings are often so laconic and condensed, presenting his schemata with note-like economy,[3] that it is sometimes difficult to discern his basic preoccupations. What is evident is that he is still loyal to a fundamentally Guillaumian approach, opposing uniquely formal analysis, and searching for the *valeur essentielle* of the linguistic element:[4]

El niño sólo oye *combinaciones de lexemas*. Intuitivamente sabe entresacar del montón de ejemplos los rasgos estables, permanentes, con que va constituyendo *su* contenido semántico fundamental para cada lexema. Este es el método que aplicamos: pasar de la infinitud de las realizaciones del discurso a la finitud relativa a las *virtualidades* en la lengua.[5]

In face of recent trends in linguistics Pottier feels his own approach, so firmly linked with semantics, has been vindicated:

Ce retour aux théories de XVIIe et XVIIIe siècles peut paraître surprenant, mais il est né d'une réaction devant les abus d'un fonctionalisme

[1] Cf. B. Pottier 1962, the most important product of his M.T. work.

[2] Cf. in particular B. Pottier (forthcoming) *b*.

[3] B. Pottier 1967*b* is a good example. Pottier claims that it is a mere "charpente d'un travail plus fouillé": in fact all but Chapter 2, "Une langue", is passed over with the utmost rapidity. Even Chapter 2 is little more than a catalogue of definitions within a framework of theory that may appear arbitrary to some. True, it is breathtakingly clear, but without more flesh to cover the bones of this skeletal treatise the uninitiated must hesitate to pass judgement on its merits.

[4] Cf. e.g. "Remarques sur les limites de l'analyse formelle", in A. Martinet 1957–62 (fest.) iii, pp. 167–70; and "Sémantique et syntaxe", in P. Gardette 1966 (fest.) pp. 399–401.

[5] "La semántica y los criterios functionales", *Actas 1 Cong. Int. Hisp. 1962* pp. 415–20.

étroit, pour qui une description (parmi d'autres) est le but de la linguistique. Dans leurs *intentions*, Harris et Chomsky ne sont pas tellement éloignés des essais de G. Guillaume à la recherche des mécanismes (sémantiques) généraux sous-tendant l'infinité des réalisations de discours. Mais la démarche est très différente. . . . La linguistique descriptive 'pure' s'épuise, tourne en rond. L'inventaire des comportements des formes est utile préalable à toute interprétation, mais reste au seuil de la science. La linguistique, discipline éminemment expérimentale, demande des hypothèses. Après avoir décrit on veut *expliquer* les fonctionnements.

A l'heure actuelle, les recherches interdisciplinaires, montrent tout le parti qu'on peut tirer d'une ouverture de la linguistique sur les autres science (humaines ou non), et du bienfait des échanges de méthodes et de perspectives. Si l'on revient à la sémantique, et à la langue-en-situation, c'est que la raison, le bon-sens ont repris le dessus. Le structuralisme traditionnel est dépassé. Il a été salutaire pour l'histoire de la discipline. Mais après les périodes réactionnaires outrées, viennent les mouvements de synthèse: c'est la *linguistique ouverte* actuelle, ouverte sur toutes les sources d'information susceptibles d'éclairer le phénomène du langage.[1]

9. *'American' or Bloomfieldian linguistics*

In the 'forties and 'fifties probably the most powerful and influential linguistic group was centred in the United States. It is common to hear these scholars referred to as the 'American School of Descriptive Linguistics'; though by no means all American linguists share the attitudes of the 'School', it is fair to say that they are almost exclusive to American-trained linguists who owed comparatively little to European theorists.[2] Some would claim that the title

---

[1] Cf. "Au delà du structuralisme en linguistique", *Critique* (February 1967), pp. 271 and 273-4. Although Pottier recognizes (private communication) "les torts des Guillaumistes . . .: chapelle, terminologie inutilement prétentieuse, intolérance", he still feels that Guillaumian theory has much to offer: "Guillaume et Chomsky se préoccupent de la langue: le dernier est loin d'avoir apporté autant! Il est curieux de voir que des foules s'enthousiasment pour des règles transformationnelles gratuites, et répugnent à concevoir un schème aussi simple que

un ⸺⟶ le ⸺⟶ ."

[2] It is sometimes maintained that the American structuralist tradition was completely independent of similar developments in Europe; it has even been thought that its proponents knew nothing of Saussure's work. Joos's comment (M. Joos 1957 (1966) p. 18) is worth quoting here: "At least half of these authors had read the *Cours*. The others got it second-hand: in an atmosphere so saturated

'American School' is little more than a geographic designation, so heterogeneous are the views of its members: however, in retrospect, after the waning of its influence, the 'Americans' do appear to share features that distinguish them from other linguistic schools of thought. It is interesting, in this connection, to compare the comments of Martin Joos in his prefaces to respectively the 1957 and 1966 editions of a collection of *Readings in Linguistics*[1] which was, unwittingly perhaps, to become the classic representative work of the school. In 1957 he wrote:

> Both Americans and Europeans are likely on each side to consider the other side both irresponsible and arrogant. We may request the Europeans to try to regard the American style as a tradition *comme une autre*, but the Americans can't be expected to reciprocate; they are having too much fun to be bothered, and few of them are aware that either side has a tradition.

In 1966 (when the volume was complemented by another covering European linguistic writings) the tone is quite different:

> In 1957 a great deal was taken for granted in American linguistics which has been called into question since. The book was first prepared simply because too much was being taken for granted. The tradition which these papers define was three decades old and still growing as rapidly as ever. Hardly anyone who counted on the American linguistic scene seemed to be outside this tradition . . . Both for intrinsic and extrinsic reasons, the development of this tradition in descriptive linguistics happened to slacken just at the time when the volume first appeared.

The 'intrinsic reasons' he suggests, are that certain features of language are not readily incorporated into the methodological framework adopted; the 'extrinsic reasons' were concerned with desertion by younger professional linguists of 'taxonomic'[2] methods for transformational-generative (Chomskyan) grammar.

with those ideas, it has been impossible to escape that. The difference is hard to detect, and it is generally unsafe to accuse a contemporary linguist of not having read the *Cours*, as had happened to me." Nevertheless, American structuralists cannot deny that there was an element of anti-European sentiment in their attitude. We may quote in this respect a comment by R. A. Hall, Jr. in *NMi* lxx (1969) pp. 192–227: "The strong anti-European feeling of many American linguists in the 1930's and 1940's had its main roots in often-times bitter personal experiences. Not a few young Americans saw, and frequently more than once, positions (for which they had been trained and were eminently qualified) snatched from under their noses and given to European refugees. Such a reaction, though by no means generous, was easily understandable in the days of the depression when any job at all was hard to come by, especially since American scholars, then as now, were not protected by citizenship-requirements of the kind prevailing in virtually all European university-systems. A frequent remark heard from our 'Group 1' was 'We'll show those Europeans we have something they never dreamed of!'".

[1] M. Joos 1957. Its fourth edition, from which I normally quote, was published in 1966, accompanied by a second volume, E. P. Hamp *et al.* (eds.) 1966.

[2] The 'American' school is unashamedly 'classificatory'—concerned first with

'American' linguistics is often called 'Bloomfieldian' (or, frequently in a pejorative context, 'neo-Bloomfieldian'), looking to
Leonard Bloomfield (1887–1949)[1] as its leader.

Leonard Bloomfield The classic handbook of the school was Bloomfield's
Language (1933), and the foundation of the Linguistic
Society of America and its mouthpiece the journal *Language* (1925
ff.) owed much to his powerful influence. Yet he himself always
disclaimed any attempt to form a 'school',[2] and indeed, by all
accounts, was a somewhat indifferent public teacher and lecturer,
exerting his influence mainly via the written word (though his
quiet, undramatic exactitude was effective in teaching small
groups).

Before 'Bloomfieldianism', however, certain distinctive traits of
American linguistics had already emerged. Interest in linguistic
structure grew mainly within the realm of social anthropology,
stimulated by the challenge presented by the multitude of 'native
American' (Indian) languages. The *International Journal of American
Linguistics*, concerned almost exclusively with American Indian
languages, was founded by the anthropologist and self-taught
linguist Franz Boas (1858–1942), who inspired Edward Sapir
(1884–1939) to widen his linguistic horizons beyond

Edward Sapir his original chosen domain of the Germanic languages. Sapir's talents and personality were such
that he exerted great influence on all who came into contact with
him, even though his one full-length book, *Language* (1921),[3]
dictated in a mere two months, is far from a technical manual like
Bloomfield's work of the same name. What it does do is to provide
stimulating insights into the structure and patterning of language
and its relationship with society and 'culture' (in the anthropological
sense). However, as R. A. Hall, Jr., puts it:[4]

> Sapir seems to have been, like Leonardo da Vinci, averse to the painstak-
> ing work of elaboration, to the *labor limae* necessary to put his conceptions

analysing out units and grouping them into classes. The term 'taxonomic' is
nowadays often used in linguistics, as in other sciences, as a derogatory term,
implying a low-level concern with mere juggling about of elements, rather than an
interest in 'explanation'. Needless to say, such an implication is a caricature of
most Bloomfieldians' point of view!

[1] Cf. especially B. Bloch's important obituary of Bloomfield in *L* xxv (1949) pp.
87–98, reprinted in T. A. Sebeok (ed.) 1966*b* pp. 508–18. Also R. A. Hall, Jr.'s,
obituary of Bloomfield in *Li* ii (1950) pp. 117–23.

[2] Cf. especially *L* xxii (1946) p. 23.

[3] Cf. also his Selected Writings (D. G. Mandelbaum (ed.) 1949). An obituary of
Sapir by C. F. Voegelin is reprinted in T. A. Sebeok (ed.) 1966*b* pp. 489–92.

[4] *ArL* iii (1951) p. 108.

into definite shape; as a result, his influence on following generations of American linguistics has been far less than that exercised by Leonard Bloomfield whose work was more systematic and afforded better methodological training.

Good commentaries on Bloomfieldian work abound[1] so perhaps it is otiose here to go over the same ground again, especially as so little of such work is applied to the Romance languages.[2] I beg the reader's indulgence, however, while I attempt to pinpoint some of the ways in which Bloomfieldians differ from other modern linguists, before I discuss the work of Romanists within the Bloomfieldian tradition.

Perhaps the most salient characteristic of the tradition is its insistence on the 'scientific' study of language, with an emphasis on empirical observation. As Bernard Bloch,[3] pointed out:

Linguistics as a science

There can be no doubt that Bloomfield's greatest contribution to the study of language was to make a science of it. Others before him had worked scientifically in linguistics, but no-one had so uncompromisingly rejected all prescientific methods, or had been so consistently careful, in writing about language, to use terms that would imply no tacit reliance on factors beyond the range of observation.

Rigorous rejection of all criteria and assumptions that were not wholly explicit became the key-note of Bloomfieldian linguistics, and its concentration on methodology and procedure was part of its attempt to break away from the woolliness of much traditional linguistic thought. Its slashing use of Occam's razor, cutting away all unnecessary hypotheses in a search for analytic simplicity and

[1] Probably the best recent survey is C. C. Fries's "The Bloomfield 'School'," in *Trends i* pp. 196–224; cf. also J. Dubois, "Grammaire distributionnelle", in *LaF* i (1969) pp. 41–8. B. Malmberg's chapter on "Modern American Linguistics", (B. Malmberg 1964 pp. 158–85) is to be recommended, but also covers non-Bloomfieldians. R. A. Hall, Jr., "American Linguistics 1925–1950", in *ArL* iii (1951) 101–25, iv (1952) 1–16, and "American Linguistics 1950–60", in *AION* vii (1965) pp. 241–60, are somewhat polemical in tone, but remain valuable surveys. A third article from his pen, "Some recent developments in American linguistics", an amplification of a lecture given in 1966, and mainly concerned with comparing Chomskyan thought with other American trends, appeared in *NMi* lxx (1969) pp. 192–227. Good student textbooks in the Bloomfieldian tradition include H. A. Gleason 1961, C. F. Hockett 1958 and A. A. Hill 1958.

[2] Bloomfield himself was a Germanist by training, but, like most of his followers, was mostly concerned with American Indian languages and English. It may be surprising to read in his 1946 survey of "21 years of the Linguistic Society", (*L* xxi–xxii pp. 1–3) that the leading topics occupying American linguists' attention during the period discussed were "comparative Indo-European grammar, the Romance languages and English", but I think it is fair to say that most of the work on Romance languages belonged to pre-Bloomfieldian traditions.

[3] *L* xxv (1949) p. 92.

elegance, appears to some to lead to a too *simpliste* rigidity. Its preoccupation with identification and classification procedures often seems arid: use of unfamiliar terminology can strike the uninitiated as pure mystification. However, it cannot be denied that the introduction into linguistic study of rigour and sober clear-thinking is largely the work of the Bloomfieldians.

Insistence on scientific descriptive statement, rejecting anecdote or 'chat', makes the written work of many Bloomfieldians particularly inaccessible to the layman: he may conclude that their austerity masks humourless unconcern with the more titillating linguistic realities. In fact many Bloomfieldians are strikingly witty in conversation and informal teaching: perhaps their comparative lack of influence outside the United States is connected with the unattractiveness of much of their written work for those who have been denied frequent personal contact with them! What is particularly repellent for generations insufficiently familiar with mathematics is the apparent reliance on quasi-mathematical techniques in analysis. Often readers fail to distinguish the form of the 'meta-language' (used to talk about language) from the content of the description, and fear that Bloomfieldians regard natural languages as in some way 'like mathematics'. Bloomfield himself, however, was quite clear about the relationship of mathematics and other sciences (including linguistic science):

Mathematics is not on a level with other sciences; it is in principle a part of every science; it is the technique of making statements in the speech-forms which elicit the most uniform response.[1]

With the insistence on the 'scientific' nature of linguistics came Bloomfield's rejection of 'mentalism' and 'metaphysics'. In *Language* he adopts a behaviourist approach to psychology, though it can be denied that his linguistic thought is in any way dependent on such an approach. What he and his disciples do insist on is strict attention to observable linguistic fact, with no reliance on vague and misleading 'intuition'. In the essentially mechanistic approach, the traditional use of 'meaning' as a criterion for linguistic analysis and description was especially criticized: so much so that horrified scholars in other traditions are often heard to exclaim that Bloomfield 'rejected meaning'. It would obviously be absurd to claim that language could exist without 'meaning something' and Bloomfield was

Anti-mentalism

[1] In "Linguistic Aspects of Science", *Philosophy of Science*, ii (1935) p. 512.

certainly not guilty of such absurdity. He did, however, insist that "meanings cannot be used for our definitions",[1] and that identification and classification of units should be carried out principally according to formal criteria, using meaning differentially (to identify units as the same or different), but not substantially. Some 'neo-Bloomfieldians' (like B. Bloch[2] and Z. S. Harris[3]), however, go further and attempt to simplify identification procedure so as to exclude meaning altogether, by relying completely on distributional criteria: in practice theirs is a fictional 'pseudo-procedure',[4] for they readily admit the utility (necessity?) of using meaning 'heuristically' or as a 'short-cut'.

Another aspect of the mechanism of Bloomfieldians is seen in their somewhat ambiguous attitude to linguistic 'structure'. Although

Structure

they are generally called 'structuralist', some European linguists would deny them that title. Certainly Bloomfieldians would reject the Saussurean concentration on *la langue*, at the expense of *la parole*, often claiming that the former is merely the linguist's abstraction from the data provided by the latter. Thus the 'structuralism' of Hjelmslev and Guillaume, as well as the teleological bias of the Prague School, would be regarded as 'metaphysical'. But Bloomfieldians differ in their estimation of the 'reality' of the 'abstractions' from the data:[5] some are 'God's truth' linguists, holding that the best analysis will indeed reflect reality, whereas some claim that it can only be a 'hocus-pocus' fiction. I remember myself being struck by a remark made by Bernard Bloch in conversation to the effect that however 'hocus-pocus' a linguist may airily claim to be, all have, in their secret hearts, to believe in 'God's truth', in order to go on with their work

---

[1] *L* vii (1931) p. 208 n.

[2] Cf. "A Set of Postulates for Phonemic Analysis" *L* xxiv (1948) pp. 5–6.

[3] Cf. Z. S. Harris 1951.

[4] Cf. on this D. Abercrombie, "Pseudo-procedures in linguistics", *ZP* xvi (1963) pp. 9–12.

[5] Bloomfield's own pronouncements appear grudgingly to incline towards 'God's truth'. Such a view might be thought to be implicit in such wary statements as this (*Journal of English and Germanic Philology* xxvi (1927) p. 444): "Our science can deal only with those features of language, de Saussure's *la langue*, which are common to all speakers of a community—the phonemes, grammatical categories, lexicon, and so on. These are abstractions, for they are only (recurrent) partial features of speech utterances. The infant is trained to these features so thoroughly that after earliest childhood the variabilities of human life no longer affect them. They form a rigid system, so rigid that without any adequate physiological information and with psychology in a state of chaos, we are nevertheless able to subject it to scientific treatment. A grammatical or lexical statement is at bottom an abstraction." On 'God's truth' vs. 'hocus-pocus', cf. especially R. A. Hall, Jr. 1964 p. 123.

at all. However, they may certainly continue to act as if the 'God's truth' did not exist!

In their attempt to establish linguistics as a science, Bloomfieldians insist on its autonomy, hence seeking severely to limit the scope of the discipline to exclude reliance on psychology, sociology, etc. As a reaction to the almost exclusively historically oriented linguistics of the 19th century, description of synchronic states is emphasized. The methodology of such description receives particular attention: Bloomfieldian 'theory' is almost wholly concerned with procedures. In particular, the sequence of procedures applied—first at the phonological level (given priority because it is more concrete and objectively more directly observable), then at the morphological, and so on—is often regarded as sacrosanct, so that 'mixing of levels' is frowned on.[1]

Linguistics as an autonomous discipline

When Bloomfieldians do concern themselves with historical problems, they largely espouse the 'regularist' and 'reconstructionist' views of the 19th-century predecessors, often applying the techniques derived therefrom to more 'exotic' language families,[2] and formulating the methods in terms of more abstract models.[3] Bloomfield himself describes the process of change in the mechanistic way familiar in neogrammarian works, that is difficult to reconcile completely with his acceptance of the findings of linguistic geography:[4]

Historical linguistics

Change in language does not reflect individual variability, but seems to be a massive, uniform, and gradual alteration, at every moment of which the system is just as rigid as at any other moment.

Some mention should be made of the 'applied' aspects of Bloomfieldian linguistics, though their importance may be due more to historical accident than to any intrinsic characteristic. During the second World War some drastic steps were necessary to remedy the neglect of language teaching that isolationism had brought to the United

Applied Linguistics

[1] Cf. K. L. Pike, "Grammatical Prerequisites to Phonemic Analysis", *Wd* iii (1947) pp. 155–72, and C. F. Hockett's criticism of Pike's views, "Two Fundamental Problems in Phonemics", *SIL* vii (1949) pp. 29–51.

[2] Cf. especially Bloomfield's own reconstruction of Proto-Algonquian in H. Hoijer (ed.) 1946 pp. 85–129, and C. F. Hockett, "Implications of Bloomfield's Algonquian Studies", *L* xxiv (1948) pp. 117–31. More recently M. R. Haas, "Historical Linguistics and the Genetic Relationship of Languages", in T. A. Sebeok (ed.) 1966a pp. 113–53.

[3] Cf. esp. H. Hoenigswald 1960.

[4] *Journal of English and Germanic Philology* xxvi (1927) pp. 444–5. Cf. also the chapter on "Dialect Geography", in L. Bloomfield 1933.

States: and an 'Intensive Language Programme' designed to cope with the problems of teaching of a great number of languages, both European and more 'exotic', was initiated in 1941, with the active co-operation of most American linguists, who also took part in the actual teaching of the Army Specialized Training Programme of 1943–44. Although many of the claims of outstanding success made about these programmes are probably exaggerated, their results were undoubtedly impressive, and helped in the dissemination of Bloomfieldian ideas among language teachers in general. The combination of insistence on *spoken* forms of language together with analysis and drilling of sentence patterns has had a lasting effect on language teaching, which has been further accentuated by the technological advances in tape-recording and so on.

I should mention, too, another aspect of the practical application of Bloomfieldian linguistics, prompted by the alleged inefficiency of the interwar American education system in teaching elementary reading and writing skills. Using phonemic theory, Bloomfield himself,[1] and others after him,[2] devised methods of teaching children to read: these methods have not, however, proved as popular as the foreign language teaching innovations mentioned above.

The number of talented linguists who adopted the 'Bloomfield style' is too great for me to wish to list them here: that the 'school' should have attracted so many brilliant minds to linguistics is in itself sufficient justification for its position in the history of linguistic thought. Special mention might be made of the 'deviationist'[3] trend represented by 'tagmemics', of which K. L. Pike[4] and E. A. Nida[5] are the most outstanding representatives: their concern with

Tagmemics the training of missionary field-workers (at the Summer Institute of Linguistics,[6] now a permanent institution with active branches in Africa as well as in the Americas), and with Bible translation, has led them to concentrate on the more practical side of linguistic description, while not neglecting theory completely.

---

[1] Cf. e.g. L. Bloomfield and C. L. Barnhart 1961.
[2] E.g. C. C. Fries 1963 and R. A. Hall, Jr. 1961b.
[3] Pike *et al.* are of course 'deviationist' only insofar as Bloch *et al.* are 'orthodox'.
[4] Cf. especially K. L. Pike 1947 and 1967.
[5] Cf. especially E. A. Nida 1943 and 1944.
[6] The Summer Institute dates from 1934: a by-product of its work has been the publication of a number of introductory manuals in linguistics. For a tagmemic study of a Romance language cf. R. M. Brend's study of Mexican Spanish (1968).

Bloomfieldians rarely concern themselves with the Romance languages, so taken up are they with the exciting vistas opened by the study of 'unknown' tongues. Only occasionally is a scholar versatile and energetic enough to range over both European and non-European languages with any degree of confidence:

Robert A. Hall, Jr. one such scholar, possessed with the gift of tongues, is Robert A. Hall, Jr., who is not only the leading 'Bloomfieldian' Romanist, but has also exercised his talents to great effect in other language domains.[1] Such a highly individualistic scholar is bound to object to the 'Bloomfieldian' label, but his 'style' is undoubtedly that of the 'classic' period of American linguistics.

Born in North Carolina in 1911 and graduating from Princeton in 1931, Hall was taught by Bloomfield, among others, at Chicago (1931–33 and 1935–36): nevertheless he admits (in private communication) that it took him some years "to realize that Bloomfield's view-point was not the 'crass materialism' it was caricatured as being". A study year in Rome during Fascism (1933–34) left him with the permanent distaste for Bertoni's 'idealist' linguistics that we have already discussed (pp. 451–5). After teaching in Puerto Rico (1937–39) Hall served at Princeton and Brown Universities successively during the war, when he worked, within the Language Programmes already described, on the analysis of Melanesian Pidgin,[2] the first of his studies on pidgins and creoles.[3] In 1946, he moved to his present home at Cornell University, where he has been a Professor of Linguistics since 1950.

Hall's abundant energy and meticulous attention to detail have produced, over and above his other scholarly works, invaluable bibliographies with which the student of Romance languages must necessarily be familiar.[4] He has also, amazingly, considering the cost in time and labour, written excellent elementary language text-books. His lively style and accuracy of thought and expression make his introductory works[5] thoroughly readable, even if their titles sometimes seem provocative.[6]

For Romanists, however, Hall is principally the leading (indeed

---

[1] Cf. especially R. A. Hall, Jr. 1944.   [2] Cf. R. A. Hall, Jr. 1948.
[3] Cf. especially R. A. Hall, Jr. 1966.
[4] Especially R. A. Hall, Jr. 1958. Also "A Bibliography of Sardinian Linguistics", *It* xix (1942) pp. 133–57.
[5] Cf. especially R. A. Hall, Jr. 1964.
[6] E.g. *Leave your Language Alone!*—later modified to *Linguistics and your Language* (R. A. Hall, Jr. 1950). One of Hall's pet bugbears is linguistic purism, which he continually attacks with great vehemence.

almost the only)[1] exponent of American descriptivism in the Romance field. His two descriptive grammars of **Descriptive works** Romance languages—*Structural Sketch 1–French* (1948) and *Descriptive Italian Grammar* (1948)[2]— have aroused the ire of many European linguists, but remain the only reasonably complete descriptions of these languages, according to modern principles. Objections centre principally around Hall's alleged neglect of sociolinguistic variation, though often it is merely the succintness of presentation and the novelty of the analysis that is disliked. Uninviting though these works appear superficially, owing to abundant use of symbolization and rejection of discursive commentary, careful study can hardly fault them within their own frame of reference. Every element of the languages is accounted for with extreme brevity and elegance: one can only applaud the author's *tour de force*, while still wondering where it can lead. For by buttoning up the languages so neatly, Hall seems to have said the last word about them, without uttering a single word of 'explanation'.[3] No overall pattern seems to emerge, nor are we any further forward in understanding or in formulating a sentence in the language.

[1] Other representatives include F. B. Agard (1958) G. L. Trager has published a few short articles concerned with Romance languages: e.g. "The Phonemes of Castillian [*sic*] Spanish", *TCLP* viii (1939) pp. 217–22: "The verb morphology of spoken French", *L* xx (1944) pp. 131–41; French morphology: personal pronouns and the indefinite article", Lxxxiv (1958) pp. 225–31. S. Saporta (cf. e.g. "Morpheme alternants in Spanish", in H. Kahane and A. Pietrangeli (eds.) 1959 pp. 15–162), appears to have recently become more Chomskyist in his approach (cf. e.g. S. Saporta and H. Contreras 1962). Another erstwhile Bloomfieldian who has 'seen the light' of Chomskyism is R. P. Stockwell (cf. e.g. R. P. Stockwell, J. D. Bowen, and J. W. Martin 1965). J. Dubois uses distributional criteria for classification in J. Dubois 1965 acknowledging his debt to Z. S. Harris 1951; in the second and third volumes (J. Dubois 1967 and 1969), his methods pertain more to transformational-generative grammar.

[2] Hall's speciality is Italian (literature as well as language) and many of his articles and monographs are concerned with that language: cf. e.g. R. A. Hall, Jr. 1942, and "Latin -*ks*- in Italian and its dialects", *L* xvii (1942) pp. 117–24; "Latin -*s*- in Italian", *L* xxiii (1947) pp. 426–9; "Initial *ts* in Italian 'zolfo' and 'zuppa', *It* xix (1942) pp. 52–5; "Italian phonemes and orthography", *It* xxi (1944) pp. 72–82, etc. He has, however, done a considerable amount of descriptive work on Romance languages other than Italian and French: e.g. "The unit phonemes of Brazilian Portuguese", *SIL* i (1943) pp. 1–6; "Occurrence and orthographical representation of phonemes in Brazilian Portuguese", *SIL* ii (1944) pp. 6–13; "Brazilian Portuguese inflection", *HR* xiii (1945) pp. 231–42; "Spanish inflection", *SIL*, iii (1945) pp. 24–36; "Classical Latin noun inflection", *Classical Philology* xii (1946) pp. 84–90.

[3] Professor Hall writes (private communication) "I don't think one's aim, in writing a descriptive grammar of the kind I did for French or Italian, should be to give 'explanation', nor yet to furnish instructions or rules for generating sentences. My favourite contrast, between maps and guide-books, holds here. One doesn't ask a map to give 'explanations'; but a good explanatory guidebook has to be based on an accurate map."

Hence we may be left with a feeling of frustration, even while marvelling at Hall's ingenuity. In French, for instance, all the complexities of liaison and morphophonemic variation are summed up in five types of alternation each of which is assigned a symbol: loss of final consonant ($\downarrow$); loss of final vowel and all that follows ($\downarrow\downarrow$); strengthening ($\square$); assibilation ($\triangle$); loss of final vowel ($\bullet$). Three sandhi-variation positions are distinguished (pre-vocalic, pre-pausal and pre-consonantal) and morphemes are assigned to an alternation-type, according to which morphophonemic alternation occurs in each sandhi-position. By analysing out such morpho-phonemic features, before proceeding to the identification and classi-fication of morphemes, we are able to use the same features as classificatory devices for different form-classes. Thus $\downarrow$ can neatly be used in the description of the alternation /lyiz-/ with /lyi-/ (e.g. *luisons* vs. *luire*) as well as of /ptit/ with /pti/ (e.g. *petite* or *petitesse* vs. *petit*). Yet we may pause to wonder whether such neat classificatory devices really reflect linguistic reality and are in tune with the intuitions of the native speaker. Admittedly Hall himself will have no truck with such vague and unreliable intuitions, but it is not surprising to find that native speakers sometimes react to his analyses with a vehemence that suggests that they feel an intimate possession has been violated.

Hall's work on historical Romance linguistics arouses less violent reactions, perhaps because being in the neogrammarian tradition it appears much less innovating than his descriptive work. His most significant contributions have been in the rigorous application of comparativist tech-niques in the reconstruction of Proto-Romance;[1] applying methods developed in descriptive linguistics, Hall reconstructs the phonemic systems of past synchronic states of the language,[2] and mainly on the basis of internal evidence, is able to postulate 'Proto-stages' intermediate between the modern Romance languages and the reconstructed 'Common Romance'. Of the 'reality' of his recon-struction, Hall appears to have no doubts—even to the extent of composing a text in the Proto-language.[3] In general he holds that *la langue* can never be a collective property, but merely a linguist's abstraction based on a collection of idiolects (the speech

Historical studies

---

[1] Especially "The reconstruction of Proto-Romance", *L* xxvi (1950) pp. 6–20 reprinted in M. Joos (ed.) 1957; and "Comparative method in Romance historical syntax", in *AL* xi (1967–68) pp. 81–8.

[2] Cf. also e.g. "Old French phonemes and orthography", *SP* xliii (1946) pp. 575–85 and "The Language of the Strasburg Oaths", *L* xxix (1953) pp. 317–21.

[3] Cf. "On Realism in Reconstruction", *L* xxxvi (1960) pp. 203–6.

habits of individuals) which can overlap in different degrees.[1] Proto-Romance would be an abstraction (a diasystem) of the same sort (though at a higher level), and not indicative of unity of speech habits among all inhabitants of the Roman Empire: indeed in his own words (private communication): "to my way of thinking all languages are diasystems anyhow, so a proto-language wouldn't be any different from any other in that respect".

Linguistic change for Hall is inevitable, given that there is always variation in usage, and that circumstances may lead to a shift in the weighting given to one variety rather than another. This view does not seem wholly consistent with his complete acceptance of the 'regularist' hypothesis of phonological change, which, however, he appears to justify mainly on the grounds that the hypothesis has proved fruitful in the establishing of historical linguistics as a science. The cause of the regular phonological change he, like the neo-grammarians, sees as an unconscious mechanical change of habits, with gradual shift in allophonic variations. I myself cannot see how such a view can be fully reconciled with a refusal to allow some degree of autonomy to the *langue* (as distinct from an agglomeration of idiolects).[2] Hall's position vis-à-vis Prague-type diachronic phonology appears broadly hostile, though he does admit the action of 'pattern pressures' or 'intra-systemic' factors in linguistic change;[3] however, he appears to use such terms to designate different types of analogical change, rather than the more positive teleological forces envisaged by the Prague diachronicists.

In his championship of regularist and reconstructionist methods, and his vigorous rejection of 'idealist' modes of thought, Hall stands apart from the mainstream of Romance linguistics since the *Iordan–Orr* era. There are signs, however, that his influence is prompting younger American Romanists[4] to take up reconstruc-

---

[1] I am grateful to Professor Hall for having shown me before publication a draft of his *Essay on Language*, (R. A. Hall, Jr. 1968) in which he expounds his views with the utmost lucidity. For him *la langue* is also a 'linguistic super-ego' "Idiolect and Linguistic Super-Ego" *SL*, v (1951) pp. 21–7.

[2] Hall writes (private communication): "Regular sound-change seems to me to be a matter of statistical regularity, much as (say) the regularity observable in such a phenomenon as the expansion of a gas; even though the behaviour of individual molecules may be unpredictable, that of a mass of molecules is predictable."

[3] "The Development of Vowel Pattern in Romance", *Li* iv (1954–55) pp. 394–406.

[4] Cf. e.g. recent work by C. S. Leonard, especially his as-yet-unpublished "The Romance Stammbaum in the West", and his "Initial Alternation in Proto-Romance", *L* xliv (1968) pp. 267–73. Another firm advocate of reconstructionist techniques, though in no way, it seems, influenced by American thought, is the Swiss, R. de Dardel (cf. especially R. de Dardel 1958 and 1965).

tionist tasks, thus bringing Romance linguistics more into line with the historical studies pursued in other fields.

10. *Other trends*

The eclipse of Romance linguistics within current general linguistic trends is especially evident when we turn to the 'school' that has exerted most influence during the last ten years—

Transforma-tional-Generative grammar
that of transformational–generative grammar (TG) —in which Noam Chomsky is the leading light.[1] Discussion of the ideas of this school is essential here, as no survey of recent linguistic thought would be complete without mention of Chomsky and his disciples, who are responsible for what has been called a 'Copernican revolution' in American linguistics. However, as so far TG theory has scarcely been applied to Romance problems(though there are signs of increasing popularity especially among French specialists[2]), I will keep the section short, relative to the overall importance of the school. Moreover, there is now a considerable number of introductions to TG, that give adequate coverage in much more detail than I would have scope for here.[3]

The feature of TG works that is most striking is their preoccupation

[1] Noam Chomsky, b. 1928 in Philadelphia, took his PhD. in linguistics in 1955. Since 1951 he has been in Cambridge, Mass. at Harvard and at M.I.T. Notable among his works are N. A. Chomsky 1957, 1964, 1965, 1966a & b, 1968 and N. A. Chomsky and M. Halle 1968.

[2] *Ls* has devoted two issues to TG: iv (1966) on "La grammaire génératrice" ed. N. Ruwet, and viii (1967) on "La phonologie générative" ed. S. A. Schane. Cf. also J. Dubois 1967 and 1969, S. A. Schane, 1968, M. Gross 1968 and R. W. Langacker, "French interrogatives: a transformational description", *L* xli (1965) pp. 587–600, and "Observations on French possessives", *L* xliv (1968) pp. 51–75. For Italian we now have: N. Costabile 1967 and M. Saltarelli (forthcoming). For Spanish, J. E. Lackstrom 1968, P. W. Klein 1968, J. S. Falk 1968, and W. W. Cressey, "Relative adverbs in Spanish: a transformational analysis", *L* xliv (1968) pp. 487–500.

[3] The best, in my view, is N. Ruwet 1967. Also to be recommended is E. Bach 1964. Romanists will also find of special interest G. Lepschy's, "La grammatica transformazionale: studi recenti", in *SSL* vi (supplement to *ID* xxix N. Ser. vi 1966) pp. 171–91; B. Grunig, "Les théories transformationnelles. Exposé critique", *LaL* 1965, 2 pp. 1–24, 1966, 1 pp. 31–101; H. Contreras 1966; B. Pottier, "La grammaire générative et la linguistique", *TLLS* vi (1968) pp. 7–26; and J. Dubois, "La dérivation en linguistique descriptive et en linguistique transformationnelle", *ibid*. pp. 27–53 and "Grammaire générative et transformationnelle" in *LaF* i (1969) pp. 49–57.

with the formal theory of grammar, with a quasi-mathematical model-building orientation. The use of mathematical type theory in linguistics will be discussed on pp. 533–5. Nevertheless, TG is not necessarily wholly theoretical;[1] yet empirical works are still comparatively scarce and fairly inadequate, so that many more traditional linguists accuse Chomskyists of losing touch with the concrete reality of living speech. Their uneasiness is often increased by the Chomskyist insistence on the necessity of studying linguistic **'Competence'** 'competence'—the inner knowledge of their lan-**and** guage that native speakers are presumed to possess—**'Performance'** rather than 'performance'—what speakers actually say. The parallel with Saussure's concentration on *langue* rather than *parole* seems obvious, though Chomsky himself is quick to point out the difference between the two theories.[2] 'Empiricist' linguists—especially of the descriptivist 'American' school—are suspicious of a method that consults native intuition, rather than 'texts'. Yet it is a fundamental feature of 'generative' grammar that it must be able to 'generate' (= 'assign a structural description to', NOT 'produce') all grammatical (or 'well-formed') sentences in the language (even when not yet pronounced) and no ungrammatical sentences. 'Grammaticality' is regarded as a self-evident concept, which is operationally discovered by examining the native speaker's intuition (usually by self-examination). Some allowance can be made for peripheral variation between native speakers, as well as for recognition of different 'degrees of grammaticality'. But the grammar must, by imitating the 'competence' of the speaker, distinguish between grammatical and ungrammatical utterances, both of which can occur in 'performance'. The possible sentences in a language are assumed to be infinite, though 'competence' must consist of a finite number of rules (as it is acquired in a relatively

---

[1] Cf. W. O. Dingwall, 1965. Notable among descriptive studies is R. B. Lees 1960. Although TG is concerned with synchronic description, some attempts have been made to relate it to historical problems: e.g. B. Sigurd, "Generative grammar and historical linguistics", *AL* x (1966) pp. 35–48; S. Saporta, "Ordered rules, dialect differences and historical processes", *L* xli (1965) pp. 218–24; E. Closs, "Diachronic syntax and generative grammar", *ibid.* pp. 402–15; and R. D. King 1969.

[2] Cf. N. A. Chomsky 1964 p. 23: "He (Saussure) was quite unable to come to grips with the recursive processes underlying sentence formation, and he appears to regard sentence formation as a matter of *parole* rather than *langue*, of free and voluntary creation rather than systematic rule (or perhaps, in some obscure way, as on the border between *langue* and *parole*). There is no place in his scheme for 'rule-governed creativity' of the kind involved in the ordinary everyday use of language." For M. Joos, however, (*Trends i* p. 17) TG is "a heresy within the neo-Saussurean tradition rather than a competitor to it".

short time by even an untutored child who hears a large number of utterances). The task of a grammar is to reproduce as closely as possible these rules, and the task of linguistics is to evaluate different grammars. The best grammar will be exhaustive (to be tested by matching it against utterances, both grammatical and ungrammatical), self-consistent (only to be achieved reliably by quasi-mathematical formalization) and the simplest (here in the sense of 'achieving most generality' NOT of 'lacking complexity').

An essential part of TG, as we have seen, is that it regards the sentence as the linguistic unit *par excellence*, and so, compared with the morphologically slanted theories we have so far examined, it is basically a theory of syntax. As well-formed sentences are infinitely variable, and as, indeed, a sentence rarely recurs twice in the same form, statistical methods are regarded as futile.[1]

Another important feature of TG is its concern with language universals—partly connected with its interest in language acquisi-

Language universals
tion (it is assumed that as children are able to build up 'competence' unaided there must be some innate bent in all human beings), as well as with its interest in 'explanation', rather than mere 'description' (so that more general statements are preferred). Here TG takes up again a non-empirical tradition in linguistics that went somewhat out of fashion in the nineteenth century.[2] In the same tradition is the distinction made between 'deep structure'[3] which allows semantic interpretation[4] and 'surface structure', which yields the phonological component of the grammar.[5]

Certain superficial traits of TG works obtrude themselves on the reader and may perhaps blind him to their basic features. Most striking is their pugnacity of tone, for TG proponents seem to prefer a 'shooting war' to 'peaceful coexistence'; as the school gains

---

[1] The reaction of some linguistic statisticians to TG is, not surprisingly, hostile: cf. G. Herdan, "The Crisis in Modern General Linguistics", *LaL* 1967, 1 pp. 27–37.

[2] Cf. especially N. A. Chomsky 1964 and 1966a.

[3] A notion to be found in *La grammaire de Port-Royal* as well as in Humboldt.

[4] A semantic theory within the framework of TG is worked out esp. by J. A. Fodor and J. J. Katz (cf. p. 463).

[5] Notable among Chomskyist phonologists is M. Halle: Cf. especially M. Halle 1959; "Phonology in Generative Grammar", *Wd* xviii (1962) pp. 54–72 (reprinted in J. A. Fodor and J. J. Katz (eds.) 1964 pp. 334–52; trans. in *Ls* viii (1967); "On the Bases of Phonology", in J. A. Fodor and J. J. Katz (eds.) 1964 pp. 324–33; and N. A. Chomsky and M. Halle 1968. P. Postal 1968 should also be noted. TG develops the Jakobsonian binary 'distinctive features' notion (cf. p. 485), but bypasses the phonemic level, passing directly from 'systematic phonemics' (i.e. morphophonemics) to 'systematic phonetics' (i.e. distinctive features).

more adherents, however, there will be doubtless less and less necessity for aggressive self-defence. Another feature that repels the uninitiated is the abundant symbolization and mathematical terminology: as I have already mentioned, formal statement is regarded as necessary to avoid self-contradiction. The existence now of introductory treatises is an aid to following more advanced TG works, and a younger, more numerate, generation of linguists will probably find them more congenial than their seniors trained in an exclusively humanist tradition. However, the 'trees' of structural description, the arrows of 'rewrites', and other symbols and abbreviations are mere conveniences, and not essential to the method.

Although harking back to Cartesianism, the roots of TG are to be found in more recent schools: in a way it is a cross between American descriptivism and Saussurean structuralism (via Z. S. Harris and Roman Jakobson respectively) with a good chunk of traditional grammar thrown in.[1] The constituent structure syntax ('Phrase Structure Grammar', PSG, in Chomskyist terms) that reached its culmination in American descriptive works[2] is an **PSG and TG** essential part of TG, though it is described in terms of 'rules' (processes) rather than of items. However PSG was found to be inadequate for the description of certain features of natural languages:[3] co-ordinated constructions are difficult to describe in terms of 'immediate constituents' and seem to require some sort of recursive rule;[4] agreement, or concord, is only clumsily describable in terms of segmental constituents and may necessitate the introduction of 'discontinuous morphemes': most

---

[1] Chomsky does not deny his debt to traditional grammar though he condemns its lack of formalism and reliance on semantic criteria. An 'independent' transformationalist, J. Lyons, Professor of Linguistics at Edinburgh, turns even further back to tradition, advocating a modified 'notional' theory of parts of speech: cf. especially J. Lyons 1968.

[2] Constituent analysis much resembles the 'parsing' of tradition: items in the string are shown to be hierarchically arranged.

[3] An unmerciful, and not wholly fair, attack on PSG in its various forms is to be found in P. Postal 1964.

[4] Such as $A \rightarrow A + A$ (where A may be expanded into A + A wherever it occurs). Thus *John, Michael, Mary, and Peter* might be generated by a recursive $N \rightarrow N + N$ rule: the disadvantage of such a rule would be that it suggests a hierarchical arrangement that is not necessarily intended by the speaker: (*John* + *Michael*) + (*Mary* + *Peter*)

important, the intuitively obvious relationship between certain sentences (like *I read the book* and *the book is read by me*) is virtually ignored by PSG, even though traditional grammar (typically semantically based) pays particular attention to this sort of feature. Z. S. Harris[1] had already recognized these limitations of PSG and advocated use of 'transformation' to supplement constituent structure analysis, by describing some structures as 'transforms' of 'kernel sentences'. Chomsky goes further, making greater use of 'transformational' rules, not only to point out the relationship between different sentence structures[2] but also to describe other features, such as morphophonological variation. He insists, moreover, that his transformational rules, unlike those of Harris and traditional grammar, are applied to abstract structures and not to concrete sentences.

One of the advantages of the transformational approach is the way it handles ambiguous sentences. *Flying planes can be dangerous*,

Syntactic Ambiguity for instance, can be derived, by transformation, from two different combinations of kernel sentences —one including the type *John flies planes* and the other, *planes fly*, hence the ambiguity. Another kind of structural ambiguity is exemplified in *John is easy to please* vs. *John is eager to please* where the same 'surface structure' overlies different 'deep structures' (of the type *X pleases John* vs. *John pleases X*). The neatness with which TG can handle such knotty, though marginal, problems is certainly attractive—though some scholars object that ambiguities *are* ambiguous (and sometimes have pronounced stylistic effect) and so to explain them away is misleading.

Chomsky acknowledges his debt to the Port-Royal grammarians, but otherwise he has been little influenced by Romance scholars.

Romanist parallels with TG However, certain parallels with his transformational approach can be detected in Romanist syntactical works, even though these lack the formal and abstract approach of TG. C. Bally's *Linguistique générale et linguistique*

C. Bally *française*[3] uses the notion of *transposition fonctionnelle* which allows *signes* of one lexical category to be

---

[1] Cf. especially Z. S. Harris, "Co-occurrence and Transformation in Linguistic Structure", *L* xxxiii (1957) pp. 283–340.
[2] Thus the differing 'surface' structures are shown to derive from the same 'deep' structure.
[3] Pp. 116 ff. Cf. *Iordan–Orr* p. 379 and N. Ruwet 1967 p. 227.

used with the grammatical function of another: for instance,

Une phrase peut devenir une proposition-terme, proposition qui, par une ou plusieurs transpositions parallèles, prend la forme du substantif, de l'adjectif ou de l'adverbe. *Je suis innocent* devient complément d'objet direct dans (*j'affirme*) *que je suis innocent*, puis (*j'affirme*) *être innocent*, et enfin (*j'affirme*) *mon innocence.*

Even though certain of the effects of Bally's *transpositions* are similar to Chomsky's *transformations*, they are, however, linked to a part-of-speech grammar that presupposes that lexical categories have an inherent grammatical function, such that, for instance a noun is 'predestined' to be used as a subject, and so in other syntactic functions it is necessarily 'transposed'.

Another Romanist scholar who made considerable use of TG-like transformations *avant la lettre* is A. Blinkenberg[1] (whose methods derive to some extent from his master, Jespersen[2]).

A. Blinkenberg Considering himself a traditionalist, by contrast with his Hjelmslevian fellow-countrymen, Blinkenberg describes syntactic functions, not only in terms of syntagmatic constituents, but also by reference to the relationship between sentences, using "l'épreuve par la transposition thématique".[3] Thus in his description of transitivity he compares sentences of the type *Pierre mange le gâteau* and *Pierre mange le soir*: the first is seen to be transitive partly because the complement *le gâteau* can be transposed to become the 'theme' of the utterance (cf. *le gâteau est mangé par Pierre*, but NOT **le soir est mangé par Pierre*).

Yet another apparent precursor of Chomsky among students of French syntax[4] is Lucien Tesnière (1893–1954).[5] Although his

---

[1] Cf. pp. 426 and 524 and A. Blinkenberg 1928–33 and 1960. Also N. Ruwet 1967 pp. 224–6, and B. Grunig, *LaL* 1965, 2 p. 3.

[2] Cf. especially O. Jespersen 1924, quoted with approval by R. B. Lees, *L* xxxiii (1957) p. 387, n. 19.

[3] Cf. A. Blinkenberg 1960, p. 68.

[4] Cf. also J. Dubois 1960, where noun and verb may sometimes be considered as variants of one 'archilexeme'. The French Indo-Europeanist E. Benveniste has also approached very close to the idea of Chomsky-type transformations (cf. the discussion of his work in N. Ruwet 1967, pp. 231–2).

[5] L. Tesnière was a pupil and collaborator of Meillet. Taking his *licence* at the Sorbonne in 1913, he served in the Great War and was taken prisoner in 1915. In 1919 he became *agrégé* in German, but after a spell in Jugoslavia (1921–24) he specialized in Slavic languages, taking his doctorate in 1952. In 1937 he succeeded Grammont at Montpellier, from 1951 holding a Chair in Comparative Grammar and Linguistics; much of his work was, however, concerned with teacher training and he never lost sight of his pedagogical purposes. A bibliography of his works from 1919 to 1952, by F. Daumas, is to be found in *O* i (1952) pp. 561–4. Cf. L. Tesnière 1943 and 1953, but his definitive work (1959) was published posthumously.

**Lucien
Tesnière**

syntactical theories are not in the mainstream of linguistic developments and have exerted comparatively little influence, they are to be reckoned with by Romanists, not only because they foreshadow ideas that were to become popular,[1] but also because of the numerous insights they provide into thorny problems of French grammar.[2]

Tesnière's approach resembles Chomsky's in according primacy to syntax, which he regards as an abstract structure, compared with

**Tesnière
and
Chomsky**

morphology which provides a mere "vêtement phonétique". Like Chomsky, too, Tesnière regards introspection as a valid method for discovery. His 'stemmata' resemble Chomsky's 'trees', in some degree, in that the linear order of a syntagm is analysed into a hierarchical structure—*connexion*—which forms *la charpente de la phrase*.[3] However, his notion of *connexion* implies essentially a dependency, not a constituent, grammar.[4] From this springs an important difference between Chomskyist analysis and that of Tesnière: whereas TG initially divides the sentence into the traditional Subject and Predicate (or rather Noun Phrase and Verb Phrase, NP + VP), Tesnière, regarding such an analysis as logical (p. 103) rather than syntactic, prefers to pick out a *nœud* which governs *subordonnés*. The highest *nœud* in the stemma—the *nœud des nœuds* or *nœud central*—is usually a verb, for instance, the sentence *mon vieil ami chante cette jolie chanson* will be depicted in a Tesnière stemma thus:

[1] The relationship of Tesnière's views to Chomsky's have been recently underlined by Martha G. Worthington, "A Precursor of the Transformational Approach to Descriptive Syntax: Lucien Tesnière", *RPh* xxi (1968) pp. 303–16 and M. Arrivé, "Les *Eléments de Syntaxe structurale*, de L. Tesnière", *LaF* i (1969) pp. 36–40. Cf. also R. H. Robins, "Syntactic Analysis", *ArL* xiii (1961) pp. 78–89 (reprinted in E. P. Hamp *et al.* (eds.) 1966 pp. 386–95; B. Grunig, *LaL* 1965, 2 pp. 5–6; N. Ruwet 1967 pp. 228–9.

[2] Tesnière is not, however, exclusively concerned with French, seeking to establish a general syntax and giving examples from a wide variety of languages.

[3] Tesnière, too, relates his notion of *connexion* to Humboldt's 'deep structure' (L. Tesnière 1959 p. 13): "C'est d'ailleurs la notion de connexion qu'exprime le nom même de la syntaxe, en grec 'mise en ordre, disposition'. Et c'est également à cette notion, purement intérieure le plus souvent, que correspond la *innere Sprachform* 'forme intérieure de la langue', de Guillaume de Humboldt."

[4] For machine translation work along 'dependency-theory' lines cf. G. Mounin 1964 pp. 162–93. Also D. G. Hays, "Dependency Theory: a Formalism and Some Observations", *L* xl (1964) pp. 511–25.

whereas PSG would represent it roughly thus:

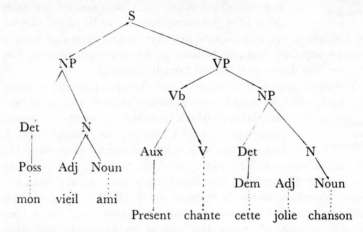

Grammatical agreement in TG would have to be described in transformational terms whereas for Tesnière "tout subordonné suit le sort de son régissant". Tesnière handles coordination under a special heading, *jonction*, allowing a horizontal relationship between *nœuds* of the same nature so that recursive rules are not called for: thus *Alfred et Bernard tombent*

Where Tesnière most resembles Chomsky, however, is in his use o the notion of *translation* to describe the relationship between sen-

'Translation'

tences, in a way that seems to anticipate Chomsky's transformations. Certainly many of the analyses of examples in terms of *translation*—which, we read, helps to "compliquer la phrase simple"—can be reformulated in transformational terms.[1]

---

[1] Tesnière, however, specifically disclaims that many ambiguities can be resolved by syntactic theory: ". . . *le train de Paris* est aussi bien celui qui va à Paris que celui qui en vient. Certes, le contexte évite le plus souvent toute ambiguïté. Mais il ne faut pas en être dupe. Lorsque le voyageur demande au chef de gare *A quelle heure arrive le train de Paris?* ou bien *A quelle heure part le train de Paris?*, ce n'est pas la préposition *de* qui exprime la direction du train, puisqu'elle sert aussi bien dans les deux cas, c'est l'emploi du verbe *arrive* dans un cas et du verbe *part* dans l'autre. Mais, en l'absence d'un contexte qui indique de quel train il s'agit, il y a bel et bien ambiguïté" (L. Tesnière 1959 p. 362). Presumably TG would seek to show that *le train de Paris* is a transform of two different kernel structures: one underlying a sentence like *Paris a un train* and the other *Le train vient de Paris*.

Nevertheless, Tesnière's grammar resembles Bally's more closely than Chomsky's, for his *translations* are more often applied to items than to structures. Indeed, in his own words:

Dans son essence, la translation consiste donc à transférer un mot plein d'une catégorie grammaticale dans une autre catégorie grammaticale, c'est-à-dire à transformer une espèce de mot en une autre espèce de mot (L. Tesnière 1959, p. 152).

Thus in *le livre de Pierre*, the noun *Pierre* becomes syntactically an adjective by the agency of the *translatif*, *de*, while conserving its semantic content.

For Tesnière, then, there are two types of syntax: the 'dynamic' or 'structural' syntax concerned with functions; and the 'static'
Static and dynamic syntax syntax of categories, or parts-of-speech. *Translation* involves a shifting of items from the static to the dynamic. Tesnière's categorial classifications appear to be largely semantic, but differ in several ways from traditional part-of-speech classification. His basic unit is the word, which can be either *plein* or *vide*: this semantic distinction is matched on the syntactic plane, in that *mots pleins* are *constitutifs* (i.e. can form a *nœud* and are autonomous[1]) while *mots vides* (including *jonctifs*, *translatifs* and *indices*) are *subsidiaires*. *Mots pleins* may be subdivided into those that indicate substance (basically nominals) and those that indicate a process (basically verbals).

Thus, although Tesnière appears to have similar ideas to Chomsky, concerning the antecedence of syntax in the speaker's intuition, and the inherent existence of some process such as *translation* in the speaker's competence, his approach is very different. Again, although superficially L. Tesnière 1959 appears formalized, with abundant diagrams, it has none of the quasi-mathematical formalism characteristic of TG: indeed its avowedly pedagogical purpose has led to a clarity of style, not to say assertiveness, which tends to avoid definition in favour of exemplification.

Another school of thought that deserves mention here, even though it has influenced Romanists but little, is that sometimes known as the 'British' or 'London' school—develop-
The British School ing the ideas of J. R. Firth (1890–1960), the holder of Britain's first chair in General Linguistics, at the

[1] Here Tesnière's model resembles that of Martinet (cf. p. 489).

London School of Oriental and African Studies.[1] The basic tenets of this school include an insistence on the need to study *both* syntagmatic *and* paradigmatic aspects of language (in Firthian terms, both *structure* and *system*). Thus Firthian phonological analysis eschews sole reliance on phonemic segmentation, preferring to link together comparatively disembodied 'phonematic' segmental units, with phonological features, 'prosodies', that

Prosodic analysis
stretch over more than one segment (typically the syllable, or the word).[2] Recognition of the utility of 'prosodic' analysis probably sprang from the problems raised by the non-European languages[3] that originally were often the domain of Firthians—languages in which such features as vowel harmony, as syllable-long labialization, aspiration, palatalization, etc., could be described only in arbitrary terms when using conventional phonemic procedures. They insist that segmental phonemic analysis, though convenient for orthographical purposes, tends to distort linguistic reality, artificially pressing a multidimensional substance into linear form.

Another basic tenet of Firthian linguistics, with similar purport, is that any linguistic act is a meaningful whole, occurring within a

Meaning and context
situation, that cannot be studied in isolation. For Firth, the study of language is principally the study of meaning, and although for methodological convenience the speech situation is analysed into different contextual levels (phonetic, lexical, morphological, syntactic, and 'situational') each of these levels is a 'level of meaning': for, as Firth often asserted, "It is part of the meaning of a Frenchman to sound like a Frenchman."

---

[1] Firth spent a good part of his life in India, teaching English, among other things. His approach may be said to be 'typically British' in that he eschewed dogmatic theory, insisting on the necessity for an 'ad hoc' approach to real problems. Most of his important works are collected in J. R. Firth 1957; cf. also 'Synopsis of Linguistic Theory, 1930–1955", in *Studies in Linguistic Analysis*, J. R. Firth 1966 (mem.), and R. H. Robins, "Obituary of J. R. Firth", *L* xxxvi (1961) pp. 191–200. An excellent survey of "General Linguistics in Great Britain 1930–1960", by R. H. Robins, is to be found in *Trends ii* pp. 11–37. Cf. also "J. R. Firth, Contextual Theory and Prosodic Phonology", in F. P. Dinneen 1967, Ch. 10, pp. 229–325, as well as D. T. Langendoen 1968.

[2] In some ways Firth's prosodies resemble Z. S. Harris's 'long components' (cf. "Phonemic Long Components", *L* xx (1944) pp. 181–205) but Firthians insist that prosodies, unlike long components, are associated with specific phonological and grammatical structures (cf. R. H. Robins, "Aspects of Prosodic Analysis", in *PDPS* i (1957) pp. 1–12 and W. S. Allen, "Aspiration in Harauti Nominals", in *Studies in Linguistic Analysis*, pp. 68–86). A selection of the most representative studies using the prosodic method is to be found in F. R. Palmer 1969.

[3] For the suggestion that some languages are better analysed in terms of phonemes, whereas others call for prosodic analysis, cf. J. Lyons, "Phonemic and non-phonemic phonology", *IJAL* xxviii (1962) pp. 127–33.

Virtually no work on Romance problems has been done within the framework of 'classic' Firthian theory. However some younger French specialists are to be found among the adherents of 'Neo-Firthian' theory, disciples of M. A. K. Halliday,[1] now Professor at University College, London, after a spell at Edinburgh where he exerted great influence on his colleagues. Halliday's theories are presented more coherently than those of Firth, whose ideas were developed completely only at the phonological level, that of *substance*. Halliday takes further his master's ideas on linguistic *form*—the two levels of grammar and lexis. He presents a model

Scale-and-category grammar known as 'scale-and-category', using the notion of fundamental theoretical categories—*class* (e.g. 'noun', 'verb', etc.), *system* (i.e. a range of possibilities within a limited choice), *unit* and *structure*. *Units* are stretches of language that carry grammatical patterns and can be *ranked* hierarchically in a *rank-scale*. *Structure* shows how a unit of one rank can be made up of units next below it in the rank-scale: *elements* of structure—like 'subject', 'complement', etc.—have a value that may be shown by the sequence in which items are arranged.

In some features, scale-and-category grammar resembles that of Tesnière: the *class* versus *structure* distinction is somewhat similar to Tesnière's *static* versus *dynamic* syntax; more notably Hallidayan *rank-shift*—when a unit at one rank operates as part of a pattern one rank further down—is a process similar to Tesnière's *translation*. More recent work in Hallidayan syntax[2] distinguishes, like TG, between surface (constituent) grammar and deep grammar, but, unlike TG, describes deep grammar in terms of distinctive syntactic features. Each feature belongs to a paradigm of two or more contrasting features—e.g. singular versus plural, declarative versus interrogative—which are called systems (hence the name 'systemic grammar' for this model). Here, as elsewhere,

Systemic grammar Hallidayan theory describes language in terms of choices. Unlike TG, it is compatible with statistical investigation, and, indeed, the Firthian notion of *collocation* which defines a 'lexical set' (= a group of items which enter into the same basic formal pattern) is a statistico-distributional one.

[1] Cf. especially M. A. K. Halliday *et al.* 1964. Cf. also the five papers by Halliday in A. McIntosh and M. A. K. Halliday 1966. Halliday's most important article is "Categories of the theory of grammar", *Wd* xvii (1962).

[2] Cf. e.g. M. A. K. Halliday, "Some notes on 'deep' grammar", *JL* ii (1966) pp. 57–67; "Notes on transitivity and theme in English", *JL* iii (1967) pp. 37–81 and R. Huddleston and O. Uren, "Declarative, interrogative and imperative in French" (to appear).

The models of grammatical description I have discussed are by no means the only ones advanced of recent years—the transformational theory of the Soviet scholar Šaumjan, and Lamb's 'stratificational grammar' are two further examples—but, on the whole, Romance linguistics remains untouched by passing fashions, so that I shall call a halt, at the risk of omitting appraisal of what may well become the most important school of the nineteen-seventies!

11. *Applied linguistics*

As linguistics has tended to become more and more theoretical and, as a discipline, more autonomous, so there has developed a somewhat heterogeneous branch of study to which the title 'applied linguistics'[1] is given. The scope of the title is not generally agreed, but nearly always knowledge of some extra-linguistic discipline is required of the 'applied linguist'. Most often the term is used for language-teaching methodology,[2] and quite frequently for translation methodology,[3] but it can also cover computational linguistics and communication engineering (for which see the next section on Mathematical and Statistical Methods), lexicography,[4] psycho-[5]

[1] The International Association of Applied Linguistics (AILA, President B. Pottier) which held its first Colloquium at Nancy in 1964 (cf. *Actes du Ie Colloque International de Linguistique Appliquée*—Nancy, Annales de l'Est, mem. 31, 1968) groups together a large number of national associations and centres. Among relevant journals we should cite *LiR, ELA, EstL, CLTA, RLA*, and the *Schedario Linguistico* of the Centro Italiano di Linguistica Applicata, Rome. A bibliographical survey: A. P. van Teslaar, "Les domaines de la linguistique appliquée", *IRAL* i (1963) pp. 50–77 and 223–78.

[2] Cf. particularly *A Language-teaching Bibliography* compiled by the English Teaching Information Centre of the British Council and the Centre for Information on Language Teaching, and supplemented quarterly by *LTA*.
So much work has been done recently in this field that it would be quite impossible to survey it here. The most important journal is *IRAL*. Here also we ought to mention that linguistics can contribute to other pedagogical problems like teaching by the medium of a non-mother tongue (e.g. J. Dakin *et al.* 1968) and the teaching of reading (e.g. L. Bloomfield and C. L. Barnhardt 1961 and C. C. Fries 1963).

[3] A bibliography, by B. Q. Morgan, is to be found in R. A. Brower (ed.) 1959 pp. 369–93; also E. and K. Delavenay 1960. Among important books we should mention J. C. Catford 1965 and E. A. Nida 1964. Periodicals include *Ba, MT, TradA*.

[4] J. Cásares 1950 and F. W. Householder and S. Saporta (eds.) 1962.

[5] Cf. especially, on psycho-linguistics, S. Saporta (ed.) 1961; R. C. Oldfield and J. C. Marshall (eds.) 1968; *Problèmes de psycho-linguistique* 1963; R. Titone 1964; C. E. Osgood and T. A. Sebeok (eds.) 1965; E. Buyssens 1960; and P. Chauchard 1956.

and bio-linguistics,[1] socio-linguistics[2] (including 'language planning'[3] and anthropological linguistics).[4]

Within the Romance sphere the problems of teaching the languages—especially French and Spanish—to foreigners most occupy the attention of applied linguists. In France the applied linguistics of French language teaching is given official encouragement, mainly through the agencies CREDIF[5] (*Centre pour la recherche et la diffusion du français* directed by G. Gougenheim and M. Rivenc) and BELC (*Bureau pour l'enseignement de la langue et de la civilisation françaises à l'étranger*), with their numerous publications and research projects.[6] In North America,[7] too, some linguists have turned their attention to the problems of teaching French—R. L. Politzer[8] (cf. p. 453) and A. Valdman[9] are outstanding examples. Naturally enough, however, Spanish occupies the attention of American applied

Language-teaching

---

[1] On bio-linguistics: C. L. Meader and J. H. Muyskens (eds.) 1962, and E. H. Lenneberg 1967. A quarterly journal of abstracts covering works on language and language behaviour from 24 different disciplines is *LLBA*, edited by the University of Michigan Center for Research on Language and Language Behaviour, in collaboration with BELC.

[2] Cf. especially M. Cohen 1956, W. Bright (ed.) 1966, A. Capell 1966, J. A. Fishman (ed.) 1968, and I. Iordan, "Concepţiă sociologică a limbajului", in *Viaţa romînească* i (1948) pp. 232–47.

[3] Sometimes called 'language engineering', cf. e.g. R. B. Le Page 1964 and V. Tauli 1968.

[4] Cf. H. Hoijer's chapter "Anthropological Linguistics", in *Trends* i pp. 110–27; Dell H. Hymes, "Notes towards a history of linguistic anthropology", *AnL* v (1963) pp. 59–103; and J. H. Greenberg 1968. On method, cf. especially D. H. Hymes (ed.) 1964. The journal *AnL* is devoted to this branch of study; *CuA* devotes considerable space to linguistics.

[5] Work on 'français fondamental' is particularly to be noted: cf. G. Gougenheim *et al.* 1964.

[6] BELC (formerly BEL) publications are too numerous to be mentioned here. It should be noted that French overseas Universities also encourage applied linguistic work, especially in the form of contrastive studies: cf. for instance CLAD (Centre de Linguistique Appliquée de Dakar) and CLAA (Centre de Linguistique Appliquée d'Abidjan).

[7] Cf. especially W. G. Moulton's survey "Linguistics and language teaching in the United States, 1940–1960", in *Trends* i pp. 82–109. From Canada we have, for instance, G. Rondeau 1965. In the USSR French and Spanish are the most frequently studied languages for teaching purposes—cf. recently papers given at a 1964 conference and published as *Métody sravnitel'no-sopostavitel'nogo izučenija sovreménnyx románskix jazykóv* (1966).

[8] Especially R. L. Politzer 1960.

[9] A. Valdman was born in 1931, received his schooling in France, taking degrees at Pennsylvania and Cornell, and is now at Indiana University. He has edited and contributed to a number of works including A. Valdman (ed.) 1966. His book on French was published in 1961.

linguists rather more,[1] though some work is also done on Italian.[2] The problems of translation[3] receive much attention in France, especially in relation to machine translation.[4] In lexicography,

Translation too, French linguists make good use of computational techniques, the two principal centres of research being Besançon (under B. Quemada)[5] and Nancy (under P. Imbs).[6]

In psycho-linguistics we should mention interest both in Rumania (especially the work of Tatiana Slama-Cazacu)[7] and in France.[8]

Psycho- and socio- linguistics A particular interest in language pathology has long been shown by French medical researchers, who frequently enlist the help of linguists.[9] In France, many linguists, including the school of Martinet (cf. p. 490) show much interest in the sociology of language use, which as *Iordan–Orr* pointed out, was always a feature of French linguistics.[10] Some recent investigations have cast light on social and regional variations in French pronunciation[11] and we may look forward to more work along these lines.

---

[1] A distinguished applied linguist who is also a Hispanist is R. Lado: cf. especially R. Lado 1963; Politzer, too, has written on Spanish: R. L. Politzer and C. N. Staubach 1961. Cf. also D. N. Cárdenas 1961, and in the Contrastive Structure Series (ed. C. F. Ferguson) R. P. Stockwell and J. D. Bowen 1965 and, also, the same authors with J. W. Martin 1965.

[2] Especially by R. A. Hall, Jr. (cf. 1961a). Also, in the Contrastive Structure Series, F. B. Agard and R. J. Di Pietro 1965 and 1966.

[3] Especially G. Mounin 1963.

[4] G. Mounin 1964, E. Delavenay 1959, and G. Gougenheim (ed.) 1968. Cf. also the work of B. Pottier (pp. 502–7) especially B. Pottier (forthcoming).

[5] Head of the *Centre d'Etude du Vocabulaire Français* at Besançon and editor of its numerous publications, including *CLe* and *BILAL*. Cf. particularly B. Quemada 1968, and p. 464.

[6] The Nancy *Centre de Recherche Pour un Trésor de la Langue Française* was founded in 1960. *LATA* is a lithographed periodical recording work at Nancy. See also P. Imbs (ed.) 1961.

[7] A distinguished psychologist, wife of the stylistician and dialectologist Boris Cazacu; cf. especially T. Slama-Cazacu 1961.

[8] For instance Andrée Tabouret-Keller, also a psychologist: cf. A. Tabouret-Keller (forthcoming). On child language we should mention particularly M. Cohen (ed.) 1962 and E. Alarcos Llorach (forthcoming). Cf. also W. F. Leopold 1952.

[9] Cf. most recently *Ls* v (1967) on "Pathologie du langage", ed. J. Dubois *et al.*

[10] Cf. M. Cohen 1956; H. Lefebvre 1966 and, most recently, *Ls* xi (1968) "La socio-linguistique", ed. J. Sumpf. Special mention should be made of 'semiology' treated as a branch of socio-linguistics among French-speaking scholars (inspired by the anthropologist Claude Lévi-Strauss): especially R. Barthes, "Eléments de sémiologie", in *Communication* iv (1964) pp. 91–135, and E. Buyssens 1967. A similar approach among Italians is represented by U. Eco. Cf. also p. 464.

[11] For instance Ruth Reichstein, "Etude des variations sociales et géographiques des faits linguistiques (Observations faites à Paris en 1956–1957)", *Wd* xvi (1960) pp. 55–95 (with a note by A. Martinet pp. 96–99) and G. Deyhime, "Enquête sur la phonologie du français contemporain", *LaL* 1967, 1 pp. 97–108, 2 pp. 57–84.

12. *Mathematical and statistical approaches*

Of recent years, numeracy has become a more important requirement for linguists than hitherto. Some of the more influential
trends, however shortlived, demand a certain familiarity with
formal notation and exact methods. No survey of linguistics in the
last thirty years can fail to discuss the development. However, as
yet, the wave has not engulfed Romance linguistics and the few
ripples to be discerned merit only a short note here. More comprehensive surveys are to be found elsewhere[1] so my remarks will
concentrate, as far as possible, on Romance works in the field.

After a brief moment of promise, when it was hoped that the
electronic computer might yield answers to intractable problems,
Statistical linguistic statistics has ceased to attract much
studies attention. It is often statisticians, not linguists, who
show great interest—witness, for instance the num-
ber of works by G. Herdan.[2] Among Romanists it is French scholars
who are most attracted by statistical problems[3] (perhaps in some
cases stimulated by the vain struggle to retain the Bull computer
firm in French hands!). I have already discussed Pierre Guiraud's
work in the field of lexical and stylostatistics (p. 448) as well as the
work of the Besançon and Nancy projects (p. 532). Perhaps
most interest centres round the possibility of applying statistical
techniques to stylistic study[4] and of using statistical data (e.g.
word-counts) for teaching purposes.

Within historical and comparative linguistics, statistical measures

---

[1] The best introductory survey of the whole field is, I think, W. Plath's chapter
in *Trends i* ("Mathematical Linguistics") pp. 21–57. Malmberg's chapter in his
review of linguistic trends (B. Malmberg 1964 pp. 186–203 (Fr. trans. 1966
pp. 278–304)) is valuable, but concerned mainly with statistics, rather than mathematics. O. S. Akhmanova *et al.* 1963, is a translation of a useful Russian textbook,
with essays on statistics, Information Theory, machine translation and glossematics.
An illuminating short introduction to the use of mathematics in linguistic study is
provided by A. G. Oettinger's "Linguistics and Mathematics", in J. Whatmough
1957 (fest.) pp. 179–86.
[2] The works of G. Herdan (1956, 1960, 1962, 1964, 1966) are especially to be
noted. We should mention here also the rather chatty journal *SMIL*. More
linguistically oriented are H. Karlgren (forthcoming) and C. Muller 1968.
[3] Cf. e.g. C. Muller and B. Pottier (eds.) 1966 and C. Muller 1964. Rumanians,
who do not disdain even comparatively crude 'counting' methods in all branches
of linguistic research also show interest in more sophisticated linguistic statistics:
see, most recently, A. Roceric-Alexandru 1968. Mention should also be made of
Spanish work (e.g. V. García Hoz 1963), as well as the Stanford project,
directed by A. G. Juilland, investigating by computer methods "The Romance
Languages and their Structures" (cf. p. 492).
[4] Cf. p. 461 and R. Posner, "The use and abuse of stylistic statistics", *ArL* xv
(1963) pp. 111–39. A recent survey, L. Dolezel and R. W. Bailey (eds.) 1968,
brings together seventeen essays by scholars in different disciplines.

of relationship have enjoyed some popularity. 'Glottochronology', a method introduced by Maurice Swadesh,[1] proposes a formula by which the degree of relationship of two languages, in terms of the date at which they are presumed to have diverged from a common ancestor, can be calculated by means of counting the proportion of cognate forms to be found in a 'basic' word-list.[2] Romanists have little recourse to this method, which is unnecessary for the study of a language family with a well-documented history: Romance material has, however, been used to cast doubt on the method itself.[3] Another measure of language relationship— Greenberg's and Householder's typological indices, based on statistical counts of morphological and syntactic features[4]—has been applied, rather more successfully, to the Romance languages,[5] though without startling results.[6]

Another fashion that seems to have come and gone without much effect on the Romance field was that for Information Theory and Cybernetics.[7] More important for linguistics today **Mathematical studies** is the current search for a formal model or theoretical description of language, using notation borrowed

[1] A particularly useful survey of glottochronology, with bibliography and comments by various authors, is that of Dell Hymes in *CuA* i (1962). For Maurice Swadesh see p. 487, n. 3.

[2] The formula used is

$$t = \frac{\log c}{2 \log r}$$

where t = elapsed time or 'time depth' (usually expressed in millennia), c = the percentage of cognate pairs, and r the 'retention rate' (which is usually assumed to be about 85%).

The derivation of this formula is to be found in R. B. Lees, "The Basis of Glottochronology", *L* xxix (1953) pp. 113–27. It is cogently criticized by C. D. Chrétien in "The Mathematical Models of Glottochronology", *L* xxxvii (1962) pp. 11–37. Certain disputable assumptions underlie the model—the most readily assailable is that the 'retention rate' of 'basic vocabulary' is more or less constant through time (cf. especially I. Fodor 1965). The word-list most frequently used contains 100 items: the suitability and universality of these items is often disputed.

[3] Cf. J. A. Rea, "Concerning the Validity of Lexicostatistics", *IJAL* xxiv (1958) pp. 145–50, and E. Coseriu, "Critique de la glottochronologie appliquée aux langues romanes", *Actes 10ᵉ Cong. (Strasbourg) 1962* pp. 87–96.

[4] Cf. J. Greenberg, "A quantitative approach to the morphological typology of language", *IJAL* xxvi (1960) pp. 178–94, and F. W. Householder, "First thoughts on syntactic indices", *ibid.* pp. 195–7.

[5] H. Contreras, "Une clasificación morfo-sintáctica de las lenguas románicas", *RPh* xvi (1963) pp. 261–8. Other quantitative approaches to Romance classification include M. A. Pei, "A new methodology for Romance classification", *Wd* v (1949) pp. 135–46; and J. E. Grimes and F. B. Agard, "Linguistic divergence in Romance", *L* xxxv (1959) pp. 598–604. Cf. also A. L. Kroeber, "Three Quantitative Classifications of Romance", *RPh* xiv (1961) pp. 189–95.

[6] One surprising result is that Spanish and Portuguese are seen to fall into different classes, though admittedly they are juxtaposed in rank-order.

[7] Especially important are C. E. Shannon and W. Weaver 1949, G. A. Miller 1951, C. Cherry 1957 and Y. Bar-Hillel 1964, as well as B. Malmberg 1963

from symbolic logic or mathematics (sometimes called 'algebraic grammar'). Language is assumed to be a well-defined algorithmic system which can be described in formal rules that admit of no exception and no external intervention. The model is thus a sort of machine that can automatically produce utterances: it will be self-confirmatory in that it can 'predict' possible utterances but not impossible ones. The relationship of this approach to the needs of mechanical translation is not far to seek (though sometimes denied by its proponents). The over-riding preoccupation of 'model-builders' is necessarily with language universals rather than particulars, and empirical data are not of prime importance to them. Not surprisingly, then, this type of approach is not popular among Romanists, finding its adherents, for the most part, in the United States (e.g. Chomsky, Lamb[1]) and in the Soviet Union (e.g. Revzin, Šaumjan[2]). In the Romance world, Rumania appears most interested in the mathematical, as in statistical, approaches.[3] In France, too, some glimmerings of interest are now appearing.[4] It is unlikely, however, that any significant advances in this field will be initiated by Romance linguists.

13. *Phonetics*

Since the publication of *Iordan–Orr*, phonetic sciences have developed

(cf. p. 538). Within the Romance world, we should mention L. Apostel *et al.* 1957. On computational linguistics cf. most recently P. L. Garvin and B. Spolsky (eds.) 1966, and D. G. Hays 1967. For a recent bibliography 1, cf. D. G. Hays *et al.* 1968.

[1] Cf. pp. 519-23, S. Lamb 1967, and N. A. Chomsky and G. A. Miller (forthcoming) but especially C. F. Hockett's essay, "Language, Mathematics and Linguistics", in T. A. Sebeok (ed.) 1966a pp. 155-304 (also published separately) in which he compares the two models. After writing the essay Hockett came to the conclusion that "all efforts at algebraic grammar, including my own, ... are foredoomed to failure" (*CuA* ix (1968) p. 128). Cf. C. F. Hockett 1968, in which he demonstrates that language is not a "well-defined system".

[2] I. I. Revzin 1962; S. K. Šaumjan (forthcoming) and "Outline of the applicational generative model for the description of language", *FoL* i (1965) pp. 189-222. Cf. also F. Papp 1966.

[3] For instance the Rumanian periodical *CLTA* is concerned wholly with this type of study. S. Marcus (S. Marcus 1966 and 1967) is perhaps the most outstanding of Rumanian linguistic mathematicians. Cf. also F. Kiefer 1968.

[4] Cf. for instance, *Ls* ix (1968) ed. M. Gross, devoted to "Modèles en linguistique".

immensely, partly due to the invention or exploitation of 'hardware'[1] which has brought experimental work more to the fore. Indeed, the increases in mechanical expertise required of phoneticians has led more and more to the establishment of phonetics as an autonomous discipline,[2] often only tangentially related to linguistics. Apart from the importance of the commercial construction of the tape-recorder (in the form now familiar, dating from 1940), the most radical new invention was that of the spectrograph (trade name "Sonagraph", circa 1945) together with the spectrograph playback (circa 1950). Thereby an added impetus was given to acoustic phonetic research,[3] which by some linguists is regarded as more relevant to language structure than the classic articulatory investigations.[4]

Among Romance countries probably France has shown most interest in phonetics; the tradition of Grammont[5] has been nobly

Phonetics in the Romance countries carried on by Pierre Fouché[6] and Georges Straka,[7] while other French phoneticians have concentrated even more on applied phonetic problems— especially

---

[1] P. R. Léon 1962 gives some account of the history of phonetic equipment, as does E. R. Moses, Jr. 1964.

[2] Though even then we may quote one of the most distinguished of present-day experimental phoneticians, Peter Ladefoged: "A phonetician has to have more talents than I have" (P. Ladefoged 1967 p. v).

[3] Introductions to acoustic phonetics designed principally for linguists include M. Joos 1948, G. Fant 1960, and P. Ladefoged 1962. A French textbook which covers acoustic and physiological aspects is J. C. Lafon 1961. A valuable survey of recent research is to be found in Ilse Lehiste (ed.) 1967. Special mention should also be made of the work on spectrography by a Romance linguist, E. Pulgram 1959. Pulgram is one of those Romance scholars who do not fit easily into any one of the categories I have described, as his interests range over early Romance history, dialectology (cf. p. 470) and the phonology especially of French (cf. especially "French/ə/: statistics and dynamics of linguistic subcodes", *Li* x (1961) pp. 305–25, and "Prosodic systems—French", *Li* xiii (1965) pp. 125–44), as well as methodology and applied linguistics. Born in Vienna in 1915, he moved to the United States in the war period and at present professes linguistics at the University of Michigan.

[4] Especially Roman Jakobson, and after him the Chomskyans.

[5] Died 1947.

[6] 1891–1967, professor of phonetics at Paris 1931–65, editor of *FM* for a considerable period. Much of his work was concerned with language history—his doctorate thesis (1924) was a historical study of his native Roussillonnais, and his most important work is a French phonological history (P. Fouché 1952). We do owe to him too, however, the invaluable treatise on modern French pronunciation: P. Fouché 1956. Mention here should be made of Marguerite Durand who was Fouché's assistant for many years, in charge mainly of experimental work at the Paris Institut de Phonétique, but whose death preceded that of the master by five years. Generations of students will remember Mademoiselle Durand's guidance in *travaux pratiques* and her publications include valuable contributions to French phonetics: cf. especially M. Durand 1936 and 1946; "La phonétique, ses buts, ses domaines", *O* ii (1953) pp. 213–24; and spectrographic studies, e.g. "De la formation des voyelles nasales", *SL* vii (1953) pp. 33–53 and "De la perception des consonnes occlusives, questions de sonorité" in *Wd* xii (1956) pp. 15–34.

[7] A Czech, born 1910, he was educated at Prague and Paris Universities. With

those of teaching French to foreigners (for instance Pierre Delattre,[1] Pierre Léon,[2] both of whom have settled in the New World). Among Spanish phoneticians the most outstanding is Tomás Navarro Tomás[3] who also settled in the United States, though for different reasons. Phonetics research is active too in Rumania[4] and to some extent in Portugal[5] but elsewhere in the Romance area, except for pedagogical treatises on individual languages,[6] descriptive phonetics tends to be neglected in favour of historical phonology.[7]

Interest in the phonology of the Romance languages as a group, rather than of any individual language, is more alive in Scandinavia than in any of the Romance countries. A valuable short survey by Göran Hammarström[8] is almost the only pan-Romance phonemic

the war he moved to Strasbourg, but spent two dreadful years in Buchenwald. After the war he at first shared his services between Brno and Strasbourg but in 1948 he moved completely to Strasbourg where he heads the Institut de Phonétique and the Centre de Philologie et de Littératures Romanes, and edits the various publications of the Centre. His works are mainly concerned with historical phonology; particularly important for Romance history are: "La dislocation linguistique de la Romania et la formation des langues romanes à la lumière de la chronologie relative des changements phonétiques", *RLiR* xx (1956) pp. 249–67, and "Observations sur la chronologie et les dates de quelques modifications phonétiques en roman et en français pré-littéraire", *RLaR* lxxi (1953) pp. 247–307. His most recent major publication on phonetics (1965) is more a collection of materials for phonetic study than a treatise properly so-called. Cf. also G. Straka (forthcoming). A recent work in experimental phonetics by a colleague of his at Strasbourg, Mme. Pèla Simon, is to be noted: P. Simon 1967.

[1] Born 1903 in France, taking his doctorate at Michigan in 1937, he has been professor of phonetics at Colorado since 1955. His most recent major publication is a collection of essays: P. Delattre 1966.

[2] Born 1926, after holding posts at Paris and Besançon now professor at Toronto his works include P. R. Léon 1962 and 1966.

[3] Born 1884, professor at Columbia from 1940 to 1952. His best known work is T. Navarro Tomás 1918; Cf. also his more recent collection of essays (1946). For a bibliography of works on Spanish phonetics and phonology cf. A. Quilis 1953.

[4] Outstanding in Rumanian phonetics, as elsewhere, is A. Rosetti (cf. esp. 1957). Work done under his direction in the Phonetics Section of the Bucharest Linguistic Institute includes experimental phonetic studies: e.g. A. Avram 1960. The periodical *FD* (ed. A. Rosetti) is partly devoted to experimental studies. Cf. also D. Macrea 1953. E. Vasiliu 1965 is an important phonological study of Rumanian.

[5] We should mention the University of Coimbra Experimental Phonetics Laboratory which since 1952 has published a journal (*Rev. Lab. Coïmbra*).

[6] For instance, A. Quilis and J. A. Fernández 1964; G. Bonfante and M. L. Porzio Gernia 1964; C. Tagliavini 1965; A. Camilli 1965.

[7] Cf. e.g. for Spanish A. Alonso 1955, D. Alonso 1962, but also S. Gili y Gaya 1958. Italian phonological studies are most often to be found within the field of dialectology. Recent Rumanian works that deserve mention here are Florica Dimitrescu 1967 and O. Nandriş 1963. For Romance historical phonology cf. pp. 416 and 492–6.

[8] Born in 1922, Professor of Phonetics at Uppsala till 1965, but now professor of Linguistics at Monash University, Australia. Much of his research has been into

description available. The Romance phonetician and phonologist who most aptly fills the slot of 'eminent scholar' in this section is, however, Bertil Malmberg, also a Swede, born in 1913 and Professor of Phonetics at Lund since 1950, editor of *Studia Linguistica* since 1947 and of *Travaux de l'Institut de Phonétique* (Lund) since 1959. Apart from his invaluable introductory book *La Phonétique*[1] and the chapter on experimental phonetics in his 1964 survey of linguistic trends,[2] he has, in 1968, as President of the International Society of Phonetic Sciences, edited the most comprehensive and authoritative survey of the present state of phonetics,[3] contributing himself an essay on "The linguistic basis of phonetics" (pp. 1-16). On Romance we owe to him an important article, "La structure phonétique de quelques langues romanes",[4] as well as several on French[5] and on Spanish (especially Spanish-American)[6] phonology. We have already mentioned several times his survey of *New Trends in Linguistics* (B. Malmberg 1964); his own linguistic views are expounded in his synthesis *Structural Linguistics and Human Communication*[7] where he shows himself eclectic between the Prague and Copenhagen schools, but more inclined to the former. Not surprisingly, he has firmer opinions on phonology than on other linguistic themes, but he is able to combine many different branches of knowledge concerning language into a "wide humanistic and scientific unity" (p. v).

[margin note: Bertil Malmberg]

---

the phonetics of dialectal Portuguese (cf. G. Hammarström 1953). His ten-page survey of the phonemic systems of the Romance languages is in L. Kaiser (ed.) 1957 pp. 279-89, but is omitted from the new edition (B. Malmberg (ed.) 1968). Hammarström's most recent major work is the synthesis G. Hammarström 1966.

[1] B. Malmberg 1954. Other introductory works on general phonetics include K. Pike 1943 and D. Abercrombie 1966. Periodicals devoted to phonetics and phonology include *MPh*, *ZP*, and *Phon*.

[2] Pp. 98-122.

[3] B. Malmberg (ed.) 1968 is a completely revised replacement for L. Kaiser (ed.) 1957.

[4] *O* xi (1962) pp. 232-46.

[5] Especially B. Malmberg 1943, and "Observations sur le système vocalique du français", *AL* ii 232-46.

[6] Cf. especially B. Malmberg 1950 and 1963a.

[7] B. Malmberg 1963b.

C. PROSPECTS FOR ROMANCE
LINGUISTICS

In spite of the antagonisms within the field of Romance linguistics, in spite of the varying theoretical predilections of its practitioners, Romance linguists still nevertheless feel that they have much in common, and that they are faced by the same problems—especially those posed by the large amount of data available, by the well-attested historical background of the languages, and by the continual influence on the languages of social institutions and inter-language contact. Perhaps more important, students of the Romance languages are conscious of a common cultural heritage that engenders some sort of 'brotherly feeling'.

We may at this juncture ask ourselves whether the discipline will preserve its coherence, or be split up and submerged variously into General Linguistic, language teaching and literary studies. Certainly the requirement for more technical know-how and more 'professionalism' in present-day linguistics militates against the humanist bias of most Romance scholars, and can tempt Romanists to abandon interest in modern developments, as being outside their competence. My own feeling is that this would in the long run be fatal to Romance linguistics, which would fail to attract talented theory-oriented younger scholars and so gradually fade out. There must therefore be encouraged, within the Romanist sphere, the existence of scholars who are primarily linguists, or 'linguisticians', concerned principally with theory and methodology but with a special interest in the Romance languages: such scholars would most naturally find their place in General Linguistics departments within the universities, but they should not lose their foothold in the more traditional Language departments, for fear that they neglect the interests of their more humanistically inclined colleagues.

Even though we may readily recognize what Romanists can learn from General Linguistics, we may wonder whether they can reciprocate by making a special contribution to linguistics, as a body of general theory and methodology. To my mind, the well-documented Romance languages should provide a testing-ground for hypotheses about language development and structure, and so bring down to earth the castles in the air constructed by theorists. In particular, Romanists can introduce into the static models of many modern linguists, the dynamic element that is so evident in Romance, where the treasure-house of literature complicates linguistic problems, as a result of the prestige of individual idiolectal contributions and of the slow rejection-rate of sub-systems. Romanists can check the unbridled theorizing of linguistic model-builders, by constantly reminding them of the individual and social factors that interfere with mechanical processes. To put it in terms of the 'schools' I have discussed, Romanists are at their best when they are 'neo-humanist' or 'neo-traditional' (of which trend the Prague school can be regarded as a special case).

Indeed, even though Romance linguistics should make room for some theoreticians, it will probably always make more appeal to humanistic-minded scholars than to rigorously 'scientific' methodologists (who can still of course find a happy hunting-ground in Romance reconstruction—both comparative and internal—but who, with the passage of time, are bound to find themselves investigating more and more subtle, or even trivial, problems). While neglect of modern linguistic developments might do irreparable harm to Romance linguistics, complete divorce from the study of Romance literature and texts would spell its doom as an identifiable sub-section within the general realm of linguistics.

APPENDIX

*Principal Periodicals, of relevance to Romance Linguistics, that have
started publication since 1937*

1939   Acta Linguistica (*Hafniensia*) (Copenhagen)
       Lingua Nostra (Florence)
       Revista de Filología Hispánica (Buenos Aires–New York, 1939–48)
       Translatøren (Copenhagen)

1940   *Modern Language Quarterly* (Seattle)

1941   *Anales del Instituto de Lingüística. Universidad Nacional de Cuyo* (Mendoza)
       Boletín de dialectología española (Barcelona)
       Cahiers Ferdinand de Saussure (Geneva)
       Cultura Neolatina (Modena)

1942   *Revista de Portugal* (Serie A: Lingua Portuguesa) (Lisbon)
       Studies in Linguistics (Buffalo, N.Y.)

1943   *University of California Publications in Linguistics* (Berkeley)

1944   *Revista de dialectología y tradiciones populares* (Madrid)
       Travaux du Cercle Linguistique de Copenhague (Copenhagen)

1945   *Bibliografia filológica portuguesa* (Lisbon)
       Boletín del Instituto Caro y Cuervo, continued as *Thesaurus* (Bogotá)
       Word (New York)

1946   *Boletim de Filología* (Rio de Janeiro)
       Symposium (Syracuse)

1947   *Estudis Romànics* (Barcelona)
       Lingua (Haarlem)
       Nueva Revista de Filología Hispánica (Mexico)
       Revista Portuguesa de Filología (Coimbra)
       Romance Philology (Berkeley)
       Romanistisches Jahrbuch (Hamburg)
       Studia Linguistica (Lund-Copenhagen)
       Zeitschrift für Phonetik, Sprachwissenschaft und Kommunicationsforschung (Berlin)

541

1948   *Românoslavica* (Prague)

1949   *Archivum Linguisticum* (Glasgow)
        Bibliographie Linguistique de l'année 19- et complément des années précédentes
           (Utrecht-Antwerp)
        Cahiers de l'Association Internationale des Etudes Françaises (Paris)
        Die Sprache (Vienna)
        Filología (Buenos Aires)

1950   *Ricerche Linguistiche* (Rome)
        Studii și Cercetări Lingvistice (Bucharest)

1951   *Acta Linguistica Academiae Scientiarum Hungariae* (Budapest)
        Archivum (Oviedo)
        Comparative Romance Linguistics (U.S.A.)
        Marche Romane (Liège)

1952   *Cahiers Sextil Pușcariu* (Bucharest)
        Limba Română (Bucharest)
        Orbis (Louvain)
        *Revista do Laboratório de Fonética Experimental da Faculdade de Letras da
           Universidade de Coïmbra* (Coimbra)
        Vie et Langage (Paris)
        Voprosy jazykoznanie (Moscow)

1953   *Jornal de Filología* (Rio de Janeiro)
        Romanica gandensia (Gand)
        *Studi mediolatini e volgari a cura dell'Istituto di Filologia romanza
           dell'Università di Pisa* (Bologna)

1954   *Filologia romanza* (Turin)
        Filologia romanza, continued as *Filologia e Letteratura* (Naples)
        Journal of the Canadian Linguistic Association (Montreal)
        Mechanical Translation (Cambridge, Mass.)

1955   *Babel: Revue Internationale de la Traduction* (Bonn–Paris)

1956   *Cercetări de Linguistică* (Cluj)
        Revue de Linguistique, continued as *Revue Roumaine de Linguistique*
           (Bucharest)
        Studia Romanica (et Anglica Zagrebiensia) (Zagreb)

1957   *Phonetica* (Basel)
        Revista de Filologie Romanică și Germanică (Bucharest, 1957-)
        Studi francesi (Turin)

1958   *Anthropological Linguistics* (Bloomington)
        Fonetică și Dialectologie (Bucharest)

1959 *Annali dell'Istituto Universitario Orientale di Napoli. Sezione Linguistica*
       (Naples)
       Cahiers de Lexicologie (Besançon)
       Ibérida (Rio de Janeiro)
       The Linguistic Reporter (Washington D.C.)

1960 *Bulletin d'Information du Laboratoire d'Analyse Lexicologique* (Besançon)
       Bulletin des jeunes romanistes (Strasbourg)
       La Traduction Automatique (The Hague, 1960–4)

1961 *Bulletin signalétique* (Section 21) *Sociologie, ethnologie* (Paris, CNRS)
       Le français dans le monde (Paris)
       Statistical Methods in Linguistics (Stockholm)

1962 *Cahiers de Linguistique Théorique et Appliquée* (Bucharest)
       Etudes de Linguistique Appliquée (Besançon)
       Linguistique appliquée et traduction automatique (Nancy)

1963 *International Review of Applied Linguistics in Language Teaching* (Heidel-
       berg)
       Linguistics (The Hague)
       Revista de Lingüística Aplicada (Concepción, Chile)
       Travaux de Linguistique et de Littérature, Strasbourg (Strasbourg)

1964 *Bulletin de la Société Roumaine de Linguistique Romane* (Bucharest)

1965 *Etudes Romanes de Brno* (Brno)
       Foundations of Language (Dordrecht)
       Journal of Linguistics (Cambridge)
       La Linguistique (Paris)

1966 *Estudios Lingüísticos* (São Paulo)
       Langages (Paris)
       Revue Romane (Copenhagen)

1967 *Folia Linguistica: Acta Societatis Linguisticae Europaeae* (The Hague)
       Glossa (Vancouver)
       Language and Language Behaviour Abstracts (The Hague)

1968 *Language Teaching Abstracts* (Cambridge U.P.)

1969 *Langue française* (Paris)

ABBREVIATIONS

Periodicals and Serial Publications

AGI	*Archivio Glottologico Italiano* (Rome, then Turin, 1873–1934, Florence, 1950–)
AION	*Annali dell'Istituto Universitario Orientale di Napoli. Sezione linguistica* (Naples, 1959–)
AL	*Acta Linguistica (Hafniensia)* (Copenhagen, 1939–)
ALH	*Acta Linguistica Academiae Scientiarum Hungariae* (Budapest, 1957–)
AmA	*American Anthropologist* (Bloomington, 1958–)
AnL	*Anthropological Linguistics* (Bloomington, 1958–)
Arch	*Archivum (Oviedo)* (Oviedo 1951–)
ArES	*Archives Européennes de Sociologie* (Paris, 1960–)
ArL	*Archivum Linguisticum* (Glasgow, 1949–)
ASNS	*Archiv für das Studium der neueren Sprachen* (Eberfeld 1846–9, Braunschweig, 1849–)
Ba	*Babel: Revue Internationale de la Traduction* (Bonn–Paris, Fédération Internationale de Traducteurs, 1955–)
BDC	*Butlletí de Dialectología Catalana* (Barcelona, 1913–1937)
BDE	*Boletín de dialectología española* (continuación del *BDC*) (Barcelona 1941–)
BDH	*Boletín de Dialectología Hispano-Americana* (Buenos Aires, 1930–)
BF	*Boletim de Filología* (Lisbon 1932–)
BFR	*Boletim de Filología* (Rio de Janeiro, 1946–)
BFP	*Bibliografia filológica portuguesa* (Lisbon, 1945–)
BH	*Bulletin Hispanique* (Bordeaux, 1899–)
Bib	*Biblos* (Coimbra, Revista da Faculdade de Letras, 1925–)
Bibl.Ling.	Comité International Permanent des Linguistes *Bibliographie linguistique de l'année 19- et complément des années précédentes* (Utrecht and Antwerp, Spectrum, 1949–)
BILAL	*Bulletin d'Information du Laboratoire d'Analyse Lexicologique* (Besançon, 1960–)
BSLP	*Bulletin de la Société de Linguistique de Paris* (Paris, 1871–)
Bull.sig.	Ministère de l'Education Nationale; Centre National de la Recherche Scientifique *Bulletin signalétique* Section 21 *Sociologie, ethnologie* (Paris, CNRS, 1961–)
CAIEF	*Cahiers de l'Association Internationale des Etudes Françaises* (Paris, 1949–)
CFS	*Cahiers Ferdinand de Saussure* (Geneva, 1941–)

544

CLe	*Cahiers de lexicologie* (Besançon, 1959–)
CLin	*Cercetări de Linguistică* (Cluj, 1956–)
CLTA	*Cahiers de Linguistique Théorique et Appliquée* (Bucharest, 1962–)
CN	*Cultura Neolatina*. Bolettino dell'Istituto di filologia romanza dell'Università di Roma (Modena, 1941–)
CSP	*Cahiers Sextil Puşcariu* (Bucharest, 1952–)
CuA	*Current Anthropology* (Chicago, 1960–)
ELA	*Etudes de linguistique appliquée* (Centre de Linguistique Appliquée de Besançon, 1962–)
ERB	*Etudes romanes de Brno* (Brno, 1965–)
EstL	*Estudios Lingüísticos* (Centro de Lingüística Aplicada, São Paulo, Brazil, 1966–)
FD	*Fonetică şi Dialectologie* (Bucharest, 1958–)
Fi	*Filología* (Buenos Aires, 1949–)
FM	*Le Français Moderne* (Paris, 1933–)
Fol	*Foundations of Language* (Dordrecht, 1965–)
FoLi	*Folia Linguistica: Acta Societatis Linguisticae Europaeae* (The Hague, 1967)
Gl	*Glossa* (Vancouver, 1967–)
HR	*Hispanic Review* (Philadelphia, 1933–)
Ib	*Ibérida* (Rio de Janeiro, 1959–)
ID	*Italia Dialettale* (Pisa, 1925–)
IJAL	*International Journal of American Linguistics* (New York, 1917–)
IRAL	*International Review of Applied Linguistics in Language Teaching* (Heidelberg, 1963–)
It	*Italica* (Evanston (Illinois), 1924–)
JL	*Journal of Linguistics* (Cambridge, 1965–)
L	*Language* (Baltimore, Linguistic Society of America, 1925–)
LaF	*Langue Française* (Paris, 1969–)
LaL	*La linguistique* (Paris, 1965–)
LATA	*Linguistique appliquée et traduction automatique* (Nancy, 1962–)
Li	*Lingua* (Haarlem, 1947–)
LiR	*The Linguistic Reporter* (Center for Applied Linguistics, Washington D.C., 1950–)
Lis	*Linguistics* (The Hague, 1963–)
LLBA	*Language and Language Behavior Abstracts* (N.Y. 1967–)
LN	*Lingua nostra* (Florence, 1939–)
Ls	*Langages* (Paris, 1966–)
LTA	*Language Teaching Abstracts* (Cambridge, 1968–)
MLQ	*Modern Language Quarterly* (Seattle, 1940–)
MLR	*Modern Language Review* (Cambridge, 1906–)
MPh	*Le Maître Phonétique* (London, 1889–)
MRo	*Marche Romane* (Liège, 1951–)
MT	*Mechanical Translation* (Cambridge, Mass., M.I.T., 1954–)
N	*Neophilologus* (Groningen, 1916–)
NMi	*Neuphilologische Mitteilungen* (Helsingfors, 1899–)
NRFH	*Nueva Revista de Filología Hispánica* (Mexico, 1947–)
O	*Orbis* (Louvain, 1952–)
PDPS	*Proceedings of the Durham Philosophical Society* (Durham, 1957–)

Phon	*Phonetica* (Basel, 1957–)
PMLA	*Publications of the Modern Language Association of America* (New York, 1889–)
PQ	*The Philological Quarterly* (Iowa City, 1922–)
RDTP	*Revista de dialectología y tradiciones populares* (Madrid, 1944–)
Rev.Lab. *Coïmbra*	*Revista do Laboratório de Fonética Experimental da Faculdade de Letras da Universidade de Coïmbra* (Coimbra, 1952–)
RF	*Romanische Forschungen* (Erlangen, 1883–)
RFE	*Revista de Filología Española* (Madrid, 1914–)
RFH	*Revista de Filología Hispánica* (Buenos Aires–New York, 1939–46)
RFRG	*Revista de Filologie Romanică şi Germanică* (Bucharest, 1957–)
RH	*Romanica Helvetica* (Monograph series; Zurich, then Berne 1935–)
RJ	*Romanistisches Jahrbuch* (Hamburg, 1947–)
RLA	*Revista de Lingüística Aplicada* (Concepción, Chile, 1963–)
RLiR	*Revue de Linguistique Romane* (Paris, 1925–)
RLR	*Revue des langues romanes* (Montpellier, 1870–)
RLu	*Revista Lusitana* (Lisbon, 1887–1938)
Ro	*Romania* (Paris, 1872–)
RP	*Revista de Portugal* Serie A: Lingua Portuguesa; (Lisbon, 1942–)
RPF	*Revista Portuguesa de Filología* (Coimbra, 1947–)
RPh	*Romance Philology* (Berkeley, 1947–)
RRL	*Revue Roumaine de Linguistique* (Bucharest, 1964–; previously *Revue de Linguistique*, 1956–63)
RR	*Romanic Review* (New York, 1910–)
RRom	*Revue Romane* (Copenhagen, 1966–)
S	*Symposium* (Syracuse, 1946–)
SCL	*Studii şi Cercetări Lingvistice* (Bucharest, 1950–)
SIL	*Studies in Linguistics* (Buffalo, N.Y., 1943–)
SL	*Studia Linguistica* (Lund–Copenhagen, 1947–)
SMIL	*Statistical Methods in Linguistics* (Stockholm, 1961–)
SN	*Studia Neophilologica* (Uppsala, 1928–)
SP	*Studies in Philology* (Chapel Hill, 1906–)
SRAZ	*Studia Romanica et Anglica Zagrebiensia* (Zagreb, 1956–, originally *Studia Romanica*)
SRo	*Studi Romanzi* (Rome, 1903–)
SSL	*Studi e Saggi Linguistici* (supplement to *ID*)
TCLC	*Travaux du Cercle Linguistique de Copenhague* (Copenhagen, 1944–)
TCLP	*Travaux du Cercle Linguistique de Prague* (Prague, 1929–39)
TLLS	*Travaux de Linguistique et de Littérature, Strasbourg* (Strasbourg, 1963–)
TPS	*Transactions of the Philological Society* (London, 1885–)
Tr	*Translatøren* (Copenhagen, 1939–)
TradA	*La Traduction Automatique* (The Hague, 1960–)
UCPL	*University of California Publications in Linguistics* (Berkeley, 1943–)
VR	*Vox Romanica. Annales Helvetici explorandis linguis romanicis destinati* (Zürich, then Berne, 1936–)

Wd	*Word* (New York, 1945–)
YWES	*The Year's Work in English Studies* (London, 1921–)
YWML	*The Year's Work in Modern Languages* (London, 1930–)
ZFSL	*Zeitschrift für französiche Sprache und Literatur* (Leipzig, 1879–)
ZP	*Zeitschrift für Phonetik, Sprachwissenschaft und Kommunikationsforschung* (formerly: *Zeitschrift für Phonetik und allgemeine Sprachwissenschaft*) (Berlin, 1947–)
ZRP	*Zeitschrift für Romanische Philologie* (Halle, 1877–)

BIBLIOGRAPHY

Books are referred to in the text by the heading used in the bibliography (author+date, or abbreviation). Periodical articles are cited in the text and are not listed in the bibliography.

D. Abercrombie 1966 *Elements of General Phonetics* (Edinburgh U.P., 1966)

Actas I Cong. Int. Hisp 1962 Actas del Primer Congreso Internacional de Hispanistas F. Pierce and C. A. Jones (eds.) (Oxford, Dolphin Books, 1964)

Actes 6ᵉ Cong. (Liège) 1951 Actes: Essais de Philologie Moderne (Paris, Les Belles Lettres, 1953)

Actes 7ᵉ Cong. (Barcelona) 1953 Actes et Mémoires (Barcelona, San Cugat del Vallès, 1955, 2 vols.)

Actes 8ᵉ Cong. (Florence) 1956 Atti (Florence, Sansoni, 1959)

Actes 9ᵉ Cong. (Lisbon) 1959 Actas do IX Congresso Internacional de Lingüística Românica (Lisboa 31 de Março-4 de Abril de 1959) (Lisbon, Centro de estudos filológicos, 1961-62, 3 vols.)

Actes 10ᵉ Cong. FILLM. 1966 Actes du Xᵉ Congres de la F.I.L.L.M. (Strasbourg) 1966 (Paris, Klincksieck, 1967)

Actes 10ᵉ Cong. (Strasbourg) 1962 Actes du Xᵉ Congres international de linguistique et philologie romanes G. Straka (ed.) (Paris, Klincksieck, 1965, 3 vols.)

Actes 11ᵉ Cong. (Madrid) 1965 Actas del 11 Congreso Internacional de Lingüística y Filología Románicas (Madrid, CSIC, 1968)

P. Aebischer 1948 *Estudios de toponimia y lexicografía románica* (Barcelona, Escuela de Filología, 1948)

F. B. Agard 1958 *Structural Sketch of Rumanian* (Baltimore, Linguistic Society of America, Language Monograph, No. 26, 1958)

F. B. Agard and R. J. Di Pietro 1965 *The Sounds of English and Italian* (Chicago U.P., 1965)

1966 *The Grammatical Structures of English and Italian* (Chicago U.P., 1966)

O. S. Akhmanova *et al.* 1963 O. S. Akhmanova, I. A. Mel'chuk, R. M. Frumkina and E. V. Paducheva *Exact Methods in Linguistic Research* (Berkeley, California U.P., 1963; English trans. by D. G. Hays and D. V. Mohr)

E. Alarcos Llorach 1950 *Fonología española, según el método de la escuela de Praga* (Madrid, Gredos, 1950, 2nd revised ed. 1954, 4th ed. 1968)

1951 *Gramática estructural (según la escuela de Copenhague y con especial atención a la lengua española)* (Madrid, Gredos, 1951)

(forthcoming) *Le langage enfantin* (Paris, P.U.F., Coll. "Le Linguiste")

548

W. S. Allen 1965 *Vox Latina—the Pronunciation of Classical Latin* (Cambridge U.P., 1965)

A. Alonso 1951 *Estudios lingüísticos. Temas españoles* (Madrid, Gredos—Biblioteca Románica Hispánica, 1951, repr. 1954, 2nd ed. 1961)

1953 *Estudios lingüísticos; temas hispano-americanos* (Madrid, Gredos, 1953)

1955 *De la pronunciación medieval a la moderna en español* (Madrid, Gredos, 1955)

A. Alonso and R. Lida 1942 *Introducción a la estilística romance* (Buenos Aires, 1942)

D. Alonso 1950 *Poesía española. Ensayo de métodos y límites estilísticos* (Madrid, Gredos, 1950)

1960–3 (fest.) *Studia Philologica. Homenaje ofrecido a Dámaso Alonso por sus amigos y discípulos con ocasión de su 60° aniversario* (Madrid, Gredos, 1960–63, 3 vols.)

1962 *La fragmentación fonética peninsular* (Madrid, CSIC, 1962)

M. Alvar 1951 *Historia y metodología lingüísticas* (Salamanca U.P., 1951)

1960 *Los Nuevos Atlas Lingüísticos de la Romania* (Granada U.P., 1960)

1961–5 *Atlas lingüístico y etnográfico de Andalucía* (Granada U.P., 1961–65, 4 vols.)

1962 *Dialectología Española* (Madrid, Cuadernos bibliográficos vii, 1962)

M. Alvar *et al.* (eds.) 1960– M. Alvar, A. Badía, R. de Balbin, L. F. Lindley Cintra (eds.) *Enciclopedia lingüística hispánica* (Madrid, CSIC, 1960–)

J. M. Anderson (forthcoming) *Readings in Romance Linguistics* (The Hague, Mouton)

L. Apostel *et al.* 1957 L. Apostel, B. Mandelbrot and A. Morf *Logique, langage et théorie de l'information* (Paris, P.U.F., 1957)

Atlas Lingüístico de la Península Ibérica (abbrev. *ALPI*) (Madrid, CSIC, 1962–)

M. T. Atzori 1953 *Bibliografia di linguistica sarda* (Florence, Valmantina, 1953)

1961 *Bibliografia di linguistica sarda (1948–1959)* (Modena, Soc. tip. editrice, 1961)

E. Auerbach 1949 *Introduction aux études de philologie romane* (Frankfurt, Klostermann, 1949, 2nd ed. 1961, English trans. *Introduction to Romance Languages and Literature*, N.Y., Capricorn Books, 1961)

R. I. Avanesov and S. B. Bernštein 1958 *Lingvističeskaja geografija i struktura jazyka. O printsipax obščeslavjanskogo lingvističeskogo atlasa* (Moscow, 1958)

A. Avram 1960 *Cercetări asupra sonorității în limba romînă* (Bucharest, Ed. Acad., 1960)

E. Bach 1964 *An Introduction to Transformational Grammars* (N.Y.–Chicago–San Francisco, Holt, Rinehart and Winston, 1964)

A. M. Badía Margarit 1951 *Gramática histórica catalana* (Barcelona, Noguer, 1951)

A. M. Badía Margarit and J. Roca Pons 1958 *Panorama de la lingüística moderna* (Introduction to J. Vendryes 1921 [1958])

W. Bahner 1956 *Beitrag zum sprachbewusstsein des 16. und 17. jahrhunderts* (Berlin, 1956, new rev. ed. 1967; Spanish trans. *La lingüística española del Siglo de Oro*)

1962 *Kurze Bibliographie für das Studium der romanischen Sprachwissenschaft mit besonderer Berücksichtigung des Französischen* (Halle, Niemeyer, 1962)

W. Bal 1966 *Introduction aux études de linguistique romane, avec considération spéciale de la linguistique française* (Paris, Didier, 1966)

K. Baldinger 1957 *Die Semasiologie. Versuch eines Überblicks* (Berlin, Akad. Verlag, 1957)

1958 *Die Herausbildung der Sprächräume auf der Pyrenäenhalbinsel* (Berlin, Akad. Verlag, 1958; Spanish trans. *La formación de los dominios lingüísticos en la Peninsula Ibérica* Madrid, Gredos, 1963)

C. Bally 1913 *Le Langage et la vie* (Geneva, Atar, 1913, rev. 2nd ed. Zurich, Niehans 1935, 3rd ed. Geneva, Droz, 1952; Spanish trans. by A. Alonso, *El lenguaje y la vida*, Buenos Aires, Losada, 1941)

1932 *Linguistique générale et linguistique française* (Paris, Leroux, 1932, rev. 2nd ed. Berne, Francke, 1944, 3rd ed. 1950; Russian trans. *Obščaja lingvistika i voprosy frantsuskogo jasyka*, Moscow, 1955)

Y. Bar-Hillel 1964 *Language and Information* (Reading (Mass.), Addison-Wesley, 1964)

R. Barthes 1967 *Système de la Mode* (Paris, Seuil, 1967)

M. Bàrtoli 1945 *Saggi di linguistica spaziale* (Turin, Rosenberg and Sellier, 1945)

S. Battaglia 1946 *Introduzione alla linguistica romanza* (Naples, Pironti, 1946)

C. Battisti 1949 *Avviamento allo studio del latino volgare* (Bari, Leonardo da Vinci, 1949)

P. Bec (forthcoming) *Manuel de philologie romane*

E. Benveniste 1966 *Problèmes de linguistique générale* (Paris, Gallimard, 1966)

V. Bertoldi 1942 *Linguistica storica. Questioni di metodo* (Naples, ed. Dante Alighieri, 1942)

G. Bertoni 1939 *Lingua e cultura* (Florence, Olschki, 1939)

Bibl. bünd.-rom. 1956 *Bibliografia des gedruckten bündnerromanischen Schriftums von 1931-1952* (Chur, Ligia Romantscha, 1956)

A. Blinkenberg 1928-33 *L'ordre des mots en français moderne* (Copenhagen, Høst, 1928-33)

1960 *Le problème de la transitivité en français moderne* (Copenhagen, Munskgaard, 1960)

1963 (fest.) *Etudes romanes dédiées à A. Blinkenberg* (Copenhagen, Munksgaard, 1963)

L. Bloomfield 1933 *Language* (New York, Holt, 1933, English ed., 1935, London, Allen & Unwin)

L. Bloomfield and C. L. Barnhardt 1961 *Let's Read; a Linguistic Approach* (Detroit, Wayne State U.P., 1961)

C. de Boer 1947 *Syntaxe du français moderne* (Leiden U.P., 1947)

T. Bolelli 1965 *Per una storia della ricerca linguistica* (Naples, Morano, 1965)

D. Bolinger 1968 *Aspects of Language* (N.Y., Harcourt, Brace and World, 1968)

G. Bonfante and M. L. Porzio Gernia 1964 *Cenni di fonètica e di fonèmatica* (Turin, Giappichelli, 1964)

H. Bourcelot 1966– *Atlas linguistique et ethnographique de la Champagne et de la Brie* (Paris, CNRS, 1966–)

E. Bourciez 1889 *Précis historique de phonétique française* (Paris, Klincksieck, 1889, 9th ed. 1958)

1967 *Eléments de linguistique romane* (Paris, Klincksieck, 5th ed. rev. by J. Bourciez, 1967)

E. and J. Bourciez 1967 *Phonétique française: étude historique* (Paris, Klincksieck, 1967; J. B.'s refurbishing of his father's *Précis historique de phonétique française*)

R. M. Brend 1968 *A tagmemic analysis of Mexican Spanish clauses* (The Hague, Mouton, 1968)

W. Bright (ed.) 1966 *Sociolinguistics* (*Proceedings of UCLA Sociolinguistics conference, 1964*) (The Hague, Mouton, 1966)

V. Brøndal 1948 *Les parties du discours* (Copenhagen, Munksgaard, 1948)

1950 *Théorie de prépositions* (Copenhagen, Munksgaard, 1950)

R. A. Brower (ed.) 1959 *On Translation* (Cambridge (Mass.), Harvard U.P., 1959)

R. A. Budagov 1961 *Problemy izučenija romanskih literaturnyh jazykov* (Moscow, 1961) trans. into Rumanian 1962 as *Problemele studierii limbilor literare romanice* (Bucharest)

E. Buyssens 1960 *Vérité et langue. Langue et pensée* (Brussels U.P., 1960)

1967 *La communication et l'articulation linguistique* (Brussels–Paris, P.U. Bruxelles–P.U.F., 1967)

J. M. Câmara Jr. 1959 *Princípios de lingüística geral* (Rio de Janeiro, Bibl. Brasileira de Filologia v, 3rd ed. 1959)

A. Camilli 1965 *Pronuncia e grafia dell'Italiano* (Florence, Sansoni, 3rd edition, 1965)

D. L. Canfield 1962 *La pronunciación del español en América* (Bogotá, Inst. Caro y Cuervo, 1962)

A. Capell 1966 *Studies in Sociolinguistics* (The Hague, Mouton, 1966)

D. N. Cárdenas 1961 *Applied Linguistics—Spanish* (Boston, Heath, 1961)

J. Cásares 1950 *Introducción a la lexicografía moderna* (Madrid, CSIC, 1950)

D. Catalán [Menéndez Pidal] 1955 *La escuela lingüística española y su concepción del lenguaje* (Madrid, Bibl. Rom. Hisp., 1955)

J. C. Catford 1965 *A Linguistic Theory of Translation* (London, O.U.P., 1965)

S. Cavaciuti 1959 *La teoria linguistica di Benedetto Croce* (Milan, Marzorati, 1959, Pub. Ist. Fil. Univ. Genova xiii)

B. Cazacu 1960 *Studii de limbă literară* (Bucharest, Ed. Acad., 1960)

1966 *Studii de dialectologie română* (Bucharest, Ed. Şt., 1966)

B. Cazacu *et al.* 1967– *Noul Atlas linguistic român pe regiuni* (Bucharest, 1967–)

Y. R. Chao 1968 *Language and Symbolic Systems* (Cambridge U.P., 1968)

S. Chase 1938 *The Tyranny of Words* (N.Y.–London, Harcourt-Methuen, 1938)

1954 *The Power of Words* (New York, Harcourt, Brace & World, 1954)

R. Chatton 1953 *Zur Geschichte der romanischen Verben für 'sprechen', 'sagen', 'reden'* (Berne, 1953, *RH* xliv)

P. Chauchard 1956 *Le langage et la pensée* (Paris, P.U.F., 1956)

C. Cherry 1957 *On Human Communication: a review, a survey, and a criticism* (Cambridge (Mass.), M.I.T. Press, 1957)

N. A. Chomsky 1957 *Syntactic Structures* (The Hague, Mouton, 1957)

1964 *Current Issues in Linguistic Theory* (The Hague, Mouton, 1964)

1965 *Aspects of the Theory of Syntax* (Cambridge (Mass.), M.I.T. Press, 1965)

1966a *Cartesian Linguistics* (New York, Harper and Row, 1966)

1966b *Topics in the Theory of Generative Grammar* (The Hague, Mouton, 1966)

1968 *Language and Mind* (New York, Harcourt, Brace & World, 1968)

N. A. Chomsky and M. Halle 1968 *The Sound Pattern of English* (New York, Harper & Row, 1968)

N. A. Chomsky and G. A. Miller (forthcoming) *L'analyse formelle des langues naturelles* trans. of two articles originally published in 1963 (The Hague, Mouton)

G. T. Clapton 1966 (mem.) *Currents of Thought in French Literature. Essays in Memory of G. T. Clapton* ed. J. C. Ireson (Oxford, Blackwell, 1966)

J. Cohen 1966 *Structure du langage poétique* (Paris, Flammarion, 1966)

M. Cohen 1950a *Le langage: Structure et évolution* (Paris, Editions sociales, 1950)

1950b *Instructions pour les voyageurs. Instructions d'enquête linguistique* (Paris Inst. d'Ethnologie, 2nd ed. 1950)

1955 *Cinquante années de recherches linguistiques, ethnographiques, sociologiques, critiques et pédagogiques* (Paris, Klincksieck, 1955)

1956 *Pour une sociologie du langage* (Paris, Michel, 1956)

1962 (ed.) *Etudes sur le langage de l'enfant* (Paris, Scarabée, 1962)

1967 *Histoire d'une langue: le français* (Paris, Editions Sociales, 3rd ed. 1967)

(fest.) (forthcoming) *Mélanges Marcel Cohen: Etudes de linguistique, ethnographie et sciences connexes offertes par ses amis et ses élèves à l'occasion de son 80ème anniversaire, avec des articles inédits de Marcel Cohen* (The Hague, Mouton)

Cong. Int. Dial. Gén. 1960 *Communications et rapports du premier Congrès International de Dialectologie Générale* S. Pop (ed.) (Louvain, A. J. van Windekens, 1964–5, 4 vols.)

H. Contreras 1966 *Sobre Gramática Transformacional* (Montevideo U.P., 1966)

E. Coseriu 1952 *Sistema, norma y habla* (Montevideo U.P., 1952)

1954*a* *Forma y sustancia en los sonidos del lenguaje* (Montevideo U.P., 1954)

1954*b* *El llamado latín vulgar y las primeras diferenciaciones romances. Breve introducción a la lingüística románica* (Montevideo U.P., 1954)

1955 *La geografía lingüística* (Montevideo U.P., 1955, another edition, 1966)

1957 *Logicismo y antilogicismo en la gramática* (Montevideo U.P., 1957)

1958 *Sincronía, diacronía e historia. El problema del cambio lingüístico* (Montevideo U.P., 1958)

N. Costabile 1967 *Le strutture della lingua italiana* (Bologna, Patròn, 1967)

J. R. Craddock (forthcoming) *The Unstressed Suffixes in the Western Mediterranean, with Special Regard to Hispano-Romance* (UCPL, 1969)

G. Cremaschi 1959 *Guida allo studio del latino medievale* (Padua, Liviana, 1959)

J. Cremona (forthcoming) *The Romance Languages* (London, Hutchinson)

M. Criado de Val 1953 *Análisis Verbal del Estilo* (Madrid, 1953, RFE, Anejo lvii)

1954 *Fisionomía del idioma español. Sus características comparadas con las del francés, italiano, portugués, inglés y alemán* (Madrid, Gredos, 1954, 2nd ed. 1957)

D. Crystal 1968 *What is Linguistics?* (London, Arnold, 1968)

J. Dakin *et al.* 1968 J. Dakin, B. Tiffen, H. G. Widdowson *Language in Education. The Problem in Commonwealth Africa and the Indo-Pakistan Sub-continent* (Oxford U.P., 1968)

R. de Dardel 1958 *Le parfait fort en roman commun* (Geneva-Paris, Droz, 1958, Publ. romanes et françaises, lxii)

1965 *Recherches sur le genre roman des substantifs de la 3ᵉ déclinaison* (Geneva, Droz, 1965, Publ. romanes et françaises, lxxxv)

A. Dauzat 1951 (fest.) *Mélanges linguistiques offerts à Albert Dauzat* (Paris, d'Artrey, 1951)

A. Dauzat and C. Bruneau 1949 *Où en sont les études de français? Manuel général de linguistique française moderne* (Paris, d'Artrey, 1949, new ed. of 1935 work with supplement for 1935-48)

M. Deanović (forthcoming) *Atlas linguistique balkanique*
(forthcoming) *Atlante Linguistico Mediterraneo*

P. Delattre 1966 *Studies in French and Comparative Phonetics* (The Hague, Mouton, 1966)

E. Delavenay 1959 *La machine à traduire* (Paris, P.U.F., 1959)

E. and K. Delavenay 1960 *Bibliographie de la traduction automatique* (The Hague, Mouton, 1960)

M. Delbouille 1964 (fest.) *Mélanges de linguistique romane et de philologie médiévale offerts à Maurice Delbouille* (Gembloux, Duculot, 1964)

P. Delbouille 1961 *La critique contemporaine devant le pouvoir suggestif des sons* (Paris, Les Belles Lettres, 1961, BFPLUL clxiii)

P. Delbouille *et al.* (eds.) 1966 P. Delbouille, P. Munot, N. Ruwet (eds.) *Méthodes de la grammaire: tradition et nouveauté* (Actes du colloque tenu à Liège du 18 au 20 novembre 1964 dans le cadre de la semaine culturelle danoise) (Paris, Les Belles Lettres, 1966, BFPLUL clxxv)

L. Deroy 1956 *L'emprunt linguistique* (Paris, Les Belles Lettres, 1956)

O. Deutschmann 1959 *Zum Adverb im Romanischen* (Tübingen, Niemeyer, 1959)

G. Devoto 1940 *Storia della lingua di Roma* (Bologna, Cappelli, 1940, 2nd ed. 1944)

  1950 *Studi di stilistica* (Florence, Le Monnier, 1950)

  1951 *I Fondamenti della storia linguistica* (Florence, Sansoni, 1951)

M. C. Díaz y Díaz 1960 *Antología del latin vulgar* (Madrid, Gredos, 1960)

H. Dieckmann 1948 *Le Philosophe* (St. Louis, 1948)

F. Dimitrescu 1967 *Introducere în fonetica istorică a limbii române* (Bucharest, Ed. Acad., 1967)

W. O. Dingwall 1965 *Transformational generative grammar—a bibliography* (Washington, D.C., Center for Applied Linguistics, 1965)

F. P. Dineen 1967 *An Introduction to General Linguistics* (New York, Holt, Rinehart & Winston, 1967)

L. Dolezel and R. W. Bailey (eds.) 1968 *Statistics and Style* (Barking, (Essex), Elsevier, 1968)

R. A. Donzé 1967 *La grammaire générale et raisonnée de Port-Royal* (Berne, Francke, 1967)

J. Dubois 1962a *Le vocabulaire politique et social en France de 1869 à 1872* (Paris, Larousse, 1962, Paris Univ. Thesis)

  1962b *Etude sur la dérivation suffixale en français moderne et contemporain; essai d'interprétation des mouvements observés dans le domaine de la morphologie des mots construits* (Paris, Larousse, 1962, Paris Univ. Thesis)

  1965 *Grammaire structurale du français: i nom et pronom* (Paris, Larousse, 1965)

  1967 *Grammaire structurale du français: ii le verbe* (Paris, Larousse, 1967)

  1969 *Grammaire structurale du français: iii la phrase et les transformations* (Paris, Larousse, 1969)

O. Ducháček 1960 *Le champ conceptuel de la beauté en français moderne* (Prague, Statui Pedagogické Nakladatelství, 1960)

  1967 *Précis de sémantique française* (Brno, 1967)

G. Dulong 1966 *Bibliographie linguistique du Canada français* (Quebec, Laval, U.P., 1966)

A. Duraffour 1939 (fest.) *Mélanges A. Duraffour* (Paris, Droz; Zurich–Leipzig, M. Niehans, 1939, RH xiv)

M. Durand 1936 *Etude expérimentale sur la durée des consonnes parisiennes* (Paris, Klincksieck, 1936)

  1946 *Essai sur la nature de la quantité vocalique* (Paris, Klincksieck, 1946)

U. Eco 1967 *Appunti per una semiologia delle communicazioni visivi* (Milan, 1967)

1968   *La struttura assente*   (Milan, Bompiani, 1968)

W. D. Elcock   1938   *De quelques affinités phonétiques entre l'aragonais et le béarnais*   (Paris, 1938)

1960   *The Romance Languages*   (London, Faber, 1960)

S. Elia   1955   *Orientaçaoes da lingüística moderna*   (Rio de Janeiro, Livraria Academica, 1955)

W. T. Elwert (ed.)   1968   *Probleme der Semantik*   (Beihefte zur *ZFSL*, N.F., H.I., 1968)

Enciclopedia italiana 1949–1960   (Rome, Ist. del E.I., 1961)

R. Engler   1968   *Lexique de la terminologie saussurienne*   (Utrecht–Anvers, Spectrum, 1968)

W. J. Entwistle   1936   *The Spanish Language (together with Portuguese, Catalan & Basque)*   (London, Faber, 1936, reprints 1948, 1951)

R. Etiemble   1964   *Parlez-vous franglais?*   (Paris, Gallimard, 1964)

A. Ewert   1933   *The French Language*   (London, Faber, 1933, 2nd ed. 1943 and later reprints)

1961 (fest.)   *Studies in Medieval French presented to Alfred Ewert in honour of his seventieth birthday*   (Oxford U.P., 1961)

J. S. Falk   1968   *Nominalizations in Spanish*   (Seattle, University of Washington, 1968, Studies in Linguistics and Language Learning, v)

G. Fant   1960   *Acoustic Theory of Speech Production*   (The Hague, Mouton, 1960)

E. de Felice   1954   *La terminologia linguistica di G. I. Ascoli e della sua scuola*   (Utrecht & Antwerp, Spectrum, 1954)

R. Fernando Retamar   1958   *Idea de la Estilística*   (Havana, Cuba, 1958)

U. L. Figge   1966   *Die romanische Anlautsonorisation*   (Bonn, Rom. Versuche und Vorarbeiten, 1966)

J. R. Firth   1957   *Papers in Linguistics, 1934–1951*   (London, O.U.P., 1957)

1966 (mem.)   C. E. Bazell, J. C. Catford, M. A. K. Halliday, R. H. Robins (eds.)   *In Memory of J. R. Firth*   (London, Longmans, 1966)

J. A. Fishman (ed.)   1968   *Readings in the Sociology of Language*   (The Hague, Mouton, 1968)

H. Flasche   1958   *Die Sprachen und Literaturen der Romaner im Spiegel der deutschen Universitätsschriften, 1885–1950*   (Bonn, Akad. Verlag, 1958)

I. Fodor   1965   *The Rate of Linguistic Change. Limits of the Application of Mathematical Methods in Linguistics*   (The Hague, Mouton, 1965)

J. A. Fodor and J. J. Katz (eds.)   1964   *The Structure of Language: Readings in the Philosophy of Language*   (Englewood Cliffs, N.J., Prentice-Hall, 1964)

P. Fouché   1931   *Le verbe français: étude morphologique*   (Paris, Klincksieck, 1931, enlarged reprint 1967)

1952   *Phonétique historique du français: introduction*   (Paris, Klincksieck, 1952, 2nd rev. ed. vol iii 1966)

1956   *Traité de prononciation français*   (Paris, Klincksieck, 1956, 2nd ed. 1959)

J. Frappier (forthcoming) (fest.)   Payer and Régnier (eds.)   *Mélanges Jean Frappier*

J. Fox and R. Wood 1968 *A Concise History of the French Language* (Oxford, Blackwell, 1968)

C. C. Fries 1963 *Linguistics and Reading* (New York, Holt, Rinehart & Winston, 1963)

G. Galichet 1967 *Grammaire structurale du français moderne* (Paris, Charles-Lavauzelle, 1967)

A. Galmés de Fuentes 1962 *Las sibilantes en la Romania* (Madrid, Gredos, 1962)

E. Gamillscheg 1951 *Französiche Bedeutungslehre* (Tübingen, Niemeyer, 1951)

V. García de Diego 1951*a* *Gramática histórica española* (Madrid, Gredos, 1951)

1951*b* *Lingüística general y española* (Madrid, CSIC, 1951)

V. García Hoz 1953 *Vocabulario usual, vocabulario común y vocabulario fundamental* (Madrid, CSIC, 1953)

P. Gardette 1950–56 *Atlas linguistique et ethnographique du Lyonnais* (Lyon, Institut de Linguistique Romane des Facultés Catholiques, Paris, Klincksieck, 1950–6, 3 vols.)

1966 (fest.) *Mélanges de linguistique et de philologie romanes offerts à Monseigneur Pierre Gardette* (Strasbourg, CNRS, 1966, in *TLLS* iv)

P. L. Garvin and B. Spolsky (eds.) 1966 *Computation in Linguistics—A Case Book* (Indiana U.P., 1966)

P. L. Garvin *et al.* (eds.) 1963 P. L. Garvin, H. Lunt, E. Stankiewicz and J. R. Krueger *Soviet and East European Linguistics*, vol. i of *Current Trends in Linguistics*, ed. T. A. Sebeok (The Hague, Mouton, 1963)

F. H. George 1964 *Teach Yourself Semantics* (London, E.U.P., 1964)

W. Giese 1962 *Los pueblos románicos y su cultura popular. Guía etnográfico folclórica* (Bogotá, Instituto Caro y Cuervo, 1962)

S. Gili y Gaya 1958 *Elementos de fonética general* (Madrid, Gredos, 3rd ed. 1958)

R. Glasser 1964 *'Sich finden' in den romanischen Sprachen* (Frankfurt, Klostermann, 1964, Analecta Romanica xv)

H. A. Gleason 1961 *An Introduction to Descriptive Linguistics* (N.Y., Holt, Rinehart and Winston, 2nd ed. 1961)

R. Godel 1957 *Les sources manuscrites du Cours de linguistique générale de F. de Saussure* (Geneva–Paris, Droz, 1957, Société de Publications Romanes et Françaises lxi)

J. González Llubera 1959 (fest.) *Hispanic Studies in Honour of J. González Llubera* F. Pierce (ed.) (Oxford U.P., 1959)

M. F. Goodman 1964 *A Comparative Study of Creole French Dialects* (The Hague, Mouton, 1964)

G. Gougenheim 1938 *Système grammatical de la langue française* (Paris, d'Artrey, 1938, 2nd ed. 1963)

G. Gougenheim *et al.* 1964 G. Gougenheim, M. Rivenc, R. Michea, A. Sauvageot *L'élaboration du français fondamental (1er degré)* (Paris, Didier, 1964)

G. Gougenheim (ed.) 1968 *Problèmes de la traduction automatique* (Paris, Klincksieck, 1968)

Gram. Lar. 1964 J-C. Chevalier, C. Blanche-Benveniste, M. Arrivé and J. Peytard *Grammaire Larousse du français contemporain* (Paris, Larousse, 1964)

La grammaire de Port-Royal. Grammaire Générale et Raisonnée 1660 (Menston, England, Scolar Press Facsimile, 1968)

M. Grammont 1895 *La Dissimilation consonantique dans les langues indo-européennes et dans les langues romanes* (Dijon, 1895)

1936 *Traité de Phonétique* (Paris, Delagrave, 1936, 7th ed. 1963)

C. H. Grandgent 1962 *An Introduction to Vulgar Latin* (N.Y., Hafner, 1962, reprint of 1934 ed.; Spanish trans. by F. de B. Moll, *Introducción al latín vulgar* Madrid, CSIC, 3rd ed. 1963)

A. Graur 1958 *Introducere în lingvistică* (Bucharest, Ed. Acad., 1958)

1960 *Studii de lingvistică generală* (Bucharest, Ed. Acad., 1960)

A. Graur and L. Wald 1965 *Scurtă istorie a lingvisticii* (Bucharest, Ed. Acad., 2nd ed. 1965)

J. H. Greenberg (ed.) 1963 *Universals of Language* (Cambridge (Mass.), M.I.T. Press, 1963, 2nd ed. 1966)

1968 *Anthropological linguistics: an introduction* (N.Y., Random House, 1968)

A. J. Greimas 1948 *La Mode en 1830* (Paris, Univ. thesis in mimeo., 1948)

1966 *Sémantique Structurale* (Paris, Larousse, 1966, Coll. "Langue et langages")

M. Grevisse 1966 (fest.) *Mélanges de grammaire française offerts à M. Maurice Grevisse pour le trentième anniversaire du 'Bon Usage'* (Gembloux, Duculot, 1966)

A. Griera 1942–68 *Atlas lingüistic de Catalunya* (San Cugat del Vallès, Instituto Internacional de Cultura Románica, 1942–68)

1949 *Dialectología catalana* (Barcelona, Instituto Cervantes, 1949)

1955–60 (fest.) *Miscelánea Filológica dedicada a Mons. A. Griera* (Barcelona, CISC and Instituto Internacional de Cultura Románica, 1955–60, 2 vols.)

M. Gross 1968 *Grammaire transformationelle du français: Syntaxe du verbe* (Paris, Larousse, 1968, Coll. "Langue et langages")

G. Guillaume 1919 *Le Problème de l'article et sa solution dans la langue française* (Paris, Hachette, 1919)

1929 *Temps et Verbe, Théorie des Aspects, des Modes et des Temps* (Paris, Champion, 1929)

1945 *L'Architectonique du temps dans les langues classiques* (Copenhagen, Munksgaard, 1945)

1962 *Langage et Science du Langage* (Paris, Nizet and Quebec, Laval U.P., 1962)

P. Guiraud 1952 *Langage et versification d'après l'œuvre de Paul Valéry. Etude sur la forme poétique dans ses rapports avec la langue.* (Paris, Klincksieck, 1952)

1953–54 *Index du vocabulaire du symbolisme* (Paris, Klincksieck, 1953–54)

1953–57 *Index du vocabulaire de la tragédie classique* (Paris, Klincksieck, 1953–57)

1954a *Les Caractères statistiques du vocabulaire* (Paris, P.U.F., 1954)

1954*b* *La Stylistique* (Paris, P.U.F., 1954, trans. into Japanese, Spanish, Norwegian, Serbo-Croat)

1954*c* *Bibliographie critique de la statistique linguistique* (revised and completed by T. D. Houchin, J. Puhvel, and C. W. Watkins, under the direction of Joshua Whatmough) (Utrecht, Spectrum, 1954)

1955 *La Sémantique* (Paris, P.U.F., 1955, trans. into Japanese, Spanish, Italian)

1956 *L'Argot* (Paris, P.U.F., 1956)

1960*a* *La Grammaire* (Paris, P.U.F., 1960, trans. into Japanese and Spanish)

1960*b* *Problèmes et méthodes de la statistique linguistique* (Paris, P.U.F., 1960)

1961 *Les locutions françaises* (Paris, P.U.F., 1961, trans. into Japanese)

1962 *La syntaxe du français* (Paris, P.U.F., 1962)

1963*a* *L'ancien français* (Paris, P.U.F., 1963)

1963*b* *Le moyen français* (Paris, P.U.F., 1963)

1964*a* *L'étymologie* (Paris, P.U.F., 1964)

1964*b* *Les mots étrangers* (Paris, P.U.F., 1964)

1965 *Le français populaire* (Paris, P.U.F., 1965)

1967 *Les structures étymologiques du français* (Paris, Larousse, 1967, Coll. "Langue et langages")

1968*a* *Les patois et dialectes français* (Paris, P.U.F., 1968)

1968*b* *Les mots savants* (Paris, P.U.F., 1968)

H. Guiter 1966 *Atlas linguistique des Pyrénées Orientales* (Paris, CNRS, 1966)

R. A. Haadsma and J. Nuchelmans 1963 *Précis de latin vulgaire* (Groningen, Wolters, 1963)

M. R. Haas (forthcoming) (fest.) *Mary R. Haas Testimonial Volume* (UCPL)

R. Hakamies 1951 *Etude sur l'origine et l'évolution du diminutif et sa survie dans les langues romanes* (Helsinki, 1951, Annales Acad. Sc. Fennicae, B lxxi, 1)

R. A. Hall, Jr. 1942 *The Italian questione della lingua* (Chapel Hill, Univ. of N. Carolina, 1942)

1943 *Melanesian Pidgin English: Grammar, Texts, Vocabulary* (Baltimore, Linguistic Society of America, 1943)

1944 *Hungarian Grammar* (Baltimore, Linguistic Society of America, Language Monograph No. 21, 1944)

1948*a* *Descriptive Italian Grammar* (Cornell U.P., 1948)

1948*b* *Structural Sketch 1—French* (Baltimore, Linguistic Society of America, Language Monograph No. 24, 1948)

1950 *Leave your Language Alone!* (New York, Linguistica Press, 1950, 2nd ed. 1960 as *Linguistics and your Language*, Doubleday)

1958 *Bibliografia della linguistica italiana* (Florence, Sansoni, 2nd ed. 1958, 3 vols. 1st supplement 1969)

1961*a* *Applied Linguistics—Italian* (Boston, Heath, 1961)

1961*b* *Sound and Spelling in English* (Philadelphia, Chilton Books, 1961)

1963   *Idealism in Romance Linguistics*   (Ithaca, Cornell U.P., 1963)

1964   *Introductory Linguistics*   (Philadelphia, Chilton, 1964)

1966   *Pidgin and Creole Languages*   (Ithaca, Cornell U.P., 1966)

1968   *An Essay on Language*   (Philadelphia, Chilton, 1968)

M. Halle   1959   *The Sound Pattern of Russian*   (The Hague, Mouton, 1959)

M. A. K. Halliday *et al.*   1964   M. A. K. Halliday, A. McIntosh and P. D. Strevens   *The Linguistic Sciences and Language Teaching*   (London, Longmans, 1964)

R. Hallig and W. von Wartburg   1952   *Begriffssystem als Grundlage für die Lexikographie*   (Berlin, Akad. Verlag, 1952, 2nd ed. 1963; cf. also W. von Wartburg and R. Hallig 1963)

J. Hamm (ed.)   1967   *Phonologie der Gegenwart*   (Graz–Wien–Köln, Böhaus, 1967)

G. Hammarström   1953   *Etude de phonétique auditive sur les parlers d'Algarve*   (Uppsala, Almqvist & Wiksell, 1953)

1966   *Linguistische Einheiten im Rahmen der modernen Sprachwissenschaft*   (Berlin, Springer, 1966)

E. A. Hammel (ed.)   1965   *Formal Semantic Analysis*   (special number of *AmA*, lxvii No. 5, ii)

E. P. Hamp   1963   *Glossary of American Technical Linguistic Usage 1925–50*   (Utrecht–Antwerp, Spectrum, 1963)

E. P. Hamp *et al.* (eds.)   1966   E. P. Hamp, F. W. Householder, R. Austerlitz   *Readings in Linguistics* ii   (Chicago, U.P., 1966)

L. C. Harmer   1954   *The French Language Today*   (London, Hutchinson, 1954)

Z. S. Harris   1951   *Methods in Structural Linguistics*   (Chicago, U.P., 1951, reprinted 1961 as *Structural Linguistics*, Phoenix Books)

B. Hasselrot   1957   *Etudes sur la formation diminutive dans les langues romanes*   (Uppsala, 1957, Uppsala Universitets Årsskrift xi)

H. A. Hatzfeld   1953   *Critical Bibliography of the New Stylistics 1900–1952*   (Chapel Hill, N. Carolina U.P., 1953, Spanish edition 1955)

1964 (fest.)   *Linguistic and Literary Studies in Honor of Helmut A. Hatzfeld*   (Washington D.C., Catholic U.P., 1964)

1966   *A Critical Bibliography of the New Stylistics Applied to the Romance Literatures, 1953–1965*   (Chapel Hill, N. Carolina U.P., 1966)

H. Hatzfeld and Y. Le Hir   1961   *Essai de Bibliographie critique de stylistique française et romane 1955–1960*   (Paris, P.U.F., 1961, 2nd ed. 1966)

A. G. Haudricourt and A. G. Juilland   1949   *Essai pour une histoire structurale du phonétisme français*   (Paris, Klincksieck, 1949; 2nd rev. ed. forthcoming, The Hague, Mouton)

E. Haugen and W. Winter (eds.) (forthcoming)   *Linguistics in Western Europe*, Vol. ix of *Current Trends in Linguistics* ed. T. A. Sebeok   (The Hague, Mouton)

J. Haust   1939 (fest.)   *Mélanges de linguistique romane offerts à J. Haust*   (Liège, Vaillant-Carmanne, 1939)

J. Haust and L. Remacle   1953–55   *Atlas Linguistique de la Wallonie*   (Liège, Vaillant-Carmanne, 1953–55)

S. I. Hayakawa 1941 *Language in Action* (New York, Harcourt, Brace and World, 3rd ed. 1941)

D. E. Hayden *et al.* (eds.) 1968 D. E. Hayden, E. P. Alworth, G. Tate *Classics in Linguistics* (London, Peter Owen, 1968)

D. G. Hays 1967 *Introduction to Computational Linguistics* (Barking, (Essex), Elsevier, 1967)

D. G. Hays *et al.* 1968 D. G. Hays, B.Henisz-Dostert and J. I. Houston *Computational linguistics: bibliography, 1967* (Sa. Monica, Rand Corp., 1968)

O. W. Heatwole 1949 *Comparative Practical Grammar of French, Spanish and Italian* (N.Y., Vanni, 1949)

P. Henríquez Ureña 1940 *El Español en Santo Domingo* (Buenos Aires, Instituto de Filología, 1940)

J. G. C. Herculano de Carvalho 1967– *Teoria da Linguagem: natureza do fenómeno lingüístico e a análise das línguas* (Coimbra, Atlântida, 1967–)

G. Herdan 1956 *Language as Choice and Chance* (Groningen, Noordhoff, 1956)
   1960 *Type-Token Mathematics, a text-book of Mathematical Linguistics* (The Hague, Mouton, 1960)
   1962 *The Calculus of Linguistic Observations* (The Hague, Mouton, 1962)
   1964 *Quantitative Linguistics* (London, Butterworth and Co., 1964)
   1966 *The Advanced Theory of Language as Choice and Chance* (Berlin–Heidelberg–N.Y., Springer, 1966)

J. Herman 1963 *La formation du système roman des conjonctions de subordination* (Berlin, Akad., 1963, VIRS xviii)
   1967 *Le latin vulgaire* (Paris, P.U.F., 1967)

J. H. Herriott 1966 (fest.) *Estudios dedicados a James Homer Herriott* (Wisconsin U.P., 1966)

A. A. Hill 1958 *Introduction to Linguistic Structures: From Sound to Sentence in English* (N.Y., Harcourt, Brace and World, 1958)

L. Hjelmslev 1959 *Essais linguistiques* (Copenhagen, 1959, *TCLC* xii)
   1943 *Omkring sprogteoriens grundlaeggelse* (Copenhagen, Munksgaard, 1943; English trans. by F. J. Whitfield, *Prolegomena to a theory of Language*, 1953, revised ed. 1961, reprint 1963, Wisconsin U.P.; French trans. *Prolégomènes à une théorie du langage*, Paris, Minuit, 1968)
   1963 *Sproget* (Copenhagen, Berlingske Forlag, 1963; French trans. *Le langage–une introduction*, Paris, Minuit, 1966, with a preface by A. J. Greimas; German trans. *Die Sprache: eine Einführung*, Darmstadt, Wissenschaftliche Buch, 1968)

C. F. Hockett 1958 *A Course in Modern Linguistics* (New York, Macmillan, 1958)
   1968 *The State of the Art* (The Hague, Mouton, 1968)

H. Hoenigswald 1960 *Language change and linguistic reconstruction* (Chicago U.P., 1960)

J. B. Hofmann 1951 *Lateinische Umgangssprache* (Heidelberg, Winter, 1951; Spanish trans. by J. Corominas, *El latin familiar*, Madrid, CSIC, 1958)

H. Hoijer (ed.) 1946 *Linguistic Structures of Native America* (New York, 1946, Viking Fund Pub. in Anth. vi)

T. E. Hope (forthcoming) *The Mutual Influence of French & Italian in the Sphere of Vocabulary from 1100 to 1900* (Oxford, Blackwell)

F. W. Householder and S. Saporta (eds.) 1962 *Problems in Lexicography* (originally published in *IJAL* xxviii: 2, 1962, Part iv; later, Bloomington, Indiana U.P., 1962)

P. Høybye 1944 *L'accord en français contemporain. Essai de grammaire descriptive* (Copenhagen, Høst, 1944)

J. Hubschmid 1949 *Praeromanica: Studien zum vorromanischen Wortschatz der Romania mit besonderer Berücksichtigung der frankoprovenzalischen und provenzalischen Mundarten der Westalpen* (Berne, 1949, *RH* xxx)

    1955 *Schläuche und Fässer: Wort und sachgeschichtliche Untersuchungen mit besonderer Berücksichtigung des romanischen Sprachgutes in und ausserhalb der Romania sowie der türkisch-europäischen und türkisch-kaukasisch-persischen Lehnbeziehungen* (Berne, 1955, *RH* xliv)

    1960*a* *Sardische Studien: Das mediterrane Substrate, mit besonderer Berücksichtigung des Baskischen und der west-östlichen Sprachbeziehungen* (Berne, 1960, *RH* xli)

    1960*b* *Mediterrane Substrate, mit besonderer Berücksichtigung des Baskischen und der westöstlichen Sprachbeziehungen* (Berne, 1960, *RH* lxx)

    1965 *Thesaurus praeromanicus. Probleme der baskischen Lautlehre und baskisch-vorromanisch Etymologien* (Berne, Francke, 1965)

J. P. Hughes 1968 *Linguistics and language teaching* (N.Y., Random House, 1968)

E. Huguet 1940 (fest.) *Mélanges de Philologie et d'Histoire littéraire offerts à E. Huguet* (Paris, Bouvin, 1945)

A. M. Huntington 1952 (fest.) *Estudios hispánicos: Homenaje a Archer M. Huntington* (Wellesley, Mass., 1952)

D. H. Hymes (ed.) 1964 *Language in Culture and Society: A Reader in Linguistics and Anthropology* (N.Y., Harper and Row, 1964)

P. Imbs 1953 *Le subjonctif en français moderne* (Paris, Les Belles Lettres, 1953)

    1960 *L'emploi des temps verbaux en français moderne* (Paris, Klincksieck, 1960)

    (ed.) 1961 *Lexicologie et lexicographie françaises et romanes. Orientation et exigences actuelles* (record of a colloquium held in Strasbourg 1957) (Paris, CNRS, 1961)

G. Ineichen and K. Reichenberger 1967–68 *Romanische Bibliographie 1963–4* (Supplements to *ZRP* lxxix–lxxx, 2 vols.)

I. Iordan 1932 *Introducere în studiul limbilor romanice. Evoluția și starea actuală a lingvisticii romanice* (Jassy U.P., 1932)

    1937 *Gramatica limbii romîne* (Bucharest, Cartea romînească, 1937, 2nd ed. 1946)

    1943 *Limba romînă actuală. O gramatică a "greșelilor"* (Jassy U.P., 1943, 2nd revised ed., Bucharest, 1948)

    1944 *Stilistica limbii romîne* (Bucharest, Inst. de ling., 1944)

    1952– *Nume de locuri romînești în Republica Populară Română* (Bucharest, Ed. Acad, 1952–)

1954 *Limba romînă contemporană. Manual pentru instituţile de invătămînt superior* (Bucharest, Ed. Acad., 1954, 2nd ed. 1956)

1958 (fest.) *Omagiu lui Iorgu Iordan cu prilejul împlinirii a 70 de ani* (Bucharest, Ed. Acad., 1958)

1962 *Lingvistica romanică: Evoluţie, curente, metode* (Bucharest, Ed. Acad., 1962)

(ed.) 1962–68 *Crestomaţie romanică* (Bucharest, 1962–68, 3 vols.)

1964 *Dos estudios de lingüística románica* (Montevideo U.P., 1964)

I. Iordan and P. Georgescu 1964 *Los estudios hispánicos en Rumania* (Bucharest, Ed. Acad., 1964)

I. Iordan, V. Guţu-Romalo and A. Niculescu 1967 *Structura morfologică a limbii române contemporane* (Bucharest, Ed. Şt, 1967)

I. Iordan and Maria Manoliu 1965 *Introducere în lingvistica romanică* (Bucharest, Ed. Didactică şi Pedagogică, 1965)

Iordan–Alvar 1967 I. Iordan 1962 (trans.) *Lingüística románica* (reelaboración parcial y notas de M. Alvar) (Madrid, Alcalá, 1967)

Iordan–Bahner 1962 I. Iordan 1962 (trans.) *Einführung in die Geschichte und Methoden der romanischen Sprachwissenschaft. Ins Deutsche übertragen, ergänzt und Teilweise neuarbeitet von W. Bahner* (Berlin, Akademie-Verlag, 1962)

Iordan–Orr 1937 *An Introduction to Romance Linguistics, its Schools and Scholars* (London, Methuen, 1937)

M. Ivić 1965 *Trends in Linguistics* (The Hague, Mouton, 1965)

J. Jaberg 1959 *Geografía lingüística. Ensayo de interpretación del Atlas Lingüístico de Francia* (Spanish trans. of 1908 *Sprachgeographie*, by A. Llorente and M. Alvar, Granada U.P., 1959)

A. Jacob 1967 *Temps et langage* (Paris, Armand Colin, 1967)

(forthcoming) *Points de vue sur le langage, textes choisis de Platon à Chomsky* (Paris, Klincksieck)

R. Jakobson 1929 *Remarques sur l'évolution phonologique du russe comparée à celle des autres langues slaves* (*TCLP* ii, 1929)

1941 *Kindersprache, Aphasia und allgemeine Lautgesetze* (Uppsala U.P., 1941; English trans. *Child language, Aphasia and Phonological Universals* The Hague, Mouton, 1968)

1956 (fest.) *For Roman Jakobson* (The Hague, Mouton, 1956)

(ed.) 1960 *The Structure of Language and its Mathematical Aspects* (Providence, American Mathematical Soc., 1960)

1962 *Selected Writings* i: *Phonological Studies* (The Hague, Mouton, 1962)

1963 *Essais de linguistique générale* (Paris, Minuit, 1963)

1967 (fest.) *To Honor Roman Jokobson* (The Hague, Mouton, 1967, 3 vols.)

(forthcoming) *Selected Writings* ii: *Word and Language* (The Hague, Mouton)

R. Jakobson, G. Fant and M. Halle 1952 *Preliminaries to Speech Analysis* (Cambridge (Mass.), M.I.T. Press, 1952)

R. Jakobson and M. Halle 1956 *Fundamentals of Language* (The Hague, Mouton, 1956)

O. Jespersen 1924 *The Philosophy of Grammar* (London, Allen and Unwin, 1924)

D. Jones 1950 *The Phoneme: its Nature and Use* (Cambridge, Heffer, 1950)

M. Joos 1948 *Acoustic Phonetics* (Baltimore, Language Society of America, Language Monograph, No. 23, 1948)

M. Joos (ed.) 1957 *Readings in Linguistics* (American Council of Learned Societies, 1957, 4th ed. 1966, Chicago, U.P.)

J. Jud 1943 (fest.) *Sache, Ort und Wort* (Zurich–Geneva, Droz-Rentsch, 1943)

A. Juilland 1961 *Outline of a General Theory of Structural Relations* (The Hague, Mouton, 1961)

F. H. Jungemann 1956 *La teoría del sustrato y los dialectos hispano-romances y gascones* (Madrid, Gredos, 1955)

H. R. Kahane and A. Pietrangeli (eds.) 1959 *Structural Studies on Spanish Themes* (Salamanca U.P., 1959, Acta Salmanticensia xii, 3)

L. Kaiser (ed.) 1957 *Manual of Phonetics* (Amsterdam, North Holland, 1957)

C. E. Kany 1945 *American Spanish Syntax* (Chicago U.P., 1945)

H. Karlgren (forthcoming) *Quantitative Linguistics* (Lund–Stockholm)

J. J. Katz and P. M. Postal 1964 *An Integrated Theory of Linguistic Descriptions* (Cambridge (Mass.), M.I.T. Press, 1964, Research Monograph No. 26)

F. Kiefer 1968 *Mathematical linguistics in Eastern Europe* (N.Y., Elsevier, 1968)

R. D. King 1969 *Historical Linguistics and Generative Grammar* (Englewood Cliffs, N.J., Prentice-Hall, 1969)

P. W. Klein 1968 *Modal Auxiliaries in Spanish* (Seattle, University of Washington, 1968, Studies in Linguistics and Language Learning iv)

A. Klum 1961 *Verbe et Adverbe* (Uppsala U.P., 1961, Studia Romanica Upsaliensia i)

A. Korzybski 1948 *Science and Sanity* (Lakeville (Conn.), Int. Non-Aristotelian Lib. Pub. Co., 3rd ed. 1948)

M. Křepinsky 1951 *Romanica I:* (1. "Du rôle de la chronologie relative dans la linguistique historique"; 2. "Les plus anciens changements phonétiques des langues romanes"; 3. "C^e après voyelle en français"; 4. "GN et NG' en français"; 5. "Tableau synoptique") (Prague, Česk. Ak., 1951)

1958 *Romanica II: La naissance des langues romanes et l'existence d'une période de leur évolution commune (latin vulgaire, période romane)* (Prague, Česk. Ak., 1958)

A. Kroeber (ed.) 1953 *Anthropology Today* (Chicago, U.P., 1953)

F. Krüger 1952 (fest.) *Homenaje a Fritz Krüger* (Mendoza, Cuyo U.P., 1952)

A. Kuhn 1951 *Romanische Philologie. Erster Teil: Die romanischen Sprachen* (Berne, Francke, 1951)

1963 (fest.) *Weltoffene Romanistik: Festschrift A. Kuhn* (Innsbruck, 1963, Innsbrucker Beiträge zur Kulturwissenschaft ix/x)

L. Kukenheim 1966 *Esquisse historique de la linguistique française et de ses rapports avec la linguistique générale* (Leiden U.P., 2nd ed. 1966)
1967– *Grammaire historique de la langue française* (Leiden U.P., 1967–)

J. E. Lackstrom 1968 *Pro-forms in the Spanish Noun Phrase* (Seattle, University of Washington, 1968, Studies in Linguistics and Language Learning, iii)

P. Ladefoged 1962 *Elements of Acoustic Phonetics* (Edinburgh–London, Oliver and Boyd, 1962)
1967 *Three Areas of Experimental Phonetics* (London, O.U.P., 1967)

R. Lado 1963 *Language Teaching: a scientific approach* (N.Y., McGraw-Hill, 1963)

R. Lado et al. (eds.) (forthcoming) *Ibero-American and Caribbean Linguistics* ed. by R. Lado, N. A. McQuown, S. Saporta and Y. Lastra, vol. iv of *Current Trends in Linguistics*, ed. T. A. Sebeok (The Hague, Mouton, 1969)

J. C. Lafon 1961 *Message et Phonétique: Introduction à l'étude acoustique et physiologique du phonème* (Paris, P.U.F., 1961)

S. Lamb 1967 *Outline of stratificational grammar* (Washington D.C., Georgetown U.P., 1967)

R. W. Langacker 1968 *Language and its structure: some fundamental linguistic concepts* (N.Y., Harcourt, Brace and World, 1968)

D. T. Langendoen 1968 *The London School of Linguistics: a Study of the Linguistic Theories of B. Malinowski and J. R. Firth* (Cambridge, Mass., M.I.T. Press, 1968)

A Language-Teaching Bibliography (Cambridge U.P., 1968)

R. Lapesa 1942 *Historia de la lengua española* (Madrid, Escelicer, 1942, rev. 5th ed. 1962)

H. Lausberg 1956–62 *Romanische Sprachwissenschaft* (Berlin, de Gruyter, 1956–62, 4 vols.)

F. Lázaro Carreter 1949 *Las ideas lingüísticas en España durante el siglo XVIII* (Madrid, CSIC, 1949)
1962 *Diccionario de Términos Filológicos* (Madrid, Gredos, 2nd ed. 1962)

R. B. Lees 1960 *The Grammar of English Nominalizations* (Indiana U.P., 1960)

H. Lefebvre 1966 *Le langage et la société* (Paris, Gallimard, 1966)

I. Lehiste (ed.) 1967 *Readings in Acoustic Phonetics* (Cambridge (Mass.), M.I.T. Press, 1967)

W. P. Lehmann 1962 *Historical Linguistics: an Introduction* (New York, Holt, Rinehart and Winston, 1962)
(ed.) 1967 *A Reader in 19th Century Historical Indo-European Linguistics* (Bloomington–London, Indiana U.P., 1967)

W. P. Lehmann and Y. Malkiel (eds.) 1968 *Directions for Historical Linguistics* (Austin, Texas U.P., 1968)

R. Lejeune 1968 (fest.) *Mélanges Rita Lejeune* (Gembloux, Duculot, 1968)

M. Lema Mourelle 1968 *La teoría lingüística en la España del siglo XIX* (Madrid, 1968)

E. H. Lenneberg 1967 *Biological Foundations of Language* (N.Y., Wiley, 1967)

P. R. Léon 1962 *Laboratoire de langues et correction phonétique* (Paris, Didier, 1962)
1966 *La prononciation du français standard* (Paris, Didier, 1966)

W. F. Leopold 1952 *A Bibliography of Child Language* (Evanston, North Western U.P., 1952)

R. B. Le Page 1964 *The National Language Question* (Oxford U.P., 1964)

G. C. Lepschy 1966 *La Linguistica strutturale* (Torino, Einaudi, 1966)

M. Leroy 1963 *Les Grands Courants de la linguistique moderne* (Paris-Brussels, P.U. Bruxelles—P.U.F., 1963; English trans. *The Main Trends in Modern Linguistics* Oxford, Blackwell, 1967, "Language and Style"; v)

S. R. Levin 1962 *Linguistic Structures in Poetry* (The Hague, Mouton, 1962)

Linguistic Theories and their Application (Council for Cultural Cooperation, 1967)

A. Llorente 1953 *Los "Principios de Gramática General" de Hjelmslev y la lingüística. Introducción a la ciencia de lenguaje* (Granada U.P., 1953)
1967 *Teoría de la lengua e historia de la lingüística* (Madrid, 1967)

P. M. Lloyd 1968 *Verb Complement Compounds in Spanish* (Tübingen, Niemeyer, 1968, *ZRP* Beiheft 116)

E. Löfstedt 1959 *Late Latin* (Oslo, Aschehoug, 1959)
1966 *Les expressions du commandement et de la défense en latin et leur survie dans les langues romanes* (Helsinki, 1966, MSNH xxix)

A. Lombard 1954–55 *Le verbe roumain, étude morphologique* (Lund, Gleerup, 1954–55, 2 vols.)
1968 (fest.) Neumann. S-G. (ed.) *Mélanges Alf Lombard* (Lund, 1968)

H. Lüdtke 1956 *Die strukturelle Entwicklung des romanischen Vokalismus* (Bonn, Rom. Sem. Univ. Bonn, 1956)

J. Lyons 1963 *Structural Semantics. An Analysis of Part of the Vocabulary of Plato* (Oxford, Blackwell, 1963, "Publications of the Philological Society" xx, reprint 1967)
1967 *The Scientific Study of Language* (Edinburgh U.P., 1967)
1968 *Introduction to Theoretical Linguistics* (Cambridge U.P., 1968)

J. P. Machado 1941 *Breve Historia da Lingüística* (Lisbon, 1942)

D. Macrea 1953 *Probleme de fonetică* (Bucharest, Ed. Acad., 1953)
1959 *Lingviști și filologi români* (Bucharest, Ed. Acad., 1959)

Y. Malkiel 1938 *Das substantivierte Adjectiv in Französischen* (Berlin, Druck, 1938, Berliner Dissertation)
1968 *Essays on Linguistic Themes* (Oxford, Blackwell, 1968, "Language and Style" vi.)
(forthcoming) *Filologia romanza e l'etimologia* (tr. Olga Devoto, rev. R. Stefanini, Florence, Sansoni)

B. Malmberg 1943 *Le système consonantique du français moderne. Etudes de phonétique et de phonologie* (Lund, Gleerup, 1943)
1950 *Etude sur la phonétique de l'espagnol parlé en Argentine* (Lund U.P., 1950)

1954 *La Phonétique* (Paris, P.U.F., 1954, 2nd ed. 1966; English trans. *Phonetics*, completely revised, New York, Dover Publications, 1963)

1963*a* *Estudios de fonética hispánica* (Madrid, CSIC, 1963)

1963*b* *Structural Linguistics and Human Communication* (Berlin–Göttingen–Heidelberg, Springer, 1963)

1964 *New Trends in Linguistics. An Orientation* (Stockholm–Lund, Nature Methods Institute, 1964, "Bibliotheca Linguistica" i) (Translation of *Nya vägar inom språkforskningen* (1959). French trans. *Les Nouvelles Tendances de la linguistique*, Paris P.U.F., 1966)

1968 (ed.) *Manual of Phonetics* (Amsterdam, North-Holland, 1968)

(forthcoming) *Phonétique générale et romane: Etudes en allemand, anglais, espagnol et français* (The Hague, Mouton)

D. G. Mandelbaum (ed.) 1949 *Selected Writings of Edward Sapir* (Berkeley, California U.P., 1949, 3rd reprint 1958)

G. Manuppella 1950 *Os estudos de Filologia Portuguesa de 1930 a 1949. Subsídios bibliográficos* (Lisbon, Centro de Estudos Filológicos, 1950)

S. Marcus 1966 *Algebraic Linguistics: analytic models* (New York, Acad. Press, 1966)

1967 *Introduction mathématique à la linguistique structurale* (Paris, Dunod, 1967)

J. Marouzeau 1950 *Précis de stylistique français* (Paris, Masson, 3rd ed. 1950)

1954 *Introduction au latin* (Paris, Les Belles Lettres, 2nd ed. 1954)

R. Martin 1966 *Le mot 'rien' et ses concurrents en français (du XIVe s. à l'époque contemporaine)* (Paris, Klincksieck, 1966)

A. Martinet 1937*a* *La Gémination consonantique d'origine expressive dans les langues germaniques* (Copenhagen, Munksgaard, 1937)

1937*b* *La Phonologie du mot en danois* (Paris, Klincksieck, 1937)

1945 *La Prononciation du français contemporain* (Paris, Droz, 1945)

1947 *Initiation pratique à l'anglais* (Lyon, IAC, 1947)

1949 *Phonology as Functional Phonetics* (London, O.U.P., 1949)

1955 *Economie des changements phonétiques, Traité de phonologie diachronique* (Berne, Francke, 1955, 2nd ed. 1964)

1956 *La description phonologique avec application au parler franco-provençal d'Hauteville (Savoie)* (Geneva, Droz–Paris, Minard, 1956, "Société de publications romanes et françaises" lvi)

1957–62 (fest.) Diego Catalán (ed.) *Miscelánea homenaje a André Martinet. "Estructuralismo e historia"* (La Laguna U.P., 1957–62, 3 vols.)

1960 *Eléments de linguistique générale* (Paris, Armand Colin, 1960; English trans. *Elements of General Linguistics* London, Faber, 1964; Spanish trans. *Elementos de lingüística general*, Madrid, Gredos, 2nd ed. 1968)

1962 *A Functional View of Language* (London, O.U.P., 1962)

1966 *La Linguistique synchronique* (Paris, P.U.F., 1966)

(ed.) 1968 *Le Langage* (Paris, Gallimard, "Encyclopédie de la Pléiade", 1968)

1969 *Le français sans fard* (Paris, P.U.F. 1969)

G. Matoré 1951 *Le Vocabulaire et la société sous Louis-Philippe* (Geneva, Droz-Lille, 1951)

　1953 *La Méthode en lexicologie: domaine français* (Paris, Didier, 1953)

　1962 *L'espace humain* (Paris, La Colombe, 1962)

　1968 *Histoire des dictionnaires français* (Paris, Larousse, 1968)

T. H. Maurer 1962 *O problema do latin vulgar* (Rio de Janeiro, Liv. Ac., 1962)

M. F. Maxfield 1941 *Rhaeto-Romance Bibliography* (Chapel Hill, N. Carolina U.P., 1941)

C. L. Meader and J. H. Muyskens (eds.) 1962 *Handbook of Biolinguistics* vol. i (Toledo–Ohio, Weller, 1962)

H. Meier 1941 *Die Entstehung der romanischen Sprachen und Nationen* (Frankfurt, Klostermann, 1941)

　1948 *Ensaios de filología românica* (Lisbon, Ed. da Rev. Port, 1948)

A. Meillet and M. Cohen 1952 *Les langues du monde* (Paris, CNRS, 1952)

R. Menéndez Pidal 1904 *Manual (elemental) de gramática histórica española* (Madrid, Suárez, 1904, rev. 6th ed. Madrid, Espasa-Calpe, 1941, subsequent reprints, 10th ed. 1958)

　1926 *Orígenes del español; estado lingüístico de la Península Ibérica hasta el siglo xi* (Madrid, Hernando, 1926, *RFE* anejo i, 3rd ed. completely recast, Madrid, Espasa-Calpe, 1950, *Obras Completas* viii 5th ed. 1964)

　1950– (fest.) *Estudios dedicados a Ramón Menéndez Pidal* (Madrid, CSIC, 1950–)

B. Migliorini 1946 *Linguistica* (Florence, Le Monnier, 1946, 4 vols.)

　1957 *Saggi linguistici* (Florence, Le Monnier, 1957)

　1960 *Storia della lingua italiana* (Firenze, Sansoni, 1960, 3rd ed. 1961; revised and extended trans. *The Italian Language*, Glasgow & N.Y., Faber, 1966)

H. Mihăescu 1960 *Limba latină in provinciile dunarene ale imperiului roman* (Bucharest, Ed. Acad., 1960)

G. A. Miller 1951 *Language and Communication* (New York, McGraw-Hill, 1951; French trans. *Langage et communication* Paris, P.U.F., 1956)

R. L. Miller 1968 *The linguistic relativity principle and Humboldtian ethno-linguistics* (The Hague, Mouton, 1968)

T. F. Mitchell 1965 *On the Nature of Linguistics and its Place in University Studies* (Leeds U.P., 1965)

C. Mohrmann 1955 *Latin vulgaire, latin des chrétiens, latin médiéval* (Paris, Klincksieck, 1955)

C. Mohrmann et al. (eds.) 1961 C. Mohrmann, A. Sommerfelt and J. Whatmough *Trends in European and American Linguistics 1930–1960* (abbrev. *Trends i*) (Utrecht–Antwerp, Spectrum, 1961)

　1963 C. Mohrmann, F. Norman and A. Sommerfelt *Trends in Modern Linguistics* (abbrev. *Trends ii*) (Utrecht–Antwerp, Spectrum, 1963)

G. Moignet 1959 *Les Signes de l'exception dans l'histoire du français* (Geneva, Droz, 1959)

　1961 *L'Adverbe dans la locution verbale. Etude de psycho-systématique française* (Quebec, Laval U.P., 1961)

1965 *Le Pronom personnel français. Essai de psycho-systématique historique* (Paris, Klincksieck, 1965)

F. de B. Moll 1952 *Gramática histórica catalana* (Madrid, Gredos, 1952)
1968 *Gramática catalana, referida especialmente a los Illes Balears* (Madrid, 1968)

A. Monteverdi 1952 *Manuale di avviamento agli studi romanzi. Le lingue romanze* (Milan, Vallardi, 1952)

E. R. Moses, Jr. 1964 *Phonetics, History and Interpretation* (Englewood Cliffs N.J., Prentice-Hall, 1964)

G. Mounin 1963 *Les Problèmes théoriques de la traduction* (Paris, Gallimard 1963)
1964 *La Machine à traduire: Histoire des problèmes linguistiques* (The Hague, Mouton, 1964)
1967 *Histoire de la linguistique des origines au XXᵉ siècle* (Paris, P.U.F., 1967)
1968 *Clefs pour la linguistique* (Paris, Seghers, 1968)
(forthcoming) *La linguistique du XXᵉ Siècle* (Paris, P.U.F., Coll. "Le linguiste")

M. J. de Moura Santos 1966 *Os estudos de lingüística românica em Portugal de 1945 a 1960* (Coimbra, Casa do Castelo, 1966, supp. to *RPF* ii)

J. W. F. Mulder 1968 *Sets and Relations in Phonology (An axiomatic approach to the description of speech)* (Oxford U.P., 1968)

C. Muller 1964 *Essai de statistique lexicale (L'Illusion Comique de Pierre Corneille)* (Paris, Klincksieck, 1964)
1968 *Initiation à la statistique linguistique* (Paris, Larousse, 1968)

C. Muller and B. Pottier (eds.) 1966 *Statistique et Analyse linguistique* (proceedings of a 1964 Strasbourg colloquium) (Paris, P.U.F., 1966)

H-F. Muller 1929 *Chronology of Vulgar Latin* (Halle, 1929)
1945 *L'époque mérovingienne. Essai de synthèse de philologie et d'histoire* (New York, Vanni, 1945)

A. McIntosh and M. A. K. Halliday 1966 *Patterns of Language* (London, Longmans, 1966)

O. Nandriş 1963 *Phonétique historique du roumain* (Paris, Klincksieck, 1963)

R. Nash 1968 *Multilingual Lexicon of Linguistics and Philology* (Paris, Klincksieck, 1968)

P. Nauton 1957– *Atlas linguistique et ethnographique du Massif Central* (Paris, CNRS, 1957–)

T. Navarro Tomás 1918 *Manual de pronunciación española* (Madrid, CSIC, 1918; 12th ed. 1965)
1946 *Estudios de fonología española* (Syracuse U.P., 1946; English trans. *Studies in Spanish Phonology*, 1968)
1948 *El español en Puerto Rico* (Puerto Rico U.P., 1948)

E. A. Nida 1943 *A Synopsis of English Syntax* (Ann Arbor, Michigan U.P., 1943, Doct. Thesis; 2nd rev. ed. The Hague, Mouton, 1966)

1944   *Morphology: the Descriptive Analysis of Words*   (Ann Arbor, Michigan U.P., 1944)
1947   *Linguistic Interludes*   (Summer Institute of Linguistics, 1947)
1964   *Towards a Science of Translating*   (Leiden, Brill, 1964)

C. K. Ogden and I. A. Richards   1923   *The Meaning of Meaning*   (London, Routledge & Kegan Paul, 1923, 10th ed. 1949, reprint 1960)
R. C. Oldfield and J. C. Marshall (eds.)   1968   *Language. Selected Writings* (London, Penguin, 1968)
R. Oroz   1954–55(fest.)   *Homenaje a Rodolfo Oroz*   (Santiago de Chile, Inst. de Filología, 1954–55)
J. Orr   1953   *Words and Sounds in English and French*   (Oxford, Blackwell, 1953)
   1953 (fest.)   *Studies in Romance Philology and French Literature presented to John Orr by pupils, colleagues and friends*   (Manchester U.P., 1953)
   1962a   *Three Studies on Homonymics*   (Edinburgh U.P., 1962)
   1962b   *Old French and Modern English Idiom*   (Oxford, Blackwell, 1962)
   1963   *Essais d'étymologie et de philologie françaises*   (Paris, Klincksieck, 1963)
C. E. Osgood and T. A. Sebeok (eds.)   1965   *Psycholinguistics: A Survey of theory and research problems*   (Bloomington, Indiana U.P., 1965)
T. Ostermann   1950   *Bibliographie der Schriften Karl Vosslers 1897–1951* (Sitzungsber. d. Bayer Ak. Wis., 1950, Phil.-hist. Abt. xi)

P8thICL 1957   Proceedings of the 8th International Congress of Linguists, Oslo, 1957   E. Sivertsen (ed.)   (Oslo, 1958)
P9thICL 1962   Proceedings of the 9th International Congress of Linguists, Cambridge, Mass. 1962   H. G. Lunt (ed.)   (The Hague, Mouton, 1964)
M. de Paiva Boléo   1946   *Introdução ao estudo da filología portuguesa*   (Lisbon, 1946)
   (ed.)   1951   *Os estudos de Lingüística Românica na Europa e na América desde 1939 a 1948*   (Coimbra, Casa do Castelo, 1951, supp. to *RPF* i)
T. R. Palfrey *et al.*   1963   T. R. Palfrey, J. G. Fucilla and W. C. Holbrook *A Bibliographical Guide to the Romance Languages and Literatures*   (Evanston, Chandler, 5th ed. 1963)
F. Palmer (ed.)   1969   *Prosodic Analysis*   (Oxford U.P., 1969)
L. R. Palmer   1955   *The Latin Language*   (London, Faber, 1955)
F. Papp   1966   *Mathematical Linguistics in the Soviet Union*   (The Hague, Mouton, 1966)
H. Pedersen   1962   *The Discovery of Language: Linguistic Science in the 19th century*   (trans. by J. W. Spargo from 1924 original and brought up to date by the translator)   (Bloomington, Indiana U.P., 1962)
M. A. Pei   1932   *The Language of the Eighth Century Texts in Northern France* (N.Y., Columbia U.P., 1932)
   1941   *The Italian Language*   (N.Y., Columbia U.P., 1941)
   1949   *The Story of language*   (Philadelphia, Lippincott, 1949, revised ed. 1969-, French trans. *Histoire du langage. Origines. Eléments constitutifs. Fonctions sociales*, Paris, Payot, 1954)

1963 *Studies in Romance Literature and Philology* (Chapel Hill, N. Carolina U.P., 1963)

1965 *Invitation to Linguistics* (Garden City, N.Y.–London, 1965)

1966 *Glossary of Linguistic Terminology* (N.Y., Doubleday, 1966)

M. A. Pei and F. Gaynor 1960 *A Dictionary of Linguistics* (London, Owen, 2nd ed. 1960, new ed. 1968)

G. B. Pellegrini 1950 *Grammatica storica spagnuola* (Bari, L. da Vinci, 1950)

J. Perrot 1953 *La Linguistique* (Paris, P.U.F., 1953)

E. Petrovici *et al.* 1940–42 *Micul altas linguistic român* (Cluj–Leipzig, Muzeul Limbii Române–Harrassowitz, 1940–42, 2 vols.)

1942 *Atlasul Linguistic Român* (Cluj–Leipzig, Muzeul Limbii Române –Harrassowitz, 1942, 2 vols and supp.)

M. Pfister 1960 *Die Entwicklung der inlautenden Konsonantengruppe -PS- in den romanischen Sprachen* (Berne, Francke, 1960, *RH* xlix)

K. L. Pike 1943 *Phonetics* (Ann Arbor, Michigan U.P., 1943)

1947 *Phonemics. A Technique for Reducing Languages to Writing* (Ann Arbor, Michigan U.P., 1947)

1967 *Language in Relation to a Unified Theory of Human Behaviour* (The Hague, Mouton, 2nd ed. 1967)

R. G. Piotrovskij 1960a *Ocherki po Stilistike Frantsuzskogo Jazyka* (Leningrad, 2nd ed., 1960)

1960b *Formirovanie artiklja v romanskih jazykah* (Moscow–Leningrad, 1960)

F. N. and R. L. Politzer 1953 *Romance Trends in 7th and 8th Century Latin Documents* (Chapel Hill, N. Carolina U.P., 1953)

R. L. Politzer 1949 *A Study of the Language of 8th Century Lombardic Documents* (N.Y., Columbia Univ. Thesis, 1949)

1960 *Teaching French—an Introduction to Applied Linguistics* (Boston, Ginn & Co., 1960)

1967a *Beitrag zur Phonologie der Nonsberger Mundart* (Innsbruck, Inst. für Rom. Phil. der Leopold-Franzens-Univ, 1967)

1967b *Foreign Language Learning: A Linguistic Introduction* (Englewood Cliffs N.J., Prentice-Hall, 1967)

R. L. Politzer and C. N. Staubach 1961 *Teaching Spanish: a linguistic orientation* (Boston, Ginn & Co., 1961)

S. Pop 1950 *La Dialectologie* (Louvain, Auteur, 1950)

1955 *Bibliographie des questionnaires linguistiques* (Louvain, Commission d'Enquête linguistique, 1955; partially published in *O* iii 1954)

1966 *Recueil posthume de linguistique et dialectologie* (Gembloux, Duculot, 1966)

S. and R. D. Pop 1959 *Jules Gilliéron. Vie, enseignement, élèves, œuvres, souvenirs* (Louvain, 1959)

M. K. Pope 1934 *From Latin to Modern French with Especial Consideration of Anglo-Norman; Phonology & Morphology* (Manchester U.P., 1934, 4 reprints to 1966)

R. Posner 1961 *Consonantal Dissimilation in the Romance Languages* (Oxford, Blackwell, 1961, "Publications of the Philological Society" xix)

1966   *The Romance Languages. A Linguistic Introduction*   (N.Y., Double-day, 1966)

P. Postal   1964   *Constituent Structure. A Study of Contemporary Models of Syntactic Description*   (Indiana U.P., 1964)

1968   *Aspects of Phonological Theory*   (New York–Evanston–London, Harper & Row, 1968)

B. Pottier   1947   *Manuel de philologie espagnole*   (Paris, dépôt Navarro, 1947)

1957–58   *Introduction à l'étude de la philologie hispanique*   (Bordeaux, 1957–8, 2 vols, 2nd ed. Paris, Payot, 1960)

1962a   *Introduction à l'étude des structures grammaticales fondamentales*   (Nancy, Faculté des Lettres et Sciences Humaines, 1962, 2nd ed. 1964)

1962b   *Systématique des éléments de relation. Etude de morphosyntaxe structurale romane*   (Paris, Klincksieck, 1962, *Bibliothèque Française et Romane publiée par le Centre de Philologie romane de la Faculté des Lettres de Strasbourg*, Série A: Manuels et Etudes Linguistiques, vol ii)

1964   *Textes médiévaux français et romans*   (Paris, Klincksieck, 1964)

1966   *Eléments de lexicologie hispano-américaine*   (U.N.E.F., 1966)

1967a   *Bibliographie américaniste: linguistique amérindienne*   (Paris: Société des Américanistes, 1967)

1967b   *Présentation de la linguistique. Fondements d'une théorie*   (Paris, Klincksieck, 1967)   (First appeared in *TLLS* v, 1967)

1968   *Lingüística moderna y filología hispánica*   (Madrid, Gredos, 1968)

(forthcoming)a   *Grammaire de l'espagnol*   (Paris, P.U.F.)

(forthcoming)b   *L'etude des langues amérindiennes*

(forthcoming)c   *Linguistique et traduction mécanique*   (Lund, "Biblioteca linguistica")

Pres. y fut. español   1964   *Presente y futuro de la lengua española   Actas de la asamblea de filología del 1 congreso de instituciones hispánicas*   (Madrid, OFINES, Ed. Cult. Hisp., 1964, 2 vols.)

Problemas . . .   1967   *Problemas y principios del estructuralismo lingüístico: coloquios . . . del xxv aniversario del CSIC*   (Madrid, Publ. *RFE* xvi, 1967)

Problèmes de psycho-linguistique   1963   (Paris, P.U.F., 1963)

Problèmes du langage   1966   (Paris, Gallimard, 1966)

Proceedings of the 5th International Congress of Phonetic Sciences   (Münster, 1964)

E. Pulgram (ed.)   1954   *Applied Linguistics in Language Teaching*   (Washington D.C., Georgetown U.P., 1954)

1958   *The Tongues of Italy. Prehistory and History*   (Cambridge (Mass.), Harvard U.P., 1958)

1959   *Introduction to the Spectrography of Speech*   (The Hague, Mouton, 1959, reprint 1964)

(forthcoming)   *Syllable, Word Nexus: a Study of Phonological Boundaries*, (The Hague, Mouton)

B. Quemada   1955a   *Le commerce amoureux dans les romans mondains (1640–1670)*   (Paris, Les Belles Lettres, 1955)

1955b   *Introduction à l'étude du vocabulaire médical (1600–1670)*   (Paris, Les Belles Lettres, 1955)

1968   *Les dictionnaires du français moderne (1539-1863) : étude sur leur histoire, leurs types et leurs méthodes*   (Paris, Didier, 1968, "Etudes lexicologiques" i)

A. Quilis   1963   *Fonética y Fonología del Español*   (Madrid, "Cuadernos bibliográficos" x, 1963)

A. Quilis and J. A. Fernández   1964   *Curso de fonética y fonología españolas* (Madrid, Instituto "Miguel de Cervantes", 1964, 2nd ed. 1966)

H. Ramsden   1963   *Weak Pronoun Position in the Early Romance Languages* (Manchester U.P., 1963)

Rec. d'ét. rom.   1959   *Recueil d'études romanes publié à l'occasion du IXe Congrès International de Linguistique Romane à Lisbonne du 31 mars au 3 avril 1959* (Bucharest, Ed. Acad., 1959)

M. Regula   1955-66   *Historische Grammatik des Französischen*   (Heidelberg, Winter, 1955-66, 3 vols.)

M. Regula & J. Jernej   1955   *Grammatica italiana descrittiva su basi storiche e psicologiche*   (Berne-Munich, Francke, 1965)

G. Reichenkron   1965-   *Historische latein-altromanische Grammatik*   (Wiesbaden, Harrassowitz, 1965-)

T. B. W. Reid   1960   *Historical Philology and Linguistic Science*   (Oxford U.P., 1960, Inaugural lecture)

J. Renson   1962   *Les dénominations du visage en français et dans les autres langues romanes*   (Paris, Les Belles Lettres, 1962)

I. I. Revzin   1962   *Modeli jazyka*   (Moscow, Nauka, 1962; English trans. by N.F.C. Owen and A.S.C. Ross, *Models of Language*, London, Methuen, 1966; French trans. *Les Modèles linguistiques*, Paris, Dunot, 1968)

H. Rheinfelder   1963 (fest.)   *Medium Aevum Romanicum. Festschrift für H. Rheinfelder*   (Munich, Hueber, 1963)

F. Rice and A. Guss   1965   *Information sources in Linguistics: a bibliographical handbook*   (Washington D.C., Center for Applied Linguistics, 1965)

M. Riffaterre   1957   *Le Style des Pléiades de Gobineau. Essai d'application d'une méthode stylistique*   (Paris, 1957)

R. H. Robins   1964   *General Linguistics: an introductory survey*   (London, Longmans, 1964)

1967   *A Short History of Linguistics*   (London, Longmans, 1967)

A. Roceric-Alexandru   1968   *Fonostatistica limbii romîne*   (Bucharest, Ed. Acad., 1968)

M. Rodrigues Lapa   1945   *Estilística da lingua portuguesa*   (Lisbon, Seara Nova, 1945)

G. Rohlfs   1949-54   *Historische Grammatik der italienischen Sprache und ihrer Mundarten*   (Berne, Franke, 1949-54, 3 vols.)   (Italian version forthcoming: *Grammatica storica della lingua italiana e dei suoi dialetti*)

1950-52   *Romanische Philologie. 1. Allgemeine Romanistik; Französische und provenzalische Philologie. ii Italienische Philologie. Die sardische und rätoromanische Sprache.*   (Heidelberg, Winter, 1950-52)

1951   *Sermo vulgaris latinus, Vulgärlateinisches Lesebuch*   (Halle-Saale, 1951, 2nd ed. Tübingen, Niemeyer, 1956)

1952   *Estudios de geografía lingüística de Italia*   (Granada, U.P., 1952)

1952   *An den Quellen der romanischen Sprachen*   (Halle, Niemeyer, 1952)

1954 *Die lexikalische Differenzierung der romanischen Sprachen: Versuch einer romanischer Wortgeographie* (Munich, Bavarische Akademie, 1954; Spanish trans. by M. Alvar, *Diferenciación lexica de las lenguas románicas*, Madrid, 1960)

1956 *Studien zur romanischen Namenkunde* (Munich, Beck, 1956)

1957 *Manual de Filología Hispánica* (Bogotá, Instituto Caro y Cuervo, 1957)

1958 (fest.) H. Lausberg and H. Weinrich (eds.) *Romanica* (Halle, Niemeyer, 1958)

1966 *Einführung in das Studium der romanischen Philologie* (Heidelberg, Winter, 1966, 2nd ed. of vol i of G. Rohlfs 1950–52, with a supplement for the years 1950–65)

1968 (fest.) R. Baehr and K. Wais (eds.) *Serta Romanica* (Tübingen, Niemeyer, 1968)

R. Rohr 1964 *Einführung in das Studium der Romanistik* (Berlin, Schmidt, 1964)

L. Romeo 1968 *The Economy of Diphthongization in Early Romance* (The Hague, Mouton, 1968)

G. Rondeau 1965 *Initiation à la linguistique appliquée à l'enseignement des langues* (Montreal, Centre éducatif et culturel, 1965)

M. Roques 1946 (fest.) *Etudes romanes dédiées à Mario Roques* (Paris, Droz, 1946)

1950– (fest.) *Mélanges de linguistique et de littérature romanes offerts à M. Mario Roques* (Paris, Didier, 1950–)

A. Rosenblat 1964 *El castellano de España y el castellano de América: unidad y diferenciación* (Caracas U.P., 1964)

A. Rosetti 1957 *Introducere în fonetică* (Bucharest, Ed. Acad., 1957, 3rd ed. 1963 rev. ed. of 1930 work written with E. Petrovici; Portuguese trans. *Introdução â Fonética*, Lisbon, Publicaões Europa-America, 1962)

1938–46 *Istoria limbii romậne* (Bucharest, Ed St., 1938–46, 4th ed. 1964)

1943 *Le mot. Esquisse d'une théorie générale* (Copenhagen, Munksgaard & Bucharest, Inst. de ling. rom., 1943, 2nd augmented ed. 1947)

1947 *Mélanges de linguistique et de philologie* (Bucharest, Institutul de Lingvistic Romînă—Copenhagen, Munksgaard, 1947)

1959 *Sur la théorie de la syllabe* (The Hague, Mouton, 1959, 2nd revised ed. 1963)

1965 (fest.) *Omagiu lui Alexandru Rosetti la 70 de ani* (Bucharest, Ed. Acad., 1965)

1967 *Linguistica* (The Hague, Mouton, 1967)

A. Rosetti and B. Cazacu 1961– *Istoria limbii romậne literare* (Bucharest, Ed. Şt., 1961–)

W. Rothe 1965 *Beiträge zur Formenbildung von lat. "esse" im Romanischen* (Bonn, Rom. Versuche und Vorarbeiten, 1965)

N. Ruwet 1967 *Introduction à la grammaire générative* (Paris, Plon, 1967)

M. Saltarelli (forthcoming) *A Phonology of Italian in a Generative Grammar* (The Hague, Mouton)

W. J. Samarin 1967 *Field Linguistics* (New York, Holt, Rinehart and Winston, 1967)

M. Sanchis Guarner 1953 *La cartografía lingüística en la actualidad y el Atlas de la Península Ibérica* (Madrid, CSIC, 1953)

K. Sandfeld 1943 (mem.) *In memoriam Kr. Sandfeld, udgiret paa 70-Aarsdagen for hans Født̶sel* (Copenhagen, Gyldendal, 1943)

E. Sapir 1921 *Language* (New York, Harcourt, Brace & World, 1921; trans. *Le Langage*, Paris, A 1953; *linguagem*, Rio, 1954, *El lenguaje*, Mexico, 1954)

S. Saporta (ed.) 1961 *Psycholinguistics: a book of readings* (N.Y., Holt, Rinehart and Winston, 1961)

S. Saporta and H. Contreras 1962 *A Phonological Grammar of Spanish* (Seattle, Washington U.P., 1962)

J. Sarrailh 1966 (mem.) *Mélanges à la mémoire de Jean Sarrailh* (Paris, Centre de Recherches de l'Institut d'Etudes Hispaniques, 1966)

S. K. Šaumjan (forthcoming) *Problems of Theoretical Phonology* (The Hague, Mouton)

F. de Saussure 1916 *Cours de linguistique générale* (abbrev. *Cours*) (Paris, Payot, 1916, 3rd ed. 1965; Ed. critique par R. Engler, Wiesbaden, Harrassowitz, 1967; Spanish trans. by A. Alonso, *Curso de lingüística general*, Buenos Aires, Losada, 1945)

A. Sauvageot 1957 *Les procédés expressifs du français contemporain* (Paris, Klincksieck, 1957)

A. Schaff 1962 *Introduction to Semantics* (Oxford, Pergamon, 1962)

F. Schalk 1955 *Somnium und verwandte Wörter in den romanischen Sprachen* (Cologne, 1955)

S. A. Schane 1968 *French Phonology and Morphology* (Cambridge (Mass.), M.I.T. Press, 1968, Research Monograph 45)

C. Schick 1960 *Il linguaggio* (Turin, Einaudi, 1960)

H. Schmid 1949 *Zur Formenbildung von 'dare' und 'stare' im Romanischen* (Berne, Francke, 1949)

H. G. Schogt 1968 *Le système verbal du français contemporain* (The Hague, Mouton, 1968)

T. A. Sebeok (ed.) 1960 *Style in Language* (Cambridge (Mass.), M.I.T. Press, 1960)
  1966a *Current Trends in Linguistics; vol iii: Theoretical Foundations* (The Hague, Mouton, 1966)
  1966b *Portraits of Linguists: A Biographical Source Book for the History of Western Linguistics 1746–1963* (Bloomington, Indiana U.P., 1966, 2 vols.)

J. Séguy 1954–66 *Atlas Linguistique et ethnographique de la Gascogne* (Paris, C.N.R.S., 1954–66, 4 vols.)

M. V. Sergievski 1952 *Vvedenie v romanskoie iazíkoznanie* (Moscow, Izd. Lit. In. Jaz. 1952)

H. Serís 1964 *Bibliografía de la lingüística española* (Bogotá, Publicaciones del Instituto Caro y Cuervo, xix, 1964)

C. E. Shannon and W. Weaver 1949 *The Mathematical Theory of Communication* (Urbana, Illinois U.P., 1949)

B. Siertsema 1955 *A Study of Glossematics. Critical survey of its fundamental concepts* (The Hague, Nijhoff 1955, 2nd revised, ed. 1965)

D. L. Sills (ed.) 1968 *International Encyclopaedia of Social Sciences* (New York, Macmillan, 1968, 17 vols.)

S. da Silva Neto 1952 *Historia da lingua portuguesa* (Rio de Janeiro, Livros de Portugal, 1952)

  1957 *Manual de Filología portuguesa* (Rio de Janeiro, Livraria Academica, 1957)

  1960 *Lingua, cultura e civilização* (Rio de Janeiro, Livraria Academica, 1960)

P. Simon 1967 *Les Consonnes françaises: mouvements et positions articulatoires à la lumière de la radio-cinématographie* (Paris, Klincksieck, 1967)

P. Skok 1940 *Osnov i romanska lingvistike* (Zagreb, 1940, 3 vols.)

T. Slama-Cazacu 1961 *Langage et Contexte* (The Hague, Mouton, 1961; trans. from *Limbaj şi context*, Bucharest, 1959)

J. Sofer 1963 *Zur Problematik des Vulgärlateins: Ergebnisse und Anregungen* (Vienna, Gerold, 1963)

E. Spang-Hanssen 1963 *Les Prépositions incolores du français moderne* (Copenhagen, Gads, 1963)

H. Spang-Hanssen 1954 *Recent Theories on the Nature of the Language Sign* (Copenhagen, 1954, *TCLC* ix)

R. K. Spaulding 1943 *How Spanish Grew* (Berkeley & Los Angeles, California U.P., 1943)

L. Spitzer 1948a *Essays in Historical Semantics* (New York, Vanni, 1948)

  1948b *Linguistics and Literary History. Essays in Stylistics* (Princeton U.P., 1948; Spanish trans. *Lingüística e historia literaria*, Madrid, 1955)

  1949 *A Method of Interpreting Literature* (Northampton (Mass.), Smith College, 1949)

  1954 *Critica stilistica e storia del linguaggio* (Bari, Laterza e Figli, 1954)

  1956 *Romanische Literaturstudien 1936–1956* (Tübingen, Niemeyer, 1956)

  1958 (fest.) *Studia philologica et litteraria in honorem L. Spitzer* (Berne, Francke, 1958)

S. Stati 1961 *Limba latină in inscripţiile din Dacia şi Scythia* (Bucharest, Ed. Acad., 1961)

A. Stefenelli 1962 *Die Volkssprache im Werk des Petron (im Hinblick auf die romanischen Sprachen)* (Vienna–Stuttgart, Braumüller, 1962, Wiener Rom. Arb. i)

D. Steible 1967 *Concise handbook of linguistics* (London, Peter Owen, 1967)

H. Sten 1952 *Les temps du verbe fini (indicatif) en français moderne* (Copenhagen, Munksgaard, 1952)

R. P. Stockwell and J. D. Bowen 1965 *The Sounds of English and Spanish* (Chicago U.P., 1965)

R. P. Stockwell, J. D. Bowen and J. W. Martin 1965 *The Grammatical Structures of English and Spanish* (Chicago U.P., 1965)

G. Straka 1965 *Album phonétique* (Quebec, Laval U.P., 1965)

  (forthcoming) *Les tendances actuelles de la prononciation française* (Paris, Klincksieck)

K. Strecker 1948 *Introduction à l'étude du latin médiéval* (Paris, Droz, 3rd trans. ed. 1948)

W. Streitberg 1924 (fest.) *Stand und Aufgaben der Sprachwissenschaft.*
　Festschrift für Wilhelm Streitberg (Heidelberg, 1924)
P. Strevens (ed.) 1966 *Five Inaugural lectures* (London, O.U.P., 1966)
Studies in Linguistic Analysis (Oxford, Blackwell *for* The Philological
　Society, 1957)

A. Tabouret-Keller (forthcoming) *Le Bilinguisme* (Paris, P.U.F. Coll.
　"Le Linguiste")
C. Tagliavini 1950 *Introduzione alla glottologia* (Bologna, Pàtron, 4th ed.
　1950)
　1959 *Le origine delle lingue neolatine. Introduzione alla filologia romanza*
　(Bologna, Pàtron, 3rd ed. 1959, reprint 1962, 4th revised ed. 1964)
　1963 *Storia della linguistica* (Bologna, Pàtron, (lithographed) 1963)
　1965 *La corretta pronuncia italiana* (Bologna, Pàtron, 1965)
V. Tauli 1968 *Introduction to a theory of language planning* (Uppsala U.P.,
　1968)
B. A. Terracini 1942 *¿Qué es la lingüística?* (Tucumán, Fac. de Filos.
　y Letras, 1942)
　1949 *Guida allo studio della linguistica storica* (Rome, Ateneo, 1949)
　1957a *Conflitti di lingua e di cultura* (Venice, Bibl. di Cultura xix,
　1957)
　1957b *Pagine e appunti di linguistica storica* (Florence, 1957)
　1963 *Lingua libera e libertà linguistica: introduzione alla linguistica storica*
　(Turin, Einaudi, 1963)
　1966 *Analisi stilistica. Teoria, storia, problemi* (Milan, Feltrinelli, 1966)
　1968 (fest.) *Linguistica e filologia. Omaggio a Benvenuto Terracini* (Milan,
　1968)
B. A. Terracini and T. Franceschi 1964 *Saggio di un atlante linguistico di
　Sardegna* (Turin, Inst. del Atlante Linguistico, 1964, 2 vols.)
L. Tesnière 1943 *Cours de syntaxe structurale* (in mimeograph, 1943)
　1953 *Esquisse d'une syntaxe structurale* (Paris, Klincksieck, 1953)
　1959 *Eléments de syntaxe structurale* (abbrev. *ESS*) (Paris, Klincksieck,
　1959, 2nd ed. 1965)
D. E. Thackray (ed.) 1967 *Research: definitions and reflections. Essays on the
　occasion of the University of Michigan's Sesquicentennial* (Ann Arbor,
　Michigan U.P., 1967)
R. Titone 1964 *La psicolinguistica oggi* (Zurich, Pas-Verlag, 1964)
K. Togeby 1951 *Structure Immanente de la langue française* (Copenhagen,
　TCLC vi, 1951, 2nd revised ed. 1965, Paris, Larousse)
　1953 *Mode, aspect et temps en espagnol* (Copenhagen, Munksgaard, 1953)
　1954 *L'Œuvre de Maupassant* (Dansk Videnstabs Forlag-P.U.F. 1954)
　1957a *Dansk Lyrik 1951-55* (Dansk laererforingen 1957)
　1957b *La Composition du roman "Don Quixote"* (Suppl. to Orbis Litterarum,
　1957)
　1960 *Litteraere renaessancer i Frankrigs middelalder* (Studier fra Sprog- og
　Oltidsforskning, 1960)
　(ed.) 1967 *La Glossématique, l'heritage de Hjelmslev au Danemark* (*Ls* vi,
　1967)

1968   *Immanence and Structure*   (Special number ii of *RRom* Copenhagen, Akademisk Forlag, 1968)

J. B. Trend   1953   *The Languages and History of Spain*   (London, Hutchinson, 1953)

Trends i & ii see C. Mohrmann *et al.* (eds.)   1961 & 1963

N. S. Trubetzkoy   1939   *Grundzüge der Phonologie*   (*TCLP* vii, 1939, 3rd ed. 1962; French trans. by J. Cantineau, *Principes de Phonologie*, 1949, rep. 1957, English trans. *Introduction to the Principles of Phonological Descriptions*, The Hague, Nijhoff. 1968)

H. J. Uldall   1957   *Outline of Glossematics*   (Copenhagen, *TCLC* x, 1957)

S. Ullmann   1951   *Principles of Semantics. A Linguistic Approach to Meaning* (Glasgow, U.P., 1951, 2nd ed. Oxford, Blackwell, 1959)

    1952   *Précis de sémantique française*   (Berne, Francke, 1952, 2nd ed. 1959; Spanish ed. *Introducción a la semántica francesa* trans. with annotations by E. Bustos Tovar, Madrid, 1965)

    1957   *Style in the French Novel*   (Oxford, Blackwell, 1957, rep. 1964)

    1960   *The Image in the Modern French Novel*   (Oxford, Blackwell, 1964)

    1962   *Semantics: an Introduction to the Study of Meaning*   (Oxford, Blackwell, 1962, reprints 1964 & 1967; Italian ed. Bologna, Il Mulino, 1966)

    1964   *Language and Style*   (Oxford, Blackwell, 1964)

V. Väänänen   1963   *Introduction au latin vulgaire*   (Paris, Klincksieck, 1963, reprint + 45 extra pages of text & commentary 1966)

    1966   *Le Latin vulgaire des inscriptions pompéiennes*   (Berlin, Abhandlungen der Deutschen Ak. der Wiss. zu Berlin, Klasse für S, L. und K, 1958 iii, 2nd rev. ed. of 1937 work; 3rd ed. 1966)

J. Vachek   1960   *Dictionnaire de linguistique de l'école de Prague*   (Utrecht–Antwerp, Spectrum, 1960)

    1964   *A Prague School Reader in Linguistics*   (Indiana U.P., 1964)

    1966   *The Linguistic School of Prague. An Introduction to its theory and practice*   (Indiana U.P., 1966)

A. Valdman   1961   *Applied Linguistics—French: a guide for teachers*   (Boston, Heath, 1961)

    (ed.)   1966   *Trends in Language Teaching*   (N.Y., McGraw-Hill, 1966)

R. Valin   1955   *Petite introduction à la psychomécanique du langage*   (Quebec, Laval U.P., 1955, in *CaLS*)

M. Valkhoff   1966   *Studies in Portuguese and Creole*   (Johannesburg, Witwatersrand U.P., 1966)

J. L. Varela   1955   *Vossler e la ciencia literaria*   (Madrid, 1955)

E. Vasiliu   1965   *Fonologia limbii române*   (Bucharest, Ed. Acad., 1965)

J. Vendryes   1921   *Le Langage...*(Paris, Michel 1921, new ed. with revised bibl. 1950; English trans. London, Routledge & Kegan Paul, 1925, 5th printing 1959; Spanish trans. with introd. by A. Badía and J. Roca, *Panorama de la lingüística moderna*, Mexico, Unión tip. ed. Hispano-Americana, 1958)

T. Vianu   1957   *Problemele metaforei şi alte studii de stilistică*   (Bucharest, Ed. Acad., 1957)

B. E. Vidos 1939 *Storia delle parole marinaresche italiane passate in francese; contributo storico-linguistico all' espansione della lingua nautica italiana* (Florence, Olschki, 1939, *BAR* Ser. II vol. xxiv)

1956 *Handboek tot de Romaanse Taalkunde* ('s-Hertogenbosch, Malmberg, 1956; Italian trans. *Manuale di linguistica romanza* Florence, Olschki, 1959; Spanish trans. *Manual de lingüística románica* Madrid, Aguilar, 1963; German trans. *Handbuch der romanischen Sprachwissenschaft* Munich, Hueber, 1968)

1965 *Prestito, espansione e migrazione dei termini tecnici nelle lingue romanze e non romanze. Problemi, metodo e risultati* (Florence, Olschki, 1965)

A. Viscardi *et al.* 1955 A. Viscardi, C. Cremonesi, E. Mozzati and M. Vitale *Preistoria e storia degli studi romanzi* (Milan, Inst. Ed. Cisalpino, 1955)

K. Vossler 1954 *Einführung ins Vulgärlatein* (Munich, Hueber, 1954)

M. L. Wagner 1941 *Historische Lautlehre des Sardischen* (Halle, Saale, 1941)

1949 *Lingua e dialetti dell'America spagnuola* (Florence, Le Lingue estere, 1949)

1951 *La lingua sarda: Forma, storia, spirito* (Berne, Francke, 1951)

1952 *Historische Wortbildungslehre des Sardischen* (Berne, Francke, 1952)

R-L. Wagner 1939 *Les phrases hypothétiques commençant par si dans la langue française des origines à la fin du xvie s·* (Paris, Droz, 1939, thesis)

1955 *Introduction à la linguistique française* (Geneva, Droz, 1947, 2nd ed. 1955, new ed. 1965, with, as a separate volume, *Supplément bibliographique*, 1947–53·

1967 *Les Vocabulaires français: 1. définitions; les dictionnaires* (Paris, Didier, 1967)

1968 *La Grammaire française* (Paris, Sédès, 1968)

W. von Wartburg 1922–68 *Französisches etymologisches Wörterbuch* (Bonn, Klopp, 1922–28, Leipzig, 1932–1940, Basel, 1955–68)

1934 *Evolution et structure de la langue française* (3rd rev. ed. Berne, Francke, 1946, 6th ed., 1962)

1938 *Die Entstehung der romanischen Völker* (Tübingen, Niemeyer, 1938, 2nd ed. 1951; French trans. *Les Origines des peuples romans*, Paris, P.U.F., 1941)

1943 *Einführung in die Problematik und Methodik der Sprachwissenschaft* (Halle, a.d.S, 1943, new ed. Tübingen, Niemeyer, 1962; French trans. *Problèmes et méthodes de la linguistique*, 1946, revised with additional chapters by S. Ullmann, 1963, and trans. into English by J. M. H. Reid, *Problems and Methods in Linguistics*, Oxford, Blackwell, 1969; Spanish trans. *Problemas y métodos de la lingüística*, Madrid, 1951)

1950 *Die Ausgliederung der romanischen Sprachräume* (Berne, Francke, 1950; Spanish trans. *La fragmentación lingüística de la Romania*, Madrid, Gredos, 1952; French trans. *La fragmentation de la Romania*, Paris, Klincksieck, 1967)

1956 *Von Sprache und Mensch* K. Baldinger and A. Thierbach (eds.) (Collected essays; Berne, Francke, 1956)

1958 (fest.) K. Baldinger (ed.) *Etymologica* (Tübingen, Niemeyer, 1958)

1968 (fest.) *Festschrift Walther von Wartburg zum 80. Geburtstag. 18. mai 1968* ed. Kurt Baldinger (Tübingen, Niemeyer, 1968, 2 vols.)

W. von Wartburg and R. Hallig 1963 *Système raisonné des concepts pour servir de base à la lexicographie. Essai d'un schéma de classement* (Berlin, Ak.-Verlag, 2nd ed. 1963, cf. also R. Hallig and W. von Wartburg 1963)

W. von Wartburg and P. Zumthor 1947 *Précis de syntaxe du français contemporain* (Berne, Francke, 1947, 2nd ed. 1958)

J. Waterman 1963 *Perspectives in Linguistics* (Chicago U.P., 1963; Translations: *Die Linguistik und ihre Perspektiven*, Munich 1966; *Breve storia della linguistica*, Florence, 1968)

U. Weinreich 1953 *Languages in Contact* (New York, Publications of the Linguistic Circle of N.Y., No. 1; also, The Hague, Mouton, 1953, rep. 1964)

H. Weinrich 1958 *Phonologische Studien zur romanischen Sprachgeschichte* (Münster, Aschendorff, 1958)

1964 *Tempus, Besprochene und erzählte Welt* (Stuttgart, Kohlhammer, 1964, Sprache und Literatur xvi)

1966 *Linguistik der Lüge* (Heidelberg, Schneider, 1966)

P. J. Wexler 1955 *La Formation du vocabulaire des chemins de fer en France* (Geneva, Droz-Lille, 1955)

J. Whatmough 1956 *Language: a modern synthesis* (N.Y., St Martin's Press, 1956)

1957 (fest.) E. Pulgram (ed.) *Studies Presented to J. Whatmough* (The Hague, Mouton, 1957)

K. A. Whinnom 1956 *Spanish Contact Vernaculars in the Philippine Islands* (Hong Kong–Oxford, 1956)

E. B. Williams 1938 *From Latin to Portuguese; Historical Phonology and Morphology of the Portuguese Language* (Philadelphia, Penn. U.P., 1938, 2nd rev. ed. 1962)

A. Zamora Vicente 1967 *Dialectología española* (Madrid, Gredos, 2nd ed. 1967)

A. Zauner 1900 *Romanische Sprachwissenschaft* (Leipzig, Göschen, 1900, 3rd rev. ed. 1914; 4th ed. (reprint) Berlin, de Gruyter 1944–5)

P. Ziff 1960 *Semantic Analysis* (Ithaca, Cornell U.P., 1960)

G. Zipf 1935 *The Psychobiology of Language* (Cambridge (Mass.), M.I.T. Press, 1965, originally published by Houghton Mifflin, 1935)

1949 *Human Behavior and the Principle of Least Effort; an Introduction to Human Ecology* (Cambridge, Mass., Addison-Wesley Press, 1949)

P. Zumthor 1963 *Langues et techniques poétiques à l'époque romane (11e–13e siècles)* (Paris, Klincksieck, 1963)

V. A. Zvengincev 1964 *Istorija jazykoznanja xix i xx vekov* (Moscow, Nauka, 3rd ed. 1964, 2 vols.)

INDEXES

Explanatory Note : Reference is to pages ; 333[1]=page 333, note 1 ; *ib.*[3]=same page, note 3 ; 333 n.=page 333, note continued from preceding page. A dash (or initials) is used to avoid repeating words.

I. SUBJECT INDEX

II WORD INDEX

III. INDEX OF PROPER NAMES